OXFORD MONOGRAPHS ON
LABOUR LAW

General Editors: Paul Davies,
Keith Ewing, Mark Freedland

INTERNATIONAL AND EUROPEAN PROTECTION
OF THE RIGHT TO STRIKE

Oxford Monographs on Labour Law

General Editors: Paul Davies, Cassel Professor of Commercial Law at London School of Economics; Keith Ewing, Professor of Public Law at King's College, London; and Mark Freedland, Fellow of St John's College, and Professor of Law at Oxford University.

This series is the first new development in the literature dealing with labour law for many years. The series recognizes the arrival not only of a renewed interest in labour law generally, but also the need for a fresh approach to the study of labour law following a decade of momentous change in the UK and Europe. The series is concerned with all aspects of labour law, including traditional subjects of study such as industrial relations law and individual employment law, but it will also include books which examine the law and economics of the labour market and the impact of social security law upon patterns of employment and the employment contract.

Titles already published in this series

The Right to Strike
K. D. EWING

Legislating for Conflict
SIMON AUERBACH

Justice in Dismissal
HUGH COLLINS

Pensions, Employment, and the Law
RICHARD NOBLES

Just Wages for Women
AILEEN MCCOLGAN

Women and the Law
SANDRA FREDMAN

Freedom of Speech and Employment
LUCY VICKERS

International and European Protection of the Right to Strike

A Comparative Study of Standards Set by the
International Labour Organization, the Council
of Europe and the European Union

TONIA NOVITZ

OXFORD
UNIVERSITY PRESS

OXFORD

UNIVERSITY PRESS

Great Clarendon Street, Oxford OX2 6DP

Oxford University Press is a department of the University of Oxford.
It furthers the University's objective of excellence in research, scholarship,
and education by publishing worldwide in

Oxford New York

Auckland Bangkok Buenos Aires Cape Town Chennai
Dar es Salaam Delhi Hong Kong Istanbul Karachi Kolkata
Kuala Lumpur Madrid Melbourne Mexico City Mumbai Nairobi
São Paulo Shanghai Taipei Tokyo Toronto

Oxford is a registered trade mark of Oxford University Press
in the UK and in certain other countries

Published in the United States
by Oxford University Press Inc., New York

© Tonia Novitz 2003

The moral rights of the author have been asserted
Database right Oxford University Press (maker)

First published 2003

British Library Cataloguing in Publication Data

Data available

Library of Congress Cataloging in Publication Data
Data available

ISBN 0-19-829854-4

1 3 5 7 9 10 8 6 4 2

Typeset by Kolam Information Services Pvt. Ltd, Pondicherry, India
Printed in Great Britain on acid-free paper by
T.J. International Ltd, Padstow, Cornwall

To my mother, Rosemary Du Plessis, and in memory of my father, David Novitz.

General Editors' Preface

The right to strike is one of the most difficult and intractable issues of modern labour law. Although recognized as a fundamental human right in international law, and indeed by the British courts, it is a fundamental right which is rarely acknowledged to its full extent, even in the domestic law of those countries which have ratified the international treaties in which it is to be found. Despite its protection in international law, the right to strike needs to be better understood, both in terms of its role and purpose, and in terms of its scope and content. This scholarly work meets that need, with Dr Novitz providing a detailed and sophisticated account of why the right to strike should be protected, and the nature and form which that protection should take.

This is an important, exhaustive, and unrivalled study of the right to strike in international law which provides a full analysis of its protection in the Council of Europe's Social Charter of 1961 and ILO Convention 87. In a highly original and careful account of the political and legal history of the right to strike in international law, Dr Novitz examines in the traveaux préparatoires the materials which have been largely neglected by international labour lawyers. The topicality of the work is enriched by her treatment of the right to strike in the European Convention on Human Rights (where there may still be some work yet to be done by the Strasbourg Court) and by her examination of the position in EU law, including the Charter of Fundamental Rights of 2000.

This is a book which will be of immense value to the legal historian, the international lawyer, and the labour lawyer, as well as those with an interest in the nature and function of social rights generally. Dr Novitz presents a study which is particularly topical and timely for British labour lawyers, not only because of the continuing debates at European level about protection for the right to strike, but also because of the United Kingdom's continued breach of both ILO Convention 87 and the Council of Europe's Social Charter of 1961. But as will quickly become clear, this is a study which will be of much wider interest and significance, illuminated as it is by numerous cases in which many different countries have also been found in breach of international human rights obligations relating to the right to strike.

PLD, KDE, MRF
13 January 2003

Preface

This book examines the extent to which the right to strike is protected under international and European law and assesses the adequacy of that protection. Its primary focus is on the International Labour Organization (ILO), the Council of Europe, and the European Union (EU), but reference is also made to the International Covenant on Economic, Social and Cultural Rights 1966. This is intended to be a statement of the relevant law as at 1 August 2002.

My study of this issue began with the aim of revealing a uniform set of principles which could serve as a basis for evaluating the adequacy of national provision for industrial action. The picture presented here is not so straightforward. There is consensus at the international level that a right to strike should be protected, but the form which this protection takes and the scope of the right itself vary between organizations and instruments.

It seems that different views have been taken of the role that a right to strike should play within national governance. Divergent institutional structures within international and European organizations have allowed one attitude to prevail within one organization that would not do so in another. Also relevant were the economic, social, and political circumstances in which these organizations were established, and in which they took decisions on the substance and interpretation of the right to strike. This book ends by considering the potential for convergence of norms in this field and the direction that this may take.

This research project began at Balliol College, Oxford, in 1992, when I commenced work on a BCL thesis analysing treatment of 'political strikes' in South Africa and the UK, and continued in my D.Phil. thesis on 'International Protection of the Right to Strike: A Comparative Study of Standards set by the International Labour Organisation and Council of Europe' which was completed in 1998. A more practical understanding of the operation of ILO and Council of Europe standard-setting and supervisory methods was gleaned from time spent subsequently as a Visiting Fellow at the International Institute of Labour Studies in Geneva and at the Council of Europe in Strasbourg. I have also sought to develop my doctoral work by extending this study to include analysis of standards set (or not set) by the European Union in this field. In this respect, I owe a great deal to my time spent as a visitor in Brussels, meeting people at the ICFTU, the ETUC, EUROFEDOP, and the European Commission. I am also very appreciative of time spent at the Robert Schuman Centre at the European University Institute, as a Jean Monnet Fellow and a Marie Curie Fellow in 2001–2. More detailed acknowledgements follow.

My personal experience has also shaped my understanding of the dimensions of the right to strike; and I believe that to speak of one's own background is appropriate. My interest in these issues dates from my experience of industrial relations in New Zealand: as a 15-year-old in my first summer job debating the merits of compulsory trade unionism with a school friend; as an 18-year-old waitress participating in a strike during negotiations over a national award; and as a lawyer when the system of collective bargaining was dismantled by the Employment Contracts Act 1991. My connection to South Africa, where I was born, has also influenced my thinking on the role of trade unions and worker solidarity in democratization. This is due to lengthy discussions with not only family and friends, but also members of the Law, Race and Gender Unit and the Labour Law Unit at the University of Cape Town. Moreover, my time in Britain and, most recently, as a Member of the Executive Committee of the Association of University Teachers at the University of Bristol has also given me an appreciation of the role that union representatives can play within the workplace.

Finally, in seminars delivered in the ILO and the EUI, concern has been expressed that my analysis of international and European law is too critical. There are some committed labour lawyers, industrial relations specialists, and trade unionists who consider that such criticism will undermine the credibility of these standards as a reference point for domestic law. I do not consider that this is the case.

I cannot see a way in which to portray the approaches of the ILO, the Council of Europe, and the European Union as entirely consistent; nor do I believe that one should try to do so. It seems important to point out the inconsistencies and inadequacies of existing international and European legal norms relating to the right to strike, so that they may be improved. That improvement can only facilitate their application at the national level. My hope is that this book will contribute to current debates over the direction that such reform should take.

T. N.
August 2002

Acknowledgements

This research project has been carried out over a considerable period of time and there are therefore many people whose assistance I must acknowledge. The first are my doctoral supervisors, Paul Davies and Keith Ewing; and my examiners, Mark Freedland and Bob Hepple. Their comments and criticism have been invaluable.

Funding for this project was provided by the Balliol College Dervorguilla scholarship and Kulkes Fund, the University of Bristol, a British Academy research grant, a Society of Legal Scholars (previously known as the Society of Public Teachers of Law) travel grant, a Jean Monnet Fellowship from the European University Institute, and the European Commission Marie Curie Fellowship. Without this financial support, its completion would not have been possible. I must also thank the School of Law at the University of Canterbury for providing me with office space in 1999, when I needed to spend time in Christchurch, New Zealand, for family reasons.

In addition, I would like to thank staff at the International Labour Organization, the International Institute for Labour Studies, the Council of Europe, and the European Commission for their assistance. Interviews with officials were conducted on the understanding that their contents would remain confidential, but they provided me with valuable insights into the ways in which these institutions operate. I am very appreciative, as well, of time taken by staff of the ICFTU, the ETUC, and EUROFE-DOP to give me their views on current developments.

I owe a great deal to assistance provided by other academics and lawyers working in the field of EU law, industrial relations, and international law. Of these, I must mention John Hughes and Sandra Fredman who were inspirational teachers. I have also gained much from the seminars and advice given by Philip Alston, Bruno de Witte, Mark Pollack, Silvana Sciarra, Helen Wallace, and other participants in the 'European Forum' during my time at the Robert Schuman Centre for Advanced Studies and the Department of Law at the European University Institute.

I would also like to thank for their help and encouragement at various stages of this project: Diamond Ashiagbor, Lizzie Barmes, Charles Barrow, Niki Best, Ben Capps, Pat Capps, Malcolm Evans, Colin Fenwick, Barry Fitzpatrick, Paul Germanotta, Victor-Yves Ghebali, John Hendy, Richard Huxtable, Hendrien Kaal, Caroline Keenan, Nadira Kenny, Claire Kilpatrick, Susan Lamb, Anne Lofaso, Gary Morton, Jill Murray, Rachel Murray, Kirsty Real, Bernard Ryan, Caroline Sawyer, Paul Skidmore,

Teresa Swift, Melanie Thomas, Karen Tickner, Lisa Tortell, and Michael Wynn. I should mention, in particular, Sally Ball, who will be greatly missed by the community of labour lawyers in the UK and elsewhere.

Further thanks are due to many other friends for their support, through good and bad days. I cannot list them all here, but I hope that they know that they are appreciated. If I should single any out, it is those who have very generously assisted my research by putting a roof over my head in my hour of need, and in this respect I owe special thanks to Louise Fonceca and Andrew Johnston.

I am also deeply indebted to my family. My parents, Rosemary Du Plessis and David Novitz, have provided me with all the love a daughter could want and their own work continues to be an inspiration to me. The ability of my brother, Julian Novitz, to write with wit, style, and flair is something that I cannot hope to emulate, but he has set me a fine example in more ways than this. I am also grateful for the support given to me by my extended family in New Zealand, Australia, South Africa, and the UK, including George and Vasso Syrpis, Khris and Abanti Mahanty, Geoff Fougere, Clare Simpson, and Jim Marshall, whose friendship has been so important.

My final thanks go to Phil Syrpis who has done more for me than I can itemize here. He has listened to my tentative thoughts and helped me to weave these into sensible arguments. He has provided swift answers to questions relating to British industrial relations and the European Union. He has provided me with source material and journal references. He has read my work, corrected my grammar, and forced me to explain myself. He has supported me when my confidence was ebbing. I am very grateful for his companionship and love.

Contents

Abbreviations

ACT/EMP	ILO Bureau for Employers' Activities
ACTRAV	ILO Bureau for Workers' Activities
AFL	American Federation of Labour
AJIL	*American Journal of International Law*
ANC	African National Congress
ASP	Agreement on Social Policy (appended to the Maastricht Treaty of European Union 1992)
BBC	British Broadcasting Corporation
BJIR	*British Journal of Industrial Relations*
BYBIL	*British Yearbook of International Law*
CCAS	ILO Conference Committee on the Application of Standards
CCFSRW	Community Charter of the Fundamental Social Rights of Workers 1989
CCP	Collective Complaints Protocol to the ESC
CCSU	Council of Civil Service Unions (UK)
CEACR	ILO Committee of Experts on the Application of Conventions and Recommendations
CEEP	Centre Européen de l'Entreprise Publique
CFA	ILO Governing Body Committee on Freedom of Association
CFI	Court of First Instance (EU)
CHARTE-REL	Committee responsible for drafting Protocols for the reform of the ESC established in 1990
CIE	Committee of Independent Experts—now known as the European Committee of Social Rights—responsible for supervision of the ESC
CMLRev.	*Common Market Law Review*
COSATU	Congress of South African Trade Unions
EC	European Community
ECOSOC	UN Economic and Social Council
ECHR	European Convention on Human Rights
ECJ	European Court of Justice
ECR	European Court Reports
ECSC	European Coal and Steel Community
ECSR	European Committee of Social Rights—previously known as the Committee of Independent Experts—responsible for supervision of the ESC
ECT	Treaty of the European Community

EDC	European Defence Community
EEC	European Economic Community
EHRR	European Human Rights Reports
EHRLR	*European Human Rights Law Review*
EIRR	*European Industrial Relations Review*
EJIL	*European Journal of International Law*
ELJ	*European Law Journal*
ELRev.	*European Law Review*
EPC	European Political Community
EPL	*European Public Law*
EPZ	Export Processing Zone
ERC	European Regional Conference (established by ILO)
ESC	European Social Charter
ETUC	European Trade Union Confederation
ETUI	European Trade Union Institute
EU	European Union
EUCFR	European Union Charter of Fundamental Rights 2000
EUROFEDOP	European Federation of Employees in Public Services
FFCC	ILO Fact-finding and Conciliation Commission on Freedom of Association
GATT	General Agreement on Tariffs and Trade
GCHQ	Government Communication Headquarters (UK)
GSP	Generalized System of Preferences
ICCPR	International Covenant on Civil and Political Rights
ICESCR	International Covenant on Economic, Social and Cultural Rights
ICFTU	International Confederation of Free Trade Unions
ICJ	International Court of Justice
ICLQ	*International and Comparative Law Quarterly*
IFCTU	International Federation of Christian Trade Unions
IFFTU	International Federation of Free Trade Unions (predecessor to the ICFTU)
IGC	Inter-Governmental Conference (EU)
IILS	International Institute for Labour Studies
IJCLLIR	*International Journal of Comparative Labour Law and Industrial Relations*
ILA	International Longshoremen's Association (US)
ILC	International Labour Conference
ILJ	*Industrial Law Journal* (UK)
ILLR	International Labour Law Reports
ILO	International Labour Organization

IRLR	Industrial Relations Law Reports
ILRev.	*International Labour Review*
JCMS	*Journal of Common Market Studies*
JEPP	*Journal of European Public Policy*
IMEC	Industrialized Market-Oriented Economy Countries (a group of States which sometimes act as a lobby group within the ILO)
IMF	International Monetary Fund
IOE	International Organization of Employers
LQR	*Law Quarterly Review*
MEP	Member of the European Parliament (EC)
MLR	*Modern Law Review*
MNE	Multinational Enterprise
NAACP	National Association for the Advancement of Colored People
NACTU	National Council of Trade Unions (South Africa)
NGO	Non-governmental Organization
NQHR	*Netherlands Quarterly of Human Rights*
OAS	Organization of American States
OAU	Organization of African Unity
OECD	Organization for Economic Co-operation and Development
OEEC	Organization for European Economic Co-operation (predecessor to the OECD)
OJ	Official Journal (EC)
OJLS	*Oxford Journal of Legal Studies*
SFTU	Swaziland Federation of Trade Unions
TEU	Treaty of European Union
TUC	Trades Union Congress (UK)
UDHR	Universal Declaration of Human Rights 1948
UEAPME	Union Européenne de l'Artisanat et des Petites et Moyennes Entreprises
UN	United Nations
UNICE	Union des Confédérations de l'Industrie et des Employers d'Europe
USSR	The Former Soviet Union
WFTU	World Federation of Trade Unions
WTO	World Trade Organization
YEL	*Yearbook of European Law*

Tables of Cases

CASES DECIDED IN DOMESTIC COURTS

CASES DECIDED BY THE EUROPEAN COMMISSION AND COURT OF HUMAN RIGHTS

CASES DECIDED BY THE EUROPEAN COURT OF JUSTICE AND COURT OF FIRST INSTANCE

CASES DECIDED BY THE COURT OF FIRST INSTANCE

CASES DECIDED BY THE EUROPEAN
COMMITTEE OF SOCIAL RIGHTS

CASES DECIDED BY THE ILO COMMITTEE ON
FREEDOM OF ASSOCIATION

CASES DECIDED BY THE INTERNATIONAL COURT OF JUSTICE

Tables of International Instruments

COUNCIL OF EUROPE

EUROPEAN UNION

INTERNATIONAL LABOUR ORGANIZATION (ILO)

ORGANIZATION OF AMERICAN STATES (OAS)

ORGANIZATION FOR ECONOMIC
CO-OPERATION AND DEVELOPMENT

OTHER UNITED NATIONS INSTRUMENTS

WORLD TRADE ORGANIZATION

1

Introduction: Why Investigate Protection of the Right to Strike?

The history of labour law is profoundly connected to the organization of workers. In the industrial sphere, workers have sought to exercise bargaining power through the combined and co-ordinated withdrawal of their labour. Within the political sphere, workers have acted collectively to persuade governments to adopt laws and policies which reflect their interests. This has been done through such means as lobbying and the formation of political parties. One result of these endeavours has been the gradual legal accommodation of a 'right to strike' in almost all States, and certainly all Western European States.[1]

The form that this legal accommodation takes differs. Within some States, this is a 'positive' entitlement to take industrial action, guaranteed as a constitutional right or as a key feature of labour legislation. Within others, this is phrased as a 'negative' liberty, such that workers and organizers are immune from what would otherwise be the legal consequences of industrial action. The scope of the entitlement (or immunity) varies from State to State. In this respect, international labour standards have tended to serve as a reference point for what could be described as the 'core' content of that right.

This is a study of those international standards. Its complexity arises from the fact that these are not altogether consistent, the reason being that they arise from diverse sources. The first and foremost source, by virtue of the 'principle of speciality',[2] remains the International Labour Organization (ILO), the United Nations (UN) agency responsible for the setting and monitoring of labour standards. Others include the UN Universal Declaration of Human Rights 1948, the International Covenant on Civil and Political Rights 1966 (ICCPR), and the International Covenant on Economic, Social, and Cultural Rights 1966 (ICESCR).[3] More prominent in

---

[1] Cf. Hepple, B. (ed.), *The Making of Labour Law in Europe: A Comparative Study of Nine Countries up to 1945* (New York: Mansell, 1986); Kelly, J., *Trade Unions and Socialist Politics* (London/New York: Verso, 1988).

[2] For a statement of this principle see *Legality of the Use by a State of Nuclear Weapons in Armed Conflict (Request by the World Health Organization for an Advisory Opinion)* (1998) 110 ILR 1.

[3] The focus in this book is on the ILO rather than the two Covenants of 1966. This is, in part, by virtue of the specialized role which the ILO plays in this sphere, recognized by the WTO in its Singapore Declaration of 13 Dec. 1996, WT/MIN96/DEC/W, para. 4. Also, the ICCPR and the ICESCR, by virtue of the jurisprudence of their supervisory bodies, have had

domestic politics, however, are the instruments adopted and jurisprudence developed by regional organizations. This book, therefore, also looks at the Council of Europe and the European Union (EU), whose engagement with human rights and social policy provide an opportunity for both transposition and distortion of ILO norms.

If one were to judge from the literature focusing on 'human resource management'[4] or the policy statements of the British 'New Labour' government,[5] one might regard such a study as irrelevant and unnecessary. It seems that we have now arrived at a juncture in industrial relations, at which the traditional methods of collective bargaining, including industrial action, are increasingly called into question. The right to strike raises not only the spectre of a fundamental conflict of interests between capital and labour, but also potential for a confrontation which involves costs to both sides. More recently, emphasis has been placed on 'corporate social responsibility', in response to which workers are asked to participate in workplace 'partnerships'. The result is intended to be greater flexibility and therefore profitability, which, at least in theory, is to benefit both workers and their employer. Labour law is being designed to encourage such partnerships, against a framework of 'individual rights'.[6] The emphasis on individual autonomy and freedom of workers arguably has the potential to undermine traditional forms of worker solidarity.

It is suggested here that such trends render study of a right to strike not irrelevant, but all the more important. Current challenges to national-level protection of the right to strike raise fundamental questions about ideal forms of 'governance' and 'democracy'. One such question is the legitimate

relatively little impact on international protection of the right to strike. The jurisprudence of the ICCPR is discussed in Part IV below at 265–327. The express, albeit limited, protection of a right to strike in Art. 8(1)(d) of the ICESCR is discussed further in Chap. 5 below at 118–9. The few observations made by the UN Committee on Economic, Social and Cultural Rights on the application of this provision also receive attention in Chaps. 11–14. These two instruments reflect the division in international human rights law drawn between protection of civil and political rights on the one hand and socio-economic rights on the other. To this extent, they are also pertinent to the arguments developed in the book, even if they are not given detailed attention. See Chap. 2 below at 41–2.

[4] See Ackers, P., and Payne, J., 'British Trade Unions and Social Partnership: Rhetoric, Reality and Strategy' (1998) 9 *International Journal of Human Resource Management* 529.

[5] See White Paper on *Fairness at Work* Cm 3968 (London: TSO, 1998), Foreword; also the description of rail strikes as 'stone age' by Tony Blair, reported in 'Why New Labour Fears These Strikes', *Guardian*, 31 Jan. 2002.

[6] An example being the Employment Relations Act 1999, discussed in Novitz, T., and Skidmore, P., *Fairness at Work: A Critical Analysis of the Employment Relations Act 1999 and its Treatment of Collective Rights* (Oxford: Hart Publishing, 2001). For a more generous analysis of the repercussions of 'Third Way' politics see Collins, H., 'Is There a Third Way in Labour Law?' in Conaghan, J., Fischl, R. M., and Klare, K. (eds.), *Labour Law in an Era of Globalization: Transformative Practices and Possibilities* (Oxford: OUP, 2002). See also Guest, D.E., and Peccei, R., 'Partnership at Work: Mutuality and the Balance of Advantage' (2001) 39 *BJIR* 207; and Rubinstein, S., 'A Different Kind of Union: Balancing Co-Management and Representation' (2001) 40 *Industrial Relations* 163.

scope of State regulatory power. Which norms should be set by central government and which (if any) by workers and employers through a collective bargaining process? To what extent should there be intervention to control the outcomes of the collective bargaining process by regulation of the ability to organize and participate in industrial action? Another key issue is how such decisions should be taken within a democratic framework. For example, is decision-making by a duly elected majoritarian legislature to be regarded as sufficient to achieve democratic legitimacy? If not, what role should be envisaged for trade unions as members of 'civil society'? There is also the more controversial, but now not unfamiliar, claim that global capitalism is eroding, not only workers' welfare,[7] but also national democratic participation.[8] This raises the further question whether such an eventuality can be avoided and, if so, how this is to be achieved.

In an era of globalization, there is an increasing tendency to look to international and regional institutions to assist in providing answers.[9] In the sphere of industrial relations, the ILO is the most obvious source of guidance. There is no ILO instrument which deals specifically with the appropriate scope of a right to strike. Nevertheless, the jurisprudence developed under ILO auspices on the subject of 'freedom of association' indicates that workers have a civil, political, and socio-economic entitlement to defend their interests through collective action. The ILO also instructs States to engage in 'tripartite' consultation with management and labour when designing legislation relating to this entitlement. This is not, however, the same message that is relayed through the Council of Europe, which recognizes a more limited right to strike. Moreover, the European Union has abstained from providing any such concrete direction.

In this book, it is suggested that differences in the approach of these organizations can be linked to the perception that each serves a distinctive function, embedded in the historical context in which its constitution was designed and has been amended. Such differences also arise from their divergent approaches to standard-setting and monitoring, which reflect a particular institutional appreciation of the appropriate forms of international and European governance. The ILO Constitution blends the notion of respect for civil liberties with recognition of the legitimacy of workers' political claims and socio-economic demands. Moreover, the

[7] Discussed by Sunmonu, H.A., 'Contemporary Challenges for Labour Standards Resulting from Globalization' in Sengenberger, W., and Campbell, D. (eds.), *International Labour Standards and Economic Interdependence* (Geneva: International Institute for Labour Studies, 1994), 110; and *Building Workers' Rights into the Global Trading System* (Brussels: ICFTU, 1999).

[8] An example being Dryzek, J.S., *Democracy in Capitalist Times: Ideals, Limits and Struggles* (New York/Oxford: OUP, 1996).

[9] See on this trend Fox, G.H., and Roth, B.R. (eds.), *Democratic Governance and International Law* (Cambridge: CUP, 2000); and Held, D., *Democracy and the Global Order: From the Modern State to Cosmopolitan Governance* (Cambridge: Polity Press, 1995).

ILO has a tripartite constitution which admits employers and workers as representatives of 'civil society', but makes negligible efforts to engage other Non-governmental Organizations (NGOs). By contrast, the Council of Europe privileges civil liberties and political freedoms at the expense of socio-economic rights. A wider range of 'civil society' is consulted on social standard-setting and can participate in the supervisory mechanisms, but their influence is minuscule compared to that possessed by the governments of its member States. Within the European Union, the European Community Treaty (ECT) seems to preclude legal regulation of the right to strike. Instead, this is ostensibly left to EU States to decide as a matter of domestic politics. The reality, however, is that there is potential for incursion of EU law into national laws relating to industrial relations.

To this extent, a 'governance' framework provides a useful basis for examining, not only the contours of the 'right to strike' as it is presented as an international legal norm to national governments, but also the internal dynamics of transnational organizations which shape the content and communication of that norm. It is for this reason that this first chapter introduces issues concerning the right to strike in the light of contemporary debates over 'good governance', which arise at both the national and international level.

What is interesting is the extent to which these institutional biases are open to challenge and change, given the active interest of many in reforming international organizations to make them the paragons of 'good governance'. Without underestimating the limitations inherent in the entrenched structures and cultural norms of each institution, it is possible that ongoing debate over ideal forms of international and European governance, within and between these organizations, may lead to a gradual convergence of approach to promotion of the right to strike. This convergence may not necessitate identical treatment of the right. There may be scope for complementary rather than the same standards. Nevertheless, the result could be greater consistency between the standards set at the global and at the European level. What the substance of the right to strike will be after such convergence remains difficult to predict. A crucial question for workers is whether there will be a 'levelling up' to ILO standards or diminishing protection of those who organize or participate in industrial action.

I.   THE RIGHT TO STRIKE: ANACHRONISTIC OR CONTEMPORARY ISSUE?

In a book on the 'right to strike', it is vital to clarify the sense in which that term is being used. In particular, legal responses to industrial action are not to be confused with the 'social phenomenon' itself.[10] Nevertheless, the

---

[10] Kahn-Freund, O., and Hepple, B., *Laws Against Strikes: International Comparisons in Social Policy* (London: The Fabian Society, 1972), 5.

pertinence of these legal responses has to be understood against the back-drop of the actual incidence of strikes in contemporary industrial relations. Moreover, it is not only the ongoing use of strikes by workers which renders this a topical subject of study, but also the impact that legal responses may have on the incidence of such action.

A.   CONTEXT AND DEFINITION

Employment is usually arranged by means of an individual contract of employment. The use of the term 'contract' suggests a consensual bargain between two parties capable of entering into mutual agreement. A worker supplies an employer's demand for labour. An employer satisfies the work-er's need for wages. However, it has been observed that this arrangement masks the underlying social reality, namely that 'the very essence of the employment problem is subordination, the very weakness of the worker'.[11] This social 'power' stems from employers' ability to affect outcomes so that their preferences take precedence over those of workers.[12] While the inter-ests of workers and employers will not always conflict,[13] where they do so it is the employer's objectives which are likely to prevail.

The financial ability to employ another suggests a degree of prosperity, which in turn gives rise to 'greater access to information, greater mobility, greater flexibility in the deployment of resources, control of the media, superior status and greater influence within society at large'.[14] This can enable employers to impose effective sanctions upon employees who fail to agree to their terms. It can also be observed that the contract of employment is less and less likely to be a contract between individuals of comparable bargaining power. More often, the employer is not another individual, but a corporation whose powers are all the more extensive. The manager who conducts the company's business is, of course, an individual, but it is unlikely that such a manager will empathize with the circumstances of the worker. The manager's personal success and career trajectory will be bound to the success of the employer and the manager's decisions will be backed by the power customarily exercised by cumulative capital. The result is that an individual employee has little opportunity to bargain over terms and

---

[11] Wedderburn, Lord, 'Labour Law and the Individual in Post-Industrial Societies' in Wedderburn, Lord, Rood, M., Lyon-Caen, A., Däubler, W., and van der Heijen, P. (eds.), *Labour Law in the Post-Industrial Era* (Dartmouth: Aldershot, 1994), 44.

[12] This definition of 'power' is derived from that used in Strange, S., *The Retreat of the State: The Diffusion of Power in the World Economy* (Cambridge: CUP, 1996), 17.

[13] E.g. 'if a firm goes bankrupt, employers and employees both suffer losses': Hyman, R., *Strikes* (4th edn., London: Macmillan, 1989), 113. However, there remain certain issues upon which employers and employees are unlikely easily to agree. They include the distribution of profits, security of employment, and control over decisions concerning work.

[14] See Burkitt, B., 'Excessive Trade Union Power: Existing Reality or Contemporary Myth?' (1981) 12 *Industrial Relations Journal* 65; also Hendy, J., and Walton, M., 'An Individual Right to Union Representation in International Law' (1997) 26 *ILJ* 205, 206.

conditions of employment, and may be vulnerable to arbitrary and unfair treatment.[15] There are exceptions where an employee possesses a valuable or rare skill, which allows that person to demand high pay, excellent working conditions, and to enjoy considerable social status. This notion of the 'affluent worker' has emerged as part of the post-Fordist split between a primary and secondary workforce,[16] but that worker is far from invulnerable. Issues of fair pay, fair treatment at work, and job security arise even for the highly skilled.[17]

Where *individual* contracts of employment allow little scope for employees to influence the conditions under which they work,[18] *collective* action appears to present a solution. Collective bargaining may take place with a number of employers at a 'sectoral' level, with a single employer or related employers at the company level, or with a manager at a particular workplace. In this manner, workers have been able to co-ordinate their demands and strategies. One tool in collective bargaining is the use or, more commonly, the threat of a 'strike'.

A 'strike' is usually taken to consist of the simultaneous and co-ordinated withdrawal of labour by workers.[19] The term is most commonly used to refer to the total cessation of work, but may also encompass a 'go slow', 'overtime ban', or any other partial stoppage of work. The productivity of an employer's business is based upon the provision of labour. The threatened or actual, partial or complete withdrawal of this vital resource may extract concessions from an employer which would otherwise not be contemplated.

Workers may take action aimed at influencing the conduct not only of their own employer but also of another person or business which will be affected by the withdrawal of their labour, for example by reason of dependence on the supplies they provide. This is known as 'secondary' action, which may be taken in 'sympathy' with another strike. The classic example, as in the case of 'the Liverpool dockers', is the refusal to cross a picket line.[20] A 'picket' is a protest organized outside the workplace (or the employer's place of business) which is designed to bring the strike to the notice of other persons and deter them from doing business with that employer. Another aim of industrial action may be to influence government policy or prompt

---

[15] This 'case for collective rights' is also made in Novitz, T., 'International Protection of the Right to Strike', Oxford D.Phil. thesis, 1998; and Novitz and Skidmore, n.6 above, 2–4.

[16] See further on this and other trends in patterns of employment Supiot, A., *Beyond Employment: Changes in Work and the Future of Labour Law in Europe* (Oxford: OUP, 2001), chap. 2.

[17] Bottomore, T., 'Citizenship and Social Class: Forty Years On' in Marshall, T.H., and Bottomore, T., *Citizenship and Social Class* (London: Pluto Press, 1992), 75–6.

[18] For a more detailed explanation see Veneziani, B., 'The Evolution of the Contract of Employment' in Hepple, n.1 above, 62–7.

[19] Hiller, E.T., *The Strike: A Study in Collective Action* (Chicago, Ill.: University of Chicago Press, 1928), 12; see also Kahn-Freund and Hepple, n.10 above, 4.

[20] See Atleson, J., 'The Voyage of the Neptune Jade: Transnational Labour Solidarity and the Obstacles of Domestic Law' in Conaghan *et al.*, n.6 above, esp. at 382–3.

legislative reform, on the basis that governments will respond to the inconvenience experienced by consumers and may make concessions to prevent further costs to business.

Strikes may be organized through trade unions or may be the result of a joint but informal decision of workers outside an institutional framework.[21] In either case, the persuasive power of a strike usually lies in collective action, which has more impact than withdrawal of labour by a solitary worker. It is for this reason that the organizers of (or participants in) a strike will often place pressure upon others to join or support the action. Sometimes this is achieved through the mechanism of union rules, which oblige trade union members to abide by a majority decision in favour of a strike. In addition, picketing and other forms of informal pressure are not uncommon. Treatment of so-called 'scabs' has been a matter of controversy, as it reveals an apparent conflict between the interests of the individual and the collectivity.[22] Linked to this is the 'free-rider' problem, namely the desire of striking workers to avoid conferring benefits on others who are unwilling to join them.[23] In part, this reluctance is due to their appreciation of risks associated with participation in industrial action. Workers intend the withdrawal of their labour to be temporary. They do not want to lose their jobs entirely, but merely to use the short-term withdrawal of their labour as a bargaining tool. They have too much to lose if they are out of work for any significant period of time. By contrast, this is not always the view taken by employers, who may wish to replace striking workers with more pliable employees.[24]

Employers have also been known to rely on their own tactical weapon, the 'lock-out'. A lock-out takes place when an employer deliberately excludes workers from their workplace, and refuses to pay them for the availability of their labour. This may be done as an offensive strategy to keep wage and other claims to a minimum, especially when bargaining is due to commence at the expiry of a collective agreement. It may even be used as a method by which unilaterally to change terms and conditions of employment.[25] An

[21] For a detailed discussion of the latter, commonly known as 'wild-cat' strikes, see Kahn-Freund and Hepple, n.10 above, 6–8. See also Jacobs, A.T.J.M., 'The Law of Strikes and Lock-Outs' in Blanpain, R., and Engels, C. (eds.), *Comparative Labour Law and Industrial Relations in Industrialized Market Economies* (5th edn., Deventer: Kluwer, 1993), 428.

[22] Shenfield, A., *What Right to Strike? With Commentaries by Cyril Grunfeld and Sir Leonard Neal* (London: Institute of Employment Affairs, 1986), 9–12.

[23] See for a classic discussion of this issue Laski, H.J., *Trade Unions in the New Society* (London: Allen & Unwin, 1950), 150.

[24] Lord Devlin took note of this point in *Rookes v Barnard* [1964] AC 1129 at 1204. See also Aaron, B., 'Methods of Industrial Action: Courts, Administrative Agencies and Legislatures' in Aaron, B., and Wedderburn, Lord (eds.), *Industrial Conflict: A Comparative Legal Survey* (London: Longmans, 1972), 83.

[25] For such strategies see Miller, K., and Woolfson, C., 'Timex: Industrial Relations and the Use of Law in the 1990s' (1994) 23 *ILJ* 209; and Thusing, G., 'Recent Developments in German Labor Law: Freedom of Association, Industrial Action and Collective Bargaining' (1998) 9 *Indiana International and Comparative Law Review* 47 at 52–7. A recent example in the UK was the lock-out of workers at Friction Dynamics after they had taken strike action for one

employer may also use a lock-out as part of a defensive strategy, in response to a strike.

It has been said that there should be a degree of parity in the legal treatment of strikes and lock-outs. For example, it was observed in 1925 that:

Whether we like it or not, we shall have in the industry of the future, on the one hand Trade Unions with the strike as their final weapon in any dispute, and on the other hand the Employers' Federation with the lock-out as their final weapon. The less frequently either weapon is used, the better for all concerned, for each is like a boomerang, capable of injuring others, and exceedingly harmful to both sides, although the side which loses tends to suffer the most.[26]

This statement appears to assume that both the strike and the lock-out are forms of 'industrial weaponry' designed to extract concessions from one's opponent in bargaining; that they are therefore equivalent and are to be treated with parity.

This can be disputed on the basis that the two are not comparable, due to the imbalance of bargaining power between the parties. Most employers will have other bargaining strategies open to them,[27] while the strike may constitute the workers' only means by which to achieve their objectives. For this reason, others have considered that the right to lock out need not be given the same priority as the right to strike, in terms of legal status.[28] This book focuses primarily on international standards relating to the workers' right to strike rather than an employer's right to lock out. In part this is due to the fact that there is little international or European jurisprudence on the appropriate legal treatment of lock-outs, but it is also because the relative importance of the strike for workers and the lock-out for employers makes these two forms of industrial weaponry distinguishable.

B.   THE INCIDENCE OF INDUSTRIAL ACTION IN THE TWENTY-FIRST CENTURY

It has been asserted, even by those who favour access to collective action, that strikes are likely to be increasingly infrequent and ineffective. This is

---

week, during which time the employer stated that he wished to imposed a 15% paycut. See 'The Wrong Friends', *Guardian*, 20 Mar. 2002.

[26] Chisholm, A., *Labour's Magna Charta: A Critical Study of the Labour Clauses of the Peace Treaty and of the Draft Conventions and Recommendations of the Washington International Labour Conference* (London: Longmans, Green & Co., 1925), 83.

[27] E.g. restructuring of a workplace, movement of plant, and dismissal of workers, as discussed in Burkitt, n.14 above. See also Hutton, W., *The State We're In* (London: Jonathan Cape, 1995), at 105; and Macfarlane, L.J., *The Right to Strike* (Harmondsworth: Penguin Books, 1981), 76.

[28] See Samuel, L., *Fundamental Social Rights: Case Law of the European Social Charter* (Strasbourg: Council of Europe Publishing, 1997), 181–3; also Committee of Experts, *The Prevention and Settlement of Industrial Conflict in the Community Member States* (the Treu Report) (Luxembourg: EC Commission, 1984), 85.

often attributed to changes in modes of work, especially in Western Europe, where the picture is drawn of a move towards a 'knowledge' economy in which workers can be given greater autonomy and responsibility for tasks than was the case in the 'Fordist' workplace.[29] There are an increasing number of 'dependent businesses' as opposed to 'dependent labour', in which workers bear the financial risks of the non-performance of a contract. One third of the working population in Britain no longer comes within the coverage of established employment-law protection.[30] More workers are employed on a part-time or temporary basis and are unlikely to achieve effective union organization as readily as those who were employed full-time in traditional industrial workplaces.[31] Such workers also tend to be women or people from ethnic minorities or immigrant communities, who may have experienced exclusion from traditional white male-dominated unions.[32] On this basis it has been asserted that 'the social and political world classically imagined by labour law is disappearing, gradually in some places and quite abruptly in others'.[33]

These structural changes to the world of work need to be addressed,[34] but it is important also to acknowledge that they are not as pervasive as has been suggested, for example, in the UK.[35] There is arguably too great a tendency to see unions as permanently in decline, and unable to address flaws concerning democratic deficits. The failure to take the interests of women and ethnic minorities into consideration 'has been shared by almost all policy-making institutions' and, to the extent that unions are actively

---

[29] Collins, H., 'Regulating the Employment Relation for Competitiveness' (2001) 30 *ILJ* 17.

[30] See Burchell, B., Deakin, S., and Honey, S., *The Employment Status of Workers in Non-Standard Employment* (London: DTI, 1999); and Collins, H., 'Independent Contractors and the Challenge of Vertical Disintegration of Employment Protection Laws' (1990) 10 *OJLS* 353.

[31] See on unconventional forms of work: Ewing, K. (ed.), *Working Life: A New Perspective on Labour Law* (London: Institute of Employment Rights, 1996), 41–58; and Barbagelata, H., 'Different Categories of Workers and Labour Contracts' in Blanpain, R. (ed.), *Comparative Labour Law and Industrial Relations* (3rd edn., Deventer: Kluwer, 1987), 427–52.

[32] See Morris, A., 'Workers First, Women Second? Trade Unions and the Equality Agenda?' in Morris, A., and O'Donnell, T. (eds.), *Feminist Perspectives on Employment Law* (London: Cavendish, 1999); and Monoghan, K., *Challenging Race Discrimination at Work* (London: Institute of Employment Rights, 2000). Both these writers argue for greater trade union engagement with issues concerning sex and race discrimination, respectively. See on the historical inadequacies of trade union organizations in this respect Pelling, H., *A History of British Trade Unionism* (London: Macmillan, 1992), 316. On challenges for trade unions more generally see Olney, S., *Unions in a Changing World: Problems and Prospects in Selected Industrialized Countries* (Geneva: ILO, 1996).

[33] Klare, K., 'Horizons of Transformative Labour Law' in Conaghan *et al.*, n.6 above, 4.

[34] They are discussed further in Chap. 15 below at 340–67.

[35] 'Traditional patterns of industrial relations, based on collective bargaining and collective agreements, seem increasingly inappropriate and are in decline': *People, Jobs and Opportunity*, Cm 1810 (London: HMSO, 1992), para. 1.15. See also Touraine, A., 'Unionism as a Social Movement' in Lipset, S.M. (ed.), *Unions in Transition: Entering the Second Century* (San Francisco, Cal.: ICS Press, 1988), 153.

seeking to address previous omissions, it may be unreasonable to seek them out as the key transgressors.[36] Moreover, there can be and have been innovative attempts by workers to organize collectively in newer non-traditional workplaces, with varying degrees of success.[37] A recent survey of US workers indicates that while workers favour 'co-operative' relations with management, they still want 'more participation and an independent say at the workplace'.[38] It has been argued by Frances Raday, and is also suggested here, that a decline in union membership, collective bargaining, or industrial action may more readily be linked to legal restriction than 'structural inevitability'.[39] It is also important to appreciate that the British story of decline[40] is not a uniform international phenomenon. This becomes apparent when one investigates further the available statistics relating to industrial action globally.

The ILO keeps and records statistics relating to the incidence of strikes, lock-outs, and other action due to industrial disputes.[41] Such statistics are compiled on the basis of national records, which are not always reliable and are sometimes not even supplied. For example, no data are available on States such as Colombia, Myanmar, and Nigeria, which are frequently criticized by ILO supervisory bodies. The statistical records that are available indicate that, between 1970 and 2000, there was a substantial decline in days

---

[36] See Raday, F., 'The Decline of Union Power—Structural Inevitability or Policy Choice?' in Conaghan *et al.*, n.6 above, 355. She also cites the ILO–ICFTU Survey, *The Role of Trade Unions in Promoting Gender Equality and Protecting Vulnerable Women Workers* (Geneva: ILO, 1999). See also ICFTU, *Trade Unions Say No to Racism and Xenophobia* (Brussels: ICFTU, 2001). For a British critique of this 'transformative' process see Healy, G., and Kirton, G., 'Women, Power and Trade Union Government in the UK' (2000) 38 *BJIR* 343.

[37] For a US example, in the care industry, see Klare, n.33 above, 20–3; and by janitors, discussed by Ontiverso, M.L., 'A New Course for Labour Unions: Identity-Based Organizing as a Response to Globalization' in Conaghan *et al.*, n.6 above. See on the potential of unions to play a transformative role in fostering a cosmopolitan workforce Piore, M., *Beyond Individualism* (Cambridge, Mass.: Harvard University Press, 1995). More generally, as regards innovative organizing among women, see Rowbotham, S., and Mitter, S. (eds.), *Dignity and Daily Bread: New Forms of Economic Organising among Poor Women in the Third World and the First* (London: Routledge, 1994).

[38] Freeman, R.B., and Rogers, J., 'What Do Workers Want? Voice, Representation and Power in the American Workplace' in Eistreicher, S. (ed.), *Employee Representation in the Emerging Workplace: Alternatives/Supplements to Collective Bargaining* (Boston, Mass./The Hague: Kluwer, 1998), 23.

[39] See Raday, n.36 above; and Raday, F., 'Constitutionalisation of Labour Law' in Blanpain, B., and Weiss, M. (eds.), *The Changing Face of Labour Law and Industrial Relations: Liber Amicorum in Honour of Professor Clyde Summers* (Baden-Baden: Nomos Verlagsgesellschaft, 1993).

[40] See Brown, W., 'The Contraction of Collective Bargaining in Britain' (1993) 31 *BJIR* 189 and Cully, M., Woodland, S., O'Reilly, A., and Dix, G., *Britain at Work: As Depicted by the 1998 Employee Relations Survey* (London and New York: Routledge, 1999).

[41] These are to be found in the Labour Statistics Database operated by the ILO Bureau of Statistics, available on http://laborsta.ilo/ (accessed last on 1 Apr. 2002). In particular, Tables 9A, 9B, 9C, and 9D are of use. These statistics are compiled with reference to the Resolution concerning statistics of strikes, lock-outs, and other action due to labour disputes, adopted by the Fifteenth International Conference of Labour Statisticians (Geneva, 1993).

lost through strikes and lock-outs in industrialized nations, such as Australia, Italy, Japan, and the UK.[42] However, this trend is far from uniform. For example, in Denmark, the number of days lost through such action has risen significantly. In certain newly industrialized States, there also seems to be a rise in the incidence of industrial action which may well coincide with the gradual growth of workers' movements in those countries.[43]

British strikes usually concern such matters as pay,[44] safety,[45] and job security.[46] The framing of 'trade disputes' around such issues seems to be, at least in part, due to the restrictions imposed by British legislation, which make the availability of 'immunities' for industrial action contingent on a narrow scope of lawful concerns. It is not lawful to organize or take part in 'political' strikes or 'secondary action' in support of claims made by workers against another employer.[47] Other motivations for industrial action are sometimes suspected. The 'New Labour' government has suggested that the wave of strikes in the British public sector reflects the attitudes of union leaders who seek to 'wreck' the introduction of 'public–private partnerships'.[48] However, unions have become cautious about the manner in which ballot papers are phrased and the ways in which the aims of strikes are publicized, seeking to avoid the taint of illegality.[49]

Elsewhere in Europe, industrial disputes also tend to centre upon pay and redundancies, particularly in the public sector.[50] Nevertheless, there is

[42] See, e.g., Table 9C, n. 41 above, which records in each year the total of days not worked, by measuring the sum of the actual working days during which work would normally have been carried out by each worker if there had been no stoppage, based on an 8-hour working day.

[43] Examples are Indonesia and Thailand. See again the statistics recorded in respect of these States in Table 9C, n. 41 above.

[44] See, e.g., 'Express Rocked by Pay Dispute', Guardian, 15 Mar. 2002; 'Strike Threat to Councils as Pay Talks Break Down', Guardian, 28 Feb. 2002; 'Union Leader Urges Council Workers to Reject Pay Offer', Guardian, 20 Mar. 2002; 'Is Local Government Slipping Down the Public Sector Pay League?', Guardian, 20 Mar. 2002.

[45] 'Strikes at Airport to be Stepped Up', Guardian, 15 Feb. 2002; 'Jobcentre Security Strike Could Spread', Guardian, 5 Mar. 2002.

[46] 'ITV News in Scotland Hit By Strike', Guardian, 30 Mar. 2000; 'Ford Faces Strike at Dagenham', Guardian, 3 Nov. 2000; 'Vauxhall Plants Hit by Strike', Guardian, 24 Feb. 2001; 'Strike Action Vote Threatens RSC Productions', Guardian, 31 Aug. 2001; 'No Strikes for Marconi', Guardian 15 Sept. 2001; 'Union Resists BT Samurai's Job Cuts', Guardian, 5 Dec. 2001; 'Red-faced Postal Chief Drops Threat of 30,000 Job Cuts', Guardian, 15 Dec. 2001; 'Transco to Cut 2,400 Jobs', Guardian, 7 Feb. 2002; 'Union Threat to IT Deal', Guardian, 14 Feb. 2002; 'Strike Threat as BA Cuts 5,800 Jobs', Guardian, 14 Feb. 2002.

[47] Trade Union and Labour Relations (Consolidation) Act 1992, s. 244. See, e.g., Mercury Communications v Scott-Garner [1983] IRLR 494; and Dimbleby & Sons v NUJ [1984] IRLR 161.

[48] 'Battle of the "Mods and Wreckers"', Guardian, 18 Feb. 2002; 'Stalemate Between Labour and Unions May Mean Permanent Rift', Financial Times, 12 Mar. 2002. This has arguably affected the UK Government's response to recent rail strikes. See, e.g., 'Fines Against Rail Companies Waived in Light of Strikes', Guardian, 7 Feb. 2002.

[49] See, e.g., the drafting of the ballot paper at issue in Associated British Ports v TGWU [1989] IRLR 291; [1989] IRLR 305; [1989] IRLR 399.

[50] See for discussion of this evidence Gall, G., 'A Review of Strike Activity in Western Europe at the End of the Second Millennium' (1999) 21 Employee Relations 357.

additional potential in certain European States for workers to use industrial action for a wider range of purposes, such as protest against labour-law reforms.[51] There is also greater scope for cross-border solidarity action, that is, action in support of another strike against another employer. Indeed, sometimes such action is taken in the framework of European-level collective bargaining, to secure a basic framework agreement with a European company or within an industry. Recourse to such action in continental Europe, rather than in Britain, may well be due to the extent to which secondary action is protected by law.[52]

Beyond Europe, unions have been actively involved in protesting against what they claim are anti-democratic practices by governments. One example was the general strike in Nigeria held in January 2002.[53] Another was the general strike initiated in Zimbabwe in March 2002, with the support of churches and national civic organizations, in protest at the manner in which elections were held and the imprisonment of the leader of the opposition.[54]

C.   THE RELEVANCE OF LEGAL RESPONSES TO INDUSTRIAL ACTION

There is no doubt that industrial action remains a contemporary 'social phenomenon', used in a variety of countries for a variety of reasons. What is less readily ascertainable is the impact which law has on the incidence of industrial action.

There are three potential legal responses to industrial action: suppression, toleration, and creation of a positive right to strike.[55] Suppression is rare but still occurs in certain States.[56] The second response, namely the creation of certain immunities from civil and criminal liability, is exemplified by UK law.[57] The inclusion of a positive right to strike is illustrated by the

---

[51] 'Italy Poised for a Shut-Down as Main Unions Begin Strike: Labour Reform Millions Against Proposals', *Financial Times*, 16 Feb. 2002. See also for discussion of the 2002 Spanish General Strike taken on 20 June 2002 in respect, *inter alia*, of the dismantling of protection for unfair dismissal, *Record of Proceedings* (Geneva: ILO, 2002) ILC, 90th Session, 17/44 per Mr Paz Lamigueiro (representative of Trade Unions International of Workers of Energy, Metal, Chemical, Oil and Allied Industries); and 12/43–12/44, per Mr Doz (workers' delegate, Spain).

[52] See Aaltonen, J., *International Secondary Industrial Action in the EU Member States* (Espoo: Metalli, 1999).

[53] 'Union Chief Held as Fuel Price Rise Fires Up Nigerians', *Guardian*, 17 Jan. 2001.

[54] 'Unions Warn of Zimbabwe Unrest', *Guardian*, 15 Mar. 2002; 'MDC Leader Charged with Treason', *Guardian*, 20 Mar. 2002; 'Jan Raath on Tsvangirai's Arrest', *The Times*, 20 Mar. 2002; 'ICFTU Calls for Solidarity Over Harassment of Zimbabwe Union Leader', ICFTU Press Release, 27 Mar. 2002.

[55] Kahn-Freund, O., *The Right to Strike: Its Scope and Limitations* (Strasbourg: Council of Europe, 1974), 3.

[56] Examples are Liberia, Myanmar, and Saudi Arabia. See ILO, *Global Report: Your Voice at Work* (Geneva: ILO, 2000), 38.

[57] See, e.g., the UK Trade Union and Labour Relations (Consolidation) Act 1992, ss. 219 and 244. For discussion of the implications of this immunity see Novitz and Skidmore, n.6 above, 130–3.

French, Greek, Italian, and Portuguese constitutions.[58] These legal responses may well be based on an appreciation of the ethical claims associated with a right to strike. For example, phrasing an entitlement to strike as a positive legal right suggests that this is a legitimate course of action. A negative immunity seems to connote a mere exception to other legal norms.[59] Nevertheless, where such immunities are generously interpreted, there may be no material difference in the consequences of this legal phrasing.[60]

There is certainly no straightforward causal relation between attempts to suppress strikes by legal means and the actual incidence of industrial action. This is evident in the context of protests against authoritarian regimes. In such circumstances, there is a possibility that an effective strike will have more impact upon the development of the law than the law has upon the outcome of a particular strike. An example is the series of strikes organized by the South African trade union organizations, the Congress of South African Trade Unions (COSATU) and the National Council of Trade Unions (NACTU), which led to the eventual repeal of the South African Labour Relations Amendment Act 1988.[61]

Nevertheless, where unions wish to play a social role within the limits of the law, legal constraints may be more influential. For example, UK prison staff have indicated that they wish to take industrial action over pay, but recognize that they are prevented by law from doing so.[62] Workers are likely to be deterred from participating in a strike if they are aware that the result of doing so, under the law, can be that they lose their jobs, suffer a term of imprisonment, are denied social security payments, or are bankrupted by civil liability.[63] Similarly, trade union organizers are less likely to instigate industrial action where the potential cost of doing so is a heavy financial penalty, the confiscation of trade union assets, or dissolution of their organization. It is also possible for the law to diminish the effect of concessions

---

[58] A thorough recent survey of constitutional protection of labour rights in the EU is to be found in Clauwaert, S., *Fundamental Social Rights in the European Union: Comparative Tables and Documents* (Brussels: ETUI, 1998).

[59] Welch, R., *The Right to Strike: A Trade Union View* (London: Institute of Employment Rights, 1991), 36; and Welch, R., 'Judges and the Law in British Industrial Relations: Towards a European Right to Strike' (1995) 4 *Social and Legal Studies* 175 at 192. See also on this debate Ewing, K.D., 'The Right to Strike' (1986) 15 *ILJ* 143 and Ewing, K.D., 'Rights and Immunities in British Labour Law' (1988) 10 *Comparative Labor Law Journal* 1; and Lord Wedderburn, *The Worker and the Law* (3rd edn., Harmondsworth: Penguin Books, 1986), 847–56.

[60] This was the view taken in Lord Donovan, *Royal Commission Report on Trade Union and Employers' Associations 1965–1968*, Cmnd. 3623 (London: HMSO, 1968), more commonly known as the Donovan Commission Report, discussed at para. 935.

[61] Discussed at length in ILO, *Report of the Fact-Finding Conciliation Commission on Freedom of Association concerning the Republic of South Africa: Prelude to Change: Industrial Relations in South Africa* (Geneva: ILO, 1992).

[62] 'Prison Staff "Ready for Industrial Action"', *Financial Times*, 18 Mar. 2002.

[63] See for discussion of individual workers' vulnerability to sanctions for participation in industrial action Ewing, 'The Right to Strike', n. 59 above, and Ewing, K.D., *The Right to Strike* (Oxford: Clarendon Press, 1991).

reached by way of industrial action. This is ably illustrated by *Universe Tankships Inc of Monrovia v ITWF*, in which a contract secured by way of industrial action was held to have been agreed under duress, and was therefore unenforceable.[64]

Furthermore, where a strike has been deemed illegal by reason of legislation or the decision of a court, this may be viewed by a government as a licence to take special action against strikers.[65] For instance, once the British miners' strike had been held to be illegal, the government could justify devoting extensive public funds to its demise.[66] In 1972, Kahn-Freund and Hepple commented somewhat optimistically that they doubted that any State, outside a totalitarian dictatorship, could suppress stoppages of work.[67] UK Conservative governments from 1979 to 1997 did their very best to contradict them.[68]

Indeed, the State may be seen as a longstanding silent participant in industrial relations. Even when the State ostensibly leaves the social partners to bargain 'autonomously', it provides the legal framework within which those negotiations can take place. For example, by refusing to modify a decision established by the courts, a legislature or executive is not necessarily acting in a manner which can be described as 'neutral' or 'impartial'. Instead, implicit consent is given to exploitation of any power imbalance which operates in favour of one of the social partners.[69] Indeed, the issues surrounding legal responses to strikes can be linked to current debates over 'governance', which continue to excite interest at national, regional, and global levels.

II.   TOPICAL ISSUES RELATING TO 'GOOD GOVERNANCE'

The notion that a State is simply ruled by top-down 'government' has gradually come to be replaced by the ideal of less coercive 'governance'.[70] The effectiveness and legitimacy of law arise, not only from the fear of

---

[64] [1983] AC 366.

[65] See Whelan, C.J., 'State Intervention, Major Disputes and the Role of Law: Contingency Planning and the Use of Troops' in Wedderburn, Lord, and Murphy, W.T. (eds.), *Labour and the Community: Perspectives for the 1980s* (London: Institute of Advanced Legal Studies, 1982), 37.

[66] *Taylor and Foulstone v NUM (Yorkshire Area)* [1984] IRLR 445. It has been estimated that the direct cost to the State of defeating the UK miners' strike was well over £3 billion, policing costs alone being over £225 million. See Hain, P., *Political Strikes: The State and Trade Unionism in Britain* (London: Viking, 1986), 139.

[67] Kahn-Freund and Hepple, n.10 above, 5.

[68] Hutton, n.27 above, 94 and 97–8.

[69] Cf. Raz, J., 'Liberalism, Autonomy and the Politics of Neutral Concern' (1982) 8 *Midwest Studies in Philosophy* 89, especially at 94–8.

[70] See for discussion of this literature Rosenau, J.N., 'Governance, Order and Change in World Politics' in Rosenau, J.N., and Czempiel, E.-O. (eds.), *Governance Without Government: Order and Change in World Politics* (Cambridge: CUP, 1992), 4; and Jachtenfuchs, M., 'The Governance Approach to European Integration' (2001) 39 *JCMS* 245.

sanction, but also the voluntary acceptance of legal norms by a variety of social actors. This involves a wider purview than that of the executive, legislature, and courts. Instead, a focus on 'governance' suggests that we look towards the ways in which norms are formulated and implemented by business interests, workers' organizations, churches, and other institutions of 'civil society'.[71] This notion of a 'decentred State' was an idea taken from the descriptive social sciences which is now given a normative dimension.[72] It is anticipated that a process of 'good governance' will achieve the support of all these interested parties and will, thereby, secure the desired end-product, that being a stable and fair society.

The content of 'good governance' is controversial. At the very least, it may be said to be the 'rule of law' which allows for law-making to be accessible, transparent, coherent, and effective.[73] Beyond this, it is often claimed that 'democracy' is becoming a universal standard. This is viewed as the result of the collapse of the Communist Soviet bloc at the end of the 1980s and the rapid move to 'democratization' by various countries. It is also said to follow from the basic precepts of international human rights law, such as the statement in Article 21(1) of the Universal Declaration of Human Rights that '[e]veryone has the right to take part in the government of his country, directly or through freely chosen representatives'.[74]

This trend raises important questions relating to the appropriate content of 'democracy', which as yet have not been authoritatively answered. Three broad models or 'variants' are suggested below. These are 'representative', 'participatory', and 'deliberative' forms of democracy. They present alternative mechanisms by which 'good governance' may be achieved: electoral representation, direct participation of interest groups, and open

---

[71] Habermas, J., *Between Facts and Norms: Contributions to a Discourse Theory of Law and Democracy* (trans. Rehg, W., Cambridge, Mass.: MIT, 1996), 367 describes 'civil society' as being 'composed of those more or less spontaneously emergent associations, organizations and movements that, attuned to how societal problems resonate in the private spheres, distill and transmit such reactions in an amplified form to the public sphere'. Mertus, J., 'From Legal Transplants to Transformative Justice: Human Rights and the Promise of Transnational Civil Society' (1999) 14 *American University International Law Review* 1335, 1337 defines this as 'the social, cultural and ethical arrangements of modern industrial society considered apart from state control'.

[72] Münch, R., *Understanding Modernity: Toward a New Perspective Going Beyond Durkheim and Weber* (London: Routledge, 1988); see also Kooiman, J. (ed.), *Modern Governance: New Government–Society Interactions* (London: Sage, 1993).

[73] See for discussion of these elements Botchway, F.N., 'Good Governance: The Old, the New, the Principle and the Elements' (2001) 13 *Florida Journal of International Law* 159. Also see Mertus, n.71 above, 1353–7.

[74] Franck, T., 'The Emerging Right to Democratic Governance' (1992) 86 *American Journal of International Law* 46; and Franck, T.M., *Fairness in International Law and Institutions* (Oxford: Clarendon Press, 1995). It is however important to be aware that Marxist theorists regarded State socialism as a more 'direct' or 'delegative' form of democracy. See for a useful examination of this claim Held, D., *Models of Democracy* (2nd edn., Oxford: Polity, 1996), chap. 4.

deliberation. Each has particular implications for legal protection of the right to strike.

A.   REPRESENTATIVE DEMOCRACY

In Western Europe, there is general familiarity with the concept of 'representative' democracy. Given the practical impossibility of securing the 'direct' democracy experienced by the Athenian *polis*, the principle of majority rule has been transposed into complex electoral systems whereby groups of voters elect candidates to represent them in national government.[75] The role of the elected government is to act in what is usually demarcated as the 'public sphere',[76] taking action for the common good that overrides the particular vested interests of certain groupings within the populace. The government is 'accountable' to the electorate in that, should there be dissatisfaction with the laws enacted or the policies pursued, it may be voted out of office at the next election. This is commonly regarded as a 'procedural' view of democracy.[77]

It may also be complemented by a more 'substantive' approach to representative democracy, according to which it is considered that, for this electoral system to be effective (and legitimate), subsidiary human rights should be protected.[78] These are commonly said to be 'civil liberties', such as freedom of speech and rights to form associations and 'political rights' of participation. Moreover, as a device to resist 'dictatorship by the majority', the interests of the minority should be protected through recognition of fundamental rights which may be written into a constitution. This democratic framework envisages a 'separation of powers' between the elected government and the judiciary. The elected government may pursue its policies by *imperium* or *dominium*, that is by law-making or public spending,[79]

---

[75]   Schumpeter, J., *Capitalism, Socialism and Democracy* (6th edn., London: Unwin, 1987), 269.

[76]   A mark of an authoritarian regime is taken to be a desire to control all aspects of citizens' personal lives, in ways that many find unpalatable. Witness George Orwell's novel *1984* (London: Secker and Warburg, 1949). However, for those critical of 'State neutrality', the distinction between the public and private spheres remains questionable. For a useful recent critique see Williams, L.A., 'Beyond Labour Law's Parochialism: A Re-envisioning of the Discourse of Redistribution' in Conaghan *et al.*, n.6 above.

[77]   Marks describes this as 'low-intensity democracy'. See Marks, S., *The Riddle of all Constitutions: International Law, Democracy and the Critique of Ideology* (Oxford: OUP, 2000), chap. 3. For use of the 'procedural' and 'substantive' terminology used here see Fox, G.H., and Nolte, G., 'Intolerant Democracies' (1995) 36 *Harvard International Law Journal* 1; also Burchill, R., 'The Developing Law of International Democracy' (2001) 64 *MLR* 123.

[78]   See Dworkin, R., *Taking Rights Seriously* (London: Ducksworth, 1977). By contrast, others have viewed constitutional protection of such rights as being in tension with a liberal democratic model, an example being Michelman, F., 'Law's Republic' (1988) 97 *Yale Law Journal* 1493 at 1499.

[79]   See Freedland, M., 'Employment Policy' in Davies, P., Lyon-Caen, A., Sciarra, S., and Simitis, S. (eds.), *European Community Labour Law—Principles and Perspectives: Liber Amicorum Lord Wedderburn* (Oxford: Clarendon Press, 1996).

but the judiciary will check that in doing so it respects the existing constitutional framework and the rights deemed essential to that framework.[80]

It has also been observed that, as suffrage became universal, socio-
economic rights such as health care and social security became established
as prerequisites of legitimate democracy.[81] Indeed, representative democracies can be seen as forming a continuum, which may be labelled 'libertarian' at one extreme and 'socialist' at the other, depending on the kinds of
socio-economic rights they respect and the extent to which these impinge on
contractual freedoms and property rights exercised through markets.
Within emergent European democracies, strikes were initially the subject
of stringent prohibitions but were gradually recognized as a permissible, or
even fundamental, entitlement of workers.[82] Within some States, a right to
strike is regarded as a useful adjunct to collective bargaining, and in others
as something akin to a right to political protest.[83] The relevance of this
categorization will be elaborated upon further in Part I.

Within the classic representative democratic model, the aim is to appoint
those who exercise government powers and to constrain such powers. Less
attention appears to be paid to the 'private' power exercised, for example,
by business. This attention deficit is perceived as problematic by those who
point to the escalation in 'globalization of market forces' that place many
aspects of the domestic economy outside national governmental control.[84]
While the definition of 'globalization' is far from straightforward, in this
context the term may be taken to encompass a number of 'component
trends', such as:

trade liberalisation and a rising volume of international trade; currency market
liberalization and an enormous increase in currency transactions; liberalization of
the rules governing foreign investment and cross-border capital flows; the emergence and dominance of multinational enterprises (MNEs); increased manufacturing in developing nations; heightened international wage competition; and steady
increases in cross-border migration.[85]

---

[80] See, e.g., the opinion of Madison CJ in *Marbury v Madison* 1 US 137 (1803) discussed by
Nino, C.S., *The Constitution of Deliberative Democracy* (New Haven, Conn., & London: Yale
University Press, 1996), chap. 7. For ongoing debate on how this is to be achieved in the US
context see Forbath, W.E., 'The Constitution and the Obligations of Government to Secure the
Material Preconditions for a Good Society: Constitutional Welfare Rights: A History, Critique
and Reconstruction' (2001) 69 *Fordham Law Review* 1821.

[81] See Marshall, T.H., *Citizenship and Social Class* (Cambridge: CUP, 1950), discussed
further in Chap. 2 below at 39–40.

[82] See Hepple, B., 'The Countries: A Short Guide' in Hepple, n.1 above, 301–29.

[83] Contrast the treatment of strikes in Germany and Italy, summarized in Clauwaert, n.58
above.

[84] See, e.g., Strange, n.12 above; Sassen, S., *Losing Control? Sovereignty in an Age of Globalization* (New York: Columbia University Press, 1996); and Trimble, P., 'Globalization, International Institutions, and the Erosion of National Sovereignty and Democracy' (1997) 95
Michigan Law Review 144, esp. at 147–8.

[85] Klare, n.33 above, 5.

Apart from the control which business may wield in politics through donations to party funding and political campaigns, influence can also now be wielded through the credible threat of 'capital flight' or the promise of 'capital investment'. Where firms flee or simply do not invest in the first place, this is likely to affect tax revenues, limiting the resources available for public schemes. Moreover, the inability to 'deliver the goods in terms of employment and income jeopardises the popularity and ultimately the legitimacy of the government'.[86] The failure of a representative democratic model to recognize the significance of other social forces has called its utility into question.

B. Participatory Democracy

The limitations of the traditional 'representative' democratic model have led to challenge from those who question whether public government can be segregated so neatly from the private societal interests.[87] An early challenge of this kind came from those who argued for greater 'participatory' democracy. Recognizing a plurality of interests in society, these writers considered that these cannot be eclipsed merely by the election of a government by a majority vote.[88] Instead, effective government should appreciate the particular expertise of different interest groups and grant them representation in decision-making. The result has been advocacy of the 'corporatist' inclusion of worker and employer representation in government in order to create a 'balance of power' between the vested interests of capital and the collective power of labour.

One motivation for direct participation of employers' organizations and trade unions is to reduce the incidence of strikes and lock-outs, which diminish 'social peace' and thereby the credibility of governments. Where trade unions are involved in centralized tripartite decision-making bodies, there is less likelihood of political strikes.[89] Indeed, it has been claimed that

---

[86] Dryzek, n.8 above, 10–12 and 25. See also Bowles, S., and Gintis, H., *Democracy and Capitalism: Property, Community and the Contradictions of Modern Social Thought* (London: Routledge and Kegan Paul, 1996), 90; and Aman, A.C., 'Symposium: Globalization, Accountability, and the Future of Administrative Law: Introduction' (2001) 8 *Indiana Journal of Global Legal Studies* 341 at 345.

[87] Black, J.K., 'What Kind of Democracy Does the "Democratic Entitlement" Entail?' in Fox, G. H., and Roth, B.R. (eds.), *Democratic Governance and International Law* (Cambridge: CUP, 2000), esp. at 529.

[88] See Kelso, W.A., *American Democratic Theory: Pluralism and its Critics* (Westport, Conn./ London: Greenwood Press, 1978), 65–87, who provides criticism from a pluralist perspective; Sartori, G., *The Theory of Democracy Revisited* (Chatham: Chatham House Publishers, 1987), 324–8, who criticizes the 'rule of legislators'; and Lukes, S., *Essays in Social Theory* (London: Macmillan, 1977), 40, who questions whether a democratic mandate arises only from majority elections.

[89] Hence Pizzorno's theory of 'political exchange' as set out in Crouch, C., and Pizzorno, A. (eds.), *The Resurgence of Class Conflict in Western Europe Since 1909* (New York: Macmillan, 1978), ii. See also Korpi, W., *The Democratic Class Struggle* (London: Routledge and Kegan

industrial action may be the best 'barometer' of the actual condition of democratic rights and the extent to which government reflects the interests of workers, as well as those of capital.[90]

The arguments associated with participatory democracy have been extended by analogy to the workplace, where workers are 'governed' by employers. It is said that, within this setting, workers must also be given the opportunity to participate more directly in the decisions that affect their working lives.[91] This school of thought arguably demonstrates the emerging appreciation of 'governance' as multi-level, rather than State-oriented.[92] Furthermore, these participatory arrangements politicize a sphere treated by liberal representative democracy as 'private'.[93] We shall see that limited experiments in workplace democracy have been introduced via voluntary 'partnership' practices within companies, as well as EC Directives and national legislation on the provision of information and consultation to workers. These are discussed further in Chapter 3, alongside arguments that a right to strike is required to supplement such mechanisms, so as to ensure meaningful participation in workplace governance.[94]

There remain certain difficulties with the application of participatory democratic theory in 'public' governance. Some are concerned that corporatism may result in the co-option of trade unions, leading to employer or State control of their activities.[95] There are also potential problems associated with accountability and criteria for participation. Clearly, an elected government is the only candidate for electoral defeat should its policies prove unpopular; but the extent to which it can be considered responsible for the outcome of tripartite decisions remains in doubt. Therefore, it has been said that there should be some way in which business and labour representatives are accountable, at least to those they purport to represent.[96] For example, there must be some suitable procedure for election

Paul, 1983), 180–3; and Bean, R., *Comparative Industrial Relations: An Introduction to Cross-National Perspectives* (London/New York: Routledge, 1985), 135.

[90] Macfarlane, n.27 above, 196; Committee of Experts, *The Prevention and Settlement of Industrial Conflict in the Community Member States* (the Treu Report) (Luxembourg: Commission, 1984), 148.

[91] E.g. see Dahl, R.A., *A Preface to Economic Democracy* (Cambridge: Polity Press, 1985), chap. 4; Pateman, C., *Participation and Democratic Theory* (Cambridge: CUP, 1970); Gould, G.C., *Rethinking Democracy* (Cambridge: CUP, 1988).

[92] For contemporary argument for this form of 'corporate governance' see Finkin, M., 'Bridging the Representation Gap' (2001) 3 *University of Pennsylvania Journal of Labor and Employment Law* 391; and Jacoby, S.M., 'Employee Representation and Corporate Governance: A Missing Link' (2001) 3 *University of Pennsylvania Journal of Labor and Employment Law* 449.

[93] Dryzek, n.8 above, 59.

[94] See Chap. 3 below, at 57–9.

[95] See De Buen Unna, C., 'Mexican Trade Unionism in a Time of Transition' in Conaghan *et al.*, n.6 above; and Stotzky, I.P., 'Substantive Self-Determination: Democracy, Communicative Power and Inter/National Labor Rights: Suppressing the Beast' (1999) 53 *University of Miami Law Review* 883 at 884–90.

[96] As regards past failings in the representative capacities of trade unions see n.32 above.

of representatives and approval of policies. The dilemma is that State regulation of the union's participatory structure may stifle its independence and its credibility may be thereby diminished. There is also the possibility that the elaboration of legal requirements will limit the efficacy of action by such organizations.[97] A further barrier to accountability under corporatist arrangements is that they lead to agreements premised on bargaining and compromise between divergent interests of parties, against a background of threatened strikes and lock-outs. What is achieved may not be the most rational solution, but one which reflects a show of power.[98]

C. DELIBERATIVE DEMOCRACY

The recent call for 'deliberative' democracy rejects the 'bargaining' aspect of traditional forms of 'participatory' democracy. Following the work of Habermas, its advocates ask for the inclusion of a more diverse range of interests in governance, reflecting the breadth of the 'life world'.[99] They also envisage the creation of an 'ideal speech situation' within which a wide range of 'civil society' actors speak freely and openly, with mutual respect, endeavouring to understand the others' point of view. In this way, the majoritarian premise of representative democracy is replaced by a more pervasive notion of equality. The aim is to transcend the particular interests of participants and reach, not a bargain, but a rational consensus on a desirable course of action.[100]

In order to achieve the 'communicative action' that this democratic dialogue envisages, a range of rights must be given to persons.[101] What these entitlements are remains the subject of debate between libertarians, liberals, and socialists. It is at least arguable that to be equipped to participate in communicative action a person should have access to a bare modicum of socio-economic welfare, as well as civil liberties and an expectation of political participation.

[97] For a review of these issues see Fredman, S., 'The New Rights: Labour Law and Ideology in the Thatcher Years' (1992) 12 *OJLS* 24, esp. 29–35; also Hepple, B., 'The Role of Trade Unions in a Democratic Society' (1990) 11 *Industrial Law Journal* (South Africa) 645.

[98] See for more detailed analysis of 'accountability' problems Zürn, M., 'Governance Beyond the Nation-State: The EU and Other International Institutions' (2000) 6 *European Journal of International Relations* 183 at 193–5.

[99] Habermas, n.71 above, 22: 'The lifeworld forms both the horizon for speech situations and the source of interpretations, while it in turn reproduces itself only through ongoing communicative actions'.

[100] Cohen, J., 'Deliberation and Democratic Legitimacy' in Hamlin, A., and Pettit, P. (eds.), *The Good Polity: Normative Analysis of the State* (Oxford: Blackwell, 1989), esp. at 17. For more detailed discussion of the 'epistemic' value of 'deliberative democracy' see Nino, n.80 above, 107–28; and Stotzky, I.P., 'Establishing Deliberative Democracy: Moving from Misery to Poverty with Dignity' (1998) 21 *University of Arkansas at Little Rock Law Review* 79.

[101] Habermas, n.71 above, 121 ff. chap. 3; and Nino, n.80 above, 136–41. See for further elaboration of Nino's theoretical work Koh, H.H., and Slye, R.C. (eds.), *Deliberative Democracy and Human Rights* (New Haven, Conn.: Yale University Press, 1999).

It seems that 'deliberative democracy' could give the State a broad mandate to include a range of interest groups in public and private dialogue. Who are suitably qualified as 'civil society' representatives and how they will be accountable for their participation in this process has yet to be settled. It does, however, appear that deliberative democracy calls into question the privileged access of workers' and employers' organizations.[102] Moreover, it seems that their industrial weaponry, including a right to strike, is to be left at the door to the debating chamber, for this would lead to bargaining rather than rational choice. Similarly, conflict within the workplace is also no longer seen as a necessary feature of employment relations. Instead, workers are called upon to lay aside their perceptions of divergent interests, and instead work together in 'partnership' with management to achieve ends which are of mutual benefit to both.[103] Within this framework, industrial action comes to be seen as too confrontational to foster the trust needed for deliberation. It becomes redundant.

Nevertheless, while the deliberative democracy model may seem attractive, its practical application remains questionable. It is difficult to conceive of a single instance when the preconceptions and particular interests of participants in a debate have been set to one side to enable an entirely rational outcome to be reached. It has been argued that decision-making by government representatives in EU committees, known as 'comitology', has come closest to achieving this objective,[104] but there are many who are sceptical of such a claim.[105] Instead, it is feared that bargaining is occurring behind the scenes, in the absence of public scrutiny and therefore accountability. Dryzek has observed that 'institutional arrangements featuring decision-making through free discussion oriented toward consensus have made more of a mark on the international system than on politics elsewhere', but also admits that this may still be 'subject to distortion and manipulation by established centres of power'.[106]

Habermas has conceded that there may be circumstances in which the interests of persons are so distinctive and intractable that bargaining is the only option. 'This is the case, namely, whenever it turns out that all

---

[102] Stotzky, n.95 above, 883.   [103] See above, at 2.

[104] Joerges, C., and Neyer, J., 'From Intergovernmental Bargaining to Deliberative Political Processes: The Constitutionalisation of Comitology' (1997) 3 *ELJ* 273; Joerges, C., and Neyer, J., 'Transforming Strategic Interaction Into Deliberative Problem-Solving: European Comitology and the Foodstuffs Sector' (1997) 4 *Journal of European Public Policy* 609; and, more generally, Joerges, C., and Vos, E. (eds.), *European Committees: Social Regulation, Law and Politics* (Oxford: Hart Publishing, 1999).

[105] See, e.g., Weiler, J.H.H., 'To Be a European Citizen—Eros and Civilization' (1997) 4 *Journal of European Public Policy* 495, esp. at 512; Weiler, J., 'Amsterdam and the Quest for Constitutional Democracy' in O'Keeffe, D., and Twomey, P. (eds.), *Legal Issues of the Amsterdam Treaty* (Oxford: Hart Publishing, 1999), and Shapiro, M., 'Administrative Law Unbounded: Reflections on Government and Governance' (2001) 8 *Indiana Journal of Global Legal Studies* 369, esp. at 372–5.

[106] Dryzek, n.8 above, 88–9.

the proposed regulations touch on the diverse interests in respectively different ways without any generalizable interest or clear priority of some one value being able to vindicate itself.'[107] This is the situation where social power situations cannot simply be neutralized. In this context, the discourse principle associated with deliberative democracy can be applied only to determine the procedures that regulate such bargaining. This, however, begs the question whether a mutual generalizable interest can be ascertained on which to base the foundation of a mutually acceptable bargaining procedure. If not, there will once more be a situation in which the necessity for bargaining arises, with the resort to threats and promises that this entails.

One is reminded here of Wedderburn's analysis of the failure to counter Hayek's neo-liberal 'economic' discourse with principles established in labour law, because they do not share the same moral precepts or notions of value.[108] If vested interests and imbalances of power are, as was suspected previously, sometimes an inevitable feature of labour politics (whether within the sphere of so-called 'public' governance or in the workplace), then the case for abandonment of a right to strike becomes weaker. Indeed, deliberative democracy theory, incorporating the notion that there can be 'an impartial point of view', represents a danger to the extent that its application can be used to cloak, and thereby legitimize, underlying cultural assumptions, economic discourse, and other sources of skewed power dynamics.

The brief overview of democratic theory provided here is intended to introduce issues which will be discussed in greater depth, particularly in Parts I and IV. It will emerge that the jurisprudence adopted by international and European organizations relating to national-level protection of the right to strike largely reflects a blend of 'representative' and 'participatory', as opposed to 'deliberative', democratic models. However, these organizations differ in their understanding of the status and ambit of such protection, according to whether they regard the right to strike as a civil, political, or socio-economic right.

III.   QUESTIONS OF INTERNATIONAL GOVERNANCE

The legitimacy of national governance is a conceptually separate issue from that of the legitimacy of 'the emerging international rules and processes by

---

[107] Habermas, n.71 above, 165. See also at 166 where he states that: '[b]argaining processes are tailored for situations in which social power relations cannot be neutralized in the way rational discourses presuppose'. See also Gutmann, A., 'The Disharmony of Democracy' in Chapman, J.W., and Shapiro, I. (eds.), *Democratic Community: Nomos XXXV* (New York: New York University Press, 1993).
[108] Wedderburn, Lord, *Employment Rights in Britain and Europe: Selected Papers in Labour Law* (London: Lawrence and Wishart, 1991), 228.

which the governance of nations is increasingly monitored and validated'.[109] Nevertheless, it is readily apparent that comparable questions relating to democratic values also arise at this level. These are pertinent to the constitutions, standard-setting capacity, and supervisory powers of international and European organizations. To the extent that such organizations seek to wield authority, reasons for deference will be sought.[110]

It is necessary to question again what are the legitimate subjects of regulation. At the transnational level, the answer is less likely to revolve around perceptions of public and private spheres,[111] but is instead complicated by issues of State sovereignty. For example, it may be pertinent to ask what kinds of entitlements should be guaranteed by international and European law as a basic minimum in States, whether these should be civil, political, or socio-economic in character, and at what level of generality these are to be set. Connected to this is the issue of who should set international and European norms and how they should be achieved.

There are also important questions to be answered as regards whether States alone should be regarded as actors in these spheres or whether a voice should be given to corporations, workers' organizations, or other NGOs. There is also no consensus on what forms of voting should be applicable. David Held has suggested that 'cosmopolitan democracy', in the form of regional 'parliaments' and a single global UN 'representative body', could be used as a model for international governance.[112] He envisages that these would operate in the context of an entrenched 'cluster of rights and obligations', which would be civil, political, and socio-economic in character, with recourse to international courts for their defence.[113] However, it is possible to dispute whether such an electoral system can be so neatly superimposed on transnational governance.[114]

Where norms are set at the international and European level, another crucial question is how they are to be enforced. What role should international supervisory bodies play in scrutinizing implementation and what sanctions should be applied? A final difficulty is how the apparent 'anarchy' of the international system is to be addressed, given the overlapping competence of international and regional organizations.

---

[109] Franck (1992), n.74 above, 50.

[110] Cf. Bodansky, D., 'The Legitimacy of International Governance: A Coming Challenge for International Environmental Law' (1999) 93 *AJIL* 596 at 600–3.

[111] Although this may yet arise in the form of tension between public and private international law: see the conclusion to Alston, P., 'The Myopia of the Handmaidens: International Lawyers and Globalization' (1997) 8 *EJIL* 435.

[112] Held, n.74 above, 353–6. See also Held, n.9 above, chap. 12. A similar proposal is made by Franck (1995), n.74 above, 478–84.

[113] Held, n.74 above, 355.

[114] Bodansky, n.110 above, 615, describes such proposals as 'unrealistic', given the absence of a world 'demos'. Cf. Weiler, J., 'European Democracy and its Critique' (1995) 18 *Western European Policy* 4, 17–19.

As in the domestic context, it is difficult to find settled or authoritative answers to these questions. Instead, the range of views outlined below is intended to provide a framework for evaluating the differences between the constitutional, standard-setting, and supervisory structures in place within the ILO, Council of Europe, and EU.

A.   IS THERE A CASE FOR INTERNATIONAL AND EUROPEAN LABOUR STANDARDS?

For many, 'internationalization' entails a loss of democratic participation, because international decisions are made so far away from those who will be affected by them.[115] Within the EU context, this concern has led to the adoption of the principle of 'subsidiarity'.[116] It might therefore seem that all domestic labour laws should be determined at the national level by actors who understand the historical context and perceive the direct social implications of their actions. These are concerns which have been at the core of debate between functionalists and federalists in the European context.[117] A case must therefore be made for standard-setting at the transnational level, demonstrating the benefits which it may be able to offer. There are at least two arguments that could be of assistance in making this case.

The first, drawing on a 'deliberative' democratic justification, is the improved quality of debate that may be achieved when controversial issues are discussed at this level. Discussion of international labour standards provides an opportunity for dialogue between national representatives who might never otherwise have the chance to meet and share experiences. Within an international or European organization it is possible to compile information and resources not available at the national level. This pool of data may allow States to devise common strategies to address particular problems or to learn from failed experiments. An international forum also forces governments to justify their policies *outside* their respective countries. This may be of particular importance in the area of 'human rights' where it may be dangerous for a State to be the sole assessor of its own compliance. Extensive communication between States allows a space for critical reflection which may be missing in the national sphere, where certain assumptions are never challenged. Participants in discussions are given a fresh

---

[115] Stein, E., 'International Integration and Democracy: No Love at First Sight' (2001) 95 *AJIL* 489 at 490.

[116] See, e.g., Bermann, G., 'Taking Subsidiarity Seriously: Federalism in the European Community and the United States' (1994) 94 *Columbia Law Review* 331 and de Búrca, G., 'Reappraising Subsidiarity's Significance After Amsterdam' (1999) *Jean Monnet Paper* 7/99, Harvard Law School. For a more general application of this principle see Abbott, K.W., and Snidal, D., 'International "Standards" and International Governance' (2001) 8 *JEPP* 345.

[117] See, e.g., Burgess, M., *Federalism and the European Union: The Building of Europe 1950–2000* (London and New York: Routledge, 2000).

perspective and, potentially, if they reach agreement, a comparative basis for criticism of their own laws.

The second argument relates to the failings of the State to protect 'representative' democracy in the light of market globalization. States may be less able to perform traditional regulatory functions, because they are aware that setting labour standards may have a negative impact on competition in trade and may make a country less attractive to business investment. These considerations can inhibit the ability of national governments and social partners to set new standards and can lead to a diminution of existing standards. An extreme example is the creation of 'export processing zones' (EPZs), in which labour standards otherwise applicable in a State cannot be relied upon by local workers. These zones have been used by developing States to attract investment by multinational enterprises (MNEs).[118] It was this concern with a downward spiral in labour standards as a result of global competition which was one reason for the establishment of the ILO in 1919.[119] One solution perceived then (and now) is to set global and regional standards for competition which arrest such a spiral, developing social governance to complement growth in global trade and investment.

That is not to say that this second argument is universally regarded as compelling. Countries in the 'North' which are comparatively more wealthy and technologically more sophisticated tend to impose higher labour standards; whereas those in the 'South' are 'weaker in all these respects'.[120] The former tend to be advocates of international regulation of such standards. Indeed, it was they who were largely responsible for the first draft of the ILO constitution. While their aims are often stated to be disinterested and are expressed in terms of concern about the universal welfare of workers, their motives have been characterized as 'protectionist', in that they seek only to protect domestic producers from overseas competition and to prevent capital flight. Workers and trade unions in the 'North' have also sought to defend hard-won employment laws and practices from what they perceive to be an external threat.[121] By contrast, those in the 'South' are reluctant to accept the imposition of internationally set labour standards which could

---

[118] See Blackett, A., 'Global Governance, Legal Pluralism and the Decentered State: A Labor Law Critique of Codes of Corporate Conduct' (2001) 8 *Indiana Journal of Global Legal Studies* 401.

[119] Barnes, G.N., *History of the International Labour Office* (London: Williams and Norgate, 1926), at 35–7; and Chisholm, n. 26 above, 10–11.

[120] See for a useful summary of this regulatory clash and dilemma Charny, D., 'Regulatory Competition and the Global Coordination of Labour Standards' in Esty, D., and Geradin, D., *Regulatory Competition and Economic Integration: Comparative Perspectives* (Oxford: OUP, 2001) at 311.

[121] See for discussion of this phenomenon in the US context Tsogas, G., 'Labour Standards in the Generalized Systems of Preferences of the European Union and the United States' (2000) 6 *European Journal of Industrial Relations* 349.

reduce the limited comparative advantage they have been able to carve out for themselves in trade and investment markets.

Some commentators have questioned whether there will be an actual 'race to the bottom' in respect of labour standards and doubt that the extreme type of 'social dumping' envisaged by the North will take place. It has been observed that there is no evidence of 'convergence toward a single lower system, but simply a slackening of the extant pre-liberalization labour regime'.[122] It is also apparent that some comparative advantage may be gained by respect for basic labour standards, including freedom of association and collective bargaining, as was observed in recent OECD studies.[123] This has given hope that it may be possible to encourage corporations to observe such standards rather than pursue a legal route to their enforcement.[124]

A sensible pro-regulatory view is that taken by Brian Langille. He suggests that, rather than seeking to harmonize labour standards to create an absolutely 'level playing field', international action should be taken to address those labour standards which are so exceptionally low as to amount to an instance of unfair competition. He links this to the 'human rights argument' for core labour standards in respect of which the claim of hidden protectionism 'rings very hollow'.[125] However, even then, there remains a need for care to be taken in the formulation and implementation of what are to be regarded as 'labour rights' so as to avoid 'protectionist' accusations. Globalization may be undermining national democratic determination of minimum labour standards, but the difficulty of securing democratic decision-making by all interested parties in global institutions also needs to be acknowledged.

B. WHAT LABOUR STANDARDS SHOULD BE SET AND AT WHAT LEVEL OF GENERALITY?

While there may be a case for standards to be set at an international level, there remains an issue as to the form that these should take. National laws are usually detailed and prescriptive. Should international laws be identical and thereby supplant these? It seems unlikely that this is desirable. After all, the international or regional standard has to cater to a broader polity than does domestic law. It may therefore be unrealistic to expect an international

---

[122] Charny, n.120 above, 312–14. Hepple, B., 'A Race to the Top? International Investment Guidelines and Corporate Codes of Conduct' (1999) 20 *Comparative Labour Law and Policy Journal* 347 at 348–50.

[123] *Trade, Employment and Labour Standards: A Study of Core Workers' Rights and International Trade* (Paris: OECD, 1996); and *International Trade and Core Labour Standards* (Paris: OECD, 2000).

[124] See, e.g., Charny, n.120 above. The central focus of this book is on the legal protection for the right to strike established at the international and regional (European) level. The possibility of pursuing this alternative agenda and the difficulties which may arise when doing so are discussed further in Chap. 15 below at 348–55.

[125] Langille, B., 'Eight Ways to Think About International Labour Standards' (1997) 31 *Journal of World Trade* 28 at 35.

or European organization to set standards which translate into a requirement of uniform practices.

This is often said to be particularly true of collective labour laws because, as Kahn-Freund observed, these legal rules are linked to the power relations peculiar to each country and cannot readily be extracted from their 'roots'.[126] Nevertheless, this case need not be overstated. An acknowledgement of cultural differences should not preclude recognition of common experience on which to base standards. 'Even recent historical work on national experiences of class formation has shown the universal presence of unions and of industrial conflict in capitalist societies'.[127] This is consistent with the emergence of new trade unions and strikes in transitional economies.[128]

In this context, it may be most appropriate for international and European law to provide a framework which enables assessment of the adequacy of national laws. We need not expect to make domestic laws governing industrial relations identical. There remains scope for deeply embedded national traditional differences to be respected so that comparable results are achieved by different means. Even Held's conception of 'cosmopolitan democracy' at the international level 'would not call for a diminution *per se* of state capacity' but is intended to complement national democratic institutions.[129] There may be a case for the creation of 'non-binding standards' or 'soft law', which provide guidance for State conduct without creating strict obligations under international or European law.[130] Examples include ILO Recommendations and the Community Charter of Fundamental Social Rights of Workers 1989. The question which hangs over such instruments is whether, in the absence of any sanction or any binding force, they are likely to influence State conduct.

C. WHO SHOULD SET THE STANDARDS?

The leading traditional view on the formation of international standards asserts that international law is based upon consent of State actors, both

---

[126] Kahn-Freund, O., 'On Uses and Misuses of Comparative Law' in his *Selected Writings* (London: Stevens & Sons, 1978), 312.

[127] Franzosi, R., *The Puzzle of Strikes: Class and Strategies in Postwar Italy* (Cambridge: CUP, 1995), 348 who cites in support of this claim Zohlberg, A., 'How Many Exceptionalisms?' in Katznetson, I., and Zohlberg, A. (eds.), *Working Class Formation* (Princeton, NJ: Princeton University Press, 1986), 397–456. See also for a similar view Locke, R., Kochlan, T., and Piore, M., 'Reconceptualizing Comparative Industrial Relations: Lessons from International Research' (1995) 134 *ILRev.* 139 at 140.

[128] See n.43 above; also as regards workers' activities in China and South Korea see ICFTU press releases: 'ICFTU condemns serious trade union rights violations in Korea', 23 Mar. 2002, and 'ICFTU Lodges Complaint with ILO Against China', 28 Mar. 2002. Both are available at www.icftu.org/.

[129] Held (1996), n.74 above, 354. See also his conclusions on the 'consolidation of democracy' in Held, n.9 above, 237–8.

[130] An advocate of such measures was Morgenstein, F., *Legal Problems of International Organizations* (Cambridge: Grotius, 1986), 119 ff.

implied over time (through custom) and express (set out in treaties and other agreements).[131] Representative democratic voting tends to be missing from the making of international law. The constitutional instruments establishing international and regional organizations are thereby always susceptible to 'watering down' through the resistance of the least enthusiastic State.[132]

Even once a constitution is created, the mode of drafting and adoption of standards by international and regional organizations raises questions of governance. Will States only be involved, as would be consistent with centrality of State consent in international law, or should a wider set of actors be engaged in this deliberative process? If States are the sole participants, one might ask whether there is to be majority voting. If so, the formula adopted for such voting will be important. One controversial question is whether each State should be given its own vote or whether voting should reflect population size or economic activity.[133]

If a wider range of participants is to be involved, the question remains who they should be. Here a key issue is whether a broad 'deliberative' framework should be adopted which includes a wide range of civil society actors, or whether it is preferable to utilize a model which provides a tripartite 'balance of power' between governments, capital, and labour. For some, the tripartite model established within the ILO is a 'participatory' practice that could be applied elsewhere, for example in relation to environmental concerns.[134] Others would view ILO tripartism as an outdated species of corporatism.[135] The ILO model remains, however, the most directly democratic participatory framework available within a UN agency. It may be more fruitful, therefore, not to abandon it but to elaborate upon it. This is the basis of arguments for a 'tripartite-plus' mode of representation within international and regional organizations. In the sphere of labour standards, this may be of particular importance as regards 'marginalized' workers, such as child labourers, victims of forced labour, domestic workers, home workers, part-time workers, and all others who find it difficult to participate within traditional union structures, but may be represented effectively through NGOs.[136]

---

[131] Teson, F.R., 'Interdependence, Consent and the Basis of International Obligation' (1989) 83 *American Society of International Law Proceedings* 547, 561.

[132] See Kirgis, F.L., 'Specialized Law-Making Processes' in Schachter, O., and Joyner, C.C. (eds.), *United Nations Legal Order* (Cambridge: CUP, 1995), i, 8.

[133] This kind of issue has arisen in respect of 'qualified majority voting' within the European Union. See Art. 205 ECT, discussed in Hosli, M., 'Coalitions and Power: Effects of Qualified Majority Voting on the Council of the European Union' (1996) 34 *JCMS* 255; and Moberg, A., 'The Nice Treaty and Voting Rules in Council' (2002) 40 *JCMS* 259.

[134] Palmer, G., 'New Ways to Make International Environmental Law' (1992) 86 *AJIL* 259 at 278–82; Trimble, n.84 above, 1967–8.

[135] Held, n.74 above, 226–32; although he does not mention the role of the ILO in global politics in Held, n.9 above.

[136] Blackett, n.118 above, 436–40; see also Cooney, S., 'Testing Times for the ILO: Institutional Reform for the New International Political Economy' (1999) 20 *Comparative Labor Law and Policy Journal* 365.

Nevertheless, there also remains a threat that NGOs may themselves threaten democratic norms through decision-making 'behind closed doors', by those who may lack expertise or training and who cannot, ultimately, be held to account for their actions.[137] We shall see that, at present, the ILO, Council of Europe, and EU differ significantly in their treatment of these issues, providing a spectrum of approaches which, it shall be suggested, have had considerable impact upon the standards that they promote.

D.   HOW SHOULD IMPLEMENTATION OF STANDARDS BE MONITORED?

In monist States, once an international instrument has been ratified, it may have direct effect in national law. 'Dualist' systems require the further step of national legislation to give such an instrument legal effect. In both instances, there may be a case for international scrutiny of enforcement which may otherwise be thwarted by the national judiciary or the legislature. How this is to be achieved is controversial.

A separation of powers between the legislature and the courts seems to have been regarded as appropriate in the context of 'representative' national-level democracy. One question is whether similar principles should be applied in the transnational sphere or whether international condemnation of failed implementation of labour standards should be a matter for political discussion. Another is whether it is appropriate to use complaints procedures, replicating domestic court proceedings, for infringement of socio-economic rights, or whether this is best reserved for the protection of civil and political rights. It will become apparent that socio-economic rights have received inferior protection under international law, but that the wisdom of this is currently under review.[138] Moreover, questions arise as to who should be able to bring complaints before such a body. Should this be an affected individual, an interested person, or an NGO? There are also concerns about who should be regarded as suitably qualified to hear cases and adjudicate upon these. Should a tripartite adjudicative model be used, as in UK employment tribunals or the ILO Governing Body Committee on Freedom of Association? Or should the adjudicator be a legal 'expert'?

There is also the problem of what is to be regarded as an appropriate 'sanction' for breach. This is a longstanding dilemma in international labour law and European social policy, for violations of labour standards

---

[137] Anderson, K., 'The Ottawa Convention Banning Landmines: The Role of International Non-Governmental Organisations and the Idea of Civil Society' (2000) 11 *EJIL* 95, 104; Kohler-Koch, B., 'Organized Interests in European Integration: The Evolution of a New Type of Governance' in Wallace, H., and Young, A. (eds.), *Participation and Policy-Making in the European Union* (Oxford: Clarendon Press, 1997), 54–6. For a broad study of the involvement of NGOs in international governance to date see Charnovitz, S., 'Two Centuries of Participation: NGOs and International Governance' (1997) 18 *Michigan Journal of International Law* 183.

[138] See Chap. 2 below at 41–6.

do not tend to lead 'to the posting of blue helmets'.[139] Hope comes from the 'self-entrapment' model. It is arguable that States which wish to participate in organizations such as the ILO, Council of Europe, and EU become trapped within a human rights discourse and that, in this fashion, denial of fundamental rights comes to be seen as inappropriate.[140] Nevertheless, the limited effectiveness of moral condemnation is widely recognized and raises the question whether anything more can be achieved. For example, are economic incentives or sanctions an acceptable means of achieving compliance? If so, how should this be imposed? If not, should the EU legal system nevertheless be utilized to ensure more effective protection of ILO standards within (or outside) Europe than has been achieved to date? This is a question which raises, in turn, the issue of the relationship between international and regional organizations.

E.   WHAT SHOULD BE THE RELATIVE ROLES OF INTERNATIONAL AND REGIONAL ORGANIZATIONS?

A last complex issue is the relative authority of different global and regional bodies to set certain standards. 'Governance in a global context exhibits one crucial feature: The absence of a central government.'[141] For example, the ILO is the acknowledged specialist UN agency which is concerned with protection of labour standards,[142] but the 'structural adjustment' programmes funded by the World Bank and International Monetary Fund (IMF), combined with their endorsement of 'Export Processing Zones' (EPZs), have resulted in the diminished application of ILO standards in certain countries.[143] Moreover, the refusal of the World Trade Organization (WTO) to address protection of core labour standards is considered by some likely to undermine respect for their authority.[144] This lack of ILO

---

[139] See *Record of Proceedings* (Geneva: ILO, 1996) ILC, 83rd Session, 194–5, per Mr Maasen (Government delegate, Germany).

[140] On the application of the 'self-entrapment' model in international human rights law generally, see Risse, T., and Ropp, S.C., 'International Human Rights Law and Domestic Change: Conclusions' in Risse, T., Ropp., S.C., and Sikkink, K. (eds.), *The Power of Human Rights: International Norms and Domestic Change* (Cambridge: CUP, 1999), discussed in Freeman, M., 'Is a Political Science of Human Rights Possible?' (2001) 19 *Netherlands Quarterly of Human Rights* 123 at 136–7.

[141] Dijkzeul, D., *The Management of Multilateral Organizations* (The Hague: Kluwer, 1997), 44.

[142] Singapore Ministerial WTO Declaration, 13 Dec. 1996, WT/MIN96/DEC/W, para. 4. See also n.3 above as regards its status *vis-à-vis* the ICCPR and ICESCR.

[143] See *Report of the Director-General: Reducing the Decent Work Deficit—A Global Challenge* (Geneva: ILO, 2001), 46.

[144] In this respect much depends on the interpretation given within WTO dispute settlement to Art. XX of the GATT. See Blackett, A., 'Whither Social Clause? Human Rights, Trade Theory and Treaty Interpretation' (1999) 31 *Columbia Human Rights Law Review* 1, esp. at 72–8; and Charnovitz, S., 'Trade, Employment and Labour Standards: The OECD Study and Recent Developments in the Trade and Labour Standards Debate' (1997) 11 *Temple International and Comparative Law Journal* 131.

influence is potentially troubling and highlights the difficulty of communication where the terms of discourse, in this case economic versus social, are
so radically different. Moreover, the economic incentives that can be offered
by the World Bank and IMF are likely to be more immediately persuasive
than the 'technical assistance' that the ILO has to offer.[145]

Comparable difficulties with competence arise at the European level,
between the EU and the Council of Europe. The former was ostensibly an
'economic union' while the latter has been more concerned with the protection of human rights, social, and cultural issues. While they share the
same flag and possess an overlapping membership, the appropriate demarcation of their functions remain unclear. Moreover, the extent to which both
these organizations will transpose or even defer to the authority of ILO
standards is uncertain. To the extent that ILO standards constitute pre-
existing obligations of Member States, they are to be respected; but it has
already been demonstrated that respect for fundamental tenets of EC law
can lead to denunciation of ILO norms.[146]

The outstanding issue is how ILO, Council of Europe, and EU approaches might come to coalesce and complement each other, rather than
conflict. While it is evident that international and European organizations
have acknowledged the importance of a right to strike, they have done so in
such divergent ways as potentially to undermine its protection.

In considering how to explain and respond to differences between ILO,
Council of Europe, and EU standards, this book does not pretend to be
comparing like with like. Transnational governance occurs at numerous
different levels.[147] Global and regional bodies clearly have different agendas
and different constitutional structures which are sensitive to their peculiar
situations. Nevertheless, it is argued in this book that there remains the
potential for greater convergence in their forms of standard setting and
supervisory methods through agreement on desirable modes of national
and transnational governance. In this manner their activities may be able

[145] Cf. Blackett, n.144 above.

[146] On the clash between ILO Convention No.89 on Night Work (Women) 1948 and EC
Council Directive 76/207 on the principle of equal treatment for men and women [1976] OJ
L39/40, see Case C–345/89 *Stoeckel* [1991] ECR I–4047. See subsequently Case C–158/91
Levy [1993] ECR I–4287. This potential clash is discussed in Kilpatrick, C., 'Production and
Circulation of EC Nightwork Jurisprudence' (1996) 25 *ILJ* 169. See also Manzini, P., 'The
Priority of Pre-existing Treaties of EC Member States within the Framework of International
Law' (2001) 12 *EJIL* 781.

[147] This book does not, e.g., draw extensively on the work currently done relating
to transnational networks, which further complicate the governance framework. See,
e.g., Slaughter, A.-M, 'The Real New World Order' (1997) 76 *Foreign Affairs* 183;
Slaughter, A.-M., 'Governing the Global Economy through Government Networks' in Byers,
M. (ed.), *The Role of Law in International Politics* (Oxford: OUP, 2000); Ladeur, K.-H.,
'Towards a Legal Theory of Supra-Nationality—The Viability of the Network Concept'
(1997) 3 *ELJ* 33; and more generally in a transatlantic context Pollack, M.A., and
Shaffer, G.C. (eds.), *Transatlantic Governance in the Global Economy* (Lanham, Mld.: Rowman,
2001).

to complement each other, so as to enhance rather than diminish protection of a right to strike.

IV. CONCLUSION: THE AIMS OF THIS INVESTIGATION

Caricatures of the right to strike as the anachronistic legacy of by-gone industrial relations are misleading. Moreover, such caricatures may also be dangerous, in that they stall otherwise constructive argument over the legitimacy of the threat or exercise of industrial action. This chapter has sought to outline the contours of this argument in the context of contemporary debates over the ideal models of 'good governance', in national, regional, and international spheres.

While the right to strike may be seen as contrary to a certain conception of 'deliberative' democracy, it has been suggested here that there are reasons to be sceptical of the practical application of this theory, such that it should not be treated as determinative of the legal status of industrial action. Instead, the right to strike may be viewed (as it has been traditionally) as complementary to 'representative' democracy, or even as a facet of 'participatory' democracy. This is the argument which is carried forward in Part I, which analyses the categorization of 'rights' as civil, political, and socio-economic within a 'democratic' framework. The extent to which the right to strike may be said to fall within such categories is considered there, as are the implications that this categorization has for the scope of such a right. This is crucial to an understanding of the differences between the jurisprudence developed in the ILO, Council of Europe, and EU concerning the legitimate scope of industrial action. This is not to say that the right to strike is to be regarded as unlimited. Part I also considers how the justifications for industrial action could be balanced against grounds for its restriction and what kinds of limitation could be regarded as appropriate.

Part II turns from problems associated with domestic governance to those of international and regional governance. It explores the difficulties associated with making express detailed provision in an international or European legal instrument. ILO Conventions and Recommendations concerning freedom of association and collective bargaining either do not mention or acknowledge only tangentially the right to strike. The right to strike has been omitted from protection under the Council of Europe's Convention on Human Rights 1950, but receives inferior protection by inclusion in a short provision set out in the European Social Charter 1961.[148] The European Union has recognized a right to strike in two declaratory Charters, one on 'the fundamental rights of workers' concluded in 1989, the other on 'fundamental rights' *per se* concluded in 2000. Nevertheless, the members

---

[148] European Social Charter 1961, Art. 6(4).

of the EU seem to have denied that organization the competence to adopt directives relating specifically to 'the right of association, the right to strike or the right to impose lockouts'.[149] It is suggested that the specific difficulties experienced by each organization can be understood in terms of their own particular constitutional foundations and standard-setting procedures, that is, their own modes of 'governance'. Forms of communication established between these organizations, especially at the inception of the two European organizations, are also examined.

Part III considers the role that supervisory bodies are able to play in protection of the right to strike and, in particular, the extent to which they may overcome the obstacles presented by the omission of an express right to strike in an international instrument. In this respect, the stance taken by the ILO Committee on Freedom of Association is contrasted with that of the Council of Europe's European Court of Human Rights. Whilst the former was able to derive a right to strike from a provision relating to 'freedom of association', the latter was not willing to do so. The approach taken by the European Court of Justice is also examined, especially in the context of its 'general principles' jurisprudence which draws on a conception of the appropriate subject matter of 'fundamental human rights'. It is suggested that the jurisprudence developed by supervisory bodies depends largely on structural factors which can, in turn, be linked to the modes of governance, that is the constitutional objectives, standard-setting procedures, and inter-institutional arrangements, outlined in Part II.

Part IV examines the jurisprudence on the actual content of the right to strike developed by international and European supervisory bodies. This is a summary of the current guidance available to States on the extent to which they may legitimately intervene in circumstances in which industrial action is taken. It is argued that there are notable points of difference between the ILO and Council of Europe which may be attributable to the limitations inherent in the wording of the European Social Charter of 1961. Nevertheless, the numerous points of agreement may fuel workers' optimism that ILO standards will be determinative of the content of the right to strike.

The final chapter provides a summary of past sources of divergence between international labour standards, but also looks ahead to future prospects for more consistent or coherent protection of a right to strike. It is acknowledged that there are potentially problematic differences between approaches to such protection taken at the international and European levels. These approaches reflect different views of human rights and appropriate forms of national governance. It is suggested that such differences stem, in turn, from structural factors peculiar to each international organization or modes of international governance. Scope for change may arise by

---

[149] This view follows from my analysis of Art. 137(6) ECT, discussed in greater detail in Chap. 7 below at 160–3.

virtue of new modes of work and globalization of markets. Neo-liberal economic policies and an emphasis on corporate self-regulation do not bode well for continued maintenance of ILO standards, let alone the extension of protection of the right to strike. Nevertheless, there is also mounting awareness that modern erosion of democratic participation and human rights protection, including provision for workers' rights, necessitates greater co-ordination between international and European organizations and combined action. The book closes by considering, to date, the specific responses of the ILO, Council of Europe, and EU to such stimuli for change.

PART I

Reasons for Legal Protection and Restriction of Strikes

Introduction

There are a multitude of reasons which may be given for protection of a right to strike. These are examined here. They can be categorized as civil, political, and socio-economic in nature. The extent to which such justifications are regarded as compelling will determine the scope and status of the right to strike, not just as a moral claim, but under international law where civil, political, and socio-economic rights tend to be treated differently. It is argued in this book that controversy over the justificatory basis for a right to strike has led to different levels of protection at the national level and, also, the adoption of different approaches by the International Labour Organization, Council of Europe, and European Union.

This Part begins by examining why the characterization of the right to strike as a civil, political, and social right is pertinent. Chapter 2 introduces the work of T.H. Marshall and discusses how his categorization of these facets of 'citizenship' influenced international and European instruments. Socio-economic rights tend to receive a lower level of protection under human rights law. Their inferior status has been defended on the basis that such rights are vague, that they are collective in nature, that they should not be regarded as universal, and that they impose positive obligations on the State in a way in which the protection of civil liberties and political rights do not. This brief chapter challenges these assumptions on various grounds, pointing also to the overlap between these species of human right which tend to be exercised in 'clusters'. However, although the inferior status of social rights is questionable, the conceptual differentiation between civil, political, and socio-economic rights remains a useful tool by which to determine the scope of the right to strike, whose ambit cannot be wider than its justificatory bases permit, and to understand its treatment under international human rights law.

Chapter 3 goes on to examine, in greater detail, the grounds for legal protection of strikes. These are, in many respects, obvious and will be familiar to the reader. The most common justification offered for legal protection of a right to strike is its role in the conclusion of collective agreements relating to terms and conditions of employment. In that context, it provides workers with the threat of an economic sanction to counter the often superior bargaining power of an employer. The aim of the workers is to extract concessions relating to pay, hours, and other matters, which the employer may otherwise be reluctant to give. Despite the so-called 'private' nature of the employment relationship, these 'socio-economic' objectives may be considered so compelling that a right to strike should be protected by law. The scope of that claim is examined here, particularly in the light of suggested alternatives to industrial action also designed to achieve these objectives, namely compulsory arbitration or mediation. Much then depends on what forms of State intervention are appropriate in the employment relationship.

Legal protection of a right to strike may also be premised on 'political' or 'democratic' principles. It can be claimed that workers have a legitimate interest in taking part in decision-making processes, when those decisions are likely to affect them. This is arguably the case regardless of whether these are taken and executed in the 'private' workplace or in the 'public' realm of State governance. The ability to have recourse to industrial action may, in both contexts, be an important incentive for the employer or the State to listen to workers' views and accord them influence over the formation of particular policies. This claim, which can arguably be linked to those usually raised in support of 'industrial democracy' and 'corporatism', is examined here. The extent to which workers should be able to challenge the policies of their employers on disinterested (or 'ideological') grounds will also be considered. This is, perhaps, more a matter of conscience and a question of free speech.

To view the right to strike as an aspect of 'free speech', 'freedom of association', or even 'freedom from forced labour' is to give it status as a fundamental 'civil liberty'. This suggests that it could be exercised whenever the worker so chose as a *prima facie* personal freedom. The entitlement to take industrial action could not be limited in terms of subject matter, such as collective bargaining or workplace governance, except where it infringed some other right or vital aspect of the public good. This illustrates how the acceptance of particular reasons for protection of a right to strike can determine the eventual scope of that protection. The extent to which one accepts the validity of each of these arguments is likely to turn on one's conception of 'good governance' and 'democratic' principles, the controversies over which were outlined in Chapter 1.

Finally, in Chapter 4 it is stressed that rights need not be absolute in character. Their force tends to be dependent on the circumstances under which they are claimed and the presence of other countervailing considerations, such as protection of the rights of others or public welfare. The reasons for protection of a right to strike therefore need to be weighed against the potential harms which industrial action can cause to employers, consumers, and others. For that reason, I also examine ongoing debates on the nature of these harms and the degree to which they should restrict legal protection of strikes. It is suggested that this is likely to depend on what one accepts to be the range and force of reasons given for protection of the right to strike outlined in Chapter 3. The relevance of this assessment should also become apparent in Part IV, which considers not only the content of, but also exceptions to the right to strike, as defined by international and European supervisory bodies.

2

The Implications of Categorizing the Right to Strike as a Civil, Political, and/or Social Right

The distinction between civil, political, and socio-economic rights will be familiar to the international human rights lawyer. However, it is a classification that stems from analysis of the constituent elements of citizenship, which were recognized first at the national level. A source commonly identified is the work of T.H. Marshall.[1]

His view was that our conception of 'citizenship' evolved from the recognition of civil liberties to the enlargement of political rights, and then to the protection of social rights. He considered that all three were essential to modern democratic governance. Civil liberties, as defined by Marshall, consist of 'the rights necessary for individual freedom', which sprang from resistance to feudalism. The 'political element' of citizenship is 'the right to participate in the exercise of political power' through a representative democracy. Social rights, stemming from universal suffrage, cover 'the whole range from the right to a modicum of economic welfare and security to the right to share to the full in the social heritage and to live the life of a civilised being according to the standards prevailing in society'.[2]

Applying this model to the right to strike, such an entitlement could be described as 'social' in so far as it promotes economic welfare and security. It can be claimed that industrial action allows workers to receive fair wages, reasonable working conditions, and, thereby, an acceptable standard of living. Marshall doubted that trade unions should be responsible for providing this basic entitlement; this was, in his view, the obligation of the

---

[1] See Marshall, T.H., *Citizenship and Social Class* (Cambridge: CUP, 1950); and Marshall, T.H., and Bottomore, T., *Citizenship and Social Class* (London: Pluto Press, 1992). For ongoing analysis of his work see Giddens, A., *Beyond Left and Right: The Future of Radical Politics* (London: Polity Press, 1994), 69–77; Habermas, J., 'Citizenship and National Identity' and Kymlicka, W., and Norman, W., 'Return of the Citizen: A Survey of Recent Work on Citizenship Theory' in Beiner, R. (ed.), *Theorizing Citizenship* (New York: State University of New York Press, 1995); Bulmer, M., and Rees, A.M. (eds.), *Citizenship Today: The Contemporary Relevance of T.H. Marshall* (London: UCL Press, 1996); and Ewing, K., 'Social Rights and Constitutional Law' [1999] *Public Law* 105.

[2] Marshall, n.1 above, 10 ff.

State. However, he did agree that as a matter of fact trade unions commonly served this function.[3] An entitlement to take industrial action could also be described as a 'political' right, in so far as a strike allows workers to participate in decision-making within the workplace. Marshall himself suggested that 'trade unionism . . . created a secondary system of industrial citizenship parallel with and supplementary to the system of political citizenship'.[4] Furthermore, there is an argument that a right to strike is necessary to democratic participation, not only within the workplace, but also within society at large. On this basis, it has been said that industrial action may, in certain circumstances, provide a legitimate means by which workers may influence the formulation of government policy.[5] Finally, the right to strike has been viewed by others as the natural extension of commonly recognized civil liberties, such as freedom of association, freedom from forced labour, and freedom of speech.[6]

The theoretical framework presented by Marshall has been challenged from a variety of perspectives. Some consider that the 'philosophically respectable concept of human rights has been muddled by an attempt to incorporate into it specific rights of a different logical category', that is, social rights.[7] Others question Marshall's account of the historical development of these rights,[8] and there are those who consider that these categories of rights are not as distinct as his analysis suggests.[9] Moreover, 'globalization' was not a concern explicitly addressed by Marshall.[10]

Nevertheless, this categorization of constitutional rights has been adopted in the field of international and European human rights law, where it has particular significance. This chapter considers current treatment of civil,

---

[3] *Ibid.*, 68–9. Cf. Kahn-Freund, O., *The Right to Strike: Its Scope and Limitations* (Strasbourg: Council of Europe Publishing, 1974), 3.

[4] Marshall, n.1 above, 44.

[5] Laski, H., *Liberty in the Modern State* (London: Faber & Faber, 1930), 125–49.

[6] See, e.g., respectively, Leader, S., *Freedom of Association: A Study in Labour Law and Political Theory* (New Haven, Conn./London: Yale University Press, 1992), 183–204; Ben-Israel, R., *International Labour Standards: The Case of Freedom to Strike* (Deventer: Kluwer, 1989), 25; and Kupferberg, S., 'Political Strikes, Labor Law and Democratic Rights' (1985) 71 *Virginia Law Review* 685. Their views shall be discussed in greater detail later within this chapter.

[7] Cranston, M., *What Are Human Rights?* (London: Bodley Head, 1973), 65; see also Vierdag, E.W., 'The Legal Nature of the Rights Granted by the International Covenant on Economic, Social and Cultural Rights' (1978) 9 *Netherlands Year Book of International Law* 69 at 73.

[8] See, e.g., Mann, M., *The Sources of Social Power: The Rise of Classes and Nation States 1760–1914* (Cambridge, CUP, 1993), ii; and Giddens, n.1 above, at 73–4. Others observe that while this historical development may be true of Britain, it is not an accurate description of other national contexts. See Rees, A. M., 'T.H. Marshall and the Progress of Citizenship' in Bulmer and Rees, n.1 above, at 14 ff.

[9] Van Hoof, G.J.H., 'The Legal Nature of Economic, Social and Cultural Rights: A Rebuttal of Some Traditional Views' in Alston, P., and Tomasevski, K. (eds.), *The Right to Food* (Utrecht: Martinus Nijhoff, 1984).

[10] Hewitt, P., 'Social Justice in a Global Economy' in Bulmer and Rees, n.1 above.

political, and socio-economic rights and its implications for protection of the right to strike. The justifications for such treatment will be examined from a critical perspective.

I. DIVERGENT PROTECTION UNDER INTERNATIONAL LAW

'Civil' and 'political' rights tend to receive comprehensive protection under international instruments, and this protection is usually reinforced by stringent reporting and complaints procedures. 'Social' (or as they are sometimes termed 'socio-economic') rights tend to be included in separate instruments, are less likely to be ratified by as many States, and are often interpreted in line with perceived economic constraints upon governments.[11]

An example is the Council of Europe, where it was decided that civil and political rights should be protected under the European Convention on Human Rights 1950 (ECHR) enforceable by recourse to a European Court of Human Rights, whereas social rights would receive inferior protection under the European Social Charter 1961 (ESC).[12] When, in 1966, the United Nations adopted the International Covenant on Civil and Political Rights (ICCPR) and the International Covenant on Economic, Social, and Cultural Rights (ICESCR), a similar approach was taken.[13] For a further recent example of disparity in treatment of socio-economic rights see the Additional San Salvador Protocol to the American Convention on Human Rights.[14] One key exception to this approach is that taken in the ILO.[15]

[11] A trend discussed by Eide, A., 'Realization of Social and Economic Rights and the Minimum Threshold Approach' (1989) 10 *Human Rights Journal* 35. See also Scheinin, M., 'Economic and Social Rights as Legal Rights' in Eide, A., Krause, C., and Rosas, A. (eds.), *Economic, Social and Cultural Rights: A Textbook* (Dordrecht/Boston, Mass./London: Martinus Nijhoff, 1995).

[12] See Novitz, T., 'Remedies for Violation of Social Rights within the Council of Europe: The Significant Absence of a Court' in Kilpatrick, C., Novitz, T., and Skidmore, P. (eds.), *The Future of Remedies in Europe* (Oxford: Hart Publishing, 2000). See also on the status of the Social Charter relative to the Convention the Opinion of Jacobs A.G. in Case C–67/96 *Albany International BV v Stichting Bedrijsfonds Textielindustrie* [1999] ECR I–5751 at paras. 142–156.

[13] Morphet, S., 'Economic, Social and Cultural Rights: The Development of Governments' Views 1941–1988' in Beddard, R., and Hill, D.M. (eds.), *Economic, Social and Cultural Rights: Progress and Achievements* (London: Macmillan, 1992); Scott, C., 'Reaching Beyond (Without Abandoning) the Category of "Economic, Social and Cultural Rights"' (1999) 21 *Human Rights Quarterly* 633.

[14] Adopted in 1988, came into force in 1999. The full text is available at www.oas.org/.

[15] See Leary, V. A., 'Lessons from the Experience of the International Labour Organisation' in Alston, P. (ed.), *The United Nations and Human Rights* (Oxford: OUP, 1992); and Leary, V.A., 'The Paradox of Workers' Rights as Human Rights' in Compa, L., and Diamond, S. (eds.), *Human Rights, Labour Rights and International Trade* (Philadelphia, Penn.: University of Pennsylvania Press, 1996).

The historical legacy of this division seems to lie in the ideological battlefield of the Cold War, played out in the international arena of diplomacy. It appears that civil and political rights symbolized respect for individual liberty and capitalist enterprise, while social and economic entitlements had become associated implicitly with the perils of Communism. Undue emphasis on the protection of the latter was considered by Western powers to be 'anti-democratic'.[16] The US Government, in particular, being one of the most influential international actors, has 'categorically denied that there is any such thing as an economic, social or a cultural human right'.[17] Nicholas Valticos once observed that this treatment of socio-economic rights 'has no logical or legal explanation but, in truth, resides in political disparities between States of different persuasions at the time of their negotiation and adoption'.[18] Nevertheless, subsequent academic commentary has sought to explain and justify the maintenance of a distinction between civil, political, and socio-economic rights, in both practical and ideological terms.[19]

II.   THE CASE FOR AND AGAINST DIFFERENTIAL TREATMENT

Four inter-related arguments have been made for the differential treatment of social rights under international law. First, it is sometimes claimed that social rights are too vague to be justiciable. There is no clear guide to when we should regard the economic welfare of a citizen as sufficiently protected.[20] Secondly, such rights tend to be regarded as 'collective' in nature, applying to a class of persons as opposed to an individual, and are

---

[16] See Fuchs, K., 'The European Social Charter: Its Role in Present-Day Europe and its Reform' in Drzewicki, K., Krause, C., and Rosas, A. (eds.), *Social Rights as Human Rights: A European Challenge* (Åbo: Åbo Akademi University Institute for Human Rights, 1994), 151; Council of Europe Parliamentary Assembly, *Additional Protocol to the European Convention on Human Rights Concerning Fundamental Social Rights*, 23 Mar. 1999, Doc. 8357, Explanatory Memorandum by Mrs Pulgar, paras. 18–19.

[17] Alston, P., 'US Ratification of the Covenant on Economic, Social and Cultural Rights: The Need for an Entirely New Strategy' (1989) XXVIII *International Legal Materials* 365. The US Government has yet to ratify the ICESCR, even though it ratified the ICCPR on 8 June 1992. Information on ratifications is available at: www.unhchr.ch/html/.

[18] Valticos, N., 'International Labour Standards and Human Rights: Approaching the Year 2000' (1998) 138 *ILRev.* 135 at 138.

[19] Examples include Cranston, M., 'Human Rights Real and Supposed', in Raphael, D. (ed.), *Political Theory and the Rights of Man* (London: Bodley Head, 1967); Vierdag, n.7 above, 103; and Foweraker, J., and Landman, T., *Citizenship Rights and Social Movements: A Comparative and Statistical Analysis* (Oxford: OUP, 1997), 14–15.

[20] See, *inter alia*, Vierdag, n.7 above, at 93; Scheinin, M., 'Economic and Social Rights as Legal Rights' in Eide, Krause, and Rosas (eds.), n. 11 above, 42 ff. Jacobs, F.G., 'The Extension of the European Convention on Human Rights to Include Economic, Social and Cultural Rights' (1978) 3 *Human Rights Review* 166, 166–7.

therefore considered to be less susceptible to enforcement by individual claimants.[21] Related to this is a third argument, that such rights are not universal and therefore, unlike civil and political rights, are not deserving of inclusion in the broader category of human rights. A fourth claim often made is that civil and political rights require minimal interference on the part of the State, whereas social rights impose positive obligations on the State to protect citizens' welfare.[22] In this sense they are suspect, for it is said that human rights should be concerned with individual autonomy, not welfare.[23] Moreover, because it is assumed that the realization of socio-economic rights involves imposing a financial burden on the State, to make social rights justiciable in the national courts would upset the accepted balance of power between the legislature and the judiciary, as the latter would be able to determine the parameters of State spending.[24] For the same reason, it is asserted that socio-economic standards imposed at an international level must be flexible enough to take into account the different resources of States. This assertion explains why social rights incorporated into international instruments are often phrased in progressive terms, as goals to be aimed at and possibly achieved over a certain period of time, depending upon the resources available. The particular importance of State discretion, over and above any usual 'margin of appreciation', is to be respected by an international supervisory body responsible for enforcing such rights.[25]

Nevertheless, each of these arguments can to some extent be rebutted. On closer investigation, the notion that social rights are inherently vague does not pass muster, for all human rights instruments contain provisions which are general in nature. A 'right to safe and healthy working conditions',[26] which is regarded as a social right, is no more vague than the civil and political right to 'freedom of expression'.[27] In both instances, States are dependent on the authoritative interpretation of a supervisory organ to elaborate on the content of such rights when applied to particular situations. For example, while there is some controversy over what the scope and content of a right to strike should be, there is no doubt that it is *capable* of definition.[28] Much will depend on the manner in

---

[21] A view discussed by Addo, M.K., 'Justiciability Re-examined' in Beddard and Hill, n.13 above, 106–7.

[22] For the classic statement of the difference between positive and negative liberty see Berlin, I., 'Two Concepts of Liberty' in Berlin, I., *Four Essays on Liberty* (Oxford: OUP, 1969) at 121–72. See also for a more recent analysis Viljanen, V., 'Abstention or Involvement? The Nature of State Obligations Under Different Categories of Rights' in Drzewicki *et al.*, n.16 above, 44.

[23] See Cranston, n.7 above.

[24] Cf. Chap. 1, at 16–17, and 29.

[25] A position discussed by Van Hoof, n.9 above, at 103–5.

[26] ESC, Art. 3; ICESCR, Art. 7(b).

[27] ECHR, Art. 10; ICCPR, Art. 19(2).

[28] See Part IV below.

which any entitlement is phrased in the context of an international instrument.[29]

Furthermore, it may be doubted whether all social rights are only 'collective' in nature and therefore not capable of enforcement by individuals.[30] Although social rights do tend to impose rights on categories of people, such as 'workers', 'children and young persons', and 'elderly persons', this need not be read in a manner which denies the individual claim of each person in such circumstances. To take the example of a right to 'paid annual leave', the individual in employment has a personal and immediate interest in ensuring that the State performs its obligations under international law, namely to ensure that employers provide paid leave.[31] Moreover, this is a right of universal application. It is true that this is a right which can be relied on only by a person in employment; however, here a comparison may be made with the right to 'a fair hearing',[32] which can be relied on solely by a person who wishes to bring a civil claim or face criminal charges. Only those people placed in such circumstances will utilize these rights, but this does not make them solely collective or merely selective in nature. This is not a useful way in which to distinguish between these different categories of rights. It will be argued below that the right to strike, to the extent that it is a socio-economic right, can be regarded as both individual and collective in nature.[33]

It is also very difficult to distinguish civil and political rights from socio-economic rights on the basis that the latter impose positive obligations as opposed to protecting negative liberties. First, those who make this claim fail to acknowledge that the protection of civil and political rights also imposes a financial burden on the State. To guard civil liberties involves the deployment of a police force, a criminal justice system, and a procedure for resolving civil claims.[34] To provide access to participation in the political process involves public provision of information, polling booths, and

---

[29] E.g., the African Charter on Human and Peoples' Rights, adopted in 1981 and entered into force in 1986, 'avoids the incremental language of progressive realization in guaranteeing economic, social and cultural rights'. See Odinkalu, C. A., 'Analysis of Paralysis or Paralysis by Analysis? Implementing Economic, Social, and Cultural Rights Under the African Charter on Human and Peoples' Rights' (2001) 23 *Human Rights Quarterly* 327 at 349. See for criticism of the wording of the ICESCR Swaminathan, R., 'Regulating Development: Structural Adjustment and the Case for National Enforcement of Economic and Social Rights' (2001) 37 *Columbia Journal of Transnational Law* 161, 182–4.

[30] Novitz, T., 'Are Social Rights Necessarily Collective Rights?—A Critical Analysis of the Collective Complaints Protocol to the European Social Charter' [2002] *EHRLR* 50. For a more jurisprudential analysis see Green, L., 'Two Views of Collective Rights' (1991) IV *Canadian Journal of Law and Jurisprudence* 315.

[31] ESC, Art. 2(2); ICESCR, Art. 7(d). See for a recent judgment that accords with this view Case C–173/99 *Broadcasting, Entertainment, Cinematographic and Theatre Union (BECTU) v Secretary of State for Trade and Industry* [2001] ECR I–4881.

[32] ECHR, Art. 6; ICCPR, Art. 14.

[33] Chap. 3, below, at 54–5.

[34] For examples along these lines see Higgins, R., *Problems and Process: International Law and How We Use It* (Oxford: Clarendon Press, 1994), 100–1.

independent scrutineers. All this is costly, as was acknowledged by the Constitutional Court of South Africa when assessing the budgetary implications of the enforcement of such rights.[35] By ignoring expenditure on civil and political rights, one implicitly prioritizes these rights over others. There arguably needs to be a fuller and more open debate on where financial priorities lie. Moreover, some of these objections do not apply to certain social rights. For example, the right to engage in collective bargaining and the right to strike require procedures to be put in place which constrain the power of the employer, but do not otherwise require public spending.[36]

III. THE OVERLAP BETWEEN CATEGORIES OF RIGHTS

Finally, it is vital to take account of the extent to which these categories of rights overlap. It may be more useful to conceptualize 'rights' as a 'cluster of legal positions' which are inter-related, entailing a blend of civil, political, and socio-economic entitlements, which may take the form of both positive obligations and negative liberties.[37] For example, a State which grants all citizens the right to vote but denies some access to education and public information provides no more than a formal right of political participation. If citizens lack the means to read or understand the ballot paper, they have no real opportunity to vote. Civil and political rights lack substance if they are not responsive to their social context.[38] It is also possible to identify a multiplicity of connections between the content of certain civil or political rights and particular socio-economic rights. For example, the right to health and safety in the workplace may be regarded as one of the many facets of the right to life, a minimum age of admission to employment is an aspect

---

[35] *Certification Judgment* (1996) 10 *BCLR* 1253, para. 77. Cited in Gutto, S.B.O., 'Beyond Justiciability: Challenges of Implementing/Enforcing Socio-Economic Rights in South Africa' (1998) 4 *Buffalo Human Rights Law Review* 79 at 92. See also Schwartz, H., 'Do Economic and Social Rights Belong in a Constitution?' (1995) 10 *American University Journal of International Law and Policy* 1233, 1240–1.

[36] Mthombeni, R., 'The Right or Freedom to Strike: An Analysis from an International or Comparative Perspective' (1990) 23 *Comparative International Law Journal of South Africa* 337 at 338. See also Schwartz, n.35 above at 1236; and Ewing, n.1 above. Eide, n.11 above, at 41, notes that human rights can place three types of obligation on States to 'respect', 'protect', and to 'fulfil'. While he acknowledges the distinction between the three, he also doubts that the fulfilment of social rights always requires public spending: they may also be 'safeguarded through non-interference by the state with the freedom and use of resources possessed by individuals', that is, through market processes.

[37] Viljanen, V., 'Abstention or Involvement? The Nature of State Obligations Under Different Categories of Rights', in Drzewicki, Krause, and Rosas (1994), n.16 above, 45 who cites Alexy's work on the 'constitutional right as a whole' (*das Grundrecht als Ganzes*). See Alexy, R., *Coherence Theory of Law* (Lund: Jurisforlaget, 1998).

[38] For further observations on this theme see Bottomore, T., 'Citizenship and Social Class: Forty Years On' in Marshall and Bottomore, n.1 above, 66–71; Ewing, K.D., 'Democratic Socialism and Labour Law' (1995) 24 *ILJ* 103 at 111.

of freedom from forced labour, and rights to join a trade union, bargain collectively, and strike may be regarded as implicit in freedom of association.

The need to recognize the close relationship between civil, political, and socio-economic entitlements has been acknowledged by various international bodies. Such rights have been described as 'equal and indivisible'; and it has been said that all require respect within a democratic State.[39] However, despite modifications to the supervisory system of the ESC and ongoing proposals for change in this context and that of the ICESCR,[40] the reality has yet to mesh with this rhetoric. More stringent protection of a right to strike is likely to be available at international law where it is regarded as a civil or political right, than if it is perceived to be socio-economic in nature. We shall see evidence of this in later chapters, when examining the Council of Europe system for protection of freedom of association and industrial action.

IV.   CONCLUSION

This chapter has endeavoured to demonstrate the difficulty of justifying the inferior treatment of socio-economic rights. Instead, it has suggested that civil, political, and socio-economic rights are alike in more respects than is commonly acknowledged. Moreover, in practice, such rights may often be exercised simultaneously in a 'cluster', rather than discretely and individually. Nevertheless, recognition of the interdependence of various categories of rights need not lead to the complete abandonment of Marshall's theoretical framework. An understanding of the traditional place of socio-economic rights within the international human rights hierarchy is of considerable assistance in understanding the ways in which international and European protection of the right to strike has developed and is developing.

---

[39] See, e.g., the Declaration on the Occasion of the 50th Anniversary of the Universal Declaration of Human Rights (adopted by the Council of Europe Committee of Ministers Meeting of Deputies on 10 Dec. 1998), para. 4. This follows on from the 1993 Vienna Declaration on Human Rights, UN Doc. A/CONF.157/24 (1993); see (1993) 32 *International Legal Materials* 1661, 1665.

[40] On the Council of Europe 'collective complaints' procedure and for further reforms see Chap. 9 below at 220–4. Note also proposals for an additional complaints protocol to be appended to the ICESCR, discussed in Alston, P., 'Draft Optional Protocol Providing for the Consideration of Communications' in Coomans, F., and Van Hoof, F. (eds.), *The Right to Complain About Economic, Social and Cultural Rights: Proceedings of the Expert Meeting on the Adoption of an Optional Protocol to the International Covenant on Economic, Social and Cultural Rights* (Utrecht: Netherlands Institute of Human Rights Studie- en Informatiecentrium Mensentrechten, 1995). A Workshop on the Justiciability of Economic, Social and Cultural Rights with Particular Reference to an Optional Protocol to the Covenant on Economic, Social and Cultural Rights was held at Palais Wilson on 5–6 Feb. 2001. A full report was submitted by the High Commissioner for Human Rights to the Commission on Human Rights at its 57th Session.

It also remains possible for the constructs of civil, political, and socio-economic rights to provide a useful basis for analysis of the underlying arguments for protection of a 'human right'. The danger inherent in complete rejection of these 'provisional' categories 'is that those social, political, cultural, and economic power relations in the international order that tend to assimilate all human rights to rights close to the heart of the privileged may become more difficult to name and challenge'.[41] For these reasons, this categorization is not only recognized as the foundation for the form and content of various international instruments discussed in subsequent chapters, but also as an analytical tool which is helpful when seeking to 'unpack' sources of controversy over protection and restriction of industrial action. For example, whether a right to strike is viewed as serving economic interests, as an extension of political participation, or as a fundamental civil liberty will affect its scope and, very probably, the extent to which it takes priority over other entitlements. Recognition of these formal categories of rights therefore underlies the remainder of Part II and provides the foundation for the analysis of international and European protection of the right to strike contained in this book.

[41] Scott, n.13 above, 644–5.

3

Reasons for Legal Protection of a Right to Strike

The potential reasons for legal protection of strikes cover a wide spectrum. They may be socio-economic in nature, may draw upon a particular understanding of rights to political participation, and may be derived from the application of commonly recognized civil liberties. These are examined below. To the extent that these diverse justifications are plausible, the right to strike may traverse conventional boundaries in international jurisprudence, indicating that certain distinctions commonly made between these categories of rights may be inappropriate.

The investigation of this range of reasons also has a further aim, which is to consider how they may determine the appropriate scope of a right to strike. For example, if an entitlement to organize or participate in industrial action is justified solely as a 'socio-economic' right, due to its role in collective bargaining, industrial action that challenges a government's environmental policy could reasonably be said to lie outside the ambit of that right; conversely, if a right to strike can be derived from an entitlement to political participation, there may be circumstances in which such action could be regarded as acceptable. A more variegated justificatory basis will give rise to a richer conception of a right to strike, which is of broader scope.

I. THE RIGHT TO STRIKE AS A SOCIO-ECONOMIC RIGHT

The case usually made for the right to strike has a socio-economic character. The ability of workers to take industrial action is said to be an important factor in the maintenance of fair wages[1] and reasonable working conditions,[2] thereby improving the economic and social welfare of a significant proportion of the population. This is premised on the understanding that there is an imbalance in bargaining power between an employer

---

[1] Hyman, R., *Strikes* (4th edn., London: Macmillan, 1989), 80.
[2] Fox, A., *Industrial Sociology and Industrial Relations*, Royal Commission Research Paper 3 (London: HMSO, 1966), 7; Flanders, A., *Management and Unions* (London: Faber & Faber, 1970), 42. Cf. Ewing, K.D., 'Citizenship and Employment' in Blackburn, R. (ed.), *Rights of Citizenship* (London: Mansell, 1993), 108.

and worker, such that in the absence of a right to strike 'collective bargaining would amount to collective begging'.[3] I shall examine the dimensions of this argument and its implications for the ambit of lawful industrial action.

A. DETERMINATION OF FAIR WAGES AND REASONABLE WORKING CONDITIONS?

A strike is an important means by which workers can seek to secure fair wages and working conditions. In this respect, legal protection of the right to strike can be viewed as the legacy of the rejection of 'sweated labour', namely a desire not to return to the long hours, low pay, exploitation of child labour, and unsafe working conditions which were prevalent in Western Europe and other industrialized countries in the nineteenth century.[4] Industrial action was used then and is used now to challenge such practices. It seems to be this social justice argument which eventually won judicial and legislative recognition of the entitlement of workers to take industrial action in these States.[5]

It has been asserted since that, now such terrible conditions of work have been eradicated, the case for the right to strike has also been eroded. For example, A.F. Utz and H.G. Schermers have observed that, in Western Europe today, the wages and standard of living are now considerably higher than they were at the beginning of the twentieth century. They consider that, for this reason, strikes are often unreasonable and therefore illegitimate.[6]

Whether wages and conditions in Western Europe are always of a sufficient level to provide Marshall's 'modicum of economic security' is, arguably, questionable.[7] Moreover, the claim made on the workers' side is that

---

[3] Jacobs, A., 'The Law of Strikes and Lock-Outs' in Blanpain, R., and Engels, C. (eds.), *Comparative Labour Law and Industrial Relations in Industrialized Market Economies* (5th edn., Deventer: Kluwer, 1993), 423.

[4] As reported not only by the politicians, but also the popular fiction of the day. See Elisabeth Gaskell's *North and South* and Charles Dickens' *Hard Times*.

[5] See the judgment of Lord Wright in *Crofter Hand Woven Harris Tweed Co. v Vietch* [1942] AC 435 at 463. For a comparable statement in the USA, see *American Steel Foundries v Tri-City Cent. Trades Council* 257 US 184 at 209 (1920), per Chief Justice Taft. Also Hepple, B. (ed.), *The Making of Labour Law in Europe: A Comparative Study of Nine Countries up to 1945* (New York: Mansell, 1986).

[6] Schermers, H.G., 'Is There a Fundamental Right to Strike? (Right to Fair Conditions)' (1989) 9 *Yearbook of European Law* 225, at 232; and Utz, A.F., 'Is the Right to Strike a Human Right?' (1987) 65 *Washington University Law Review* 732, 744.

[7] See Marshall, T.H., *Citizenship and Social Class* (Cambridge: CUP, 1950) discussed in Chap. 2 above. E.g., in the UK, research undertaken in preparation for the introduction of a minimum wage revealed considerable poverty amongst those in employment, due to the level of wages: Gosling, A., 'Minimum Wages: Possible Effects on the Distribution of Income' in Employment Policy Institute, *Implementing a National Minimum Wage in the UK* (London: EPI, 1997).

they are interested in more than a mere 'basic living wage'.[8] For example, the introduction of a minimum wage by the British Labour Government has not led trade unions to the abandonment of collective bargaining. This is because workers do not seek simply to evade poverty, but to enhance their standard of living and social well-being.[9] They are not asking only for a bare subsistence wage and bearable working conditions, but terms of employment which reflect their skills and experience.[10] They may also wish to appeal to broader egalitarian principles, claiming a share of the profits which an employer makes from the hire of their labour. Furthermore, workers are concerned not only with preventing debilitating effects on their health and home life, but also facilitating enjoyment of their working environment and their time outside work.[11]

The opposing argument, on the employer's side, is that it is unreasonable to allow workers to impose their view of what will constitute 'fair' wages and working conditions on employers by taking industrial action. Allowing workers to make their own assessment forces employers to pay more than they can afford and inconveniences the public at large.[12] The question, then, is whose conception of 'fair working conditions' will prevail and by what means?

In the context of this dilemma, Utz and Schermers argue that the answer lies, not in legal protection of a right to strike, but in more direct State intervention in the setting of terms and conditions of employment, via compulsory arbitration or mediation. Utz takes the harder line, arguing that industrial action is unacceptable and that compulsory arbitration and conciliation should be introduced in its place.[13] Schermers concedes that industrial action could be taken as a last resort, but only when compulsory mediation procedures have failed.[14] The arguments for and against these claims are considered here.

1.   Compulsory Arbitration

Compulsory arbitration was notably used as a substitute for collective bargaining in the Antipodes. In Australia, the introduction of the federal Conciliation and Arbitration Act 1904 reassured those concerned by the mass strikes of the 1890s that industrial action of this magnitude could

[8] Marshall, A., 'A Fair Rate of Wages' in Pigou, A.C. (ed.), *Memorials of Alfred Marshall* (London: Macmillan, 1925), 212.

[9] Solow, R.M., *The Labor Market as a Social Institution* (Oxford: Blackwell, 1990), 22; and the European Social Charter 1961, Preamble.

[10] Marshall, n.7 above, at 71–2.

[11] *Strike and Structural Change: The Future of the Trade Unions' Mobilisation Capacity in Europe* (Brussels: ETUI, 1993), 42.

[12] See Shenfield, A., *What Right to Strike? With Commentaries by Cyril Grunfeld and Sir Leonard Neal* (London: Institute of Economic Affairs, 1986).

[13] Utz, n.6 above.

[14] Schermers, n.6 above.

never reoccur.[15] The trade unions, suffering in the aftermath of this action, saw arbitration as a mechanism by which to ensure that workers received some minimal guarantees (and believed that the process would promote trade union membership).[16] Previously, a distinction was drawn between a 'dispute of right' and a 'dispute of interest'. The former was a dispute over the appropriate interpretation of a binding agreement relating to terms and conditions of employment. This could be the subject of a case heard before an arbitration panel or a court. By contrast, a 'dispute of interest' consisted of an argument over what those terms and conditions of employment should be. This was not settled by judicial or other forms of arbitration, but was left to bargaining between the parties. The legislation introduced in Australia undermined this distinction.

The new conciliation and arbitration system, which was designed to reduce the number of strikes, was not entirely successful. One problem seems to be that parties are more likely to abide by an agreement freely entered into rather than one imposed by a third party.[17] The value of labour may be best known to the two players in the market rather than an arbiter appointed by the State. If the arbiter's decisions are viewed as inadequate by either party, industrial conflict may result, despite its illegality.[18] There is also a danger that a quasi-legal process may lead to a more conflictual approach, as the 'legalism' of the procedure alienates the parties. Both sides may then be reluctant to make concessions for fear of 'establishing a new floor or ceiling for arbitration'.[19]

Moreover, the State is not an impartial arbiter. State appointees may have their own agenda in arbitration proceedings. In Australia, the government's 'wage policy' was a key factor affecting the content of awards provided by its centralized arbitration mechanism.[20] States in general

---

[15] Macken, J.J., *Australian Industrial Laws: The Constitutional Basis* (2nd edn., Sydney: Law Book Company, 1980), 84–5.

[16] Rawson, D.W., 'The Law and the Objects of Federal Unions' (1981) 23 *The Journal of Industrial Relations* (Australia) 295 at 296. A similar mechanism was adopted in New Zealand. See Deeks, J., and Boxall, P., *Labour Relations in New Zealand* (Auckland: Longman Paul, 1989), 24–46; Nolan, D.R., 'RIP: Compulsory Labour Arbitration in New Zealand (1894–1984)' (1991) 12 *Comparative Labour Law Journal* 411, 414–23; and Novitz, T., 'New Zealand Industrial Relations and the International Labour Organisation: Resolving Contradictions Implicit in Freedom of Association' (1996) 21 *New Zealand Journal of Industrial Relations* 119, 125–8.

[17] Kahn-Freund, O., and Hepple, B., *Laws Against Strikes: International Comparisons in Social Policy* (London: The Fabian Society, 1972), 29–30.

[18] Cf. the discussion of the problem of 'real wages' in Mulvey, C., 'Alternatives to Arbitration: Overview of the Debate', in Blandy, R., and Niland, J. (eds.), *Alternatives to Arbitration* (London/Sydney: Allen & Unwin, 1986), 13–18.

[19] Kahn-Freund and Hepple, n.17 above, at 29–30. Again, cf. Mulvey, n.18 above, at 19–20.

[20] *Australian Industrial Relations Law and Systems: Report of the Committee of Review* (Canberra: Australian Federal Government, Apr. 1985), ii, 229–32; Nolan, n.16 above, comments at 445 that having created the arbitration system and having forced the parties to use it, New Zealand politicians 'could not then deny that wage-fixing was a political process'.

are likely to be concerned with preservation of economic stability, as well as attraction of foreign investment, and may therefore represent the interests of business rather than those of workers.[21] Also, the party political sympathies of the government in question may make some difference.[22]

It may seem desirable to have the State provide, by way of legislation, minimum terms and conditions of employment, as well as standards of conduct within the workplace; and to set the ground rules for collective bargaining, including industrial action. However, it seems more dangerous for State appointees actually to set workers' terms and conditions of employment through arbitration.

2. Compulsory Mediation

Schermers' proposal of compulsory mediation may seem to be a more attractive solution. In theory, such a procedure deters the parties to an industrial dispute from engaging too swiftly in conflict and provides time for an amicable settlement. Moreover, proponents of 'reflexive' labour law may prefer this procedural solution to one which allows the State to intervene in the setting of substantive labour standards.[23] Nevertheless, there may be grounds for concern, as regards both the delay that mediation may entail and the controls which the State may exercise over the parties through this medium.

The delay associated with mediation may serve the employer's interests as opposed to those of the worker. Support for a strike may be eroded when little is seen to be accomplished over a significant period of time. Furthermore, the period designated for mediation may give employers the opportunity to engage in subsidiary tactics to dissuade workers from engaging in such action. Also, the outcomes of any mediation procedure put in place are likely to be determined by what the parties perceive to be their alternative available options, such as the ease with which industrial action can be taken should such methods fail. Ultimately, the State will designate the methods by which workers and their organizations may take action to challenge existing terms and conditions of employment, and any penalties to which they may be subject. In addition, any statutory standards that will govern the employment relationship, in default of any agreement being reached, may also determine the outcome of this 'mediation'.

Interestingly, there are parallels between Schermers' suggested approach and that taken in South Africa during the apartheid years, when trade

---

[21] See, e.g., the intervention by Prime Minister Bob Hawke in the pilots' dispute of 1989–90, discussed in Smith, G.F., 'From Consensus to Coercion: The Australian Air Pilots Dispute' (1990) 32 *The Journal of Industrial Relations* (Australia) 238.

[22] See Hain, P., *Political Strikes: The State and Trade Unionism in Britain* (London: Viking, 1986), 20–6; Hyman, n.1 above, 167–9.

[23] See Rogowski, R., and Wilthagen, T., *Reflexive Labour Law: Studies in Industrial Relations and the Employment Regulation* (Deventer: Kluwer, 1994).

unions which called industrial action were required to attend compulsory mediation and conciliation. This was a fairly obvious attempt to diminish the unions' bargaining power.[24] This experience suggests that such requirements should sometimes be viewed critically. It may be preferable for the State to make voluntary mediation and arbitration available where industrial disputes arise, rather than to make this a precondition for a lawful strike.

B.   THE IMPACT OF THIS JUSTIFICATORY BASIS ON THE SCOPE OF THE RIGHT TO STRIKE

If the alternatives suggested by Utz and Schermers are rejected in favour of collective bargaining, it does not follow that the right to strike will have a broad scope. Where a socio-economic rationale centred on conclusion of a collective agreement is regarded as the *sole* justification for a right to strike, workers should be able to strike only in pursuit of improved terms and conditions of employment. Strikes aimed at changing managerial policy related to the profitability of the business or organization of work does not seem to come within the scope of this right, but must be justified on some other ground.[25] Moreover, strikes aimed at changing government policy could not be justified upon this basis.

Approached from the perspective of collective bargaining, the right to strike may be viewed as a *collective* right.[26] Ruth Ben-Israel takes this approach, arguing that the right to strike can be exercised only collectively; individual withdrawal of labour has little persuasive force.[27] She also observes that strikes usually require some degree of co-ordination, so that it makes sense to confer the right to strike on workers' organizations, rather than their individual members.[28] This would mean that, as far as a trade union is concerned, its individual members will have either a duty to strike or a duty not to strike in accordance with the decision made within the organization—'never a right to strike'.[29] If the right to strike is only a means by which to achieve the inclusion of certain terms and conditions in a collective agreement, this may be desirable, at least in terms of efficacy. However, it is a less desirable view if the right to strike can also be justified on political grounds or as an extension of other civil liberties.

---

[24] See Labour Relations Act No. 28 of 1956 (SA), s. 65(1)(d).

[25] Cf. discussion of 'objectionable purposes' in Macfarlane, L.J., *The Right to Strike* (Harmondsworth: Penguin Books, 1981), 36.

[26] *Ibid.*, 20; Schermers, n.6 above, 230; and Von Prondzynski, F., *Freedom of Association and Industrial Relations: A Comparative Study* (London: Mansell, 1987), 106 and 233.

[27] Ben-Israel, R., 'Is the Right to Strike a Collective Human Right?' (1981) 11 *Israel Yearbook of Human Rights* 195, 214.

[28] *Ibid.*, 200.

[29] Macfarlane, n.25 above, 20–1.

Another problem is that Ben-Israel's argument relies on a view of trade unions as entirely democratic and representative in their membership. There are difficulties with the wholesale adoption of this assumption. As was observed in Chapter 1, workers are not necessarily a homogeneous group. Those who work from home on a part-time or on a casual basis often do not have ready access to trade union membership and may wish to take industrial action on their own initiative. Moreover, trade unions have, at least in the past, failed to represent adequately the interests of women and ethnic minorities.[30] These workers may, despite their notional membership of a trade union, wish to take action to protect their particular interests which appear to be overlooked by the upper echelons of trade union management. Solidarity and, therefore, organization in a trade union seem the more desirable course of action. Nevertheless, to the extent that membership is limited or where unions do not adequately represent their members, the option should arguably be there for workers outside this institutional structure to claim a right to strike for purposes of bargaining with their employer; or at least there should be scope swiftly to form a trade union which reflects their interests. It is even possible that the availability of such action to individual workers, outside the scope of trade union endorsement, will prompt trade unions to review their decision-making procedures, their bargaining agendas, and their recruitment strategies. The right to strike, even when justified solely in socio-economic terms, as a tool in collective bargaining, may therefore be viewed as a right possessed by individual workers, to be exercised in combination with like-minded persons, as well as within the confines of what the State has designated as legitimate trade union structures.[31]

A further issue is the extent to which workers should be able to rely on their 'socio-economic' interests as a basis for taking 'secondary action', that is, a strike designed to affect the policies adopted by someone other than their immediate employer. There is arguably a case for legal protection of such action where the employer is artificially divided into a number of discrete corporate entities or 'buffer companies', so as to avoid broader-based collective representation amongst its workforce which would be likely to give the workers more bargaining power.[32] It is also arguable that secondary industrial action should be able to be taken in defence of socio-economic interests of workers at the sectoral level, or within a 'European company', in the

---

[30] Chap. 1 above, at 9–10.

[31] Subject, of course, to the exceptions set out in Chap. 4 below.

[32] See the comments on Rupert Murdoch's UK activities in Simpson, B., 'Trade Union Immunities' in Lewis, R. (ed.), *Labour Law in Britain* (Oxford: Blackwell, 1986), 176–9; also see *Dimbleby & Sons Ltd v NUJ* [1984] IRLR 161; [1984] ICR 386. See for criticism of the UK position, *Report of the Committee of Experts on the Application of Conventions and Recommendations* (Geneva: ILO, 1999) ILC, 87th Session, 290–1, discussed in Chap. 4 below, at 76–7.

context of Europe-wide collective bargaining.[33] The smaller the workplace or the bargaining unit, the more difficult it may be to influence the conduct of one's own employer or standards within an industrial sector. Arguments that 'sympathy' action should be lawful stem from a broad view of the benefits of solidarity in achieving the socio-economic goals of workers.

A final question is how broadly the scope of legitimate 'socio-economic' objectives of workers can be construed. For example, if workers are entitled to strike to improve terms and conditions which impact upon their daily welfare, can they not take action to seek to improve the minimum wage set by the State or the labour laws relating to the consequences of dismissal? These claims can also be extended to circumstances in which workers are dependent upon the State for key provision of other aspects of their welfare, such as health, education, and social security. These questions are considered further in this chapter, when considering the legitimacy of strikes aimed at challenging government policy.

II. THE RIGHT TO STRIKE AS A POLITICAL RIGHT

The term 'political strike' customarily denotes a key exception to legal protection which would otherwise be extended to those who organize or participate in industrial action. Indeed, it is a term associated with illegality and disapprobation.[34]

The reason is that 'political strikes' are viewed as disruptive of democratic processes. My contention is that it is inappropriate to speak of 'political strikes' as if they constituted an amorphous mass of iniquity, for strikes may be capable, not only of undermining, but also of facilitating democratic participation. In this context, it is important to identify the senses in which diverse forms of industrial action are viewed as political. These are, arguably, threefold.

First, a strike can be said to be 'political' in so far as it challenges the traditional balance of power between capital and labour in any particular enterprise or industry.[35] Industrial action that challenges traditional powers

---

[33] See Germanotta, P., and Novitz, T., 'Globalisation and the Right to Strike: The Case for European-Level Protection of Secondary Action' (2002) 18 *IJCLLIR* 67; Bruun, N., and Veneziani, B., 'The Right or Freedom to Transnational Industrial Action in the European Union' in *A Legal Framework for European Industrial Relations* (Brussels: ETUI, 1999); and Aaltonen, J., *International Secondary Action in the EU Member States* (Espoo: Metalli, 1999).

[34] *Sherard v AUEW* [1973] ICR 421 at 435 per Roskill LJ. See also Kahn-Freund, O., Davies, P., and Freedland, M., *Labour and the Law* (3rd edn., London: Stevens & Sons, 1983), 315.

[35] See Hain, n.22 above, 20; and Williams, M., 'Control at All Costs: South African Security Legislation and the Trade Unions' (1989) 30 *Harvard Journal of International Law* 477 at 479 who states that when the worker 'joins the union he enters into a power relationship with the employer, and whether through strike action or negotiations, that worker has engaged in a political act'.

of managerial prerogative, for example as regards restructuring, is an illustration of this phenomenon. It is suggested here that there may be an argument for protection of the right to strike as an aspect of 'industrial democracy'.

Secondly, the adjective 'political' can be used to describe actions taken by reason of ideological convictions relating to the achievement of social justice. Strikes which challenge an employer's environmental practices or trading partners would come within this category. Here, workers are not acting in their own direct interests, but in line with what they consider to be fundamental ethical beliefs. By taking an extended view of workers' legitimate interests or by mounting an argument based on 'freedom of speech', it may be possible to provide a democratic justification for protection of a right to strike in these circumstances.

Finally, the term 'political' is most commonly applied to those actions which are connected with or are designed to affect the operation of government. Strikes which have such aims are generally regarded as the most alarming. Nevertheless, I shall examine the controversial argument that the ability to take such industrial action can sometimes be justified in democratic terms; both in the context of 'protest strikes' against totalitarian regimes and even, potentially, against Western European 'democratic' government.

A.   THE RIGHT TO STRIKE AS A FACET OF INDUSTRIAL DEMOCRACY

Traditionally, collective bargaining has been concerned solely with determining wages and working conditions. Other matters, such as decisions about 'production programming, workshop layout and the technology and design of plant equipment', were viewed exclusively as matters for management and not of concern to workers.[36] However, the question has arisen whether this should be regarded as the sole ambit of their legitimate concerns. It has been suggested that the right to strike can do more than merely ensure the material well-being of workers.[37] Industrial action can also provide workers with an opportunity to participate in decisions concerning management of the workplace and can thereby influence policies which affect their daily lives.

It has become increasingly common for workers to claim, in their work situations, some version of the rights they now enjoy in the political field.[38] These claims appear to have been broadly accepted by States and

[36] Macfarlane, n.25 above, 69.

[37] See Ewing, n.2 above, 100; and Laski, H., *A Grammar of Politics* (London: Faber & Faber, 1938), chap. 3.

[38] See, e.g., Dahl, R.A., *A Preface to Economic Democracy* (Cambridge: Polity Press, 1985), chap. 4; Pateman, C., *Participation and Democratic Theory* (Cambridge: CUP, 1970); Gould, G.C., *Rethinking Democracy* (Cambridge: CUP, 1988). Cf. Narveson, J., 'Democracy and Economic Rights' in Frankel Paul, E., Miller, F.D., and Paul, J. (eds.), *Economic Rights* (Cambridge: CUP, 1992).

employers, who have introduced various forms of 'worker participation' into workplace decision-making.

Collective bargaining is one of the oldest forms of worker participation, but is considered by many employers today to be too confrontational.[39] They prefer alternative methods, such as consultation of worker representatives, profit-sharing schemes, or appointment of worker directors.[40] Within the European Community, provision is made for workers to be informed and consulted on various issues.[41] These more co-operative initiatives seem to be designed to avoid industrial conflict and focus upon the shared interests or 'partnership' of employers and workers.[42] They also tend to use the language of personal 'empowerment' and 'social responsibility', taken from grassroots egalitarian organizations; but it has been observed that the procedures established do not usually challenge the fundamental basis of property ownership, or managerial control.[43]

It has been claimed that, as a result of these initiatives, the sphere of unchallenged managerial prerogative has diminished.[44] A different view is taken by those who fear that current forms of workforce participation allow only token involvement of workers in the decision-making process, so that their actions do little more than legitimate decisions taken by management. Wolfgang Däubler has observed that participation in management decision-making can become an 'exercise in futility' where worker representatives are choosing, at best, between 'various forms and procedures for maximising profits'.[45] For example, the information and consultation procedures established by the EC may provide workers with remarkably little influence over

[39] Fox, A., *Man Mismanagement* (2nd edn., London: Hutchinson, 1985), chap. 5.

[40] For a discussion of the various forms of worker participation see Ewing, n.2 above, 110–13. Also see *Workers' Participation in Decisions within Undertakings* (Geneva: ILO, 1981), chap. 2, 'Varieties of Participation'.

[41] See, e.g., EC Framework Directive on Health and Safety 89/391 [1989] OJ L183/1; EC Directive on Collective Redundancies 98/59 [1998] OJ L225/16; and EC Directive on Acquired Rights 2001/23 [2001] OJ L82/116.

[42] Note, e.g., that in 'works councils', the employee representatives are required to work with management 'in a spirit of co-operation', which, judging from the German works councils experience, seems to preclude strikes. See the UK Transnational Information and Consultation of Employee Regulations 1999, SI 1999/3323. Cf. Däubler, W., 'Co-determination: The German Experience' (1975) 4 *ILJ* 218 at 225.

[43] Rothschild, J., 'Obscuring But Not Reducing Managerial Control: Does TQM Measure up to Democracy Standards?' (1999) 20 *Economic and Industrial Democracy* 583 at 610–11. See also Guest, D.E., and Peccei, R., 'Partnership at Work: Mutuality and the Balance of Advantage' (2001) 39 *BJIR* 207.

[44] For a recent UK survey see 'Partnership at Work: A Survey' (1997) 645 *IRS Employment Trends* 3. For a review of US claims relating to the desirability of 'partnership' see Kochan, T., and Osterman, P., *The Mutual Gains Enterprise: Forging a Winning Partnership among Labor, Management and Government* (Boston, Mass.: Harvard Business School Press, 1994); Heckscher, C., *The New Unionism: Employee Involvement in the Changing Corporation* (Ithaca, NY: ILR Press, 1996).

[45] Däubler, W., 'The Employee Participation Directive—A Realistic Utopia?' (1977) 14 *CMLRev.* 457 at 473.

decision-making in matters concerning collective redundancies, unless they possess some external source of bargaining power. Lord Wedderburn, commenting on European developments, has delivered the following warning: '[t]he right to consult must be measured alongside the right, in law or practice, to negotiate. Without the constraints of autonomous collective bargaining, management prerogative can turn consultation into a highway for personalised contracts.'[46] If it is the threat of industrial action which provides employers with an incentive to respond to workers' concerns, then any effective form of industrial democracy 'should include the right of workers at the shop-floor level to put pressure on management, even if they are represented on a board by a workers' director'.[47] A right to strike can therefore be regarded as an appropriate supplement to effective worker participation in decision-making within the enterprise.

The consequences of accepting this supplementary justification for the right to strike are significant. If the right to strike is justified on the basis of industrial democracy, and not merely as a means by which to ensure fair working conditions, the scope of the right to strike will be broader. Workers may be able to take industrial action, not only when their own wages or working conditions are directly at stake, but when they are opposed to the way in which an enterprise is being run or the decisions management has made. In reliance upon this justification, workers could strike in protest against choices made to increase profit margins through reorganization of the workplace.

B.   IDEOLOGICAL STRIKES AGAINST EMPLOYER POLICIES

At various times, workers have been willing to engage in industrial action for reasons unconnected with their own immediate concerns or financial interests. The motivation for their action often has an ideological basis and broad social implications.[48] There are many examples. In the United States, the International Longshoremen's Association (ILA) refused to load and unload goods destined for or originating in the Soviet Union following the invasion of Afghanistan. The union's protest was predominantly aimed at their employer's continued trade with the Soviet Union whose actions they viewed as morally culpable.[49] Similarly, in the 1970s an Australian

---

[46] Wedderburn, Lord, 'Consultation and Collective Bargaining in Europe: Success or Ideology?' (1997) 26 *ILJ* 1, 32.

[47] Betten, L., *The Right to Strike in Community Law: The Incorporation of Fundamental Rights in the Legal Order of the European Communities* (Amsterdam/New York/Oxford: North-Holland, 1985), 120. Similar sentiments are expressed by Wedderburn, n.46 above, at 26–30.

[48] Kupferberg, S., 'Political Strikes, Labor Law and Democratic Rights' (1985) 71 *Virginia Law Review* 685, 743.

[49] See *International Longshoremen's Association v Allied International Inc* 465 US 212 (1982); *Jacksonville Bulk Terminal Inc v International Longshoremen's Association* 457 US 702 (1982); Lee-Ching, D., 'Labor Law I: Judicial Intervention in Politically Motivated Work Stoppages' [1983] *Annual Survey of American Law* 411; and Kupferberg, n.48 above.

construction workers' union embarked upon 'green bans' industrial action to protect the environment. The New South Wales Builders' Labourers Federation refused to take jobs constructing a luxury complex on undeveloped bush land, on the 'green belt' of Sydney, respecting community opposition to this project.[50] A British example was the threat made on behalf of members of the Association of Broadcasting Staff to the British Broadcasting Corporation (BBC) that the union's members would take 'whatever industrial action necessary' to prevent the 1977 FA Cup Final being relayed via satellite to South Africa.[51] The strikes in these cases were not directly connected to workers' own self-interest and had minimal relevance to their terms and conditions of employment. They were taken for reasons of conscience and aimed at policies of their employer which did not directly concern their own interests.

When workers strike with the express aim of influencing employers' policies with regard to some matter other than their own working conditions, they impinge even more directly on matters which are conventionally the subject of managerial prerogative. Traditionally, the owners of capital were considered to be entitled to do what they wished with their property and to delegate such authority to their managers, subject only to considerations relating to the welfare of their workers.[52] Any ethical decisions relating to the conduct of trading were to be made by the employer without reference to the preferences of the workers.

There are at least two bases on which it may be possible to regard industrial action of this type as being defensible in democratic terms. The first relies on an extended view of the socio-economic or other legitimate interests of workers. The second is that considerations of a social character should be permitted to influence the market-led decisions often taken by employers.

In certain cases, courts have been prepared to extend the concept of workers' 'self-interest', so as to accommodate industrial action taken on a principled stance. This is an attempt to relate the right to strike back to the socio-economic interests of the workers. An example is *Scala Ballroom (Wolverhampton) Ltd v Ratcliffe*, where workers protested against a 'colour bar' which excluded certain customers from their workplace, a ballroom. The Court of Appeal found that the refusal of members of the Musicians' Union to perform in the ballroom did not constitute actionable conspiracy. The Court's reasoning was that the musicians were merely protecting the livelihood of members of the union, a great many of whom were people of

---

[50] See Thomas, P., *Taming the Corporate Jungle* (Sydney: NSW Branch of the Australian Building Construction Employees and Builders' Labourers' Federation, 1973).

[51] *BBC v Hearn* [1977] ICR 685 (CA).

[52] Collins, H., 'Market Power, Bureaucratic Power and the Contract of Employment' (1986) 15 *ILJ* 1, 14.

colour.[53] In such circumstances, it may be preferable for the court openly to acknowledge that, while these types of strikes do not relate to workers' material self-interest, legitimately defensible interests of a different kind are at stake. Such strikes could be considered justifiable on the grounds of individual conscience and moral autonomy or as an extension of free speech.[54] Indeed, a strike may be viewed as an aspect of acting as a responsible citizen, a role which cannot simply be suspended during working hours.[55]

On another level, we could view this form of industrial action as a means by which to allow the values of the 'life world' to permeate the capitalist 'system'.[56] In relation to the Sydney 'green bans', one writer has noted that: '[c]onstitutional democratic procedures had not decided how to develop Sydney before the labourers stepped in; profit-making builders had. The green bans may be understood, therefore, as taking one step further a union goal traditionally applied to setting wages and other conditions of employment: substituting a conscious group decision for a market determination seemingly independent of human will.'[57] There are suggestions that multinational companies will soon, if they do not already, operate outside the control of domestic laws and regulation.[58] Action by workers taken on ethical as well as straightforwardly self-interested grounds could constrain their operations, making such corporations aware, not only of the potential for short- or long-term profit, but also of certain social issues which concern the majority of those who work for them.

C. STRIKES THAT CHALLENGE GOVERNMENT POLICY

Strikes have been called in various States, such as Poland,[59] South Africa,[60] Nigeria,[61] and most recently Zimbabwe,[62] in pursuit of representative

[53] [1958] 3 All ER 220 per Hodgson LJ at 223–4.

[54] See for arguments of this nature Werhane, P.H., *Persons, Rights and Corporations* (Englewood Cliffs, NJ: Prentice-Hall, 1985).

[55] It should also be possible to place limits upon the objectives of strikers where these are anti-democratic, such as where a trade union seeks to exclude a portion of the workforce on the basis of sex or race.

[56] Cf. Habermas, J., *Between Facts and Norms: Contributions to a Discourse Theory of Law and Democracy*, trans. Rehg, W. (Boston, Mass.: MIT, 1997), discussed in Chap. 1 above, at 20.

[57] Kupferberg, n.48 above, 743.

[58] See Chap. 1 above at 17–18.

[59] See *Report of the Commission Instituted Under Article 26 of the Constitution of the ILO to Examine the Complaint on the Observance by Poland of Conventions Nos. 87 and 98* (Geneva: ILO, 1984), para. 491.

[60] See *Gana v Building Manufacturers Ltd t/a Doorcor* (1990) ILJ (SA) 561, at 570–1. Also *Report of the Fact-Finding and Conciliation Commission on Freedom of Association concerning the Republic of South Africa* (Geneva: ILO, 1992).

[61] See *Case No. 1793 (Nigeria)*, 295th Report of the ILO Committee on Freedom of Association (1994), para. 567; Committee of Inquiry established 26 Mar. 1998: see GB271/18/5 and ILO Press Releases ILO/91/13 and ILO/98/29. This was discussed further in Chap. 12, below, at 300.

[62] Chap. 1 above, at 12.

democratic government. The withdrawal of labour has a detrimental effect on the profits of business and the economy as a whole, indirectly placing pressure on the State to accede to workers' demands. It is a more effective form of protest than marching in the streets. Also, 'if one is dealing with a highly repressive or autocratic regime, it is not difficult, in terms of democratic theory, to justify the use of the strike weapon to secure the overthrow of the Government or major changes in the constitution'.[63] Indeed, trade unions past and present have been said to 'play a crucial role in the fight for democracy all over the world'.[64]

A non-democratic government would be unlikely to take legal measures to protect strikes aimed at challenging its policies or mode of government, but it remains possible for international organizations to intervene in defence of such strikes. The difficulty faced by international organizations in this kind of situation is that international law is traditionally built upon consensus among States and is therefore unlikely to support overtly revolutionary acts.[65]

Industrial action with such a revolutionary purpose arises in extreme circumstances and is relatively rare. A more interesting question is whether strikes aimed at influencing government policy should be permitted in an ostensibly democratic State. It is said that political issues should be exposed, debated, decided, and legislated upon in the open political arena of Parliament, and those involved at the centre of the political process be accountable to the electorate.[66] If strikes can be used to influence government policy, governments can no longer act upon the views of the majority of the people they purport to represent. As Schermers noted:

In a democratic society where decisions are based on the wishes of the majority of the population political strikes are unacceptable. One cannot tolerate that a relatively small group of persons in key positions can force a democratic government into a policy not wanted by the majority.[67]

This objection rests on a firm belief in the model of majoritarian 'representative' democracy outlined in Chapter 1.[68]

Such an objection may, however, be overcome if it is accepted that government by elected representatives is not sufficient to secure democratic participation. Pluralist theorists who advocate 'participatory democracy'

---

[63] Macfarlane, n.25 above, 158–9.

[64] See Hepple, B., 'The Role of Trade Unions in a Democratic Society' (1990) 11 *Industrial Law Journal* (South Africa) 645.

[65] See Chap. 1 above, at 27–8.

[66] Shenfield, n.12 above, 55. Note that a similar view is taken in Germany. See Weiss, M., 'Germany', in Blanpain, R. (ed.), *International Encyclopaedia of Labour Law and Industrial Relations* (Deventer: Kluwer, 1977–), v. For a discussion of this view see Laski, H.J., *Liberty in the Modern State* (London: Faber & Faber, 1930), 127–35.

[67] Schermers, n.6 above, 231.

[68] See Chap. 1 above, at 16–18.

consider that centralized political power is neither a reality nor desirable. Despite the existence of an elected government, interest groups compete for political influence, and it is more desirable to place these interest groups upon an even footing than to pretend that they do not exist. If this alternative account of democratic participation is accepted, employers and workers can be regarded as two interest groups, which can and should have input into government policy.[69] All governments require 'at least the passive acquiescence of these pressure groups', but 'in an economy based upon private ownership the power of industrial and financial capitalists is greater than those of any other class'.[70] If there is to be some balance between the relative political influence of capital and labour, there may be a case for legal recognition of strikes which seek to influence government policy.

Free movement of capital is widely accepted. At present, employers, whether they be companies or individuals, possess the potential to undermine governments by closing factories and moving capital overseas, when they consider that a government's economic or social policies are unsatisfactory.[71] It has been argued that workers should have the parallel freedom to withdraw their labour. Roger Welch has written:

Imagine the howls of protest if legislation was passed to force employers to stay in business; yet this is effectively what the current law does to employees in preventing them from obtaining the support of unions for withdrawing their labour if a dispute is regarded by a court as having a significant political dimension.[72]

If one accepts this argument, there appears to be a case for strikes aimed at influencing government policy, even where this is a government elected by a majority of the people.[73]

The drawback of this theory is, however, that it skips from a description of current power relations within modern democracies to a normative assumption that this is the manner in which they *should* operate. It seems worth considering whether any negative consequences will follow from labour seeking to maintain this precarious 'balance of power' in the political sphere by means of industrial action.[74]

---

[69] *Ibid.*, 18–20.

[70] Burkitt, B., 'Excessive Trade Union Power: Existing Reality or Contemporary Myth?' (1981) 12 *Industrial Relations Journal* (UK) 65, 70; and Dahl, n.38 above, 60. See also Laski, H., *Trade Unions in the New Society* (London: Allen & Unwin, 1950), 22–3.

[71] Burkitt, n.70 above, 70 discusses the reality of 'capital strikes' when state actions transgress financial interests. See Chap. 1 above, at 17–18.

[72] Welch, R., *The Right to Strike: A Trade Union View* (London: Institute of Employment Rights, 1991), 9–10.

[73] At least in so far as those organizing a strike, usually trade unions, are representative of the workers in question.

[74] Note that it remains difficult to assess how this elusive 'balance of power' or 'equilibrium' is to be determined. See 'The New Democracy' in Lukes, S., *Essays in Social Theory* (London: Macmillan, 1977), 44–5.

The most obvious danger is that, if capital and labour are allowed to stage a battle over government policy, other interest groups within 'civil society' with less bargaining power may be deprived of democratic participation. For this reason, Macfarlane has suggested that a distinction can be drawn between 'protest strikes' and 'coercive strikes'. He describes 'protest strikes' as 'those strikes designed merely to draw attention to the extent or depth of feeling against a particular government law, policy or action' while 'coercive strikes' are 'designed to force the government to change that policy'. It follows that 'protest strikes', but not 'coercive strikes', should be permissible in a democratic society.[75]

This may be a difficult distinction to make, but a code of conduct for protest strikes could be of some assistance. One South African labour lawyer, Chris Albertyn, has suggested three such limitations which could be applied to South African 'political stay-aways':

(i) that the strike should concern political issues in which workers have a special interest as workers, and not merely an interest as citizens;

(ii) that the strike should be of a predetermined and limited duration (no longer than three days); and

(iii) that the union should give reasonable notice to the employer (perhaps as much as fourteen days' notice).[76]

The first of these limitations is difficult to reconcile with my earlier discussion of a right to strike on the grounds of a collective social conscience, for example against apartheid or on environmental issues. One may be sceptical whether it is possible to demarcate the sphere of workers' interests in the manner Albertyn suggests.[77] The second limitation ties in with Macfarlane's distinction between 'protest' and 'coercive' strikes. As Albertyn states, 'a political strike of limited duration achieves the legitimate purpose: protest and publicity of workers' opposition to the government's programme'. It does not seek to depose government.[78] Finally, the third limitation is consistent with the strikers' apparent aims. If the purpose of the political strike is not to harm the employer but to express opposition to government policy, then steps should be taken to cause minimal inconvenience and cost to the employer. The application of these limitations may not be entirely straightforward, but they do however raise the prospect of defensible legal protection of a 'political strike', aimed solely at protesting against government policy within ostensibly democratic States.

[75] Macfarlane, n.25 above, 149.
[76] Albertyn, C., 'Political Strikes' (1993) 10(2) *Employment Law* (South Africa) 40.
[77] See Laski, n.66 above, 148 who describes 'such a definition of spheres' as 'impossible of achievement'.
[78] Albertyn, n.76 above, 41.

III.   THE RIGHT TO STRIKE AS A CIVIL LIBERTY

Those advocating international protection of a right to strike have been well aware of the difference in status between 'socio-economic' rights and 'civil liberties' under certain national constitutions and international human rights instruments. Their response has been to forge a link between the right to strike and more commonly recognized civil liberties, the prime example being freedom of association.[79]

It has been argued that collective bargaining and the right to strike are not just the 'mundane creation of the legislative branch concerned primarily with mundane matters of material well-being', but that 'the freedoms claimed by workers... are amongst the oldest liberties in our tradition of liberal democratic social relations'.[80] This section considers the extent to which it is possible to make a logical connection between the right to strike and established civil liberties, such as freedom of association, freedom from forced labour, and freedom of speech.

A.   FREEDOM OF ASSOCIATION

The right to strike receives express protection under the European Social Charter 1961 and the International Covenant on Economic and Social Rights 1966, but these instruments deal exclusively with socio-economic rights and possess minimal persuasive force. By contrast, freedom of association is commonly recognized as a fundamental civil liberty, and as such is guaranteed under instruments such as the European Convention on Human Rights 1950, the International Covenant on Civil and Political Rights 1966, and the Constitution of the ILO. To claim that the right to strike is derived from or inextricably linked to freedom of association is to claim the greater degree of protection commonly afforded to the latter.

Strictly speaking, a 'freedom' can be distinguished from a 'right'. The difference, in theory, is that a right imposes correlative duties on others while a freedom is merely the absence of a duty. A 'freedom' can be understood as the opposition of obstruction, from either the State or private persons. Nevertheless, 'freedom of association' can be regarded as a basis for imposing obligations upon others. Indeed, the same could be said to be true of freedom of speech and freedom from forced labour.[81]

---

[79] This fundamental rights approach seems to have been adopted in France and Italy. See Kahn-Freund, O., *The Right to Strike: Its Scope and Limitations* (Strasbourg: Council of Europe, 1974), 3.

[80] Beatty, D., and Kennett, S., 'Striking Back: Fighting Words, Social Protest and Political Participation in Free and Democratic Societies' (1988) 67 *Canadian Bar Review* 573, 598.

[81] See Von Prondzynski, F., 'Freedom of Association and the Closed Shop' (1982) 41 *Cambridge Law Journal* 256 at 263–4. See also Chap. 2 above, at 42–5.

Ferdinand von Prondzynski once described freedom of association as 'no more than a useful shorthand expression for a bundle of rights and freedoms relating to membership of associations'.[82] Freedom of association can be regarded as a civil right in that, where an individual wishes to associate with others, there is to be 'protection against arbitrary interference by the State or private parties'.[83] Freedom of association can also be viewed as a political right, 'because political interests can be effectively championed only in community with others'.[84] Moreover, freedom of association has a social function, as it enables the collective defence of workers' interests. This spectrum of possible justifications could, therefore, be said to parallel that potentially applicable to the right to strike.

Freedom of association is most commonly regarded as safeguarding individual civil liberty. It is an extension of the principle that people may do whatever they wish as long as they do not harm others. Accordingly, an individual should be free to join an organization and to act in association with others, as long as no harm is caused by doing so.[85] Freedom of association was initially claimed for the protection of groups created for religious, scientific, and charitable purposes.[86] Protection of individual freedom of conscience appears to have been its primary aim. Gradually, this freedom to form associations was extended to other spheres, one of these being the industrial sphere.[87]

At first 'the simultaneous combination among workers' in trade unions generated alarm. '[I]n accordance with the concept of the free play of supply and demand which then prevailed it was strictly penalised.'[88] Certain governments went so far as to prohibit workers' organizations.[89] Nevertheless, over the past century, the right to form trade unions has been recognized by the vast majority of governments in Western industrial countries.

[82] Von Prondzynski, n.26 above, 27. For a similar, but earlier, view of the multiple ambiguity of this term see Nicod, J., 'Freedom of Association and Trade Unionism: An Introductory Survey' (1924) 9 *ILRev.* 467 at 468.

[83] Nowak, M., *UN Covenant on Civil and Political Rights: CCPR Commentary* (Kehl/Strasbourg/Arlington, Vir.: Engel, 1993), 385.

[84] *Ibid.*

[85] 'On Liberty' in Mill, J.S., *Utilitarianism* (Warnock, M. (ed.), Glasgow: Fontana Press, 1962), 138. See also for a more contemporary formulation of that principle Sheppard, T., 'Liberalism and the Charter: Freedom of Association and the Freedom to Strike' (1996) 5 *Dalhousie Journal of Legal Studies* 117 at 125 ff.

[86] Jenks, C.W., *The International Protection of Trade Union Freedoms* (London: Stevens & Sons, 1957), 14. Alkema, E., 'Freedom of Associations and Civil Society' in Council of Europe, *Freedom of Association Proceedings* (Strasbourg: Council of Europe Press, 1994), 58–9.

[87] E.g., the provision concerning freedom of association in Art. 11(1) of the European Convention on Human Rights 1950 expressly includes 'the right to form and join trade unions'.

[88] Nicod, n.82 above, 468.

[89] Chisholm, A., *Labour's Magna Charta: A Critical Study of the Labour Clauses of the Peace Treaty and of the Draft Conventions and Recommendations of the Washington International Labour Conference* (London: Longmans, Green & Co., 1925), 77 and Hepple, n.5 above, App. I, 'The Countries: A Short Guide', 301–29.

The liberal state, 'which recognised the right of association and of assembly in general, could not indefinitely maintain the paradox of forbidding a certain category of citizens from combining and meeting'.[90]

Individual choice and the freedom to dissociate have been recognized as essential aspects of freedom of association.[91] However, it has long been argued that the individualistic conception of freedom of association should be modified in the context of trade union affiliation and collective bargaining.[92] In this context, freedom of association can be viewed as having a particular purpose over and above the protection of an individual's desire to meet, study, or worship with others; that purpose being to redress long-standing inequalities of bargaining power between employer and worker. Through membership of trade unions, workers can appoint representatives to voice their opinions, argue their case in collective bargaining, and organize industrial action. In other words, freedom to associate allows workers to participate in making those decisions which affect their working environment and thereby their working lives.[93] It is a means by which to secure recognition of workers' political, social, and economic interests.

Those who regard freedom of association solely as a civil liberty commonly hold that the right to strike does not come within its ambit by virtue of Mill's 'harm principle'.[94] Strikes inflict economic harm upon employers in an attempt to force them to modify their position in negotiations. Strikes may also involve placing pressure upon other workers; first, upon members of the existing workforce to join the strike, and secondly, upon other workers outside the workplace not to replace striking workers. For these reasons, it is said that strikes impinge on individual liberty. Those who view freedom of association as an individual right, even though it is exercised collectively, tend to conclude that where the individual is in tension with the community the individual must prevail.[95]

Sheldon Leader has challenged this conventional narrow view of freedom of association. He considers that freedom of association means more than the individual right to join and act within an association. Rather, it is the 'freedom of persons to do collectively what they are allowed to do individually'.[96] In other words, individuals should not have less freedom as a group

---

[90] *Freedom of Association: Report and Draft Questionnaire*, ILC, 10th Session (Geneva: International Labour Office, 1927), 12.

[91] E.g., the Universal Declaration of Human Rights 1948, Art. 20(2) states that 'no one may be compelled to belong to an association'.

[92] See, e.g., Jenks, n.86 above, 63.

[93] See above, at 57–9.

[94] Cf. Mill, n.85 above.

[95] Accordingly, the freedom *not* to associate takes precedence over the freedom to associate. Cf. de Tocqueville, A., *Democracy in America*, transl. Lawrence, G. (New York: Harper and Row, 1996), 177: 'freedom of association has become a necessary guarantee against the tyranny of the majority . . .'.

[96] See Leader, S., *Freedom of Association, A Study in Labour Law and Political Theory* (New Haven, Conn./London: Yale University Press, 1992), 23 and 200.

than they have individually. He phrases this claim essentially as an individual right, in 'the language of equal protection'.[97] The right to strike can then be explained in the following terms. If an individual is legally entitled to refuse to work then the co-ordinated withdrawal of labour should be permitted. As an individual is free to withdraw his or her services for any reason whatsoever without civil or criminal liability, this gives rise to a wide-ranging right to strike.[98]

Leader's argument is however more problematic than it may at first appear. While an individual who withdraws his or her labour may be immune from criminal liability or liability in tort, that individual breaches his or her contract of employment by non-performance, thereby giving the employer the option to terminate the contract or seek an alternative form of relief.[99] Even if the worker's aim in leaving is to obtain better terms and conditions of employment from that employer, at least in English common law the employer is entitled to sever the contractual nexus. On the other hand, workers who go on strike claim that the contract of employment has been or should be suspended and that their jobs continue to belong to them while they temporarily cease to perform them. Moreover, an individual worker may be required to pay contractual damages as an 'exit price' from work. Leader's response is that 'if we can see that the right to strike which is carved out of the restrictions of tort and crime expresses the principle behind a fundamental right to associate, then we are entitled to turn back to contract and demand that it express the same principle'.[100] Nevertheless, this rejoinder does not rely on Leader's earlier symmetry argument. Indeed, he seems to be arguing from the *descriptive* (the state of the law of tort and criminal law in the twentieth century) to the *normative* (what the law of contract should be). He requires some further reasons to support his argument, and this suggests that questions other than those of symmetry are at issue here.

A more promising argument is that, in the industrial context, freedom of association has a second-order justification that gives it particular force and scope in the context of employment. Combination in a trade union is a function of individual liberty, but its desirability, as perceived by trade union members, is also connected to the political, social, and economic sphere within which the trade union operates. Freedom of association allows workers to form trade unions, which in turn provide a basis for

[97] *Ibid.*, 189.

[98] Note that Leader's argument relates only to legal immunity for those participating in strikes. He does not explain why the organizer of a strike should receive such immunity. Individuals who encourage others to withdraw their services can be liable in tort. See, e.g., *Lumley v Gye* (1853) 2 E & B 216 and *South Wales Miners' Federation v Glamorgan Coal Co. Ltd* [1905] AC 239 (although the impact of liability in tort has been mitigated since by industrial legislation in the UK).

[99] Leader, n.96 above, 189. See for a similar claim that of Beatty and Kennett, n.80 above, 590–2.

[100] Leader, n.96 above, 204.

collective bargaining. This is the means by which workers can overcome the limitations inherent in individual contracts of employment and participate in making those decisions which affect their lives and their society. To the extent that the right to strike assists workers in the achievement of these goals, it may be viewed as the logical extension of freedom of association in the workplace. Similarly, the freedom to associate may be regarded as a freedom which can be exercised even without formal membership of a trade union, where workers perceive the value of employing a joint bargaining strategy to achieve objectives which are socio-economic (or even political) in character. If the right to strike can be linked in this manner to respect for freedom of association, a broad entitlement to strike may arise in relation to all those matters in respect of which it is accepted that workers have a legitimate interest.

B.   Freedom from Forced Labour

A worker's entitlement to freedom from forced labour is recognized in Article 427 of the Treaty of Versailles 1919 and in the precept under international law that 'no one shall be held in slavery or servitude'.[101] The principle of freedom from forced labour is usually seen as applicable only to individual workers and their right to refuse to work for a particular employer. The question is whether, as Ben-Israel has claimed, freedom from forced labour provides a justification for the right to strike.[102]

When strikers withdraw their labour, no criminal sanction is usually imposed for the failure to perform an employment contract.[103] However, injunctions against organizers and dismissal of participants may make it difficult for a striker to resist the compulsion to work.[104] Some governments also impose additional economic sanctions for participation in strikes, such as disentitlement to social security benefits or loss of tax rebates, which may effectively keep an individual at work.[105]

Nevertheless, the claim made by Ben-Israel has yet to receive widespread recognition or acceptance. For example, the United States Supreme Court failed to make any connection between a right to organize or take part in industrial action and the Thirteenth Amendment to the Constitution,

---

[101] Universal Declaration of Human Rights 1948, Art. 4. See also ILO Conventions Nos. 29 and 105 on the Elimination of All Forms of Forced and Compulsory Labour (1930 and 1957).

[102] Ben-Israel, R., *International Labour Standards: The Case of Freedom to Strike* (Deventer: Kluwer, 1988), 25. To some extent this argument can also be linked to Leader's argument that a right to strike can be based on the freedom of individual workers to withdraw their labour.

[103] Kahn-Freund and Hepple, n.17 above, 7–8 consider that this argument lacks persuasion for that reason.

[104] Ben-Israel, n.102 above, 25.

[105] Kupferberg, n.48 above, 734. See also on individuals' vulnerability in the event of a strike Ewing, K.D., *The Right to Strike* (Oxford: OUP, 1991).

which prohibits involuntary servitude. There is no constitutional protection of a right to strike in the USA.[106] In 1926, Justice Brandeis upheld a state statute imposing imprisonment and a fine for inducing a work stoppage in Kansas coal mines.[107] Subsequently, the Supreme Court has upheld an absolute prohibition of strikes in the public sector despite constitutional challenges.[108]

There are various reasons for questioning the alleged connection between freedom from forced labour and a right to strike. First, freedom from forced labour is an individual freedom involving individual choice. This freedom allows a worker to decide for whom he or she will work, in what job, and for what length of time. By contrast, the right to strike may be exercised in the context of collective bargaining or political protest. It has little to do with a worker's personal antipathy towards a certain employer or a certain job. Moreover, a strike involves only a temporary withdrawal of labour. Usually, strikers fully intend to return to their jobs when their terms are met. They are not so much asking for the freedom not to work, rather demanding the freedom to work on their own terms. In *Legislating for Conflict*, Simon Auerbach concluded that the technical thrust of the no slavery argument can be met so long as the law does not allow an *individual* to be forced to work—'a condition which might be fulfilled notwithstanding the presence of restrictions on the legality of organizing *collective* withdrawals of labour'.[109]

In response, it could be argued that the distinction between freedom not to work and the freedom to work on one's own terms is not as clear-cut as certain commentators suggest. Above all, the principle of freedom from forced labour requires us to regard labour as something more than a mere commodity to be bought and sold. It follows that slavery is the archetypal example of forced labour. But what of the early master and servant relationship, whereby labourers were not allowed to terminate relationships with their masters at will and were therefore forced to work under whatever conditions their masters dictated? A similar case could be made in respect of indentured labour in early colonial society, which in many regards resembled slavery. Forced labour may best be understood, not in terms of a stark division between slavery and freedom, but as a continuum.[110] The scale of freedom necessary to avoid forced labour in industrial relations will never be

---

[106] Gorman, R., *Labor Law: Unionization and Collective Bargaining* (St Paul, Minn.: West Publishing Co., 1976), 210–11.

[107] *Dorchy v Kansas* 272 US 306 (1926). For an analysis of this case see Pope, J.G., 'Labor's Constitution of Freedom' (1997) 106 *Yale Law Journal* 941 at 1022–4.

[108] See, e.g., *United Federation of Postal Workers v Blount* 325 F Supp. 879 (DDC), affirmed 404 US 802 (1971). See also Hanslowe, K.L., and Acierno, J.L., 'The Law and Theory of Strikes by Government Employees' (1982) 67 *Cornell Law Review* 1055.

[109] Auerbach, S., *Legislating for Conflict* (Oxford: Clarendon Press, 1990), 203–4.

[110] Cf. Ben-Israel, n.102 above, 24–5.

easily ascertainable. On the basis of such arguments, freedom from forced labour could provide one further justification for legal recognition of a right to strike.

If freedom from forced labour is accepted as one of the grounds for protection of a right to strike this may have important repercussions upon the scope of this right. Injunctions which force workers to return to work or suffer criminal sanctions could be regarded as unreasonable violations of individual liberty. Moreover, if freedom from forced labour is a basis for protection of the right to strike, this protection should be 'agnostic' as to the reasons given by workers for the withdrawal of their labour.[111] For example, strikes aimed at influencing government policy could be regarded as *prima facie* legitimate. Nevertheless, it is apparent from the jurisprudence developed within international and European organizations that they do evaluate the legitimacy of industrial action with reference to its aims and objectives.[112] The right to strike has yet to be treated as synonymous with freedom from forced labour, but there remains a possibility that it provides a second-order justification for jurisprudence relating to the sanctions imposed on those who organize and participate in strikes.[113]

C. FREEDOM OF SPEECH

Freedom of speech is another widely recognized civil liberty, protected in international instruments[114] and national constitutions.[115] Strikes are used to express workers' opinions and therefore are on a par with 'expressive conduct', which may be protected as speech.[116] However, strikes have the capacity to cause substantial financial loss to employers and there has been considerable debate whether, as a consequence, industrial action should forfeit the protection extended to other forms of speech.

It has been suggested that this need not present an insurmountable barrier to legal protection,[117] given the precedent set in a decision of the US Supreme Court in *NAACP v Claiborne Hardware Co.*,[118] where a consumer boycott was found to warrant constitutional protection in the United States on the grounds of freedom of speech.

---

[111] Beatty and Kennett, n.80 above, 590.   [112] See Chap. 12 below.

[113] See Chap. 14 below.

[114] E.g., ICCPR 1966, Art. 19; and ECHR 1950, Art. 10.

[115] See, e.g., the First Amendment to the United States Constitution. On its relevance in the employment context see Wheeler, H.N., 'Employee Rights and Industrial Justice' (1994) 28 *Bulletin of Comparative Labour Relations* 9 at 13.

[116] Cf. *United States v O'Brien* 391 US 367 (1968); and *Tinker v Des Moines School Dist.* 393 US 503 (1969).

[117] See Kupferberg, n.48 above; and Webb, J.F., 'Political Boycotts and Union Speech: A Critical First Amendment Analysis' (1988) 4 *Journal of Law and Politics* 579.

[118] 458 US 886 (1982).

In *Claiborne*, the National Association for the Advancement of Colored People (NAACP) organized a boycott placing pressure upon local civic and business leaders to take steps to promote racial equality. Their action was considered to constitute a form of political expression and therefore was protected as speech.[119] Considering whether the government should be able to restrict the boycott, on account of the economic loss which it caused, the Court found that the boycott had aims which outweighed the inconvenience or harm caused to other members of the public. The NAACP, by seeking to remove racial segregation in a Mississippi town, were trying to put a constitutional right into effect.

A strike seems to be no more coercive than a successfully organized economic boycott. If the harm caused by the latter can be justified by reference to the aims of the boycott, cannot the harm caused by a strike be justified by reference to the aims of the strike? For example, if the aim of a strike were to end racial prejudice within a workplace,[120] would it not merit protection as speech? This question has yet to come before the US Supreme Court, but it seems that the Court would answer this question in the negative.

Reluctance to equate treatment of strikes with economic boycotts under free speech principles was apparent from the judgment of Justice Powell in *International Longshoremen's Association v Allied International Limited*.[121] In that case, the International Longshoremen's Association (ILA) had refused to load and unload goods destined for or originating in the Soviet Union, following the invasion of Afghanistan. The Court stated briefly that the coercive effects of the union's conduct excluded its members from protection under the First Amendment. There were many other ways in which the union and its individual members could express their opposition to their employer's trade relations and Russian foreign policy 'without infringing upon the rights of others'. The judge was not interested in a content dependent assessment of the speech in question. This has come to be known in the US context as the 'labor exception', which 'prohibits what would be regarded as perfectly legitimate protest activity by any other social group'.[122] It seems that it is only through coalitions with other community groups that unions may engage in protected boycotts.[123]

---

[119] *Ibid.*, at 908.
[120] Cf. *Scala Ballroom (Wolverhampton) Ltd v Ratcliffe* [1958] 3 All ER 220 (CA), discussed above, at 60.
[121] 456 US 212 (1982). See also for discussion of this case law Atleson, J., 'The Voyage of the *Neptune Jade*: Transnational Labour Solidarity and the Obstacles of Domestic Law' in Conaghan, H., Fischl, R.M., and Klare, K. (eds.), *Labour Law in an Era of Globalization: Transformative Practices & Possibilities* (Oxford: OUP, 2002), 390–2.
[122] Ontiveros, M.L., 'A New Course for Labour Unions: Identity-Based Organizing as a Response to Globalization' in Conaghan *et al.*, n.121 above, 426.
[123] Pope, J.G., 'Labor-Community Coalitions and Boycotts: The Old Labor Law, the New Unionism and the Living Constitution' (1991) 60 *Texas Law Review* 889.

The finding in the *ILA* case is inconsistent with that in *Claiborne*, where the ready availability of alternative forms of speech was not an issue. Other avenues were open to the NAACP, but the frustrations experienced by the Association had led to the promotion of the boycott. It is arguable that these frustrations may be analogous to those often experienced by workers, within both the workplace and society at large. In certain totalitarian societies, strikes are taken where workers have no other means by which to convey their views to the government, or indeed to other citizens.[124] It is also possible that, on an everyday level, the background threat of industrial action moderates employers' treatment of their workers, such that it becomes easier for workers to voice concerns within the enterprise. Freedom of speech could therefore be associated with broader democratic justifications for a right to strike.

[124] *Report of the Fact-Finding and Conciliation Commission on Freedom of Association concerning the Republic of South Africa* (Geneva: ILO, 1992), 41 noted the role of trade unions in 'default of other outlets for attention to urgent social and economic reform'.

4

Reasons for Restriction of Strikes

There are various potential justifications for the right to strike, spanning the traditional social, political, and civil dimensions of citizenship. The right to strike has even received acknowledgement from such an unlikely source as Hayek, who has conceded that 'everybody ought to have a right to strike'. However, he has added to this statement the proviso that the exercise of this right must not impinge upon others' rights.[1] He recognizes a bare freedom to strike but considers that legal protection of industrial action should be circumscribed by the harms which strikes cause to employers, to other workers, to consumers, and to society at large. Such alleged harms are discussed below, alongside present debate over the extent to which they are to be regarded as good grounds for restriction of strikes.

I. HARMS TO EMPLOYERS

The productivity of an employer's business is dependent upon various factors, one of which is the constant and reliable provision of labour. When workers attempt to extract concessions from employers by withdrawing this vital resource, they affect the employer's business. It has been claimed that the actual costs imposed by strikes have been over-estimated. The loss of working days caused by a strike is usually made good, by either overtime or a spontaneous rise in production.[2] Nevertheless, while these costs may be smaller than they are commonly purported to be, it must be conceded that strikes inflict a significant degree of financial loss upon an employer. A strike usually has other objectives, but this is its inevitable by-product.

Some have argued that strikes also cause harm to employers, because they impinge upon employers' liberty. Strikers usually claim that they are

---

[1] Hayek, F.A., *1980s Unemployment and the Unions: Essays on the Impotent Price Structure of Britain and Monopoly in the Labour Market* (2nd edn., London: Institute of Economic Affairs, 1984), 51. Cf. Mill's treatment of the 'harm principle' in Mill, J.S., 'On Liberty' in Mill, J.S., *Utilitarianism* (Warnock, M. (ed.), Glasgow: Fontana Press, 1962), discussed in Chap. 3 above, at 66–7.

[2] This is said to follow the release of 'psychological tension'. See Hyman, R., *Strikes* (4th edn., London: Macmillan, 1989), 37, who cites the Donovan Commission Report. See Donovan, Lord, *Royal Commission on Trade Unions and Employers' Associations 1965–1968*, Cmnd 3623 (London: HMSO, 1968), 111. Hyman also cites a study completed in 1970 relating to the national coal strike of 1912. Apparently, it cost the industry 11% of its annual working time, but only 4% of its expected annual output.

entitled to cease working and to return to their jobs when they choose to do so. They may oppose the employer's use of other workers, protesting by way of a picket. If legal recognition of a right to strike protects workers' rights to return to their jobs, a right to strike restricts an employer's freedom to enter into new contracts with other potential workers. This restriction of freedom of contract has been described as inconsistent with the liberty of 'free men in a free society'.[3]

It follows that anyone seeking to justify international protection of a right to strike must give reasons which counterbalance the financial costs and loss of liberty suffered by employers in the course of strikes. From the arguments reviewed earlier in Chapter 1 and this Part, it seems that such reasons are available. For example, it may be argued that strikes are an essential means by which to achieve the 'social well-being' of workers. Should the law fail to recognize a right to strike, the costs for *workers*, in terms of diminished wages and poorer conditions of employment, may be considerable. Some compromise must be made in a 'clash of rights' situation. It may therefore be appropriate to restrict employers' freedom of contract in certain re-spects, so as to accommodate the interests of workers. Where this com-promise should lie is more controversial. One suggestion has been that strikers should give employers some warning of their intention to take industrial action. What constitutes reasonable notice may however be less easily agreed upon.[4]

It is possible that industrial action may affect people who are not in direct dispute with the workers. Manufacturers may be affected indirectly, for example where the failure of a supplier to provide a component part affects their ability to produce their own goods. Also, a sympathy strike may have the inadvertent effect of penalizing an employer who is unable to exercise any control over the actions of the employer at the centre of the dispute.[5]

It has been suggested that the worst harms to 'innocent employers' could be prevented if sympathy strikes or 'secondary action' were forbidden.[6] However, bans on strikes in support of a dispute with another employer

---

[3] Shenfield, A., *What Right to Strike? With Commentaries by Cyril Grunfeld and Sir Leonard Neal* (London: Institute of Economic Affairs, 1986), 12. Cf. Fisher, W., and McDonald, J., 'State Anti-Strikebreaker Laws: Unconstitutional Interference with Employers' Right to Self-Help' (1985) 3 *Hofstra Labor Law Journal* 59.

[4] For argument on this under UK legislation see Novitz, T., and Skidmore, P., *Fairness at Work: A Critical Analysis of the Employment Relations Act and its Treatment of Collective Rights* (Oxford: Hart Publishing, 2001), 141–7. See for recent UK developments on this issue *National Union of Rail, Maritime and Transport Workers v London Underground Ltd* [2001] IRLR 228 discussed in Wedderburn, Lord, 'Underground Labour Injunctions' (2001) 30 *ILJ* 206. Cf. *Westminster CC v UNISON* [2001] IRLR 524.

[5] Discussed by Kahn-Freund, O., and Hepple, B., *Laws Against Strikes: International Comparisons in Social Policy* (London: The Fabian Society, 1972), 32–4.

[6] It is clear, e.g., that this was the attitude adopted by the 1979–97 Conservative Government. See Department of Trade and Industry, *Industrial Action and Trade Unions* (London: DTI, 1996), at para. 1.3.

overlook the initial aims of industrial action. Individual workers and small groups of workers tend to have limited bargaining power in their negotiations with their employer. For example, if a workplace consists of five workers, the impact of any industrial action taken by these five workers is likely to be minimal. By contrast, solidarity across workplaces (perhaps within a particular neighbourhood or within the industry in which they are employed), and the threat of larger scale collective action may bring an employer to the bargaining table.

Developments in the UK during the 1980s illustrate the effects of restricting immunity for secondary action. Employers' response to this legislative change was to take steps artificially to divide their workforce, creating ostensibly separate 'buffer companies'.[7] There is also an argument that, in response to the growth of global markets and transnational corporate entities, worker solidarity should extend beyond this situation to encompass Europe-wide or international campaigns for the achievement of social and economic objectives.[8]

II.   HARMS TO OTHER WORKERS AND THE UNEMPLOYED

The financial loss experienced by an employer as a result of a strike may have detrimental effects on workers within that enterprise. The worst possible scenario is that an otherwise profitable business folds, leading to the loss of jobs. Another possibility is that an employer may decide that it will be less expensive to manufacture overseas, in another country where labour costs will be lower. Once again, the result would be a loss of jobs. Nevertheless, it is doubtful whether workers would take industrial action where they were in possession of reliable information that the probable result was closure or transfer of the plant. There may be a few instances in which short-sighted action is taken, but it is unlikely that this is a general trend. In fact, it is arguable that workers and their organizations, fearing job losses, have increasingly conciliatory and co-operative in dealings with management.[9]

It has also been argued that strikes are ultimately coercive. When a trade union calls a strike, it is difficult for a member to resist the call and act as a 'scab'.[10] However, when workers join a trade union for the collective defence of their interests, they also agree to abide by the union rules as regards

---

[7] See Chap. 3 above, at 55–6.

[8] E.g., see Hepple, B., 'Protection of Outsiders' in Lapping, B. (ed.), *Laws Against Strikes: International Comparisons in Social Policy* (London: Fabian Society, 1972), 33. See further Chap. 15 below, at 347.

[9] Supiot, A., *Beyond Employment: Changes in Work and the Future of Labour Law in Europe* (Oxford: OUP, 2001), at 112–4.

[10] Shenfield, n.3 above, 9.

when industrial action will be taken. As long as trade unions provide adequate democratic representation of all their members, there is little reason to fear coercion of a trade union member. Balloting requirements can ensure some degree of fairness in the decision to take industrial action. This was one of the reasons given for the introduction of compulsory ballots in the UK, although it was widely suspected that was merely another mechanism by which a Conservative government sought to curb trade union bargaining power.[11] Nonetheless, those engaged in research into this area have suggested that, in fact, strike ballots may be useful in promoting the legitimacy of a strike, as well as strengthening the perception that trade unions were democratically representative and accountable to their members.[12] Ballots also give an employer an indication of the strength of commitment to industrial action, and therefore sometimes an added incentive to settle a dispute before the strike takes place.

It has also been alleged that industrial action succeeds only in raising the living standards of a small group of workers at the expense of others seeking work. The decline of trade union membership over the past twenty years has led to suggestions that trade unions now represent only a minority of the existing and potential workforce and do not act in the interests of the majority. In Britain, for example, the 31 per cent of the workforce still represented by trade unions remains privileged relative to other insecure and marginalized workers.[13] Strikes may also cause disruption to other manufacturing operations and may lead to job losses in those industries.[14] Furthermore, it is said that a successful strike achieving higher wages will mean that fewer jobs are available to those seeking work. The claim is that 'excessive wages reduce profits and thus investment, thereby reducing employment through a shrinking of productive capacity'.[15] In other words, strikes are a reflection of the greed of a minority of relatively privileged workers, whose actions have detrimental consequences for other workers.

What remains curious is that empirical studies have been unable to draw any concrete link between unemployment and a right to strike in pursuit of

---

[11] See Elgar, J., and Simpson, B., *Industrial Ballots and the Law* (London: Institute of Employment Rights, 1996). Recent cases suggest that it may be having the effect desired by past Conservative governments. See *RJB Mining (UK) Ltd v NUM* [1997] IRLR 621; and *Midland Mainline v National Union of Rail, Maritime and Transport Workers* [2001] IRLR 813.

[12] Balloting also strengthened internal administration within trade unions: Elgar and Simpson, n.11 above, 20–1. Also see Undy, R., Fosh, P., Morris, H., Smith, P., and Martin, R., *Managing Trade Unions: The Impact of Legislation on Trade Union Behaviour* (Oxford: OUP, 1996), 260–1.

[13] See Hutton, W., *The State We're In* (London: Jonathan Cape, 1995), 105–10.

[14] Schermers, H.G., 'Is There a Fundamental Right to Strike? (Right to Fair Conditions)' (1989) 9 *Yearbook of European Law* 225, 226.

[15] Discussed and refuted in *Report of the Director-General: Promoting Employment* (Geneva: ILO, 1995), 78.

higher wages.[16] A report by the Director-General of the International Labour Organization, entitled *Promoting Employment* and released in 1995, indicated that the two are unrelated.[17] This view has been supported by OECD reports which have asserted that economic growth can actually be linked to 'improvements in association and bargaining rights'.[18] This view has also been taken by a range of academic commentators.[19]

III. HARMS TO CONSUMERS

Strikes also have the potential to cause harm to consumers. For example, following a strike, employers may offset their financial losses by raising the price of goods. The consumer may therefore come to regard price increases as the direct result of a strike.[20] Consumers may also experience delays in acquiring goods or services for the duration of a strike.

Usually these harms are relatively trivial. It has been observed that one may reasonably expect people to put up with inconvenience or annoyance as a price that has to be paid if other people are allowed to exercise their rights,[21] but 'it is not reasonable that they should suffer serious threats or injury to their lives or liberties'.[22] What is crucial is that members of the public are able to receive those goods and services essential for their survival. It is therefore to be supposed that recognition of consumers' interests need not preclude protection of a right to strike. It is only where essential goods or services are withheld by reason of a strike that there is cause for concern. For example, where there is a shortage of food, transport, and communications, and health services, there may be a case for government intervention.[23]

---

[16] Deakin, S., and Wilkinson, F., 'The Law and Economics of the Minimum Wage' (1992) 19 *Journal of Law and Society* 379, 386–8; Hutton, n.13 above, 99–103. These conclusions are consistent with the views of Solow, R.M., *The Labor Market as a Social Institution* (Oxford: Blackwell, 1990), 28.

[17] *Report of the Director-General: Promoting Employment* (Geneva: ILO, 1995), 76–88. Cf. *Record of Proceedings* (Geneva: ILO, 1996) International Labour Conference, 83rd Session, Resolutions, 6–13.

[18] *Trade, Employment and Labour Standards: A Study of Core Workers' Rights and International Trade* (Paris: OECD, 1996); and *International Trade and Core Labour Standards* (Paris: OECD, 2000).

[19] E.g., see Campbell, D., 'Labour Standards, Flexibility and Economic Performance' in Wilthagen, T. (ed.), *Advancing Theory in Labour Law and Industrial Relations in a Global Context* (Amsterdam: Royal Netherlands Academy of Arts & Sciences, 1998), 229. See also below, at 81.

[20] Utz, A.F., 'Is the Right to Strike a Human Right?' (1987) 65 *Washington University Law Quarterly* 732.

[21] Cf. McCarthy, W., 'The Notion of the Public Interest in Labour Disputes: A Note' in Wedderburn, Lord, and Murphy, W.T. (eds.), *Labour and Community: Perspectives for the 1980's* (London: Institute of Advanced Legal Studies, 1982), 118.

[22] Macfarlane, L.J., *The Right to Strike* (Harmondsworth: Penguin Books, 1981), 179.

[23] *Ibid.*, 136–40. Macfarlane also suggests that education comes within this category (owing to the long-term rather than short-term effects of missing a key period of schooling). In addition, if members of the police force, the courts, or other public administrators go on strike, alternative arrangements may have to be made by government.

The solution to this problem is not necessarily a prohibition of strikes in essential services. For example, where governments can maintain a minimum level of services without endangering public health and safety, strikes can be permitted. It is conceded that, in some circumstances, the maintenance of a minimum service will not be sufficient to prevent harm to the public. Then there could be a case for prohibiting all strikes, in so far as a fair system of arbitration and conciliation is provided.[24]

IV. HARMS TO PUBLIC WELFARE

There are at least two ways in which strikes could be said to harm public welfare or society at large. First, it could be argued that legal recognition of a right to strike undermines the efficient working of the free market and thereby obstructs productivity and economic growth. Secondly, it has been suggested that certain forms of industrial action are detrimental to democratic institutions and therefore should not be condoned by law. These arguments are considered here.

A. DO STRIKES UNDERMINE ECONOMIC EFFICIENCY AND PRODUCTIVITY?

Advocates of 'free-market' economic policies are opposed to any kind of interference in the labour market, whether at a national[25] or an international[26] level. They place their faith in the 'market mechanism' as a means of mediating individual interests and thereby achieving greater economic prosperity without the use of force or coercion.[27]

Government regulation is criticized upon the basis that it interferes with market forces. Moreover, trade unions are regarded as illegitimate 'worker cartels', which raise the price of labour 'above the level which would prevail under conditions of unregulated competition', with potentially disastrous consequences.[28] Trade unions are said to inhibit productivity, boost inflation, and promote unemployment. Hayek and others have, on this basis, argued for an end to trade union 'privileges' and a return to common law

---

[24] *Ibid.*, 137.   [25] See Hayek, n.1 above.

[26] See Addison, J.T., and Siebert, W.S., 'The Social Charter of the European Community: Evolution and Controversies' (1991) 44 *Industrial and Labor Relations Review* 597.

[27] Hayek, F.A., *Law, Legislation and Liberty: A New Statement of the Liberal Principles of Justice and Political Economy* (London: Routledge and Kegan Paul, 1976), ii, 'The Mirage of Social Justice', 64–5, and 118; and Posner, R., *The Economics of Justice* (Boston, Mass.: Harvard University Press, 1983), 60–76 and 91. This view is very similar to that taken by economic individualists in the early 19th century. See Macfarlane, n.22 above, 30. However, the opinions of free market enthusiasts do diverge. E.g., Hayek bases his theories upon a 'policy of freedom'; whereas Posner is concerned largely with maximizing wealth.

[28] Epstein, R.A., 'A Common Law for Labor Relations' (1988) 92 *Yale Law Journal* 1357, 1362; Posner, n.27 above, 990–1. Cf. Deakin, S., and Wilkinson, F., 'Rights vs Efficiency? The Economic Case for Transnational Labour Standards' (1994) 23 *ILJ* 289 at 293.

principles of contract as a means by which to govern the employment relationship.[29] Trade unions reinforce their demands by threatening or engaging in industrial action. Therefore, it can be assumed that economists of the neo-classical school, who are hostile to both State intervention and trade union activity, would also be unwilling to endorse legal protection of a · right to strike.[30]

These economic arguments have had considerable impact upon both international and domestic labour standards over the last twenty years.[31] Nevertheless, they are not immune to criticism. It can be argued in response that 'free-market' policies are not necessarily conducive to either economic prosperity or liberty.

There is insufficient evidence to support the claims of 'free-market' enthusiasts. Contrary to Hayek's assertions, empirical studies suggest that trade union activity and higher wages are not correlated to unemployment.[32] Nor does it seem that deregulationary policies are automatically a recipe for economic success.[33] One can see why this might be. Hayek assumes that individual decisions rationally made for the good of a particular enterprise will benefit society as a whole, but this seems unlikely, given that the short-term interests of a particular employer may conflict with the long-term interests of the industry as a whole.[34]

If collective bargaining is not accompanied by a legally recognized right to strike the outcome may be lower wages or cheaper labour; but this does not necessarily result in higher productivity or competitiveness. Instead, low wages may merely allow an inefficient business to hide its managerial, organizational, and other inadequacies, while increasing the dependency of waged workers on social security. It has therefore been argued that collective bargaining and a right to strike force managers 'to adopt more productive systems rather than to try to become competitive at the expense of the worker'.[35]

Hayek's response would be that even if the market does not always yield the most productive result, it is to be preferred to any other means of regulation because it not only enhances economic wealth, but also enhances individual liberty. 'It virtually eliminates the use of force and the coercion of

---

[29] Epstein, n.28 above.

[30] One example is Hayek, n.1 above, at 52, who says that the 'legalised powers of the unions have become the biggest obstacle to raising the living standards of the working-class as a whole'.

[31] *Report of the Director-General: Promoting Employment* (Geneva: ILO, 1995), 88–9; Wedderburn, Lord, *Employment Rights in Britain and Europe: Selected Papers in Labour Law* (London: Lawrence and Wishart/Institute of Employment Rights, 1991), 228.

[32] Hutton, n.13 above, 102. See *Trade, Employment and Labour Standards: A Study of Core Workers' Rights and International Trade* (Paris: OECD, 1996), 105 and 111–2.

[33] Deakin and Wilkinson, n.28 above, 308.

[34] See Hyman, n.2 above, 91.

[35] Marshall, R., *Unheard Voices: Labor and Economic Policy in a Competitive World* (New York: Basic Books, 1987), 112; Deakin and Wilkinson, n.28 above, 294.

men by other men', in marked contrast to 'the inexorable subjection to superiors which is an essential and indispensable ingredient of socialism and monopoly'.[36] However, he assumes that in the absence of intervention by the State, the employment relationship does not involve 'subjection to superiors'. Hayek concedes that 'in the past' there were situations in which workers had virtually no bargaining power, owing to a lack of mobility. Local managers could exercise an almost dictatorial power over workers.[37] Similarly, Posner notes that, in bygone days, workers may have been disadvantaged in collective bargaining for a number of reasons; for instance where workers were ignorant of their alternative employment opportunities, where workers would incur heavy costs in changing jobs, and where employers conspired to depress wages.[38] Both Hayek and Posner would assert that these conditions do not exist today. For example, the car ensures a degree of mobility and workers are aware of alternative jobs. Neither writer acknowledges the existence of certain other factors which indicate that subordination is the very essence of the employment relationship.[39] Moreover, it is arguable that these factors have been further exacerbated in Western Europe by unemployment[40] and the possibility of utilizing non-unionized labour in developing countries.[41] Also, rapid technological change has led to diminished job security, and therefore workers may be prepared to accept lower wages to retain jobs.[42] A so-called 'free-market' regime, which excludes any protection of the right to strike, is unlikely to be conducive to the liberty of workers. Hayek seems to be more concerned with the liberty of employers.

Finally, one could question whether lawmakers should rely upon economic arguments alone, when considering the desirability of a right to strike. Indeed, this may not be possible. Political values will always underlie

---

[36] Hayek, n.1 above, 41.

[37] *Ibid.*   [38] Posner, n.27 above, 991.

[39] Wedderburn, Lord, 'Labour Law and the Individual in Post-Industrial Societies' in Wedderburn, Lord, Rood, M., Lyon-Caen, A., Däubler, W., and Van der Heijen, P., *Labour Law in the Post-Industrial Era* (Dartmouth: Aldershot, 1994), 44; Wheeler, H.N., 'Employee Rights as Human Rights' (1994) 28 *Bulletin of Comparative Labour Relations* 9, at 12–13.

[40] The latest available statistics for 'developed (industrialised) countries—Major Europe' indicated that the average unemployment rate ranges from 2.4% in Luxembourg to 16% in Spain. See *World Employment Report 2001* (Geneva: ILO, 2001). The statistics available on http://europa.eu.int/comm/eurostat/ indicate that in the 'Euro-zone' unemployment is at 8.3%, while in the 15 Member States the average unemployment rate is 7.6%.

[41] Sunmonu, H.A., 'Contemporary Challenges for Labour Standards Resulting from Globalization' in Sengenberger, W., and Campbell, D. (eds.), *International Labour Standards and Economic Interdependence* (Geneva: International Institute for Labour Studies, 1994), 110. Wedderburn, Lord, 'Labour Law and the Individual in Post-Industrial Societies' in Wedderburn, Rood, Lyon-Caen, Däubler, and Van der Heijen, n.39 above, at 13; Hutton, n.13 above, 12–19.

[42] *Report of the Director-General: Defending Values, Promoting Change* (Geneva: ILO, 1994), 21. Cf. Lewis, R., 'Reforming Industrial Relations: Law, Politics and Power' (1991) 7 *Oxford Review of Economic Policy* 60, 62.

economic theory. For example, Hayek appeals to the 'market' as a good in itself, but also as an instantiation of 'liberty'. The latter is not so much an 'economic', but a 'social', value. Supply, demand, and the rules of exchange within a market are ultimately shaped by a country's social system and values. It is for government and, indeed, the international community as a whole to determine how a market is constructed and the values which it reflects. The plea of 'neutrality' is unconvincing.[43]

It is also self-evident that the labour market can be distinguished from other markets trading in different commodities.[44] It is true that the labour market is an economic institution, but by reason of the commodities traded within this particular market, it is also a social and a political institution. Not only the commercial aspirations of employers are at stake here, but also the social needs, the political rights, and the civil liberties of workers.[45] These seem to be relevant considerations when considering whether a right to strike should be recognized.

B.   CAN STRIKES THREATEN DEMOCRATIC INSTITUTIONS?

Democracy is widely regarded as an ideal to which modern States should aspire. The result has been the development of central political institutions which purport to reflect these aspirations.[46] Chapter 3 considered democratic justifications for 'political strikes',[47] but there are in addition two further types of strike which are often termed 'political' because they have the potential to undermine democratic institutions. One is the 'public sector' strike, that is, industrial action taken by workers employed directly by the State. The second is a 'political impact' strike, that is, industrial action which is likely to have so detrimental a political impact that it can undermine the ability of a democratically elected body to govern. Each shall be considered in turn.

1.   Public Sector Strikes

The traditional view of public sector employment was that, as state servants, workers owed absolute loyalty to their employer.[48] The State as employer should be answerable to the legislature and not to external interest groups

---

[43] Cf. Raz, J., 'Liberalism, Autonomy and the Politics of Neutral Concern' (1982) 8 *Midwest Studies in Philosophy* 89, 94–8; and Langille, B., 'Eight Ways to Think about International Labour Standards' (1997) 31 *Journal of World Trade* 27, 52–3.

[44] Solow, n.16 above, 30.

[45] Deakin and Wilkinson, n.28 above, 308; Hutton, n.13 above, 101.

[46] Although the extent to which they do so remains the subject of debate. See Chap. 1 above, at 14–22.

[47] Chap. 3 above, at 56–64.

[48] Hepple, B., 'Labour Law and Public Employees in Britain' in Wedderburn and Murphy, n.21 above, 69.

such as trade unions.[49] Industrial action in the public sector, even when this is concerned only with negotiation of a collective agreement concerning terms and conditions of employment, is regarded as being an attempt to influence State decision-making, inherently political, and therefore unlawful.

As Kahn-Freund and Hepple have noted, this view appears to be mistaken as it is based upon a false premise which confuses 'the role of the State as an employer and as a political entity'. In reality, 'the public worker has no more opportunities than his counterpart in private industry to influence the election of legislatures and the political responsibility of ministers'.[50]

It has also been claimed that in a private employment situation an employer's means are constrained within objective limits, 'determined by the necessity to remain competitive in the market for its product'. In State employment, there is no such limit and demands could expand indefinitely.[51] This scenario seems improbable, given that wages in the private sector will provide some reference point for the wages of government workers. Indeed, in their negotiations with the State over pay and conditions, it seems that public sector workers are most in need of some kind of bargaining leverage. Viewed as an adversary in collective bargaining, the State is an exceptionally powerful employer. It is able to introduce or invoke legislation to control the activities of both public and private sector workers, to determine terms and conditions of employment, and to mitigate the impact of industrial disruption, options not open to employers in the private sector.[52] The State's concerns also extend beyond those of the classic private employer. These interests are primarily political rather than commercial,[53] so that there may not be the same concern where revenue lost in quashing a strike exceeds a union's claim. Few private employers could afford to make tactical decisions of this sort.[54] If workers are to redress imbalances in collective bargaining within the public sector, they should be

[49] Fredman, S., and Morris, G., 'Is There a Public/Private Labour Divide?' (1993) 14 *Comparative Labor Law Journal* 115; Zanghi, C., 'Freedom of Association and Social Democracy' in Council of Europe, *Freedom of Association Proceedings* (Strasbourg: Council of Europe Press, 1994), 146–7.

[50] Kahn-Freund and Hepple, n.5 above, 20. Cf. Laski, H.J., *Liberty in the Modern State* (London: Faber & Faber, 1930), 135–8; and Powers McGuire, J., 'A Comparison of the Right of Public Employees to Strike in the United States and Canada' [1987] *Labor Law Journal* 304, 304–5.

[51] Zanghi, n.49 above, 147.

[52] Fredman and Morris, n.49 above, 124; Fredman, S., and Morris, G., 'Public or Private? State Employees and Judicial Review' (1991) 107 *LQR* 298, 310. See also Sheppard, T., 'Liberalism and the Charter: Freedom of Association and the Right to Strike' (1996) 5 *Dalhousie Journal of Legal Studies* 117, who at 158 considers that 'this is why the freedom to strike must be more vigilantly guarded [i.e. protected] in their case'.

[53] Summers, C., 'Public Employee Bargaining: A Political Perspective' (1974) 83 *Yale Law Journal* 1156, 1159; Hepple, n.48 above, 68.

[54] Fredman and Morris, n.49 above, at 124.

entitled to engage in industrial action. Moreover, it has been argued that the trend towards privatization in the public sector should prompt lawmakers to reconsider the conventional conceptual distinction between the public and private employer.[55]

This is not to say that other arguments cannot be made for restricting industrial action in the public sector. For example, there may be a case for limiting the right to strike where public sector workers are responsible for providing an essential service.[56] Also, for similar reasons, it could be argued that the police, the army, and high-ranking government officials, whose absence would create a national emergency, should be prevented from taking industrial action. However, both these arguments for restriction of the right to strike are concerned with the nature of the services provided by public sector workers rather than their status as servants of the State. The grounds for regarding public sector strikes as anti-democratic *per se* seem to be spurious.

2. Political Impact Strikes

The other question is what is the appropriate response to a strike whose aims are clearly concerned with well-recognized legitimate subjects of collective bargaining, but which is likely to have a severe negative impact on the credibility of the government.[57] Whether a strike in fact forces a government to change or abandon a policy may be dependent more on impact than intent.[58]

The tendency of modern government to intervene in economic policy (and accordingly the supply of goods and services) means that most industrial action will have a political aspect, whether or not this is intentional. As Hyman notes, 'every important trade union struggle over wages or conditions has today a political dimension since it impinges directly on government economic strategy'.[59] Moreover, the issue of impact does not work only one way. Aspects of State economic policy affect workers in relation to their wages, job security, and opportunity for employment.

General strikes, strikes in the public sector, and strikes in essential services are sometimes said to have a 'political impact' capable of undermining

[55] Neal, A.C., 'Public Sector Industrial Relations: Some Developing Trends' (2001) 17 *IJCLLIR* 233.

[56] Indeed, these two categories will often overlap. See *Committee of Experts' General Survey on Freedom of Association and Collective Bargaining* (Geneva: ILO, 1994) at 61, para. 136.

[57] Welch, R., *The Right to Strike: A Trade Union View* (London: Institute of Employment Rights, 1991), 10. See also Kahn-Freund, O., Davies, P., and Freedland, M., *Labour and the Law* (3rd edn, London: Stevens & Sons, 1983), 317; Wedderburn, Lord, 'Industrial Action, the State and the Public Interest', in Aaron, B., and Wedderburn, Lord (eds.), *Industrial Conflict: A Comparative Legal Survey* (London: Longmans, 1972), 321; Betten, L., *The Right to Strike in Community Law: The Incorporation of Fundamental Rights in the Legal Order of the European Communities* (Amsterdam: North-Holland, 1985), 150–78.

[58] Auerbach, S., *Legislating for Conflict* (Oxford: Clarendon Press, 1990), 83.

[59] Hyman, n.2 above, 176–7.

democratic government. A general strike challenges a government's author-ity, irrespective of the limited aims of the strike leaders themselves.[60] A strike in the public service may undermine government controls over the State's infrastructure and the services which are provided to the public. Finally, a strike in 'essential services', such as fire-fighting and hospitals, could have severe repercussions on the economy, society, and thereby the government in power.

If the maintenance of a centralized democratic government is considered desirable, these potential harms must be acknowledged. Yet, once again, appreciation of these harms can be balanced against opposing benefits associated with legal protection of a right to strike. As noted above, it seems reasonable to protect members of the public by placing certain restrictions upon strikes in essential services. There may also be grounds for State intervention in cases of a national emergency. Nevertheless, it is self-evident that there would be no effective protection of the right to strike if embarrassment caused to a government could, alone, prevent workers striking.

[60] Macfarlane, n.22 above, 155.

Conclusion: A Potentially Rich Justificatory Basis

The right to strike is most often described as a socio-economic right. However, careful examination of alternative justifications for the right to strike indicates that this entitlement may also serve a vital political function and be linked to the protection of civil liberties. Acceptance of these diverse justifications turns on one's view of the ideal form of 'democratic governance' at the national level. It is possible, on this basis, to take a 'holistic' view of the right to strike, which crosses the traditionally accepted boundaries between different categories of human rights.[1]

The importance of the relative status of social, political, and civil rights should become apparent in Part II, which analyses the attempts made to incorporate a right to strike into a legal instrument under the auspices of the ILO, the Council of Europe, and the European Union. Controversy over the relationship between freedom of association and the right to strike will be considered further in Part III, which examines the role played by international and European supervisory bodies.

Another controversial issue is the scope of the right to strike, which is dependent on the recognition of certain justifications for its legal protection. If industrial action is viewed solely as a means by which to negotiate over terms to be set out in a collective agreement, its ambit may be very limited. On this basis, legal protection of the right to strike should extend only to industrial action aimed at achieving higher wages or improved working conditions. By contrast, if industrial action can be justified in terms of democratic participation or as an extension of existing civil liberties, it then becomes possible to endorse strikes aimed at challenging managerial decisions and even government policy. However, the right to strike can also be circumscribed according to the weight given to the alleged harms caused by industrial action, as was indicated in Chapter 4. The analysis here forms the basis for further exploration of jurisprudence relating to the ambit of the right to strike discussed in Part IV.

---

[1] The term 'holistic' is borrowed from Leary, V., 'Lessons from the Experience of the International Labour Organisation' in Alston, P. (ed.), *The United Nations and Human Rights: A Critical Reappraisal* (Oxford: OUP, 1992), at 590, where she comments that the ILO has 'made a major contribution to theory and practice by its "holistic" or integrated approach to human rights'.

There is potentially a rich, variegated justificatory basis for a right to strike, which could give rise to broad legal protection. The extent to which the justifications enumerated here are accepted within international and European organizations is likely to depend, as it tends to do in the domestic sphere, on the values embedded in the relevant constitutional framework, the procedures for setting of standards, and the extent to which particular vested interests are represented in those standard-setting procedures. Part II will examine these dynamics of international and European norm-setting in greater depth and their implications for protection and restriction of strikes.

PART II
Inclusion of the Right to Strike in International Instruments

Introduction

As early as 1838, arguments were made for the adoption of international treaties to promulgate labour standards.[1] From the beginning of the twentieth century onwards, a number of conventions were signed and ratified by States relating to such standards.[2] Nevertheless, as we shall see, protection of the 'right to strike' through inclusion in a multilateral instrument has proved problematic; so much so that the first time this was achieved was in the European Social Charter of 1961.[3]

Treaties are often regarded as the key building-blocks of international law,[4] but an entirely treaty-oriented view could lead one to overlook the role of international and regional organizations in facilitating the consensus upon which instruments are based. It has been observed that these bodies, 'themselves the creatures of multilateral treaties, have . . . assumed increasing prominence in the last half of this century'.[5] This Part examines the extent to which the International Labour Organization, Council of Europe, and the European Union have adopted instruments which contain provisions recognizing the right to strike, while seeking to explain the difficulties they have faced in doing so.

It will be suggested that the difficulties experienced by each organization are palpably different, because each body adheres to its own particular model of transnational governance. This is evident from even the most cursory analysis of their divergent constitutional backgrounds, which determine their objectives and circumscribe the scope of their legitimate activities. This is also apparent from the methods by which instruments are adopted in each organization and the role of various participants in that 'standard-setting' process.

The ILO Constitution does not draw any stark division between 'civil and political' rights and 'socio-economic' rights.[6] By contrast, the Council of Europe Statute is indicative of a desire to distinguish 'Western values' from those of Eastern European socialist States. This planted the seeds for a distinction between civil and political rights on the one

---

[1] Butler, H., *The International Labour Organization* (Oxford: OUP, 1939), 3.

[2] See also Shotwell, J.T., *The Origins of the International Labour Organization* (New York: Columbia University Press, 1934), i, 'History', 127–98.

[3] ESC 1961, Art. 6(4).

[4] See the Statute of the International Court of Justice 1945, Art. 38.

[5] Charney, J.I., 'Universal International Law' (1993) 87 *AJIL* 529, at 529.

[6] See Chap. 2 above, at 41.

hand and socio-economic rights on the other. The result was divergent protection of freedom of association and the right to strike, as well as disparate decisions from ILO and Council of Europe supervisory bodies. The ILO sees freedom of association and the right to strike as inseparably linked. The Council of Europe views the two as capable of being connected but ultimately distinguishable.[7] When looking at the present EC Treaty, we have to remember its origins as the 1957 Treaty of Rome, the objectives of which were focused more on economic goals than social aspirations. It is only gradually that the scope of European Community (and now European Union) concerns has been extended. This, too, has had an impact on the protection of a right to strike under the auspices of EU law. There is also, obviously, an important difference between the ILO role as a global organization whose focus is on international labour standards and the parts played at the regional level, respectively, by the Council of Europe and the EU. The European organizations also seek to demarcate their respective competencies in this field.

In addition, methods of standard-setting peculiar to each organization provide a framework for understanding their decisions. The ILO adopts international instruments containing labour standards through a process involving the tripartite participation of government, worker, and employer representatives. This arguably lends authority to the Conventions and Recommendations that they adopt, which reflect the interests of workers and employers as well as governments. Such a decision-making procedure can also lead to reluctance in standard-setting on contested issues. Wholesale opposition from either the workers' group or the employers' bloc within the ILO has, at different times, stalled initiatives relating to industrial action. In these respects, the ILO is unlike other UN agencies and differs from the Council of Europe and EU.

At root level, the promulgation of labour standards in the two European organizations depends on the consent of Member States. Within the Council of Europe, consent is given or withheld in the Committee of Ministers. This has led to the adoption of instruments which arguably reflect the concerns of State bodies rather than the social partners. Whereas within the Council of Europe civil and political rights are given priority; within the European Union there is something of a role reversal. The remit of the EC Treaty is such that particular socio-economic rights, such as free movement of persons or equal pay, have historically received greater attention. The right to strike is not amongst these entitlements, which arguably have more of an economic than a social basis. This right has been recognized only in declaratory instruments. It seems that the decisions taken unanimously by Member States at Inter-Governmental Conferences concerning reform of the EC and EU Treaties will continue to be of crucial importance, given the

---

[7] In this respect, there are important links to be made between this Part and Part III below.

apparent exclusion of industrial action from protection under EC social policy.[8] What is emerging instead is the determination of the EU and its Member States to impose 'core labour standards', including the 'right to strike', upon third countries through trade and aid incentives. The implications of this course of action for relations between the ILO, Council of Europe, and European Union are considered further at the conclusion of this Part.

---

[8] By virtue of Art. 137(6) EC Treaty, discussed in Chap. 7 below, at 160–1.

5

Standard-setting in the ILO

'Today the right to strike is essential to a democratic society, so one might justifiably wonder why there is no ILO Convention or Recommendation on the subject.'[1] This may be regarded as an over-exaggeration, for a number of ILO instruments refer tangentially to such a right; but the fact remains that no ILO Convention or Recommendation deals systematically with the right to strike, expressly requiring States to take active steps to protect industrial action. This chapter considers the reasons for this apparent anomaly.

One could seek to explain this state of affairs in terms of the 'constitutional objectives' of the ILO. However, these are very general and could readily encompass protection by the Organization of a right to strike. Instead, the explanation may lie with the peculiar tripartite structure of the Organization, which does not lend itself to standard-setting on issues where employer and worker opinion conflict. The constitutional objectives of the ILO and the form of its standard-setting mechanisms arguably made the adoption of conventions concerning freedom of association imperative. These were, in turn, to provide the basis for protection of a right to strike, by virtue of the jurisprudence developed by ILO supervisory bodies, which also made reference to the terms of the ILO Constitution. In the light of this jurisprudence, workers' representatives within the ILO expressed adamant opposition to any suggestion by employers of further standard-setting in the field of dispute settlement, that might reduce the scope of this protection.

I. CONSTITUTIONAL OBJECTIVES

The ILO is a global organization[2] whose essential concern is the promotion and protection of labour standards. The ILO Constitution has evolved over three crucial stages: first, its emergence as an international organization at the end of World War I; secondly, its renewal as a UN agency in 1945, following World War II; and, thirdly, its survival post the close of the Cold War, following the 'democratization' and 'liberalization' of Central and

---

[1] Gernigon, B., Odero, A., and Guido, H., 'ILO Principles concerning the Right to Strike' (1998) 137 *ILRev.* 441 at 479–80.

[2] At the time of writing, the ILO has 175 members. See for the current list www.ilo.org/public/english/standards/relm/ctry-ndx.htm.

Eastern Europe.[3] Nevertheless, at each stage, the same constitutional themes arose.

The first of these is 'social justice', which was viewed as a means by which to ensure global stability and 'universal peace'. This is the political dimension of the ILO Constitution; for the victorious at Versailles wanted to ensure that the new 'world order' which they had established would not be undermined by social grievances which could lead to political instability. Moreover, this desire to protect the dignity as well as the material well-being of workers can, in retrospect, be seen as an important precursor to the eventual recognition of labour standards as 'human rights' in other international conventions. The second is the prevention of a downward spiral in the protection of labour standards through international co-operation. This could be regarded as the economic dimension of the puzzle. The ILO was the first international organization which systematically tried to regulate the terms of free trade, so that countries would not engage in 'unfair' competition on the basis of inferior labour standards. Problems associated with this ambition will also be discussed here. The third and final theme is the importance of 'freedom of association' and its link to trade union and employer representation. The embodiment of this notion in the tripartite structure of the ILO Constitution was significant.

A.   THE FIRST STAGE: POST WORLD WAR I

The Peace Conference of 1919 set up a Commission on International Labour Legislation,[4] dominated by representatives from industrialized States.[5] The ILO Constitution was designed to complement the overall peace settlement and the formation of a League of Nations. The end result could be viewed cynically in terms of the vested interests of these few, chiefly European, nations,[6] were it not for the more idealistic intervention of Samuel Gompers, president of the American Federation of Labour (AFL), who was elected President of the Commission by its members.[7]

---

[3] This analysis draws on discussion of this constitutional framework in the context of 'working time' regulation in Murray, J., *Transnational Labour Regulation: The ILO and EC Compared* (The Hague: Kluwer, 2001), especially at 35–47.

[4] For the terms of reference see *Report and Minutes of the Commission on International Labour Legislation, Peace Conference, Paris 1919* (Rome: Tipografia, 1921), p. v. See also O'Higgins, P., 'International Standards and British Labour Law' in Lewis, R. (ed.), *Labour Law in Britain* (Oxford: Blackwell, 1986), 575.

[5] Barnes, G.N., *History of the International Labour Office* (London: Williams and Norgate, 1926), 38.

[6] Alcock, A., *History of the International Labour Organisation* (London: Macmillan, 1971), 3–16.

[7] *Report and Minutes of the Commission on International Labour Legislation*, n.4 above, 47–8. See also proceedings of the Commission, related by Edward Phelan (later to become a Director of the ILO) in Shotwell, J.T., *The Origins of the International Labour Organization* (New York: Columbia University Press, 1934), i, 127–98.

The final agreed text of Part XIII of the Treaty of Versailles consisted of two sections, Section I, 'Organization of Labour', contained the Preamble, which set out the ILO's constitutional aims, and Articles 387–426, which determined the manner in which the Organization was to operate. The 'International Labour Conference' was to be the primary standard-setting body; a 'Governing Body' was established to exercise executive powers; and both were to receive administrative assistance from a newly established 'International Labour Office' led by a 'Director'.[8] Section II, 'General Principles', consisted of Article 427, which established 'nine guiding points' of 'special and urgent importance'.[9]

The first theme which emerged from the Preamble was that of 'social justice'. The founders of the ILO sought to establish 'universal peace', and recognized that such a peace could be established only 'through the promotion and development of social justice'.[10] The intention was to ensure a basic level of protection for workers, so that they did not, in their despair, turn to Bolshevik revolution.[11] It was with this objective in mind that Section II of the new ILO Constitution stated that 'labour should not be regarded merely as a commodity or article of commerce'.

The second theme was that of 'fair competition'. The Preamble to Part XIII recognizes that 'the failure of any nation to adopt humane conditions of labour is an obstacle in the way of other nations which desire to improve the conditions in their own countries'. The UK Government Representative, George Barnes, had dwelt on this concern in the negotiations at Versailles and stated subsequently:

Labour regulation had become a necessity in order to safeguard the relatively high standards of life in the advanced countries . . . . That . . . is an insular sort of argument to use in favour of an organization with humanitarian outlook, but at least it is a practical one. . . . The need had arisen for levelling out industrial competition between nations by raising the conditions of labour in the lower-paid countries.[12]

It seems that industrialized States hoped to use the ILO as a vehicle by which to maintain their competitive advantage on world markets or, at least,

---

[8] Later to become the 'Director-General'.

[9] See Thomas, A., 'Preface' in *The International Labour Organization: The First Decade* (London: Allen & Unwin, 1931), 31.

[10] *ILO Report of the Director-General: Defending Values, Promoting Change* (Geneva: ILO, 1994), 25. This was an objective which was recognized by the grant of the Nobel Peace Prize to the ILO on its 50th anniversary in 1969. Cf. Ghebali, V.-Y., *The International Labour Organization: A Case-Study on the Evolution of UN Specialised Agencies* (Dordrecht: Martinus Nijhoff, 1989), 62–5.

[11] Imber, M., *The USA, ILO, UNESCO and IAEA: Politicization and Withdrawal in the Specialised Agencies* (London: Macmillan, 1989), 43. See also Barnes, n.5 above, at 80.

[12] *Ibid.*, 35–7 and 45–7. See for a similar view Chisholm, A., *Labour's Magna Charta: A Critical Study of the Labour Clauses of the Peace Treaty and of the Draft Conventions and Recommendations of the Washington International Labour Conference* (London: Longmans, 1925), 10–11. Cf. Ghebali, n.10 above, 14.

to prevent such advantage being undermined by lower labour standards. Whether such a course of action can be regarded as defensible depends on the basis on which Western States intended to object to these lower labour standards. A distinction can be drawn between advantage which is derived from merely different processes of production involving different treatment of workers and that which arises where the treatment of workers is morally repugnant. The argument can be (and has been) forcefully made that the former is legitimate while the latter is not.[13] The requirement that labour laws be harmonized or treatment of workers 'equalized' (for example that wages be identical) could fairly be characterized as 'protectionist', that is, designed to protect Western labour markets from legitimate sources of competition. By contrast, the setting of minimum or 'humane' standards reflecting what is regarded by an international community as an unacceptable source of competitive advantage seems positively desirable.[14] This competitive agenda did, however, 'permeate the constitution and subsequent history of the ILO',[15] providing scope for continued debate.

A third principle of 'special and urgent importance' was recognition of 'the right of association for all lawful purposes by the employed as well as by the employers'. This guarantee was fundamental to the 'tripartite' structure of the organization, which envisaged extensive participation from representatives of employers' organizations and organized labour.[16] The reference to 'lawful purposes' disappointed workers, for it appeared to present States with the option to declare illegal various acts of worker concertation, such as strikes and other forms of industrial action.[17] This provision was to be deleted by subsequent constitutional amendments.

As the first Director of the ILO, Albert Thomas, observed, 'institutions are living things' and 'all codification is abstract'. Texts may continue to exist while the reality becomes something quite different.[18] For example, the gradual change in ILO membership meant that there would be some change in the Organization's activities. Initially, the support and cooperation of European States was perceived as central to the ILO. It was observed that:

If [the ILO] is not supported by the great industrial countries of Europe, it must assuredly lose in moral prestige, because for good or ill those countries lead the

---

[13] See for an excellent exposition of these arguments Langille, B., 'Eight Ways to Think About International Labour Standards' (1997) 31 *Journal of World Trade* 27.

[14] Provided that the methods used for scrutiny of the enforcement of such standards are fair and impartial and that the sanctions for non-compliance take account of the circumstances of States' particular circumstances. See for an introduction to this debate Chap. 1 at 25–6.

[15] Butler, H., *The International Labour Organization* (Oxford: OUP, 1939), 7–8.

[16] ILO, *Digest of Decisions of the ILO Committee on Freedom of Association* (4th edn., Geneva: ILO, 1996), 1.

[17] Alcock, n.6 above, 36.

[18] Thomas, A. 'The International Labour Organisation: Its Origins, Development and Future' (1921) 1 *International Labour Review* 5 at 7.

world in labour and industrial activities generally. Above all else, the International Labour Organisation must justify itself to the European organised industrialised democracies.[19]

This situation changed when the United States joined in 1934 and became a vital member, paying a significant proportion of the budget.[20] Nevertheless, the Treaty of Versailles was used as a key point of reference, circumscribing the limitations of ILO competence,[21] until the ILO reformulated and elaborated upon its constitutional objectives in the Declaration of Philadelphia 1944.

B.   The Second Stage: Post World War II

Towards the end of World War II, representatives from Member States reviewed the constitutional objectives of the ILO. Concentration camps, in which not only genocide but also forced labour was rife, had caused international concern. In this context, workers' rights came to be viewed as human rights; they stemmed from a recognition of human dignity.[22] When the ILO reconvened in 1944, the plan was to ensure adoption of a 'solemn declaration' by the Conference, which 'would serve to mark a turning point in the history of the Organisation by reformulating its objectives in the new perspective of a changed world situation'.[23]

The ensuing Declaration of Philadelphia 1944 recognized the potential for connection between civil liberties, democratic participation, material well-being, and economic security.[24] Its signatories seem to have assumed that civil, political, and socio-economic rights were indivisible. Indeed, a similar assumption appears to underlie the United Nations Universal Declaration of Human Rights of 1948.[25]

---

[19] Barnes, n.5 above, 79.

[20] Butler, n.15 above, 16–18; also see Alcock, n.6 above, 118–33.

[21] The Governing Body in 1921 'drew attention to the necessity of limiting' the activities of the ILO 'and keeping them strictly within the bounds defined by the Treaty with regard to international legislation': Thomas, n.18 above, 18. See also Anon., 'The First Year of the International Labour Organisation' (1921) 1 *ILRev.* 23.

[22] Declaration of Philadelphia 1944, Art. II(a). This approach was emphasized again in the 1970 Resolution relating to civil liberties and workers' rights: see ILO, *Record of Proceedings* (Geneva: ILO, 1970), International Labour Conference, 54th Session, 733–6.

[23] *Future Policy, Programme and Status of the International Labour Organisation* (Montreal: ILO, 1944), Report I to be presented at the ILC, 26th Session, 3.

[24] See Leary, V.A., 'Lessons from the Experience of the ILO' in Alston, P. (ed.), *The United Nations and Human Rights: A Critical Reappraisal* (Oxford: OUP, 1992), 591.

[25] See UNGA Resolution 217 A (III) of 10 Dec. 1948; ILO, *Report of the Committee of Experts on the Application of Conventions and Recommendations: General Report and Observations concerning Particular Countries*, Report III (Part IA) (Geneva: ILO, 1998) ILC, 86th Session, 16–17, cited in Swepston, L., 'Human Rights and Freedom of Association: Development through ILO Supervision' (1998) 137 *ILRev.* 169, 169.

The Declaration of Philadelphia stressed again that 'labour is not a commodity'.[26] Economic and financial policies, whether national or international, should be accepted 'only insofar as they may be held to promote and not to hinder' the achievement of the Organization's fundamental objective.[27] The ability of the ILO to scrutinize rather than respond to the perceived dictates of economic policy was also an important addition to its competence.[28] In this way, 'social justice' was given priority over competitive regulation.[29]

At the same time, the Declaration emphasized the importance of 'freedom of association', on the basis that it was 'essential to sustained progress'.[30] Also advocated was 'effective recognition of the right of collective bargaining, the co-operation of management and labour in the continuous improvement of productive efficiency, and the collaboration of workers and employers in the preparation and application of social and economic measures'.[31] The social partners, 'enjoying equal status with those of governments', were to join with them in 'free discussion and democratic decision with a view to promotion of the common welfare'.[32] It appears that 'freedom of association' was regarded as an important means by which to secure both collective bargaining and political participation.

The Declaration was later annexed to the Constitution and, at the same time, Section II of the original Constitution contained in the Treaty of Versailles was abolished. Following the Declaration, the ILO became an officially recognized agency of the United Nations (UN).[33] It was to be left to carve out its competence *vis-à-vis* the other manifestations of the UN, such as the Economic and Social Council (ECOSOC) and the Bretton Woods institutions.[34]

In the post-war period, the survival of the ILO depended on its ability to demonstrate its 'global', as opposed to its European or US, credentials. This was the 'challenge of universality' identified by Wilfred Jenks, another

---

[26] Declaration of Philadelphia 1944, Art. I(a).

[27] *Ibid.*, Art. II(c).

[28] *Future Policy, Programme and Status of the International Labour Organisation*, n. 23 above, 7–10.

[29] See Ghebali, n.10 above, at 62–3, 78–80, and 81–6.

[30] Declaration of Philadelphia 1944, Arts. I(b) and III(e).

[31] Swepston, n.25 above, 170.

[32] Declaration of Philadelphia 1944, Art. I(d).

[33] The text of the agreement between the UN and the ILO can be found in XXIX No. 4 *Official Bulletin* 15 Nov. 1946, 293. See for the substance of these negotiations Alcock, n.6 above, 188–204; and Sohn, L.B., 'The Contribution of the International Labour Organization to the Development of the Concept of Economic, Social and Cultural Rights' in Dupuy, R.-J. (ed.), *Mélanges en l'Honneur de Nicolas Valticos* (Paris: Editions A. Pedone, 1999).

[34] Alcock, n.6 above, 188–202; Jenks, C.W., 'Co-ordination in International Organization: An Introductory Survey' (1951) 28 *BYBIL* 29 at 43–8. See also ILO, *Future Policy, Programme and Status of the International Labour Organisation*, n. 23 above, chap. II of which anticipates such difficulties.

ILO Director-General, as a key constitutional principle.[35] Such 'universality' required some sensitivity to a range of national circumstances. While the need for a 'margin of appreciation' in the application of ILO standards had long been recognized by the original ILO Constitution, this perceived need became more pressing as membership of the Organization rapidly increased. The difficulty was the potential dilution in standards that this entailed.[36]

In addition, the decision-making process became more susceptible to domination by views unpalatable to Western powers. The inclusion of Eastern bloc members, such as Soviet Russia in 1954, posed problems for European and US control of the Organization.[37] This was exacerbated by decolonization.[38] The USA was soon confronted with a majority vote which was often hostile to its agenda; and in 1977 withdrew from membership of the ILO, leaving the Organization financially embarrassed and with its influence weakened.[39] From World War II onwards, there have been other cases of withdrawal, involving states such as Yugoslavia, Venezuela, Lesotho, South Africa, Albania, and Poland, but none had such a stark impact as the US withdrawal, which forced the ILO to cut its budget by 21.7 per cent entailing the loss of 230 posts.[40]

One of the reasons that the USA gave for its withdrawal was the increasing 'politicization' of the ILO. It objected to an anti-Israeli resolution and made 'a generalised accusation of anti-Western sentiment and ideology'. The USA called on the ILO to act only as a 'technical agency' and to avoid entering the arena of the 'political'.[41] This was said to be implicit in the ILO's constitutional role.

In the ILO's history, the term 'political' has been used, in a pejorative fashion, to refer to a wide range of concerns, including harassment, *ultra vires* actions, reference to extraneous matters, double standards, and mismanagement. Most commonly, the term 'politicization' is used in circumstances in which the International Labour Conference or an ILO

---

[35] Jenks, C.W., 'The Challenge of Universality' (1959) 53 *American Society of International Law Proceedings* 85.

[36] Note in particular the controversial 'flexibility' clause, which has been introduced into particular Conventions in order to ensure that 'universal' ILO standards cater for the special domestic circumstances of its members. Okogwu, G.C., 'Labour Standards Across Different Levels of Development' in Sengenberger, W., and Campbell, D. (eds.), *International Labour Standards and Economic Interdependence* (Geneva: IILS, 1994), 154–7.

[37] See Alcock, n.6 above, 318–37; Imber, n.11 above, 51–2. There were also logistical problems, given the absence of independent employer and worker representatives. See further Alcock, n.6 above, 284–305.

[38] On the role of the Group of 77 within the ILO see Ghebali, n.10 above, 41–2.

[39] Schlossberg, S.I., 'United States Participation in the ILO' (1989) 11 *Comparative Labor Law Journal* 48, 68–71; Imber, n.11 above, 65–6.

[40] See Ghebali, n.10 above, 110–16.

[41] See Alcock, n.6 above, 288; Schlossberg, n.39 above, 68–71; Imber, n.11 above, 59–66. See also Betten, L., *International Labour Standards: Selected Issues* (Deventer: Kluwer, 1993), 9; and Ghebali, n.10 above, 25–7.

supervisory body has criticized, not only a State's regulation of labour relations, but also its mode of government.[42] However, it seems that allegations of 'politicization' tend to be made selectively, as is illustrated by the ILO's response to South Africa. From 1961 onwards, the International Labour Conference took steps to censure the practice of apartheid in South Africa. The ILO was engaged in condemnation of a particular political system, but few were concerned by this, as apartheid was then almost universally condemned by the world community.[43] Perhaps the notion of 'politicization' is itself spurious. To separate the political system of apartheid from the employment conditions of black workers in South Africa would have been a ludicrous exercise. Labour relations cannot be neatly extrapolated and isolated from the political system within which they operate; nor is it likely that an international organization can maintain an apolitical stance. Nevertheless, as a consequence of continuing pressure from government and employer representatives at the International Labour Conference, various ILO organs have demonstrated their reluctance to appear 'politicized'.[44]

C.   The Third Stage: Post the Cold War

At the end of the Cold War, the ILO appeared to stall as an international organization. One aspect of its initial function had been to prevent the spread of Communism by delivering 'social justice' to workers. Now that this was a diminishing threat, the role and function of the ILO in the international community came into question. Furthermore, the implosion of the Soviet bloc and the collapse of the planned economies of the Eastern bloc were viewed by some as vindicating the capitalist ideal and signalling 'the end of history'.[45]

This was compounded by the economic crisis which followed the boom period of the 1970s and was attributed to the failure of mixed economies. Trade union involvement in industrial policy-making and standard-setting, as well as government intervention, was called into question.[46] The 1980s was

---

[42] E.g., following ILO criticism of the Polish Government's suppression of the Solidarity trade union movement, 8 Eastern bloc countries complained that this entailed criticism of the Polish political system and was therefore a misuse of the ILO's supervisory bodies for political purposes. See Press Release, ILO 2194, UN, 7 Dec. 1984.

[43] *Report of the Fact-Finding and Conciliation Commission on Freedom of Association concerning the Republic of South Africa* (Geneva: ILO, 1992). At the 1993 ILC, delegates congratulated the ILO on its stance regarding South Africa. See *Record of Proceedings* (Geneva: ILO, 1993) ILC, 80th Session, 22nd and 23rd Sittings at 21/1–21/20.

[44] An example is the introduction of Standing Orders which provide for 'preliminary screening of political resolutions'. See Ghebali, n.10 above, 201–2. The reluctance of ILO supervisory bodies to appear 'politicized' will be considered further in Chap. 12.

[45] For the classic statement of this view see Fukuyama, F., *The End of History and the Last Man* (New York: Free Press, 1992); also see Chap. 1 above, at 15.

[46] Jacobi, O., *Economic Crisis, Trade Unions and the State* (London: Croom Helm, 1986), 65.

a period when radical deregulatory or 'free market' policies were introduced by governments; the UK being a prime example.[47] Unemployment was also seen to be a key issue in Western industrialized countries, leading to a call for a diminution of wages and working conditions, so that such States could attract capital investment. The overall result was that the pertinence of ILO norms, including the principle of trade unionism or freedom of association, was questioned by Member States[48] and an employers' lobby whose strength was increasing.[49] This caused a crisis 'as satisfaction with the ILO's work was inevitably linked to the budgetary request presented to the Conference annually'.[50] The Director-General of the ILO responded by initiating studies of the continuing relevance and efficacy of ILO standards.[51]

One result of international criticism of ILO standards was the 1997 amendment to the ILO Constitution, which allows abrogation of any Convention 'if it appears that the Convention has lost its purpose or that it no longer makes a useful contribution to attaining the objectives of the Organisation'.[52] However, there was not a wholesale abandonment of the fundamental tenets of the ILO Constitution.

Subsequent studies on globalization and unemployment, undertaken by the International Labour Office, were radical in their findings, challenging libertarian views on the role of labour standards in the global marketplace. They argued that, far from inhibiting prosperity, recognition of 'core labour standards' would enhance the creation of employment and assist economic growth.[53] Reports produced by the OECD

---

[47] See Brown, D., and McColgan, A., 'UK Employment Law and the International Labour Organisation: The Spirit of Co-operation' (1992) 21 *ILJ* 265; Ewing, K.D., *Britain and the ILO* (2nd edn., London: Institute of Employment Rights, 1994).

[48] See, e.g., during the International Labour Conference of 1995, Mr Barrot, Minister of Labour, Social Dialogue, and Participation in France, requested that priority be given to employment rather than collective bargaining. See *Record of Proceedings* (Geneva: ILO, 1995) ILC, 82nd Session, 8/11–8/12. See also the comments of Mr Melkert, Minister of Social Affairs for the Netherlands at the same conference, at 8/21.

[49] Cordova, E., 'Some Reflections on the Overproduction of International Labour Standards' (1993) 14 *Comparative Labor Law Journal* 138. For the current activities of the Bureau for Employers' Activities (or ACT/EMP as it is known internally within the ILO), see www. ilo.org/public/english/dialogue/actemp/.

[50] Bellace, J.R., 'The ILO Declaration of Fundamental Principles and Rights at Work' (2001) 17 *IJCLLIR* 269 at 271.

[51] See *Report of the Director-General: Defending Values, Promoting Change* (Geneva: ILO, 1994); See *Report of the Director-General: Promoting Employment* (Geneva: ILO, 1995).

[52] Instrument for the Amendment of the Constitution of the ILO 1997, Art. 1, inserting ILO Constitution Art. 19(9). See for discussion of the implications of this amendment *Report of the Committee on the Application of Standards* (Geneva: ILO, 2001), paras. 57–61.

[53] See also the research carried out under the auspices of the IILS, attached to the ILO. In particular, see Feis, H., 'International Labour Legislation in the Light of Economic Theory' in Sengenberger and Campbell, n.36 above; Figueiredo, J.B., and Shaheed, Z. (eds.), *Reducing Poverty through Labour Market Policies* (Geneva: IILS, 1995); Campbell, D., and Sengenberger, W. (eds.), *Creating Economic Opportunities: The Role of Labour Standards in Industrial Restructuring* (Geneva: IILS, 1994).

concurred.[54] A change in attitude could also be attributed to the aftermath of the Asian financial crisis of the 1990s.[55] The scene was set for the ILO to establish its place as a social mediator in the process of globalization.

In 1998, a new Declaration on Fundamental Principles and Rights at Work was adopted at the International Labour Conference. This Declaration, unlike the Declaration of Philadelphia, does not have constitutional status, but has set in motion a new ILO agenda. Langille has gone so far as to describe the 1998 Declaration as 'a third "constitutional moment" for the ILO—a moment of renewal and reaffirmation by the virtually global membership of basic constitutional values and commitment to social justice on the basis of economic progress'.[56]

The Preamble to the 1998 Declaration is reminiscent of the 1944 Declaration, in that it recognizes that social progress is not to be sacrificed to economic growth. Instead, there is a need for the ILO to promote 'strong social policies, justice and democratic institutions'. Moreover, the 1998 Declaration states that certain core labour standards are fundamental and 'embodied in the Constitution of the Organization'. These workers' rights may have been developed in 'the form of specific rights and obligations in Conventions', but by virtue of the Declaration all Member States, whether or not they have ratified the relevant Convention, 'have an obligation arising from the very fact of membership in the Organization' to respect, promote, and realize these rights in good faith.[57] Although the Declaration does not itself have constitutional status, it indicates how the ILO Constitution is to be interpreted.

The adoption of this instrument followed in the wake of the 1995 Copenhagen World Summit on Social Development which had declared the importance of protecting 'basic workers' rights'.[58] The 1996 WTO Ministerial Declaration in Singapore rejected the introduction of a global 'social clause', that is, compliance with labour standards as a precondition for trade access, but did advocate the protection of 'core international labour standards', stating that the ILO was the appropriate body to set such standards and monitor compliance.[59] The resultant ILO Declaration

---

[54] *Trade, Employment and Labour Standards: A Study of Core Workers' Rights and International Trade* (Paris: OECD, 1996); and *International Trade and Core Labour Standards* (Paris: OECD, 2000).

[55] See Tsogas, G., 'Labour Standards in the Generalized System of Preferences of the European Union and the United States' (2000) 6 *European Journal of Industrial Relations* 349 at 349.

[56] Langille, B., 'The ILO and the New Economy: Recent Developments' (1999) 15 *IJCL-LIR* 229 at 232.

[57] ILO Declaration of Fundamental Principles and Rights at Work and its Follow-Up, Art. 2.

[58] See para. 54(b) of the Programme of Action adopted by the Copenhagen Summit. For acknowledgement of this source see doc GB.267/LILS/5, para. 16.

[59] WTO Ministerial Conference Singapore 1996—Final Declaration 13 Dec. 1996 WT/MIN96/DEC/W, para. 4.

takes the form of an elaborate compromise between governments from the North and South and, likewise, between interested worker and employer lobbyists.[60] This is apparent from the list of 'rights' recognized as core or constitutional ILO standards and the references to international trade competition within the instrument.

The list of rights which are designated as 'fundamental' is tightly circumscribed, and apparently narrower than that envisaged some years previously.[61] Nevertheless, the use of a 'human rights' or 'fundamental rights' rhetoric asserts the universal character of those selected and liberates the discussion from the dictates of economic efficiency.[62] Moreover, 'freedom of association' is again explicitly guaranteed, alongside elimination of forced labour, prohibition of child labour, and the principle of non-discrimination.

The text of the 1998 Declaration reveals the tension between those who wished to use the instrument as a means by which to set fair terms of competition for international trade and those who wished to resist any form of protectionism.[63] There are echoes of 'the economic dimension' of the first ILO Constitution of 1919 identified above; but there is also a counter-balance in the explicit provision made for less wealthy States. Article 1 of the 1998 Declaration states that 'the specific circumstances' of States must be considered when assessing compliance. Consistent with this is Article 5, which stresses that 'labour standards should not be used for protectionist trade purposes' and that, in the context of the Declaration and follow-up procedure, 'the comparative advantage of any country should in no way be called into question'.[64] Instead, the current Director-General, Juan Somavia, hopes to open the way for 'a more substantive policy debate on development issues and rights at work within the ILO'. The aim is to target appropriate recipients of technical assistance rather than simply condemn State conduct.[65]

In conclusion, it seems that the Constitution of the ILO has survived three historical episodes with the essence of its initial mandate intact. 'Social

---

[60] See Murray, n.3 above, at 219; also the *Record of Proceedings* (Geneva: ILO, 1998), ILC, 86th Session, Report of the Committee on the Declaration of Principles, and the subsequent discussion by the same Committee on 'Submission, Discussion and Adoption'.

[61] Contrast the list contained in Art. 2 of the 1998 Declaration with that proposed 4 years before, in Bartolomei de la Cruz, H.G., 'International Labour Law: Renewal or Decline?' (1994) 10 *IJCLLIR* 201, 211–13. Indeed, the now limited 'core' could be regarded as a retreat from protection of more wide-ranging standards. See Hepple, B., 'New Approaches to International Labour Regulation' (1997) 26 *ILJ* 353 at 358.

[62] Bellace, J., 'The ILO Declaration of Fundamental Principles and Rights at Work' (2001) 17 *IJCLLIR* 269, at 272–3; and McCrudden, C., and Davies, A., 'A Perspective on Trade and Labour Rights' (2000) 21 *Journal of International Economic Law* 43 at 50–2.

[63] See *Report of the Director-General: The ILO, Standard-Setting and Globalisation* (Geneva: ILO, 1997); abbreviated version published in (1997) 13 IJCLLIR 143; and *Report of the Director-General: Decent Work* (Geneva: ILO, 1999), 14–15.

[64] See for analysis of this debate Langille, n.56 above.

[65] *Report of the Director-General: Decent Work* (Geneva: ILO, 1999), 8.

justice' in the form of 'decent work' remains at the heart of ILO object-ives.[66] The prevention of unfair competition in trade (where this is based on violation of core labour standards) also remains an important (if controver-sial) theme of current ILO debates. Finally, the principle of 'freedom of association' seems to have withstood the challenges of the latter part of the twentieth century and emerged as an almost universally recognized 'core labour standard'. This has enabled the tripartite structure of the ILO to survive. Moreover, pressure is still placed on Member States to use tripartite consultative processes at the national level for the implementation of ILO standards.[67]

II.   TRIPARTITE STANDARD-SETTING

The ILO performs various roles. For example, the International Labour Office, its secretariat, provides 'technical assistance' and other advisory services. It also initiates and sponsors research, promoting the exchange of information and experience through publications, data banks, meetings, and seminars. However, it is the standard-setting capacity of the ILO that has traditionally been regarded as central to its function. Indeed, it has been observed that 'the need for international labour legislation . . . was the main reason for the setting up of the ILO'.[68]

The peculiar feature of ILO standard-setting, which distinguishes this process from that in many other international organizations, is its tripartite character. Even though ratification of international conventions is ultim-ately dependent upon State consent, the drafting, voting, monitoring, and enforcement of labour standards within the ILO is the joint responsibility of employer, worker, and State representatives.

The executive organ of the ILO is the Governing Body, which has general responsibility for co-ordinating the activities of the Organization. In par-ticular, the Governing Body sets the agenda for the annual International Labour Conference (ILC), which performs the key standard-setting role.[69] The Governing Body also appoints the Director-General, who provides

---

[66] As is evident from the 'strategic objectives' set out on the ILO website. See http://webfusion.ilo.org/public/db/bureau/program/objectives/.

[67] ILO, *General Survey concerning the Tripartite Consultation (International Labour Standards) Convention 1976 (No. 144) and the Tripartite Consultation (Activities of the International Labour Organisation) Recommendation, 1976 (No. 152)* (Geneva: ILO, 2000), presented at the ILC, 88th Session.

[68] Ghebali, n.10 above, 204.

[69] The Governing Body also decides on the action that should be taken on the basis of resolutions passed at the Conference (ILO Constitution, Art. 14). It analyses the budget, financial estimates, and accounts submitted by the Director-General for adoption by the Conference (ILO Constitution, Art.13). It decides on the date and agenda of regional and technical conferences and on what action should be taken on the basis of their reports. It also fulfils an important role in the application of Conventions and recommendations by Member States.

strategic guidance for the Organization in the form of policy proposals.[70] The Governing Body currently consists of fifty-six persons, twenty-eight of whom represent governments. There are fourteen employer representatives and fourteen worker representatives.[71]

The tripartite constitution of this executive body is also significant, for it means that the agenda set for the ILC, which is bound to affect the substance of instruments adopted within the Conference, is determined not by States acting alone, but by States in agreement with employer and worker representatives. While a State can raise objections to a particular matter being on the agenda, if there is a two-thirds majority at the ILC in favour of discussing the matter, this objection can be overridden.[72]

The ILC is the key legislative body which has the power to conclude Conventions and adopt Recommendations. ILO Conventions create legal obligations which are binding on States which ratify them.[73] By contrast, Recommendations create 'soft' rather than 'hard' law, and merely set standards which are intended to provide guidance for governments in their national legislation or administrative practice.[74] Recommendations are often adopted that supplement and parallel Conventions.[75]

The tripartite structure of the ILO allows employer and worker representatives to vote at the ILC upon the adoption of Conventions and Recommendations. To allay States' fears that government representatives could be outvoted by workers' and employers' delegates, national delegations consist of one worker, one employer, and two government representatives.[76] 'It was felt that unless the preponderating voice was with the governments, the conference might tend to become a debating society, and its resolutions would not command the official authority without which they would not be carried into practical effect'.[77] There is also a requirement that conventions and recommendations be passed with a two-thirds majority which ensures that more than one representative faction must approve of the measure in

---

[70] ILO Constitution, Art. 8.   [71] *Ibid.*, Art. 7(1).

[72] Dunning, H., 'The Origins of Convention No. 87 on Freedom of Association and the Right to Organize' (1998) 137 *ILRev.* 149 at 156–7.

[73] As was observed by the Permanent Court of International Justice in an Opinion of 1926 on the competence of the ILO's jurisdiction. See PCIJ, Series B No. 13, at 16–17: 'Each Member is free to adopt or reject any proposal of the Organisation either for a national law or for an international Convention'.

[74] Kirgis, F.L., 'Specialized Law-Making Processes', in Schachter, O., and Joyner, C.C. (eds.), *United Nations Legal Order* (Cambridge: CUP, 1995), i, 143–4.

[75] Ghebali, n.10 above, 210. See also on the preparatory stages of standard-setting Swepston, L., 'Supervision of ILO Standards' (1997) 13 *IJCLLIR* 327, at 330–1.

[76] The Chairman, Samuel Gompers, had proposed equal voting rights for each of the three groups but was outvoted, for reasons which shall become apparent below. See Dunning, n.72 above, 155.

[77] Butler, n.15 above, 9; cf. the views expressed in *Report and Minutes of the Commission on International Labour Legislation*, n.4 above, 81–6, 88–90, 94–102.

question.[78] Divergence in the positions taken by national governments on labour-related matters means that it is often also necessary for employers and workers to reach a compromise on the content of a proposed instrument. Revision of these tripartite procedures was considered in 1945, but ultimately rejected as too controversial and potentially destructive of the delicate but workable power balance which had already been established.[79]

Employers and workers tend to vote in separate blocks which have become known as the 'employers' group' and the 'workers' group'. They usually compete to win government representatives' votes. The employers' group receives administrative support from the Bureau for Employers' Activities (or ACT/EMP), while the workers' group tends to operate through the Bureau for Workers' Activities (ACTRAV). They therefore have the resources to research issues and develop proposals which may sway the ILC.

In addition, the Committees elected by the ILC to deal with particular matters are tripartite. They consist of employer, employee, and government representatives in equal proportions. These Committees include the Drafting Committee for Conventions and Recommendations, the Resolutions Committee, the Selection Committee, and the vital Credentials Committee (which assesses whether employer and worker delegates are sufficiently representative of employers' and workers' organizations within the State concerned). The task of these Committees is to report back to the plenary meeting of the Conference, which then votes on the proposals they make.[80] There is therefore tripartite engagement at each stage of the standard-setting process.

It is notable that in 1919 this was a radical new development. 'All official international conferences in the past had consisted exclusively of government delegates.'[81] This had meant that 'discussions took place in the pure, but thin, atmosphere of academic abstraction'.[82] The aim was to utilize the knowledge and experience of employers and workers to create adequate regulations and ensure their effective implementation. This form of decision-making was intended to give the ILO's work 'a broader basis of social consensus' and a degree of moral authority.[83]

---

[78] ILO Constitution, Art. 19. Moreover, a vote is not valid if the number of votes cast for and against is less than half the number of delegates attending the Conference (ILO Constitution, Art. 17(3)).

[79] Ghebali, n.10 above, 126–7. See also *Record of Proceedings* (Geneva: ILO, 1945) ILC, 27th Session, 55–8, 445–9.

[80] Betten, n.41 above, 17–18.

[81] Butler, n.15 above, 8.

[82] Thomas, n.18 above, 9.

[83] *Record of Proceedings* (Philadelphia, Penn.: ILO, 1944) ILC, 26th Session, per Mr Tixier (Government delegate, France) at 48.

Tripartism has additional significance, due to the peculiar requirements that follow the adoption of an ILO convention by the ILC. Even where the representatives of a particular State have voted against the adoption of a measure, that State will be obliged to present the convention to the appropriate national body which has power to give effect to the text. 'Submission to the competent authorities' must normally be achieved within a year. All members must inform the ILO Director-General of the measures they have taken to secure approval of the domestic legislature. If the domestic legislature approves the convention, the State is required to ratify it and to see that it is effective. Moreover, even if the domestic legislature does not approve the ILO convention, the member is obliged to report the extent to which its law and practice are consistent with the convention, 'stating the difficulties which prevent or delay the ratification of the Convention'.[84] Accordingly, it has been observed that 'a State—merely by being a member of the ILO—incurs significant responsibilities, and subjects itself to peer pressure, regarding not only those Conventions which it ratifies, but also those of which it disapproves'.[85] Worker and employer interests also receive effective protection within this process. Bearing this in mind, it becomes evident that the tripartite standard-setting procedures set in place by the ILO place a subtle but tangible restriction on State sovereignty.

The tripartite structure of the ILO would therefore seem to be a useful strategy by which to ensure that States do not unduly obstruct the adoption of international labour standards. This form of standard-setting ensures that the content of ILO conventions is not reduced to that acceptable to the least enthusiastic State party.[86] Nevertheless, this system still relies on alliances between States and the employers' or the workers' group; and it is arguable that this structure does provide scope for workers and employers, rather than only States, to obstruct the adoption of ILO instruments on particular subjects; the right to strike appears to be one of these.

III.   ILO INSTRUMENTS ON FREEDOM OF ASSOCIATION AND THE RIGHT TO STRIKE

The ILO Constitution, as amended by the Declaration of Philadelphia, arguably rendered inevitable the setting of ILO standards on 'freedom of association'. Tripartism depended on the effective protection of this freedom for both employers' and workers' organizations. The ILO became increasingly embarrassed by the lack of any mechanism by which to criticize those States which violated this core principle.

---

[84] ILO Constitution, Art. 19(2) and (5). See also Swepston, n.25 above, 332.
[85] Kirgis, n.74 above, 115.
[86] Cf. Chap. 1 above, at 27–8.

It is therefore not so surprising that there was eventual agreement on the two 'core' ILO Conventions relating to freedom of association. These were Convention No. 87 Concerning Freedom of Association and Protection of the Right to Organise 1948 and Convention No. 98 Concerning the Application of the Principles of the Right to Organise and to Bargain Collectively 1949. They are now designated as among the ILO's 'fundamental' or 'basic human rights Conventions'[87] and have received amongst the highest levels of ratification.[88] By 1951, agreement was also reached on special procedures for scrutinizing complaints relating to freedom of association, through the ILO Fact-Finding and Conciliation Commission on Freedom of Association (FFCC) and the tripartite Governing Body Committee on Freedom of Association (CFA).[89]

What is more surprising is that it took the ILO thirty years to achieve this. It seems that this delay was due to the early determination of the workers' group to push simultaneously for standard-setting on freedom of association alongside the right to strike, which they saw as indistinguishable. Moreover, the workers' group was unwilling to make the compromises, such as recognition of the negative right to disassociate, which would have satisfied the employers' contingent and won greater State support. It was only in the wake of World War II, namely a global crisis in the protection of human rights and an institutional crisis in terms of ILO competence, that compromises were made which would secure the acceptance of Conventions Nos. 87 and 98.

There remains no ILO convention that explicitly requires Member States to take particular steps to ensure protection of the right to strike. From 1948 onwards, the majority of workers' representatives appeared to be resigned to omitting the subject of industrial action from ILO standard-setting. By the 1990s, the workers' group was actively opposed to employers' proposals for a convention on industrial dispute settlement, which could circumscribe the scope of the right to strike. In this later period of opposition to further ILO intervention in this field, the jurisprudence developed by the ILO CFA was in all probability a significant factor,

---

[87] An early example of this status is the Declaration adopted on 25 June 1970, reported in *Record of Proceedings* (Geneva: ILO, 1970) ILC, 54th Session, 733–6.

[88] See for ratification of all ILO Conventions: www.ilo.org/. At the time of writing, ILO Convention No. 87 has received 140 ratifications and Convention No. 98 has received 151 ratifications. This compares to ILO Convention No. 29 on Forced Labour which has the highest number of ratifications (160) and ILO Convention No. 138 on the Minimum Age of Admission to Employment which has the lowest number of ratifications for a 'fundamental' convention (117).

[89] See on the creation of the FFCC *Record of Proceedings* (Geneva: ILO, 1950) ILC, 33rd Session, App. XII, 564; and Nafziger, J.A.R., 'The International Organization and Social Change: The Fact-Finding and Conciliation Commission on Freedom of Association' (1969) 2 *New York University Journal of International Law and Politics* 1. On the creation of the CFA see *Sixth Report of the ILO to the UN* (Geneva: ILO, 1952) App. V. The activities of these supervisory bodies are discussed further in Chap. 8 below, at 188–91.

since this supervisory body recognized early on that the right to strike was an essential aspect of freedom of association and criticized State conduct on this basis.[90]

This section examines these developments in some detail. The aim is to provide not only a historical outline of these events and the debates that surrounded them, but also a tentative analysis of the factors which led to the present outcome.

A. POST WORLD WAR I: THE FIRST WORKER PROPOSALS FOR PROTECTION OF FREEDOM OF ASSOCIATION AND THE RIGHT TO STRIKE

At the very first ILO International Labour Conference in Washington, the issue of freedom of association and the right to strike was raised by workers' representatives from Belgium and Japan.[91] From 1920 onwards, protests were lodged with the ILO relating to State violation of these principles,[92] but the ILO was unable to take any action.[93] The Organization could intervene only where there was a convention on the subject matter of a complaint and there was no convention on freedom of association or the right to strike.

Nevertheless, it was widely recognized that the *status quo* was unsatisfactory, given that the very Constitution of the ILO relied on the prior effective protection of freedom of association by the Member States. In 1923, the workers called for an enquiry to see whether Members were indeed acting in accordance with this principle, and this request was agreed to by the Governing Body.[94]

The result was the preliminary 'Nicod Report' of 1924 that addressed the issue of freedom of association in tandem with industrial action, indicating that its author regarded the two as linked. No value judgements were made as to the practices in ILO Member States, but there was an endeavour to find a 'mean' which might provide the foundation for ILO standards relating to the constitutional guarantee of freedom of association.[95] On this basis, it was agreed that further study was required, both providing an

---

[90] See for an early example *Case No. 28 (UK–Jamaica)*, 2nd Report of the CFA, para. 68. For further discussion of the development of this principle see Chap. 8 below, at 192–6.

[91] *Record of Proceedings* (Washington, DC: ILO, 1919) ILC, 1st Session, 52 and 160–3.

[92] E.g., apart from early complaints made by the workers' representative from Japan, complaints were also received from workers' representatives of the Kingdom of Serbs, Croats, and Slovenes, Hungary, and Spain. See *Record of Proceedings* (Geneva: ILO, 1924) ILC, 6th Session, 151–2, 158; *Freedom of Association: Report and Draft Questionnaire* (Geneva: ILO, 1927) ILC, 10th Session, 138–9.

[93] See the restrictive jurisdiction of the ILO set down in Treaty of Versailles, Art. 409.

[94] *Minutes of the 20th Session of the Governing Body of the International Labour Office* (Geneva: ILO, 1923), 520 ff.

[95] Nicod, J., 'Freedom of Association and Trade Unionism: An Introductory Survey' (1924) 9 *ILRev.* 467.

accurate statement of facts and examining judicial practice 'in order to see how the laws were applied in various countries'.[96]

This cautious approach provoked some frustration amongst the workers. Complaints continued to be made in the ILC by workers' representatives who asked that 'freedom of association' be placed on the Conference agenda.[97] They considered that this issue would be linked to protection of the 'right to strike'.[98]

Many governments were not so enthusiastic about the measures proposed by workers, which would enhance the power of organized labour. Their preferences tended to lie in the compulsory arbitration and conciliation model that had been introduced in Australia.[99] For example, in 1924, the government delegate for Finland requested 'that the International Labour Office devote attention, in its programme of research, to the question of settlement of labour disputes and the methods employed in various countries for the organisation of conciliation and arbitration in such disputes'.[100] This latter Resolution was adopted by the Conference, but it was also determined that the subject of freedom of association should be set down for the 1927 ILC, and the Office was asked to prepare a Report and Questionnaire in preparation for the Conference discussions.[101]

The preamble to the Report placed before the International Labour Conference in 1927 acknowledged the 'special difficulties' arising from international protection of freedom of association. 'Many of the legal conceptions which have governed the development of Continental law and jurisprudence on the subject are foreign to Anglo-Saxon law and jurisprudence and vice versa.' However, these difficulties were ultimately deemed superficial, being associated more with legal terminology than practicalities, for the report concluded that 'the practical problems to be solved are similar in all countries'.[102] In the view of the International Labour Office, even at this early stage, there was an 'intimate relationship between the right to combine for trade purposes and the right to strike'.[103] In its Conclusions, the Report made a strong case for international legislation on both.[104]

---

[96] *Minutes of the 22nd Session of the Governing Body of the International Labour Office* (Geneva: ILO, 1924), 141–3.

[97] *Record of Proceedings* (Geneva: ILO, 1924) ILC, 6th Session, 538–9.

[98] *Ibid.*, 158, which sets out the statement by the workers' representative of the Kingdom of Serbs, Croats, and Slovenes that respect for 'freedom of association' would enable trade union officials to organize strikes without imprisonment.

[99] See Chap. 3 above, at 51–3.

[100] *Record of Proceedings* (Geneva: ILO, 1924) ILC, 6th Session, 538.

[101] *Minutes of the 32nd Session of the Governing Body of the International Labour Office* (Geneva: ILO, 1926), App. II, 294.

[102] *Freedom of Association: Report and Draft Questionnaire* (Geneva: ILO, 1927) ILC, 10th Session, 9.

[103] *Ibid.*, 75.   [104] *Ibid.*, 138 and 143.

The 1927 ILC had to decide, as a preliminary measure, how to draft the questionnaire which would survey the views of Member States. A tripartite Conference Committee on Freedom of Association was established for this purpose. It was composed of twelve representatives from each of the three groups of the Conference. These negotiations on the questionnaire ultimately failed, because workers would not accept a draft which made too many concessions.[105] In particular, they were opposed to any assertion that the freedom to associate included the negative right not to join an association. There was heated debate in which it was said that if the needs of workers were not met, they might altogether abandon co-operation with governments and employers under the auspices of the ILO.[106] This extreme threat was intended to play on States' fears of Bolshevik revolution, but did not have the desired result. State and employer delegates held fast. Despite recourse to an 'emergency meeting', no agreement could be reached. The proposal to insert the question of freedom of association on the Agenda of the 1928 Conference was therefore rejected by sixty-six votes to twenty-eight.[107]

Nevertheless, a Resolution was adopted unanimously concerning 'collective labour disputes', namely: '[t]he International Labour Office requests the Governing Body to consider the possibility of placing the question of "the solution of collective labour disputes" on the Agenda of an early Session of the Conference'.[108] This was considered to be distinct from the survey on 'freedom of association'; although there were still workers' representatives who challenged this distinction.[109] The successful adoption of this Resolution may also have stemmed from its ambiguity. Workers may have seen this as an opportunity to secure protection of a right to strike, whereas the then Director of the ILO and many government representatives saw this as a means by which to set standards on alternative forms of dispute resolution.[110] From this point onwards, within the ILC and Governing Body, consideration of the potential for protection of 'freedom of association' was formally segregated from the issue of the right to strike.

In 1930, the Governing Body reopened the question of freedom of association, establishing yet another Committee to investigate the potential for adoption of a Convention on this subject.[111] However, the proposal was

[105] *Record of Proceedings* (Geneva: ILO, 1927) ILC, 10th Session, i, 268–70 and 374.

[106] *Ibid.*, 281.

[107] *Ibid.*, 384–9.

[108] *Ibid.*, 680. There was no opposition to this Resolution, proposed by a government delegate. See *ibid.*, 330–1.

[109] *Ibid.*, i, 341, where the Uruguay workers' representative stated that there were three vital elements of freedom of association: individual liberty, freedom of organization, and the right to strike.

[110] *Ibid.*, ii, 'Report of the Director Presented to the Conference', 231–3.

[111] *Minutes of the 50th Session of the Governing Body of the International Labour Office* (Geneva: ILO, 1930), 646–8 and 678; and *Minutes of the 55th Session of the Governing Body of the ILO* (Geneva: ILO, 1931) 716–23, App. IX, Annex A, 'Note on Freedom of Association'.

not carried forward, despite the positive recommendations of the Committee and its Chairman.[112] It may be that this issue was perceived as being too sensitive so soon after the debacle of the 1927 ILC.

A parallel development was the investigation into compulsory conciliation and arbitration as a way of settling industrial disputes, which was likely to call into question the wisdom of legal protection of a right to strike. The inquiry conducted by the Office reached fruition in 1933 with a Report titled *Conciliation and Arbitration in Industrial Disputes*. The Report consisted of 'a comparative analysis of the legislation of various countries on the conciliation and arbitration procedure adopted for the prevention and settlement of trade disputes concerning the fixing of working conditions'.[113] However, there is evidence to suggest that the writers of the Report in the International Labour Office were ambivalent about the benefits of these procedures as an alternative to traditional methods of securing collective agreements. For example, the Report observed that '[w]orkers often object to conciliation and arbitration for the reason, based on a criticism both of their technique and of their politico-legal consequences, that they are calculated to endanger the existence of trade organisations by taking from them and transferring to the State one of their principal objects, the achievement of favourable conditions by their own efforts, and by depriving them of the right to strike'.[114] The Report's conclusions were that success in the implementation of such a system depends on whether the system of conciliation and arbitration is 'essentially in keeping with the general legal system' of a particular country.[115] No further action was taken by the ILO on the basis of this Office Report; nor was the matter placed on the ILC agenda. The potential for international labour legislation on the right to strike does not appear to have been re-evaluated until the 1940s and, even then, it was sidelined in favour of a focus on freedom of association.

B.   Post World War II: Renewed Trade Union Pressure

After World War II, there was renewed pressure for the adoption of an ILO convention on freedom of association. This stemmed in part from the emphasis placed on this principle in the Declaration of Philadelphia 1944 and the resolutions adopted by the 1946 Third Conference of American States, held in Mexico City. The latter had requested the Governing Body to place the question of freedom of association on the agenda of other Regional Conferences and the International Labour Conference.

---

[112] *Minutes of the 61st Session of the Governing Body of the International Labour Office* (Geneva: ILO, 1933), 23–5.

[113] *Conciliation and Arbitration in Industrial Disputes* (Geneva: ILO, 1933), p. v.

[114] *Ibid.*, 133–4. Cf. Chap. 3 above, at 51–4.   [115] *Ibid.*, 138.

In 1947, the World Federation of Trade Unions (WFTU) and the American Federation of Labour (AFL) submitted memoranda to the Economic and Social Council (ECOSOC) of the United Nations, requesting that ECOSOC consider the 'guarantees for the exercise and development of trade union rights'—or rather the lack of such guarantees. Their memoranda drew attention to 'allegations of infringements of trade union rights in a large number of countries... which called for the intervention of the competent organs of the United Nations and the ILO to ascertain the truth of these allegations and obtain redress'.[116]

The WFTU requested that a Committee on Trade Union Rights be established by ECOSOC, which could then take measures on the basis of the Committee's recommendations. The AFL, by contrast, requested action by the ILO. The WFTU represented the interests of socialist countries in diluting the power of the ILO, whereas the AFL, in the tradition of Samuel Gompers, was an ardent liberal supporter of the continuation of an ILO endeavour.[117] In response, on 24 March 1947, ECOSOC adopted a resolution transmitting the memoranda to the ILO with a request that the Organization place the issue of trade union rights on the agenda at the next International Labour Conference.[118]

This was an instance of the Cold War game played out through the United Nations system, for it 'provided a forum within which each of the protagonists could expound the virtues of its own economic and social system and attack that of the other'.[119] The ECOSOC decision was an important concession in favour of the Western capitalist bloc which the ILO was seen to represent at that time. Apart from the political considerations which made it wise for the ILO to include this subject in the 1947 Conference Agenda, it was obliged to do so under Article III of its Agreement with the UN.[120] The new role of the ILO as a UN agency meant that the issue could no longer be evaded.

The memorandum submitted by the AFL directly raised the question: '[t]o what extent is the right of workers and their organizations to resort to strikes recognized and protected?'[121] The AFL seems to have been seeking confirmation that there was a link between freedom of association (which had received recognition from the international community) and the right to strike.

---

[116] *Record of Proceedings* (Geneva: ILO, 1950), ILC, 33rd Session, App. XII, 563–6.

[117] Dunning, n.72 above, 159–60.

[118] *Record of Proceedings* (Geneva: ILO, 1947) ILC, 30th Session, App. X, 566; Ben-Israel, R., *International Labour Standards: The Case of Freedom to Strike* (Deventer: Kluwer, 1988), 37–9 and 48.

[119] Alcock, n.6 above, 252. For the substance of arguments made by the UK, the USA, and the USSR see *Freedom of Association and Industrial Relations* (Geneva: ILO, 1947), Report VII, ILC, 30th Session, 7–11.

[120] *Freedom of Association and Industrial Relations* (Geneva: ILO, 1947), Report VII, ILC, 30th Session, Geneva, 2.

[121] See Ben-Israel, n.118 above, 38–9.

The issues raised by the memoranda and ECOSOC were initially the subject of a Report by a Conference 'Committee on Freedom of Association' formed by the International Labour Office.[122] The Report outlined the historical problems associated with freedom of association and surveyed current legislation and practice. The right to strike was mentioned several times in the Conference Committee's Report and was referred to in the Report's conclusions referring to public sector employment and voluntary conciliation.[123] The Report was adopted unanimously by the 1947 Conference and a Resolution Concerning Freedom of Association and Protection of the Right to Organise and Bargain Collectively was passed. It is, however, interesting that the ILC Resolution made no mention of the right to strike, giving an early indication that the explicit question asked by the AFL might go unanswered.

The ILO then distributed to all members a summary report of the proceedings in 1947 and circulated a questionnaire, asking for the views of all member governments on further action.[124] ECOSOC approved of these actions, calling on the ILO to continue in this vein and to adopt one or several conventions on this subject.[125] The General Assembly also asked that the ILO create the necessary machinery to monitor implementation of trade union rights and freedom of association.[126]

A Report prepared by the International Labour Office in preparation for the 1948 Conference provided detailed information relating to the 'law and practice' of various countries together with a questionnaire. This Report did not mention the right to strike, except in relation to the adoption of international legislation relating to conciliation and arbitration. Given the diversity of national practice, the Office suggested that to take measures on conciliation and arbitration for industrial dispute settlement was not advisable.[127]

At the 1948 Conference, another Committee on Freedom of Association and Industrial Relations was established, which drafted and secured the adoption of Convention No. 87.[128] As in 1927, the question arose whether

[122] *Record of Proceedings* (Geneva: ILO, 1947) ILC, 30th Session, App. X, 566. This body is not to be confused with the later Governing Body Committee on Freedom of Association, which screened complaints relating to freedom of association.

[123] *Freedom of Association and Industrial Relations* (Geneva: ILO, 1947), 30–4, 46, 52, 73–4.

[124] The text of the questionnaire can be found in *Freedom of Association and Protection of the Right to Organise* (ILO, 1947) Questionnaire, prepared for ILC, 31st Session, San Francisco, 1948, 15–17.

[125] United Nations, Economic and Social Council: E/533. Also see *Freedom of Association and Protection of the Right to Organise* (ILO, 1948) Report VII prepared by the ILO for ILC, 31st Session, San Francisco, 2–3.

[126] UNGA A/C 3/166 and A/444. See Chap. 8 below, at 188–91.

[127] *Industrial Relations: Application of the Principles of the Right to Organise and to Bargain Collectively, Collective Agreements, Conciliation and Arbitration, and Co-operation between Public Authorities and Employers' and Workers' Organisations* (ILO, 1947) Report VIII(1) prepared for ILC, 31st Session, San Francisco, 92–124.

[128] *Record of Proceedings* (ILO, 1948) ILC, 31st Session, First Report of the Committee on Freedom of Association, 473.

freedom of association included the freedom to disassociate, and whether this negative freedom should be protected in an international instrument. Several employers' representatives wanted an express guarantee that there would be no compulsion to organize. Other worker and government members expressed concern at this view. The UK, in particular, feared that this would prevent what was regarded domestically as legitimate industrial action, where workers refused to work with other workers who were not prepared to join the union.[129] This provision was accordingly excluded from the final draft, at the joint request of workers' and government representatives.

The issue of industrial action also faded from view.[130] It was raised only in relation to debates concerning conciliation and arbitration procedures,[131] public sector strikes,[132] and industrial action in pursuit of a closed shop.[133] Ben-Israel suggests that members of the Office assumed, as did others present at the Conference, that the right to strike was included in the more general guarantee of freedom of association.[134] However, apart from the preparatory Report on Convention No. 87, there is little evidence to confirm this supposition.

Certainly, the government representatives of certain socialist countries did not take inclusion of the right to strike for granted. At one point in the discussion on Convention No. 98 in 1949, Polish and Czech government representatives expressed concern that there was nothing in the draft prohibiting the victimization of striking workers.[135] Their pressure for some

[129] *Record of Proceedings* (ILO, 1948) ILC, 31st Session, 489–90; *Application of the Principles of the Right to Organise and to Bargain Collectively* (Geneva: ILO, 1948), Report IV(1) prepared for ILC, 32nd Session, 1949, 4–6, 'Extracts from the Report of the Conference Committee'. This seems ironic, given the subsequent stance of the UK Conservative government in proceedings before the European Court of Human Rights in *Young, James and Webster v UK* (1982) 4 EHRR 38, discussed in Chap. 9 below, at 232–6.

[130] At the International Labour Conference between 1947 and 1949, no amendment expressly establishing or denying the right to strike was adopted. ILO, *Committee of Experts' General Survey on Freedom of Association and Collective Bargaining* (Geneva: ILO, 1994), 63.

[131] *Record of Proceedings* (ILO, 1947), App. X, 563, para. 20 and 565, para. 25; ILO, *Record of Proceedings* (ILO, 1948) ILC, 31st Session, App. X, 478; ILO, *Record of Proceedings* (Geneva: ILO, 1949) ILC, 32nd Session, App. VII, 468 and 470; Alcock, n.6 above, 256–9; Ben-Israel, n.118 above, 39.

[132] See the comments of Mr Veiga, government delegate, Portugal, in *Record of Proceedings* (ILO, 1948) ILC, 31st Session, 15th Sitting, 232.

[133] *Record of Proceedings* (ILO, 1948), App. XI, 490; ILO, *Record of Proceedings* (Geneva: ILO, 1949) ILC, 32nd Session, App. VII, 466.

[134] Ben-Israel, n. 118 above, 45.

[135] ILO, *Record of Proceedings* (Geneva: ILO, 1949) ILC, 32nd Session, 315, where the workers' adviser for Poland, Mr Szynarowski, stated that '[t]he Convention as a whole could be used also by the employers and by some Governments as an anti-strike weapon. Strikes, that is, the union's activity during working hours, are not covered by the Convention, and it would seem that, according to its provisions, the workers taking part in a strike are victimised'. See also Alcock, n.6 above, 259. Note however that Socialist Eastern bloc states later expressed the view that the exercise of the right to strike was unnecessary under a Communist state. See *Case No. 148 (Poland)*, 22nd Report of the CFA (1956), para. 66; and *Case No. 111 (USSR)*, 23rd Report (1956), para. 4.

explicit guarantee of protection for participants in industrial action seems consistent with the later debate surrounding the inclusion of a right to strike in the UN International Covenant on Economic, Social and Cultural Rights 1966 (ICESCR). In that context, socialist countries also argued for a right to strike, while countries such as the United Kingdom and France rejected their proposals. Only when three South American countries indicated their support for the inclusion of the provision for a right to strike did the Western countries allow the amendment.[136] This suggests that the beginnings of a Cold War division and the developing ideological opposition between East and West may have been responsible for Western States' opposition to the inclusion of a right to strike in an ILO Convention in the International Labour Conferences of the late 1940s.

Another possible reason for the failure to include a right to strike in Conventions Nos. 87 and 98 may have been the workers' group itself. It has been observed that the majority of workers' representatives were afraid that 'the safeguarding of the right to strike within the ILO Conventions would inevitably require setting its limitations'. By the end of World War II, worker organizations had consolidated their *de facto* position and strength in most ILO Member States. Trade unions, use of industrial action, and the political wing of the labour movement had secured workers unprecedented rights (or immunities).[137] Owing to the tripartite structure of the International Labour Conference, workers' representatives were often forced to compromise in order to secure the votes of employer and government representatives. If a detailed right to strike were to be incorporated into any Convention, the necessity of compromise meant that this right would be more limited than that already recognized in many States. Therefore, workers' reluctance to see a lesser right guaranteed in the international sphere may account for the failure to incorporate a right to strike into Conventions Nos. 87 and 98. By contrast, workers had no such voice in the drafting of the ICESCR, which reflected the primacy of and divisions between the ideological positions held by Western and Eastern bloc States.

It is worth noting that inclusion of the right to strike in the ICESCR has not been significant for its global protection. One reason is the wording of Article 8(1)(d), under which the Contracting Parties merely undertake to ensure 'the right to strike, provided that it is exercised in conformity with the laws of the particular country'. There is no apparent scope on the face of this document for criticism of the laws of the Member States.[138] However,

[136] Ben-Israel, n.118 above, 43–6.
[137] See French, J.D., 'The Declaration of Philadelphia and the Global Social Charter of the United Nations 1944–45' in Sengenberger and Campbell, n.36 above, 19.
[138] In this respect, it is similar to the initial provision made for 'freedom of association' under the first ILO Constitution included in the Treaty of Versailles. See above at 98.

as we shall see in Part IV, the Committee on Economic, Social, and Cultural Rights has overcome this apparent impediment and has criticized State conduct relating to industrial action where this deviates from ILO standards.[139]

By contrast, despite the absence of specific provision for protection of a right to strike, the content and influence of ILO Conventions Nos. 87 and 98 are far-reaching.[140] Convention No. 87 on Freedom of Association and Protection of the Right to Organise 1948 guarantees the right of workers and employers not only to establish and join organizations,[141] but also 'to organise their administration and activities'.[142] While the rights provided for in the Convention are to be exercised with due respect to 'the law of the land', that law 'shall not be such as to impair; nor shall it be so applied to impair, the guarantees provided for in this Convention'.[143] Moreover, States are not merely to tolerate the existence of such organizations but must take 'all necessary and appropriate measures to ensure that workers and employers may exercise freely the right to organise'.[144] Under Convention No. 98 on the Right to Organise and Bargain Collectively 1949, workers are to be protected from anti-union discrimination and workers' organizations are to be protected from acts of interference with their establishment, functioning, or administration.[145] The State also has an obligation to introduce machinery and measures 'appropriate to national conditions' to facilitate such organization and promote negotiation of collective agreements.[146]

The status of Convention No. 87, in particular, is also recognized in the UN Covenants of 1966. Article 22(3) of the ICCPR and Article 8(3) of the ICESCR state that nothing in those provisions authorizes a State to prejudice, by its legislation or applicable law, its obligations under Convention No. 87.[147]

---

[139] See, e.g., *Concluding Observations: Trinidad and Tobago 17/05/2002 E/C.12/1/Add.80*, paras. 35 and 43; and *Concluding Observations: Bulgaria 9/12/99 E/C.12/1/Add.37*, para. 16.

[140] See Apps. 1 and 2 for the full text of Conventions Nos. 87 and 98, respectively.

[141] ILO Convention No. 87 1948, Art. 2.

[142] *Ibid.*, Art. 3.

[143] *Ibid.*, Art. 8. Cf. again the narrow guarantee of 'freedom of association' in the first ILO Constitution, discussed above at 98.

[144] ILO Convention No. 87 1948, Art. 11.

[145] Employers and employers' organizations receive the same protection. See ILO Convention No. 98 1949, Arts. 1 and 2.

[146] ILO Convention No. 98 1949, Arts. 3 and 4.

[147] This was by reason of an amendment submitted by the UK and the Netherlands. Again, it is not clear why the amendment was accepted or why this ILO Convention was singled out in this fashion. See for detailed analysis of the *travaux préparatoires*, Ben-Israel, n.118 above, at 80–1; and Craven, M., *The International Covenant on Economic, Social and Cultural Rights: A Perspective on its Development* (2nd revd edn., Oxford: Clarendon Press, 1998) at 260. It is probably on account of this provision that the Committee on Economic, Social, and Cultural Rights, responsible for interpretation of the ICESCR, has tended to defer to ILO standards. The Committee has also recommended ratification of ILO Convention No. 87. See, e.g., *Concluding Observations: Morocco 1/12/00 E/C.12/1/Add.55*, para. 22. For the text of those provisions see App. 3.

The ILO Committee on Freedom of Association took the view that the right to strike is an essential aspect of freedom of association, guaranteed not only in Conventions Nos. 87 and 98 but also in the ILO Constitution.[148] This approach was subsequently adopted by the ILO Committee of Experts on the Application of Conventions and Recommendations (CEACR), which is, *inter alia*, responsible for scrutinizing compliance with Conventions Nos. 87 and 98.[149] In this respect, the broad and general terms of those instruments have been helpful to workers.

It appears that all factions have been happy to include, in other instruments, supplementary provisions affirming the existence of the right to strike. Article 7 of the Voluntary Conciliation and Arbitration Recommendation No. 92 of 1951 states that none of its provisions should be interpreted as limiting the right to strike.[150] Also, Article 1 of the Abolition of Forced Labour Convention No. 105 of 1957 specifies that forced or compulsory labour is prohibited 'as a punishment for having participated in strikes'. In addition, various resolutions of the International Labour Conference have referred to the right to strike.[151]

C. Post Cold War: Employer Attempts to Place 'Dispute Resolution' on the International Labour Conference Agenda

After a long moratorium on the subject of the right to strike, the issue was raised again in 1992, when employer members of the Governing Body suggested that 'the settlement of labour disputes' would be an appropriate subject for the agenda of the International Labour Conference. The employers' motivation for proposing discussion of this issue seems to have been the limitation of the right to strike. The broaching of this matter at a time when there was a general trend towards curtailing of labour standards is unlikely to be coincidental.[152]

For example, in the 1995 Governing Body meeting on this issue, an employer representative stated that he envisaged regulation whereby the

---

[148] *Freedom of Association: Digest of Decisions and Principles of the Freedom of Association Committee of the Governing Body of the ILO* (4th edn., Geneva: ILO, 1996), para. 477. See Chap. 8 below, at 192–6.

[149] *Committee of Experts on the Application of Conventions and Recommendations: General Survey on Freedom of Association and Collective Bargaining* (Geneva: ILO, 1994), paras. 175 and 179.

[150] See *Date, Place and Agenda of the International Labour Conference* GB.262/92–2.E95/v.2 (Geneva: ILO, 1995), 38.

[151] Resolutions of the International Labour Conference referring to the right to strike include the Resolution concerning the Abolition of Anti-Trade Union Legislation 1957 and the Resolution Concerning Trade Union Rights and their Relation to Civil Liberties 1970.

[152] See above, at 102–3.

right to strike would be viewed as a 'last resort'.[153] He also directly acknowledged workers' apprehension 'that the regulation of arrangements for the settlement of labour disputes would lead to a restriction of workers' or unions' rights', but did little to assuage these fears. The employers' group was not opposed to international recognition of the right to strike *per se*, if it could restrict its scope and impose limitations upon its exercise as part of a dispute settlement procedure. There are also indications that in taking this step employers hope to achieve protection for employers' lock-outs equivalent to that recognized at present for workers' entitlement to strike.[154] Moreover, given the privileged status of Conventions Nos. 87 and 98 under the 1998 Declaration, distancing the right to strike from coverage by their provisions could well diminish the scope of its protection.[155]

For these reasons, the workers' group within the ILO opposed employer initiatives. It appreciated that a significant degree of protection for the right to strike had already been secured, owing to the jurisprudence developed by ILO supervisory bodies. In a time of declining union influence, an ILO instrument on this subject could undermine these principles. It was not prepared to risk this. The International Labour Office was also hesitant to give its wholehearted support to the employers' proposal. Its reports appreciated that this was a 'sensitive field' and that 'it may not be feasible for new provisions to go beyond the rather general terms contained in ... existing Recommendations'.[156] In 1996, the Employer Vice-Chairman sought to reassure the workers that the settlement of labour disputes was being proposed only 'as an item for general discussion and not for a potential instrument, for which it was unsuited, as national practice varied widely in accordance with local tradition'.[157] Nevertheless, the workers' group remained resistant to allowing this matter to come onto the Conference agenda, in whatever form.[158]

In the first report of the International Labour Office on *Proposals for the Agenda of the 90th Session of the International Labour Conference (2002)*, the discussion of 'new trends in the prevention and resolution of labour disputes' was once again proposed. No mention was made in this document of

---

[153] *Minutes of the 262nd Session of the Governing Body of the International Labour Organization* GB. 262/PV/Rev (Geneva: ILO, 1995), 1st Sitting, I/3. This is consistent with the stance taken in Schermers, H., 'Is There a Fundamental Right to Strike? (Right to Fair Conditions)' (1989) 9 *Yearbook of European Law* 225, discussed in Chap. 3 above, at 51–4.

[154] *Report of the Committee on the Application of Standards* (Geneva: ILO, 1999) ILC, 87th Session, para. 113; discussed in Chap. 8 below, at 200–3.

[155] See above, at 104–5.

[156] *Report Prepared for the 262nd Session of the Governing Body of the International Labour Organization* GB.262/92–2.E95/v.2 (Geneva: ILO, 1995), 40.

[157] *Minutes of the 267th Session of the Governing Body of the International Labour Organization* (Geneva: ILO, 1996) GB.267/PV, II/2.

[158] *Ibid.*, per Mr Brett at II/6.

the right to strike, and the only proposal was for general discussion on the issue.[159] In consultations, the Office found that the employers' group and fifty-six governments supported the proposal, while only three governments opposed it.[160] Nevertheless, in the face of opposition from the workers' group, it appears that there will be no progress on this initiative.

The Summaries of Governing Body decisions in 1999 indicate that the Governing Body responded to the Office report by requesting law and practice reports or more detailed proposals on matters other than labour dispute settlement; it seems that this item did not make the shortlist.[161] The subsequent Office reports presented to the Governing Body on the agendas of the 2002 and 2003 Conferences did not mention this subject at all.[162] Instead, as we shall see in Chapter 8, the employers' group is trying to put pressure on the International Labour Conference to place this matter on the agenda by challenging the authority of CFA jurisprudence and Committee of Experts' recommendations relating to the right to strike.[163] For the meantime, however, it seems that government delegates are reluctant to play an active role in the employers' campaign, for this would entail resiling from long-established ILO principles. In this context, although tripartism enabled new proposals to be triggered, it also operated in such a manner as to block action by the Governing Body and prevent the right to strike coming on to the ILC agenda. Workers' interests were reflected in the decision not to pursue the inclusion of a right to collective action in an ILO instrument.

In 2000, there was however a suggestion by the International Centre for Trade Union Rights (ICTUR) that it was time to revise and modernize the content of ILO Conventions Nos. 87 and 98.[164] The aim of doing so would be to clarify the rights upon which workers can rely. This would, presumably, entail recognition of the right to strike. Whether the findings of the ICTUR study will change the attitude of the workers' group within the ILO

[159] *Proposals for the Agenda of the 90th Session of the International Labour Conference 2002* GB.276/2 (Geneva: ILO, 1999), paras. 213–222.

[160] *Ibid.*, para. 224.

[161] *Restricted Minutes of the 276th Session of the Governing Body of the International Labour Organization* GB 276/2 (Geneva: ILO, 1999), Second Sitting, para. 14.

[162] *Report Presented to the Governing Body on Date, Place and Agenda of the 90th Session (2002) of the Conference* (Geneva: ILO, 2000) GB 277/2/1; *Agenda of the 90th Session (2002) of the Conference* GB.279/3 (Geneva: ILO, 2000); *Date, Place and Agenda of the 91st Session (2003) of the Conference* BD.280/2 (Geneva: ILO, 2001); *Proposals for the Agenda of the 92nd Session (2004) of the International Labour Conference* GB282/2/1 (Geneva: ILO, 2001).

[163] Part II of the Report of the Committee on the Application of Standards in *Record of Proceedings* (Geneva: ILO, 2001) ILC, 89th Session, 19 Part 2/21. See also Chap. 8 below, at 200–3.

[164] Ewing, K.D., and Sibley, T., *International Trade Union Rights for the New Millennium* (London: Institute of Employment Rights, 2000); and Ewing, K.D., 'Modernising International Labour Standards: Globalisation, Multinationals and International Trade Union Rights' (2000) 50 *Federation News* 109, at 112–13.

has yet to be seen; much may depend upon workers' perception of their influence within the ILC.

IV. CONCLUSION

In conclusion, it seems that the constitutional objectives of the ILO are wide-ranging. They allow for standard-setting on matters concerned with global protection of 'social justice' and 'fair competition'. Moreover, given the prominence accorded to 'freedom of association', in both the first ILO Constitution contained in the Treaty of Versailles and the subsequent Declaration of Philadelphia, it was perhaps inevitable that further ILO Conventions relating to freedom of association would be adopted, in due course, by the International Labour Conference. Nevertheless, the necessity to reach agreement within a tripartite standard-setting body, including worker, employer, and government representatives, significantly delayed this process. The momentum for standard-setting was found only after World War II, when external institutional pressures and humanitarian concerns combined to ensure that such action was taken.

By contrast, systematic protection of a 'right to strike' in an ILO instrument, although initially sought by worker representatives and later employer representatives, was not achieved. Prior to 1945, this may have been due to the preference of certain governments for the imposition of a compulsory conciliation and arbitration procedure. After 1945, it seems that the principle that workers be entitled to take industrial action was not so contested, but that the employer bloc wished to place further restrictions upon the circumstances in which the right was exercised. An awareness of this controversy and the possible dilution of their existing freedoms meant that workers did not press for standard-setting in this field in the period from 1947 to 1949. They were rewarded by ILO supervisory bodies, which found that a right to strike was, in any case, an essential aspect of freedom of association and was to be protected accordingly. From 1992 onwards, the workers' group therefore actively opposed employer initiatives which might have led to more stringent limitations on industrial action; and won sufficient allies among government representatives to keep this topic off the Conference agenda. In this manner, tripartism constrained ILO standard-setting on the right to strike, but arguably did so to the benefit of workers' interests.

6

Adoption of Human Rights Instruments in the Council of Europe

The first multilateral instrument to contain an explicit provision requiring protection of the right to strike was the European Social Charter 1961 (ESC), adopted under the auspices of the Council of Europe. This was arguably an important initiative in terms of the prominence thereby given to this entitlement. Nevertheless, its importance should not be over-rated. The right set out in Article 6(4) of the ESC was strictly circumscribed. Moreover, the limitations of the supervisory procedure attached to the Charter were significant, especially when compared with the quasi-judicial process established for the enforcement of the European Convention on Human Rights 1950 (ECHR). The right to strike was regarded merely as one of a number of socio-economic rights, of inferior status to civil and political rights, which were to receive the greater protection.

This chapter charts the historical background to the adoption of these two instruments. It begins with analysis of the constitutional objectives set out in the Statute of the Council of Europe. It is suggested that, given the open nature of this text, which could easily be subject to flexible interpretation, the exclusion of socio-economic rights from a single human rights instrument is not readily explicable. It may be that the broad terms of the Statute were interpreted narrowly in the light of the perceived imperatives of a 'Cold War' stand-off with Eastern Europe,[1] but it is also probable that the standard-setting mechanisms established by that Statute had a role to play. The United Kingdom, in particular, was unwilling to allow itself to be bound by an instrument which restricted the scope of its autonomy in the social field and, given a standard-setting process which required unanimity, was successful in limiting both the content and scope of the Council of Europe human rights instruments.

---

[1] Council of Europe Parliamentary Assembly, *Additional Protocol to the European Convention on Human Rights Concerning Fundamental Social Rights*, 23 Mar. 1999, Doc.8357, Explanatory Memorandum by Mrs Pulgar, paras. 18–19.

I.   CONSTITUTIONAL OBJECTIVES

Whereas the ILO is a global organization solely concerned with workers' rights, the Council of Europe is a regional organization possessing broader social and political aims. The latter is not a specialist in labour relations, but has developed an expertise in human rights, as well as competence in a range of political, economic, social, and cultural matters. While the creation of the ILO was prompted by the desire for peace following World War I, the formation of the Council of Europe was inspired by the desire for peace in Europe after World War II. Previously, European leaders had met only on an *ad hoc* basis. This standing inter-governmental conference[2] was to ensure that conflict was averted swiftly. Through co-operative initiatives channelled via the Council, it was hoped that the common aspects of European cultural heritage would bind nations together and give them a sense of unity. These very broad aims are evident from the discussions that preceded the establishment of the organization and the text of the Council of Europe Statute itself.

In 1946, speaking in Zurich, Winston Churchill set out his vision for Europe. He wanted to 'recreate the European family', which he considered shared a common cultural inheritance, and 'to build a kind of United States of Europe'. The aim was not to compete with the competence of the United Nations, but to fortify its strength by constructing, in particular, a permanent alliance of France with Germany. The first step would be 'to form a Council of Europe'.[3] At the Hague 'Congress of Europe', Churchill was the President of Honour and, before some 750 delegates from nineteen European States, elaborated further on this theme. He claimed that a European 'democratic culture' could be secured through international co-operation and that this was imperative, even at the potential sacrifice of national sovereignty. Moreover, he argued for a European Assembly and a 'Charter of Human Rights' as essential to the creation of European peace.[4] That others found this vision compelling is evident from the discussions and Resolutions at the Hague Congress.[5] Both the 'Political' and 'Cultural' Resolutions advocated the adoption of a 'Charter of Human Rights' and the creation of a 'Supreme Court' 'with adequate sanctions for the implementation of this Charter'.[6]

---

[2] Robertson, A.H., *The Council of Europe as an Organ of Inter-governmental Co-operation* (Strasbourg: Council of Europe, 1954), 73.

[3] *Churchills Ansprache an die akademische Jugend der Welt*, 19 Sept. 1946, Zurich, unpublished, copy read at Council of Europe archives, Strasbourg. See for analysis of this speech by the first leader of the Council of Europe Consultative Assembly, Spaak, P.-H., *Strasbourg: The Second Year* (London: OUP, 1952), 12.

[4] *The Grand Design: A Speech by the Right Hon Winston S. Churchill at the Congress of Europe* (London: United Europe Movement, 1948).

[5] *Congress of Europe: May 1948: Verbatim Report*, Plenary Sessions (The Hague, 1949).

[6] *Congress of Europe: The Hague—May 1948 Resolutions* (London: European Movement, 1948), 5–7 and 12–14.

Churchill's vision of European unity was taken a step further when the Brussels Treaty was signed in 1948 by France, the UK, Belgium, the Netherlands, and Luxembourg. It stated their intention to co-operate within 'Western Europe', presumably in opposition to the emergent Eastern European bloc. A further Convention for 'European Economic Co-operation', establishing the OEEC, was signed in Paris that same year.[7]

The treaty constituting the Statute of the Council of Europe was signed by ten States in May 1949.[8] The new organization was to consist of a Committee of Foreign Ministers acting as a decision-making organ, a Consultative Assembly representing the views of national parliaments, and a Secretariat providing administrative support. Through inter-governmental co-operation, this Council was intended to prevent the reoccurrence of fascism and other totalitarian forms of government that might threaten European stability.

The Preamble to the founding document reflects the concerns high-lighted by Churchill in Zurich and the Hague; namely, the 'pursuit of peace' through 'international co-operation' and the 'moral heritage' of the peoples of Europe which are 'the true source of individual freedom, political liberty and the rule of law'. With these objectives in mind, 'and in the interests of economic and social progress', it was necessary to form a closer association between European States. This is emphasized again in Article 1, which states that the 'Aim of the Council of Europe' is to be pursued by 'discussion of questions of common concern and by agreements and common action in economic, social, cultural, scientific, legal and administrative matters and in the maintenance and realisation of human rights and fundamental freedoms'. Whereas the ILO Declaration of Philadelphia privileges social over economic progress, no such priority is apparent on the face of this instrument.[9]

The reference to 'the rule of law', 'human rights', and 'fundamental freedoms' suggests that a human rights convention was one of the primary items on the Council's agenda. Under Article 3 of the Statute, all Members had to accept these principles and 'collaborate sincerely and effectively in the aim of the Council'. Under Article 4, any European State deemed to be able and willing to fulfil Article 3 may be invited to become a Member. The reference to 'individual freedom' in the Preamble did not bode well for the inclusion of socio-economic rights within the definition of 'human rights', which are usually (albeit often unjustifiably) viewed as 'collective' in

---

[7] For useful background information on these see Council of Europe, *The Union of Europe: Its Progress, Problems and Prospects, and Place in the Western World* (Strasbourg: Council of Europe, 1951), 5–14. The OEEC was the predecessor to the current Organization on Economic Co-operation and Development (OECD). See www.oecd.org/.

[8] These were Belgium, France, Luxembourg, the Netherlands, the UK, Ireland, Italy, Denmark, Norway, and Sweden. See Statute of the Council of Europe, Preamble. By 1951, Germany, Greece, Iceland, and Turkey had also joined the Council.

[9] See Chap. 5 above, at 100.

nature.[10] Otherwise, however, there was no clear indication from the text of the Statute that a stark division would be made between the treatment of civil and political rights on the one hand and socio-economic entitlements on the other.

The Statute did refer to the obligations of European States 'to participate in the work of the United Nations and other organisations or unions';[11] and in 1951 a further Resolution was adopted by the Committee of Ministers, which gave that Committee the power, on behalf of the Council of Europe, to conclude agreements with 'any intergovernmental organisation' on matters within the Council's competence.[12] A few months later, such an agreement was concluded between the Council of Europe and the ILO. This stated that the ILO was willing to co-operate with all its Member States, either severally or through regional organizations to implement global labour standards. It also envisaged, *inter alia*, the possibility that the Council of Europe might wish to convene European conferences of a tripartite nature. In such circumstances, the Committee of Ministers could ask the ILO Governing Body for assistance.[13]

It is interesting that, in comparison with the ILO, the Council of Europe saw little need to review its constitutional aims at the end of the Cold War. The terms of its Statute seem to have been sufficiently generous to enable Central and Eastern European countries to obtain membership, in so far as they were prepared to accept the civil liberties and notions of 'democratic' political participation that had previously characterized Western European democracies.[14] The 1993 Vienna Declaration merely elaborated upon Article 4, requiring that new members undertake to sign the ECHR and accept the Convention's supervisory machinery in its entirety within a short period.[15] The omission of the European Social Charter from mention in this context might seem peculiar, given the simultaneous reference to 'the indivisibility and universality of human rights', but reflects the present status of socio-economic rights within the Council of Europe, which have yet to be elevated to the position of civil and political rights guaranteed under the Convention.

---

[10] See Chap. 2 above, at 41–6 and Chap. 3 above, at 54–5.

[11] Statute of the Council of Europe, Art. 1(c).

[12] Resolution Adopted by the Committee of Ministers at its Eighth Session, May 1951, Res. (51) 30F.

[13] Agreement between the Council of Europe and the ILO, Nov. 1951, Res. (51) 38, Art. 3. The establishment of such a conference would however depend entirely upon the goodwill of the Governing Body, and the conference itself would have no powers of decision binding upon the Council of Europe. See for further discussion of the content of this instrument Jenks, C.W., *The International Protection of Trade Union Freedoms* (London, Stevens & Sons, 1957), 72–3.

[14] As at 1 August 2002, there were 44 Members of the Council of Europe. See on the process of enlargement of the Council of Europe Leuprecht, P., 'Innovations in the European System of Human Rights Protection: Is Enlargement Compatible with Enforcement?' (1998) 8 *Transnational and Contemporary Problems* 313 at 325–33.

[15] Vienna Declaration of 9 Oct. 1993, available on http://cm.coe.int/ta/decl/1993/Vienna%20Summit%20Declaration.htm.

II.   THE CENTRALITY OF STATE CONSENT

The 1948 Hague Congress was attended, not only by government leaders and representatives of political parties, but also by 'chiefs of industry and prominent trade unionists'. This was described by Churchill as 'a representative grouping' of various facets of European life.[16] As the Council of Europe was a new form of regional organization of 'a character [then] unparalleled in modern legal theory';[17] there was potential for the Preparatory Commission, responsible for designing the standard-setting mechanisms, to include the participation of such interest groups. However, this was not proposed. Instead, the standard-setting process is dominated by government representatives through the Committee of Ministers, with the parliaments of Member States being able to make only a limited contribution to this process.

The Committee of Ministers is made up of the Ministers of Foreign Affairs of Member States or those Ministers' deputies; and its meetings are usually held in private.[18] This body makes binding decisions on the internal organization and arrangements of the Council of Europe.[19] It also has the power to set up advisory and technical committees and to make a range of resolutions and recommendations to Member States.[20] Most importantly, this is the body which considers the 'conclusion of conventions or agreements' and 'the adoption by governments of a common policy with regard to particular matters'.[21]

Previously, a decision on the opening for signature of a Convention or Agreement had to be unanimous, but since 1993 such a decision may be taken by a two-thirds majority of the representatives casting a vote and a majority of the representatives entitled to sit on the Committee.[22] It is then open to individual States to sign this instrument and agree to be bound by it. States are bound by a Council of Europe instrument only once they have ratified it and, even then, their acceptance of the obligations it imposes will be subject to any reservations they have made. In this respect, despite the statement in the Statute that the aim is 'greater unity' between European States, it was observed by early commentaries that the sovereignty of States had been safeguarded.[23] There is usually no obligation to submit the

[16] *The Grand Design*, n. 4 above, 4.

[17] *Report of the Preparatory Commission of the Council of Europe*, Paris, 13 July 1949, 5.

[18] Statute of the Council of Europe, Arts. 14 and 21.

[19] *Ibid.*, Art. 16.

[20] *Ibid.*, Art. 17 ff. The most significant of these for our purposes is the Steering Committee on Human Rights (CDDH) which provides technical advice on human rights instruments and policies.

[21] *Ibid.*, Art. 15.

[22] Resolution on Majorities Required for Decisions of the Committee of Ministers, adopted by the Committee of Ministers, 92nd Session, May 1993, Res. (93) 27.

[23] *The Union of Europe: Its Progress, Problems, Prospects and Place in the Western World* (Strasbourg: Council of Europe, 1951), 40.

instrument to a competent authority, as there is within the ILO, but 'a system has been introduced, on a selective basis, whereby the Committee requests governments to inform it of the action taken to implement them'.[24]

The Parliamentary Assembly (previously entitled the Consultative Assembly) is the Council's deliberative body, authorized to discuss any matter falling within the Council's jurisdiction and to make recommendations to the Committee of Ministers.[25] Representatives of the Parliamentary Assembly are elected by the parliaments of Member States.[26] There is no specific representation of any interest group such as workers' or employers' organizations in the Assembly, but different subject areas are dealt with by specialist committees, which are lobbied by NGOs. There are also loose coalitions between political parties.[27] At the time the Council of Europe was established, the creation of such an Assembly was seen as a radical departure from previous purely inter-governmental structures. However, even then it was observed that relations between this body and the Committee of Ministers were problematic.[28] This can be observed in debates over which of the two should be regarded as responsible for drafting the final authoritative text of the European Social Charter. As we shall see, it is the Committee of Ministers that has prevailed.

The Secretariat of the Council of Europe performs a role comparable to that of the International Labour Office within the ILO. It provides administrative assistance to both the Committee of Ministers and the Assembly.[29] The staff of the Secretariat are expected to be politically neutral.[30] Nevertheless, it is notable that its head, the Secretary-General, is primarily responsible to the Committee of Ministers. If the Parliamentary Assembly requires assistance that would exceed its budget, such requests are to be referred to the Committee of Ministers.[31]

This institutional structure is such that, typically, instruments are drafted and adopted without direct involvement of workers or employers. There is no evidence that worker or employer representatives were consulted over the content of the European Convention on Human Rights, although

---

[24] *The Parliamentary Assembly: Procedure and Practice* (8th edn., Strasbourg: Council of Europe, 2001), 34. See, e.g., reports requested under the ESC 1961 on provisions that have not yet been adopted, discussed in Chap. 9 below, at 217.

[25] Statute of the Council of Europe, Art. 23.

[26] *Ibid.*, Art. 25(a).

[27] At present there are five political groups: the Socialist Group (SOC); the Group of the European People's Party (EPP/CD); the European Democratic Group (EDG); the Liberal, Democratic and Reformers Group (LDR); and the Group of the Unified European Left (UEL). See http://stars.coe.fr/.

[28] Jenks, C.W., 'Co-ordination in International Organization: An Introductory Survey' (1951) 28 *BYBIL* 29, 49–50.

[29] Statute of the Council of Europe, Art. 36.

[30] *Ibid.*, Art. 36(e).

[31] *Ibid.*, Arts. 37 and 38.

informal consultation may have taken place behind the scenes.[32] The one exception has been the drafting of the European Social Charter and amendments to that Charter. The tripartite conference held to discuss the appropriate form and content of the Charter had been recommended by the Assembly, on the insistence of the trade union lobby in reliance on the terms of the Council's Agreement with the ILO.[33] Nevertheless, the conclusions reached in the tripartite conference were not binding upon the Council of Europe. The final decision was left with the Committee of Ministers.[34] If ultimate control over the adoption of labour standards lies with government representatives, the content of such standards is less likely to reflect the views of the social partners.

III.   COUNCIL OF EUROPE INSTRUMENTS CONTAINING PROVISIONS PROTECTING FREEDOM OF ASSOCIATION AND THE RIGHT TO STRIKE

The Council of Europe has the capacity to exercise influence over labour standards in Europe via two key instruments. These are the ECHR and the ESC. There is some overlap between the two instruments, both of which recognize 'freedom of association' or the right to join and act as a member of a trade union.[35] However, only the ESC expressly recognizes a right to strike.[36] It should be acknowledged from the outset that these two instruments are not of equal status within the Council of Europe. The ESC has been largely overshadowed by its predecessor. In comparison with the Convention, the Charter has been 'little known, rarely referred to and often ignored in practice'.[37] There are various reasons for this.

---

[32] E.g., when the Committee on Legal and Administrative Questions gave its opinion on what was to be the guarantee of 'freedom of association' in ECHR 1950, Art. 11, it made express reference to the importance of the 'closed shop' in various Member States. See *Report presented by M. Teitgen on behalf of the Committee on Legal and Administrative Questions on the establishment of a collective guarantee of essential freedoms and fundamental rights*, Consultative Assembly of the Council of Europe, First Ordinary Session, 15th Sitting, 5 Sept. 1949, Doc. 77, para. 10.

[33] Above, at 128. See also *ESC Travaux Préparatoires* (Strasbourg: Council of Europe, 1952–61), iii, Part I, Section IV, Consultative Assembly of the Council of Europe, Eighth Ordinary Session, 14 Apr. 1956, Draft Recommendations and Reports, Doc. 488 in 'Draft Recommendation on a European Economic and Social Conference'; and iv (1957), Part I, Section IV, Committee of Ministers, Report of the Social Committee, Fourth Session, 11 Feb. 1957, CM(57)24 on the views of the ILO representative.

[34] *Tripartite Conference: Record of Proceedings* (Geneva: ILO, 1959), 168; See Council of Europe, Treaties and Reports Series, *Additional Protocol to the European Social Charter (No. 128) and Explanatory Report*, 14, para. 7; Council of Europe, Treaty and Reports Series, *Revised European Social Charter and Explanatory Report*, 37, para. 3.

[35] ECHR, Art. 11; and ESC 1961, Art. 5.

[36] *Ibid.*, Art. 6(4).

[37] Hepple, B., '25 Years of the European Social Charter' (1989) 10 *Comparative Labor Law Journal* 460 at 460.

One is the way in which the socio-economic entitlements set out in the ESC are phrased. They are not all guaranteed as minimum standards. Instead, Contracting Parties are often under an obligation only to *promote* these rights.[38] Moreover, whereas the ECHR requires the immediate and complete guarantee of all rights included in the instrument, there is no such requirement under the ESC. Within certain boundaries, Article 20 of the ESC 1961 provides contracting parties with the option to choose which obligations they wish to adopt.[39] For example, it remains possible to be a party to the Charter without actually agreeing to be bound by Article 6(4) which requires States to recognize the right to strike.[40]

Another reason is the coverage of the two instruments. Once party to the ECHR, a State is bound by all the provisions contained in the Convention, which the government is obliged to 'secure to everyone within their jurisdiction'.[41] By contrast, the Appendix to the ESC states that 'foreigners' are covered by the Charter only 'insofar as they are nationals of other Contracting Parties lawfully resident or working regularly within the territory of the Contracting Party concerned'. Third-country nationals lawfully resident in a contracting State are entitled to the guarantees set out in the ECHR, but not necessarily those rights contained in the ESC.[42]

In addition, it seems that the supervisory machinery created in respect of the ECHR and the ESC played a vital role in determining their respective status. The ECHR established a procedure whereby Contracting Parties and victims might bring complaints, which could fall ultimately for determination by a European Court of Human Rights. By contrast, until 1998, no complaints procedure was available under the Charter and the new procedure now in operation does not allow for individual claims. Although various reforms have been made to Charter control mechanisms, no body responsible for supervising the implementation of Charter rights merits the

---

[38] See, e.g., ESC 1961, Art. 6(1)–(3).

[39] ESC 1961, Art. 20(2) requires that each Contracting Party consider itself bound by at least 5 of the 'core' Arts. contained in Part II of the Charter. These are Arts. 1, 5, 6, 12, 13, 16, and 19. In addition a Contracting Party is required to consider itself bound by such a number of Arts. or numbered paras. contained in Part II of the Charter as it may select, provided that the total number of Arts. or numbered paras. is not fewer than 10 Arts. or 45 numbered paras. These must be notified to the Secretary General of the Council of Europe. Cf. the extension of the number of core Arts. under Part II, Section A of the Revised Social Charter 1996 (RSC).

[40] Austria, Greece, Luxembourg, and Turkey are all parties to the Charter but have not accepted Art. 6(4). This provision has also been partially excluded by Germany (in relation to pensionable civil servants, judges, and soldiers), by the Netherlands (in relation to civil servants only), and by Spain (to the extent that there is conflict with its Constitutional provisions relating to the armed forces, public officials, and essential services): Samuel, L., *Fundamental Social Rights: Case Law of the European Social Charter* (Strasbourg: Council of Europe, 1997), App. III, 448–9.

[41] ECHR 1950, Art. 1.

[42] This leaves migrant workers vulnerable, but note that under the Revised Social Charter 1996 Contracting Parties do have an obligation to treat refugees and stateless persons no less favourably than their own nationals, although there is no such requirement for third-country nationals generally. See Appendix to the Revised Social Charter (1996), paras. 1–3.

status of a 'Court', nor are litigants relying on Charter rights given access to the existing European Court of Human Rights. Enforcement of justiciable civil and political rights can be contrasted with the mere monitoring of socio-economic objectives.[43] The implications of these supervisory regimes will be considered further in Chapter 9. For the time being, it is sufficient to observe that the interaction of these three factors is such that, by virtue of inclusion in the ESC as opposed to the ECHR, provision made for protection of the right to strike is less effective than might otherwise have been the case.

A. EXCLUSION OF 'SOCIAL RIGHTS' FROM THE TEXT OF THE EUROPEAN CONVENTION ON HUMAN RIGHTS (ECHR)

The creation of a 'Declaration of Rights', enforced by an independent European Court, was the initial aim of the founders of the Council of Europe.[44] This Declaration was to evolve into a European Convention on Human Rights.[45] The key available precedent in the drafting process was the UN Universal Declaration of Human Rights 1948 (UDHR) which proclaimed that all persons were entitled to a combination of civil, political and socio-economic rights.[46] On this basis, arguments were made within the Council of Europe that its human rights instrument should be drafted in a similar manner.

An Irish representative made the following eloquent plea:

this Council should ask the Committee, which is to be appointed to examine the question, to take into consideration, not merely the Declaration of Human Rights made by the United Nations, not merely the Declaration of Human Rights made by the European Parliamentary Union, but also the Philadelphia Resolution of the ILO, so that by marrying these three concepts of human rights we may be able to evolve for Europe a Convention which will beget the respect, not merely of this Council, not merely of Governments, but of every man and woman who loves freedom in any part of the world today.[47]

He was supported in this by other Irish and by French delegates.[48] However, they proved to be unsuccessful.

---

[43] See Novitz, T., 'Remedies for Violation of Social Rights within the Council of Europe: The Significant Absence of a Court' in Kilpatrick, C., Novitz, T., and Skidmore, P. (eds.), *The Future of Remedies in Europe* (Oxford: Hart Publishing, 2000), esp. at 232.

[44] *Manual of the Council of Europe: Structure, Function and Achievements* (Strasbourg: Council of Europe, 1970), 8.

[45] Weil, G.L., *The European Convention on Human Rights: Background, Development and Prospects* (Leiden: A.W. Sythoff, 1963), 22–4.

[46] UDHR 1948, Arts. 22–26 deal with what are now regarded as typical socio-economic rights. Also see Art. 28 which states that: '[e]veryone is entitled to a social and international order in which the rights and freedoms set out in this declaration can fully be realized'.

[47] *ECHR Travaux Préparatoires* (Strasbourg: Council of Europe, 1949–50), i, Preparatory Commission of the Council of Europe, Committee of Ministers, Consultative Assembly, 11 May 1949–8 Sept. 1949 (The Hague, 1975), per Mr Norton (Ireland) at 130.

[48] *Ibid.*, per Mr Everett (Ireland), 102–6 and M. Jacquet (France), 136.

The strongest opposition came from the UK delegation, which considered that 'such rights would...be too controversial and difficult of enforcement'.[49] One UK representative also asked the question:

What I want to know is whether it is part of human rights that a man shall be allowed to strike. Is it or is it not? I can imagine our Court, duly set up, and our Commission of Human Rights being asked to determine whether or not inside a democracy a man is entitled to lead a strike, even if it be for mischievous purposes. What is the answer? The truth is that there is no answer, and to try to pretend that a European Commission or a European Court can decide this is a nonsense.[50]

There was no mention of a right to strike in the UDHR, and there seems to have been no other discussion whether it should be included in the new Convention.

What seems to have been most persuasive was the UK position that the inclusion of socio-economic rights 'would jeopardise the acceptance of the Convention'.[51] Unanimous agreement was required if the Committee of Ministers of the Council of Europe was to adopt the Convention, and therefore the co-operation of the UK was vital. If the UK warned that inclusion of social rights would jeopardize the Convention's adoption, this could be read as an implicit threat. The matter was off the agenda.

The Assembly Committee on Legal and Administrative Questions stated subsequently that it expected that social rights would be protected at some time in the future. It was 'necessary to begin at the beginning and to guarantee political democracy in the European Union and then to co-ordinate our economies, before undertaking the generalisation of social democracy'.[52]

A year after this concession was made, the issue of social rights arose again, this time in relation to proposals to include in the final draft of the Convention a right to property and a right of parents to make choices relating to education of their children. UK representatives opposed the inclusion of such rights on the grounds that they were social, as opposed to civil or political in character, and accordingly that they were too broad to be susceptible to judicial interpretation.[53] Once again, it was an Irish representative who pointed to the flaws in the UK position, observing that their arguments 'might equally be used to justify the exclusion from the list of human rights many of those which have been incorporated in the Convention', such as those rights set out in Articles 9–12.[54] There were however

---

[49] *Ibid.*, per Sir David Maxwell-Fyfe (UK), 116.
[50] *Ibid.*, per Mr Nally (UK), 148.
[51] *Ibid.*, per Sir David Maxwell-Fyfe (UK), 116.
[52] *Ibid.*, 194, para. 5.
[53] *ECHR Travaux Préparatoires*, n. 47 above, v, per Sir David Maxwell-Fife (UK) 222–4; vi, per Mr Roberts (UK), 88 and Mr Mitchison (UK), 94.
[54] *Ibid.*, per Mr MacEntee (Ireland), 310.

some who were unhappy that the rights to property and education were the only social rights that were to be protected.[55] Finally, a compromise was reached in the Committee of Ministers, which agreed to the inclusion of these rights in a subsequent Protocol, rather than the main text of the Convention.[56]

Protection of 'freedom of association' was viewed as a civil and political right appropriate for inclusion in the ECHR, following the precedent set by Articles 20 and 23 of the UDHR.[57] The first paragraph of Article 11 of the ECHR states that '[e]veryone has the right to freedom of assembly and to freedom of association with others, including the right to form and to join trade unions for the protection of his interests'. It therefore seems possible to interpret the scope of freedom of association as having particular application to workers' organizations and their activities. This provision is, however, subject to a second paragraph which states that '[n]o restrictions shall be placed on the exercise of these rights other than such as are prescribed by law and are necessary in a democratic society in the interests of national security or public safety, for the prevention of disorder or crime, for the protection of health or morals or for the protection of the rights and freedoms of others'. Moreover, this Article is not to 'prevent the imposition of lawful restrictions on the exercise of these rights by members of the armed forces, of the police or of the administration of the State'.[58]

It is worth noting that this decision of the Council of Europe may have influenced the form of the proposed UN human rights instrument. At the time that the Universal Declaration of Human Rights was adopted, the UN General Assembly had also adopted a resolution requesting that ECOSOC ask the Commission on Human Rights to draft a covenant on human rights protection.[59] It was only in 1950, having already prepared a draft and in the face of controversy over the method of enforcement of the covenant, that the Commission and ECOSOC sought to separate protection of civil and political rights from that of socio-economic and cultural entitlements. The initial response of the General Assembly was that this was inappropriate, as

[55] *ECHR Travaux Préparatoires*, n. 47, above, vi, per Mr Rolin (Belgium) 124.

[56] *ECHR Travaux Préparatoires*, n. 47 above, vii, 44. Other rights have subsequently been added by means of Protocols 4, 6, and 7, but the inclusion of social rights remains controversial.

[57] See *ECHR Travaux Préparatoires*, n. 47 above, i, Report presented by M. Pierre-Teitgen in the name of the Committee on Legal and Administrative Questions on the draft resolution which recommends to the Member States of the Council of Europe the establishment of a collective guarantee of fundamental rights and liberties (now Doc.77 of the Consultative Assembly, First Session, 15th Sitting, 5 Sept. 1949), at 196, para. 8; and iv, Committee of Experts—Committee of Ministers, Conference of Senior Officials 8 June 1950–17 June 1950, Commentary on the Single Text of the Convention Proposed by the Conference, 262.

[58] See App. 4; also Chap. 13 below, at 306–7.

[59] GA Res. 217E (III), 10 Dec. 1948, discussed by Ben-Israel, R., *International Labour Standards: The Case of Freedom to Strike* (Deventer: Kluwer, 1988), at 71–2; and Craven, M., *The International Covenant on Economic, Social and Cultural Rights: A Perspective on its Development* (2nd revd. edn., Oxford: Clarendon, 1998), at 16–18.

such rights were 'interconnected and interdependent'.[60] However, the precedent set by the Council of Europe, which had after all succeeded in the adoption of one human rights instrument, seems to have prevailed. By 1952, the General Assembly was prepared to accept that there would be two separate covenants, one on civil and political rights and the other on economic, social, and cultural rights.[61] These were both finally adopted, after much deliberation, on 16 December 1966. Just as the drafters of the ECHR paid attention to the text of the UN Declaration, the Human Rights Commission in the course of drafting these two instruments took account of the deliberations in the Council of Europe.

B.   THE DRAFTING (AND REDRAFTING) OF THE EUROPEAN SOCIAL CHARTER (ESC)

The creation of a European Social Charter involved extensive research, prolonged negotiations, and the repeated drafting and redrafting of texts.[62] There was considerable tension between those who would rather the document merely entailed a statement of intent and those who wanted a strong charter which would place parties under legal obligations to fulfil its provisions, accompanied by an effective system of enforcement.[63] This tension was reflected in an internal institutional struggle between the Assembly and the Committee of Ministers for control of the drafting process and its ultimate outcome. Within the Assembly, there were also divisions between the Committee on Social Questions and the Committee on Economic Questions.

It is evident that the ILO served as a reference point for this initiative. It was the means by which the trade union movement, represented by the International Federation of Free Trade Unions (IFFTU) and the International Federation of Christian Trade Unions (IFCTU), managed to place pressure on the Committee of Ministers to accommodate its views. However, as we shall see, the trade union movement was not entirely successful in this regard. Express protection of a right to strike was secured, but in such a way that the scope of that right was significantly limited; not only by virtue of the restricted scope and application of the ESC, but also in terms of the narrow wording of the relevant provisions.

---

[60] GA Res. 421(V), 4 Dec. 1950.   [61] GA Res. 543(V), 5 Feb. 1952.

[62] *European Social Charter and European Economic and Social Council Draft Recommendation*, Consultative Assembly of the Council of Europe, 7th Ordinary Session, 26 Oct. 1955, Doc. 403, Explanatory Memorandum, paras. 10–15.

[63] Mower, A.G., *International Co-operation for Social Justice: Global and Regional Protection of Economic/Social Rights* (London/Westport, Conn.: Greenwood Press, 1985), 188–90; Robertson, A.H., *The Council of Europe* (2nd edn., London: Stevens & Sons, 1961), 144; The Council of Europe, *The European Social Charter: Origin, Operation and Results* (Strasbourg: Council of Europe, 1991), 11–13.

1. Initial Debates Over the Adoption of a Social Complement to the ECHR

By 1952, the then Consultative Assembly was pushing for the Council of Europe to adopt a 'large-scale and long-term social programme'. On receipt of a Recommendation from the Assembly, the Committee of Ministers instructed the Secretary-General to provide an advisory memorandum outlining what activities the Council of Europe might properly carry out in the social sphere.[64]

The Secretary-General argued for the adoption of a 'European document' containing the principles 'that characterise Western democracies in the social field'.[65] In harmony with Article 1 of the Statute of the Council of Europe, it was proposed that member governments 'should declare that European Society is based on respect for the dignity of man and has as its aim the improvement of his living conditions'.[66] A European Social Charter was to 'lay down general principles and their limitations clearly defined as was done in the Human Rights Convention in respect of civil and political rights'.[67] Certain social rights in question were enumerated in this initial memorandum. For example, the charter was to recognize the importance of industrial relations and collective bargaining.[68] Although the Secretary-General conceded that social policy would primarily be the concern of national authorities, it was envisaged that a charter would provide the opening for further co-operation between Member States in this field.[69] Some objectives of the Charter, presented in the Memorandum, look remarkably similar to those stated in the Treaty of Rome 1957 and eventually pursued by the European Union. These included 'harmonisation of social legislation and practice', abolition of discrimination 'on grounds of nationality between nationals of Members of the Council in relation to social rights', and the 'free movement of persons between Member countries'.[70]

This memorandum received a mixed response from the Committee of Experts appointed to report to the Committee of Ministers on this issue. For example, the UK representative considered that 'any single instrument could deal with social "rights" only in the most general way'. To give effect to social principles required their elaboration 'in a series of detailed

---

[64] *ESC Travaux Préparatoires* (Strasbourg: Council of Europe, 1952–62), i, Section IV, Consultative Assembly of the Council of Europe, Fifth Ordinary Session, 18 Sept. 1953, Official Report of the Committee of Social Questions, Draft Opinion and Subsequent Debate, Doc. 188.

[65] *Ibid.*, Section I, Memorandum by the Secretariat-General of the Council of Europe on the Role of the Council of Europe in the Social Field, Strasbourg, 16 Apr. 1953, SG(53)1, para. 3.

[66] *Ibid.*, para. 5.

[67] *Ibid.*, para. 17.

[68] *Ibid.*, para. 7.

[69] *Ibid.*, para. 13.

[70] *Ibid.*, para. 14.

instruments' which was best left to international specialized agencies, such as the ILO.[71]

Despite this initial opposition, the Committee of Ministers finally adopted a resolution stating that it would 'endeavour to elaborate a European Social Charter'.[72] It established a special Social Committee, composed of Senior Officials from the appropriate departments of Government Ministers, to carry out this task.[73] Simultaneously, although no mention had been made of the Assembly's role in this process, the Assembly subsequently began to draft a 'Social Charter' under its Committee of Social Rights. The Governmental Social Committee then wrote to the President of the Assembly asking for a postponement of debate on the Assembly's draft Social Charter, but the Assembly refused to desist, claiming dual competence on this issue.[74] After much deliberation within the Assembly, a Recommendation concerning a 'European Convention on Social and Economic Rights' was transmitted to the Committee of Ministers in 1956.[75]

There were to be significant differences between the Assembly and the Committee of Ministers on the form and content of the ESC. For example, the Assembly considered that the Charter should set out 'social principles that correspond to individual rights'.[76] Government representatives within the Social Committee appointed by the Committee of Ministers were initially more reluctant to make the Charter 'binding' on States.[77]

Trade unions placed considerable pressure on both the Council of Europe bodies to adopt a Social Charter which stated aims akin to the ILO Declaration of Philadelphia. For example, the IFCTU asked that the instrument include a declaration from States that they regarded 'economic policy, not as

[71] *ESC Travaux Préparatoires*, n.64 above, i, Section III, Report of the Ad Hoc Committee of Social Experts to the 13th Session of the Committee of Ministers, 12 Sept. 1953, CM (53) 99.

[72] *Ibid.*, Section V, Committee of Ministers, 14th Session, Draft Report of the Third Meeting, 20 May 1954, CM (54) CR 3 Provisional.

[73] *Ibid.*, Section VI, Subsection I, Consultative Assembly, Sixth Ordinary Session, Special Message of the Committee of Ministers, 20 May 1954, Doc. 238.

[74] *Ibid.*, Section VI, Subsection II, Consultative Assembly, Committee on Social Questions (Second Session) Minutes, 22 Sept. 1954, AS/Soc (6) PV 7; and iii, Part I, Section I, Consultative Assembly, Committee on Economic Questions: European Social Charter and European Economic and Social Council, 28 Feb. 1956, AC/EC(7)24, Provisional.

[75] *ESC Travaux Préparatoires*, n.64 above, iii, Part I, Section IV, Recommendation 104, 26 Oct. 1956.

[76] *ESC Travaux Préparatoires*, n.64 above, i, Section VI, Subsection II, Consultative Assembly Committee on Social Questions, Second Session, 17 Sept. 1954, Preparation of a European Social Charter: Preliminary Draft Report submitted by the Chairman of the Committee, AS/Soc (6) 11, Draft Opinion on the Elaboration of a European Social Charter, para. 6.

[77] The one exception seems to have been the Greek government representative who considered that social rights had the potential to acquire comparable status with the guarantees contained in the Convention: *ESC Travaux Préparatoires*, n.64 above, i, Section VII, Social Committee Minutes of First Meeting, 4–5 Oct. 1954, CE/Soc(55)1.

an end in itself, but as a means of achieving social objectives'.[78] Moreover, they wanted the Charter to be, not only a statement of aims, but also an instrument placing obligations on States. In line with ILO precedent, they also wished to 'take part in the preparation of the European Social Charter'. They lobbied for final drafting of the Charter at a tripartite Conference, as provided for in the Agreement between the ILO and Council of Europe. In addition, they argued for the introduction of a tripartite Economic and Social Council in the Council of Europe which would, in part, play a role in supervising implementation of the Charter but would also be engaged in more active policy-making.[79] For example, the IFCTU observed that 'workers' organisations in most countries feel that employers' groups more easily gain hearing in governmental and political circles than they themselves do' and 'that certain economic or social decisions may be swayed by covert arguments to which they have no opportunity of replying'. For these reasons, they suggested that it would be worthwhile destroying the foundations of such a belief by establishing a tripartite decision-making body.[80]

The introduction of an Economic and Social Council, which shall be discussed further in the context of supervisory processes in Chapter 9,[81] was briefly considered in a draft produced by the Assembly Committee on Social Questions. However, its creation was contested by the Assembly Committee on Economic Questions, which considered that this 'would introduce an undesirable element of syndicalism and corporatism in European politics'.[82] It was suggested that, in its place, an Economic and Social Conference comprising both national and international organizations representing employers, workers, consumers, and professional groups could be held regularly to discuss European economic and social problems. The Assembly adopted this latter suggestion,[83] but it was not accepted by the Committee of Ministers.

[78] *ESC Travaux Préparatoires*, n.64 above, ii, Part I, Section I, Views of the International Federation of Christian Trade Unions presented to the Consultative Assembly Committee on Social Questions, 1 Mar. 1955, AS/Soc (6) 22.

[79] *Ibid.*, Part I, Section II. Consultative Assembly Committee on Social Questions Working Party for the preparation of a draft European Social Charter, Minutes of Meeting held on 29–30 Apr. 1955, AS/Soc I (6) PV 1. This body would 'define what measures should be taken by the Governments to achieve their declared objectives and to supervise the execution of such measures'.

[80] *ESC Travaux Préparatoires*, n.64 above, iii, Part I, Section III, Memorandum by the International Federation of Christian Trade Unions, 10 Feb. 1956, AS/Soc(7)27.

[81] See Chap. 9 below, at 216–7.

[82] *ESC Travaux Préparatoires*, n.64 above, iii, Part I, Section III, Consultative Assembly Committee on Economic Questions, European Social Charter, Draft Minutes, 23 Jan. 1956, AS/Ec(7)23.

[83] *Ibid.*, Part I, Section IV, Consultative Assembly of the Council of Europe, Eighth Ordinary Session, 14 Apr. 1956, Draft Recommendations and Reports, Doc. 488, 'Report of M. Haekkerup on a European Economic and Social Council'.

2.   Inclusion of the Right to Strike and the Impact of the Tripartite Conference

From the first draft of the Social Charter, produced by the Consultative Assembly, there was mention of a right to strike. This was, however, exceptionally limited, being confined to circumstances in which workers considered that their rights to fair, stable, and satisfactory conditions of work were not met or the entitlement of children and young persons to protection were not recognized.[84] Nevertheless, the explicit recognition of a right to strike was welcomed by trade union representatives.[85]

Its inclusion in the Charter seems to have been accepted by virtue of reference to ILO standards. The Assembly Committee on Social Questions observed that ILO Conventions and Recommendations made no mention of a right to strike, but they were aware of the reference to such a right in an ILO Recommendation and the jurisprudence already developed by the ILO Governing Body Committee on Freedom of Association.[86] They therefore considered this initiative to be compatible with ILO obligations accepted by European States.

The content of the entitlement to strike was however still the subject of some controversy. In the Assembly, certain delegates asked for reassurance that this guarantee would be subject to reasonable limitations.[87] There was also a suggestion in a later draft that the exercise of the right should be linked to provisions relating to conciliation and arbitration established for the settlement of industrial conflict. However, the General Affairs Committee of the Assembly was reluctant to 'declare itself in favour of or opposed to voluntary or obligatory arbitration' and decided against including such a requirement in the provision relating to 'collective action', included in its draft Charter.[88] After a number of draft provisions incorporating a right to strike, the final draft merely stated that '[t]he High Contracting Parties

[84] *ESC Travaux Préparatoires*, n.64 above, ii, Part I, Section II, Consultative Assembly Committee on Social Questions, Working Party for the Preparation of a Draft European Social Charter, Preliminary Draft of Social Charter submitted by Secretariat of the Committee, 19 Apr. 1955, AS/Soc I (6) 1, Part II, Section C, Art. 6.

[85] *Ibid.*, Part I, Section II Supplementary Memorandum by the International Federation of Christian Trade Unions presented to the Consultative Assembly Committee on Social Questions, 21 Apr. 1955, AS/Soc (6) 27.

[86] *ESC Travaux Préparatoires*, n.64 above, iii, Part I, Section III, Consultative Assembly, Committee on Social Questions, Fifth Session, Excerpt of a Comparative Analysis of Part II of the Draft European Social Charter in the Light of the Instruments of the International Labour Organization, 5 Mar. 1956, AS/Soc(7)32.

[87] *ESC Travaux Préparatoires*, n.64 above, ii, Part II, Section III, Consultative Assembly, Seventh Ordinary Session, *Official Report*, 16th Sitting, 21 Apr. 1955, per M. Federspiel (Denmark) and per Mme. Weber (Germany).

[88] *ESC Travaux Préparatoires*, n.64 above, iii, Part I, Section II, Consultative Assembly, Committee on General Affairs. Fifth Meeting, Social Charter and Economic and Social Council: Draft Report, 6 Aug. 1956, AS/AG(8)16.

recognise the right to strike. They undertake to encourage the use of agreed machinery for the settlement of labour disputes'.[89]

A right to strike was not mentioned in the first Committee of Ministers draft.[90] Later there was a limited provision, under which States were to recognize the right of workers and employers to 'collective action in cases of conflict of interest'.[91] There was also deliberate avoidance of any requirement that a conflict be resolved first through conciliation or arbitration.[92]

In 1958, it was the Committee of Ministers' draft that was discussed and approved at a tripartite conference convened in Strasbourg by the ILO, at the request of the Council of Europe.[93] Despite this apparently innovative procedure, the final decision on the form and content of the ESC was taken by the Committee of Ministers. As Mr Veysey, the government delegate for the UK and member of the Committee of Ministers, commented at the close of the Tripartite Conference, the Conference was not 'called to draft and adopt the European Social Charter but to express its views . . . on the draft prepared on behalf of the Committee of Ministers, in order that the latter might be able to draw upon the collective wisdom and to benefit from the combined advice of all three parties'.[94] While the Committee of Ministers would carefully consider the suggestions made at the Conference, the final power of standard-setting lay with the respective governments of Member States, not employer and worker representatives.

At the conference, worker representatives proposed that an express right to strike be included in the Charter. Their proposal was endorsed by the Social Committee of the Assembly,[95] but was opposed by employer and numerous State representatives. These opponents accepted in principle that express provision could be made for a right to strike, but only if certain conditions were met. First, such a right could be exercised only in respect of conflicts of interests rather than conflicts of rights. Secondly, industrial action should be permissible only where this did not violate agreements

[89] Ibid., Part I, Section IV, Consultative Assembly, Eighth Ordinary Session, European Social Charter: Draft Recommendation, 27 Sept. 1956, Doc. 536.

[90] Ibid., Part I, Sections II and III: Social Committee, Third Session, Preliminary Draft of Arts. for Possible Inclusion in a European Social Charter, 27 Apr. 1956, CE/Soc (56) 7; and Social Committee, European Social Charter: Draft Texts Drawn up by the Social Committee and by the Working Party, 31 Oct. 1957, CE/Soc(57)19.

[91] ESC Travaux Préparatoires, n.64 above, iv, Social Committee, Report of the Working Party Appointed to Draft Arts. for a European Social Charter, 12 Apr. 1957, CF/Soc(57)5, App. IV. See also ILO, Comparison of the Provisions of the Draft European Social Charter with the Corresponding ILO Standards (Geneva: ILO, 1958), 32–7.

[92] Ibid., Part I, Section IV, Social Committee, Report, 31 July 1957, CM(57)107, para. 89 which records the submissions of the French delegation that such procedures should not be a precondition for exercise of the right to strike.

[93] Tripartite Conference Convened by the International Labour Organization at the Request of the Council of Europe: Record of Proceedings (Geneva: ILO, 1959), hereafter 'Tripartite Conference'.

[94] Ibid., 168.   [95] Ibid., 138, 205–6.

previously entered into.[96] As pressure mounted, the workers' delegation also conceded that 'the exercise of the right to strike might be made subject to the condition that possibilities of conciliation and arbitration had been exhausted', adding that this followed from 'the order of the paragraphs in Article 6, which dealt with the right to strike only after dealing with consultation, negotiation, conciliation and arbitration'. Finally, the workers pointed to Article 31 and the Appendix to the Charter, which together would meet the concerns of governments and employers.[97]

3. The Content of the Right to Strike set out in the ESC

At first glance, it might seem that the Assembly and workers' organizations achieved their objectives. The ESC became a formally binding document containing express protection of the right to strike. However, the supervisory procedure attached to it was such that it would receive little notice and less respect. Until these control mechanisms were reformed in the 1990s, the Charter was to lead 'a twilight existence'.[98] Furthermore, while the result of the tripartite conference was the historic recognition of a right to strike in an international instrument, this was a right of limited ambit. Article 6(4) of the ESC 1961, which provides for a right to strike, must be read in conjunction with Article 5 which sets out the content of 'the right to organise' and the preceding provisions of Article 6 which outline 'the right to bargain collectively'. In addition, note should be taken of the Appendix, and Article 31 which circumscribe its scope.[99]

Article 5 states that '[w]ith a view to ensuring or promoting the freedom of workers and employers to form local, national or international organisations for the protection of their economic and social interests and to join these organisations, the Contracting Parties undertake the national law shall not be such as to impair, nor shall it be applied to impair, this freedom'. There is not the same positive obligation placed on States to take active steps to promote the right to organize as there is under Article 11 of ILO Convention No. 87 or Articles 3 and 4 of ILO Convention No. 98.[100] Moreover, no acknowledgement is made of the ways in which such organizations may promote civil and political rights.

Article 6 concerns only 'the right to bargain collectively', as is evident from its title. It too seems concerned only with protection of a limited conception of workers' socio-economic interests. Article 6(3) requires States 'to promote the establishment and use of appropriate machinery for conciliation

---

[96] Anon., 'The European Social Charter and International Labour Standards' (1961) 84 *ILRev.* 354 at 364–5.

[97] *Tripartite Conference*, n.93 above, 206–7.

[98] Harris, D.J., 'A Fresh Impetus for the European Social Charter' (1992) 41 *ICLQ* 659; see also Chap. 9, at 217–24.

[99] See App. 5 for the full text of these provisions.

[100] See Chap. 5 above, at 119.

and voluntary arbitration for the settlement of labour disputes'. The extent to which such procedures may be treated as a legitimate precondition for exercise of the right to strike is ambiguous. Article 6(4) itself recognizes only 'the right of workers to collective action in cases of conflicts of interest, including the right to strike, subject to obligations that might arise out of collective agreements previously entered into'. The reference to conflicts of interest suggests again a rationale for strike action associated only with collective bargaining.[101] The limitation imposed via collective agreements stems from the insistence of employers' organizations at the tripartite conference that the Charter 'mention duties as well as rights', including the 'rules and conditions of work' laid down in collective contracts.[102]

Like Article 11 of the ECHR, Article 6(4) remains subject to express limitations. The Appendix to the ESC 1961 states that '[i]t is understood that each Contracting Party may, insofar as it is concerned, regulate the exercise of the right to strike by law, provided that any further restriction that this might place on the right can be justified under Article 31'. The latter adopts a formulation comparable to Article 11(2), in that permissible restrictions or limitations are to be 'prescribed by law' and 'necessary in a democratic society for the protection of the rights and freedoms of others or for the protection of public interest, national security, public health or morals'.

The content of Article 31 is arguably not so problematic, as it indicates that there should be parity in the treatment of rights under the Convention and the Charter. Of greater concern is the relatively narrow scope of the wording of Article 6(4) and the context within which it arises in the instrument. This perhaps illustrates the dilemma faced by workers' organizations when contemplating incorporation of a right to strike in a multilateral instrument, other than in the most general terms. Explicit recognition of such an entitlement has potential political significance, but may also confine its scope in ways which are inappropriate to its application in a modern social context.

In Part IV, we shall see that the ESC supervisory bodies have since departed from some of the restrictions apparent in the wording of the Charter, arguably affording the right to strike greater protection than was intended originally. For example, the ability to impose compulsory arbitration has been construed narrowly, even in relation to public-sector strikes.[103] To some extent this attempt of supervisory bodies to breathe life into European protection of a right to strike is consistent with the sentiments expressed in Article 32 of the ESC 1961, which seems to defer

---

[101] See Chap. 3 above, 52.

[102] *ESC Travaux Préparatoires*, n.64 above, iv, Part I, Section IV, Social Committee, Sixth Session, 10 Feb. 1958, CM(58)18, App. III, per M. Waline on behalf of the International Organization of Employers.

[103] See Chap. 11 below, at 280–1; and Chap. 13 below, at 304–10.

to the host of the tripartite conference, the ILO. This provision states that '[t]he provisions of this Charter shall not prejudice the provisions of domestic law or of any bilateral or multilateral treaties, conventions or agreements which are already in force, or may come into force, under which more favourable treatment would be accorded to the persons protected'. Nevertheless, ESC supervisory bodies have still been hampered by the limitations of the text adopted finally by the Committee of Ministers and the monitoring process that has been applied to the Charter.[104]

4.   Subsequent Proposals, Amendments, and Recommendations

Despite being praised at the time and regardless of Assembly proposals that this become an annual event,[105] the 1958 tripartite conference was an experiment that was never repeated by the Council of Europe and the ILO together. The revision and 'revitalization' of the Charter utilized a different process. At the 1990 Rome Conference, a Committee for the European Social Charter (the CHARTE-REL Committee) was created. CHARTE-REL had a broad-based membership, including representatives of the Parliamentary Assembly, the ILO, supervisory bodies established under the ESC, as well as employer and worker organizations.[106] Although it is clear that the social partners were consulted over the content of these reforms, it is not clear how much influence they had over the final drafts of the Turin Amending Protocol of 1991, the Protocol Providing for a System of Collective Complaints 1995 (CCP), and the Revised Social Charter of 1996 (RSC). The final decision on the adoption of these instruments still lay with the Committee of Ministers, that is, with the Foreign Ministers of the Member States.[107] The ILO was however an enthusiastic proponent of the CCP, which it views as having similarities with 'the procedures of the ILO'.[108]

---

[104] See Chap. 9 and Part IV below.

[105] *ESC Travaux Préparatoires*, n.64 above, iii, Part I, Section IV, Consultative Assembly of the Council of Europe, Eighth Ordinary Session, 14 Apr. 1956, Draft Recommendations and Reports, Doc. 488, 'Report of M. Haekkerup on a European Economic and Social Council'. See also Mower, n.63 above, 191–2; Robertson, n.63 above, 145.

[106] Pucci di Benisichi, P., 'Reforms of the Charter since 1989—Reform of the Supervisory Machinery and Reform of the Rights Guaranteed', in *The Social Charter of the 21st Century* (Strasbourg: Council of Europe, 1997), 43–9. See also Fuchs, K., 'The European Social Charter: Its Role in Present-Day Europe and its Reform' in Drzewicki, K., Krause, C., and Rosas, A. (eds.), *Social Rights as Human Rights: A European Challenge* (Åbo: Åbo Akademi University Institute for Human Rights, 1994), 151–2; and *Record of Proceedings* (Geneva: ILO, 1996) ILC, 83rd Session, 14/20.

[107] See Council of Europe, Treaties and Reports Series, Additional Protocol to the European Social Charter (No. 128) and Explanatory Report, 14, para. 7; Council of Europe, Treaty and Reports Series, Revised European Social Charter and Explanatory Report, 37, para. 3.

[108] *Report of the Committee of Experts on the Application of Conventions and Recommendations: General Report and Observations Concerning Particular Countries* (Geneva: ILO, 1996), 13, para. 40. Also see the comments of Betten, L., 'The Protection of Fundamental Social Rights in Europe', in Smith, J., and Zwaak, L. (eds.), *International Protection of Human Rights: Selected Topics* (Utrecht: Martinus Nijhoff, 1995), 46 at 57.

The Explanatory Note to the RSC states that it had been agreed 'that the reform would involve taking account both of developments in social and economic rights as reflected in other international instruments and in the legislation of member states'.[109] In the light of this, one might have expected that there was cause to rephrase the limited provision for the right to strike created in 1961, but this was not done. It was proposed that acceptance of the provisions currently set out in Article 20, which set out the minimum but flexible content of the Charter for each ratifying State, should all be made mandatory. This would mean making obligatory acceptance of Article 6, and thereby a right to strike.[110] However, the proposal was not adopted and, as the minutes of CHARTE-REL remain confidential (the *travaux préparatoires* to the Revised Charter are not yet publicly available), there is no accessible information as to the reasons. Instead, under the RSC, Article 6 is now one of nine core Articles, from which the Contracting Party has to select at least six as binding obligations.[111]

It is evident that there is still some tension between the Assembly and the Committee as to the future protection of socio-economic rights within the Council of Europe. In 1998, an Assembly Recommendation on 'The Future of the European Social Charter' revived a much earlier proposal made in 1978.[112] The Assembly is now asking that either a 'parallel European Court of Social Rights' be established or that individual rights should be transferred from the Charter to the Convention 'in order to create the basis for stricter legal observance'.[113] In a subsequent Recommendation of 1999 on an 'Additional Protocol to the European Convention on Human Rights Concerning Fundamental Social Rights', the Assembly asked that, as a preliminary step, the Committee of Ministers should carry out a survey to examine which social rights are guaranteed by constitutions of Member States and are considered enforceable in national courts. The end result was to be an optional Protocol to the Convention setting out certain social rights which would be justiciable before a court.[114]

The Committee of Ministers responded only in 2001, stating that it was not 'at this stage' in favour of setting up a European Court of Social Rights.

---

[109] See *Explanatory Reports to the Revised European Social Charter and to the Additional Protocol of 1995 providing for a system of collective complaints* (Strasbourg: Council of Europe, 1996), para. 7.

[110] ECSR, *Sixth Report on Certain Provisions of the Charter which Have Not Been Accepted* (Strasbourg: Council of Europe Publishing, 1998), 7. See above, at 132.

[111] Revised European Social Charter 1996, Part III, Art. A(1)(b).

[112] Parliamentary Assembly, *Recommendation No. 839* (Strasbourg: Council of Europe, 1978). Cf. Harris, 266.

[113] Parliamentary Assembly, *Recommendation No. 1354 on the Future of the European Social Charter* (Strasbourg: Council of Europe, 1998), para. 18. See also the Report Doc. 7980, 12 Jan. 1998.

[114] Parliamentary Assembly, *Recommendation No. 1415 on An Additional Protocol to the European Convention on Human Rights Concerning Fundamental Rights* (Strasbourg: Council of Europe, 1999). See also the Reports Doc. 8357, 23 Mar. 1999, and Doc. 8433, 2 June 1999.

Rather, it considered that priority should be given to the ratification and implementation of the new collective complaints procedure and the RSC. As regards the inclusion of some of the rights contained in the ESC in the ECHR, the Committee of Ministers, 'while not excluding this possibility in due course', considered that priority should be given to consolidating the mechanisms of the Charter.[115] Reference was made to the revision and update of the European Convention on Human Rights, and an observation that it was open to the Steering Committee for Human Rights (CDDH) to take note of the Assembly recommendations.[116] However, there is no indication that this body has taken the matter further.[117] The consequence is that the Council of Europe is left with a weak instrument protecting a right to strike of narrow scope.

IV.   CONCLUSION

The constitutional aims of the Council of Europe were broad and far-reaching. So much so that, as we shall see in Chapter 7, they provided a basis for the genesis of the European Communities, the predecessors of the modern European Union. The determination of the Council of Europe not to engage in protection of socio-economic rights, comparable to provisions for the guarantee of civil and political rights, does not necessarily follow from its foundational Statute. This omission can more readily be explained by the inter-governmental character of standard-setting mechanisms within the Council of Europe and the context in which standard-setting took place.

The centrality of State consent meant that the most reluctant State could play a significant role in limiting the content and scope of certain instruments. It seems that the UK government was determined to protect the autonomy of its social policy and resist what it may have seen as nascent federalization. Churchill had contemplated greater political union and economic interdependence of France and Germany, but he had not, as was noted acerbically by Paul-Henri Spaak, committed the UK to full participation in that project.[118]

The *travaux préparatoires* of both the ECHR and the ESC highlight the role played by the UK, but it remains possible that this State was not the sole guest to spoil the party. Given the Cold War context, socio-economic

[115] Decision of the Committee of Ministers (Deputies), *Future of the European Social Charter and Additional Protocol to the European Convention on Human Rights Concerning Fundamental Social Rights—Parliamentary Assembly Recommendations 1354 (1998) and 1415 (1999)*, CM/Del/ Dec(98)645/4/4 and (99)677b/3.1, 18 Apr. 2001, 'Appendix to the Reply', para. 23 I, ii.

[116] *Ibid.*

[117] See as regards the lack of notable progress Council of Europe, *Statutory Report*, 'Chapter 4: Human Rights' for 2001 and 2002. The only change to the content of the ECHR was the adoption of Protocol No. 13 on the abolition of the death penalty in all circumstances, adopted on 21 Feb. 2002.

[118] Spaak, n.3 above, 9–14. See also, above at 126.

rights seem to have been viewed with distrust by a significant number of Western European governments which associated these with the curtailment of freedom in Eastern Europe. It also seems that the absence of meaningful tripartite participation in decisions concerning the adoption of instruments made it less likely that there would be an outcome sympathetic to workers' interests.

This was to have repercussions for the scope and efficacy of that right. A right to strike was not included in the ECHR alongside 'freedom of association', but relegated in the ESC to the tail end of a set of provisions relating to collective bargaining, conciliation, and arbitration. If included in the ECHR, the right to strike would have been binding on all signatories to the instrument. Under the ESC, this need not be the case.[119] The limitations of the supervisory process which accompany the ESC will be discussed further in Chapter 9, but it suffices to note here that this too was likely to determine the influence of its provisions. Moreover, the actual wording of Article 6(4) provides a right to strike which is narrowly circumscribed. It is more restrictive than that which the ILO supervisory bodies endorse. So, while on one level the inclusion of a right to strike in a legal instrument is significant, it is not quite the achievement it might superficially seem.

[119] See above, at 132 and 145.

7

Setting Social Standards for and Beyond the European Union

The setting of social standards in the EU has been limited by the terms of the Treaty of Rome 1957 which forms the basis of the current Treaty Establishing the European Community (or ECT).[1] Initially, promotion of labour standards was stalled by the concentration of the ECT on economic goals, which were intended to bring about the indirect improvement of social conditions. It was only by means of a series of Treaty amendments that competence on social matters was acquired incrementally. However, the potential for EC protection of freedom of association or a right to strike still appears to be excluded. Unanimous agreement between EU Member States, resulting in further Treaty amendment, seems to be required, if there is to be any express inclusion of such a right in a legally binding EU instrument.

Nevertheless, there does seem to be consensus within the Union that the right to strike is a 'core labour standard' and a 'fundamental right'. This is evident from declaratory instruments adopted by the Member States and EU institutions. In addition, respect for 'freedom of association' may be required of beneficiaries of EU trade preferences and development aid. In this sense, the EU acts in tandem with Member States as an external 'enforcer' of labour standards, even if it refuses to legislate upon these internally.

I. THE ORIGINS OF EU CONSTITUTIONAL OBJECTIVES

The 'Economic and Social' Resolution adopted at the Hague Conference of 1948 was prescient of many of the initiatives that have since been taken in the European Union. This resolution contained recommendations for the 'mobility of labour', 'unification of currencies', and 'co-ordination of social legislation'.[2] The signing of the Treaty of Rome in 1957 can be regarded as

---

[1] Previously, this was known as the Treaty Establishing the 'European Economic Communities' (or EEC Treaty), but this title was changed by the Maastricht Treaty of European Union 1992 (TEU) to 'European Community' (EC Treaty). Under the TEU, the EC became one of three pillars of EU activity, the second pillar being 'Common Foreign and Security Policy' and the third being 'Justice and Home Affairs', now (post the amendments made by the Amsterdam Treaty 1997) 'Police and Judicial Co-operation in Criminal Matters'.

[2] *Congress of Europe: The Hague—May 1948 Resolutions* (London: European Movement, 1948), 8–11.

the result of frustration experienced by certain European States as it became apparent that the Council of Europe was unlikely to achieve any of these goals. It had become clear that the Assembly would have little influence over the unanimous decision-making of the Committee of Ministers. The Council of Europe was, essentially, an inter-governmental organization.[3] The reluctance of the UK Government and other 'functionalists' to cede sovereignty to that European organization swiftly came to be regarded by many as a 'crisis'.[4]

In 1950, the French Foreign Minister, Robert Schuman, called for the creation of a coal and steel community which would involve the surrender of national control over these industries to an independent, supranational High Authority. The Schuman Plan, prepared by Jean Monnet, was debated within the Council of Europe Consultative Assembly, where there was more support for this initiative than in the Committee of Ministers.[5] The result was that six States signed the Treaty instituting the European Coal and Steel Community (ECSC) at Paris in April 1951. These were France, Germany, Italy, the Netherlands, Belgium, and Luxembourg.[6] Plans for more ambitious forms of political union, namely the European Defence Community (EDC) and a European Political Community (EPC), foundered.[7] In their place was to be the creation of a 'European Economic Community', which was to build on the success of the ECSC.

Preparation for the EEC initiative entailed examination of the potential connection between the economic objectives of this new organization and protection of labour standards within Europe. In this respect, assistance was provided by the ILO, which had already established the mechanism of the 'European Regional Conference' (ERC) to monitor and respond to industrial and social problems.[8] A group of ILO experts, headed by Bertil Ohlin, was formed specifically to study the potential social effects of European economic integration.[9] The Ohlin Committee considered that social welfare

---

[3] Zurcher, A.J., *The Struggle to Unite Europe, 1948–1958: An Historical Account of the Development of the Contemporary European Movement from its Origin in the Pan-European Union to the Drafting of Treaties for Euratom and the European Common Market* (New York: New York University Press, 1958), 55.

[4] Spaak, P.-H., *Strasbourg: The Second Year* (London: OUP, 1952), 7 and 24. See for another contemporary analysis of these tensions Robertson, A.H., *The Council of Europe as an Organ of Inter-governmental Co-operation* (Strasbourg: Council of Europe, 1954), 94–6.

[5] Council of Europe, *The Council of Europe and the Schuman Plan* (Strasbourg: Council of Europe, 1952), esp. 6–12.

[6] See *The Union of Europe: Its Progress, Problems, Prospects, and Place in the Western World* (Strasbourg: Council of Europe, 1951), 14–15 and 18.

[7] See Griffiths, R.T., *Europe's First Constitution: The European Political Community 1952–1954* (London: Federal Trust, 2000), 62–3 and 91; and Robertson, A.H., 'The European Political Community' [1952] *BYBIL* 383 at 385–7.

[8] The first such conference was held in 1955. See for an analysis of the tensions surrounding the establishment of the ERC Murray, J., *Transnational Labour Regulation: The ILO and EC Compared* (The Hague: Kluwer, 2001), 80–1.

[9] Report of a Group of Experts, *Social Aspects of European Economic Co-operation* (ILO: Geneva, 1956).

could be promoted by greater economic integration, which would reward efficient production and promote consumer welfare. It doubted 'whether in most countries the existence or absence of collective bargaining and differences in the strength of trade unions appreciably affect relative wages, patterns of production and of international trade, even where there is a measure of protection'.[10] It did not therefore 'consider it necessary or practicable that special measures to "harmonise" social policies or social conditions should precede or accompany measures to promote greater freedom of international trade'.[11] Instead, minimum standards should be set in accordance with basic ILO standards, an example given being equal pay.[12]

The attitude of the Ohlin Committee broadly corresponded to that of the ECSC, which possessed auxiliary powers to address abnormally low labour conditions for competitive reasons, but had found it unnecessary to exercise these.[13] It also had the effect of reserving for the ILO and the Organization's ERC the role of setting global and European-level labour standards.[14] The ILO recommendations were broadly accepted in the Treaty of Rome's 'White Paper', otherwise known as the 'Spaak Report', adopted by 'the Six' in 1956.[15]

The Spaak Report set out the essential objectives of European integration; that is, free movement of goods, services, establishment, and labour. A common tariff would also be imposed upon goods originating outside the borders of the Member States. This was expected to result in the improvement, and indeed the gradual harmonization, of social conditions in Member States. The issue of labour standards arose only in relation to regulation of the terms of 'fair competition', once again a major motivating factor for transnational standard-setting in the social field.[16] Nevertheless, it is evident from the final text of the 1957 Treaty of Rome that the scope of these 'distortions' was expected to be minimal. The key concession to the fears of the French that they would suffer competitive disadvantage due to their superior labour standards was Article 119 (now Article 141), which provided for equal pay of men and women.[17] France, in fact, never sought to rely on this provision, and there was even speculation that it would not

---

[10] *Ibid.*, 29.   [11] *Ibid.*, 40.

[12] See for analysis of this requirement Fredman, S., 'Social Law in the European Union' in Craig, P., and Harlow, C. (eds.), *Lawmaking in the European Union* (The Hague/London: Kluwer, 1998), 387–8.

[13] Diebold., W., *The Schuman Plan: A Study in Economic Co-operation 1950–1959* (New York: Praeger, 1959).

[14] Murray, n.8 above, 81.

[15] Discussed in Davies, P., 'The Emergence of European Labour Law' in McCarthy, W. (ed.), *Legal Intervention in Industrial Relations* (Oxford: OUP, 1992), 319; Barnard, C., 'EC "Social Policy" ' in Craig, P., and de Búrca, G. (eds.), *The Evolution of EU Law* (Oxford: OUP, 1999), 480; and Barnard, C., *EC Employment Law* (2nd edn., Oxford: OUP, 2000), 3–4.

[16] See Chap. 1 above, at 25–6; also Chap. 5 above, at 97–8.

[17] Davies, n.15 above, 323.

become operational.[18] This might have been the case were it not for the response of the European Court of Justice to the litigation brought by Gabrielle Defrenne.[19]

A basic co-operation agreement was concluded between the ILO and the EEC in 1958, which was supplemented in 1961. Extended co-operation has been achieved by means of 'an exchange of letters' at various junctures between the ILO Director-General and the President of the European Commission, the most recent of which took place in 2001.[20] Moreover, Article 234(1) of the Treaty of Rome (now Article 307 ECT) established that the provisions contained therein would not affect 'the rights and obligations arising from agreements concluded before the entry into force of this Treaty'. However, to the extent that such agreements were not compatible with the Treaty, the Member State or Member States concerned are obliged to eliminate incompatibilities.

II. FINDING A TREATY BASE FOR SOCIAL POLICY MEASURES

The Treaty of Rome established what was a new form of European governance.[21] At the helm of the new organization was a Council, consisting of the national Ministers of Member States, which was given powers to make regulations, issue directives, take decisions, formulate recommendations, and deliver opinions. A Commission was established to make policy proposals and to monitor compliance with the Treaty and delegated legislation, by both the Communities and Member States. This body was to have considerably more autonomy and influence than the Council of Europe Secretariat. A Consultative Assembly, later to be renamed the European Parliament, was to provide its views on Commission proposals. Moreover, a European Court of Justice (ECJ) was to determine complaints relating to non-compliance with the Treaty and delegated legislation. This was an extension of the role of the Court of Justice already established under the ECSC. These institutions were supplemented by an Economic and Social Committee, an advisory body comprising various members of civil society, but constituted with the achievement of a tripartite balance of power in mind.[22] The Com-

---

[18] See for discussion of this provision Kahn-Freund, O., 'Common Law and Civil Law— Imaginary and Real Obstacles to Assimilation' in Cappelletti, M. (ed.), *New Perspectives for a Common Law of Europe* (Leiden: EUI/Sijthoff, 1978).

[19] Case 43/75 *Defrenne v Sabena* [1976] ECR 455.

[20] The most recent took place on 14 May 2001. The text of these is available at http:// europa.eu.int/comm/employment_social/news/2001/jun/letter1_en.html and http:// europa. eu.int/comm/employment_social/news/2001/jun/letter2_en.html.

[21] See for a more detailed outline of this institutional framework as at 1957 Murray, n.8 above, 84.

[22] See Zellantin, G., 'The Economic and Social Committee' (1962) 1 *JCMS* 22. For a critique of its modern incarnation see Smismans, S., 'An Economic and Social Committee for the Citizen or a Citizen for the Economic and Social Committee' (1999) 5 *European Public Law* 557.

mittee in charge of the Social Fund was more truly tripartite, consisting of 'representatives of governments, trade unions and employers' organisations'.[23]

This has remained the broad constitutional basis of the first pillar of the Union, although there have been some significant modifications to the roles of these bodies and additional structural changes.[24] One such change was the creation of a Court of First Instance, to reduce the workload of the ECJ.[25] Another, more significant, development was the introduction of 'social dialogue', to the extent that the social partners now play a key role, not only in the development of sectoral standards, but also in the formulation of EC directives.[26] In addition, the transformation of the EC into part of a broader European Union led to the introduction of a further tier of institutional apparatus. There is, for example, a 'European Council', which consists of the heads of government of Member States and meets at least twice a year. Its task is to 'provide the Union with the necessary impetus for its development and define the general political guidelines thereof'.[27]

However, this institutional framework is of limited relevance for our purposes, owing to the restricted treaty base for measures relating to social policy and, in particular, protection of freedom of association and the right to strike. It is only by treaty amendment, that is the unanimous consent of all EU Member States, that this can be changed.

A. The Limitations of the Treaty of Rome 1957 and the Single European Act 1987

In the preamble to the Treaty of Rome 1957 it was declared that one of the essential objectives of the European Economic Communities was to improve the living and working conditions of their peoples. By way of contrast with the ILO and the Council of Europe, the *travaux préparatoires* were never

---

[23] See Treaty of Rome 1957, Art. 124; now ECT, Art. 147.

[24] For an updated summary, see http://europa.eu.int/comm/dg10/publications/brochures/move/instit/euwork/txt_en.html#1.

[25] See Brown, L.N., and Kennedy, T., *Brown and Jacobs' The Court of Justice of the European Communities* (London: Sweet & Maxwell, 2000), chap. 5. The role of the CFI is also discussed in Chap. 10 below, at 248.

[26] See ECT, Arts. 137–139. For analysis of the dynamics of social dialogue see, *inter alia*, Treu, T., 'European Collective Bargaining Levels and Competences of the Social Partners' in Davies, P., Lyon-Caen, A., Sciarra, S., and Simitis, S. (eds.), *European Community Labour Law: Principles and Perspectives: Liber Amicorum Lord Wedderburn* (Oxford: OUP, 1996); Jacobs, A., and Ojeda-Aviles, A., 'The European Social Dialogue—Some Legal Issues' in ETUI, *A Legal Framework for European Industrial Relations* (Brussels: ETUI, 1999) and Syrpis, P., 'Social Democracy and Judicial Review in the Community Order' in Kilpatrick, C., Novitz, T., and Skidmore, P. (eds.), *The Future of Remedies in Europe* (Oxford: Hart Publishing, 2000).

[27] TEU, Art. 4.

disclosed, so the intentions of the drafters remain a matter for speculation.[28] Nevertheless, the underlying assumption seems to have been that 'if one could remove all artificial obstacles to the free movement of labour, goods and capital, this would in time ensure the optimum allocation of resources throughout the Community, the optimum rate of economic growth, and thus an optimum social system'.[29] The title on Social Policy contained in the 1957 Treaty was remarkably limited. Article 117 reinforced the commitment of Member States to the improvement of social standards, but provided no basis for the Council to make regulations or directives for their protection. Article 118 provided a limited role for the Commission to promote 'close co-operation between Member States in the social field', but this was to entail 'making studies, delivering opinions and arranging consultations' rather than proposing specific EEC legislation.[30] Article 119 made provision for equal pay but set out no means for the implementation of this principle. On the whole, social policy was perceived as a matter for domestic politics and not the legitimate subject of Community concerns.

It was argued by Wolfgang Däubler that, despite the limited treaty base for social policy measures, the Treaty of Rome could provide the impetus for reform of domestic labour laws, such as, for example, German laws governing strikes. He referred to Article 5 which set out the commitment of Member States to fulfil objectives of the Treaty of their own accord, placing an onus on national legislators and judges to work towards upwards harmonization. He also cited Article 3(h) which required harmonization of all national provisions so far as is necessary for functioning of the common market. His view was that, on this basis, German courts were obliged to move in the direction of more strike-friendly initiatives taken in other Member States.[31] This plea was, however, unsuccessful. German courts adhered to the more limited and rigid national constitutional foundation for protection of the right to strike.[32]

Member States initially seemed content with the narrow scope of European social policy, but the Commission was less convinced. The Commission's First General Report of 1958 recognized that 'in the future the Community will be judged by a large part of public opinion on the basis

---

[28] Engel, C., 'The European Charter of Fundamental Rights: A Changed Political Opportunity and its Normative Consequences' (2001) 7 *ELJ* 151 at 151.

[29] Shanks, M., 'The Social Policy of the European Communities' (1977) 14 *CMLRev.* 375 at 375.

[30] These were only 'procedural powers', as was evident from Joined Cases 281, 283, 285, 287/85 *Germany, UK and others v Commission* [1987] ECR 3203.

[31] Däubler, W., *Der Streik im offentlichen Dienst* (Tübingen: Mohr, 1971), 188; and Däubler, W., and Hegge, H., *Koalitionsfreiheit* (Baden: Nomos, 1976), 132–3; cited in Jacobs, A., 'Towards Community Action on Strike Law' (1978) 15 *CMLRev.* 133 at 147.

[32] See 'Germany' in Swabey, J., and Groushko, M., *Secondary Industrial Action: The Right to Strike and to Take Secondary Action in the EU Member States* (Brussels: Watson Wyatt, 1996). See also Clauwaert, S., *Fundamental Social Rights in the European Union: Comparative Tables and Documents* (Brussels: ETUI, 1998), 196–8.

of its direct and indirect successes in the social field'. By the late 1960s, it was evident that the indirect success hoped for had not been realized. Achievement of EEC economic objectives did not necessarily assure social welfare. It was time to take more direct steps to give the Union a 'human face'.[33]

In 1972, following widespread social unrest and the election of social democratic governments in Europe, came the Declaration of Heads of Government in Paris.[34] The leaders of the then Member States declared that they attributed 'the same importance to energetic proceedings in the field of social policy as to the realisation of the economic and financial union'. They also stated that the conclusion of European-level collective agreements should be made possible.[35] This change of heart culminated in the adoption of the Social Action Programme of 1974–6, but this Programme made no mention of Community intervention in the field of industrial action, even though it was difficult to see what form collective bargaining at the European level could take without a European-level guarantee that workers possessed the right to strike in pursuit of such agreements.[36]

The legislative measures proposed under the first Social Action Programme relied on the capacity for the adoption of social measures under Articles 100 (now Article 94) and 235 (now Article 308) of the EC Treaty, two legal bases not specific to social policy. Article 100 authorized the Council, acting unanimously, to issue directives requiring the approximation of Member State laws in so far as they directly affect the establishment of the common market. This was to be the basis for early directives relating to collective redundancies, transfers of undertakings, insolvency, and health and safety.[37] Article 235 also authorized the Council, acting unanimously, to take appropriate measures to achieve a Community objective where the Treaty had not granted the necessary powers. This provision has been used more sparingly, but provided the basis for directives such as those on equal pay and equal treatment of men and women.[38] There were however two further logistical problems. The first was that the extensive use of these supplementary legislative provisions would defy 'the general principle requiring legislation pursuant to specific powers'.[39] The second

[33] Shanks, n.29 above, 383.

[34] Streek, W., and Schmitter, P., 'From National Corporatism to Transnational Pluralism: Organised Interests in the Single European Market' (1991) 19 *Politics and Society* 133, 138.

[35] Declaration of the Heads of State and Government of the Member States, Paris, 20 Oct. 1972, EC Bull. 10/72, 19–20.

[36] Bull., Supp. 2/74. See Shanks, n.29 above, 377.

[37] See, e.g., Council Directives 75/129 [1975] OJ L48/29, 77/187 [1977] OJ L61/26, 80/987 [1980] OJ L283/23, and 77/576 [1977] OJ L229/12.

[38] See Council Directives 75/117 [1975] OJ L45/19 and 76/207 [1976] OJ L39/40.

[39] Ebsen, I., 'Social Policy in the European Community Between Competition, Solidarity and Harmonization: Still on the Way from a Free Trade Area to a Federal System' (1996) 2 *Columbia Journal of European Law* 421 at 432.

more practical difficulty was that unanimity on social policy was difficult to achieve, conferring considerable power on the most reluctant State which could seek to avert the adoption or dilute the content of labour standards.

Attempts were nevertheless made to secure protection of a right to strike under these more general legal bases.[40] In 1974, a Member of the European Parliament (MEP) tabled an amendment to a draft Resolution of the Parliament on the Communication from the Commission to the Council on multinational undertakings. This was to request 'that European legislation should eliminate the obstacles existing in certain countries to manifestations of solidarity between trade unions, in particular those taking the form of sympathy strikes'.[41] The response was not favourable. Lipservice was paid to the right of workers to manifest their solidarity in this manner, but ultimately the amendment was rejected, obtaining the support of only the socialist and communist groups.[42] Again, in 1976, the Parliament was spurred into action by the actions of Hertz Rent-A-Car, which tried to use its German drivers to supplant the labour of Danish workers who were striking against its Danish subsidiary. This time the European Parliament adopted a resolution in which it urged the Commission to take the necessary steps to prevent similar abuses of the right of workers to free movement.[43] The Commission did not respond with enthusiasm to this proposal, answering a subsequent written question from another MEP with the observation that the right to strike does not affect and is not affected by the principle of freedom of establishment.[44]

The requests of MEPs received more support from academic commentators. In 1977, Antoine Jacobs observed that the rise of the multinational company within Europe provided a case for EEC protection of transnational industrial action.[45] In a similar vein, Lammy Betten put forward concrete proposals for a regulation concerning the prohibition of cross-border bootlegging and diversion of goods and services in the Community in the course of an industrial conflict.[46] There was, however, no proposal from the Commission for the creative use of the existing treaty bases to achieve these ends. The Commission did authorize a study by industrial

[40] These are recorded in Jacobs, n.31 above, at 142; and Betten, L., *The Right to Strike in Community Law: The Incorporation of Fundamental Rights in the Legal Order of the European Communities* (Amsterdam: North-Holland, 1985), 117–8.

[41] Bull. Supp. 8/73.

[42] Annex to OJ of 1974, Debates of the European Parliament, 12 Dec. 1974, 228–30.

[43] Doc. EP 424/76.

[44] [1977] OJ C214/18. No attention was paid to fears expressed earlier that 'free movement of goods' could be used to break strikes. See Cox, R.W., 'Social and Labour Policy in the EEC' (1963) 1 *BJIR* 5 at 9.

[45] Jacobs, n.31 above, drawing on the arguments of Wedderburn, K.W., 'Multinational Enterprise and National Law' (1972) 1 *ILJ* 16.

[46] Betten, n.40 above, chap. 8.

relations experts of 'the prevention and settlement of industrial disputes', but it appears that no action was taken on this basis.[47]

The Single European Act of 1987 did little to change this situation. In a time of neo-liberal market dominance this is perhaps not surprising. Moreover, it seems that the UK, under the Conservative government led by Margaret Thatcher, was unwilling to make any concessions in this regard.[48] Article 100a provided for qualified-majority voting in respect of measures aimed at the establishment and functioning of the common market, but provisions relating to 'the rights and interests of employed persons' were expressly excluded from its coverage. One development of note was the introduction of Article 118a, which extended qualified-majority voting to the adoption of minimum standards in the field of health and safety.[49] Another was the formal recognition in Article 118b of 'social dialogue' between management and labour at the European level, which was to be assisted by the Commission. This might be seen as promising from the perspective of European-level collective bargaining, but offered nothing in practice as regards protection of a right to strike.[50]

B.   THE COMMUNITY CHARTER OF THE FUNDAMENTAL SOCIAL RIGHTS OF WORKERS 1989

During the 1980s, the trade union lobby through the European Trade Union Confederation (ETUC), alongside a number of MEPs, continued to argue for greater protection by the EC of fundamental rights and freedoms, including socio-economic rights.[51] In 1989, the Economic and Social Committee argued for 'certain social rights' to be laid down as a matter of urgency. These were to include the 'right of freedom of association and the right to organise, including recourse to collective action'.[52] It considered

---

[47] Committee of Experts, *The Prevention and Settlement of Industrial Conflict in the Community Member States* (the Treu Report) (Luxembourg: Commission, 1984). A further report was also commissioned by the Commission in 1992 but has not been widely published: Wedderburn, Lord, *Freedom of Association and Community Protection: A Comparative Enquiry into Trade Union Rights of the European Community and into the Need for Intervention at Community Level* (Luxembourg: European Commission, 1992). That report proposed that a Recommendation concerning freedom of association be adopted as an interim step towards tentative Community regulation in this field.

[48] Davies, n.15 above, 332.

[49] See for attempts made to broaden the scope of EU social policy through a generous interpretation of these provisions Fitzpatrick, B., 'Straining the Definition of Health and Safety?' (1997) 26 *ILJ* 115. See also Case C–84/94 *UK v Council* [1996] ECR I–5755.

[50] Cf. Lo Faro, A., *Regulating Social Europe: Reality & Myth of Collective Bargaining in the EC Legal Order* (Oxford: Hart Publishing, 2000), who suggests that social dialogue has been devised to serve regulatory and legitimacy objectives rather than European-level collective bargaining.

[51] For a summary of these initiatives see Betten, L., 'Towards a Community Charter of Fundamental Social Rights' (1989) 1 *NQHR* 77, at 81–4.

[52] *Opinion of the Economic and Social Committee on Community Basic Social Rights* [1989] OJ C126, 4–9.

that to 'ensure concurrent economic and social development on a Community scale', there must be 'a set of fundamental social guarantees ... to boost Community action to secure the extension and effective application of citizens' rights and prevent competition being distorted as a result of differing conditions'.[53] Later that year, government representatives of eleven (of the then twelve) Member States, became signatories to the Community Charter of the Fundamental Social Rights of Workers (CCFSRW), which expressly acknowledged the significance of freedom of association and the right to strike as fundamental social rights.

The UK, as was its wont, abstained from any commitment to this instrument. However, it is also possible that 'British intransigence' provided an excuse for other States to dilute its provisions and effect.[54] For example, this was initially intended to be a Charter for 'citizens', but the final draft refers only to the rights of 'workers'.[55] Moreover, although the Parliament had wished to incorporate the Charter into Community law,[56] the final result was only a 'solemn proclamation' with declaratory effect.

In many respects, the preamble to the 1989 CCFSRW reflects the assumptions of the drafters of the Treaty of Rome that 'the completion of the internal market is the most effective means of ... ensuring maximum well-being in the Community'. It states that 'inspiration should be drawn' from ILO Conventions and the European Social Charter 1961 of the Council of Europe. However, it is clear that this does not require the immediate translation of the principles set out in these instruments into Community law. 'By virtue of the principle of subsidiarity', the primary responsibility for implementation of these social rights is said to lie with the Member States, and only 'within the limits of its powers' with the European Community.

Point 11 of the CCFSRW sets out the basic principle of freedom of association, applicable to both workers and employers, including the freedom to join a trade union for the 'defence of their economic and social interests'. This includes the freedom to join or not to join a trade union 'without any personal or occupational damage being suffered'. This is a formulation similar to that of Article 11 of the ECHR, except in so far as it places on a par positive and negative freedom of association.[57] Point 12 sets out the right to negotiate and conclude collective agreements, including at the inter-occupational and sectoral level. The right to resort to 'collective action', including the right to strike, is set out in Point 13. This entitlement remains subject to 'the obligations arising under national regulations and collective agreements'. This

---

[53] Ibid., 6, para. 9.

[54] Silvia, S.J., 'The Social Charter of the European Community: A Defeat for European Labor' (1990–91) 44 Industrial and Labour Relations Review 626 at 638.

[55] Bercusson, B., 'The European Community's Charter of Fundamental Social Rights of Workers' (1990) 53 MLR 624 at 626.

[56] [1991] OJ C96/61 and [1989] OJ C120/5.

[57] This may perhaps be explained as a response to the judgment of the European Court of Human Rights in Young, James and Webster v UK (1982) 4 EHRR 38. See Chap. 9 below, at 232–4.

restrictive wording is reminiscent of that of Article 6(4) of the European Social Charter 1961, except that it demands even greater deference to domestic legislation.[58] Moreover, 'in order to facilitate the settlement of industrial disputes the establishment and utilisation at the appropriate levels of conciliation, mediation and arbitration procedures should be encouraged in accordance with national practice'. What the appropriate level of conciliation, mediation, or arbitration may be is not elaborated upon.[59]

The CCFSRW may have lacked binding force, but the instrument was intended to be 'implemented'. This is evident from Title II. Primarily, as was stressed in Point 27, this implementation was 'the responsibility of Member States'. In addition, Point 28 invited the Commission to make proposals for the adoption of legal instruments relating to 'those rights which come within the Community's area of competence'. Points 11 to 13 did not appear to come within this competence. In the Action Programme devised by the Commission for the implementation of the CCFSRW, it was said explicitly that no Community initiative would be proposed on freedom of association and the right to strike. Instead, 'the problems arising from the application of these principles must be settled directly by the two sides of industry, or where appropriate, by the Member States'.[60] This was, however, to be supplemented by a review procedure under Point 29, which stated that the Commission was to provide an annual report 'on the application of the Charter by the Member States and by the European Community'. The process of review was possibly intended by those in favour of a more rigorous and extensive European social policy to be a supervisory mechanism which would inspire concern and lead to further initiatives. This did not prove to be the case, at least in respect of freedom of association or rights to collective action.

From 1992 onwards, reports were provided by the Commission pertaining to the application of the CCFSRW. These tended to follow the same pattern. Part I of each report considered application of the 1989 Charter by the EC, while Part II outlined its application by Member States. Each report began by stressing three 'cardinal principles': 'subsidiarity', 'diversity', and 'the preservation of the competitiveness of undertakings'. There was no mention of freedom of association or the right to strike in Part I of these reports. There was only a statement, in the context of a section on the 'information, consultation and participation of workers', that '[i]n this field, more so perhaps than others, it is important to stress the respect shown for the social partners'

---

[58]   Cf. Chap. 6 above, at 143.

[59]   The full text of CCFSRW, Points 11–14, is provided in App. 6.

[60]   COM(89)568 final, Brussels, 29 Nov. 1989, para. 6. All that was proposed was a 'Communication on the role of social partners in collective bargaining'. See for analysis of the limitations of this programme Wedderburn, Lord, 'Labour Standards, Global Markets and Labour Laws in Europe' in Sengenberger, W., and Campbell, D. (eds.), *International Labour Standards and Economic Interdependence* (Geneva: IILS, 1994), 248.

bargaining autonomy'.[61] Part II merely assimilated the reports provided by Member States, including information that they had provided relating to collective bargaining and strikes. The Commission highlighted issues of controversy, but was not critical of national legislation.[62]

C.   Explicit Exclusion of the 'Right to Association' and the 'Right to Strike' from Social Policy Post 1992

In 1992, an important initiative was taken to overcome the social policy deadlock. This was an agreement between the then twelve Member States to append an 'Agreement on Social Policy' (ASP) to the Maastricht Treaty on European Union which would be binding on all but the UK. This received the support of the social partners, whose draft was 'taken over virtually verbatim' and constituted Articles 3 and 4 of the ASP relating to 'social dialogue'.[63] The ASP set out the competence of the Council to adopt social policy directives which would bind the eleven Member States, both by qualified majority voting and by unanimity. However, Article 2(6) expressly stated that its provision would not apply to, *inter alia*, 'the right of association, the right to strike or the right to impose lock-outs'. The Commission initially did not intend to exclude any area of social policy from the ambit of these provisions and proposed that the right to strike be among the subjects upon which a directive could be adopted unanimously.[64] It seems that the exclusion was decided upon by the Member States, perhaps in the hope that the UK could, thereby, be persuaded to accede to its provisions, but more probably because the majority 'were untroubled by the prospect of inactivity in these areas'.[65]

The expansion of EC social competence by the ASP, despite its 'twin-track' nature, resulted in a flurry of renewed interest in the labour law field. The Commission began to explore the policies that might be pursued and, in particular, how the economic objectives of the Union could be reconciled with the pursuit of improved social welfare.[66] In particular, the 1994 White Paper on Social Policy presented the prospect of a 'European social model'

---

[61] *First Report on the Application of the Community Charter of the Fundamental Social Rights of Workers* (1992) in *Social Europe* 1/92, 21. See also *Second Report on the Application of the Community Charter of the Fundamental Social Rights of Workers* (1993) in *Social Europe*, Supp. 1/93, 14; and *Third Report on the Application of the Community Charter of the Fundamental Social Rights of Workers*, COM(93)668 final, 13.

[62] See, e.g., the analysis of Belgian legislation relating to the right to strike which does not change in any of the reports.

[63] See *Social Europe* 2/95 and Bercusson, B., *European Labour Law* (London: Butterworths, 1996), 544 ff.

[64] Bull. Supp. 2/91, 126–31.

[65] Ryan, B., 'Pay, Trade Union Rights and European Community Law' (1997) 13 *IJCLLIR* 305 at 309.

[66] See COM(94)551 and COM(94)333, discussed by Kenner, J., 'European Social Policy—New Directions' (1994) 10 *IJCLLIR* 56.

based on 'democracy and individual rights, free collective bargaining, the market economy, equality of opportunity for all and social welfare and solidarity'.[67] Nevertheless, there was no great change of stance on the question of freedom of association or the right to strike.

The Council response, namely the Resolution on Social Policy in 1994, merely recognized once again that 'particular attention should be paid to existing systems, traditions and practice in the Member States', especially as 'the national identity of the Member States is particularly defined by their individual paths to solidarity within society and social balance'.[68] Subsidiarity and diversity were, in this manner, presented as the reasons for legislative inactivity within the Union. On the subject of freedom of association, the 1994 Resolution proved to be outward rather than inward looking. Although the need for regulation on this matter to secure fair competition within the Union was considered unnecessary, the Resolution stated that 'the Union's international competitiveness must be strengthened'. While protectionism was apparently ruled out, it was considered necessary to embark on a dialogue with major competitors to set fair rules of competition so that 'any economic success is used for the purpose of suitable social progress'. This course of action was to be pursued through such bodies as the ILO and the World Trade Organization (WTO) 'for the future organization of international trade and above all for combating forced and child labour and securing freedom of association and collective bargaining'.[69]

A change of government in the UK led to a new readiness to be bound by the ASP. The ASP is now incorporated in Articles 137 to 139 of the EC Treaty, following the Treaty of Amsterdam 1997. However, the exclusion of the rights to association, strike, and lock-out still stands, owing to Article 137(6). This is perhaps surprising given that Article 136, a revised version of the former Article 117, refers for the first time to the Council of Europe's Social Charter of 1961 and the 1989 Community Charter of Fundamental Rights, both of which contain express guarantees of collective bargaining and a right to strike. There would therefore appear to be 'a mismatch between the EC's Title on Social Policy and the two Charters'.[70] Despite this obvious anomaly, no substantive change was made to Article 137(6) by the Treaty of Nice 2000.[71]

The text of the Amsterdam Treaty also sanctioned the protection of human rights, adding a further paragraph to Article F, now Article 6(1) of the TEU. This states that '[t]he Union is founded on the principles of

[67] COM(94)333, para. 3.

[68] Council Resolution of 6 Dec. 1994 on certain aspects of a European social policy: a contribution to economic and social convergence in the Union [1994] OJ C368/6, Preamble.

[69] *Ibid.*, para. 9. See on the further development of this policy below at 167–70.

[70] Barnard, n.15 above, 18.

[71] [2001] OJ C80/1, signed on 26 Feb. 2001 and at the time of writing still in the process of ratification by Member States. All that has changed as regards freedom of association and the right to strike is that Art. 137(6) becomes Art. 137(5).

liberty, democracy, respect for human rights and fundamental freedoms'. Moreover, in the event of 'the existence of a serious and persistent' breach of this provision by a Member State, a new Article 7 TEU empowers the Council, acting by unanimity (excluding the vote of the Member State in question), to suspend certain of the rights of that State.[72] While such action could in theory extend to breaches of freedom of association and the right to strike, this has yet to be established in practice. It is perhaps made more doubtful by the terms of Article 6(2) TEU which refers only to 'fundamental rights, as guaranteed by the European Convention on Human Rights ... and as they result from the constitutional traditions common to the Member States, as general principles of Community law'.[73] No mention is made of other international human rights instruments, such as the European Social Charter. In any case, the Article 7 procedure has yet to be invoked in any context and seems to be, at least at present, only of symbolic significance.

It is conceivable that a directive setting out a right to strike could be adopted under Article 94 (ex Article 100) or Article 308 (ex Article 235) of the EC Treaty, but the principle that the specialized treaty base should prevail makes this course of action unlikely and potentially open to challenge by Member States.[74] The right to strike has been recognized incidentally in the 'Monti' Regulation, where it is acknowledged as an exception to rules pertaining to free movement of goods.[75] This was due to intensive lobbying by the European Trade Union Confederation (ETUC) and the timely intervention of the European Parliament.[76] Nevertheless, the 'Monti' Regulation leaves the determination of the content of the 'right to strike' to be defined by national laws. There is no European-level definition or protection of such a right. Giovanni Orlandini has recently questioned whether this mention of the right to strike in an EC instrument, albeit significant, will be sufficient to ensure that the exercise of industrial action is not progressively limited by the project of market integration.[77] When phrased in negative terms as an exception, whose scope is defined only by national laws, the right to strike is likely to receive only the most nominal protection.

---

[72] See the analysis of this provision in Schermers, H.G., 'Human Rights in the European Union after the Reform of 1 November 1998' (1998) 4 *European Public Law* 335 at 340. See also Lenaerts, K., 'Fundamental Rights in the European Union' (2000) 25 *ELRev.* 575.

[73] For more on the 'general principles' jurisprudence of the European Court of Justice see Chap. 10 below, at 250–8.

[74] Ryan, n.65 above, 310–16.

[75] Council Regulation 2679/98 [1998] OJ L337/8, Art. 2.

[76] See *Report on Transnational Trade Union Rights in the European Union*, Committee on Employment and Social Affairs, Mrs Ria Oomen-Ruijten, 20 Mar. 1998, A4–0095/98, PE 223.118/fin.

[77] Orlandini, G., 'The Free Movement of Goods as a Possible "Community" Limitation on Industrial Conflict' (2000) 6 *ELJ* 341, at 358. See also Chap. 10 below, at 253–5.

It remains arguable that the introduction of a right to strike is desirable. The introduction of such an entitlement would be consistent with the increasing emphasis in European social policy on collective agreements. The relatively recent EC mechanism of social dialogue,[78] the potential for implementation of EC Directives by collective agreement,[79] and the broad provision made for 'workplace agreements' under the Working Time and Parental Leave Directives[80] indicate that it is expected that EC Member States will take measures to promote collective bargaining. It is difficult to see how such bargaining can be meaningful without potential recourse to industrial action.[81] Moreover, as more European companies emerge, there is an increased likelihood of transnational bargaining and industrial conflict. On this basis the European Parliament has called for inclusion of basic trade union rights into the ECT.[82]

In the Presidency Conclusions at the Laeken Council, mention was made of 'the importance of preventing and resolving social conflicts, and especially transnational social conflicts'. The Commission was invited to submit a discussion paper relating to voluntary mediation mechanisms.[83] A report has been submitted by Fernando Valdés Dal-Ré on this matter, but no recommendations have been made on the transnational aspect of the right to strike.[84]

It seems that Treaty amendment is the sole means by which the current state of affairs can be changed. The difficulty is that this demands unanimity or a return to the less desirable 'twin-track' Social Europe.

D.   THE EU CHARTER OF FUNDAMENTAL RIGHTS 2000

The EU Charter of Fundamental Rights (EUCFR) was proclaimed at the meeting of the European Council held in December 2000 at Nice. This instrument has also been approved by the Parliament and the Commission. Its drafting was unusual in that it involved a more open deliberative process

---

[78] See above, at 153.

[79] See Case 143/83 *Commission v Denmark* [1985] ECR 427, para. 8 and Case 235/84 *Commission v Italy* [1986] ECR 2291, para. 20. See also provision made for implementation by management and labour in the Works Councils Directive, Council Directive 94/45 [1994] OJ L254/64, Art. 14.

[80] Council Directives 93/104 [1993] OJ L307/18, Art. 17 and 96/104 [1996] OJ L145/9, Annex, Cll. 2 and 3.

[81] See Chap. 1 above, at 5–8 and 20–2, and Chap. 3 above, at 57–9. For elaboration of this argument see Germanotta, P., and Novitz, T., 'Globalisation and the Right to Strike: The Case for European-Level Protection of Secondary Action' (2002) 18 *IJCLLIR* 67 at 78–82. See also Wedderburn, n.60 above, on the same theme.

[82] European Parliament Resolution on Transnational Trade Union Rights in the European Union, A4-0095/1998, 2 July 1998, para. 13.

[83] *Laeken Council Presidency Conclusions*, 15 Dec. 2001, 'Fleshing Out the European Social Model', para. 25.

[84] Valdés Dal-Ré, F., 'Synthesis Report on Conciliation, Mediation and Arbitration in European Union Countries', presented to the European Commission, Mar. 2002.

than had been undertaken previously by the EU. The 'Convention' responsible for this process contained not only heads of State, but also representatives of the European Parliament and national parliaments. The Ombudsman, representatives of the Economic and Social Committee, the Committee of the Regions, representatives of civil society (including trade unions), and applicant countries did not participate in the final decision-making but were able to contribute their views at public hearings.[85]

The Charter's preamble is more daring than the 1989 CCFSRW. It stresses the indivisibility of human rights which span categories previously demarcated as civil, political, and socio-economic. It also dwells on 'citizenship' of the Union, as opposed to the mere status of the 'worker' as an economic unit. Even non-citizens who find themselves in a situation governed by Community law are able to rely on certain of its provisions.[86]

These rights encompass 'freedom of association', recognized in Chapter II of the EUCFR on 'Freedoms'. Article 12(1) states: '[e]veryone has the right to freedom of peaceful assembly and to freedom of association at all levels, in particular in political, trade union and civic matters, which implies the right of everyone to form and to join trade unions for the protection of his or her interests'.[87] As in Article 11 of the ECHR, freedom of association is linked to trade union freedom. Negative freedom of association is not guaranteed, at least on the face of the document; although this provision is understood as having the same meaning as the equivalent provision in the ECHR.[88] This right is also said in the explanatory note to be based on Point 11 of the CCFSRW 1989, which does expressly protect the right to dissociate.[89] To the extent that there is any difference between the ECHR and the CCFSRW it is not clear which is to prevail. All that we are told is that the EUCFR is not intended to limit or adversely affect human rights and fundamental freedoms recognized in other international agreements, the ECHR, and Member States' constitutions.[90] ILO instruments, the ESC 1961, and the CCFSRW presumably come within this category, even if they are not regarded as being as worthy of mention as the ECHR.[91] However, this wording may betray the implicit accepted hierarchy of these human rights instruments.

[85] See de Búrca, G., 'The Drafting of the European Union Charter of Fundamental Rights' (2001) 26 *ELRev*. 126; and Miller, V., 'Human Rights in the EU: The Charter of Fundamental Rights' (2000) House of Commons Research Paper 00/32 at 24–31.

[86] Lenaerts, K., and De Smijter, E.E., 'A "Bill of Rights" for the European Union' (2001) 38 *CMLRev*. 273 at 278. With the exception of 'Citizens' Rights', e.g., in Chap. V of the EUCFR.

[87] The full text of EUCFR, Arts. 12 and 28 is provided in App. 7.

[88] See EUCFR, Art. 52(3).

[89] *Charter of Fundamental Rights of the European Union: Explanations Relating to the Complete Text of the Charter* (Luxembourg: Official Publications of the EC, 2001), 30.

[90] EUCFR, Art. 53. See on the controversy over the drafting and implication of this provision Liisberg, J.B., 'Does the EU Charter of Fundamental Rights Threaten the Supremacy of Community Law?' (2001) 38 *CMLRev*. 1171.

[91] See in this respect the recent plea within the Council of Europe that EU Member States take account of Charter standards when implementing EC directives: CIE, *Conclusions XIV–1* (1998), 27–8.

A 'right of collective bargaining and action' is set out in Chapter IV which states the rights arising under the heading of 'Solidarity'. Article 28 states: '[w]orkers and employers, or their respective organisations, have, in accordance with Community law and national laws and practices, the right to negotiate and conclude collective agreements at the appropriate levels and, in cases of conflicts of interest, to take collective action to defend their interests, including strike action'. This is a provision which is said to be based on Article 6 of the ESC and on the CCFSRW, rather than ILO instruments. It is similar to the CCFSRW in terms of its deference to national laws and practices. The explanatory note makes it plain that this is not to be regarded as a basis for EC protection of transnational collective bargaining or industrial action: '[c]ollective action, including strike action, comes under national laws and practices, including the question of whether it may be carried out in parallel in several Member States'.[92]

As would be the case under the ECHR or the ESC, these rights are not intended to be absolute. They are circumscribed by Article 52 which states that '[a]ny limitation on the exercise of the rights and freedoms recognised by the Charter must be provided for by law and respect the essence of those rights and freedoms'. This provision refers to 'the principle of proportionality', a feature of jurisprudence developed by both the European Court of Human Rights and the European Court of Justice. This principle is to be applied so that limitations are permissible 'only if they are necessary and genuinely meet objectives of general interest recognised by the Union or the need to protect the rights and freedoms of others'.

The mention of social rights in the Charter was a matter of some controversy and can be seen as a victory for those who lobbied hard for their inclusion. Of particular influence appears to have been the Reports of Experts appointed by the European Commission to present their views on this issue. The first was the *'Comité des Sages'* of 1996, which argued for the inclusion in the Treaty of a minimum core of rights, followed by a consultation process for their further elaboration. Its report stressed the indivisibility of civil, political, and social rights.[93] Support for the 'indivisibility' thesis can also be found in the reports of a further *Comité des Sages*, which established a human rights project at the European University Institute.[94] The third link in this chain was the Expert Group on Fundamental Rights commissioned by the Employment and Social Affairs Directorate-General of the Commission. This group, led by Spiros Simitis, argued that:

---

[92] *Charter of Fundamental Rights of the EU: Explanations*, n.89 above, 46.

[93] *For a Europe of Civic and Social Rights: Report by the Comité des Sages* chaired by Maria Lourdes Pintasilgo (1996). A copy of this report can be found in Betten, L., and MacDevitt, D. (eds.), *The Protection of Fundamental Social Rights in the European Union* (The Hague: Kluwer, 1996). For the summary of proposals see 244–6.

[94] See *Leading by Example: A Human Rights Agenda for the European Union for the Year 2000: Agenda of the Comité des Sages and Final Project Report* (Florence: EUI, 1998). See also Alston, P. (ed.), *The European Union and Human Rights* (Oxford: OUP, 1999).

Indivisibility... demands, first and foremost, a meticulous review of civil rights in order to address and incorporate matters traditionally dealt with in a closed category of social rights. Where adaptation and completion of civil rights is not possible, formulation of new rights will be needed, as is particularly the case with collective rights, such as the right to resort to collective actions.[95]

As useful and influential as the principle of indivisibility could be, recommendation for inclusion of a right to collective action was not elaborated upon further in this report. The ETUC and the Platform of European Social NGOs sought to remedy this situation, arguing in particular for the introduction into the Charter of a transnational right to strike, including a right to take secondary action.[96] They observed that without the recognition of such a right attempts to engage in European-level collective bargaining could be thwarted. However, they were to be disappointed. The legality of secondary or sympathy action will still be determined by Member States at the domestic level.

In terms of its legal effect, the 2000 Charter is merely another solemn proclamation which is addressed 'to the institutions and bodies of the Union with due regard for the principle of subsidiarity and to the Member States only when they are implementing Union law'. Article 51 makes it clear that the EUCFR 'does not establish any new power or task for the Community or Union, or modify powers and tasks defined by the Treaties'. This is 'an instrument of constitutional review of Union acts, which does not affect national legislation directly'.[97] It seems that the Charter is merely designed to codify the 'fundamental rights' to which the European Court of Justice may already have reference when determining the legality of Community or Union action, or the legality of Member State action in the context of EU law.[98] Speculation continues about the potential legal effect of the Charter after the 2004 European Council.[99] There remains, for example, the possibility that it

---

[95] *Affirming the Fundamental Rights in the European Union: Report of the Expert Group on Fundamental Rights* (Luxembourg, European Commission: Employment and Social Affairs, 1999), 22.

[96] *Contribution by Three Trade Unions (LO, TCO and SACO) in Sweden*, CHARTE 4355/00, CONTRIB 219, 13 June 2000; Proposed Amendment to Article 34 submitted by Dr Sylvia-Yvonne Kaufmann, CHARTE 4405/00, CONTRIB 262, 6 July 2000; *Contribution by the Working Group of the Platform of European Social NGOs*, CHARTE 4434/00, CONTRIB 288, 31 Aug. 2000; and *Contribution of the European Trade Union Confederation and the Platform of European Social NGOs*, with comments and a working paper on Convention document 45, CHARTE 4460/00 CONTRIB 314, 8 Sept. 2000.

[97] Betten, L., 'Current Developments: European Law: Human Rights' (2001) 50 *ICLQ* 690 at 695.

[98] *Charter of Fundamental Rights of the EU: Explanations*, n.89 above, 73. The requirement to respect fundamental rights is to be binding on Member States only when they act in the context of Community law. See Chap. 10 below, at 251.

[99] See McCrudden, C., 'The Future of the EU Charter of Fundamental Rights' and de Búrca, G., 'Human Rights: The Charter and Beyond' (2001) Jean Monnet Working Paper Series No. 10/01. For the view of the Commission see COM(2000)644.

will be incorporated into either or both of the EC and EU Treaties.[100] For the time being, the 2000 Charter is not likely to be the basis for an EU instrument protecting freedom of association or a right to strike.

III.   TRADE AND AID CONDITIONALITY

While there has been reluctance to take specific measures to promote protection of freedom of association and the right to strike within the EU, there has been a greater willingness to do so beyond its boundaries. This is a policy that has taken some time to develop. Initially, the international promotion of labour standards was considered a matter for the foreign policy of Member States, not the EC or EU. For example, Western European States played a key role in the creation of the ILO and its revitalization after World War II.[101] While the EC later acquired ILO observer status, States retained their membership and their voting rights. There was a time when Member States' autonomy in this field was contested by the Commission, which perceived the danger that EC and international legal obligations could clash. An eventual accommodation was reached, whereby the EC could claim exclusive competence to represent Member States in the social field only where EC law harmonized national laws. Shared competence could be claimed in areas where the EC was engaged in setting minimum standards.[102] Moreover, Heads of State gradually came to perceive the utility of collective representation by the EC in relation to labour standards, as well as trade, as was reflected in the Council Resolution of 1994.[103]

The European Commission has argued for the WTO to secure enforcement of core labour standards by linking compliance to trade access. The Council and Commission have both strenuously denied that this would serve 'protectionist' purposes, as is claimed by developing and newly-industrialized States which oppose such measures.[104] They have however

---

[100] Vitorino, A., 'The Charter of Fundamental Rights as a Foundation for the Area of Freedom, Security and Justice', Exeter Paper in European Law No. 4 (Centre for European Studies, University of Exeter, 2001), 16.

[101] See Chap. 5 above, at 96–9.

[102] See *Opinion 2/91* regarding ILO Convention No. 170 on Chemicals at Work, Decision of 19 Mar. 1993 [1993] ECR I–1061; see also [1993] CMLR 800 and the discussion by Vedder, C., and Floz, H.-P. (1994) 5 *EJIL* 452. For an example of such a clash see the 'nightwork' cases, discussed by Kilpatrick, C., 'Production and Circulation of EC Nightwork Jurisprudence' (1996) 25 *ILJ* 169.

[103] For e.g. Council Resolution of 6 Dec. 1994 on certain aspects of a European Social Policy [1994] OJ C368/6 discussed above at 161. Cf. the more controversial debate over the content of the 'Common Commercial Policy' set out in Art. 133 ECT, which arose in *Opinion 1/94* re WTO Agreement [1994] ECR I–5267, discussed in Meunier, D., and Nicolaidis, K., 'Who Speaks for Europe? The Delegation of Trade Authority in the EU' (1999) 37 *JCMS* 477.

[104] Communication from the Commission to the Council, the European Parliament, and the Economic and Social Committee, *Promoting Core Labour Standards and Improving Social Governance in the Context of Globalization*, COM(2001)416, hereafter 'Promoting Core Labour Standards', 11 and Annex 1 which sets out the Council conclusions of 1999.

failed to persuade these States of their disinterested motives. No such measures were adopted at the WTO Ministerial meetings held at Singapore, Seattle, or Doha.[105]

In this respect, the EC seems to have taken matters into its own hands. It requires compliance with core labour standards, as set out in the 1998 ILO Declaration on Fundamental Principles and Rights at Work, within the 'Generalized System of Preferences' (GSP) and in bilateral trade and aid agreements. The GSP is a mechanism under which industrialized States can grant non-reciprocal preferences to developing nations. This constitutes an exception to the principle of 'most favoured nation status' under the General Agreement on Tariffs and Trade (GATT) now regulated through the WTO. ILO Conventions Nos. 87, 98, and 138[106] have been included in the GSP as a basis for preferential trade access. Provision has also been made for EU temporary withdrawal of such preferences where the beneficiary country allows the practices of slavery or, forced labour or is seeking to export goods made by prison labour.[107]

In addition, the EU has received WTO dispensation to enter into certain preferential aid and trade agreements, which introduce social conditionality. An example is the 2000 Cotonou Agreement, the successor to the Lomé Conventions,[108] which confirms the parties' commitment to 'core labour standards' and states that one of the aims of co-operation will be to 'respect... basic social rights', although this is not to be used for 'protectionist purposes'.[109] Agreements like Cotonou are ostensibly multilateral in character, but as it is the incontrovertible bargaining power of the EU in such a context that leads to the insertion of social clauses into these instruments and it is only the other parties to the agreement which have to comply with these clauses, the EU can be regarded as acting unilaterally to protect core labour standards, including freedom of association.[110]

It is not entirely clear whether the right to strike is to be protected as a facet of freedom of association. The Global Report on Freedom of Association, adopted under the 'follow-up' to the ILO 1998 Declaration, con-

---

[105] See Summers, C., 'The Battle in Seattle: Free Trade, Labor Rights and Societal Values' (2001) 22 *University of Pennsylvania Journal of International Economic Law* 61. See also Doha 2001 WTO Ministerial Briefing Notes available at www.wto.org/english/thewto_e/minist_e/min01_e/brief_e/brief16_e.htm.

[106] ILO Convention No. 138 on the Minimum Age for Admission to Employment 1973.

[107] Council Regulation 2820/98 [1998] OJ L357/1, Arts. 8–21. See for details of these special incentives in terms of tariffs WTO, *Trade Policy Review: European Union 2001*, WT/TPR/S/72 (Geneva: WTO, 2000) i, 36, Box II.5.

[108] See for discussion of its content and effect the Commission Staff Working Document D(2001) 32947 at 88 ff. The provisional WTO Decision of 14 Nov. 2001, WT/MIN(01)/15, on its status is available at www.wto.org/english/thewto_e/minist_e/min01_e/mindecl_acp_ec_agre_e.htm.

[109] Cotonou Agreement 2000, Arts. 25 and 50.

[110] McCrudden, C., and Davies, A., 'A Perspective on Trade and Labour Rights' (2000) 21 *Journal of International Economic Law* 43, at 53–4.

sidered that the two were closely connected and commented specifically on the treatment of industrial action in States.[111] This follows from the previous findings of ILO supervisory bodies.[112] Given the enforcement of other forms of conditionality by the EU to date, much may depend in practice upon contingent political and economic circumstances rather than matters of principle.[113]

The European Commission apparently considers that the fundamental principles and rights at work identified in the 1998 ILO Declaration already 'apply in their entirety to the countries of the EU'.[114] The aim is ostensibly to export the 'European social model'.[115] This is correct to the extent that EU Member States are all members of the ILO and have ratified ILO Conventions Nos. 87 and 98. Nevertheless, despite Commission rhetoric, EU Member States have a far from perfect record of compliance with ILO standards. ILO supervisory bodies have repeatedly found that UK legislation is in breach of 'freedom of association' under the core Conventions, Nos. 87 and 98.[116] German treatment of civil servants and Portuguese imposition of compulsory arbitration have also been the subject of criticism.[117] These EU States do not themselves abide by the recommendations of ILO supervisory bodies and yet these are, apparently, to be used as the basis for suspension of trade benefits or aid provision to other States.

EU Member States do not seem unduly concerned by this state of affairs; nor do they appear to see any contradiction in the path mapped in terms of international enforcers of labour standards and the limited powers of the EU. Criticism, if it does come, is more likely to arise externally, perhaps within the context of the WTO dispute procedure which provides a forum for challenges from those States excluded from agreements or disadvantaged by arrangements. Much will therefore depend upon whether the conduct of the EU is defensible under Article XX, that is, the 'general exceptions' clause of GATT.

The assumption seems to be that violations elsewhere are 'proportionately' worse than those which take place in EU Member States. There may

---

[111] *Your Voice at Work* (Geneva: ILO, 2000) ILC, 88th Session, esp. at 38. See also Chap. 8 below, at 203–6.

[112] See Chap. 6 above, at 120 and Chap. 8 below, at 192–203.

[113] See for discussion of inconsistent application of political conditionality Smith, K.E., 'The Use of Political Conditionality In the EU's Relations with Third Countries', EUI Working Paper SPS No. 97/7. See also Tsogas, G., 'Labour Standards in the Generalized Systems of Preferences of the European Union and the United States' (2000) 6 *European Journal of Industrial Relations* 349, who at 362 observes that, despite Pakistan's refusal to allow EU investigation of its labour practices, Member States did not take action, fearing the implications for their trade connections.

[114] *Promoting Core Labour Standards*, n.104 above, 11.

[115] *Ibid.*, 10.

[116] On the UK see CEACR Individual Observations Concerning Conventions Nos. 87 and No. 98 (UK) 2000, 2001, and 2002.

[117] See ILOLEX at www.ilo.org. See also Part IV below.

be instances where this is so, such as where all workers are precluded from access to industrial action. Nevertheless, there remains a risk that EU trade conditionality will be regarded as discriminatory and will lie outside Article XX if EU compliance with core labour standards does not measure up to that required of other States, in which case its practices may be regarded as 'a disguised restriction on international trade'.[118] There could therefore be some additional and previously unanticipated impetus for the EC to provide basic protection for freedom of association and, potentially, the right to strike.

IV. CONCLUSION

The initial objectives expressed in the Treaty of Rome emphasized the achievement of economic progress as a precursor to social welfare. The latter was expected to follow without additional legislative intervention at the European level, except in circumstances where lower labour standards were unfairly used as a means to achieve a competitive advantage. Failure to regulate protection of freedom of association and a right to strike stems, in part, from the assumption in the Ohlin Report that this was an unlikely source of competitive advantage. Since 1957, there has been continued resistance to the creation of EC legislation on these matters, by virtue of the principle of subsidiarity. It is said that this is a matter best regulated at the national level, with due regard to the diversity of industrial relations systems within the Member States.

This deference seems to spring from the resistance of Member States to EC social policy. They have been impervious to lobbying by the ETUC and recommendations made by the European Parliament. As standard-setting on freedom of association and industrial action seems to require an amendment of the EC Treaty, the control lies entirely in the hands of the Member States. They have proved unwilling to accept the argument that the growth of European corporations and transnational collective bargaining requires EC-level protection of a right to strike.

The EU Charter of Fundamental Rights does demonstrate a degree of respect for the human rights instruments adopted by the Council of Europe. However, despite the rhetoric of 'indivisibility' of such rights, greater emphasis is placed on compliance with the European Convention on Human Rights than the European Social Charter. The EUCFR is also of doubtful legal effect and can, in any case, be relied upon only as a shield against EU infringement of human rights norms or failure by Member States to comply

---

[118] See Marceau, G., 'A Call for Coherence in International Law: Praises for the Prohibition Against "Clinical Isolation" in WTO Dispute Settlement' (1999) 33 *Journal of World Trade* 87 and Blackett, A., 'Whither Social Clause? Human Rights, Trade Theory and Treaty Interpretation' (1999) 31 *Columbia Human Rights Law Review* 1, 72–8.

with such norms in the application of EU law. It cannot be relied upon to alter the industrial relations systems or laws of Member States.

Perhaps ironically, the attention of the EU (and its Member States) has been diverted to the global stage. Respect for freedom of association, in compliance with ILO Conventions Nos. 87 and 98, is now used as a means by which to determine who receives EU (and Member State) trade preferences and development aid. This policy is based on the assumption that all EU Member States satisfy these requirements, an assumption that on the basis of findings of ILO supervisory bodies is ill-founded. Given this, there may yet be pressure upon the EU to reconsider this stance and impose effective minimum standards within the Union as well as outside its borders. Otherwise, it may be difficult to defend the legitimacy of the Union's role in global social governance. However, at present, there is no clear indication that this is appreciated by the Member States in whose hands this decision lies.

Conclusion: Explanations of Divergent Approaches

This Part has examined the divergent approaches taken by the ILO, Council of Europe, and European Union to protection of the right to strike. The Council of Europe has adopted a European Social Charter, Article 6(4) of which makes express provision for the right to strike. Contracting Parties may opt to be bound by this Article, which has privileged status within that instrument. Within the EU, only declaratory instruments recognize the entitlement of workers to take collective action. The ILO has been even more circumspect. No ILO instrument has been adopted which provides systematic protection or even a definition of the scope of the right to strike. As we shall see in Chapter 8, this entitlement has instead been treated by ILO supervisory bodies as a logical extension of guarantees of freedom of association contained in the ILO Constitution and ILO Conventions Nos. 87 and 98.

It has been suggested that these differences stem in part from the constitution of each organization. The historical context of their origins and their very purpose differ dramatically. This has led to distinctive institutional understandings of the role to be played by each organization in transnational governance. The ILO has a remit to set international labour standards on a global scale, but is aware that these can be set as minimum standards only at a broad level of generality. This has arguably led to the very general provisions in ILO Conventions Nos. 87 and 98 which ILO supervisory bodies were required to apply to specific situations. The Council of Europe Statute emphasizes the protection of individual freedom and the commonality of Western European values, presumably in opposition to the Communist Eastern European bloc. Civil and political rights have received more attention and respect than socio-economic rights. To the extent that a right to strike is understood as falling solely within the latter category, it will receive inferior protection under the auspices of the Council. The European Union, by contrast, has its origins in the Treaty of Rome 1957 which was signed with the objective of economic integration in mind. This is one reason why the EU has only gradually and incrementally accommodated the development of a social policy, from which the right to strike is still excluded. Instead, compliance with freedom of association is required by the EU of third States and receives some acknowledgement in instruments which are not binding upon the Member States.

Moreover, the methods of standard-setting particular to each organization provide some explanation of the differences between the content of the instruments which they have promulgated. Within the ILO, not only States but also national worker and employer representatives play a role in the setting of standards. This gives these interest groups an opportunity to contribute directly to decisions on the content and adoption of instruments. Workers and employers are often able to resist compromise where this does not accommodate their baseline bargaining positions. Opposition from first the employers' group and then the workers' group appears to have operated to prevent express detailed protection of the right to strike in an ILO instrument. Weighing up the pros and cons of this omission, the workers' group concluded that there was no cause for concern, given the jurisprudence of the ILO supervisory bodies. Indeed, the workers' group went so far as to reject further standard-setting by the ILO in the field of 'dispute settlement'.

The adoption of instruments in the Council of Europe is done by State actors alone, initially by unanimity and now by a two-thirds majority within a Committee of Ministers. The Parliamentary Assembly can make recommendations and trade unions may lobby, but they have no say in this final decision. This means that instruments which are adopted (if they are adopted) tend not to place onerous social-policy obligations on States. A case in point is the right to strike set out in the European Social Charter 1961 which places arguably only minimal, narrowly circumscribed duties on those States which elect to be bound by that provision. The trade union movement represented in the Council of Europe at a tripartite conference, organized by the ILO, argued enthusiastically for written recognition of this right, only to find that the cost of doing so was high.

The EU prides itself on a more complex form of European governance, reflecting the early federalist aspirations of its founders. The European Parliament has increased in influence beyond the Council of Europe's Assembly, and the operation of a 'social dialogue' mechanism in standard-setting is also innovative. However, in the absence of any legal base in the EC or EU Treaty for the adoption of measures of the right to strike, and given the express exclusion of use of Article 137 of the EC Treaty for this purpose, control over standard-setting resides again with the Member States. The right to strike receives explicit recognition in the Community Charter of the Fundamental Rights of Workers 1989 and the EU Charter of Fundamental Rights 2001, but both of these instruments take the form of what is described as 'soft law'. They have moral or persuasive force, but do not, on their face, create binding legal obligations. Where the right to strike has entered the legislative and judicial framework, it is as an exception to other established entitlements under the EC Treaty, such as freedom of movement or fair competition.[1] Trade unions and academics continue to

---

[1] See Chap. 7 above, at 162; and Chap. 10 below, at 253–7.

argue for EU protection of a transnational right to strike. Arguably, if this were formulated through the process of social dialogue, workers could exert significant influence over the content of Community legislation on this issue and might perhaps avoid concessions made by trade unions in the drafting of the European Social Charter. However, before this becomes a possibility, all EU Member States first need to consent to such a change. Impetus for consent might be forthcoming if the EU continues to pursue its current policies relating to trade preferences and development aid, but only if it is embarrassed in this regard.

These organizations have been analysed individually, but it should be apparent that each is aware of the policies of the others. The EU institutional framework is in certain ways defined in opposition to the Council of Europe from whence it sprung, the EU Charter on Fundamental Rights is designed to be consistent with the European Convention on Human Rights, and ILO standards provide the basis for EU conditionality. This interaction poses interesting questions, many of which cannot definitively be answered. For example, it would be interesting to know the extent to which the revitalization of the European Social Charter from 1990 onwards, which is usually linked to the end of the Cold War and the enlargement of the Council of Europe, is also a response to the introduction of a Community Charter of Fundamental Rights of Workers 1989 which was considered to threaten the status of the ESC.[2] Interesting issues may also arise in respect of EU enforcement of 'freedom of association' via the GSP and aid agreements. In doing so, the EU has the potential either to assist or to detract from the universal protection of ILO standards. There is tremendous scope for co-operation between these organizations, but also potential for competition.

Part III will go on to consider the extent to which supervisory bodies within the ILO, Council of Europe, and EU have influenced the extent to which the right to strike is protected internationally. It is suggested that such bodies operate within constraints set by the international instruments under which they are established and wider perceptions of their legitimate role generated, at least in part, by the constitutional objectives of the organizations themselves. While there is often some awareness of the jurisprudence developed by another organization, in their supervisory role these bodies reflect and arguably perpetuate these crucial differences of approach.

[2] Betten, L., 'Towards a Community Charter of Fundamental Social Rights' (1989) 1 *NQHR* 77, 85 ff.

PART III

The Roles Played by Supervisory Bodies in Protection of a Right to Strike

Introduction

On the international and European stages, there are at least two key roles that supervisory bodies can play in protection of the right to strike. One is the application of express provisions guaranteeing this right set out in a multilateral instrument. An example is the operation of the control mechanisms established under the European Social Charter 1961 (ESC) in relation to Article 6(4). A second is the interpretation of provision made for 'freedom of association' as encompassing a right to strike. This is done by ILO supervisory bodies, when considering the scope of the constitutional entitlement to 'freedom of association' and the appropriate construction of ILO Conventions Nos. 87 and 98.

This Part considers the ingredients for effective action by supervisory bodies at the international and European levels. It suggests that the control mechanisms available in respect of the ESC are less than satisfactory and seeks to explain why. It also examines how the connection between freedom of association and the right to strike came to be recognized within the ILO and the reasons other supervisory bodies, such as the European Court of Human Rights and the European Court of Justice, have yet to adopt this view.

International and European control mechanisms tend to take two distinctive forms. The first is the 'reporting' model, which relies on scrutiny of reports sent by governments and other interested parties on the extent of State compliance with the relevant norm. The second is the 'complaints' model which focuses on the circumstances of the person (or persons) affected by the wrongdoing of a particular State. Both possess their respective merits. Complaints may highlight the injustice done to a particular individual or a particular sector of the population. They may attract public attention and prompt action for redress of the grievance. By contrast, reporting may deliver more information than the occasional complaint and is arguably less confrontational.[1] It removes the onus on the victim of a violation to bring an action and is less reliant on their possession of the resources to do so. It has the potential to make governments reflect on their conduct (and defend it) upon a regular basis, which may also lead to legal reforms and changes in domestic policy without external prompting.

---

[1] Landy, E., *The Effectiveness of International Supervision: Thirty Years of ILO Experience* (London: Stevens & Sons, 1966), 210.

Nevertheless, it is possible to thwart the application of either a reporting or a complaints procedure, so that it ceases to be effective. This may be done by governments which evade provision of accurate information or indeed any information at all. At this stage, it may be desirable to supplement these procedures by investigatory missions by Commissions of Inquiry, where this is feasible. An effective mission will still require the co-operation of the government in question.

The efficacy of reporting and complaints procedures can also be thwarted from the outset by their institutional design. For example, the extent to which individuals and groups have access to the procedure will be important, as will the time it takes to complete. A procedure which requires too many lengthy stages of review, and which therefore involves considerable delays, may tax the patience of participants and is unlikely to be of significant value in evaluating or influencing State conduct. Significant breaches of workers' rights may go unnoticed, without reprimand for too great a period of time. We will see that this has been a failing of the European Social Charter reporting mechanism.

Also pertinent, in terms of institutional design, will be the function that States perform in the supervisory process. Where States are able to control whether or not recommendations or sanctions are issued, they are given the opportunity to act as judge in their own cause. There may even be a hint of bias where it is the governments of Member States which appoint the supervisory body by which their conduct will be assessed. It has been suggested that this body should be appointed by a wider representative grouping, such as a parliamentary assembly or a tripartite committee. This ideal is difficult to achieve, for although international and European legal norms are designed to restrain State action, their currency remains reliant upon State co-operation, without which they could not exist. However, again, this is one respect in which the credibility of the ESC supervisory process has been undermined.

Another key concern is the form that the supervisory body itself should take. Certainly, its members should possess the expertise required for scrutiny of State conduct, especially in the particular field of social rights. Moreover, and perhaps most importantly, this body should be impartial and independent. It can be argued that true impartiality is unobtainable,[2] but that a balance of vested interests is the best that can be hoped for. Where employment rights are at issue, the tendency has been, both in the international and the domestic spheres, to achieve this balance through the creation of a tripartite body, consisting of worker, employer, and govern-

[2] See, in particular, the American Realist and Critical Legal Studies traditions. Useful extracts from the works of key theorists from the first jurisprudential school can be found in Fisher, W.W., and Horwitz, M.J. (eds.), *American Legal Realism* (Oxford: OUP, 1993). For an overview of the contributions made by both schools see Duxbury, N., *Patterns of American Jurisprudence* (Oxford: OUP, 1997).

ment representatives.[3] With such a constitution, the body in question cannot then be accused of pursuing any agenda particularly favourable to one of these groups. The expertise criterion is also met by the specialized experience of its members, especially when assisted by an independent chair, who can provide guidance on legal issues. The alternative is judgment by a body resembling a 'court of law', in which legal experts of proven experience evaluate the claims of the parties. This title may not be entirely merited, for a supra-national body is unlikely to possess the same powers as its domestic counterparts.[4] There will be no police available to enforce its judgments; only reliance upon State co-operation.[5] Nevertheless, the label of a 'Court' has the advantage of imbuing the organ with the 'socio-linguistic insignia' of hierarchy and status associated with the national institution it is designed to replicate.[6] One could however question whether a 'legalistic' approach to social policy is ideal, especially if the judiciary lacks experience or understanding of the dynamics that underlie modern industrial relations.[7] It is for this reason that many prefer the jurisprudence developed by a tripartite body, for example within the ILO, to that of the European Court of Human Rights.

A final issue is the extent to which the findings of supervisory bodies need be considered formally binding upon States. Their legal status will depend upon treaty interpretation and customary international law, that is, the provision made for such bodies in international instruments and the manner in which their findings are treated by States over time. It is well established that the findings of the European Court of Human Rights on compliance with the European Convention on Human Rights 1950 (ECHR) are binding,[8] but this is not the case in respect of the conclusions and reports of the European Committee of Social Rights on compliance with the ESC.[9]

---

[3] See the constitution of the ILO CFA discussed in Chap. 8 below, at 190. In the UK context, the creation of industrial tribunals is typical of this attempt. See McKee, J., 'Legalism in Industrial Tribunals' (1986) 15 *ILJ* 110; and MacMillan, J., 'Employment Tribunals: Philosophies and Practicalities' (1999) 28 *ILJ* 33.

[4] Leary, V.A., 'The Paradox of Workers' Rights as Human Rights' in Compa, L., and Diamond, S.F. (eds.), *Human Rights, Labor Rights and International Trade* (Philadelphia, Penn.: Philadelphia University Press, 1996), 41.

[5] Schermers, H.G., *International Institutional Law* (Alphen aan der Rijn: Sijthoff and Noordhoff, 1980), 683.

[6] Cf. Goodrich, P., *Legal Discourse: Studies in Linguistics, Rhetoric and Legal Analysis* (London: Macmillan, 1987), 171; and Shapiro, M., 'The European Court of Justice' in Craig, P., and de Búrca, G. (eds.), *The Evolution of EU Law* (Oxford: OUP, 1999), 327–8. See also Novitz, T., 'Remedies for Violation of Social Rights within the Council of Europe: The Significant Absence of a Court' in Kilpatrick, C., Novitz, T., and Skidmore, P. (eds.), *The Future of Remedies in Europe* (Oxford: Hart Publishing, 2000), 236.

[7] One might also wish to note that lack of judicial sympathy for a right to strike in the UK: see, e.g., *Crosville Wales Ltd v Tracey (No. 2)* [1997] IRLR 691 at 698 on the subject of compensation for dismissal of a striker, which Lord Nolan considers to be unfair to the employer.

[8] ECHR 1950 (prior to amendment by Protocol 11), Arts. 49–54 and (post amendment by Protocol 11), Arts. 41–46.

[9] See below, at 223.

Control mechanisms at this level tend, in any case, to rely most upon moral condemnation as the key form of censure, their aim being to embarrass those States which fail to comply with their international obligations. Even then, the necessity to maintain State co-operation has led supervisory bodies to demonstrate a degree of respect for State autonomy and, in particular, national political structures and certain aspects of domestic policy.[10] Criticism is often subtle rather than overt.

It should also be observed that the multiplicity of supervisory regimes, to be found in the ILO, Council of Europe, World Trade Organization (WTO), other regional organizations, and the UN system as a whole can create tension and confusion. It remains entirely possible that one institution will condemn a course of conduct while another will not. These differences have the potential to undermine the 'authority' of particular supervisory bodies and their conclusions.

The ILO has deployed a wide range of flexible, inter-related procedures, including analysis of State reports, the hearing of collective complaints, and investigation by a Commission that will visit the State concerned. There is no quasi-judicial procedure under which an individual can seek a remedy for breach of labour standards. However, the tripartite structure of control mechanisms mean that, within this Organization at least, their findings on breach of workers' rights and recommendations for future conduct receive considerable attention and respect.

The complaints procedure for enforcement of the ECHR is widely regarded as effective, by virtue of the potential range of applicants and the binding quality of the judgments that it generates. The difficulty, however, is that its capacity to protect collective rights of workers remains doubtful. The European Court of Human Rights considers industrial action to be a potential aspect of freedom of association, but has concluded that a right to strike is *not necessary* to the effective exercise of this freedom. Instead, this right is labelled a mere socio-economic right, through its inclusion in the ESC. Its status is diminished by virtue of the reporting procedure for assessing the implementation of that instrument, which has limited influence. Various reforms have been made to this procedure, including the introduction of a collective complaints procedure. Nevertheless, it is doubtful that these have truly remedied all the defects previously associated with supervision of the ESC. States have held too great a stranglehold over this control mechanism for it to gain credibility or recognition.

In the context of the European Union, the European Court of Justice is an effective and influential supervisory body, by virtue not only of its judicial form, but also the principles which it has developed relating to the suprem-

---

[10] See, e.g., Parliamentary Assembly of the Council of Europe, *Report on the European Social Charter: A Political Reappraisal*, 12 Sept. 1985, Doc. 5453, 14, which recognizes that the Committee of Ministers is hesitant to condemn 'a whole policy'.

acy of EU law. Nevertheless, this Court cannot hear complaints relating to failure of States to implement a right to strike. This seems to be beyond its jurisdiction, since no EC directive or regulation explicitly requires this of a Member State. Instead, there is potential for the right to strike provided for by national laws to become vulnerable to the encroachment of basic tenets of EU law which are associated with market integration. However, the ECJ plays two additional functions, in which there is potential for protection of a right to strike. The first is in relation to treatment of EU officials, who may make complaints where there is a violation of the Staff Regulations. In the context of these 'staff cases', the importance of a right to associate has been recognized, but no definitive position has been reached on the scope or status of the right to strike. Secondly, through its 'general principles' juris-prudence, the ECJ can restrict EU action, constrain Member State behav-iour when implementing EU law, and, in its interpretive role, limit the scope of EC law, on the basis that there would otherwise be a breach of a 'fundamental right'. There is potential for a right to strike to be recognized by the ECJ as being such a right, alongside freedom of association. We shall see, however, that the ECJ has not yet done so.

It will be argued here that whether an international or European super-visory body recognizes the right to strike as implicit in freedom of associ-ation follows, not so much from the structural form of the control machinery (although this does influence its effectiveness), but from the constitutional objectives and ethos of the organization within which it operates. The jurisprudence of the ILO Committee on Freedom of Associ-ation corresponds to the perception of its members that its adoption is consistent with the fundamental aims of the Organization, as set out in its constitutional instruments. The reluctance of the European Court of Human Rights to do the same stems from the extant demarcation between civil and political rights guaranteed under a European Convention on Human Rights and socio-economic rights protected under a European Social Charter. The difficulty is that, in accepting the status quo, the Court seems to overlook pre-existing obligations of Member States within the ILO. Moreover, given the superior control mechanism attached to the Convention, the judgments of the Court which touch on socio-economic rights are likely to take precedence over the findings of Charter supervisory bodies. The European Court of Justice also exercises caution in the protec-tion of freedom of association and the right to strike under its 'general principles' jurisprudence. In part, this is due to the few cases which have raised the question whether these are to be regarded as 'fundamental rights'. It is also readily observable that extension of this jurisprudence to provide protection of the right to strike is not essential for the ECJ to perform its traditional objectives of promoting the common market and fair competi-tion. Since Member States have resisted the definition of the right to strike or its protection under an EC directive, the ECJ seems unwilling to take this

8

A Panoply of Supervisory Procedures in the ILO

The ILO has established a number of different methods for supervising the enforcement of international labour standards. These include the analysis of State reports, as well as complaints procedures. In addition, ILO experts may visit a State so as to examine the extent of compliance. Indeed, one strength of ILO supervision lies in the 'panoply' of multiple overlapping supervisory methods which tend to supplement and reinforce one another.[1] Another lies in the tripartite nature of the ILO Committee on Freedom of Association (CFA).

There is no explicit guarantee of the right to strike in the ILO Constitution or conventions. No link is made between freedom of association and the right to strike at this standard-setting stage. However, the creation of the CFA led to the recognition of such a connection, which has since been acknowledged by the Committee of Experts and other ILO supervisory organs.

The absence of any express guarantee of a right to strike in an ILO instrument may seem to pose a problem. Initially, it was contemplated that the fundamental purpose of the ILO 'should be attained mainly through legislative activities'.[2] How then can the ILO endorse a right to strike, if not via a Convention or Recommendation? This was a question initially asked by States, which were reluctant to acknowledge the force of decisions reached by the CFA relating to the scope of the right to strike. For example, at the International Labour Conference in 1983, the government representative of the USSR 'doubted that the principles enunciated by the Committee on Freedom of Association could constitute a recognised body of jurisprudence since only Conventions could constitute legal instruments'.[3] However, as was recognized by commentators early on, 'although the judicial function was not envisaged as the primary means for attaining the fundamental purpose of the ILO, it would be erroneous to suppose that this function is outside the scope of the activities of the Organisation'.[4] The

---

[1] Swepston, L., 'Supervision of ILO Standards' (1997) 13 *IJCLLIR* 327, 341.

[2] Osieke, E., 'The Exercise of the Judicial Function with respect to the International Labour Organization' (1974–1975) LXVII *BYBIL* 315. Cf. Valticos, N., 'The Sources of International Labour Law: Recent Trends' in Heere, W. (ed.), *International Law and its Sources: Liber Americorum Maarten Bos* (Deventer: Kluwer, 1988), 179.

[3] *Record of Proceedings* (Geneva: ILO, 1983) ILC, 69th Session, 31/11, para. 46.

[4] Osieke, n.2 above, 315.

interpretation of treaties may involve looking behind the text to what is implicitly as well as what is explicitly guaranteed. This section considers how the CFA and other ILO supervisory bodies came to take this position.

It is argued here that ILO jurisprudence may be defended with reference to constitutional principles and basic principles of treaty interpretation. What is perhaps curious is that, despite the degree of consensus on this jurisprudence within the institutional structure of the ILO, the connection between freedom of association and the right to strike does not receive the same degree of recognition in other contexts.

I. BASIC PROCEDURES FOR MONITORING IMPLEMENTATION OF ILO STANDARDS

Compliance with ratified ILO Conventions and Recommendations is monitored through reports provided by Member States, which can be supplemented by observations from national employer and worker organizations.[5] Analysis of these reports involves a two-tier procedure. First, the ILO Committee of Experts on the Application of Conventions and Recommendation ('CEACR' or 'Committee of Experts') provides a technical examination of the State reports and subsequent observations. The now twenty members of the Committee of Experts are appointed by the tripartite Governing Body.[6] CEACR conclusions are published, regardless of the embarrassment they may cause to States, but they are not legally binding, for this is not the end of the supervisory process. After the CEACR has provided its comments, selected cases are publicly discussed by the Conference Committee on the Application of Standards ('CCAS' or 'Conference Committee'). This is the second tier of the procedure. In the CCAS, State representatives are given an opportunity to explain the reasons for discrepancies between national law and practice and obligations deriving from ILO Conventions.[7] Instances of serious breach are then identified. In the past this was achieved via the use of a 'special list',[8] which has since been replaced by the 'special paragraph'.[9]

---

[5] ILO Constitution, Art. 22. From 1993 onwards, a system was introduced whereby detailed State reports must be given every two years in respect of 'priority Conventions' and every five years on other Conventions. In 2001–2 the CEACR received 195 observations from employers' and workers' organizations. See *General Report of the Committee of Experts on the Application of Conventions and Recommendations* (Geneva: ILO, 2002), paras. 12 and 117.

[6] The CEACR was established with eight members: *ibid.*, para. 10.

[7] The Conference Committee consists of approximately 200 representatives of employers, workers, and governments, in equal numbers. See for an early description of its operation Johnston, G.A., *The International Labour Organization: Its Work for Social and Economic Progress* (London: Europa Publications, 1970), 100–2.

[8] Discussed by Landy, E.A., *The Effectiveness of International Supervision: Thirty Years of ILO Experience* (London: Stevens & Sons, 1966), 170.

[9] There is no settled criterion for selection of individual cases, so this remains a matter over which there is considerable debate. See *Report of the Committee on the Application of Standards* (Geneva: ILO, 2001), ILC, 89th Session, paras. 17–18.

This supervisory process was established in 1926 and has just celebrated its seventy-fifth anniversary. Apparently, 'in the early years, some governments took umbrage at reporting, viewing this as a form of interrogation which infringed their sovereignty'.[10] Gradually, however, it was recognized that some such form of mutual control is both reasonable and necessary, with the result that the majority of States make no objection to furnishing such information. There do however remain certain States which have ratified conventions but do not provide the necessary reports;[11] and the reporting procedure is currently under review so as to encourage compliance.[12]

In recent times, this reporting procedure has been extended further to cover certain non-ratified conventions. This was due to the campaign launched by the ILO in 1995, designed to encourage ratification of the then seven designated 'core' or 'fundamental' conventions.[13] These were Conventions Nos. 87 and 98 on Freedom of Association and Collective Bargaining (1948 and 1949); Conventions Nos. 29 and 105 on the Elimination of All Forms of Forced and Compulsory Labour (1930 and 1957); ILO Convention No. 138 on the Minimum Age for Admission to Employment (1973); and ILO Conventions Nos. 100 and 111 on the Elimination of Discrimination in Respect of Employment and Occupation (1957 and 1958). States were asked to report on their efforts to comply with these standards, regardless of ratification, by virtue of the discretionary power provided by Article 19(5) of the ILO Constitution. This selection of core rights and the introduction of a procedure for their scrutiny were the forerunners to the 1998 ILO Declaration on Fundamental Principles and Rights at Work and the 'follow-up procedure' now in operation.[14]

In addition, any question or dispute related to interpretation of the Constitution of the ILO (or of ILO instruments) can be submitted to the International Court of Justice.[15] Only rarely has the ICJ been called upon to give judgment on these matters—namely on four occasions between 1922 and 1932.[16] No case has been brought before the ICJ concerning freedom of association or the right to strike.

---

[10] Butler, H., *The International Labour Organization* (Oxford: OUP, 1939), 29.

[11] For discussion of this phenomenon see *General Report of the Committee of Experts on the Application of Conventions and Recommendations* (Geneva: ILO, 2002), paras. 86–102. For a concrete example see *CEACR: Individual Observation concerning Convention No. 87—The Former Yugoslav Republic of Macedonia* (2002): 'The Committee notes with regret that, since the entry into force in respect of The former Yugoslav Republic of Macedonia of this Convention in 1992, the Government's first report has still not been received'.

[12] See Chap. 15 below, at 359–61.

[13] This was decided by the ILO Governing Body at its 264th Session (Nov. 1995). See most recently for confirmation of this 'fundamental' status the discussions of the ILO Governing Body at its 282nd Session (Nov. 2001). Note that to this list is now added ILO Convention No. 182 on the Worst Forms of Child Labour 1999. There are also four designated 'priority' Conventions, see www.ilo.org/public/english/standards/norm/whatare/priority/index.htm.

[14] Discussed in Chap. 5 above, at 102–6; and below, at 203–6.   [15] ILO Constitution, Art. 37.

[16] Blanpain, R. (ed.), *International Encyclopaedia of Labour Law and Industrial Relations* (Deventer: Kluwer, 0000), Case Law Vol.4, ICJ–5; Osieke, n.2 above, 316–9.

Complaints may be made to the ILO itself through a number of procedures. Under Article 24 of the Constitution, employer and worker representatives can make 'representations' that a State has not implemented the standards contained in a Convention which it has ratified. Under Article 26, 'complaints' can be made by governments who have ratified the same Convention, delegates to the Conference and the Governing Body itself.[17] In addition, two special procedures have been created in respect of freedom of association.

II. CREATION OF SPECIAL MACHINERY FOR COMPLAINTS RELATING TO 'FREEDOM OF ASSOCIATION'

While debating the adoption of ILO conventions on the subject of freedom of association and collective bargaining, the 1948 International Labour Conference adopted a Resolution which requested the ILO Governing Body to enter into consultation with the UN for the purpose of examining what changes in existing supervisory machinery were necessary to ensure that these rights were safeguarded.[18] Conventions Nos. 87 and 98 were adopted prior to but in anticipation of this consultation.[19]

The International Labour Office suggested that an additional organ be created to consider complaints from governments, trade unions, and employers' organizations relating to the violation of freedom of association. These complaints would be screened by the Governing Body and then referred to a new Fact-Finding and Conciliation Commission on Freedom of Association (FFCC).[20] The task of the FFCC would be to carry out investigations, preferably in the country concerned, on questions of fact raised by complaints. ECOSOC agreed that it would forward to the Governing Body all allegations concerning infringement of trade union rights received from governments, trade unions, or employers' organizations against ILO Member States.[21] Also, ECOSOC decided to accept the services of the FFCC on behalf of the UN. 'Consequently, on occasion, cases concerning States which at the time were members of the United Nations but not of the ILO have been referred to the Commission, with the consent of the governments concerned.'[22]

The introduction of this procedure was discussed and voted upon at the 1950 ILC, but it was agreed, following concerns raised by the South African

---

[17] Complaints made by States tend to be rare. See Swepston, n.1 above, 338–9.

[18] *Record of Proceedings* (Geneva: ILO, 1948) ILC, 30th Session, App. X, 486.

[19] *Ibid.*, App. XI, 492.

[20] *Record of Proceedings* (Geneva: ILO, 1950) ILC, 33rd Session, App. XII, 564.

[21] Ben-Israel, R., *International Labour Standards: The Case of Freedom to Strike* (Deventer: Kluwer, 1988), 48–9.

[22] See *Report of the Director-General* (Geneva: ILO, 1984), 40.

and Australian governments,[23] that recourse to the FFCC would require the consent of the State named in the allegations. However, 'if an infringement was alleged to have occurred in a State that had ratified Conventions Nos. 87 and 98, the Governing Body could decide under Article 26 of the ILO Constitution, to refer the matter to a Commission of Inquiry rather than an FFCC', *without* the permission of the government concerned.[24]

Almost two years after the FFCC had been established, there had yet to be investigation of a single complaint, as no State would consent to its intervention.[25] By 1951 the Governing Body was already considering how this complaints procedure might be made more effective.[26]

All along it was envisaged that the Governing Body would be responsible for screening complaints before referring these to the FFCC. It was decided that this procedure should be rationalized by creating a special Committee of the Governing Body which would specialize in examining these complaints. Given the apparent failings of the FFCC procedure, certain members of the Governing Body became interested in establishing an influential Committee which would be capable of expressing an opinion on compliance with freedom of association obligations, without first having to secure State consent.[27]

The Governing Body Committee on Freedom of Association (or CFA) was to be entrusted with the preliminary examination of allegations concerning trade union rights submitted to the ILO. The Committee would be required to determine whether cases were worthy of further examination and whether the Governing Body should attempt to secure the consent of the government concerned to refer the case to the FFCC. It was not necessary that a *prima facie* case had been made out; it was sufficient that the complaint was worthy of further investigation.[28] The FFCC was to be retained and, indeed, cases are still referred to commissions of inquiry established under this title.[29]

[23] *Sixth Report of the International Labour Organization to the United Nations* (Geneva: ILO, 1952), App. V, Reports of the Governing Body Committee on Freedom of Association, 171–2. See also ILO, *Record of Proceedings* (1950) ILC, 33rd Session, App. XII.

[24] An example was the *ad hoc* Commission established for the purpose of investigating violations of ILO standards in Poland. See ILO, *Report of the Commission instituted under Article 26 of the Constitution of the ILO to Examine the Complaint on the Observance by Poland of Conventions Nos. 87 and 98* (1984) LXVII Official Bulletin, Series B, Special Supplement, para. 491. In 1998 complaints were also made under Art. 26 concerning the observance by Nigeria and Colombia of ILO Conventions Nos. 87 and 98. See GB 271/18/5 and GB 273/15/2.

[25] Indeed, it was not until 1964 that a State was prepared to do so: Swepston, L., 'Human Rights and Freedom of Association: Development through ILO Supervision' (1998) 137 *International Labour Review* 169 at 175.

[26] See, e.g., *Minutes of the 117th Session of the Governing Body* (Geneva: ILO, 1951), 45.

[27] *Ibid.*, per Mr Jouhaux at 46 and Mr Delaney at 47.

[28] *Sixth Report of the International Labour Organization to the United Nations*, n.23 above, App. V, Reports of the Governing Body Committee on Freedom of Association, 169–74.

[29] An example is the *Report of the Fact-Finding and Conciliation Commission on Freedom of Association concerning the Republic of South Africa: Prelude to Change: Industrial Relations in South Africa*, Official Bulletin, Special Supplement, Vol. LXXV, Series B.

Although objections were raised again by the South African government,[30] the Governing Body appeared confident that it was acting constitutionally. ECOSOC and the International Labour Conference had already accepted that, as part of the FFCC procedure, the Governing Body would screen complaints relating to freedom of association. The Governing Body considered itself entitled to make these modifications to its internal procedure 'without further reference to the Economic and Social Council or the International Labour Conference'.[31] It was on this basis that the members of the CFA were appointed. Membership consisted of three government, three worker, and three employer representatives, to be assisted in reaching decisions by an independent chairperson.[32]

This remains only a collective complaints procedure. An individual worker or employer cannot bring matters to the attention of the CFA, without organizational assistance from a trade union or employers' association with the appropriate credentials. These must be either a national organization directly interested in the matter or an international organization with ILO consultative status, or another international organization whose affiliates are directly affected by the matters raised by the complaint.[33] Nevertheless, the circumstances of an individual can provide the basis for a complaint, and the CFA has been willing to make recommendations in respect of the treatment of certain named persons.[34]

In 1955, a further constitutional challenge to the competence of the CFA was made in *Case No. 102 (South Africa)*.[35] The South African government had not ratified Conventions Nos. 87 and 98 and therefore objected to a complaint being heard before the CFA. The Committee responded that, by virtue of the Constitution, all ILO Members were bound to abide by the principle of freedom of association. The CFA also relied upon Article 19(5) of the ILO Constitution, which states that ILO Members can be required to report to the Director-General on the position of their law and practice in relation to unratified Conventions.[36]

The CFA cannot hear direct oral evidence from affected persons, and is therefore reliant on second-hand information provided by the complainant and the State in question. In 1964, in response to the frustrations this can cause, a procedure was adopted for the Governing Body to authorize visits by a

[30] *Minutes of the 117th Session of the Governing Body* (Geneva: ILO, 1951), 49.
[31] *Sixth Report of the International Labour Organization to the United Nations*, n.23 above, App. V, Reports of the Governing Body Committee on Freedom of Association, 88, para. 8.
[32] It has retained this structure to the present date.
[33] *Handbook of Procedures Relating to International Labour Conventions and Recommendations* (Geneva: ILO, 2002), para. 80; also *Procedures of the Fact-Finding and Conciliation Commission and the Committee on Freedom of Association for the Examination of Complaints Alleging Violation of Freedom of Association* (Geneva: ILO, 2002), para. 34.
[34] *Case No. 2111 (Peru)*, 326th Report of the CFA (2001), para. 451 at para. 477(c).
[35] *Case No. 102 (South Africa)*, 15th Report of the CFA (1955), para. 128.
[36] *Ibid.*, paras. 130–132. See above, at 187, for subsequent use of this power.

direct contacts mission, if the State agrees, which can attempt to ascertain the accuracy of information submitted to the CFA.[37] The CFA will then make further recommendations on the basis of the report made by the mission.[38] This was a mechanism also adopted by the Committee of Experts in 1968.[39]

In the CFA's first report, it became apparent that similar issues would arise requiring the formulation of general principles and that interpretation of the term 'freedom of association' would be required. The CFA observed that it had been 'impressed by the extent to which the same questions constantly recur in different cases' and submitted to the Governing Body certain criteria by which the Committee had been 'guided in considering individual cases and will, subject to any views which the Governing Body may express, continue to follow in examining further cases'.[40]

In seeking to enforce the constitutional guarantee of freedom of association and ensure implementation of Conventions Nos. 87 and 98, the CFA has elaborated on the substance of workers' rights contained in these instruments, developing its own distinctive jurisprudence. Its decisions are unanimous and therefore reflect a position reached, sometimes with difficulty, within a tripartite structure. The result is that statements of principle, once agreed upon, tend to be repeated verbatim in subsequent cases.

These principles have been summarized in the regularly revised *Digest* of CFA decisions[41] and have emerged as a 'veritable code of conduct' for ILO member states.[42] The perceived utility of this process is evident in the sheer number of complaints which have come before the CFA.[43] Nevertheless, the CFA itself remains aware of the need for continued improvements in its procedure and hopes that in future its conclusions will receive improved publicity.[44]

If the tripartite Governing Body approves the recommendations made by the CFA, the FFCC, or another *ad hoc* Commission, it will transmit these recommendations to the State concerned. In addition, the Governing Body will endeavour to ensure that States found to be in violation of ILO standards receive 'technical assistance' from the International Labour Office so as to make the necessary changes to their domestic legislation.[45]

[37] Note the refusal of Venezuela to accept such a Commission, communicated to the CFA on 11 Apr. 2002, discussed in 328th Report of the CFA (2002), para. 9.

[38] See, e.g., the Report of the Direct Contacts Mission to Guatemala, included in *Case No. 2122 (Guatemala)*, 326th Report of the CFA (2001), para. 82 at para. 84.

[39] See *General Report of the Committee of Experts on the Application of Conventions and Recommendations 2002* (Geneva: ILO, 2002), para. 12.

[40] *Sixth Report of the International Labour Organization to the United Nations* (Geneva: ILO, 1952) App. V, Reports of the CFA, 175. See also Valticos, n.2 above, 194.

[41] The latest was published in 1996 by the International Labour Office. See *Freedom of Association: Digest of Decisions and Principles of the Governing Body Committee on Freedom of Association* (4th edn., Geneva: ILO, 1996), hereafter 'CFA Digest of Decisions'.

[42] Servais, J.-M., 'ILO Standards on Freedom of Association and their Implementation' (1984) 123 *ILRev.* 765, 772.

[43] In 2002, these number well over 2,000 cases.

[44] 327th Report of the CFA (2002), paras. 18–26.   [45] See Swepston, n.1 above, 341.

III.   RECOGNITION OF A RIGHT TO STRIKE IN CASES DECIDED BY THE COMMITTEE ON FREEDOM OF ASSOCIATION (CFA)

Initially, the CFA was reluctant to comment on the right to strike. This may be attributable to the tripartite constitution of the Committee, which makes consensus difficult to reach. However, by 1960 if not before, the Committee was adamant that the right to strike is a necessary aspect of freedom of association and that therefore all complaints relating to industrial action come within its jurisdiction. This is the principle that it asserts today. The evolution of this jurisprudence is examined here, alongside the reasons why it may have taken this form. The influence of these principles on the findings of other ILO supervisory bodies is also outlined.

A.   THE GRADUAL EVOLUTION OF CFA JURISPRUDENCE

In the First Report of the CFA, two cases mentioned strike activity, but no principles were formulated relating to the legitimacy of industrial action. For example, *Case No. 2 (Venezuela)*, concerned the dissolution of forty-six petroleum unions, following a strike which broke out on oil fields following the expiry of a collective agreement. The CFA, in making its conclusions, noted only that the dissolution of these trade unions had not been submitted to the proper courts. The Committee made no general comment on a right to strike.[46] No information is available on the background negotiations between employer, employee, and government delegates on the Committee at that time. It is however possible that the CFA was merely uncertain of its role and was therefore unwilling to take diplomatic risks by formulating new principles on the right to strike.

It was only in the Second Report that any general principle was stated. In *Case No. 28 (UK–Jamaica)*, the WFTU alleged that the Jamaican government (then under the control of the UK) had used police, reinforced by troops, to break strikes and prevent public meetings. The CFA stated that 'the right to strike and that of organising trade union meetings are essential elements of trade union freedoms'.[47] Nevertheless, in this actual case, the Committee refrained from criticizing the government's conduct, as 'in view of the explanation provided by the Government', it did not seem that the complainant had sufficient evidence to support the claim.[48] The CFA had boldly propounded a principle, but had managed to avoid the political consequences associated with condemning the conduct of a powerful and influential nation, the UK.

---

[46] *Case No. 2 (Venezuela)*, 1st Report of the CFA (1952), para. 119.
[47] *Case No. 28 (UK–Jamaica)*, 2nd Report of the CFA (1952), para. 68.
[48] *Ibid.*, para. 69.

This first statement was much more forthright than those which immediately followed. In *Case No. 5 (India)*, the complainant alleged that whenever industrial disputes arose, the Indian government, under the guise of maintaining law and order, resorted to the arrest and detention of trade union members and organizers. The CFA pointed out that the complainant had made no reference to specific cases in which the right to strike had been prohibited and that therefore there was insufficient information to warrant further examination of the case. The Committee merely observed that '*in most countries* strikes are recognised as a legitimate weapon of trade unions in furtherance of their members' interests'.[49] Also, the Committee added that strikes are regarded as legitimate in these countries only 'so long as they are exercised peacefully and with due regard to temporary restrictions placed thereon (for example, cessation of strikes during conciliation and arbitration procedures, refraining from strikes in breach of collective agreements)'.[50]

This seems to have been an accurate observation. A unanimous resolution of the Governing Body of the ILO dated 4 March 1955 had established a Committee to report on the 'Freedom of Employers' and Workers' Organisations'. The Report indicated that some States placed limited restrictions on general strikes, strikes in essential services, or strikes in the public sector. Others placed procedural restrictions on strikes, or limited the legitimate aims of strike activity. However, virtually no country placed a total prohibition on the right to strike—the exceptions being Portugal and Turkey.[51] Still, it seems surprising that in this context the CFA should make a descriptive rather than a normative statement. Furthermore, pointing out that a right to strike is recognized 'in most countries' falls somewhat short of the CFA's earlier statement that the right to strike was an essential element of trade union freedom.

From 1954 to 1956, the CFA's response to strike action varied greatly from case to case. In some cases, the Committee would merely state that 'it is not called upon to give an opinion on the question as to how far the right to strike in general should be regarded as constituting a trade union right'.[52] The reason given was that such an entitlement was not specifically dealt with in Conventions Nos. 87 and 98.

In *Case No. 102 (South Africa)*, the right to strike had been denied to 'African workers'.[53] The Committee noted that the Declaration of

[49] *Case No. 5 (India)*, 4th Report of the CFA (1952), para. 18.

[50] *Ibid.*, para. 18.

[51] *Report of the Committee on Freedom of Employers' and Workers' Organizations* (Geneva: ILO, 1956), Vol. XXXIX, *Official Bulletin* No. 9, 475. However, the Committee declined to consider 'the general question of the existence in law of a "right to strike" or a "right to lockout" or the meaning of these terms'. This is consistent with the CFA's reluctance to comment on the existence of such a right at that date.

[52] *Case No. 60 (Japan)*, 12th Report of the CFA (1954), para. 53; *Case No. 102 (South Africa)*, 15th Report (1955), para. 75; *Case No. 73 (British Honduras)*, 17th Report (1956), para. 72.

[53] *Case No. 102 (South Africa)*, 15th Report of the CFA (1955), para. 77.

Philadelphia now included in the ILO Constitution stated that 'all peoples everywhere' were entitled to social justice. It decided that there was no universal entitlement to take industrial action, making precisely the same statement as that quoted above. However, the Committee concluded that if, within a country, a right to strike was generally accorded to workers or their organizations, 'there should be no racial discrimination with respect to those to whom it is accorded'.[54] It may seem surprising that the Committee did not take an opportunity to comment upon the importance of protection of the right to strike, given its earlier comments in *Case No. 28*, especially as the entire tone of this report was condemnatory. This case reflects the uncertain state of CFA principles on the right to strike at this particular point in time.

By and large, the Committee settled on an ambiguous formula, evident in cases such as *Case No. 47 (India)* and *Case No. 50 (Turkey)*. In these cases the CFA commented that, although Convention No. 87 did not deal with the right to strike, such a right 'is generally accorded to workers and their organisations'.[55] In each of these cases the Committee decided that 'the case as a whole' did not call for further examination by the Governing Body.

Nevertheless, the meaning of the term 'generally' seems to have shifted, initially indicating that the right *was* accepted 'in most countries', to meaning that the right *should* be recognized, subject to certain exceptions. This is evident from *Case No. 148 (Poland)*, in which the International Confederation of Free Trade Unions (ICFTU) claimed that, although there was no law in Poland prohibiting the right to strike, official disapproval meant that it was almost impossible to take such action. The Central Trade Union Organ had adopted a resolution in 1947 in which it recognized that there could be no strikes in Poland, and stated that it would view any industrial action as improper and harmful.[56] The CFA reviewed its past case law on this question, stating that 'in a number of cases the Committee has recognised in general terms the importance of the right to strike', citing *Case No. 47 (India)* and *Case No. 50 (Turkey)*. While the Committee used the same formulation as previously, commenting that 'the right to strike is generally admitted as an integral part of the general right of workers to further their economic interests', it recommended that the Governing Body take note of its conclusions and convey these to the Polish government. The stance taken by the CFA on Polish industrial relations seems to indicate that, over time, the Committee became more committed to the protection of a right to strike. This commitment is also evident from the CFA's decision in *Case No. 111 (USSR)*.[57]

---

[54] *Ibid.*, para. 154.
[55] *Case No. 47 (India)*, 6th Report of the CFA (1952), para. 724; *Case No. 50 (Turkey)*, 6th Report of the CFA (1952), para. 864.
[56] *Case No. 148 (Poland)*, 22nd Report of the CFA (1956), para. 66 at para. 97.
[57] *Case No. 111 (USSR)*, 23rd Report of the CFA (1956), para. 4.

The report on *Case No. 111 (USSR)* spans over ninety pages and forms the entirety of the twenty-third Report of the CFA. A small part of this report is devoted to the right to strike. In its 'Conclusions', the Committee appears to draw upon the conclusions stated in the Polish case. The Soviet government had given formal reassurances that there was no official sanction against strikes and that industrial action would not be regarded as absenteeism. The CFA reaffirmed that the right to strike 'is generally regarded as an integral part of the general right of workers and their organisations to defend their economic interests' and recommended that the Soviet government inform its workers that no penalties would be imposed upon those who took industrial action.[58] The CFA also requested that the USSR provide further information concerning the action which was to be taken on the basis of the Committee's recommendations and suggested that if the Governing Body did not receive 'satisfactory information', it should seek the consent of the USSR to refer the case to the FFCC.

It is interesting that the active promotion of a right to strike should begin with a response to the situation in Eastern bloc countries. One may wonder whether these findings were influenced by the development of Cold War politics. This condemnation of Communist States may have been what finally reconciled employer and certain State representatives on the CFA to protection of the right to strike. Such criticism was no doubt warranted, but is also ironic as Poland and the USSR were strong advocates of trade union rights in Western states and had argued for the inclusion of a right to strike in ILO and UN instruments.[59] The USSR could not therefore respond by denying that the right to strike should be guaranteed as a workers' right.

CFA criticism of the USSR in *Case No. 111* was met with a furious response, which is recorded in the Minutes of the 133rd Session of the Governing Body. Nevertheless, the Soviet government representative did not deny its obligations to protect a right to strike. Instead the USSR made a point of claiming that active steps had been taken to acquaint Soviet worker representatives and others with Soviet labour legislation.[60]

In the aftermath of *Case No. 111*, the CFA began to assert its entitlement to address complaints relating to the right to strike. In *Case No. 163 (Burma)* and *Case No. 169 (Turkey)*, the CFA stressed that 'allegations relating to prohibitions of the right to strike are not outside its competence when the question of freedom of association is involved'.[61] The suggestion was that freedom of association and the right to strike were linked.

---

[58] *Ibid.*, at para. 227(8).   [59] See Chap. 5 above, 117–18.

[60] *Minutes of the 133rd Session of the Governing Body* (Geneva: ILO, 1956), Fifth Sitting, Mr Arutiunian, 49–50.

[61] *Case No. 163 (Burma)*, 27th Report of the CFA (1958), para. 46 at para. 51; or 'in so far as such prohibitions affect the exercise of trade union rights': see *Case No. 169 (Turkey)*, 28th Report (1958), para. 297.

In the 1958 case on Turkish industrial relations, the Committee expressed its disappointment that Turkey had not made the legislative changes it had undertaken when responding to the complaint made in *Case No. 50*. The CFA recommended that the Governing Body request the Turkish government to provide further information on the progress made.[62] Contrasting the Committee's approach in the two cases, this decision seems to indicate a move towards a more proactive approach.

Then, in 1960, the CFA committed itself to considering the merits of cases concerning the right to strike, regardless of whether the strike would be considered unlawful in the country concerned. The starting point was *Case No. 170 (France–Madagascar)*,[63] where a strike relating to national economic policy was declared illegal by the General Inspectorate of Labour in Madagascar. The Committee decided that the strike was aimed at changing government policy and that therefore the restriction was justified. However, 'the mere fact of a strike being regarded as unlawful in a country would not be sufficient to cause the Committee to refrain from examining the merits of the case'.[64] The conditions that have to be fulfilled under the law to render a strike to be lawful must be reasonable.[65]

The result is that the ILO Committee on Freedom of Association has ever since been willing to criticize any State which has not taken sufficient steps to ensure protection of the right to strike. Indeed, this right is regarded as 'one of the essential means through which workers and their organisations may promote and defend their economic and social interests'.[66] It is protected as a vital element of freedom of association, albeit subject to certain restrictions. A more detailed outline of this extensive jurisprudence on the right to strike is examined in Part IV.

B.   REASONS FOR THE ADOPTION OF THIS PRINCIPLE

The development of this principle may be attributed to a desire to follow recent international trends. In 1961 a provision guaranteeing the right to strike was included in Article 6 of the European Social Charter. In 1966 a similar provision was included in Article 8 of the International Covenant on Economic and Social Rights of Workers. However, CFA findings concerning the right to strike narrowly preceded these developments. It is therefore possible to make the inverse argument; namely, that the Committee's active promotion of a right to strike was, at least in part, responsible for the later

---

[62] *Case No. 169 (Turkey)*, 28th Report of the CFA (1958), para. 297.

[63] *Case No. 170 (France–Madagascar)*, 37th Report of the CFA (1960), para. 12.

[64] *Ibid.*, at para. 41.

[65] A similar approach was taken in *Case No. 172 (Argentine Republic)*, 41st Report of the CFA (1960), para. 105 at para. 157. See also *Case No. 208 (Ivory Coast)*, 46th Report (1961), para. 8 at para. 15; and *Case No. 143 (Spain)*, 47th Report (1961), para. 66.

[66] *CFA Digest of Decisions*, n.41 above, para. 475. See for a recent full reiteration of this principle *Case No. 1581 (Thailand)*, 327th Report (2002), para. 111.

recognition of the right in these two international instruments. Rather than speculate on this chain of events, it may be preferable to consider the conclusions reached by the CFA in the light of standard principles of treaty interpretation.

According to the Vienna Convention and indeed customary international law, the CFA was obliged to interpret the term 'freedom of association' in good faith and in accordance with its ordinary meaning.[67] There are, however, times when reference to the ordinary meaning may not be the most fruitful course of action,[68] such as where a straightforward definition is not readily ascertainable. This is the difficulty which arises when seeking to ascertain the ordinary meaning of 'freedom of association', which can be interpreted in two quite different ways.[69]

One view is that freedom of association should be regarded as a civil liberty. A guarantee of freedom of association means only that a person is free to join an organization and associate with others. This is an individual liberty, not a collective entitlement. Therefore, the actions of the collectivity are not themselves protected under this head. Strikes, in particular, are viewed as coercive and restrictive of the individual choices of others. They are not regarded as a legitimate extension of this liberty.

The CFA has taken another approach to interpretation of freedom of association, specific to the context of the workplace. The Committee recognizes that combination in a trade union may be a function of individual liberty, but this liberty has little meaning if workers are unable to pursue their own interests within such organizations. Worker solidarity allows workers to overcome the limitations inherent in individual contracts of employment, to achieve fair conditions of employment, and to participate in making decisions which affect their own lives and society at large. In the absence of a right to strike, it remains difficult (if not impossible) for workers to achieve these goals. From this premise stems the CFA view that freedom of association implies not only the right of workers and employers freely to form organizations of their own choosing, but also the right to pursue collective activities for the defence of workers' occupational, social, and economic interests.[70]

Thus the CFA did not disregard the 'ordinary meaning' of the term freedom of association. Instead, the Committee recognized the ambiguity

[67] Vienna Convention on the Law of Treaties 1969, Arts. 31 and 32. The Convention came into force on 27 Jan. 1980, after the Committee had heard over 1,000 decisions. However, the principles of customary international law, which the Vienna Convention was intended to codify, were relevant. See, inter alia, Golder v UK, 1 EHRR 524 (1975); Beagle Channel Arbitration (Argentina v Chile) (1979) 52 ILR 93 at 124.

[68] See Legal Consequences for States of the Continued Presence of South Africa in Namibia (South West Africa) Notwithstanding Security Council Resln 276 (1970) (1976) 49 ILR 3; also (1971) ICJ Reports 16 at 185.

[69] See Chap. 3 above, at 65–9.

[70] CFA Digest of Decisions, n.41 above, paras. 447 and 473.

of the term and its connotations in the particular sphere of labour relations, which entitled the Committee to look at the context in which the term was used and the purpose of relevant international instruments.[71] The first, and most obvious, is the ILO Constitution, which contains the primary guarantee of freedom of association, upon which the CFA bases its jurisdiction.

The present ILO Constitution comprises Part XIII of the Treaty of Versailles 1919 and the supplementary Declaration of Philadelphia 1944. Neither instrument contains any explicit guidance on the appropriate interpretation of the guarantees of freedom of association. Nevertheless, it is possible to isolate certain aims expressed in these constitutional documents which appear to have guided the CFA in making its decisions. As noted previously, the primary aim of the ILO is 'social justice', which is to take precedence over other economic goals.[72] It is apparent from the ILO Constitution that social justice involves the improvement of conditions of work[73] and the ability of workers to participate in making the decisions which affect their working lives, either by means of collective bargaining or tripartite consultation.[74] The CFA says that it has made direct reference to these constitutional goals when interpreting the constitutional provision for freedom of association.[75] Examination of the ILO Constitution therefore goes some way to explaining how the CFA came to draw this link between freedom of association and the right to strike.

In addition, the CFA has said that it considers that 'it should be guided in its task, among other things, by the provisions that have been approved by the Conference and embodied in the Conventions on freedom of association, which afford a basis for comparison when particular allegations are examined'.[76] The two most relevant Conventions for this purpose are Conventions Nos. 87 and 98, now recognized as encapsulating 'core' ILO principles.

Convention No. 87 has been relied upon as the predominant basis for protection of the right to strike. Article 3 of this Convention states that workers' and employers' organizations are to have the right 'to organise their administration and activities and to formulate their programmes'. Under Article 10, the term 'organisation' is said to mean 'any organisation of workers or of employers for furthering the interests of workers and employers'. Industrial action can be said to be one of many 'workers'

---

[71] Vienna Convention on the Law of Treaties 1969, Arts. 31(2) and (3).

[72] Preamble to Part XIII of the Treaty of Versailles 1919 and Declaration of Philadelphia 1944, Art. II(c). See also Chap. 5 above, at 97 and 100.

[73] Preamble to Part XIII of the Treaty of Versailles 1919 and Declaration of Philadelphia 1944, Arts. II(a), II(b), III(d), III(g) etc.

[74] Declaration of Philadelphia 1944, Arts. I(d) and III(e).

[75] *CFA Digest of Decisions* (3rd edn., Geneva: ILO, 1985), paras. 23 and 53; and 4th edn., n.41 above, paras. 1–3.

[76] *CFA Digest of Decisions* (1985), n.75 above, 2; Committee of Experts on the Application of Conventions and Recommendations, *General Survey on Freedom of Association and Collective Bargaining* (Geneva: ILO, 1994), hereafter 'CEACR General Survey', 65.

activities' protected under Article 3, and indeed it is described by the CFA as an 'essential means' of furthering workers' interests in accordance with Article 10.[77] Convention No. 98 has been used not so much as a basis for recognition of the right to strike, but for the principle that workers should be protected from sanctions when taking industrial action. This is due to Article 1, paragraph 1 of which states that 'workers shall enjoy adequate protection against acts of anti-union discrimination in respect of their employment'.

The remaining question is whether there is any supplementary material, which would have assisted the CFA in reaching its conclusions.[78] As noted above, the *travaux préparatoires*, namely the *Records of Proceedings* for International Labour Conferences between 1947 and 1949, are of remarkably little assistance in this regard.[79] Given the absence of any clear guidance on legislative intent, the manner in which the CFA has forged a connection between freedom of association and the right to strike may seem bold to some, but is defensible with reference to fundamental principles of treaty interpretation.

C. ACCEPTANCE OF THIS PRINCIPLE BY OTHER ILO SUPERVISORY BODIES

Within the ILO, the Governing Body has routinely endorsed CFA findings.[80] The Director-General's reports have also contained principles developed by the Committee.[81] The FFCC has applied CFA principles to its investigations, one example being the 1992 report on industrial relations within the Republic of South Africa.[82] In addition, when a legislative problem has arisen and the country concerned has ratified the Conventions to which a complaint refers, the CFA can draw the matter to the attention of the Committee of Experts on the Application of Conventions and Recommendations (CEACR). The latter will follow the development of the situation during the regular examination of the reports submitted by the government concerned, in relation to the Convention in question.[83] The

---

[77] *CFA Digest of Decisions* (1985), n.75 above, para. 363. The CFA's attitude on this point is also discussed in Hodges-Aeberhard, J., and de Dios, O., 'The Principles of the Committee on Freedom of Association Concerning Strikes' (1987) 126 *ILRev.* 543, 548. See also Chap. 5 above, at 120; and App. 1.

[78] Ris, M., 'Treaty Interpretation and ICJ Recourse to *Travaux Préparatoires*: Towards a Proposed Amendment of Articles 31 and 32 of the Vienna Convention on the Law of Treaties' (1991) 14 *Boston College International and Comparative Law Review* 111 at 112.

[79] See Chap. 5 above, 114–20.

[80] See, e.g., the conclusion of the Governing Body's debate on the CFA's recommendations in respect of *Case No. 111 (USSR)*, 23rd Report of the CFA (1956) in ILO, *Minutes of the 133rd Session of the Governing Body* (1956) International Labour Office, Geneva, Fifth Sitting, 54.

[81] See, e.g., *Report of the Director-General: Human Rights—A Common Responsibility* (Geneva: ILO, 1988), 19.

[82] *Report of the Fact-Finding Conciliation Commission on Freedom of Association concerning the Republic of South Africa* (Geneva: ILO, 1992) at 93–4 and 180–1.

[83] See, e.g., *General Report of the Committee of Experts on the Application of Conventions and Recommendations* (Geneva: ILO, 2002) ILC, 90th Session, para. 47.

CEACR also provides 'General Surveys' on freedom of association and collective bargaining under Article 19 of the ILO Constitution. There was a risk that the principles developed by the Committee of Experts might clash with those formulated by the CFA,[84] but instead the CEACR has arrived at the same conclusions, albeit at a slightly slower pace.

The 1959 CEACR *General Survey* suggested that the prohibition of strikes in the public sector might 'constitute a considerable restriction on the potential activities of trade unions' and therefore could be contrary to Article 10 of Convention No. 87.[85] In another *General Survey* of 1973,[86] the CEACR used Convention No. 87 as a basis from which to state its concern over restriction of the industrial action, but did not make a positive statement in favour of the right to strike. This state of affairs had changed by 1983. A *General Survey* of that year endorsed the formulation of the right to strike adopted by the CFA, namely that 'the right to strike is one of the essential means available to workers and their organisations for the promotion of their economic and social interests'.[87] This statement was repeated in the *General Survey* produced by the Committee of Experts in 1994.[88] In 2002, the CEACR *General Report* recognized that the CFA had been 'the origin of a number of important decisions setting forth the principles according to which freedom of association should be applied in different circumstances' and, *inter alia*, its significant impact as regards 'recognition of the right to strike'. It was said that the Committee of Experts 'attaches great importance to the permanence of the privileged links it has with the Committee on Freedom of Association'.[89]

The adoption by the CEACR of CFA jurisprudence has been criticized by employer delegates in the ILO Conference Committee, but notably only within the last decade. In 1994, the employers' group set out what it now regards as the authoritative statement of its opposition to recognition of the right to strike under ILO Conventions Nos. 87 and 98.[90] Employer representatives have stated that they do not accept that the text of these Conven-

---

[84] Cf. past clashes between the ECSR and the Governmental Committee responsible for supervising the implementation of the European Social Charter 1961. See below, at 218.

[85] *CEACR General Survey* (Geneva: ILO, 1959), para. 68; *CEACR General Survey* (Geneva: ILO, 1994), 65.

[86] *CEACR General Survey* (Geneva: ILO, 1973), 44–5 at para. 107 states that 'a general prohibition of strikes constitutes a considerable restriction of the opportunities open to trade unions for furthering and defending the interests of their members (Article 10 of Convention No. 87) and of the right of trade unions to organise their activities (Article 3)'.

[87] *CEACR General Survey* (Geneva: ILO, 1983), 62, para. 200.

[88] *CEACR General Survey* (Geneva: ILO, 1994), 64–5, paras. 146–147. See for a reiteration of its acceptance of jurisprudence recognizing the right to strike and its 'privileged links' with the CFA *General Report of the Committee of Experts on the Application of Conventions and Recommendations* (Geneva: ILO, 2002), paras. 19–20.

[89] *General Report of the Committee of Experts on the Application of Conventions and Recommendations* (Geneva: ILO, 2002), paras. 19–20.

[90] *Record of Proceedings* (Geneva: ILO, 1994) ILC, 81st Session, 25/31–41.

tions can give rise to a global, detailed and precise, absolute and unlimited entitlement to take industrial action. They also assert that this approach has deterred ratification of that Convention.[91] In this, the employers have yet to be explicitly supported by any government representative, but it should also be noted that only a very few government representatives have voiced support for the position of the CEACR on this point.[92]

The workers' group has responded by asking why employers have only now changed their stance, identifying a 'striking inconsistency' between this position and that which the employers' group took prior to 1989, when it fully supported this principle and the position still taken by employer representatives in the CFA.[93] The workers have suggested that if the employers' group was so concerned it could take the matter to the ICJ; nor do they consider it feasible to claim that the Committee of Experts' interpretation deterred ratification, since Conventions Nos. 87 and 98 have had among the highest numbers of ratifications.[94] Moreover, the workers consider that it is significant that the Committee of Experts, being 'composed of independent persons coming from all the continents [have] confirmed the position of the Committee on Freedom of Association concerning the right to strike'.[95]

Initially, this challenge to the CEACR jurisprudence seemed to make little difference. In practice, the employers' group would refer to its position, as stated in the 1994 ILC *Record of Proceedings*, but would ultimately agree to issue a special paragraph in cases where there were blatant violations of freedom of association, including the right to strike.[96] This was presumably because employer members of the Committee on the Application of Standards were prepared to acknowledge that 'the principle of industrial action ... [did form] part of the principles of freedom of association'.[97] They accepted that a right to strike for workers was deserving of protection, alongside a right to lock out for employers, and as such could be recognized as an integral part of international customary law. It should not be abolished or unduly restricted. What they objected to was only the

[91] *Report of the Committee on the Application of Standards* (Geneva: ILO, 1999) ILC, 87th Session, para. 113. For a more general warning by the employers of extension of provisions through interpretation see *Report of the Committee on the Application of Standards* (Geneva: ILO, 2000) ILC, 88th Session, para. 25.

[92] Those which have include Denmark, Finland, Germany, Iceland, Norway, and Sweden. See *Record of Proceedings* (Geneva: ILO, 2000) ILC, 88th Session, 23/70; and *Record of Proceedings* (Geneva: ILO, 2001) ILC, 89th Session, 2/22–3.

[93] *Report of the Committee on the Application of Standards* (Geneva: ILO, 1999) ILC, 87th Session, para. 121.

[94] *Report of the Committee on the Application of Standards* (Geneva: ILO, 2000) ILC, 88th Session, paras. 28–29. See also Chap. 5 above, at 110.

[95] *Record of Proceedings* (Geneva: ILO, 2002) ILC, 90th Session, 28/11.

[96] See, e.g., Part II of the Report of the Committee on the Application of Standards in *Record of Proceedings* (Geneva: ILO, 2000) ILC, 88th Session, 23/69 and 23/71.

[97] *Record of Proceedings* (Geneva: ILO, 1997) ILC, 85th Session, 19/35.

implicit protection of such a right under ILO Conventions in which it was not specifically mentioned.

However, in the last two years this debate has become more heated. In the 2001 Conference Committee on the Application of Standards the employers' group declined to support the recommendations of the Committee of Experts on the subject of protection of the right to strike in Belarus and Colombia. It was subsequently accused by worker members of hypocrisy, given its support for condemnation of restriction of industrial action during the Cold War period: 'The arguments that employer members used today were the same arguments put forward by the Soviet regime to undermine the ILO supervisory system ... Hence, the worker members had no choice but to believe that the attack by worker members on the Committee of Experts was based on political rather than legal grounds. This stand smacked of opportunism, as politics often did'.[98] The employers replied by observing that they had never made any positive statement in favour of a right to strike which they had objected to as far back as 1953. This seems somewhat specious, given that the jurisprudence of the CFA and CEACR on this point was developed some time after this date and that the employers had been in the majority of the Conference Committee which had approved recommendations made to States regarding the right to strike up to 1993.

The employers' group has also recently downplayed the significance of CFA jurisprudence, regarding that Committee to be only 'a conciliation, mediation and fact-finding body' with *no* legal mandate. Its sole role was to inform the Governing Body of reported infringements of freedom of association. It could provide no basis for the interpretation of ILO Conventions Nos. 87 and 98.[99] This view has been fiercely resisted in 2002 by the workers' group[100] and the Committee of Experts itself.[101]

The employers' agenda seems to be to force the right to strike onto the Conference agenda. During its demonstration of non-co-operation in 2001, the employers' members 'recalled that they had asked for this issue to be put on the agenda of the Conference on several occasions but nothing had ever happened', adding that 'this was probably because of the fears of the possible results of such a discussion'.[102] It was said that 'were this matter

[98] Part II of the Report of the Committee on the Application of Standards in *Record of Proceedings* (Geneva: ILO, 2001) ILC, 89th Session, 19 Part 2/20–1.

[99] Part II of the Report of the Committee on the Application of Standards in *Record of Proceedings* (Geneva: ILO, 2001) ILC, 89th Session, 19 Part 2/21–2.

[100] *Record of Proceedings* (Geneva: ILO, 2002) ILC, 90th Session, 28/11 and 30/8. Also see *Record of Proceedings* (Geneva: ILO, 2001) ILC, 89th Session, at 17/19, per Mr Parrot (workers' delegate, Canada): 'We have only one thing to say to employers and government who are tempted to follow this idea. The right of association and collective bargaining include the right to strike. We cannot and will not compromise on this.'

[101] *General Report of the Committee of Experts on the Application of Conventions and Recommendations* (Geneva: ILO, 2002), para. 19.

[102] Part II of the Report of the Committee on the Application of Standards in *Record of Proceedings* (Geneva: ILO, 2001) ILC, 89th Session, 19 Part 2/21.

to be placed on the Conference agenda, the workers might be surprised to discover how liberal the employers could be on the issue of the right to strike and lockouts'.[103] Here the linking of workers' strikes to employers' lock-outs is significant, for it suggests that they should receive identical treatment. Such a claim fails to recognize the separate and distinctive justificatory basis of each form of collective action.[104] Moreover, given the privileged status of Conventions Nos. 87 and 98 as core or fundamental ILO instruments, distancing the right to strike from coverage by their provisions might well diminish the present priority given to protection of this entitlement.[105] For the meantime, however, it seems that government delegates are reluctant to play an active role in the employers' campaign, for this would entail resiling from long-established ILO principles and, tacitly, undermining the authority of the Committee of Experts.

IV.   THE FOLLOW-UP TO THE ILO DECLARATION ON FUNDAMENTAL PRINCIPLES AND RIGHTS OF WORKERS 1998

The latest addition to existing ILO supervisory procedures was the 'follow-up mechanism' set out in the Annex to the 1998 ILO Declaration on Fundamental Principles and Rights of Workers. The Declaration is not 'a substitute for the established supervisory mechanisms', but provides an additional means by which to scrutinize State compliance with fundamental workers' rights, regardless of ratification of ILO Conventions.

The 'follow-up' has two facets. The first is an 'annual review' of the extent to which those Member States which have not ratified one of the core Conventions comply with the standards contained therein. This replaced the special reporting system which was introduced in 1995 in respect of core ILO Conventions.[106] The second is a 'global report' which is to provide a 'dynamic global picture' inclusive of all States, relating to each category of the core labour standards. There is to be one global report per year for a four-year period; after which time the process will be reviewed. Freedom of association and collective bargaining were the focus of the global report for the year 2000, entitled *Your Voice at Work*. A global report on forced labour was presented in 2001 and the global report on child labour was released in 2002. The global report on discrimination should follow in 2003.[107] These are to be compiled by a 'Group of Experts', whose members' credentials are comparable to those of the Committee of Experts and which is also appointed by the tripartite ILO Governing Body.

---

[103] *Ibid.*, 19 Part 2/24.   [104] See Chap. 1 above, at 7–8.

[105] See Chap. 5 above, at 104–5.   [106] See above, at 187.

[107] See for the full text of these Reports to date www.ilo.org/public/english/standards/decl/publ/reports/index.htm.

The aim of the follow-up procedure has been not so much to expose violations of core labour standards, but more to examine the underlying factors which led to such violations. It is thought that if these factors can be identified, then it may be possible for the State in question to tackle them, preferably with the assistance of the ILO and other international organizations.[108] The ILO Director-General, Juan Somavia, has stated that the Declaration is intended to 'strengthen and support the ILO's technical cooperation activities as a whole'.[109] The budget allocated for such assistance over this four-year period is in the region of at least $US 45 million.[110] These reports not only criticize State conduct, but also assess the effectiveness of ILO action. The Legal Adviser to the Committee on the Declaration of Principles has gone so far as to say that 'the mechanism has a promotional objective; not a supervisory one'.[111]

What is uncertain is whether this process will aid protection of the right to strike. The CFA has long held that this entitlement is inextricably linked to 'freedom of association and the effective recognition of the right to collective bargaining', which are set out expressly as fundamental rights in the 1998 Declaration. However, it is not apparent from records of debates over the drafting of the Charter that there was clear consensus on this issue.[112] It was stressed at that time that the 'fundamental rights' listed did not mean the specific provisions of 'core' conventions, such as ILO Conventions Nos. 87 and 98, but merely their general principles.[113]

The annual reviews have sought only general information on compliance with the 1998 Declaration. The right to strike has not been explicitly mentioned in the questionnaire submitted by the International Labour Office to States.[114] Nevertheless, certain States did submit information on

---

[108] ILO Declaration of Fundamental Principles and Rights at Work and its Follow-Up 1998, Art. 3.

[109] Report of the Director-General, *Decent Work* (Geneva: ILO, 1999), 8.

[110] Trebilcock, A., 'The ILO Declaration on Fundamental Principles and Rights at Work: A New Tool' in Blanpain, R., and Engels, C. (eds.), *The ILO and the Social Challenges of the 21st Century: The Geneva Lectures* (The Hague: Kluwer, 2001), 110.

[111] *Report of the Committee on the Declaration of Principles: Discussion in Plenary* (Geneva: ILO, 1998), ILC, 86th Session, para. 78. See also *Report of the Committee on the Declaration of Principles: Submission, Discussion and Adoption* (Geneva: ILO, 1998), ILC, 86th Session, 3, per Mr Moher (Government delegate, Canada): 'follow-up is purely promotional in nature and therefore is not, and cannot be, punitive or complaints-based'.

[112] See Trebilcock, n.110 above, 108.

[113] *Report of the Committee on the Declaration of Principles: Discussion in Plenary* (Geneva: ILO, 1998), ILC, 86th Session, paras. 205–213; and *Report of the Committee on the Declaration of Principles: Submission and Adoption* (Geneva: ILO, 1998), ILC, 86th Session, 6, per Mr Potter (employers' delegate, US): 'the Declaration does not impose on Member States the detailed obligations of Conventions that they have not freely ratified, and does not impose on countries that have not ratified the fundamental Conventions the supervisory mechanisms that apply to ratified Conventions'.

[114] See *Annual Review* (Geneva: ILO, 2000), Annex 5: 'Report Forms for the Annual Reports: Report Form on Freedom of Association and the Effective Recognition of the Right to Collective Bargaining', 52. This document is available on www.ilo.org/public/english/standards/relm/gb/docs/gb277/d1–index.htm.

the right to strike with their reports, noting the restrictions that they placed on such a right. For example, the Republic of Korea reported that teachers were not permitted to take industrial action.[115] A dispute arose when the ICFTU wished to contribute its comments to the annual review, it not being evident from the wording of the 1998 Declaration whether their observations could be receivable. It was decided by the International Labour Office and the Group of Experts that such comments were admissible, on the basis that the ICFTU was a representative international trade union organization, with the capacity to study and accumulate accurate information on the conduct of States. Data provided by the ICFTU on industrial action, which was not corroborated by State reports, was thereby included in the annual review.[116] This proved important, given the low reporting rate for the annual review, which still lies at approximately 70 per cent. Nevertheless, this information could not be presented in the form of complaints and the summaries contained in the first annual review did not appear to make any judgment on the findings. This was left to the global report on *Your Voice at Work*. It is only subsequent to that report that the annual review has contained more critical commentary on the right to strike.[117]

Your Voice at Work connected freedom of association and the effective right to collective bargaining to workers' participation in workplace decision-making and freedom of speech. It claimed that 'good governance of the labour market based on respect for these principles and rights can contribute to stable economic, social and political development'.[118] The report therefore illustrated, once again, the capacity for ILO supervisory mechanisms to recognize the overlap between civil, political, and socio-economic entitlements. There was, in particular, an express link to 'democratic values'.[119] The document sought to identify the best and worst State practices in the context of globalization, while identifying targets for ILO technical assistance.

The right to strike was explicitly mentioned in Part I of this global report. It was said to be 'the logical corollary of the effective realization of the right to collective bargaining', because where it does not exist 'bargaining risks being inconsequential—a dead letter'.[120] *Your Voice at Work* stressed that the right to strike was only a narrow right, which is to be exercised as a 'last resort' subject to certain listed 'restrictions'. In this respect, the view taken of the legitimate scope of industrial action is potentially more circumscribed

---

[115] *Ibid.*, Annex 6: 'Information from Reports', para. 23.

[116] *Ibid.* See, e.g., the information provided on Jordan, Qatar, Vietnam, and China.

[117] See *Review of Annual Reports under the Follow Up to the ILO Declaration on Fundamental Principles and Rights at Work* (2001) GB 280/3/2 on 'Freedom of Association and the Effective Recognition of Collective Bargaining'.

[118] *Your Voice at Work* (Geneva: ILO, 2000) ILC, 88th Session, 'Executive Summary', p. vii.

[119] *Ibid.*, 2, para. 6; and 25–38.   [120] *Ibid.*, 37, para. 101.

than that recognized by the CFA,[121] but it may be a mistake to read too much into these few paragraphs. The report continued by naming, in a critical fashion, various States that place excessive restrictions on industrial action and impose severe penalties on participants in strikes. This received a negative reaction from the US employers' delegate, who observed that 'the Declaration is not designed to address detailed legal questions derived from the relevant Conventions themselves such as . . . the delineation of the right to strike'.[122]

Part II of *Your Voice at Work* lacked any detailed analysis of how the ILO might be able to assist in remedying specific breaches of the right to strike. Moreover, the right to strike was not specifically mentioned when the 2001 ILC set out the 'principal hurdles to be addressed' in respect of the follow-up on freedom of association and collective bargaining.[123] Nevertheless, ILO technical advisory services provided to Cambodia seem to have addressed issues relating to industrial action and an ILO mission has recently assessed Bulgaria's legislation and practice on the right to strike.[124] It therefore appears that industrial action does come within the remit of the 'follow-up' procedure and is receiving some attention.

V. CONCLUSION: GLOBAL EFFECTIVENESS OF STANDARDS

In 1957, C. Wilfred Jenks predicted that the decisions of the CFA had the potential to 'harden into customary international law', as they became accepted international doctrine.[125] Decisions on freedom of association made by the CFA and the Committee of Experts have long been respected within the ILO. What is less readily ascertainable is their impact on domestic legal systems and the conduct of States.

The ILO CEACR seems confident of the impact that its findings (and those of the CFA) have on States. For example, its 2001 general report on the application of standards identified forty-six new cases in which governments had made changes to their law and practice, following the comments given by the CEACR. Since 1964, there have been 2,276 instances in which the Committee has expressed satisfaction with the progress achieved since its criticisms were received. The CEACR claimed that 'these results are tangible proof of the effectiveness of the supervisory system'.[126] However, failure to

---

[121] Cf. Part IV below.

[122] *Record of Proceedings* (Geneva: ILO, 2000) ILC, 88th Session, 11/3, per Mr Potter, US employers' delegate.

[123] *Record of Proceedings* (Geneva: ILO, 2001) ILC, 89th Session, 2/1.

[124] *Record of Proceedings* (Geneva: ILO, 2002) ILC, 90th Session, 6/2 and 6/5.

[125] Jenks, C.W., *The International Protection of Trade Union Freedoms* (London: Stevens & Sons, 1957), 561–2.

[126] *General Report of the Committee of Experts on the Application of Standards 2001* (Geneva: ILO, 2001), para. 224.

respond to requests for reports and to reply to the comments of the supervisory bodies have also been observed.[127] The CEACR is also aware of the problematic failure of certain States even to ratify Conventions Nos. 87 and 98.[128]

There is no readily accessible source of statistical information which would allow us to assess the impact of criticism relating to, in particular, freedom of association and protection of the right to strike. There are success stories, such as South Africa, where the Nationalist government eventually conceded that labour laws should be modified in accordance with ILO standards, and where a 'right to strike' was included in the interim Constitution before the ANC government came to power.[129] A more recent example is that of Guatemala, which received an ILO mission in April 2001 and has now, by legislative decree, amended provisions which unduly restricted the right to strike.[130] By contrast, there are also States like the US and UK, which seem happy to blithely ignore their failure to comply with ILO Conventions and the recommendations made by supervisory bodies.[131]

One difficulty may be the lack of any sanction greater than the potential embarrassment of States. Ultimately, the ILC can vote to expel a State that has been consistently recalcitrant in its response to ILO criticism, but this occurs rarely.[132] If the principle of universality is to be taken seriously, the ILO cannot afford to expel too many States; nor can it arguably afford to expel its greatest funders regardless of their stance on freedom of association and the right to strike.[133]

---

[127] *General Report of the Committee of Experts on the Application of Standards 2002* (Geneva: ILO, 2002), paras. 86–102.

[128] *General Report of the Committee of Experts on the Application of Standards 1999* (Geneva: ILO, 1999), para. 162: 'The Committee reminds the Governments of the great importance of ratifying ILO freedom of association Conventions, given that the principles on which those instruments are based form one of the foundations of tripartism and should be at the heart of any democracy.' On this basis the Committee addressed an 'urgent appeal' to non-ratifying States.

[129] This was s. 27(4) of the interim South African Constitution and is now s. 23(2)(c) of the 1996 Constitution. See, *inter alia*, Brassey, M., *Labour Relations under the New South African Constitution* (Cape Town: Labour Law Unit, 1994) and Tajgman, D., *International Labour Standards in Southern Africa* (Cape Town: Labour Law Unit, 1994).

[130] Discussed in the Director-General's Report, *ILO Programme Implementation 2000–01* (Geneva: ILO, 2002), 17.

[131] For US failure to protect the right to strike of public sector workers in North Carolina. see *Record of Proceedings* (Geneva: ILO, 2002) ILC, 90th Session, 28 Part 2/60. See also generally Compa, L., 'Workers' Freedom of Association in the United States under International Human Rights Standards' (2001) 17 *IJCLLIR* 289; Gross, J.A., 'A Human Rights Perspective on United States Labour Relations Law: A Violation of the Right of Freedom of Association' (1999) 3 *Employee Rights & Employee Policy Journal* 65; Ewing, K.D., *Britain and the ILO* (2nd edn., London: Institute of Employment Rights, 1994); and Novitz, T., 'International Promises and Domestic Pragmatism: To What Extent will the Employment Relations Act 1999 Implement International Labour Standards Relating to Freedom of Association?' (2000) 63 *MLR* 379.

[132] The most recent example is Myanmar (Burma). See ILO, *Resolution on the Widespread Use of Forced Labour in Myanmar*, ILC, 87th Session (ILO: Geneva, 1999), available on www.ilo.org/public/english/10ilc/ilc87/com-myan.htm.

[133] See Chap. 5 above, at 101–2.

Incentives for change are offered in the form of 'technical assistance' from the International Labour Office, which normally takes the form of skilled legal or economic advice from staff rather than funding for programmes. In this respect, the endeavours of the ILO have at times clashed with those of the World Bank and IMF, whose 'structural adjustment programmes' have often been more concerned with deregulating than regulating labour markets.[134] In addition, the development of Export Processing Zones (or EPZs), in which a State's standard labour laws will not apply, have also been endorsed by the Bretton Woods institutions. This also poses problems for the enforcement of ILO standards.[135] In this context, developing States are placed in a difficult position; yet it seems that ILO standards may have no greater hold over the more wealthy countries who can afford to comply, but who simply refuse to do so.

The fundamental principle that a right to strike should be protected is accepted in almost every State. There remain a few exceptional deviations from this premise, such as Liberia, Myanmar, and Saudi Arabia,[136] but generally it is only the scope of that right that remains the subject of controversy. It is in this respect that States such as the USA and UK continue to deviate from CFA principles and CEACR recommendations. Issues surrounding the ambit of legitimate industrial action will be considered further in Part IV.

What is also of interest is the response of States to ILO derivation of right to strike from respect for freedom of association. While no State has seriously challenged ILO jurisprudence on this point, this is not a view which has been uniformly adopted outside the ILO.

For example, the Privy Council judgment in *Collymore v Attorney General of Trinidad and Tobago*[137] and that of the Supreme Court of Canada in *Reference Re Public Service Employee Relations Act* (the '*Alberta Reference Case*') depart from principles established by the ILO.[138] The effect of both these judgments was to exclude the right to strike from constitutional protection as a facet of freedom of association. Also, in a communication linked to the latter case, the UN Human Rights Committee deviated from

---

[134] See ILO, *Report of the Director-General: Reducing the Decent Work Deficit—A Global Challenge* (Geneva: ILO, 2001), ILC, 89th Session, 46.

[135] *Report of the Committee on the Application of Standards* (Geneva: ILO, 2001), ILC, 89th Session, paras. 175–176.

[136] *Your Voice at Work* (Geneva: ILO, 2000), ILC, 88th Session, 38, para. 103. Liberia, e.g., has ratified Conventions Nos. 87 and 98 but refuses to repeal a law enacted in 1980 banning all strikes. See *Case No. 1219 (Liberia)*, 241st Report of the CFA (1985), para. 551; and the latest Committee of Experts Individual Observation Concerning Convention No. 87 (Liberia) (2002).

[137] [1970] AC 539. See for further discussion of this case and those below Hendy, J., 'The Human Rights Act, Article 11 and the Right to Strike' [1998] *EHRLR* 582 at 598 and 603–6.

[138] (1987) 38 DLR (4th) 161, discussed in Beatty, D., and Kennett, S., 'Striking Back: Fighting Words, Social Protest and Political Participation in Free and Democratic Societies' (1988) 67 *Canadian Bar Review* 573; and Sheppard, T., 'Liberalism and the Charter: Freedom of Association and the Right to Strike' (1996) 5 *Dalhousie Journal of Legal Studies* 117 at 135–51.

ILO principles when a majority of its members decided that 'freedom of association', guaranteed under Article 22 of the International Covenant on Civil and Political Rights 1966, did not necessarily imply a right to strike.[139] This decision was reached on the basis of the *travaux préparatoires*, which revealed extensive deliberations on the subject of inclusion of the right to strike in the International Covenant on Economic, Social and Cultural Rights. This was taken to indicate that such a right did not arise under Article 22. This conclusion was reached, despite the express reference in Article 22 to ILO Convention No. 87 and condemnation of the statute in question by the ILO CFA.[140]

That is not to say that these decisions were all taken unopposed. In the *Alberta Reference Case* Dickson CJ dissented from the majority view on the grounds that 'if freedom of association only protects the joining together of persons for common purposes, but not the pursuit of the very activities for which the association was formed, then the freedom is indeed legalistic, ungenerous, indeed vapid'.[141] This was also the tenor of the dissenting opinion in the Human Rights Committee, which stated that the exercise of the right of freedom of association requires 'that some measure of concerted activities be allowed; otherwise it could not serve its purposes'.[142] Nevertheless, however persuasive the ILO view has been within the ILO, it does not seem to have gained the universal acceptance hoped for and anticipated by ILO supervisory bodies. The Council of Europe provides a further illustration of departure from ILO jurisprudence on this point.

---

[139] See Human Rights Committee, 28th Session, Communication No. R.26/118/1982, *JB et al. v Canada*, 28th Session.

[140] *Case No. 893 (Canada)*, 194th Report of the CFA (1980).

[141] (1987) 38 DLR (4th) 161 at 227.

[142] These concerted activities should include holding meetings, collective bargaining or the right to strike, as these are all activities in which 'a trade-unionist may engage in to protect his interests'. See Communication No. R.26/118/1982, *J.B. et al. v Canada*, App., Individual Opinion, 38, given by Rosalyn Higgins, Rjsoomer Lallah, Andreas Mavrommatis, Torkel Opsahl, and Amos Wako.

9

Divergent Remedial Mechanisms in the Council of Europe

The official Council of Europe position is that civil, political, and socio-economic rights are 'universal, indivisible, interdependent and interrelated'.[1] There is however a marked disparity between this rhetorical claim and the reality of mechanisms utilized for their implementation and review.

Protection of human rights within the Council of Europe differs according to whether the right in question is protected under the European Convention on Human Rights 1950 (ECHR) or the European Social Charter 1961 (ESC). The level of protection for civil and political rights under the former is far superior to that provided for social rights under the latter. This is significant because the right to strike is expressly protected only under the ESC.

The limitations of the ESC supervisory proceedings suggest that findings of the European Court of Human Rights will have greater influence than those of the European Committee of Social Rights. This is problematic, because although the European Court of Human Rights is not a specialist in labour law issues and does not consider the right to strike to be an essential aspect of freedom of association under Article 11 of the ECHR, its case law does touch upon the legitimacy of industrial action. It will be argued here that the status quo is unfortunate, in so far as it may lead to greater emphasis being placed on negative 'freedom' than positive rights to 'association'.

I. THE CONTRAST BETWEEN THE EUROPEAN CONVENTION ON HUMAN RIGHTS AND THE EUROPEAN SOCIAL CHARTER

Whereas the ILO has created a variety of supervisory procedures which function co-operatively and interdependently, there is a stark contrast between ECHR and ESC remedial mechanisms. The availability of a complaints procedure was initially restricted to the ECHR, and implementation of the ESC was monitored only by analysis of State reports. Their operation was clearly demarcated and distinct.

---

[1] Declaration on the Occasion of the 50th Anniversary of the Universal Declaration of Human Rights, adopted by the Committee of Ministers on 10 Dec. 1998 at the 651*bis* meeting of the Ministers' Deputies, para. 4.

Reforms made to ESC supervisory mechanisms have improved their efficacy, but they still do not compare favourably with those provided for by the ECHR. An example is the relative status of the findings of the key supervisory bodies. The judgments of the European Court of Human Rights prevail over State interests and must be deferred to by the Committee of Ministers, which is responsible for overseeing their execution. The conclusions and reports of the European Committee of Social Rights (ECSR), a Committee of Independent Experts responsible for supervision of the ESC, are less influential. It is possible for the Governmental Committee and the Committee of Ministers to decide not to follow the recommendations of the ECSR and preserve State discretion in the 'social' field. Moreover, individual cases may be heard and compensation to victims granted under the ECHR. This is not contemplated under the ESC.

It is also worth observing that, despite initial proposals inspired by ILO procedures, there is no tripartite supervisory mechanism available within the Council of Europe, under either the ECHR or the ESC. This may have affected the status of findings relating to the ESC, which lack judicial authority. NGOs can play a limited role in the Charter supervisory process. These include, but also go beyond, workers' and employers' organizations. There is therefore potential for a wider range of participants than contemplated by the tripartite structure of the ILO. However, these NGOs possess much less influence than do States within the Council of Europe, or even trade unions and employers within the ILO. This dominance of representation of State interests in the supervision of socio-economic rights reflects the greater emphasis on inter-governmental decision-making within the Council of Europe.[2]

A.   THE EUROPEAN COURT and COMMISSION of HUMAN RIGHTS UNDER THE ECHR

The notion of a European Charter of Rights, enforceable by individuals and States before a European Court, seems to have been one of the key motivations for the creation of the Council of Europe.[3] Nevertheless, the resistance of certain States to any cession of sovereign control meant that there was no mention of an authoritative court which would hear individual complaints in the 1949 Statute of the Council of Europe. This issue was addressed later in the course of drafting the ECHR. This section traces the development of supervisory mechanisms under this instrument to the adoption of Protocol 11 in 1998.

---

[2] Discussed in Chap. 6 above, at 129–31.

[3] See *The Grand Design: A Speech by the Right Hon. Winston Churchill at the Congress of Europe* (London: United Europe Movement, 1948); and *Congress of Europe: the Hague—May 1948 Resolutions* (London: European Movement, 1948), 5–7 and 12–14.

In 1950, the establishment of a European 'court' which considered individual complaints was novel and therefore, to some, alarming. Traditionally, only States had constituted legitimate subjects of international law and therefore held a monopoly on the ability to make complaints before international tribunals. One contemporary commentator observed that this was 'the first time in history' the individual was to be recognized as having 'direct access to an international instance before which he can bring his case against a government'.[4] Also, no such court had been previously created at a regional level. The only potentially useful comparator was the International Court of Justice.[5] Various delegates, including those from the UK, expressed their opposition to the creation of a judicial organ under the ECHR.[6] Others, such as the French, insisted that if a European human rights instrument were to be effective, a supervisory mechanism had to be developed which was comparable to that available in national legal systems. 'In domestic law the protection of rights depended upon the existence of courts. The international position could not be different.' There had to be a right of individuals to bring a petition against a State before competent judges, who would provide a final judgment on legal principles and, where necessary, award compensation to the victim.[7]

Eventually, a compromise was sought and obtained, whereby Contracting Parties were not obliged to allow individual petition or accede to the jurisdiction of the Court but could do so by a declaration under Articles 25 and 46 respectively.[8] It took time for there to be a critical mass of declarations, so that the European Court of Human Rights began sitting only in 1959. Prior to this date, the European Commission played a key role in resolving State complaints and achieving 'friendly settlement'. In addition, the Committee of Ministers could embark on 'political settlement of complaints'.[9]

Yet what was once strange and threatening has since become a matter of course. As the composition of the Court has evolved, its credibility has been

---

[4] Robertson, A.H., *The Council of Europe: Its Structure, Functions and Achievements* (London: Stevens & Sons, 1956), 168. See also Janis, M., 'Individuals as Subjects of International Law' (1984) 17 *Cornell International Law Journal* 61.

[5] This is evident from the Draft Statute of the European Court of Human Rights which contained many provisions based on the Statute of the International Court of Justice. See Weil, G.L., *The European Convention on Human Rights: Background, Development and Prospects* (Leyden: Sythoff, 1963), 26.

[6] See, e.g., *ECHR Travaux Préparatoires* (Strasbourg: Council of Europe, 1949–50), iii, 268.

[7] *Ibid.*, i, 194–202 per M. Teitgen; ii, 172–82 per M. Bidault; and iv, 114 and 138 per M. Chaumont. See also Robertson, A.H., 'The European Convention for the Protection of Human Rights' (1950) 27 *BYBIL* 145.

[8] Moreover, even then, an application was admissible before the Court only where domestic remedies had been exhausted. See ECHR prior to amendment by Protocol 11, Arts. 13, 26, and 60. Cf. Drzemczewski, A., 'The European Human Rights Convention: A New Court of Human Rights in Strasbourg as of November 1, 1998' (1998) 55 *Washington and Lee Law Review* 697, 715. See now the essential admissibility criteria set out in Art. 35.

[9] Cf. Tomkins, A., 'The Committee of Ministers: Its Roles Under the European Convention on Human Rights' [1995] 1 *EHRLR* 49.

enhanced.[10] All States Parties now accept the right of individual petition and the jurisdiction of a single permanent Court by virtue of Protocol 11,[11] which entered into force on 1 November 1998. There is no longer a European Commission on Human Rights, but its role in 'friendly settlement' and in scrutinizing the admissibility of applications is now performed by the Committees and Chambers of the Court. The Protocol also abolished the role of the Committee of Ministers in 'political settlement', so that 'a fully judicial system prevails'.[12] The Court now consists of a number of judges equal to that of the Contracting Parties to the Convention and reflects this national diversity. Judges are elected for a period of six years, but may be re-elected. When considering whether to make a declaration of inadmissibility, the judges sit in committees of three. More complex decisions on the admissibility and merits of a case are taken by Chambers of seven judges. Where a case raises a serious question relating to interpretation of the ECHR or where there could be a departure from previous precedents, the Chamber may relinquish jurisdiction in favour of a Grand Chamber, made up of seventeen judges. There is no obligation to reach decisions by consensus, and the dissenting opinions in one case may influence the decision in the next.[13] This practice can be contrasted with the delivery of unanimous opinions by the European Court of Justice.[14]

The judgments of the European Court of Human Rights have long received considerable attention and respect. Such a judgment cannot 'annul, repeal or modify any legislation or individual decision of a competent State', but the Court is empowered to determine whether a domestic administrative act, court decision, or law is in breach of the ECHR and, in giving reasons, may specify the obligations incumbent upon the State concerned.[15] The Court may also make provision for compensation to an injured party.[16]

The findings of the Court may be regarded as having the status of customary international law. It has been observed that 'sometimes a

---

[10] This is largely due to Protocols 5, 8, and 11 to the ECHR. On qualification of the judges see the ECHR prior to amendment by Protocol 11, Art. 39, now the ECHR, Arts. 21 and 22. See also Schermers, H.G., 'Election of Judges to the European Court of Human Rights' (1998) 23 *ELRev.* 568.

[11] See for a summary of the content of Protocol 11 Drzemczewski, A., 'A Major Overhaul of the European Human Rights Convention Control Mechanism: Protocol 11' (1995) VI(2) *Collected Courses of the Academy of European Law: The Protection of Human Rights in Europe* 206; and Schermers, H.G., 'The Eleventh Protocol to the European Convention on Human Rights' (1994) 19 *ELRev.* 367.

[12] Salcedo, J.A.C., 'The European System of Protection of Human Rights' in Carpi, F., and Orlandi, C.G. (eds.), *Judicial Protection of Human Rights at the National and International Level: International Congress on Procedural Law for the Ninth Centenary of the University of Bologna September 22–24 1998* (Bologna: University of Bologna, 1999), i, 364.

[13] ECHR post amendment by Protocol 11, Arts. 19–51.

[14] Discussed in Chap. 10 below, at 248.

[15] Salcedo, n.12 above, 374–6.

[16] ECHR post amendment by Protocol 11, Arts. 41–46. Note also the capacity of the Court to provide advisory opinions, previously under Protocol No. 2 and now, post amendment by Protocol 11, Arts. 47–49.

happy (or unhappy) confluence of political decisions, social attitudes, and individual actors and actions makes possible the kind of breakthrough that converts *ad hoc* decision-making bodies into legal tribunals and turns acquiescence into legal obligation'. It has been claimed that it is this 'extraordinary phenomenon' which we may now be observing in the European human rights system.[17] This is consistent with the views of other commentators, who dwell on the authoritative nature of the judgments handed down by the Court.[18] Like the ECHR provisions themselves, the judgments of the Court are regarded as binding under international law, but do not have direct effect in the courts of the Contracting States.[19] The Committee of Ministers has no actual sanctions at its disposal to ensure the obedience of recalcitrant States, but relies on international embarrassment. It would be reluctant to exercise the ultimate penalty of expulsion from the Council of Europe.

B.   REPORTING and COLLECTIVE COMPLAINTS UNDER THE ESC

In records of debates relating to the drafting of the ESC it is possible to detect a tussle between certain Member States, which did not wish to cede any control over national determination of social standards, and others, which expressed concern that the neglect of social rights could defeat their common democratic project.[20] The result was a further compromise, according to which social rights were set out in a European Social Charter, and even elaborated upon in subsequent Protocols, but whereby crucial limitations were placed on the supervisory mechanisms which monitored their implementation. This section traces the development of these mechanisms under the ESC, comparing these with those established under the ECHR.

1.   Initial Decisions on Supervisory Machinery Appropriate to a Social Charter

Early proposals for a Council of Europe Social Charter, formulated by the Consultative Assembly, envisaged that both a reporting mechanism and a complaints procedure would be made available. Enforcement of this instrument would be linked to enforcement of the ECHR, by finding a role for the European Commission on Human Rights in both procedures. The Consultative Assembly would then give its opinion on the Commission's report,

---

[17] Janis, M., Kay, R., and Bradley, A., *European Human Rights Law* (Oxford: OUP, 1995), 8.

[18] Gomien, D., Harris, D., and Zwaak, L., *Law and Practice of the European Convention on Human Rights and the European Social Charter* (Strasbourg: Council of Europe, 1996), 19; Heffernan, L., 'A Comparative View of the Individual Petition Procedures under the European Convention on Human Rights and the International Covenant on Civil and Political Rights' (1997) 19 *Human Rights Quarterly* 78 at 95.

[19] Cf. the effect of EC law, discussed in Chap. 10 below, at 246.

[20] Mower, A.G., *International Co-operation for Social Justice: Global and Regional Protection of Economic/Social Rights* (Westport, Conn., Greenwood Press, 1985), 187–93. See also Chap. 6 above, at 133–46.

and finally the Committee of Ministers, on the recommendation of the Assembly, could make recommendations directly to the State itself or take other measures (such as convening a European conference on a particular matter).[21] There were, however, fears from the trade union movement that such a procedure would be 'so slow and cumbersome that it would never achieve its purpose'.[22] As we shall see, these fears were not without foundation.[23]

The Assembly's revised proposals did not seek to simplify or shorten the procedure but rather introduced a further role for an Economic and Social 'Council' or 'Conference'. This body would 'define what measures should be taken by the Governments to achieve their declared objectives' and 'supervise the execution of such measures'.[24] In other words, it would play a role in the enforcement of Charter rights as well as a policy-directing function. It would consist of ninety-three members, one third of whom would represent employers, one third the workers, and one third independent occupations and the general interest. It was however still envisaged that 'the important task of investigating and checking the measures taken by the signatory States under the terms of the Charter could be entrusted to the European Commission of Human Rights which includes eminent specialists in social law among its members'.[25]

The involvement of the European Commission on Human Rights was eventually rejected. This was possibly on the basis that the result might be an overload of work and, one suspects, what was regarded as a disproportionate degree of power for this supervisory body. Moreover, there seems to have been an assumption that the ECHR and ESC dealt with discrete subject matters which could be addressed independently.[26]

---

[21] *ESC Travaux Préparatoires* (Strasbourg: Council of Europe, 1952–62) ii, Section II, Consultative Assembly Committee on Social Questions, Working Party for the Preparation of a Draft European Social Charter, Preliminary Draft of Social Charter submitted by Secretariat of the Committee, 19 Apr. 1955, AS/Soc I (6) 1, Part III, Arts. 1–5. See also Consultative Assembly, European Social Charter and European Economic and Social Conference Draft Recommendation (1955) Doc. 403.

[22] *Ibid.*, ii, Part I, Section II, Memorandum by the Secretariat of the European Regional Organization of the International Confederation of Free Trade Unions presented to the Consultative Assembly Committee on Social Questions, 20 Apr. 1955, AS/Soc (6) 26.

[23] See below, at 218.

[24] *Ibid.*, ii, Part I, Section II, Consultative Assembly Committee on Social Questions Working Party for the preparation of a draft European Social Charter, Minutes of Meeting held on 29 Apr. 1955, AS/Soc I (6) PV 1.

[25] *Ibid.*, ii, Part I, Section III, Consultative Assembly Committee on Social Questions Working Party for the preparation of a draft European Social Charter, Memorandum by the Secretariat of the Committee on the Preliminary Draft of Social Charter drawn up by the Working Party, 23 May 1955, AS/Soc I (6) 3. See also Chap. 6 above, at 139.

[26] *Ibid.*, iii, Section IV, Consultative Assembly, Economic Social Charter and European Economic and Social Conference, Draft Recommendations and Reports, presented on behalf of the Committee on Social Questions (1956) Doc 488, Report by M. Heyman, 22.

Despite awareness of the precedent set by the ILO and acknowledgement of the significance of sectional interests,[27] the introduction of a tripartite supervisory body was also not favoured by the Assembly. It was considered preferable for there to be 'more democratic' parliamentary representation.[28] There was vocal worker support for the involvement of a tripartite body in the supervisory process at the 1958 tripartite conference.[29] However, the workers did not win the Assembly's full support and the Committee of Ministers maintained its opposition to such an initiative. The procedure devised by the latter allowed for an ostensibly legal interpretation of the text of the Charter, but was designed to ensure the maximum political control by States over the supervisory process.

2. The Procedure Instigated by the ESC 1961

There was no complaints mechanism in the 1961 Charter. Contracting Parties were obliged only to provide reports on the extent of their compliance with Charter obligations they had adopted.[30] National trade unions and employers' organizations were given the opportunity to comment on such reports. Afterwards a Committee of Independent Experts (now renamed the European Committee of Social Rights or ECSR) conducted a legal assessment of compliance with Charter provisions.[31] These were usually unanimous, although sometimes dissenting opinions were given.[32] The ECSR, appointed by the Committee of Ministers,[33] was also assisted by a representative from the ILO.[34] The governmental reports, the supplementary

[27] *Ibid.*, ii, Part II, Section III, Consultative Assembly, Seventh Ordinary Session, Official Report, 15th Sitting, per Mr Cornish (Ireland) and M. Harlem (Minister of Social Affairs, Norway), 16th Sitting, per M. Federspiel (Denmark) and M. Birkelbach (Germany).

[28] *Ibid.*, ii, Part II, Section III, Consultative Assembly, Seventh Ordinary Session, Official Report, 15th Sitting, per Mr Cornish (Ireland), 16th Sitting, per M. Federspiel (Denmark) and, on the benefits of governance by Ministers representing elected governments, Mr Nicolson (UK).

[29] *Record of Proceedings: Tripartite Conference Convened by the ILO at the request of the Council of Europe, Strasbourg 1–12 December 1958* (Geneva, International Labour Office, 1959), at 76 per Mr Eggerman (representative of the International Federation of Christian Trade Unions), at 82 per Mr Ventejol (workers' delegate, France), and at 84 per Mr Alders (workers' delegate, Netherlands).

[30] See ESC 1961, Arts. 21–23. States can also, on occasion, be required to report on provisions that they have not yet adopted. See for a recent example of this practice ECSR, *Sixth Report on Certain Provisions of the Charter which Have Not Been Accepted* (Strasbourg, Council of Europe Publishing, 1998).

[31] ESC 1961, Arts. 24–25.

[32] See ECSR, *Conclusions XIII-4*, 453–7 and *Conclusions XIV-2*, 791–3.

[33] See for criticism of this power *Record of Proceedings: Tripartite Conference*, n.29 above, 76 and 82. See also Berenstein, A., 'The System of Supervision of the European Social Charter' in Betten, L., Harris, D., and Jaspers, T. (eds.), *The Future of European Social Policy* (Deventer: Kluwer, 1989), 42.

[34] This practice has continued until the present date. The reports of the ECSR are called 'Conclusions', the dates for which are not commonly cited in academic work or Council of Europe publications. The reason is that the deliberations of the Committee may continue over more than a year and are sometimes published long after the conclusions were reached. Moreover, changes to the reporting system make the citation of dates difficult. For further elaboration of the supervisory cycles associated with the procedure see App. 8.

reports, and the 'Conclusions' of the ECSR were subsequently examined by a Governmental Committee, consisting of ministerial representatives. The Governmental Committee was also attended by representatives of international organizations of employers and workers (such as the IOE, ETUC, and UNICE) who could not vote but could act in a consultative capacity. The reports of the ECSR and Governmental Committee were subsequently examined by the Assembly, which gave its own opinion. Finally, the Committee of Ministers had the discretion to issue recommendations by a two-thirds majority vote to States which had violated a guarantee of the Charter.[35]

This was a lengthy, complicated process. On average it took between four and six years for a supervisory cycle to be completed. Trade unions and employers' organizations appeared distinctly underwhelmed by its efficacy. This was reflected in their apathy in supplying observations supplementing State reports.[36] It was a procedure whereby Ministers of State possessed control over both membership of the Committee of Experts and the ability to undermine their findings when this was politically convenient. ECSR findings were often disregarded by the Governmental Committee, whose decisions, largely based on political considerations, were given precedence by the Committee of Ministers.

For example, the Governmental Committee was, at first, opposed to any finding that a Contracting State was in breach of Article 6(4) of the European Social Charter, which sets out the scope of protection of the right to strike. The argument presented by the Governmental Committee was that Article 6(4) requires only that States 'recognize' rather than 'undertake to recognize' the right to strike. It was claimed that this indicated that all Members of the Council of Europe at the date of drafting recognized the right to strike, although different definitions of the right to strike co-existed at that time in Western Europe. 'There was nothing in the *travaux préparatoires* or the wording of Article 6, paragraph 4, to justify the supposition that the authors of the Charter wished to favour one definition over another and to formalise it in a text.'[37] The Governmental Committee concluded that the ECSR should observe State practice in this field without criticism, unless there had been a radical departure from State norms existing at the time that the Charter was drafted. This was not a position which could easily be sustained in the light of enlargement of the Council of Europe's membership and is not held today, but it is an interesting reminder of how

[35]   ESC 1961, Arts. 26–9.

[36]   In ECSR, *Conclusions XIV-I*, 22 it was noted by the ECSR that supplementary observations were provided only by German, Dutch, Portuguese, Spanish, and Swedish trade unions. This can be contrasted with the conduct of the social partners within the ILO, where they have showed themselves willing and able to submit observations. See *Report of the Committee of Experts on the Application of Conventions and Recommendations* (Geneva, International Labour Office, 1999), ILC, 87th Session, 43–4. The ECSR also has regard to ILO, EC, and OECD publications.

[37]   ECSR Governmental Committee, *Report 10(1)*, 13–15.

Ministers of State exercised a stranglehold on the ESC supervisory mechanism.

It should also be observed that Council of Europe Member States which had not ratified any part of the Charter were, during this period, able to participate in the determination whether the Committee of Ministers would issue a recommendation relating to State non-compliance with Charter provisions. Bearing in mind all these factors, it is not so surprising that, for over thirty years, no recommendation was directed to a State by the Committee of Ministers.[38]

3. Recent Reforms to Charter Supervisory Machinery

By 1989, radical political and social changes were taking place in Central and Eastern Europe, and the decision had been taken to expand the membership of the Council of Europe. The Committee of Ministers was confronted with two alternatives. Either they could abandon the social rights dimension of their democratic project or it was necessary to 'revitalize' the ESC.[39] The result was the adoption of a spate of additional Protocols. Some were designed to supplement the existing Charter rights.[40] Others were concerned with modification of the supervisory machinery. There was to be both improvement of the existing reporting mechanism and the creation of a new collective complaints procedure. However, there was no planned co-ordination with the system already developed for enforcement of the ECHR.

The Turin Amending Protocol of 1991 revised various facets of the reporting procedure. This Protocol has received a significant number of ratifications, but has yet to enter into force, as it requires the unanimous acceptance of all contracting parties to the 1961 Charter.[41] In the meantime, various facets of the Protocol have been introduced, following a decision to this effect by the Committee of Ministers on 11 December 1991. The Committee of Ministers retained its power to appoint members to the ECSR, despite Article 3 of the 1991 Protocol, which confers such a power on the Assembly,[42] but other aspects of the reporting procedure have been modified and improved.

The length of the supervisory procedure has been addressed by removing reference to the Assembly as a step in the supervisory process; instead the

---

[38] See Shrubsall, V., 'The European Social Charter: Employment, Unions and Strikes' in Beddard, R., and Hill, D.M. (eds.), *Economic, Social and Cultural Rights: Progress and Achievements* (London: Macmillan, 1992), 154.

[39] *The Social Charter of the 21st Century: Colloquy Organised by the Secretariat of the Council of Europe 14–16 May 1997* (Strasbourg: Council of Europe, 1998), per M. di Benisichi at 43–9 and per M. Lidal at 71. See Chap. 6 above, at 144–6.

[40] Additional Protocol to the European Social Charter 1988 and the Revised Social Charter 1996.

[41] Protocol Amending the European Social Charter 1991, Art. 8.

[42] For objections to this omission see Parliamentary Assembly, *Recommendation No. 1354* (1998), para. 19.

Assembly will hold periodic debates on what it considers to be vital issues concerning enforcement of the Charter.[43] The Governmental Committee has also revised its working methods in accordance with Article 4 of the Protocol, giving the ECSR exclusive competence to make the necessary technical assessments of compliance with the Charter.[44] However, the Governmental Committee does retain a role in so far as it may advise the Committee of Ministers on the subject of recommendations, with reference to 'social, economic and other policy considerations'. Finally, the Committee of Ministers has adopted new voting procedures under Article 5 of the Protocol. A two-thirds majority is still required for the making of recommendations, but States which have not ratified the Charter are not allowed to vote. Since this procedure was put in place, the Committee of Ministers has issued a number of recommendations to States which have contravened Charter provisions.[45] These modifications represent an improvement in the reporting procedure; but, taken as a whole, this remains a largely political, as opposed to a legal, process, deferential to State interests.

4. The Operation of the Collective Complaints Procedure

Potentially more significant was the Collective Complaints Protocol 1995 (CCP), which came into force in 1998 for ratifying States.[46] 'The idea of setting up a system of collective complaints for the European Social Charter along the lines of the existing International Labour Organization (ILO) arrangements [was] not new (see, for example, Recommendation 839 (1978) of the Parliamentary Assembly),'[47] but it was the first time that it had been put into practice. The complaints procedure was to complement the existing reporting mechanism, but would increase participation by worker, employer, and non-governmental organizations. They would be able to bring complaints, rather than merely submitting observations. It would also be much shorter, ensuring a swift response to legitimate concerns relating to enforcement of the ESC.[48] However, there are still numerous differences between the ESC and ECHR complaints machinery. These are enumerated here, since they reveal the relative lack of efficacy of this new procedure.

[43] Protocol Amending the European Social Charter 1991, Art. 6. The first such debate in the Assembly was held on 7 Oct. 1992.

[44] See ESC Governmental Committee, *13th Report (III)*, 11–13; and ESC Governmental Committee, *15th Report (I)*, 11.

[45] See for a list of Committee of Ministers ESC Recommendations on the Council of Europe's web site at www.coe.int/t/E/Committee_of_Ministers/public/Documents/#TopOf-Page. For comment on this change in approach see Betten, L., 'Committee of Ministers of the Council of Europe Call for Contracting States to Account for Violations of the European Social Charter' (1994) 10 *IJCLLIR* 147.

[46] See also RSC 1996, which came into force on 1 July 1999 for ratifying States, which in Art. C preserves the normal supervisory arrangements for the ESC, and in Art. D provides for collective complaints where the Contracting Parties to the RSC have ratified the CCP.

[47] *Explanatory Report to the 1995 Additional Protocol Providing for a System of Collective Complaints* (Strasbourg: Council of Europe, 1995), para. 1.

[48] *Ibid.*, para. 2.

First, only 'unsatisfactory application of the Charter' is at issue under the CCP; whereas applications under the Convention are made in respect of 'a violation of rights'.[49] The latter is implicitly a much more serious matter. The decision of the Committee of Independent Experts to rename itself the 'European Committee of Social Rights' does stress that Charter provisions entail 'rights'. While this invokes the powerful rhetoric of entitlement, the reality is that these provisions are not to be regarded as justiciable in the same sense as ECHR rights. Moreover, this Committee has never claimed the title of a 'Court', and any claim to such status is undermined by the restrictive wording and procedure contained in the CCP.

Secondly, there is no right of individual complaint under the CCP. Complaints may be made by certain trade unions, employers' organizations, and non-governmental organizations (NGOs). The fact that NGOs are given standing is said to 'highlight the originality of the European Social Charter as compared to other equivalent international systems'.[50] This makes sense to the extent that certain Charter provisions are concerned with matters other than labour laws. However, national NGOs do not have the same automatic right to bring complaints as do national trade unions. Instead, States have the option to allow national NGOs to bring complaints under Article 2. The complainant must be 'representative' and particularly 'qualified' in issues covered by the Charter and the complaint.[51] Victims of a violation have no independent right to utilize this process. To defend their social rights, they are required to join or form organizations. The instrument fails to acknowledge that adequate representation will not always be achieved. Moreover, it appears from the Explanatory Report accompanying the CCP that 'because of their collective nature, complaints may only raise questions concerning non-compliance of a State's law or practice with one of the provisions of the Charter'. 'Individual situations' will not be regarded as the legitimate subject of a complaint.[52]

It is possible that the ECSR jurisprudence will gradually depart from these narrow limits. As David Harris, previously a member of the ECSR, has observed, consideration of individual circumstances would be consistent with the practice of the ILO CFA, which explicitly criticizes violations of individual rights, as well as national law and State practice.[53] Decisions of the ILO Committee often refer to and make recommendations in respect of individuals who are dismissed, arrested, detained, executed, or in any

[49] ECHR post amendment by Protocol 11, Art. 34.

[50] *Explanatory Report to the 1995 Additional Protocol Providing for a System of Collective Complaints*, n.47 above, para. 18.

[51] *Ibid.*, para. 26.

[52] *Ibid.*, para. 31. Also see Parliamentary Assembly, *Opinion No. 167 (1993) on the draft second additional protocol of the Social Charter of the Council of Europe providing for a system of collective complaints*, para. 4.

[53] See *Social Charter of the 21st Century*, above n.39, per Mr Harris, 101–5.

other way harmed. Indeed, it is this human element which brings its decisions to life and maintains its relevance.[54] It is potentially open to the ECSR to take the same line, and the presence of an ILO observer may have some influence in this regard. However, there is no indication from the collective complaints already heard under the ESC that the ECSR is willing to do so.[55]

Thirdly, the conclusions reached by the ECSR, after hearing the complaint, are not binding upon the State concerned. The ECSR must decide on admissibility, collect information on the complaint, and draw up a 'report'.[56] The report from this Committee is then transmitted to the Committee of Ministers, the complainant, Contracting Parties to the Charter, and the Parliamentary Assembly. It can be made public at the same time as the Committee of Ministers' resolution on the report, or four months after the Committee of Ministers received the report. This gives the report a degree of prominence, even though the procedure itself is conducted behind closed doors,[57] but its effect turns upon the response of the Committee of Ministers.

Article 9 of the CCP provides that, if the ECSR report presents a finding of 'unsatisfactory application of the Charter', the Committee of Ministers 'shall' adopt, by a two-thirds majority, a recommendation addressed to the Contracting Party concerned. This use of mandatory language, the notion that this *must* be done, is recognized and stressed in the Explanatory Report.[58] However, the Committee of Ministers has now demonstrated that in making a Recommendation to a State under the CCP it may take account, not only of the report submitted by the ECSR, but also of further representations made by the government in question. The Recommendation then issued can be such that a State is merely called upon to give a full account of additional considerations in its next report on the implementation of the ESC.[59] It should also be noted that, if the Committee of Ministers considers that the ECSR report raises new issues, it can decide, again by a two-thirds majority, to consult the Governmental Committee.[60] The Committee of Ministers has not yet taken the latter option of reference to the Governmental Committee, and it may be that there would be recourse to this

---

[54] See Chap. 8 above, at 190.

[55] A full list of complaints to date is available at www.humanrights.coe.int/cseweb/GB/GB3/GB31.htm.

[56] CCP, Arts. 6–8.

[57] *Explanatory Report to the 1995 Additional Protocol Providing for a System of Collective Complaints*, n.47 above, paras. 43–44. Cf. the Rules of Procedure adopted by the ECSR contained in *Conclusions XIV-1*, 29.

[58] *Explanatory Report to the 1995 Additional Protocol Providing for a System of Collective Complaints*, n.47 above, para. 46.

[59] Committee of Ministers Resolution ResChS(2001)6, adopted on 5 Apr. 2001 concerning *Complaint No. 7/2000 International Federation of Human Rights Leagues v Greece*.

[60] CCP, Arts. 8–9. The Governmental Committee could conceivably persuade the Committee of Ministers not to make such a recommendation.

route only in the most exceptional circumstances.[61] Still, the very existence of this option compares unfavourably with the procedure provided by the ECHR, under which Contracting Parties are bound by judgments of the Court and the Committee of Ministers merely supervises their execution.[62]

A fourth important difference between the ECHR and ESC complaints mechanisms is that, whereas the European Court of Human Rights may 'afford just satisfaction' to an injured party, this does not appear to be contemplated by the CCP. There is no specification of what the recommendation by the Committee of Ministers should contain, but both the Explanatory Report and the Parliamentary Assembly envisage that recommendations will be directed to changes in domestic law and practice rather than compensation for an individual victim.[63] This follows from the lack of standing of individual complainants and the failure to consider individual situations.

Finally, the limited legal status of recommendations made under the CCP must be recognized. The ESC places legally binding obligations on Contracting Parties, to the extent that they have adopted provisions contained in the Charter.[64] However, it seems from the text of the CCP that recommendations made by the Committee of Ministers will not be regarded as binding in international law.[65] Whereas Contracting Parties to the ECHR 'undertake to abide by the final judgment of the Court in any case to which they are parties',[66] no such obligation is imposed on a Contracting State in respect of a report issued by the ECSR. Even where a Recommendation is issued by the Committee of Ministers, all the State concerned is required to do is 'provide information on the measures it has taken to give effect to the . . . Recommendation' in its next report under the ESC.[67]

It therefore seems doubtful that the operation of the collective complaints procedure, as envisaged in the CCP, will transform the ESC into an instrument of equivalent status to the ECHR. There have been only twelve complaints to date, since the Protocol came into force on 1 July 1998.

---

[61] Arguably, this opportunity came in relation to *Complaint No. 8/2000 Quaker Council for European Affairs v Greece*, where the ECSR report contained two strong dissenting opinions. However, the Committee of Ministers apparently chose not to avail itself of this option. See Committee of Ministers Resolution ResChs(2002)3.

[62] ECHR post amendment by Protocol 11, Art. 46.

[63] See, in particular, Parliamentary Assembly, Opinion No. 167 (1993) on the draft second additional protocol of the Social Charter of the Council of Europe providing for a system of collective complaints, paras. 4 and 5.

[64] See the first para. of the app. to the ESC 1961, relating to Part III. See also for recognition of the binding nature of ESC Art. 6(4) in the Netherlands, *NV Dutch Railways v Transport Unions FNV, FSV and CNV* (1986) 6 International Labour Law Reports 3. In that case Art. 6(4) was found to be a 'self-executing provision of international law that was binding upon everyone in the Netherlands' and capable of enforcement in the domestic courts, by virtue of the 'monist' nature of the Dutch Constitution. Cf. Chap. 1 above, at 29.

[65] This is conceded by Harris, n.53 above, at 108.

[66] ECHR post amendment by Protocol 11, Art. 46(1).

[67] CCP, Art. 10.

A call for a larger ECSR[68] has been met by expanding the membership of the Committee,[69] but the size of its administrative support in the Charter section remains negligible compared to that utilized by the European Court of Human Rights. The Parliamentary Assembly has adopted two Recommendations calling for further amendment of the ESC, creating either a 'parallel European Court of Social Rights' or enforcement of certain social rights through the European Court of Human Rights.[70] The first initiative had the provisional support of the ECSR,[71] but both have subsequently been rejected by the Committee of Ministers, whose interest for the time being lies only in supporting the operation of the collective complaints procedure and rationalizing the operation of the ECHR control mechanism.[72]

II. CASES DECIDED BY THE EUROPEAN COMMISSION AND COURT OF HUMAN RIGHTS RELATING TO FREEDOM OF ASSOCIATION

Article 11 of the ECHR guarantees every person 'freedom of association with others', including the 'right to form and join trade unions for the protection of his interests'. There is no express mention of a right to strike in Article 11. However, given the development of ILO jurisprudence, it was arguably open to the European Commission and Court of Human Rights to establish that this entitlement was an essential element of freedom of association. They did not do so.

The European Commission of Human Rights was willing to refer to ILO Conventions when deciding cases. For example, in *X v Ireland*,[73] the Commission stated that 'when interpreting the meaning and scope of freedom of association in Article 11 in relation to trade regard should be had to the meaning given to this term in the International Labour Organisation Convention of 1948 (No. 87) concerning Freedom of Association and the Right to Organise'.[74] In addition, the Commission's report on the *National Union of Belgian Police* case pointed out that ILO Conventions were ratified by almost all the parties to the European Convention on Human Rights.[75] The Commission added that:

[68] ECSR, *Conclusions XIV-I* (1998), 21. Cf. *Conclusions XIV-2* (1998), 23.

[69] It has been agreed in principle by the Committee of Ministers (Deputies) at its 751st meeting on 2 and 7 May 2001 that the membership of the ECSR could be expanded from 9 members to 15. 3 members have been appointed immediately with 3 more to follow. See Committee of Ministers Resolution ResChs(2001)7.

[70] See Chap. 6 above, at 145.

[71] ECSR, *Conclusions XIV-1* (1998), 26–7; and *Conclusions XIV(2)* (1998), 28–9.

[72] See Chap. 6 above, at 145–6; and Chap. 15 below, at 366.

[73] *X v Ireland* (1971) XIV Yearbook European Commission of Human Rights 198.

[74] *Ibid.*, at 220–2.

[75] 1 EHRR 578 (1979). *Proceedings of the Colloquy about the European Convention on Human Rights in relation to other International Instruments for the Protection of Human Rights* (Strasbourg: Council of Europe, 1979), 40.

They reflect widely accepted labour law standards which are elaborated and clarified by competent organs of the ILO. As they are a body of special rules binding also on European states, they should not be ignored in the interpretation of Article 11 if the European Convention is to keep pace with the dynamic context of international labour standards and if its concepts are to remain in harmony with the concepts used in international law and practice.[76]

The Court has also, from time to time, referred to ILO standards and the decisions of ILO supervisory bodies in its judgments.[77] However, neither the Commission nor the Court has been prepared to follow the decisions of ILO supervisory organs on the question of the link between freedom of association and the right to strike.

The reluctance of the Commission and the Court to protect trade union rights is demonstrated by decisions reached on access to consultation and participation in collective bargaining. In these cases, a generous margin of appreciation is given to States. There has been partial recognition of the right to strike as an aspect of freedom of association, but this does not extend to the ILO position that such a right is necessary to the effective exercise of this freedom. This disinclination for promotion of collective rights in the industrial relations context can be contrasted with enthusiasm for protection of the individual right *not* to associate. This section ends by considering the potential for a clash between positive and negative freedom of association and how this may impact upon protection of the right to strike in the Council of Europe.

A. Reluctance to Protect Trade Union Rights under Article 11 of the ECHR?

The right to form a trade union imposes a positive duty upon the State to ensure that trade unions are able to enjoy the freedoms guaranteed under Article 11. However, the Court's restrictive interpretation of Article 11 means that there are relatively few trade union freedoms which the State is obliged to protect.[78] On various occasions, the Court has found against trade unions which have claimed the right to consultation, the right to collective bargaining, and the right to strike.

This approach was initially justified by reference to the separate provision made for such rights under the European Social Charter. For example, in the *Belgian Police* case, the applicant union claimed that the right to consultation was implicit in freedom of association. The Court found that

---

[76] The quotation is taken from the *Publications of the Court*, Series B., vol. 18, 42–5. See also *Cheall v UK* (1986) 8 EHRR 74.

[77] *Gustafsson v Sweden* (1996) 22 EHRR 409; and *Wilson, NUJ and Others*, Appl. Nos. 30668/96, 30671/96, & 30678/96, judgment of 2 July 2002, unreported.

[78] Forde, M., 'The European Convention on Human Rights and Labor Law' (1983) 31 *American Journal of Comparative Law* 301, 331–2.

Article 6(1) of the ESC could bind states only 'to promote' consultation and therefore did not give rise to a 'real right' to consultation. Even if it did so, the Court did not consider that this meant that Article 11 of the ECHR should be interpreted to protect such a right. Obligations under the ESC were regarded merely as optional, by virtue of Article 20 of that instrument. 'Thus it cannot be supposed that such a right derives by implication from Article 11 . . . of the 1950 Convention, which incidentally would amount to admitting that the 1961 Charter took a retrograde step in this domain.'[79]

Here, the Court relied on the traditional distinction drawn between civil liberties and social rights, emphasized by the drafters of the ECHR.[80] Nonetheless, the Court's approach does not seem altogether consistent with the intentions of those responsible for drafting the European Social Charter. It does seem doubtful that the drafters of the ESC envisaged that the instrument would not enhance protection of trade union rights, but would give the Court reason to interpret Article 11 in a more restrictive manner.[81]

For example, the Court could have found some connection between protection of freedom of association and the right to engage in collective bargaining. After all, a 'bare right' to join a trade union means little unless, through the union, one is able to participate in collective bargaining.[82] The Court has yet to find that protection of collective bargaining is required under Article 11.

The leading authority is the *Swedish Engine Drivers' Union* case,[83] which concerned the Swedish government's refusal to enter into a collective agreement with the applicant union. The government preferred to reach an agreement with a larger, more representative organization, on the understanding that the agreement would automatically apply to the applicant's members. The applicant had already agreed, in principle, to the actual terms included in that agreement. On these facts, the Court denied that the applicant had any right to enter into a separate collective agreement with the government. The Court left open the question whether there could be a positive right to collective bargaining. In a recent case, *Schettini v Italy*, the Court has confirmed that it is legitimate to exclude certain less representative trade unions from collective bargaining, as long as this exclusion is not discriminatory.[84]

Although the tenor of the Court's judgment in the *Swedish Engine Drivers' Union case* is ambivalent on the subject of an overarching right to engage in

---

[79] *National Union of Belgian Police v Belgium*, 1 EHRR 578 (1979), para. 38.

[80] Cf. Chap. 6 above, at 133–6.

[81] What is perhaps curious is the readiness of the Court to refer to the ESC and the jurisprudence of the then Committee of Independent Experts in supporting the principle of negative freedom of association. See below, at 242 and *Sigurjonsson v Sweden* (1993) 16 EHRR 462 at para. 34.

[82] See Wedderburn, Lord, 'Freedom of Association or Right to Organise? The Common Law and International Sources' in Wedderburn, Lord, *Employment Rights in Britain and Europe: Selected Papers in Labour Law* (London: Lawrence & Wishart/Institute of Employment Rights, 1991), 151; and also Chap. 1 above, at 5–6.

[83] 1 EHRR 617 (1979).   [84] Appl. No. 29529/95, Decision of 9 Dec. 2000, unreported.

collective bargaining or conclude a collective agreement, the Court has cited the case in subsequent judgments as authority for the proposition that Article 11 does not encompass a right to collective bargaining or to enter into a collective agreement.[85] Again, there is a stark contrast between the Court's views and those expressed within the ILO on the relationship between freedom of association and collective bargaining.[86]

What is more promising is the recent decision of the European Court of Human Rights in *Wilson, the NUJ and others v UK*, a case concerning discrimination against trade union members who seek active participation in collective bargaining.[87] The ILO Committee of Experts and the ECSR under the ESC had condemned UK legislation which enabled employers to give bonuses and increased wages to workers who opted out of collective bargaining, on the basis that this obstructed the ability of trade unions to defend their members' interests.[88] The European Court of Human Rights also found that 'by permitting employers to use financial incentives to induce employees to surrender important union rights, the [UK had] failed in its positive obligation to secure the enjoyment of rights under Article 11'.[89] The judgment does however reiterate the Court's standard position that collective bargaining 'is not indispensable for the effective enjoyment of trade union freedom' and that 'the Contracting States enjoy a wide margin of appreciation as to how trade union freedom may be secured'.[90]

This is consistent with past interpretation of Article 11(2). For example, in the *Belgian Police* case, the Court stated that, although trade unions did have a 'right to be heard' under Article 11, this did not equate to a right of consultation, as it was for each State, 'in the exercise of its power of appreciation', to choose the means by which to achieve that end.[91] The

---

[85] See *Gustafsson v Sweden* (1996) 22 EHRR 409, para. 52.

[86] *Freedom of Association: Digest of Decisions and Principles of the Freedom of Association Committee of the Governing Body of the ILO* (4th edn., Geneva: ILO, 1996), hereafter 'CFA Digest of Decisions', at para. 782, which states that collective bargaining 'constitutes an essential element in freedom of association'.

[87] Appl. Nos. 30668/96, 30671/96 & 30678/96, judgment of 2 July 2002, unreported. See the press release issued by the Registrar on the hearing, 30 Jan. 2002. For the background to this case see *Wilson v Associated Newspapers; Palmer v Associated British Ports* [1995] IRLR 258, discussed in Ewing, K.D., 'Dancing with the Daffodils?' (2000) 50 *Federation News* 1 and Novitz, T., 'International Promises and Domestic Pragmatism: To What Extent will the Employment Relations Act 1999 Implement International Labour Standards Relating to Freedom of Association' (2000) 63 *MLR* 379, 389–93.

[88] *ILO Committee of Experts on the Application of Conventions and Recommendations* (Geneva: ILO, 2000), 'Individual Observation Concerning Convention No. 98 United Kingdom'; and ESC European Committee of Social Rights, *Conclusions XV-I*: 'Conclusions concerning Articles 1, 5, 6, 12, 13, 16 and 19 of the Charter in respect of the United Kingdom', released in Dec. 2000. See also, previously, Council of Europe, Committee of Ministers Recommendation No. RChS(97)3, 15 Jan. 1997.

[89] *Wilson, the NUJ and others v UK*, n.77 above, para. 48.

[90] *Ibid.*, para. 44.

[91] *National Union of Belgian Police v Belgium*, 1 EHRR 578 (1979) at para. 39. See also Yourow, H.C., *The Margin of Appreciation Doctrine in the Dynamics of European Human Rights Jurisprudence* (The Hague/Boston, Mass./London: Kluwer, 1996), 40–1.

Court looked to see whether there was any consistent European practice as regards consultation of workers and, deciding that there was not, refused to impose such a requirement upon Contracting States.[92] This broad margin of appreciation is justified on the basis of the diversity of industrial relations systems in Europe.[93] This breadth should, nevertheless, be contrasted with the narrow margin of appreciation allowed to States in certain cases where negative freedom of association has been at issue.[94]

It should also be noted that Article 11(2) allows lawful restrictions to be placed on the exercise of freedom of association by certain categories of persons. These persons are 'members of the armed forces, of the police or of the administration of the State'. The latter category of persons was interpreted broadly by the Commission in an application brought by the Council of Civil Service Unions (CCSU) against the UK government. The civil servants at Government Communications Headquarters (GCHQ) in Cheltenham had, for the past thirty-seven years, been permitted to join the CCSU, but were prohibited from doing so after participating in industrial action. The Commission followed the UK courts, and upheld the government's prohibition on the ground that the staff in question were 'members of the administration of the State'.[95] The Commission refused to go further and examine whether the measures taken were proportionate to the threat which trade union membership at GCHQ would pose to national security.[96] This case has been the subject of some criticism,[97] but the principles it sets out still stand.

---

[92] A similar approach was taken in the *Swedish Engine Drivers' Union* case, n.83 above. See Lewis-Anthony, S., *The Right to Freedom of Peaceful Assembly and to Freedom of Association as Guaranteed by Article 11 of the European Convention on Human Rights* (Strasbourg: Council of Europe, 1992), 15. See for further discussion of the 'consensus principle' Bernhardt, R., 'Thoughts on the Interpretation of Human-Rights Treaties', in Matscher, F., and Petzold, H., *Protecting Human Rights: The European Dimension: Studies in Honour of Gerald J. Wiarda* (2nd edn., Cologne/Bonn/Berlin: Carl Heymanns Verlag KG, 1990), 67; and Jones, T., 'The Devaluation of Human Rights under the European Convention' [1995] *Public Law* 430 at 440–2.

[93] Kahn-Freund, O., 'On Uses and Misuses of Comparative Law' in Kahn-Freund, O., *Selected Writings* (London: Stevens & Sons, 1978), 312. See Chap. 1 above, 26–7.

[94] See *Young, James and Webster v UK* (1982) 4 EHRR 38 and *Sigurjonsson v Iceland* (1993) 16 EHRR 462, discussed further below, at 232–4. Indeed Jones, n.92 above, 440–1, comments on the 'unpredictability' of the consensus principle as a determining factor for the margin of appreciation.

[95] In the sense that the Commission was satisfied that the action taken by the Government was in accordance with national law and not arbitrary. See Jacobs, F.G., and White, R.C.A., *The European Convention on Human Rights* (2nd edn., Oxford: OUP, 1996), 244–5.

[96] *Council of Civil Service Unions v UK* (1988) 10 EHRR 269. This was also the view taken by the ECSR in *Conclusions X-I*, 68–9. See Ewing, K.D., 'Social Rights and Human Rights: Britain and the Social Charter—the Conservative Legacy' [2000] *EHRLR* 91 at 100–1.

[97] See, e.g., Ewing, K.D., 'Freedom of Association and Trade Union Rights' in Harris, D.J., and Joseph, S. (eds.), *The International Covenant on Civil and Political Rights and United Kingdom Law* (Oxford: Clarendon Press, 1995), 475; and Fredman, S., and Morris, G., 'Freedom of Association' (1988) 17 *ILJ* 105.

By contrast, the ILO Governing Body Committee on Freedom of Association had found that the ban imposed by the Conservative Government in 1984 was contrary to Article 2 of Convention No. 87;[98] and the UK was consequently the subject of repeated criticism from the ILO Committee of Experts.[99] It was in response to ILO recommendations and domestic pressure, that in 1997, just two weeks after gaining office, the Foreign Secretary, Robin Cook, restored to workers at Government Communication Headquarters (GCHQ) in Cheltenham the right to join a trade union of their choice.[100] The Council of Europe's Commission of Human Rights would have been content with the status quo.

B.   PARTIAL RECOGNITION OF A RIGHT TO STRIKE

In the light of this reluctance to intervene so as to protect trade union rights, it is not surprising that the Court has been hesitant to recognize that Article 11 gives rise to a right to strike. What is more surprising is the claim made by the Court in *Schmidt and Dahlström v Sweden*;[101] namely, that its decision was reached with reference to ILO standards and the requirements of the European Social Charter.[102]

The applicants, Schmidt and Dahlström, were State officials and members of Swedish trade unions. Their trade unions had organized selective strikes while attempting to secure a collective agreement. Neither of the two applicants was required to take part in any strike. Eventually, a collective agreement was drawn up between the Swedish 'National Collective Bargaining Office' and two other trade unions. By Swedish law, this collective agreement became applicable to all workers, including the applicants. However, the agreement was designed to reward members of unions who had not gone on strike. The two applicants were thereby exempt from retrospective benefits to which other workers were entitled. The applicants claimed that this state of affairs would 'discourage them from henceforth availing themselves of their right to strike', as an 'organic right', included in Article 11.[103]

---

[98]   *Case No. 1261 (UK)*, 234th Report of the CFA (1984), para. 343, at paras. 361–364; Ewing, K.D., *Britain and the ILO* (2nd edn., London: Institute of Employment Rights, 1994), chap. 6; and Morris, G., 'Freedom of Association and the Interests of the State' in Ewing, K., Gearty, C., and Hepple, B. (eds.), *Human Rights and Labour Law* (London/New York: Mansell, 1994), 45–9.

[99]   See, e.g., *Report of the Committee of Experts* (Geneva: ILO, 1985) ILC, 71st Session, 193–8 and *Report of the Committee of Experts* (Geneva: ILO, 1996) ILC, 83rd Session, 165.

[100]   In June of 1997, the ILO Conference Committee welcomed the Labour Government's decision to rectify the situation. See *Record of Proceedings* (Geneva: ILO, 1997) ILC, 85th Session, 19/100.

[101]   1 EHRR 632 (1979).

[102]   Cf. Van Dijk, P., and Van Hoof, G.J.H., *Theory and Practice of the European Convention on Human Rights* (Deventer: Kluwer, 1984), 326–7.

[103]   1 EHRR 632 (1979), para. 36.

The Court conceded that the right to strike was one important means by which union members protect their occupational interests, but it expressed the view that there were also *other* avenues.[104] This was not an entitlement 'expressly enshrined in Article 11' and could be subjected by national law to 'regulation of a kind that limits its exercise in certain instances'.[105] The applicants were said to have retained 'their personal freedom of association'.[106] Here the Court seems to have taken a view of 'freedom of association', which aims at protecting an individual's liberty to join an association rather than the ability to act in association with others.

This finding cannot readily be reconciled with the recent decision of the Court in *Wilson*,[107] and does not sit easily with the views expressed by the ILO Committee on Freedom of Association. The CFA has stated repeatedly that discrimination in favour of non-strikers (or, one can assume, members of a union who do not go on strike) is 'a major obstacle to the right of trade unionists to organise their activities' and a breach of freedom-of-association principles.[108]

In *Schmidt and Dahlström*, the Court seemed to suggest that the action of the State, as employer, was justified because employers also have 'the right to resort to collective action' in defence of their own interests.[109] In doing so, the Court equated collective action by employees and employers in a manner contrary to the views of the ECSR, the Governmental Committee, and the Parliamentary Assembly, responsible for interpretation and enforcement of Article 6 of the European Social Charter.[110]

Nevertheless, the precedent set by *Schmidt and Dahlström* was followed by the Commission in *S v Federal Republic of Germany*, where it was found that dismissal of an employee following a strike which breached a no-strike rule did not constitute a breach of Article 11.[111] Similarly, the Commission found in *NATFHE v UK* that the requirement imposed on trade unions to name members expected to participate in a strike did not breach Article 11.[112] Once again, it was observed that the right to strike was not expressly enshrined in Article 11 and could be subjected to limitations by national law. In addition, the Commission reached the conclusion that divulging the names of members did not constitute a restriction of industrial action, since the employer would find out the names of strikers after the strike, and so this

---

[104] *Ibid.*, para. 33.   [105] *Ibid.*, para. 36.   [106] *Ibid.*, para. 35.

[107] See above, at 227.   [108] *CFA Digest of Decisions*, n.86 above, para. 605.

[109] 1 EHRR 632 (1979), para. 36. Cf. European Commission of Human Rights, *Stock-taking on the European Convention on Human Rights: A Periodic Note on the Concrete Results Achieved under the Convention* (Strasbourg: Council of Europe, 1982), 149–51.

[110] All three deny that there is 'full legal equality' between the right to strike and collective action taken by an employer, such as a lock-out. See Samuel, L., *Fundamental Social Rights: Case Law of the European Social Charter* (Straşbourg: Council of Europe, 1997), 181–3.

[111] *S v Federal Republic of Germany* (1984) 39 DR 237; Lewis-Anthony, n.92 above, 14.

[112] *National Association of Teachers in Further and Higher Education v UK* (1998) 25 EHRR CD 122. See also (1998) 6 *EHRLR* 773–4.

would not materially affect their position. This reveals a fairly naïve view of industrial relations, since disclosure of names would not only enable the employer to counter the effects of a strike by arranging replacement workers and alternative means of production, but could also provide the employer with the opportunity to threaten or coerce these workers into abandoning such action.

The most recent decision on admissibility of a case relating to the right to strike was taken by the Court in *UNISON v UK*.[113] In this case, it was argued that the right to strike, and thereby freedom of association, was unjustifiably restricted by virtue of the narrowly defined immunities for industrial action provided under UK statutes. The industrial action in question had been called in order to influence the terms of transfer of an undertaking in the health service. UK courts had issued an injunction to prevent the strike taking place, on the basis that the aims of the action did not come within the statutory immunity. This was said to be not a legitimate 'trade dispute', because it related to future terms and conditions with an as yet unspecified future employer.

The European Court of Human Rights accepted that the guarantees sought by the union calling the strike would not only protect hypothetical future employees, but would also have provided existing members with additional protection of their interests. 'The proposed strike must be regarded therefore as concerning the occupational interests of the applicant's members in the sense covered by Article 11 of the Convention.' Moreover, the prohibition of the strike was considered to be a restriction on the union's power to protect those interests.

Nevertheless, this restriction was found by the Court to be justified under Article 11(2) because it pursued a legitimate aim: the 'rights of others', that is, the right of the employer to pursue the most effective delivery of the health service. The necessity of the measure was not established by the Court. Instead, the Court merely stated that it did not believe the rights of workers to engage in collective bargaining over terms and conditions of employment or to take future industrial action had been affected. Workers had not been placed 'at any real or immediate risk of detriment or of being left defenceless against future attempts to downgrade pay or conditions'. They could take industrial action later when this became a genuine threat. The Court therefore concluded that the State had not exceeded the margin of appreciation accorded to it and that the application was manifestly unfounded.

[113] App. No. 53574/99, Decision of 10 Feb. 2002, unreported. This decision was taken by a Chamber of the Court, following abolition of the Commission, due to the entry into force of Protocol 11 to the ECHR. Cf. *University College London Hospital NHS Trust v UNISON* [1999] IRLR 31.

This decision is, at one level, promising. It goes further than any other in terms of its recognition that the right to strike is linked to workers' entitlement to pursue their occupational interests under Article 11. However, it is evident that the only legitimate interests of a trade union recognized by the court are strictly 'occupational'. The legitimate aims of a strike did not extend to resistance to privatization or to protection of other workers. This can be contrasted with the broader formulation of 'economic and social' interests referred to by ILO supervisory bodies, discussed below in Chapter 12. Moreover, a very broad margin of appreciation was applied in this case, such that the necessity of measures taken to restrict industrial action was not questioned. This is then a very weak right to strike, especially when contrasted with the Court's bolder protection of negative freedom of association.

C.   PROTECTION OF NEGATIVE FREEDOM OF ASSOCIATION
AND ITS IMPLICATIONS

Negative freedom of association is also not recognized expressly in the ECHR. This was arguably a significant decision on the part of the drafters. The Committee on Legal and Administrative Questions, responsible for drafting the ECHR, used as the basis for its text the UN Universal Declaration of Human Rights,[114] Article 20(2) of which states that 'no person shall be compelled to belong to an association'. The *travaux préparatoires* reveal that this provision was deliberately excluded from the ECHR. The reason was that several members of the Council of Europe allowed or even promoted 'closed shops', as a means by which to promote collective bargaining and ensure adequate terms and conditions of employment for workers within their respective countries. The drafters evidently thought it desirable to allow the status quo to continue.

Almost thirty years later, the European Court of Human Rights decided to depart from this position in *Young, James and Webster*. The case for doing so was put most forcefully in the 'Concurring Opinion' which accompanied the main judgment. This said that:

The negative aspect of freedom of association is necessarily complementary to, and a correlative of and inseparable from its positive aspect. Protection of freedom of association would be incomplete if it extended to no more than its positive aspect. It is one and the same right that is involved.[115]

---

[114] *ECHR Travaux Préparatoires*, n.6 above, Report presented by M. Pierre-Henri Teitgen in the name of the Committee on Legal and Administrative Questions on the draft resolution which recommends to the Member States of the Council of Europe the establishment of a collective guarantee of fundamental rights and liberties (now Doc. 77 of the Consultative Assembly, First Session, 15th Sitting, 5 Sept. 1949), 196, para. 8.

[115] *Young, James and Webster v UK* (1982) 4 EHRR 38; see Concurring Opinion of Judges Ganshof van der Meersch, Bindschedler-Robert, Liesch, Gölcüklü, Matscher, Pinheiro Farinha, and Pettiti.

However, the main judgment was more cautious. It stated that the Court's conclusions were affected by the facts peculiar to this case, namely the apparent injustice done to the three workers who, on principled grounds, refused to become members of a trade union. Young, James, and Webster had been employees of British Rail prior to agreement upon a 'closed shop' and were not trade union members. If the Court had found that compulsory membership was permissible, these employees would be forced to leave their employment for refusing to become union members. This was considered to be too strong a compulsion to join a union and inconsistent with the notion of 'freedom'.[116] The judgment did observe that compulsion to join a particular trade union may not always be contrary to the Convention, conceding that Article 11 may 'not guarantee the negative aspect of freedom on the same footing as the positive aspect'.[117]

The Court's judgment in this case is also interesting on the subject of the exceptions provided by Article 11(2). It took a strict view of the phrase, 'necessary in a democratic society', contained in the limitations clause. A 'closed shop' might have certain desirable or useful outcomes, but this did not fulfil the criterion of 'necessity' under Article 11(2).[118] There was little recognition of the wide margin of appreciation allowed to States when the positive aspect of freedom of association, involving protection of trade union rights, was at issue. The fact that Denmark (and to a more limited extent France) also permitted 'closed shops' was not taken into consideration, even though this would have indicated that there was no common 'European standard' which had been breached.[119]

This decision deliberately and expressly chose to disregard the *travaux préparatoires* of the ECHR and thereby the political will of the Member States and Contracting Parties.[120] Nevertheless, the recognition of negative freedom of association has been defended in subsequent judgments of the Court, on the basis that 'the Convention is a living instrument which must be interpreted in the light of present-day conditions'.[121] It was also approved by the then Committee of Independent Experts, now renamed the European Committee of Social Rights, responsible for interpretation of the European Social Charter.[122]

Other responses to the Court's decision in *Young, James and Webster* have been mixed. Some have praised the decision on the basis that the closed

---

[116] (1982) 4 EHRR 38, para. 55.

[117] *Ibid.*

[118] *Ibid.*, at para. 63. It should be noted that the then Conservative government did not attempt to justify the existence of a 'closed shop' in the UK. See also Yourow, n.91 above, 136–40.

[119] See Samuel, n.110 above, 119–23. See above, at 227–8.

[120] (1982) 4 EHRR 38, para. 52.

[121] *Sigurjonsson v Iceland* (1993) 16 EHRR 462, para. 35.

[122] See, e.g., ECSR, *Conclusions XIII-1*, 26.

shop placed unreasonable constraints upon individual liberty.[123] This has not convinced those who are apprehensive of the emphasis which the judgment placed upon individual autonomy in the sphere of collective labour relations.[124] My concern is that the Court's enthusiasm for protection of negative freedom of association may undermine protection of the right to strike.

The issue is whether the Court will regard industrial action, which interferes with negative freedom of association, as a violation of Article 11. Will the Court give priority to the positive or to the negative aspect of freedom of association? This problem has been considered in two cases, *Sibson v UK*[125] and *Gustafsson v Sweden*.[126]

In the first, Sibson had been the branch secretary of a union, but had been dismissed from this post following a decision that he had been involved in defrauding members. He then joined a rival union. The members of his former union at his workplace subsequently voted in favour of a closed shop and threatened a strike if the employer did not respect this. The employer and the union agreed that the strike threat would be lifted if Sibson either rejoined the union or commenced work at another of the employer's depots. The applicant declined to accept either alternative and was dismissed. His claim was that his negative freedom of association guaranteed by Article 11 had been violated. The Commission declared the application admissible, but decided by eight votes to six that there had been no violation of Article 11. The Court considered that the facts of this case could be distinguished from those in *Young, James and Webster* as Sibson did not have 'any specific convictions as regards trade union membership'.[127] Moreover, the applicants in *Young, James and Webster* were faced with a threat of dismissal involving loss of livelihood, while Sibson had the option of moving to work in another of the employer's depots. Therefore, the Court decided, by seven votes to two, that there was no infringement of Article 11.

The claim brought by Gustafsson originated as one of two applications, *Englund and Others v Sweden* and *Gustafsson v Sweden*, which arose from a single set of facts.[128] For three years, Gustafsson had employed the two Englund sisters, along with others, at his youth hostel and restaurant. The

---

[123] See the statements made by representatives at the seminar organized by the Council of Europe, held at Rejkavik, 26–28 Aug. 1993, *Freedom of Association Proceedings* (Strasbourg: Council of Europe, 1994), e.g., at 7.

[124] Examples include Forde, n.78 above; Wedderburn, n.82 above, 138. See, in particular, Wedderburn of Charlton, Lord, *Freedom of Association and Community Protection: A Comparative Enquiry into Trade Union Rights of the European Community and into the Need for Intervention at the Community Level* (Luxembourg: European Commission, 1992), at 225, citing Kahn-Freund, O., *Labour and the Law* (2nd edn., Stevens & Sons, London, 1977), 196.

[125] (1994) 17 EHRR 193.

[126] (1996) 22 EHRR 409.

[127] (1994) 17 EHRR 193, para. 29.

[128] See Vol V(II), *Human Rights Digest* (Mar.–Apr. 1994), 101–2. Also see Novitz, T., 'Negative Freedom of Association' (1997) 26 *ILJ* 79.

two sisters did not belong to the relevant workers' union, nor did Gustafsson belong to the relevant employers' union. Accordingly, he was not bound by a collective agreement between the employers' and employees' unions. He also declined to enter into a substitute agreement directly with the workers' union. Both agreements would have obliged Gustafsson to ensure that all his workers were employed under certain minimal terms and conditions of employment, to contribute to certain insurance policy schemes, and to employ only union members. In 1987, the union instituted industrial action against Gustafsson's establishment. None of Gustafsson's workers took part in any industrial action, but delivery of groceries to the restaurant and collection of refuse were stopped. In 1988, Gustafsson had requested government intervention, invoking Article 11 of the Convention. However, in 1989 this request was dismissed; and the relevant courts refused to exercise their powers of judicial review. The sympathy strikes continued intermittently until 1991, when Gustafsson sold his restaurant. He claimed that the industrial action was the chief reason for the sale.

In their applications to the Commission, both the workers and the employer claimed, *inter alia*, that the lack of State protection against unjustified industrial action violated their negative freedom of association. The workers' claim was subsequently dismissed on the basis that the industrial action in question did not prevent them from remaining unorganized employees, nor did it affect their terms and conditions of employment.[129] It was only Gustafsson's case that went on to final determination by the Court.

The Commission viewed Gustafsson's claim favourably because it considered that the principle of negative freedom of association could be extended to encompass a right to refuse to engage in collective bargaining. Although it was acknowledged that Article 11 was also designed to protect positive freedom of association, on the facts of this case it was said that the trade union in question had abused this freedom. One determinative factor appears to have been the severe financial loss caused by the union's industrial action. This is a curious finding, as most strikes will cause some form of financial loss,[130] and it would be surprising if every such action constituted an abuse of trade union freedom. Another key consideration seems to have been that Gustafsson's own employees were opposed to the union's action.[131] If the union had acted on behalf of members whose economic or social conditions would have been improved by the collective agreement, the Commission indicated that the 'harsh measures' taken could have been justified. The desire to promote collective bargaining generally, and thereby secure greater bargaining power for a greater number of employees, was not

[129] *Englund v Sweden* (1994) 77–A DR 10.
[130] See Chap. 1 above, at 6; and Chap. 4 above, at 75.
[131] Only one of his employees was a member of the union, and she had provided a statement to the effect that, in her view, the union's action was unnecessary.

considered to be a permissible reason for industrial action.[132] A final decisive factor was that, on the facts before the Commission, it appeared that Gustafsson's workers were not disadvantaged by the terms of their agreement with him, when compared to their entitlements under the collective agreement. The result was that the Commission decided, by thirteen votes to four, that Sweden had infringed Article 11 by failing to provide Mr Gustafsson with sufficient legal protection or adequate redress for his loss.

However, the European Court of Human Rights took a different view, albeit by a slim majority.[133] As there was no right to enter into a collective agreement, following the *Swedish Engine Drivers' Union* case, there could be no negative right not to enter into a collective agreement. The Court's majority judgment emphasized the importance of finding a 'proper balance' between the positive and negative aspects of freedom of association guaranteed under Article 11.[134] The Court pointed to widespread international recognition of 'the legitimate character of collective bargaining', citing, *inter alia*, Article 6 of the European Social Charter and ILO Conventions Nos. 87 and 98.[135]

The Court seems to be prepared to acknowledge that a State is entitled to refuse to intervene to protect negative freedom of association where, as in the present case, legitimate industrial action is taken by a trade union. The action taken by the union against Gustafsson was viewed as legitimate, largely due to evidence produced at the last available opportunity by the Swedish government to the effect that the terms under which Gustafsson's workers were employed were less favourable than those provided by the collective agreement.[136] The Court also stated that, in cases such as this, States should be allowed a wide margin of appreciation 'in view of the sensitive character of the social and political issues involved in achieving a proper balance between the competing interests'.[137] This statement appears to deviate from the stricter approach taken in *Young, James and Webster*.

The outcomes in *Sibson* and *Gustafsson* might reassure proponents of a right to strike. However, nowhere in these two judgments is the view expressed that the right to strike could itself be regarded as a facet of freedom of association, protected under Article 11. Moreover, the majority's decision in *Gustafsson* seemed to turn on an unfortunate refusal to

---

[132] Cf. ECSR, *Conclusions I*, 183, which found that industrial action aimed generally at securing trade union recognition or collective bargaining is *prima facie* legitimate. See also *Conclusions XII-1*, 130–2 concerning the UK's removal of statutory immunity for secondary action; and the legitimate aims of industrial action recognized in *CFA Digest of Decisions*, n.86 above, paras. 479–489.

[133] (1996) 22 EHRR 409.

[134] *Ibid.*, para. 45.

[135] *Ibid.*, para. 53.

[136] The outcome of the case was subsequently challenged on this basis, but that challenge was ultimately rejected. See Request for Revision, allowed 13 Oct. 1997 and dismissal of the application, 11 Sept. 1998.

[137] (1996) 22 EHRR 409, para. 45.

recognize a link between freedom of association and collective bargaining. The artificiality of such a narrow construction was pointed out by Judge Martens in his dissenting judgment. Martens observed that freedom of association refers to freedom not only to join an organization but also to enter into contractual or quasi-contractual relations with others. Accordingly, freedom of association should encompass the freedom to enter into collective bargaining, while negative freedom of association must include the refusal to enter into a collective agreement.[138]

This dissenting opinion also highlights the potential threat posed by Gustafsson's application. Judge Martens identified that 'what is at stake is a conflict between two fundamental rights, that of the trade union relying on its positive freedom of association and that of the employer who invokes his negative freedom of association'. Given that these two rights conflict, Judge Martens argued for an individualistic interpretation of Article 11, observing that 'the Convention purports to lay down fundamental rights of the individual and to furnish the individual an effective protection against interferences with these rights'. His view was that, as a result, the employer's negative right not to engage in collective bargaining should 'in principle' take precedence over the trade union's right to take industrial action. Moreover, Judge Martens foresaw that, were freedom of disassociation given this priority, radical consequences would follow. The result would be that it would not be possible to 'justify the use of collective action in order to compel an individual employer to join an employers' association or to be otherwise integrated into the system of collective bargaining'.[139] Five other judges took a similar view. It may therefore be too early to say with any certainty that the relative priority of negative freedom of association and the right to strike, under Article 11, has been settled. This opinion delivered by Judge Martens exposes the danger posed by the principles which underlie the judgments of the European Court of Human Rights. In order for protection of a right to strike to be maintained within the Council of Europe, some priority must be given to collective action ahead of negative liberty.

D. REASONS FOR ADOPTION OF THESE PRINCIPLES

International law requires supervisory bodies to interpret relevant treaty Articles in good faith, in accordance with the ordinary meaning to be given to the term in question.[140] The European Commission and Court of Human Rights did not disregard the 'ordinary meaning' of freedom of association, but they have not been prepared to recognize that the term may have additional connotations in the context of industrial relations. The

---

[138] *Ibid.*, Dissenting Opinion of Judge Martens joined by Judge Maatscher.
[139] *Ibid.*
[140] Vienna Convention on the Law of Treaties, Art. 31(1).

reluctance of the Court to appreciate that Article 11 of the ECHR gives rise to a right to engage in collective bargaining or a right to strike suggests that the Court has limited enthusiasm for the protection of trade union rights. Moreover, efforts to ensure the protection of negative freedom of association reveal a greater interest on the defence of individual autonomy than collective solidarity. Whether the Court and the Commission were correct to adopt such a narrow construction of 'freedom of association' must be decided by reference to the context in which the term was used and the purpose of the ECHR.[141]

In the *Wemhoff* case, the Court commented that, given that the ECHR was a law-making treaty, it was 'necessary to seek the interpretation that is most appropriate in order to realise the aim and achieve the object of the treaty'.[142] As the text and purpose of the European Convention on Human Rights are different from those of the ILO Constitution and ILO Conventions, one might expect the Court to produce a different interpretation of 'freedom of association'. The ECHR is phrased generally in terms of individual rights; whereas the ILO has been concerned with the protection of both individual and collective rights.[143] Just as the Preamble to the Statute of the Council of Europe refers to 'individual freedom', so the initial aim of the ECHR was to 'guarantee the fundamental *personal* and civic rights essential for the maintenance of democracy'.[144] The argument runs that the Court's decisions on freedom of association are therefore consistent with other rights recognized under the ECHR, which tend to focus upon personal freedom rather than collective action. Moreover, the guarantee of 'freedom of association' contained in Article 11 alongside 'freedom of assembly' has a broad scope. It is intended to extend beyond the field of labour relations. In this sense, this instrument is very different from the European Social Charter and the ILO Constitution.

However, this approach to trade union rights sits oddly with the Court's general acknowledgement that many of the civil and political rights contained in the Convention have implications of a social or economic nature. For example, in the *Airey* case of 1979, the Court found 'that the mere fact that an interpretation of the Convention may extend into the sphere of social and economic rights should not be a decisive factor against such an

[141] Vienna Convention on the Law of Treaties 1969, Arts. 31(2) and (3). Cf. McDougal, M.S., Lasswell, H.D., and Miller, J.C., *The Interpretation of International Agreements and World Public Order: Principles of Content and Procedure* (New Haven, Conn.: New Haven Press, 1994), pp. xl–xlix; and Ris, M., 'Treaty Interpretation and ICJ Recourse to *Travaux Préparatoires*: Towards a Proposed Amendment of Articles 31 and 32 of the Vienna Convention on the Law of Treaties' (1991) 14 *Boston College International and Comparative Law Review* 111.

[142] *Wemhoff v Federal Republic of Germany*, 1 EHRR 55 (1979), para. 8.

[143] Hepple, B., 'Freedom to Form and Join or not to Join Trade Unions' in *Freedom of Association Proceedings*, n.123 above, 165.

[144] From the proposal made at The Hague Congress in May 1948 reported in the *Manual of the Council of Europe: Functions and Achievements* (Strasbourg: Council of Europe, 1978), 261 (my emphasis).

interpretation; there is no watertight division separating that sphere from the field covered by the Convention'.[145] The Court has also been willing to find that the freedoms protected under the ECHR may require governments to take positive action, devoting resources to the maintenance of those freedoms, again blurring the conventional distinction between civil, political, and socio-economic rights.[146]

Furthermore, Article 11 should be interpreted in a manner consistent with other provisions contained in the ECHR.[147] In particular, Article 11 should be read alongside Article 60 of the Convention. Article 60 states that nothing in the Convention 'shall be construed as limiting or derogating from any of the human rights and fundamental freedoms which may be ensured by any other agreement' to which a Contracting State is a party. This provision requires that the ECHR be interpreted in accordance with Contracting Parties' obligations under the ILO Constitution and ILO Conventions. Members of the ILO are required to respect freedom of association by virtue of the ILO Constitution as well as Conventions Nos. 87 and 98. The responsibility for interpreting the guarantee of 'freedom of association' contained therein lies with the ILO Committee on Freedom of Association and the Committee of Experts. Where the European Court of Human Rights makes decisions which contradict the principles promulgated by the two ILO Committees, the Court is construing the Convention in a manner which limits a fundamental freedom contained in agreements to which Member States are a party. The Court is therefore interpreting Article 11 in a way which is inconsistent with Article 60. This is yet another factor which indicates that the Court's decisions on trade union related issues are problematic.

The final aids to interpretation of international treaties are the *travaux préparatoires*, to which parties may appeal when the meaning of a treaty cannot be ascertained by the means outlined above. Those who oppose the Court's attempts to protect negative freedom of association may wish to appeal to records of debates preceding the adoption of the ECHR, which indicate that the Member States never intended to undermine the protection of the 'closed shop'.[148] Those who oppose the protection of a right to strike under Article 11

---

[145] *Airey v Ireland*, 2 EHRR 305 (1980). In this case, the Court found that Airey had been deprived of her right of access to the Court under ECHR Art. 6(1) when the State did not provide her with the financial aid necessary to afford a solicitor. See for the expression of similar sentiments in relation to Art. 8 *McGinley and Egan v UK* (1998) 27 EHRR 1, para. 101.

[146] E.g., in response to the 'freedom of assembly' limb of Art. 11, the Court has been prepared to place a positive obligation upon government to protect peaceful demonstrations. See *Plattform 'Ärzte für das Leben'* (1991) 13 EHRR 204. See also Viljanen, V., 'Abstention or Involvement? The Nature of State Obligations under Different Categories of Rights' in Drzewicki, K., Krouse, C., and Rosas, A. (eds.), *Social Rights as Human Rights: A European Challenge* (Åbo, Finland: Åbo Akademi University Institute for Human Rights, 1994), 44 and 58–9; and Tennjford, F., 'The Social Charter—An Instrument of Social Collaboration in Europe' [1962] *European Year Book* 71 at 79–80.

[147] Vienna Convention on the Law of Treaties, Art. 31(2).

[148] See above, at 232.

may wish to point to the *travaux préparatoires* as evidence that this never came within the contemplation of the Convention's drafters.[149]

The desirability of appeal to legislative intent has long been the subject of jurisprudential debate. This is also the subject of an on-going argument between international lawyers.[150] Those who defend the Court's decision to protect the negative as well as the positive aspects of freedom of association have declared that the ECHR is a dynamic 'living instrument', which should not be bound by the intentions of its drafters fifty years ago.[151]

It does seem desirable that those interpreting the Convention be responsive to 'modern convictions and conditions'.[152] Whether this is sufficient to account for the Court's decision that negative freedom of association was included in Article 11 will remain a matter for debate. It could also be argued that, if the Court is to be truly responsive to present-day conditions and modern views, it should give precedence to the opinions expressed at the Ministerial Conference on Human Rights in Rome on 5 November 1990. This Conference called for recognition of 'the indivisible nature of all human rights, be they civil, political, social or cultural'.[153] This is however yet to be a feature of ECHR jurisprudence.

III.   CONCLUSION: IMPLICATIONS FOR EFFECTIVENESS OF 'SOCIAL RIGHTS'

It could be said that the attitude adopted by the European Commission and Court of Human Rights to the protection of the right to strike is of little concern, given the existence of a separate Council of Europe document, the European Social Charter, which was intended to complement the European Convention on Human Rights.[154] At the time the Charter was drafted, the inclusion of an express right to strike in an international instrument was considered to be a crucial, and an innovative development in international labour law. At the 1958 tripartite conference this was seen as a clear recognition of the importance of the right to strike.[155] The inclusion of

---

[149]   See Chap. 3 above, at 133–6.

[150]   Largely between the 'Textualist' and the 'Intention' schools, although there are others. See, e.g., Johnstone, I., 'Treaty Interpretation: The Authority of Interpretive Communities' (1991) 12 *Michigan Journal of International Law* 371; McDougal, Lasswell, and Miller, n.141 above, pp. lxii–lxix; and Ris, n.141 above.

[151]   See *Sigurjonsson v Iceland* (1993) 16 EHRR 462, para. 35. For a similar view see Yourow, n.91 above, 139–40.

[152]   Bernhardt, R., 'Thoughts on the Interpretation of Human-Rights Treaties' in Matscher and Petzold, n.92 above, 69–71.

[153]   This call is now recorded in the Preamble to the Revised Social Charter. See *The Social Charter of the 21st Century*, n.39 above, per M. Heringa at 192.

[154]   Mower, n.20 above, 187; Tennjford, n.146 above, 72; *Proceedings of the Colloquy about the European Convention on Human Rights in relation to other International Instruments for the Protection of Human Rights* (Strasbourg: Council of Europe, 1979), 26.

[155]   *Tripartite Conference: Record of Proceedings*, n.29 above, 175.

the right to strike in the Charter indicates widespread acceptance of the principle that workers are entitled to take industrial action and can lead to binding obligations on Contracting Parties which ratify this provision. However, the failure of both the drafters and the supervisory bodies to make a connection with the guarantee of freedom of association contained in the ECHR has resulted in diminished protection of the right to strike.

The European Committee of Social Rights is more than capable of delivering competent guidance on the subject of the right to strike and related issues. In this, it has been assisted by ILO experts. Its sizeable jurisprudence, although not as extensive as that of the ILO Committee on Freedom of Association, merits attention.[156] The problem is that the ECSR, at least in its prior incarnation as the Committee of Independent Experts, did not have the final word on interpretation and application of Charter provisions. This was commandeered instead by a Governmental Committee, which now has a more limited competence but remains in operation. Moreover, the Conclusions reached by the ECSR have not necessarily led to the adoption of recommendations by the Committee of Ministers. The control mechanism in operation in respect of the ESC is hampered by State control. Its influence is also curtailed by the dominance of the supervisory procedures established under the ECHR.

The refusal of the European Court of Human Rights to recognize that a right to strike is necessary to effective protection of freedom of association seems to contradict the findings of other bodies responsible for supervision of the European Social Charter. The provisions contained in the European Social Charter do not make any express connection between the right to organize and join a trade union under Article 5 and the right to engage in collective bargaining (including the right to strike) under Article 6. However, in 1992, when commenting on the requisitioning of public-sector workers to replace striking manual workers, the ECSR found that the conduct of the German government constituted a violation of both Articles 5 and 6.[157] This could be viewed as an implicit acknowledgement that the two are inter-related. The Parliamentary Assembly has also observed in the course of its role in supervision of the ESC that collective action is 'an essential element of freedom of association'.[158]

This is problematic because, as the case of *Gustafsson* illustrates, when the Court hears a case concerning negative freedom of association, it will often

---

[156] See Part IV below.

[157] See the comments of Mr Fuchs in *Freedom of Association Proceedings*, n.123 above, 187; and ECSR, *Conclusions X-II*, 98–9. See also the ECSR view that referral of a collective dispute to compulsory arbitration at the request of only one of the parties can constitute a restraint on the right to trade union activities in contravention of Art. 5 ESC as well as a breach of the right to strike guaranteed under Art. 6(4). ECSR, *Conclusions XV-I (Malta)*, 4 and 6.

[158] Parliamentary Assembly of the Council of Europe, 41st Ordinary Session, *Opinion No. 145 (1989) on the first stage of the tenth supervisory cycle of the application of the European Social Charter*, para. 9.

be faced with issues relating to consultation, collective bargaining, and industrial action.[159] In such cases, the members of the Court will be deciding, albeit indirectly, on the status of trade union rights. Cases like *NATFHE* and *UNISON* suggest that the Court does not possess more than a limited understanding of the dynamics of industrial relations and ILO standards.[160] It may be more advisable for the Court to seek guidance from the specialized organs responsible for enforcement of the European Social Charter, which are assisted by an ILO observer.

However, at present, it seems that where there is a divergence of opinion the judgments of the Court are likely to prevail. For example, in 1975 the ECSR simply agreed to be bound by whatever decision the court reached in *Schmidt and Dahlström*.[161] Deference to the opinions of the Court is also evident from the Conclusions of the ECSR following the *Young, James and Webster* case. Previously, the Committee had ruled that governments could not impose compulsory trade unionism, but that it was permissible for workers themselves to negotiate a 'closed shop' with their employers.[162] The ECSR received the Court's decision in *Young, James and Webster* with some apprehension, and did not reach a final conclusion on the question of negative freedom of association until its next supervision cycle.[163] However, at its Eighth Supervisory Session, the Committee adopted this principle and subsequently recommended to states that failure to guarantee negative freedom of association would be a violation of Article 5 of the Charter.[164]

It has been claimed that the ESC supervisory mechanisms have influenced that of the Court. An example is said to be *Sigurjonsson v Iceland*, where the Court cited the Conclusions of the ECSR.[165] However, this seems an optimistic rather than an accurate interpretation of that judgment, which follows almost to the letter the principles set out by the Court itself in *Young, James and Webster*.[166] Since these cases were heard, the ECSR has become a more staunch opponent to the closed shop than the European Court of Human Rights ever dared to be,[167] but it seems that the origin of its enthusiasm lies with the sentiments of the Court rather than its own initiative.

It is possible that the influence of the European Committee of Social Rights will increase as the new collective complaints system for Charter violations comes into effect, and is further improved. As Harris notes, 'the

---

[159] See above, at 234–7.
[160] See above, at 230–1.
[161] ECSR, *Conclusions IV*, 47.
[162] ECSR, *Conclusions I*, 31.
[163] See Samuel, n.110 above, 116–23.
[164] See, e.g., the Committee's criticism of Denmark in ECSR, *Conclusions IX-1*, 47.
[165] See *Social Charter of the 21st Century*, n.39 above, per M. Heringa at 219.
[166] (1982) 4 EHRR 38.
[167] See, e.g., criticism of Denmark in ECSR, *Conclusions XIV-1*, 177; France at 252–3; and Ireland at 413.

future of the European Social Charter as an international treaty-based instrument for the protection of economic and social rights in Europe is brighter than could possibly have been foreseen just a year or two ago'.[168] Yet, even if the influence of this Committee does increase, there will still be a need to avoid the development of two parallel but conflicting lines of authority. There is therefore a strong case for the Committee of Ministers to revisit the recommendations made in 1998 and 1999 by the Parliamentary Assembly, calling for a more integrated and effective system for the enforcement of social rights.[169] One possibility may be to create a tripartite Court of First Instance to hear cases relating to labour-related issues, in which a member of the European Committee of Social Rights sat as an independent chairperson, with appeal to the European Court of Human Rights on points of law. The Committee of Ministers, however, seems reluctant to consider or devote resources to further structural change under the ESC. If it does, there may yet be scope for the Council of Europe to follow the example set by the ILO, which recognizes the integration of civil, political, and economic rights and thereby the connection between freedom of association and the right to strike.

[168] Harris, D., 'A Fresh Impetus for the European Social Charter' (1992) 41 *ICLQ* 659, 676.

[169] See above, at 224.

10

Judicial Circumspection in the EU

Neither freedom of association nor the right to strike receives explicit protection under any EC legislation, apart from non-binding declaratory instruments. This means that, generally, not only is there no potential role for the European Court of Justice in enforcing protection of the right to strike, but no possibility for the Court to imitate ILO supervisory bodies and craft protection of such a right from the basis of a guarantee of freedom of association. Some have viewed it as a shame that the ECJ plays no greater role in the transposition and enforcement of international labour rights in Europe, given the peculiar efficacy of this supervisory process.[1] This leaves the right to strike, protected under national laws, vulnerable to incursions by other facets of EC law, designed to achieve market integration. As was observed in Chapter 7, these include the principles of free movement of goods and removal of barriers to competition.[2] 'The question is how far the Community rules relating to the integration of national markets constitute a constraint on the law-making powers in the social field which the Member States in principle retain.'[3]

There are two alternative paths through which the jurisprudence of the ECJ may touch on and, indeed, shape the extent to which a right to strike is protected. The first is through 'staff cases', that is complaints brought before the Court by EU officials who claim that there has been a breach of the 'Staff Regulations' which form the basis of their contract of employment. The second is via the 'fundamental rights' jurisprudence developed by the Court, which limits the scope of EC law, circumscribes the activities of EU institutions, and even restricts Member States when implementing EC law. This 'fundamental rights' jurisprudence has the potential to be used as a defence against the aggressive application of market integration principles to national laws.

Nevertheless, the ECJ has been relatively circumspect in taking either path. The Court seems reluctant to establish the scope of a right

---

[1] Wedderburn, Lord, 'Labour Standards, Global Markets and Labour Laws in Europe' in Sengenberger, W., and Campbell, D. (eds.), *International Labour Standards and Economic Interdependence* (Geneva: IILS, 1994); and Germanotta, P., and Novitz, T., 'Globalisation and the Right to Strike: The Case for European-Level Protection of Secondary Action' (2002) 18 *IJCLLIR* 67 at 81.

[2] Chap. 7 above, at 156 and 162–3.

[3] Davies, P., 'Market Integration and Social Policy in the Court of Justice' (1995) 24 *ILJ* 49 at 50.

to strike and has provided no legal definition of its content.[4] This reticence can be contrasted with judicial activism in the fields of gender equality and the internal market.[5] Indeed, the bold adoption of doctrines of direct (and indirect) effect, together with the *Francovich* principle of liability, has established the superior status of provisions of the EC Treaty, Regulations, and Directives, which national courts are instructed to apply in preference to domestic laws.[6] That these laws could implement other international obligations appears to be of limited relevance. Article 307 (ex Article 234) of the EC Treaty states that the prior obligations of States arising under international agreements before 1 January 1958 or their accession to the Union remain unaffected by provisions of the Treaty. However, the second paragraph of this Article states that 'to the extent that such agreements are not compatible with this Treaty, the Member State shall take all appropriate steps to eliminate the incompatibilities established', evidently by renouncing these prior obligations.[7]

The limited development of the Court's jurisprudence can be accounted for by the very few cases in which the Court is called on to decide these issues, by virtue of restrictions placed on individual *locus standi*. It is also possible that the attitude of the ECJ reflects the sparse Treaty bases for social policy, especially in respect of freedom of association and the priority given to the European Convention on Human Rights as a source of 'fundamental rights'. This section examines potentially relevant case law and considers the extent to which the status quo is sustainable.

I. JURISDICTION OF THE EUROPEAN COURT OF JUSTICE

The jurisdiction of the European Court of Justice is established in Articles 220 to 245 of the EC Treaty. Actions may be brought against a Member

---

[4] See, e.g., Case 70/86 *Commission v Greece* [1987] ECR 3545; and Case C–338/89 *Organisationen Danske Slagterier v Landbrugsministeriet* [1991] ECR I–2315, in which the ECJ considered whether industrial action should amount to a case of *force majeure* in the context of an application for the extension of an export licence. This is to be determined by whether such action was reasonably in the contemplation of the applicant for the licence at the time the application was made. No comment on the legitimacy of industrial action or otherwise was provided.

[5] See, on gender equality, Kilpatrick, C., 'Gender Equality: A Fundamental Dialogue' in Sciarra, S. (ed.), *Labour Law in the Courts: National Judges and the European Court of Justice* (Oxford: Hart Publishing, 2001); and, on the internal market, Maduro, M.P., *We The Court: The European Court of Justice and the European Economic Constitution: A Critical Reading of Article 30 of the EC Treaty* (Oxford: Hart Publishing, 1998).

[6] Case 26/62 *Van Gend en Loos* [1963] ECR 10; Case C–106/89 *Marleasing SA v La Comercial International de Alimentacion* [1990] ECR I–4135; Joined Cases C–6 & C–9/90 *Francovich and Bonifaci v Italy* [1991] ECR I–5357; further elaborated in Joined Cases C–46 & C–48/93 *Brasserie du Pêcheur v Germany; The Queen v Secretary of State, ex p. Factortame* [1996] ECR I–1029.

[7] See for application of this policy Kilpatrick, C., 'Production and Circulation of EC Nightwork Jurisprudence' (1996) 25 *ILJ* 169. The issue is also discussed briefly below, at 254.

State for infringement of EC law by the Commission under Article 226 (ex Article 169) ECT and by another Member State under Article 227 (ex Article 170) ECT. Article 230 (ex Article 173) ECT allows the Court to review the legality of acts of Community institutions. In this context, both Member States and Community institutions have standing to bring actions. An individual can also institute proceedings in such cases against a decision addressed to them or an issue which is of individual and direct concern, although this has tended to be defined narrowly.[8] There is an additional argument that trade unions may have standing as 'privileged applicants', to the extent that they are legitimate participants in the creation of EC law, but this point has not been settled.[9] The most common form of intervention in the field of social policy is through the preliminary reference procedure, whereby domestic courts may seek guidance from the ECJ on interpretation of EC law under Article 234 (ex Article 177) ECT.[10] This is, however, dependent upon the enthusiasm of national courts for utilizing this procedure. 'It is solely for the national court before which the dispute has been brought, and which must assume responsibility for the subsequent judicial decision, to determine in the light of the particular circumstances of the case both the need for a preliminary ruling in order to enable it to deliver judgment and the relevance of the questions which it submits to the Court.'[11] An individual worker or trade union cannot rely upon access to a hearing before the ECJ by this means.[12]

---

[8] The classic statement of access for 'non-privileged applicants' was set out in Case 25/61 *Plaumann & Co v Commission* [1963] ECR 95. This may however be changed in the light of the test approved by the CFI in Case T–177/01 *Jégo-Quéré et Cie v Commission*, Judgment of 3 May 2002, not yet reported: '[a] person is to be regarded as individually concerned by a Community measure of general application that concerns him directly, if the measure in question affects his legal position, in a manner which is both definite and immediate, by restricting his rights or by imposing obligations on him. The number and the position of other persons who are likewise affected by the measure, or who may be so, are of no relevance in that regard.'

[9] This would require building upon the principles stated in Case C–70/88 *European Parliament v Council* [1990] ECR I–2041, paras. 20–28 and Case T–585/93 *Stichting Greenpeace Council (Greenpeace International) v Commission* [1995] ECR II–2205, para. 59. However, note that where there is no such participation it seems that this exclusion cannot be challenged by this means: see Case T–135/96 *UEAPME v Council* [1998] ECR II–2335; discussed in Syrpis, P., 'Social Democracy and Judicial Review in the Community Order' in Kilpatrick, C., Novitz, T., and Skidmore, P. (eds.), *The Future of Remedies in Europe* (Oxford: Hart Publishing, 2000); and Bernard, N., 'Legitimising EU Law: Is the Social Dialogue the Way Forward? Some Reflections Around the UEAPME Case' in Shaw, J. (ed.), *Social Law and Policy in an Evolving European Union* (Oxford: Hart Publishing, 2000).

[10] See Sciarra, S., 'Integration Through Courts: Article 177 as a Pre-federal Device' in Sciarra, n.5 above.

[11] A reiteration of the principles governing the preliminary reference procedure, taken from Case C–415/93 *Union Royale Belge des Sociétés de Football Association ASBL v Bosman* [1995] ECR I–4921, Judgment, at para. 59.

[12] Duvigneau, J.L., 'From Advisory Opinion 2/94 to the Amsterdam Treaty: Human Rights Protection in the European Union' (1999) 25 *Legal Issues of European Integration* 61, at 66.

The Court is composed of fifteen judges, who are of fifteen different nationalities, appointed for an initial, but renewable, term of six years.[13] These judges usually hear cases in six Chambers, but the most important cases are heard by the full Court. Judgments of the Court are unanimous and are therefore often notorious for reflecting subtly the underlying compromises between judges whose legal grounding is in different national systems. These judgments of the ECJ are binding on Member States, which may be subjected to a financial penalty for non-compliance.[14]

The judges are aided by eight Advocates General, who act as independent advisers to the Court, providing reasoned submissions on cases which supplement those of the interested parties.[15] These tend to be more detailed than judgments given and can provide an insight into the reasons for some of the Court's decisions.

The workload of the Court has grown considerably as the competence of the EC and its membership have expanded. One attempt to address the strain placed on the ECJ was the creation of a 'Court of First Instance' to hear, *inter alia*, competition cases, anti-dumping cases, cases arising from the application of the ECSC, and cases concerning the application of the Staff Regulations. In respect of such subject-matter, the ECJ has been converted to an appellate body.[16] With this one exception, 'the judicial system of the Community has not changed essentially since the founding of the Community'.[17]

II. STAFF CASES

Staff cases consist of actions taken by EU officials against the institutions that employ them. Since 1989, these cases have been heard by the Court of First Instance, with appeals to the ECJ on points of law. This jurisdiction arises by virtue of Article 236 (ex Article 179) ECT and covers 'any dispute between the Community and its servants within the limits and under the conditions laid down in the Staff Regulations or the Conditions of Employment'.[18]

Article 24a of the Staff Regulations provides that EU officials 'shall be entitled to exercise the right of association; they may in particular be

[13] Art. 221 (ex Art. 165) ECT. This seems to have provided the model for Protocol 11 to the ECHR, discussed in Chap. 9 above, at 214.
[14] Art. 228 (ex Art. 228) ECT.
[15] Art. 222 (ex Art. 166) ECT. The ninth AG was only temporary. Note also that the parties are not given the opportunity to comment on the AG's opinion.
[16] Art. 225 (ex Art. 168a) ECT. See Brown, L.N., and Kennedy, T., *Brown and Jacobs: The Court of Justice of the European Communities* (5th edn., London: Sweet & Maxwell, 2000), chap. 5. Note the amendment of Art. 225 by the Treaty of Nice 2000; also the creation of 'judicial panels' under a new Art. 225a, which should also assist in alleviating the workload of the ECJ.
[17] Jacobs, F., 'Introducing the Court's Paper' in Dashwood, A., and Johnston, A. (eds.), *The Future of the Judicial System of the European Union* (Oxford: Hart Publishing, 2001), 9.
[18] See Brown and Kennedy, n.16 above, chap. 9.

trade union members'. Unions have been recognized by Community institutions, acting in the capacity of employers. One key question which has arisen in this context is the extent to which staff unions have standing in 'staff cases', that is, complaints brought by their members. The remedy provided by Article 91 of the Staff Regulations is available only to officials and other employees. For this reason, in two key cases, *Kortner*[19] and *Syndicat Général*,[20] it was held by the ECJ that the direct action brought by a staff association under Article 91 was inadmissible.

However, these two cases do, *obiter*, establish principles of use to trade unions which wish to undertake collective action in defence of their members' interests. In *Kortner*, it was stated by the Court 'under the general principles of labour law, the freedom of trade union activity recognised under Article 24a of the Staff Regulations means not only that officials and servants have the right without hindrance to form organisations of their own choosing, but also that these associations are free to do anything lawful to protect the interests of their members as employees'.[21] The reference to what is 'lawful' does limit the ambit of this principle significantly. It is therefore necessary to find other routes for action which are sanctioned by EC law. The Court indicated that what was then the second paragraph of Article 173 of the EC Treaty (now the fourth paragraph of Article 230) could provide one such route for the union to acquire standing, providing that the conditions set out therein were met. In other words, the union could institute proceedings in cases concerning staff, to the extent that a decision was addressed to it or the decision addressed to another person was of 'direct and individual concern' to that union.[22] In addition, the union had the entitlement, under Article 37 of the Statute of the Court, to intervene in disputes submitted to the Court, to the extent that it could establish a 'legitimate interest in the result of any case'. What it could not do was bring a direct action under Articles 90–91 of the Staff Regulations.[23] *Syndicat Général* concerned a challenge by a trade union to deductions from staff pay following strikes. The same principles were reiterated. In addition,

---

[19] Case 175/73 *Union Syndicale, Massa and Kortner v Commission* [1974] ECR 917, Judgment, para. 18.

[20] Case 18/75 *Syndicat Général du Personnel des Organismes Européens v Commission* [1974] ECR 933, Judgment, at para. 22.

[21] Case 175/73 *Union Syndicale, Massa and Kortner v Commission* [1974] ECR 917, Judgment, para. 14.

[22] See, however, for a very narrow construction of this entitlement Case T–96/92 *Comité Central d'Entreprise de la Société Générale des Grandes Sources and others v Commission* [1995] ECR II–1213; Case T–12/93 *Comité Central d'Entreprise de la Société Anonyme Vittel and others v Commission* [1995] ECR II–1247; and Case T–189/97 *Comité d'Entreprise de la Société Française de Production and others v. Commission* [1998] ECR II–335.

[23] Case 175/73 *Union Syndicale, Massa and Kortner v Commission* [1974] ECR 917, Judgment, at paras. 16–22.

Advocate General Trabucchi indicated that to allow the union such standing would be consistent with ILO Convention No. 87.[24]

These pronouncements were elaborated upon in *Maurissen*.[25] There the ECJ recognized the entitlement of trade unions to perform various functions on behalf of their members. 'Community institutions must allow trade unions and staff associations to fulfil their proper role, *inter alia* by keeping officials and servants informed, representing them . . . and participating in consultations . . . on all matters affecting staff, and may not treat them differently without justification'.[26] Nevertheless, the Court was reluctant to impose on the employer any obligation to facilitate trade union activity apart from time off to be given to representatives to attend meetings. There was no obligation placed on Community institutions or bodies to make their messenger services available to trade unions. More recently, in the judgment of the Court of First Instance in *Dunnett*, it has been confirmed that staff representatives should be consulted on matters which concern the financial interests of staff, 'under a general principle of labour law common to all Member States'. This must be 'such as to have an influence of the substance of the measure adopted', be timely, and *bona fide*. However, this does not amount to a 'right of co-decision'. Managerial prerogative is to be left intact.[27]

The 'staff cases' seem promising, in that it is possible to detect in these cases some judicial support at the Community level for trade unions and for collective action in defence of the interests of trade union members. It could be assumed that industrial action in defence of workers' interests comes within the ambit of these principles, but there is no unequivocal express endorsement of a right to strike in these judgments.[28]

III.   THE 'FUNDAMENTAL RIGHTS' JURISPRUDENCE OF THE ECJ

In the first cases that it heard, the European Court of Justice refused to examine the compatibility of EC actions with fundamental human rights.[29]

---

[24] Case 18/75 *Syndicat Général du Personnel des Organismes Européens v Commission* [1974] ECR 933 AG's Opinion at 948. This is indeed consistent with Art. 7 of ILO Convention No. 87 which concerns legal personality of trade unions.

[25] Cases C–193 & C–194/87 *Maurissen and European Public Service Union v Court of Auditors* [1990] ECR I–95.

[26] *Ibid.*, Judgment, para. 15.

[27] Case T–192/99 *Dunnett, Hackett and Calvet v European Investment Bank* [2001] ECR II–813, IA–65, II–313, paras. 89–90.

[28] Cf. Hendy, J., 'The Human Rights Act, Article 11 and the Right to Strike' [1998] *EHRLR* 582, 592–5; and Wedderburn, Lord, *Freedom of Association and Community Protection: A Comparative Enquiry into Trade Union Rights of the European Community and into the Need for Intervention at the Community Level* (Luxembourg: European Commission, 1992), 158–64.

[29] Jacqué, J.P., 'The Convention and the European Communities' in Macdonald, R. St. J., Matscher, F., and Petzold, H. (eds.), *The European System for the Protection of Human Rights* (Dordrecht: Martinus Nijhoff, 1993), at 890.

This refusal seems to stem from the assumption that the European Communities were to serve primarily economic ends. However, the challenge to the supremacy of EC law by the Constitutional Court of the Federal Republic of Germany led to a swift change of stance.[30] In the *Nold II* case, the Court made its classic statement that it would have regard to 'fundamental rights' when scrutinizing the application of EC law. These rights were said to consist of those contained in the European Convention on Human Rights 1950, those set out in other international instruments, and those derived from the constitutional traditions of Member States.[31] This jurisprudence was formally endorsed by the European Parliament, the Council, and the Commission in a 'Common Declaration' of 5 April 1977.[32] The civil and political rights set out in the ECHR have always taken primacy, as is reflected in Article 6(2) of the Treaty on European Union.[33]

These fundamental rights constrain the actions of the EU, for unless EU action is in compliance with these, it will lack legal validity. Moreover, the scope of EC law, such as, for example, the basic provisions contained in the EC Treaty, is to be determined with reference to such general principles. It has also been established that Member States, when acting within the scope of EC law, must respect fundamental rights.[34] This jurisprudence has had the incidental effect of precluding the EC legal regime from review under the supervisory machinery established in respect of the ECHR.[35]

The Court has long regarded 'social' rights as being capable of recognition as fundamental rights. For example, in *Defrenne (No. 3)*, the ECJ made reference to the elimination of discrimination on grounds of sex contained

---

[30] *Bundesgerichtshof*, order of 8 Oct. 1967 in BVerGE 1967, 223. The Constitutional Court had found that it had jurisdiction to scrutinize EC law to ensure that it was compatible with German constitutional rights set out in the Basic Law. See Case 11/70 *Internationale Handelsgesellschaft v Einführ- und Vorratsstelle Getreide* [1970] ECR 1125, which reasserted the primacy of ECJ entitlement to scrutinize whether there was conformity with the fundamental rights which formed 'an integral part of the general principles of Community law'. See paras. 3 and 4 of the Judgment.

[31] Case 4/73 *Nold KG v Commission* [1974] ECR 491 at para. 13.

[32] Joint Declaration of 5 Apr. 1977 [1977] OJ C103/1. See also EC Bull. 3/77, 5.

[33] See Chap. 7 above, at 162.

[34] This is usually taken to apply to national implementing or derogating legislation. See, e.g., Case C–5/88 *Wachhauf v Bundesamt für Ernährung und Forstwirtschaft* [1989] ECR 2609. Nevertheless, the scope of review of Member States' actions remains the subject of some controversy, on which see Binder, D.S., 'The European Court of Justice and the Protection of Fundamental Rights in the Community: New Developments and Future Possibilities in Expanding Fundamental Rights Review to Member State Action' (1995) Jean Monnet Working Paper Series 4/95 (Cambridge, Mass.: Harvard, 1995).

[35] The European Court of Human Rights has stated that, to the extent that the EU legal regime provides equivalent protection of human rights, there will be no question of accepting an application under the ECHR. See *Matthews v UK* (1999) 28 EHRR 361. An application cannot in any case be brought against the EC or EU under the ECHR, since neither is a party to that instrument. Nor could an application be brought against an EU Member State when implementing EC law, to the extent that it lacked discretion to do so. See, e.g., App. No. 13258/87, *M & Co. v FRG* (1990) 64 DR 138.

in both the European Social Charter 1961 and ILO Convention No. 111.[36] In *Bosman*, the ECJ recognized that the principle of freedom of association, enshrined in Article 11 of the ECHR, was 'one of the fundamental rights which, as the Court has consistently held . . . are protected under the Community legal order'.[37] However, it did not elaborate on the scope of this freedom and the right to strike was not at issue in that case.

It has been asserted that the Court's recognition of principles is best regarded as extending in 'concentric circles' from the core civil and political rights contained in the ECHR to merely 'aspirational social rights'.[38] This assertion seems speculative, for limitations on standing and judicial access have created a situation whereby 'the [C]ourt has not had the means to elaborate comprehensive set of rights'.[39] Nevertheless, it may be significant that the ECJ has referred rarely to instruments containing social rights.[40]

In 1978, Antoine Jacobs flagged the possibility that the right to strike could be recognized as a fundamental right by the ECJ.[41] He recognized that, if the right to strike had been enshrined in the ECHR, it would have been more immediately obvious that it came within the scope of this jurisprudence. Nevertheless, he suggested that, even though this was not the case, there were two other bases on which the right to strike could be regarded as a fundamental right. First, such a right is expressly protected in other international instruments, such as the ICESCR 1966 and the European Social Charter 1961. Secondly, the right to strike is referred to explicitly in the Constitutions of Member States of the Community, namely France, Greece, Italy, Portugal, Spain, and Sweden.[42] There has not, however, been any definitive statement provided by the ECJ about the status of the right to strike as a 'fundamental right' under the general principles of Community law. It seems that its exclusion from the ECHR

---

[36] Case 149/77 *Defrenne v Sabena (No. 3)* [1978] ECR 1365, paras. 26–27. See also Szyszczak, E., 'Social Rights as General Principles of Community Law' in Neuwahl, N.A., and Rosas, A. (eds.), *The European Union and Human Rights* (The Hague: Kluwer/Martinus Nijhoff, 1995), 211.

[37] Case C–415/93 *Union Royale Belge des Sociétés de Football Association and Others v Bosman and Others* [1995] ECR I–4921, Judgment, para. 79.

[38] Lenaerts, K., 'Fundamental Rights to be Included in a Community Catalogue' (1991) 16 *ELRev.* 367 at 376.

[39] Weiss, M., 'Fundamental Social Rights for the European Union' (1997) 18 *Industrial Law Journal* (South Africa) 417 at 423.

[40] See Betten, L., 'The EU Charter on Fundamental Rights: A Trojan Horse or a Mouse?' (2001) 17 *IJCLLIR* 151 at 157, who observed that, since 1989, the only case in which the ECJ has referred to the 1989 Community Charter of the Fundamental Social Rights of Workers was Case C–84/94 *UK v Council* [1996] ECR I–5755. Also it was alleged in the Report of the Expert Group on Fundamental Rights, *Affirming Fundamental Rights in the European Union: Time to Act* (Brussels: European Commission DG for Employment and Social Affairs, 1999), 14, that status is given to the ECHR in preference to the ESC and ILO Conventions.

[41] Jacobs, A., 'Towards Community Action on Strike Law' (1978) 15 *CMLRev.* 133, 144–6.

[42] See Clauwaert, S., *Fundamental Social Rights in the European Union: Comparative Tables and Documents* (Brussels: ETUI, 1998).

and from recognition under the case law of the European Court of Human Rights has had an unfortunate 'knock on' effect.

This is potentially problematic, given the extensive reach of principles relating to free movement of goods and the removal of barriers to competition, enshrined in the EC Treaty. Recent case law demonstrates that collective labour laws could well come into conflict with these principles. Given the reticence of the Court on the subject of the right to strike, it is difficult to predict the extent to which national laws can be preserved in opposition to their application.

A.   POTENTIAL CONFLICT BETWEEN FREE MOVEMENT OF GOODS AND PROTECTION OF A RIGHT TO STRIKE

Free movement of goods is essential to the construction of a common market, as is evident from Articles 28 to 31 (ex Articles 30–37) of the EC Treaty and has been recognized by the ECJ.[43] It is a fundamental treaty principle. As far back as 1963, it was predicted that a clash could arise between national protection of industrial action and the principle of free movement of goods, given the potential for the former to affect the latter.[44] This issue has not been addressed directly by the Court. However, concern arose following the judgment delivered by the ECJ in *Commission v France*.[45]

This case was brought by the Commission under Article 226 (ex Article 169) ECT, after a Spanish complaint. The action was also supported by the UK. It concerned the behaviour of French farmers, who had initiated a campaign resisting the sale of agricultural products which originated outside France. The French State claimed that it could not be held responsible for the actions of private citizens. However, the Court took note of the fact that repeated violent acts committed by the farmers had received little response from the French government, despite previous criticism from the Commission. The case itself was initiated after three lorries carrying fruit and vegetables from Spain were attacked in Southern France and the police did not intervene. The ECJ found that the actions of the French government amounted to a violation of Article 28 (ex Article 30) of the EC Treaty which prohibits quantitative restrictions upon imports. In reliance on Article 10 (ex Article 5) ECT the Court considered that France had failed to take 'all appropriate measures' to meet its Treaty obligations. The measures taken were described 'as manifestly inadequate to ensure freedom of intra-Community trade'.[46] Although this case concerned vandalism and 'violent

---

[43]   See Joined Cases 2 & 3/62 *Commission v Belgium and Luxembourg* [1962] ECR 791.

[44]   Cox, R., 'Social and Labour Policy in the EEC' (1963) 1 *BJIR* 5, at 9. It has also been argued that there may be a clash between free movement of persons and the right to strike, where persons are recruited across the border to replace strikers. See Chap. 7 above, at 156–7.

[45]   Case C–265/95 *Commission v France* [1997] ECR I–6961.

[46]   *Ibid.*, Judgment, para. 52.

acts' by farmers, it was unclear whether industrial action (such as stoppage of work or a picket) which affected the free movement of goods would also be caught under by the judgment. The Court had said that 'apprehension of internal difficulties cannot justify a failure by a Member State to apply Community law correctly',[47] and it was not clear what the ambit of this principle would be. The trade union movement was aware that it was not impossible for EU Member States to be required to adhere to EC law rather than established ILO standards, given the mass denunciation of ILO Convention No. 89 of 1948 which was found to be contrary to the principle of gender equality enshrined in the EC Equal Treatment Directive.[48]

An answer has yet to come from the Court. In the meantime, the 'Monti Regulation', adopted in 1998, has created a mechanism whereby the Commission can intervene in order to prevent obstacles to trade. After long debate and much political wrangling, the effect of this Regulation was tempered by Article 2, which states that it is not to 'be interpreted as affecting in any way the exercise of fundamental rights as recognised in Member States, including the right or freedom to strike. These rights may also include the right or freedom to take other actions covered by the specific provisions governing industrial relations systems in Member States'.[49] This seems to provide exceptions for various forms of industrial action, including picketing, but only to the extent that these are protected under national laws.

The wording of the provision indicates that the scope of the right to strike is to be determined by the Member States rather than defined at the Community level. This is consistent with the wording of Article 28 of the EU Charter of Fundamental Rights.[50] The Court has yet to hear a case in which it is required to consider the application of this provision, but it will be interesting to see whether it will defer entirely to national laws. Arguably, it cannot do so and will also have to address the legitimacy of the laws and action in question.

Giovanni Orlandini has surmised that it will be difficult for the Court to shelter behind a lack of legislative competence in the sphere of industrial action. 'In order to determine whether there is a breach of Community law or not, what has to be assessed is the "well-foundedness" of the justification adopted; if based on alleged protection of a fundamental right, it is that right that is brought before the Court's judgment, to assess the value it may take in the Community system, and the "reasonableness"

[47] *Ibid.*, Judgment, para. 55.
[48] See Council Directive 76/207 on the Principle of Equal Treatment for Men and Women [1976] OJ L39/40. See Case C–345/89 *Stoeckel* [1991] ECR I–4047; Case C–151/91 *Levy* [1993] ECR I–4287; and Case C–13/93 *Minne* [1994] ECR I–371. These cases are discussed in Kilpatrick, n.7 above.
[49] See Chap. 7 above, at 162.
[50] Discussed in Chap. 7 above, at 165.

of appeal to it in the case under consideration.'[51] There is accordingly still some potential for EC law to restrict the access of European workers to the exercise of the right to strike. Indeed, the very existence of this potential may erode the spaces for industrial conflict, such as, for example, in the transport sector.[52]

B. POTENTIAL CONFLICT BETWEEN COMPETITION RULES AND INDUSTRIAL ACTION

Workers tend to engage in collective bargaining and industrial action, so as to secure collective agreements. Their aim in doing so is to place pressure upon an employer to restrain competition over terms and conditions of employment. Similarly, employers may benefit from entering into agreements which 'cushion' them against competition for manpower.[53] Where national laws permit a right to strike to restrain competition, one might expect such laws to be overridden by EC rules on competition set out in Articles 81–86 (ex Articles 85–90) of the EC Treaty. This was the situation in the *Merci* case, where a strike by dockworkers delayed and thereby deterred the free movement of goods.[54] No mention was made in that judgment of the importance of protecting the right to strike as a 'fundamental right', but this may well have been because the point was tangential to the central issue in that case, the monopoly exercised over dockwork.

In *Albany International*,[55] the ECJ was faced with a comparable problem in the area of pensions. A Dutch supplementary pension scheme was created by collective agreement and, on the request of the parties to the agreement, affiliation to that scheme could be made compulsory by the relevant Minister within that industrial sector. This was a preliminary reference case in which the Court was asked to rule on whether it should be possible for an employer to opt out of the scheme, established by collective agreement, and extended by the State to cover an entire sector.

Advocate General Francis Jacobs analysed the jurisprudence of the ECJ to date on the subject of collective action. He considered that no fundamental right to collective bargaining existed. He cited the judgment of the European Court of Human Rights in the *Swedish Engine Drivers' Union* case,[56] and noted the inferior status of the European Social Charter in

[51] Orlandini, G., 'The Free Movement of Goods as a Possible "Community" Limitation on Industrial Conflict' (2000) 6 *ELJ* 341 at 351.

[52] *Ibid.*, at 362.

[53] See Evju, S., 'Collective Agreements and Competition Law: The *Albany* Puzzle and *van der Woude*' (2001) 17 *IJCLLIR* 165 at 165.

[54] Case C–179/90 *Merci Convenzionali Porto di Genova SpA v Siderurgica Gabrielli SpA* [1991] ECR I–5889. See the discussion of this case by Davies, n.3 above, 64–6.

[55] Case C–67/96 *Albany International BV v Stichting Bedrijfsfonds Textielindustrie* [1999] ECR I–5751.

[56] See above, at 226–8.

which a right to collective bargaining was recognized.[57] By contrast, he did consider that the right to strike and freedom of association were 'fundamental rights'. He added that '[i]n my view, the right to take collective action in order to protect occupational interests in so far as it is indispensable for the enjoyment of freedom of association is also protected by Community law'.[58] In this respect, he relied on the statements made in *Bosman*[59] with regard to freedom of association and *Maurissen*[60] with regard to trade unions. It seems that he considered that judgments given in 'staff cases' could provide the foundation for the elaboration of a broader fundamental rights jurisprudence on labour issues. He did not however elaborate upon what the scope of a right to strike might be. Neither did the Court in its subsequent judgment, which focused solely on whether a collective agreement constituted a legitimate exception to the application of EC competition rules.

The ECJ did not consider whether the right to collective bargaining was or was not a fundamental right; nor was there any need on the facts of the case to determine the status of the right to strike. Instead, the Court reached its conclusions on the basis of the wording of Article 81 (ex Article 85) and its interpretation of the EC Treaty as a whole. The judgment recognized that 'certain restrictions of competition are inherent in collective agreements between organisations representing employers and workers', but that 'the social policy objectives pursued by such agreements' would be seriously undermined if management and labour were to be subject to Article 81 when adopting measures to improve conditions of work and employment. On this basis, the Court concluded that 'agreements concluded in the context of collective negotiations between management and labour in pursuit of such objectives must, by their very nature and purpose, be regarded as falling outside the scope of Article 85(1) of the Treaty'.[61] This principle has been applied in subsequent cases,[62] and a similar line has been taken by the Court in the *Van der Woude* case,[63] which concerned supplementary health insurance, arranged in a comparable fashion to the supplementary pension

---

[57] Case C–67/96 *Albany International BV v Stichting Bedrijfsfonds Textielindustrie* [1999] ECR I–5751, Opinion, paras. 130–65.

[58] *Ibid.*, Opinion, para. 159.

[59] Case C–415/93 *Union Royale Belge des Sociétés de Football Association and Others v Bosman and Others* [1995] ECR I–4921, Judgment, paras. 79 and 80.

[60] Cases C–193 & C–194/87 *Maurissen and European Public Service Union v Court of Auditors* [1990] ECR I–95, paras. 11–16 and 21.

[61] See for detailed analysis and criticism of the Court's reasoning Vousden, S., 'Albany, Market Law and Social Exclusion' (2000) 29 *ILJ* 181.

[62] Joined Cases C–115–117/97 *Brentjens' Handelsonderneming BV v Stichting Bedrijfspensioenfonds voor Handel in Bouwmaterialen* [1999] ECR I–6025; and Case C–219/97 *Maatschappij Drijvende Bokken BV v Stichting Pensioenfonds voor de Vervoer- en avenderijven* [1999] ECR I–6121. A medical specialists' pension fund, established outside collective bargaining, has been found to be an undertaking within the meaning of Articles 81 and 82 ECT, but not necessarily to be in breach of these provisions. See Joined Cases C–180/98–184/98 *Pavlov and Others v Stichting Pensioenfonds Medische Specialisten* [2000] ECR I–6451.

[63] Case C–222/98 *Van der Woude v Stichting Breatrixoord* [2000] ECR I–7111.

provision at issue in *Albany*. These decisions demonstrate the ability of the ECJ to temper market liberalism within a market order.

Still, the demarcation of what is the legitimate subject-matter of a collective agreement covered by this exclusion remains relatively vague. In *Albany*, Advocate General Jacobs expressed the view that, to be excluded from competition law requirements, collective agreements should be concluded in 'good faith', should deal with 'core subjects of collective bargaining such as wages and working conditions', and should not 'directly affect third parties or markets'.[64] In *Van der Woude*, Advocate General Fennelly resisted the third condition suggested by Advocate General Jacobs. He considered that the objectives of such an agreement were not limited to 'matters that the parties to the agreement are capable of carrying out themselves'. This would be an undue restriction which would 'undermine the solidarity inherent in collective bargaining'.[65] Nevertheless, this statement was not explicitly endorsed by the Court.

C.   Speculation on the Impact of the EU Charter of Fundamental Rights 2001

What has caused immense frustration within the EU is that, while the ECJ acknowledges almost any alleged human right as being protected under the EU legal order, 'it hardly ever defines what the reach of that right actually is'.[66] One key objective of the EU Charter of Fundamental Rights 2000 (EUCFR) was to enhance the visibility of these rights. Freedom of association and the right to strike are now guaranteed, respectively, under Articles 12 and 28 of the EUCFR. Nevertheless, it is not clear to what extent this will have an impact upon the existing jurisprudence of the ECJ relating to fundamental rights.

There was a suggestion that the Charter would be regarded as having more than mere declaratory status, as it had been the subject of agreement by the 'institutions and bodies of the Union' to which it was addressed under Article 51(1).[67] However, this optimism must be qualified by the statement in Article 51(2) that the Charter 'does not establish any new power or task for the Community or the Union, or modify powers and tasks defined by the Treaties'.[68]

---

[64] Case C–67/96 *Albany International BV v Stichting Bedrijfsfonds Textielindustrie* [1999] ECR I–5751, Opinion, at paras. 193–194.

[65] Case C–222/98 *Van der Woude v Stichting Breatrixoord* [2000] ECR I–7111, Opinion, paras. 25, 27, and 30.

[66] Von Bogdandy, A., 'The European Union as a Human Rights Organization? Human Rights and the Core of the European Union' (2000) 37 *CMLRev*. 1307 at 1330.

[67] Lenaerts, K., and de Smijter, E., 'A Bill of Rights for the European Union' (2001) 38 *CMLRev*. 273 at 299.

[68] Betten, n.322 above, 162–3; de Búrca, G., 'The Drafting of the European Union Charter of Fundamental Rights' (2001) 26 *ELRev*. 126, 136–7; and Goldsmith, Lord, 'A Charter of Rights, Freedoms and Principles' (2001) 38 *CMLRev*. 1201.

In the *BECTU* case, Advocate General Tizzano commented on the legal status of the EU Charter of Fundamental Rights 2001. He observed that the EUCFR does not have 'genuine legislative scope in the strict sense', but considered that 'the fact remains that it includes statements which appear in large measure to reaffirm rights which are enshrined in other instruments'. Its clear purpose is to act as a 'substantive point of reference' for all EU institutions involved, including the ECJ. It was on this basis that he referred to the EUCFR as confirming the claim that a right to paid annual leave constitutes a fundamental right which should be protected under EC law.[69] This approach to the application of the 2000 Charter has been followed by other Advocates General[70] and the Court of First Instance.[71] This has, however, yet to be the sole ground on which an Opinion or a CFI judgment is based. We have also still to see whether such reasoning will be adopted by the ECJ, if there is an appeal on legal grounds from the judgments of the CFI. It is arguable that, as Lammy Betten claims, the higher Court will resist providing such confirmation until there is a political decision by Member States to afford the EUCFR legal status and much may depend on the form such status will take.[72]

IV. CONCLUSION:
INFLUENCE VIA THE BACK DOOR?

The European Court of Justice has no ostensible jurisdiction to enforce the protection of a right to strike in Member States, by virtue of the lack of EC law on this subject. However, there remains the potential for the Court to develop its influence through the 'back door'. This can occur when a litigant challenges national labour laws which clash with corresponding EC law. This is a prospect which many view with concern and trepidation, for this will not be a representative democratic process, but the opposite. It may allow the desires of the populace, as expressed in national political processes within each State, to be subsumed by the economic goals of European market integration as perceived by the ECJ.[73]

---

[69] Case C–173/99 *Broadcasting, Entertainment, Cinematographic and Theatre Union (BECTU) v Secretary of State for Trade and Industry*, AG's Opinion, 8 Feb. 2001, [2001] ECR I–4881, paras. 26–28.

[70] Opinion of Jacobs AG in Case C–377/98 *Netherlands v European Parliament and Council of the EU*, Opinion of 14 June 2001, [2001] ECR I–7079; and Geelhoed AG in Case C–413/99 *Baumbast v Secretary of State for Home Department*, Opinion of 5 July 2001, not yet reported.

[71] As regards the right to 'good administration' and the right to an 'effective legal remedy' set out in EUCFR, Arts. 41 and 47 respectively, see Case T–198/01R *Technische Glaswerke*, Judgment of 4 Apr. 2002, not yet reported, para. 85; and Case T–177/01 *Jégo-Quéré et Cie v Commission*, Judgment of 3 May 2002, not yet reported.

[72] Betten, L., 'Human Rights' (2001) 50 *ICLQ* 690, at 694 and 697.

[73] Maduro, M.P., 'Never on a Sunday—What Has (EU) Law Got to Do With It?' in Sciarra, n.5 above, at 281 and 288. See also Bruun, N., *Trade Union and Fundamental Rights in the EU: A Discussion Document on Strategies for the Future* (Stockholm: TCO, 1999), 3.

The ability of the ECJ to recognize and preserve national laws relating to collective bargaining is demonstrated by the *Albany* case, but the threat of decisions which restrict access to the right to strike remain. This concern is exacerbated by an awareness of the likely litigants in such cases. To date, strategic litigation has been taken by MNEs and 'business firms with time on their hands'.[74] If there is to be preservation of national labour laws in the light of this threat, cases will need to be brought by other social actors. This may, however, require further relaxation in standing rules.[75] The adequacy of the ECJ as a forum for the determination of fundamental rights, particularly those arising in the sphere of labour relations, has also been called into question.[76]

For the time being, the ECJ seems hesitant to reach any definitive stance on the status of the right to strike as a facet of 'freedom of association' under the Staff Regulations or as a 'fundamental right' in its own terms. Doing so may require litigants whose legal representatives encourage the Court to have regard to ILO Conventions and the European Social Charter, and not merely the ECHR. The danger is that the ECJ will decide independently of the findings of other international supervisory bodies on the scope and content of the right to strike, as it has been known to do in the past in relation to other rights set out in the ECHR.[77] Given the Court's limited experience in the labour law field, due to the restrictions on EU competence to date, this may be a cause for concern.

The European Commission has suggested that decisions on whether a third State, not a Member of the EU, which is receiving EU trade preferences or aid benefits is in violation of 'core' international labour standards, such as freedom of association, should be decided by ILO supervisory bodies.[78] One might wonder whether there is a similar case for delegating authority to, or at least following the precedents set by, the ILO as regards the right to strike. An alternative might be to set up some form of comparable, even tripartite, body which provided authoritative advice on labour rights, at least at first instance. Finally, it should be observed

---

[74] De Witte, B., 'The Past and Future Role of the European Court of Justice in the Protection of Human Rights' in Alston, P. (ed.), *The European Union and Human Rights* (Oxford: OUP, 1999), at 883; and Maduro, n.73 above, 290.

[75] Ward, A., 'Amsterdam and Amendment to Article 230: An Opportunity Lost or Simply Deferred' in Dashwood, A., and Johnston, A., *The Future of the Judicial System of the European Union* (Oxford: Hart Publishing, 2001). For the recent reformulation of individual entitlement to standing see Case T–177/01 *Jégo-Quéré et Cie v Commission*, Judgment of 3 May 2002, not yet reported.

[76] Birk, R., 'The European Social Charter and the European Union' in Blanpain, R. (ed.), *The Council of Europe and the Social Challenges of the XXIst Century* (The Hague: Kluwer, 2001), at 48.

[77] De Witte, n.74 at 878–82.

[78] EC Communication from the Commission to the Council, the European Parliament, and the Economic and Social Committee, *Promoting Core Labour Standards and Improving Social Governance in the Context of Globalization*, COM(2001)416 final, 18 July 2001, 14.

Conclusion: Structural Constraints on Supervisory Initiatives

The effectiveness of transnational supervisory bodies in protecting a right to strike is likely to be affected by the form of the control mechanism, for example how the reporting or complaints procedure is designed and whether its authoritative status derives from its resemblance to a court or its tripartite constitution. The ability to initiate protection of a right to strike on the basis of express provision for protection of 'freedom of association' seems most likely to depend upon how these control mechanisms are situated within the larger constitution of the international or European organization. Members of these supervisory bodies are likely to be sensitive to the constraints of constitutional texts. Moreover, because they, unlike national courts, rely heavily upon the co-operation of the constituent members of their organization, they may be even more conscious of the political dynamics which underlie the judgments that they make.

The authority of the ILO supervisory bodies stems, in part, from their specialist expertise in the field of labour law. The ILO Committee on Freedom of Association also derives further status from its tripartite structure. The latter provides decisions which are the result of an accord between employer, worker, and government representatives, that is, those with vested interests in the outcome of these cases. While it could be claimed that a wider range of participants in these decisions would be desirable, representing other elements of civil society, this remains the one forum where government representatives or appointees do not alone hold sway in making a final determination of compliance. Nevertheless, complaints procedures which closely resemble national 'court' proceedings are also widely viewed as authoritative. The European Court of Human Rights and the European Court of Justice could be said to exemplify this model. Cases can be brought by an individual or a collective entity, to be heard by an impartial judiciary, whose judgment is final and binding.

ILO supervisory bodies have been willing to derive protection of the right to strike from the bare guarantee of 'freedom of association' in constitutional documents and ILO Conventions. One might ask whether this is the result of its tripartite structure, as opposed to a more 'legalistic' reading which might be adopted by an international 'court'. There is no evidence here to support the proposition that its membership is decisive. This seems all the more improbable when one recalls how tripartite decision-making in the International Labour Conference blocked the adoption of an instrument on the right to strike. It is more likely that the explanation lies elsewhere, most probably in the way in which the members of ILO supervisory bodies identify with and feel the need to act upon the particular institutional objectives of that organization. The jurisprudence of the ILO CFA can be defended on principles of international law, with recourse to the Vienna Convention on the Law of Treaties, on the basis of its constitutional framework. This is not necessarily because its members reason in a legalistic fashion; rather, they are placed within a context where they perceive it to be their function to adhere to the primary institutional values set out in these texts.

By contrast, the longstanding divide between the European Convention on Human Rights and the European Social Charter, set up within the Council of Europe, has proved problematic for effective protection of a right to strike. The European Court of Human Rights could have adopted a different view of the provision governing freedom of association contained in Article 11 of the ECHR, which would have been consistent with basic principles of treaty interpretation, but the institutional context created a judiciary which had imbibed a notion of human rights as the exercise of individual negative liberty, rather than collective positive freedom. It has been suggested here that a major structural overhaul, such as integration of these two instruments or their control mechanisms, may yet be required to remedy this situation. The alternative is the maintenance of the status quo, whereby the incidental pronouncements of the European Court of Human Rights on the status of trade union rights take apparent priority over the conclusions of the European Social Rights Committee. This seems to be to the detriment of workers' social protection.

One might have hoped for more within the European Union, given its broad socio-economic objectives. However, the European Court of Justice has been placed in a peculiar position. It has no basis on which to enforce Member State implementation of a right to strike, as this is not the subject of any binding EC instrument. This makes national laws relating to industrial action, even when they comply with ILO standards, vulnerable to the application of other EC treaty provisions or directives, such as those relating to free movement of goods or barriers to competition. The ECJ can correct such a trend only through exercise of its fundamental rights jurisdiction. Thus far, one Advocate General has been willing to commit himself to recognition of the right to strike as a fundamental right. The ECJ has not done so. This may be due to the perceived goals of the EU. A right to strike does not immediately seem a necessary incident of an 'integration project'.[1] In such circumstances, positive protection of such a right is left to the Member States, and the Court is, arguably, more likely to play a role in its erosion. We have yet to see the extent to which the 2000 Charter of Fundamental Rights will remedy this situation. Much may depend upon the legal status lent to the Charter. Indeed, in conclusion, it seems that supervisory bodies do not tend to act radically or autonomously to protect a right to strike. Instead, they tend to reflect and amplify Member States' decisions on the objectives of that particular organization and the structures within which those objectives are to be achieved.

[1] Bengoetxea, J., MacCormick, N., and Soriano, L.M., 'Integration and Integrity in the Legal Reasoning of the European Court of Justice' in de Búrca, G. (ed.), *The European Court of Justice* (Oxford: OUP, 2001).

Part IV

Jurisprudence Relating to the Scope of the Right to Strike

Introduction

It is generally acknowledged that a right to strike should be protected under international law and that, albeit perhaps imperfectly, this protection is reiterated and elaborated upon within European organizations. We have seen that this may be achieved by inclusion of an express right in instruments, such as the International Covenant on Economic, Social, and Cultural Rights 1966 (ICESCR), the European Social Charter 1961 (ESC), the Community Charter of the Fundamental Rights of Workers 1989, and the European Union Charter of Fundamental Rights 2000. There is also capacity for protection of this right as a facet of freedom of association, as we have seen within the International Labour Organization (ILO) and (to a much more limited extent) under the European Convention on Human Rights 1950 (ECHR). There is, however, one further outstanding question, which remains controversial. This is what the scope of the right to strike should be.

This Part outlines the actual jurisprudence developed by international and European supervisory bodies on the subject of the right to strike. In particular, it examines four key dimensions of the right to strike which determine its scope: first, its existence and basic exercise; secondly, the objectives which are regarded as permissible; thirdly, responses to public welfare considerations; and, finally, the sanctions which are considered unacceptable.

At the global level, this study primarily involves reference to the findings and recommendations made by the ILO supervisory bodies. The observations made by the UN Committee on Economic, Social, and Cultural Rights under Article 8(1) of the ICESCR are fewer, tend to be less detailed, and usually defer to ILO standards and case law. However, where appropriate, the conclusions of the UN Committee will also be considered. Within the EU, the European Court of Justice has not commented in any detail on the scope of the right to strike, which has been left to determination by national laws. The European Court of Human Rights has likewise shied away from elaborating on the ambit of lawful industrial action, although its views on related matters may be relevant to the extent that they have influenced the ESC control mechanism. Under the ESC, it has been the European Committee of Social Rights (ECSR), previously known as the 'Committee of Independent Experts', which has developed a series of principles intended to provide guidance for States on collective action. Its findings also receive attention here, alongside the sometimes obstructive interventions of the Governmental Committee.

It is apparent that, on the whole, ILO supervisory bodies seek to protect a right to strike of broader scope than that envisaged by the ECSR. This is not to say that they are enthusiastic about industrial conflict. For example, the ILO Committee on Freedom of Association considers that 'it is important that both employers and trade unions bargain in good faith and make every effort to reach an agreement; moreover genuine and constructive negotiations are a necessary component to establish and maintain a relationship of confidence between the parties'.[1] Nor has the ILO promulgated 'a comprehensive and unlimited right to strike', as has been alleged by certain members of the employers' group.[2] ILO supervisory bodies have long accepted that legitimate limitations may be placed upon such a right,[3] and these exceptions will be considered here. Nevertheless, it seems that the ILO supervisory bodies utilize a broader, more variegated justificatory basis for protection of the right to strike, such that it is seen simultaneously as a civil, political, and socio-economic right. This allows the ILO to conceive of the use of industrial action by a wide range of persons, for a broad set of objectives. The UN Committee on Economic, Social, and Cultural Rights has a less developed jurisprudence, but tends to follow the views of ILO bodies, in accordance with the status granted to ILO Convention No. 87 under Article 8(3) of the ICESCR.

By contrast, the ECSR is hampered by the restrictive wording of Article 6(4) of the ESC, which allows a right to strike to arise only in 'cases of conflicts of interests' in the context of 'collective bargaining', 'subject to obligations that might arise out of collective agreements previously entered into'. This is subject to a general exception clause set out in Article 31 of the ESC, which allows restrictions to be placed on the right to strike to the extent that these are 'prescribed by law and are necessary in a democratic society for the protection of the rights and freedoms of others or for the protection of public interest, national security, public health or morals'.

In addition, the ESC supervisory process has been such that the Governmental Committee, representing government interests, was previously able to make opposing recommendations to those of the ECSR, thereby detracting from the force of the findings of the Expert Committee. Moreover, this weak control mechanism has been overshadowed by the more authoritative

---

[1] *Freedom of Association: Digest of Decisions and Principles of the Freedom of Association Committee of the Governing Body of the ILO* (4th edn., Geneva: ILO, 1996), paras. 815 and 817. See for application of this principle *Case No. 2127 (Bahamas)*, 327th Report of the CFA, para. 174 at para. 195; and *Case 2122 (Guatemala)*, 326th Report (2001), para. 302 at para. 316.

[2] *Record of Proceedings* (Geneva: ILO, 1994) ILC, 81st Session, 25/33, para. 121; *Record of Proceedings* (Geneva: ILO, 1997) ILC, 85th Session, 19/30–19/31, para. 87 and 19/35–19/36, para. 100.

[3] See for an early example of this recognition *Case 170 (France–Madagascar)* 37th Report of the CFA (1960), para. 12 at para. 41.

decisions of the European Commission and Court of Human Rights, which apparently took a narrow view of the legitimate scope of the right to strike. Nevertheless, with the assistance of an ILO observer, the ECSR has been able to overcome many of these obstacles. Since the supervisory process was revised in 1991, Recommendations have been issued by the Council of Europe Committee of Ministers which closely reflect the concerns of ILO supervisory bodies. Therefore, despite initial discrepancies, it is possible to detect a gradual convergence of approach.

11

Existence and Exercise of the Right to Strike

Supervisory bodies in the International Labour Organization (ILO) have been adamant that, in every State, a 'right to strike' should be protected under domestic laws. In this, Contracting Parties to the International Covenant on Economic, Social, and Cultural Rights 1966 (ICESCR) and the Council of Europe's European Social Charter 1961 (ESC) concurred. This chapter examines the international and European jurisprudence concerning the existence of the right to strike and the basic constraints that may be placed on its exercise. Its focus is on decisions taken under the ILO and ESC supervisory mechanisms, but attention will also be paid to the few observations made by the United Nations (UN) Committee on Economic, Social, and Cultural Rights under the ICESCR relevant to these issues.

The chapter begins by outlining the types of industrial action covered by this entitlement and the kind of legal protection which is to be considered acceptable. It emerges that States are given considerable discretion concerning how such protection is provided. Legal protection of industrial action may be phrased in terms of either a 'right' or a 'freedom', as long as workers and organizers are not unduly penalized for their actions. There is, in this sense, some attention paid to the principle of 'subsidiarity' and respect for the particularities (and peculiarities) of national systems of industrial relations.[1]

The question whether the right to strike is an individual or a collective right is more controversial.[2] The text of Article 8(1) of the ICESCR and Article 6(4) of the ESC seems to indicate that it should be regarded as an individual right which can be exercised collectively. This has been the view of the European Committee of Social Rights (ECSR) which, as a 'Committee of Independent Experts', provides a technical assessment of ESC implementation. In the past, ECSR views had little impact, given the resistance of the Governmental Committee to any criticism of State conduct on this issue. This was an instance of State control, which was to limit the efficacy of the ESC supervisory process. However, since the reforms undertaken in 1991, the Governmental Committee has altered its position and the Council of Europe Committee of Ministers has issued recommendations on this matter.[3]

---

[1] See Chap. 1 above, at 24 and 26–7.   [2] See Chap. 3 above, at 54–5.
[3] See Chap. 9 above, at 220.

ILO supervisory bodies initially took a cautious view, accepting the choice made by some States to give to established trade unions the sole entitlement to call industrial action. Nevertheless, States may not allocate this function only to trade union federations or confederations, as this may limit the ability of smaller groupings of workers to initiate industrial action. Moreover, persons who call a peaceful 'wild-cat' strike should receive protection from dismissal. On this (and other issues) the principles stated by ILO supervisory bodies have developed over time, such that there is protection of the worker's entitlement to strike at least equivalent to that available under the ESC.

No international or European supervisory body has commented in any detail, or at length, on what is understood to be the justificatory basis of the right to strike. Determining the views of supervisory bodies involves 'detective work' and careful analysis of their decisions. What we do know is that they do not consider that the right to strike can be rendered unnecessary by the existence of compulsory arbitration mechanisms.[4] These are permissible only in exceptional circumstances, such as, for example, when the provision of essential services is at risk. It is arguable that this principle can be linked to the ILO view that the right to strike is based on more than an entitlement to fair wages and working conditions; but it is also possible that this principle merely reflects general scepticism about whether compulsory arbitration can secure fair wages and working conditions.

Compulsory mediation may, however, be considered permissible, within limits.[5] International and European supervisory bodies agree that certain preconditions may be placed on the exercise of the right to strike. A conciliation, mediation, or 'cooling off' period will be considered acceptable where this is designed to encourage the parties to reach agreement without recourse to industrial action. A balloting requirement may also be imposed where this would promote democratic decision-making within a trade union. Such procedural requirements should not, however, be such as to preclude access to collective action entirely. Where the delays involved in compulsory mediation or a 'cooling off' period are too lengthy or the thresholds for a successful strike ballot are too high, national legislation will be criticized.

Collective agreements have been known to contain provisions which, for the term of the agreement's duration, impose a binding 'peace obligation'. This is a subject on which ILO supervisory bodies appear to differ from the ECSR. Both accept that such an obligation can be introduced through agreement by employers and workers. However, they disagree on the scope of its effect. The ILO Committee of Experts on the Application of Conventions and Recommendations (CEACR) considers that such a provision should not operate to prevent 'protest strikes', aimed at changing

---

[4] See Chap. 3 above, at 51–3.   [5] *Ibid.*, at 53–4.

government policy on economic and social issues. By contrast, the ECSR considers that a 'peace obligation' can apply to any industrial action for the period in question, taken for any reason. This may be due to the wording of Article 6(4) of the ESC, which provides a more restrictive formulation of the right to strike than that adopted within the ILO.

One key difference between ILO and ESC supervisory processes has been the efficacy of the former when compared to the latter, largely owing to the refusal of the ESC Governmental Committee to endorse the findings of the ECSR. However, over the past decade reforms to the ESC control mechanism have led to a more cohesive approach by the supervisory bodies. Today, it is more likely to be the textual limitations inherent in Article 6(4) which are the significant source of discrepancies between ESC and ILO jurisprudence, as we shall see here and in later chapters.

I.   DEFINITION OF A STRIKE

For the definition of a 'strike', it makes sense to look first at those international instruments which recognize the right to strike. The difficulty is that political compromise between State Parties to international instruments can lead to the inclusion of broad, general provisions, which then fall for interpretation by supervisory bodies. For example, Article 8(1)(d) of the ICESCR refers only to 'the right to strike' and does not expressly state whether this should extend to a partial stoppage of work, such as a go-slow, work-to-rule, or sit-in. The view has been expressed that these should therefore also be regarded as being encompassed within the more narrowly worded 'right to strike', even though the Committee on Economic, Social, and Cultural Rights has yet to express an opinion on this point.[6] By contrast, Article 6(4) of the ESC clearly covers 'collective action' generally, of which the right to strike is only one instance.[7] There is no doubt that partial work stoppages fall within the coverage of that provision, if not within 'the right to strike' *per se*.

There is no ILO Convention which explicitly guarantees the right to strike; instead, ILO supervisory bodies derive this entitlement from the broad provision for freedom of association and the right to organize set out in the ILO Constitution and ILO Conventions Nos. 87 and 98.[8] On this basis, they advocate that 'any work stoppage', 'however brief and limited', should be considered a strike. This is because, whatever its form, the aim of the withdrawal of labour is an activity designed to further workers' interests

---

[6] Craven, M., *The International Covenant on Economic, Social and Cultural Rights: A Perspective on its Development* (2nd revd. edn., Oxford: Clarendon Press, 1998), 279.

[7] See, e.g., on use of this provision to protect 'lock-outs', which do not necessarily receive the same status as 'strikes', Samuel, L., *Fundamental Social Rights: Case Law of the European Social Charter* (Strasbourg: Council of Europe, 1997), 181–3; and Casey, N., *The Right to Organise and Bargain Collectively: Protection within the European Social Charter* (Strasbourg: Council of Europe, 1996), 73–6.

[8] See Chap. 8 above, at 192–9.

in accordance with Articles 3 and 10 of ILO Convention No. 87. 'Restrictions as to the forms of strike action can only be justified if the action ceases to be peaceful.'[9] Moreover, even in the absence of a work stoppage *per se*, respect for freedom of association is said to entail protection of workers' rights to assemble peacefully, so as to protest against the conduct of an employer or government.[10] ILO bodies have, therefore, been prepared to apply the same principle of protection to pickets and workplace occupations, that is, that restrictions should be limited to cases where the action ceases to be peaceful.

The UN Committee on Economic, Social, and Cultural Rights has taken its obligations to promote protection of the right to strike fairly literally. It has advocated the establishment of such a right in either domestic legislation or the national constitution. In particular, it has questioned the utility of a 'freedom to strike' for workers. This is evident from its observations on the UK in 1997 and 2002. On both occasions the Committee said that it considers 'failure to incorporate the right to strike into domestic law' to constitute a breach of Article 8 of the ICESCR.[11] It has been observed that the Committee 'was taking an excessively strict line on this question',[12] for it should not matter whether there is a 'right' or 'freedom' to strike, as long as there is adequate protection of those who organize and participate in industrial action. This may be the principle that the Committee intended to promote for, in the case of the UK, it observed that the legal position is unacceptable, since industrial action is regarded as a breach of contract, which makes workers vulnerable to dismissal.[13]

This is closer to the position taken by ILO CFA, which accepts that the protection of industrial action may take the form of an immunity rather than a right, as long as 'no one is penalized for carrying out or attempting to carry out a legitimate strike'.[14] In doing so, the Committee has shown itself willing to defer to decisions taken at the national level on the most appropriate way in which to provide for this entitlement. All that the CFA views as a matter for concern is the extent to which workers' ability to take industrial

---

[9] Committee of Experts on the Application of Conventions and Recommendations, *General Survey on Freedom of Association and Collective Bargaining* (Geneva: ILO, 1994), hereafter 'CEACR General Survey', paras. 173–174; and Gernigon, B., Odero, A., and Guido, H., 'ILO Principles concerning the Right to Strike' (1998) 137 *ILRev.* 441 at 458. See, e.g., *Case No. 2082 (Morocco)*, 328th Report of the CFA (2002), para. 464 at 470, from which it is evident that the CFA considers that a workplace 'sit-in' can be covered by the right to strike; and *Case No. 2090 (Belarus)*, 326th Report (2001), para. 210 at para. 242, which concerns a union's entitlement to picket without the penalty of deregistration.

[10] *Freedom of Association: Digest of Decisions and Principles of the Freedom of Association Committee of the Governing Body of the ILO* (4th revd. edn., Geneva: ILO, 1996), hereafter 'CFA Digest of Decisions', paras. 459–472.

[11] *Concluding Observations of the Committee on Economic, Social and Cultural Rights: UK* 4 Dec. 1997 E/C.12/1/Add.19, para. 11; and *Concluding Observations: UK* 17 May 2002, E/C.12/1/Add.79, para. 16.

[12] Craven, n.6 above, 280.   [13] See Chap. 14 below, at 319.

[14] *CFA Digest of Decisions*, n.10 above, paras. 590–597.

action is limited. This involves careful scrutiny of national laws and their application, so as to ensure that they are consistent with the principle of freedom of association and the collective promotion of workers' economic and social interests. The ECSR also considers that the form that domestic legal protection takes is unimportant; what is crucial is that any limitations placed on the right to strike do not contravene the guarantees contained in Articles 6 and 31 of the ESC.[15]

II.   AN INDIVIDUAL OR A COLLECTIVE RIGHT?

One fundamental question posed by Otto Kahn-Freund was: 'does the right to strike vest in unions, individuals or both?'[16] The answer to this question is likely to turn on what one understands to be the justificatory basis for the right to strike. In Chapter 3, I noted that where a right to strike is viewed in terms of its role in collective bargaining it is often seen as a collective right to be exercised by trade unions. This, however, assumes that trade unions are sufficiently representative of all those parts of the workforce who may wish to take industrial action; or, in the alternative, that there are no insuperable barriers to the swift formation by workers of a trade union so that they can exercise such a right effectively, should they wish to do so. Where these conditions are not met, or if the right to strike is regarded as a legitimate means of voicing political protest, then it may make more sense to regard this as an individual right linked to a person's conscience.[17] Different States have taken different views of this matter. Germany, for example, treats the right to strike solely as a collective right to be exercised by trade unions for collective bargaining purposes. Italy recognizes workers' entitlement to 'protest strikes' on matters concerning economic and social policy.[18] The issue for international and European supervisory organs is the extent to which they should try to alter national regimes which determine the character of the right to strike.

Article 8(1) of the ICESCR refers to the rights of 'everyone' to form and join trade unions, as well as the right of 'trade unions' to form federations and function freely, but does not state who is entitled to exercise the right to strike. It has been suggested that this indicates that the right is to be regarded as individual in nature.[19] However, it should be noted that there is no statement made by the Committee on Economic, Social, and Cultural Rights which would definitively establish this principle.

[15] *Conclusions XII-1*, 131; and *Conclusions XIV-1*, 805.

[16] Kahn-Freund, O., *The Right to Strike: Its Scope and Limitations* (Strasbourg: Council of Europe, 1974), 5.

[17] See Chap. 3 above, at 54–5.

[18] See Clauwaert, S., *Fundamental Social Rights in the European Union: Comparative Tables and Documents* (Brussels: ETUI, 1998).

[19] Craven, n.6 above, 278.

In 1977, Kahn-Freund stated that the right to strike contained in Article 6(4) ESC 'must be considered as being conferred on an individual and not as a member of a trade union'. This followed from the fact that the right to bargain collectively, guaranteed under Article 6, was an individual right and not confined to employees' or employers' organizations.[20] The ECSR has also found that States which prohibit strikes on the ground that they are not organized by a trade union are in breach of Article 6(4).[21] 'All workers must be allowed to call a strike, even outside a trade union framework.'[22] Just as 'an ordinary group of workers' without any special legal status may engage in such bargaining, 'it can and should be given the right to strike . . . so that it can effectively exercise its right to bargain collectively'.[23] For example, under French law, if a strike has been called by a representative trade union, each worker may, individually, decide to join all or part of the strike; but the very requirement that the strike must be initiated by a representative trade union is considered by the ECSR to amount to a restriction of the right to collective action that is not compatible with Article 6(4) of the ESC.[24] It seems, however, that there will be no breach of the individual right to strike, if workers can 'easily and without undue delay form a trade union for the purpose of calling a strike'.[25]

The notion that the right to strike should not be the sole prerogative of trade unions was, in the past, questioned by the Governmental Committee. For example, when the ECSR criticized Iceland's restrictions on the right to strike, on the ground that the power to call a strike lay entirely with a trade union, the Governmental Committee commented that:

Iceland was not the only country to restrict the right to initiate strikes to trade unions. It appeared indeed that this applied to all the Nordic countries and possibly others as well, and it would therefore be unjust to single Iceland out for criticism.[26]

The Governmental Committee decided to take no further action until the ECSR had been able to ascertain the situation in other Contracting Parties. This response of the Governmental Committee illustrates the way in which government representatives were able to obstruct the dissemination of standards by independent experts, until in 1991 changes were made to the

---

[20] Council of Europe, *Symposium on the European Social Charter and Social Policy Today* (Strasbourg: Council of Europe, 1977), 35–6. See also Prof. Sinay's comments at 37. Cf. Betten, L., *The Right to Strike in Community Law: The Incorporation of Fundamental Rights in the Legal Order of the European Communities* (Amsterdam: North Holland, 1985), 198.

[21] ECSR, *Conclusions I*, 185; *Conclusions II*, 28–9; *Conclusions IV*, 48–51; *Conclusions VIII*, 96; *Conclusions XIII-1*, 155–6; *Conclusions XIV-1*, 301.

[22] ECSR, *Conclusions XIV-1*, 662.

[23] ECSR, *Conclusions IV*, 50; *Conclusions XII-2*, 115; *Conclusions XIII-2*, 282; *Conclusions XV-1*, 201–6.

[24] ECSR, *Conclusions XV-1*, 254–7.

[25] ECSR, *Conclusions XV-1*, 475–82; *Conclusions XV-1, Second Addendum (Germany)*, 27–30.

[26] ESC Governmental Committee, *Report 13(1)*, 94, para. 459.

enforcement procedure.[27] There has been no further comment on Icelandic law,[28] but the Governmental Committee has since been prepared to issue a warning to Germany on the basis that the right to call a strike should not be the sole prerogative of a trade union; and a Recommendation has since been issued by the Committee of Ministers in this regard.[29] It now seems that the principle initially stated by the ECSR will stand as a basis for criticism of the conduct of Contracting Parties.

By contrast, the ILO initially refused to find that States breached the principle of freedom of association by 'making a right to strike the sole preserve of a trade union organisation'.[30] The CFA did not require that this constraint be placed upon the right to strike, but allowed States to do so. This was because, early on, the CFA appears to have accepted that the right to strike serves only a limited social function, namely assisting workers in collective bargaining;[31] or it may be that this follows from the derivation of the right to strike from Convention No. 87 which relates to protection of 'workers' organizations' and their activities.[32] However, in practice it seems that the ECSR and ILO supervisory bodies endorse similar principles.

In the 1994 *General Survey*, the Committee of Experts observed that strike action is a collective right exercised by a group of persons who decide not to work in order to have their demands met. Yet the interests and agency of the workers who make up that group are to be respected. For this reason, the CEACR has been reluctant to approve the allocation of the decision to call a strike to national trade union federations and confederations. These bodies should not be banned from calling strikes, but should not be the sole organizations authorized to do so.[33] This is because taking this decision away from the workers affected could stifle access to industrial action.[34]

A comparable approach was taken by the CFA in *Case No. 1759 (Peru)*,[35] where workers were dismissed for calling a twenty-four-hour work stoppage, without being 'accredited trade union representatives'. The stoppage was never carried out, although a hunger strike did follow. The CFA found that 'even though the strike was not decided by a trade union executive representing more than the majority of workers', the dismissal of the seven

[27] See Chap. 9 above, at 219–20.

[28] Arguably, there has been no need to do so, by virtue of amendments made to the Trade Unions and Industrial Disputes Act in May 1996 by Act No. 75/1996, which, at least in theory, provide scope for individual exercise of the right to strike, as noted in the State Report submitted by Iceland under the ICESCR, 26 June 1997 E/1990/6/Add.15, para. 44.

[29] ESC Governmental Committee, *Report 13(2)*, 41–3, paras. 178–186; and Committee of Ministers Recommendation RChS(98)2.

[30] *CFA Digest of Decisions*, n.10 above, para. 477.

[31] See Chap. 12 below, at 290–1.

[32] See App. 1 below.

[33] Cf. *CFA Digest of Decisions*, n.10 above, para. 478.

[34] See, e.g., CEACR, *Individual Observation concerning Convention No. 87 (Egypt)* (Geneva: ILO, 2002); for a similar view taken by the UN Committee on Economic, Social, and Cultural Rights: see *Concluding Observations: Tunisia* 14 May 1999, E/C.12/1/Add.36, para. 15.

[35] *Case No. 1759 (Peru)*, 294th Report of the CFA (1994), para. 335.

workers was contrary to the principles of freedom of association.[36] It seems that dismissal is not an acceptable response to a call for a strike, even where the requisite trade union consent is absent. To this extent, there will be protection of those who organize wild-cat strikes.[37]

III. THE POTENTIAL FOR ABROGATION OF THE RIGHT: IS COMPULSORY ARBITRATION AN ACCEPTABLE ALTERNATIVE TO INDUSTRIAL ACTION?

There is consensus at the international and European level that where there is a dispute over 'rights', for example on the appropriate interpretation of a legally binding collective agreement, recourse should be had to the courts rather than industrial action. This is apparent from the wording of Article 6(4) of the ESC which refers to an entitlement to take collective action only 'in cases of conflicts of interests'. The ILO CFA has also agreed that '[t]he solution to a legal conflict as a result of *a difference in interpretation of a legal text* should be left to the competent courts. The prohibition of strikes in such a situation does not constitute a breach of freedom of association'.[38]

A separate and distinct question is whether it should be permissible for a government to require conflicts of interests to be referred to compulsory arbitration. Chapter 3 outlined the argument made by Utz, that provision of compulsory arbitration could abrogate the need for protection of a right to strike. This argument is based on the premise that industrial action is merely a means by which to ensure that workers receive fair conditions of employment. If this can be secured by arbitration, there need be no right to strike.[39]

Cases decided in 1961 and 1962 suggested that the CFA had adopted this position. For example, the Committee stated that 'utilisation of compulsory conciliation and arbitration in industrial disputes before a strike is called' and other provisions of this type 'cannot be regarded as an infringement of freedom of association'.[40] In *Case No. 274 (Libya)*, the CFA added only that 'where strikes by workers are restricted or prohibited, such restriction or prohibition should be accompanied by the provision of conciliation procedures and of independent and impartial arbitration machinery whose awards are in all cases binding on both sides'.[41] This might seem to indicate

---

[36] *Ibid.*, 343.

[37] *CFA Digest of Decisions*, n.10 above, para. 497 states that restrictions on wild-cat strikes will be justifiable only if the strike ceases to be peaceful.

[38] *CFA Digest of Decisions*, n.10 above, para. 485.

[39] Utz, A.F., 'Is the Right to Strike a Human Right?' (1987) 65 *Washington University Law Quarterly* 732. This argument was considered in Chap. 3 above, at 50–3.

[40] *Case No. 208 (Ivory Coast)*, 46th Report of the CFA (1961), para. 8 at para. 15.

[41] *Case No. 274 (Libya)*, 60th Report of the CFA (1962), para. 281(g). This case concerned the restriction of strikes in public-sector employment, but it seemed that the principle was of more general application.

that restriction of strike activity is permissible as long as alternative forms of dispute resolution are available.

In *Case No. 294 (Spain)*,[42] the Spanish government admitted that it had suppressed a miners' strike, but argued that conciliation and arbitration procedures would suffice as alternatives to industrial action. At this point, the CFA elaborated upon its earlier position, explaining its earlier recommendation in the following terms:

> The Committee must explain in this respect that the recommendation in question refers not to the restriction of the right to strike as such but to the restriction of that right in essential services or in the public service, in relation to which the Committee has stated that adequate guarantees should be provided to safeguard workers' interests.[43]

From this date, it became clear that the right to strike is indeed an integral aspect of freedom of association and may be restricted only with good reason, such as in the public service, essential services, or in the event of an acute national crisis.[44]

The CFA has since indicated repeatedly that States 'should endeavour to give priority to collective bargaining as the means of determining employment conditions'.[45] For example, in its response to a complaint heard by the CFA in 1999, the Chinese government argued that 'mediation and arbitration systems which preclude the right to strike adequately and appropriately reflect the requirements of Chinese society and the fundamental interests of the broad mass of workers'. The CFA was not convinced and reiterated that 'it has always considered the right to strike to be one of the essential means through which workers and their organisations may promote and defend their economic and social interests', recommending that Chinese legislation be amended accordingly.[46] A similar principle has been adopted by the CEACR.[47]

ILO supervisory organs have never explicitly provided the reasons for their antagonism to compulsory conciliation and arbitration as an alternative to protection of industrial action. However, there are at least three reasons why they could choose to adopt this approach. First, there is the argument that compulsory arbitration does not provide useful outcomes for workers or employers, in that it chills negotiations, interferes with market forces, and puts both parties at the mercy of an arbitrator who can never be

---

[42] *Case No. 294 (Spain)*, 66th Report of the CFA (1963), para. 481.

[43] *Ibid.*, para. 485.

[44] See for confirmation of this principle *Case No. 1937 (Zimbabwe)*, 326th Report of the CFA (2001), para. 171; and *Case No. 1845 (Peru)*, 302nd Report (1996), para. 495 at paras. 511–513. See also Chap. 13 below.

[45] *Case No. 1576 (Norway)*, 279th Report of the CFA (1991), para. 91, at para. 116. See, more recently, *Case No. 1973 (Zimbabwe)*, 327th Report (2002), para. 130 at para. 130.

[46] *Case No. 1930 (China)*, 316th Report of the CFA (1999), para. 341 at para. 361.

[47] *CEACR General Survey*, n.9 above, para. 153. See, e.g., CEACR, *Individual Observations concerning Convention No. 87 (Algeria), (Belarus), (Haiti) and (Jamaica)* (Geneva: ILO, 2002).

as acquainted with the issues as the parties themselves.[48] Secondly, there is the danger that arbitration will allow the State too great control over workers' wages and conditions of employment. Appreciation of this danger may well have had some impact upon the outcome in the seminal case, *Case No. 294 (Spain)*.[49] Finally, if there are other justifications for protection of a right to strike which extend beyond the ambit of collective bargaining, namely to provide workers with a political voice or agency within the workplace, then compulsory arbitration cannot be an acceptable alternative to the right to strike.

Just as ILO bodies have decided that compulsory arbitration will not usually suffice as an alternative to the right to strike, so too the ECSR has concluded that where a government 'has the power to impose compulsory arbitration and thus to prohibit strikes in an unlimited manner', it is in breach of its obligations under Article 6(4).[50] The imposition of compulsory arbitration is permissible only where the relevant conditions laid down in Article 31 of the Charter are met.[51] Otherwise, the imposition of compulsory arbitration is viewed as 'a restraint on a fundamental trade union prerogative' in violation of Article 5 as well as Article 6 of the ESC.[52]

Potentially, Article 31 might seem to provide a rather broad basis for restriction of the right to strike, since industrial action is likely to impinge on the property rights of employers and could be said to damage the 'public interest' in the supply of goods and services. Nevertheless, the ECSR has tended to interpret this exception in a restrictive fashion.

For example, the Norwegian government imposed compulsory arbitration to end a strike by oil workers in the North Sea. The government had taken this action only thirty-six hours after the work stoppage began. The ECSR took note of the recommendations of the ILO CFA (*Case No. 1576 (Norway)*) which had expressed doubts about the compelling need for such arbitration, and found that this intervention was unacceptable.[53] The 'absence of any limitation on the government's power to intervene in strike action and the consequent absence of any protection of workers' constituted a breach of Article 6(4), 'since without such protection there is no real recognition for the right to strike as required by this provision of the Charter'.[54] The ECSR findings were, in this case, upheld by the Gov-

---

[48] Benjamin, P., 'The Big Ban Theory: Strikes in Essential Services' (1989) 6 *Employment Law* (South Africa), 44–66. Cf. Chap. 3 above, at 52–3.

[49] *Case No. 294 (Spain)*, 76th Report of the CFA (1964), para. 285.

[50] See for a recent example of the application of this principle to industrial relations in Portugal ECSR, *Conclusions XIII-3*, 280–1.

[51] ECSR, *Conclusions X-1*, 74–5.

[52] ECSR, *Conclusions XIV-1*, 526; *Conclusions XV-1*, 407–8.

[53] ECSR, *Conclusions XIII-1*, 158–9. See also *Conclusions X-1*, 7–8; *Conclusions XII-1*, 130. This was also consistent with the findings of the UN Committee on Economic, Social, and Cultural Rights set out in *Concluding Observations: Norway*, 1 Dec. 1997, E/C.12/1995/18, para. 224 which expressed concern at the existence of legislative powers to impose compulsory arbitration.

[54] ECSR, *Conclusions XIII-3*, 141–2.

ernmental Committee, which took the view that the government could not have had sufficient time 'to assess the economic and social implications of the strike and to consult the social partners before taking the decision to resort to compulsory arbitration'. This was not a complete refusal to countenance compulsory arbitration as an alternative to industrial action. However, at least the Governmental Committee did not detract from the conclusions of the ECSR and decided to propose that a recommendation be addressed to Norway on this point.[55] The Norwegian government has since imposed compulsory arbitration again on oil workers.[56] While the ECSR has held that such intervention can potentially be justified under Article 31 of the Charter, it considered that this was not possible in the specific circumstances of this case, where protection of public interest and safety was not truly at stake. The Governmental Committee has now issued another warning to Norway on this basis.[57]

IV. PRECONDITIONS FOR EXERCISE OF THE RIGHT

All supervisory bodies at the international and European levels have accepted that governments may impose some procedural restrictions upon the exercise of the right to strike. These may include compulsory conciliation, a period of notice, and a strike ballot. Such procedures may be required by legislation or a legally enforceable collective agreement. The extent to which they can constrain exercise of the right to strike is considered in this section.

It should be noted at the outset that the imposition of these preconditions is subject to certain limitations. 'The conditions that have to be fulfilled under the law in order to render a strike lawful should be reasonable and in any event not such as to place a substantial limitation on the means of action open to trade union organizations.'[58] For example, strikes should not be rendered illegal on the basis of 'minor procedural flaws'.[59] Nor should the procedural stages 'be so complex or slow that a lawful strike becomes impossible in practice or loses its effectiveness'.[60] Moreover, the determination whether or not the procedural criterion for lawful industrial action has been met is to be made by the judiciary or some other independent

[55] By 11 votes in favour, one against, and four abstentions. See ESC Governmental Committee, *Report 13(1)*, 98, para. 476.

[56] ECSR, *Conclusions XIV-1*, 621–3; *Conclusions XV-1*, 430–8.

[57] ESC Governmental Committee, *Report 15(1)*, 66, para. 267.

[58] *CFA Digest of Decisions*, n.10 above, para. 498.

[59] CEACR, *Individual Observation concerning Convention No. 87 (Russian Federation)* (Geneva: ILO, 2001).

[60] CEACR, *Individual Observation concerning Convention No. 87 (Swaziland)* (Geneva: ILO, 2001), citing *CEACR General Survey*, n.9 above, para. 171. See also *Concluding Observations of the Committee on Economic, Social and Cultural Rights: Bolivia*, 21 May 2001, E/C.12/1/Add.60, para. 18.

authority, not by a government ministry.[61] The restrictions to be placed on these procedural preconditions are also discussed below.

First, a strike may be delayed temporarily until procedures for negotiation, conciliation, and mediation have been exhausted.[62] The CEACR asserts that this is 'compatible with Article 4 of Convention No. 98 which encourages the full development and utilization of machinery for the voluntary negotiation of collective agreements'.[63] It is also consistent with the emphasis placed on promotion of such machinery by Article 6(2) of the ESC. If industrial conflict can be resolved by negotiation rather than by means of a strike, this is advantageous to employers, employees, the government, and indeed society at large. Nevertheless, delay for these purposes is not to be used as a means by which to prevent workers' eventual recourse to industrial action. The period of time set aside must not be too lengthy, reference to conciliation must not be compulsory, and workers must still be able to call a strike once this period of time has expired.[64]

Secondly, national governments are entitled to lay down a requirement that those who intend to take industrial action provide their employers with a reasonable period of notice.[65] This has been said to amount to a 'cooling off period', which may encourage the parties to an industrial dispute to reach a settlement without recourse to strike action, with all its potentially harmful effects.[66] This period of notice may also minimize some of the harsher disruptive effects of a strike, allowing the management of a business to inform its customers of future inconvenience, and giving other businesses the opportunity to make alternative arrangements.[67] However, 'the period of advance notice should not be an additional obstacle to bargaining, with workers in practice simply waiting for its expiry in order to be able to exercise their right to strike'.[68] So, if the period of time allocated for voluntary conciliation is itself lengthy, it may be unreasonable to impose a long notice or waiting period upon workers who wish to strike. The content of the notice given must also be reasonable. For example, the CEACR has found that a requirement that the duration of a strike be announced when giving notice unduly restricts the right of workers' organizations to organize their activities and formulate their programmes in full freedom.[69]

---

[61] CEACR, *Individual Observation concerning Convention No. 87 (Colombia)* (Geneva: ILO, 2000).

[62] *CFA Digest of Decisions*, n.10 above, para. 501; ECSR, *Conclusions I*, 38; Samuel, n.7 above, 162.

[63] *CEACR General Survey*, n.9 above, para. 171.

[64] *CFA Digest of Decisions*, n.10 above, para. 500; *CEACR General Survey*, n.9 above, para. 171.

[65] *CFA Digest of Decisions*, n.10 above, para. 502; *CEACR General Survey*, n.9 above, para. 172.

[66] *CFA Digest of Decisions*, n.10 above, paras. 504 and 505. ECSR, *Conclusions I*, 38. See also Kahn-Freund, O., 'Labour Relations and International Standards: Some Reflections on the European Social Charter' in *Miscellanea W.J. Ganshof van der Meersch* (Paris/Brussels: Librarie Générale de Droit et Jurisprudence/Establissements Emile Bruylant, 1972), 149.

[67] See Chap. 4 above, at 76.

[68] *CEACR General Survey*, n.9 above, para. 172.

[69] CEACR, *Individual Observation concerning Convention No. 87 (Belarus)* (Geneva: ILO, 2002); CEACR, *Individual Observation concerning Convention No. 87 (Russian Federation)* (Geneva: ILO, 2001).

Thirdly, national legislation requiring a strike ballot can be regarded as acceptable.[70] Strike ballots may be useful to a number of interest groups in different ways. They may be useful to trade unions in that they may strengthen perception of a strike's legitimacy. They may also protect the majority of workers in a workplace, enterprise, or industry, where such workers do not want to be coerced into taking industrial action desired by a minority. Moreover, such ballots can provide employers with an indication of the strength of worker feeling on a particular issue and thereby provide an incentive to respond with an appropriate settlement before a strike is called. From a more cynical perspective, balloting requirements can be used as a means by which to delay industrial action; and may also provide grounds for an employer to challenge the legality of industrial action so as to acquire an order requiring a return to work.[71] International and European supervisory bodies are eager to ensure that such ballots are not used as a crude mechanism to prevent industrial action. Legislative provisions imposing balloting requirements will be criticized when they are too complex or restrictive in nature.[72] Moreover, the threshold for approval must not be too high.[73] For example, the ILO CFA has criticized the requirement that a decision to strike must be taken by a two-thirds majority; it being more appropriate that this be determined by a bare majority of those who wish to vote.[74]

Finally, a collective agreement may impose legitimate procedural limitations on the exercise of the right to strike. These may include the requirement that industrial action not be taken for the duration of the collective agreement. However, different views have been taken by the ILO's CEACR and the Council of Europe's ECSR on the application of such 'peace obligations'.

The ILO CEACR has recognized that, in some States, a collective agreement is viewed as a 'social peace treaty of fixed duration' and that, during the term of a collective agreement, strikes are prohibited. This is said to be acceptable in so far as the parties have access to 'impartial and rapid arbitration machinery for individual and collective grievances'.[75] Even then, during the term of a collective agreement, workers should always be able to take industrial action aimed at protesting against the social and

[70] *CFA Digest of Decisions*, n.10 above, paras. 511 and 514; *CEACR General Survey*, n.9 above, para. 170; ECSR, *Conclusions II*, 187.

[71] See Chap. 4 above, at 78; and Chap. 14 below, at 321–2.

[72] *CFA Digest of Decisions*, n.10 above, paras. 498 and 499; applied in *Case No. 1989 (Bulgaria)*, 316th Report of the CFA (1999), para. 163 at para. 189. In respect of the UK, in particular, see ECSR, *Conclusions XII-1*, 131.

[73] CEACR, *Individual Observation concerning Convention No. 87 (Slovakia)* (Geneva: ILO, 2002); ECSR, *Conclusions XIII-2*, 280–1; and *Concluding Observations of the Committee on Economic, Social and Cultural Rights: Dominican Republic*, E/C.12/1990/SR.44, para. 73, discussed by Craven, n.6 above, at 282.

[74] CEACR, *Individual Observations concerning Convention No. 87 (Honduras)* and *(Sao Tome)* (Geneva: ILO, 2002); CEACR, *Individual Observation concerning Convention No. 87 (Mexico)* (Geneva: ILO, 2001).

[75] *CEACR General Survey*, n.9 above, para. 167.

economic policy of the government.[76] This principle arguably demonstrates an appreciation of the range of potential reasons for exercise of the right to strike, including arguably its broader 'political' function.

The ECSR has said that a moratorium on strike action stemming from a collective agreement should apply only to matters contained in the agreement and to members of the trade union covered by the agreement.[77] It is, however, permissible for a collective agreement to contain considerable restrictions on the right to strike, even if they would be unacceptable when imposed directly by legislation. This is because such restrictions are 'imposed by mutual consent of the parties concerned for the purpose of limiting recourse to such action in the interests of the community or the users of essential services'.[78] There is no suggestion that a protest against the economic or social policy of a government could provide the legitimate basis for industrial action while a 'peace obligation' is in operation.[79]

The position taken by the ECSR on this issue may stem from the wording of Article 6(4) of the ESC, which states that the right to strike must be 'subject to obligations that might arise out of collective agreements previously entered into'. This is phrased as an absolute obligation and seems to be treated by the ECSR as such. Moreover, the title of Article 6 is 'the right to bargain collectively' and the provision is concerned only with the 'effective exercise' of this right. As we shall see in Chapter 12, the ECSR has construed 'collective bargaining' in a broad sense, but has yet to endorse the use of protest strikes to promote and defend workers' general economic and social interests. In this respect, its jurisprudence can be contrasted with that of ILO supervisory bodies.

---

[76] *Ibid.*, para. 166.   [77] ECSR, *Conclusions VII*, 40; *Conclusions XV-1*, 430–8.

[78] ECSR, *Conclusions VIII*, 98; *Conclusions XIII-2*, 283; and *Conclusions XIII-3*, 138. See also Casey, n.7 above, 62–3, paras. 185–187.

[79] ECSR, *Conclusions XV-1*, 149–57.

12

Permissible Objectives of a Strike

There is yet to be agreement between international and European supervisory bodies on the objectives that a strike may legitimately pursue. It is possible to identify no fewer than three distinctive approaches to this issue. The first is that the exercise of the right to strike should be restricted to the aim of achieving a collective agreement. There is reason to believe that this is the opinion of the European Court of Human Rights and would be the preference of Advocate General Jacobs, in the light of his advice to the European Court of Justice (ECJ). Different views are held by specialist supervisory bodies under the European Social Charter (ESC) and within the International Labour Organization (ILO). The European Committee of Social Rights (ECSR) has adhered to the wording of Article 6 of the ESC, which links the right to strike to 'the right to bargain collectively'. ILO supervisory bodies have taken a third position, namely that workers are entitled to take industrial action to defend their 'economic and social interests'.[1]

All three of these approaches are examined here. It seems that the first is most closely connected to the conception of the right to strike as a socio-economic right, aimed only at securing improved terms and conditions of employment for workers, which would then be incorporated into a collective agreement. The second has a slightly broader scope, for it entails the pursuit of any objective on which there could be collective negotiation. This legitimates industrial action taken in relation to matters which have traditionally been regarded as coming within the sphere of managerial prerogative, such as collective dismissals and co-determination. The third stance taken by the ILO is interesting, for while the formula for assessing whether a strike's aims are legitimate has remained the same, its application has been extended over time. Today the 'economic and social interests' of workers are understood as encompassing a wide range of concerns, which relate to government as well as employer policies. It seems that the right to strike has become associated with rights of political participation and the protection of civil liberties. This last is therefore the most generous approach.[2]

What is not permissible is the exercise of the right to strike for 'purely political' purposes. On this point, all international and European supervisory bodies agree. The difficulty, however, lies in defining what is an illegitimate

---

[1] The UN Committee on Economic, Social, and Cultural Rights has yet to express an opinion on this issue.

[2] See the analysis of reasons for protection of a right to strike in Chap. 3 above.

'political strike'. This is the issue which is examined in the last part of this chapter. Since this definitional problem has not been addressed in any detail by the ECSR, my focus here is on ILO jurisprudence. We shall see that strikes which protest against employer policies on ideological grounds may be permissible. Strikes which challenge key elements of government policy have also been found to be acceptable in the context of protest against totalitarian regimes, on the ground that their motives are mixed. To this extent, there are indications that ILO supervisory bodies regard the right to strike not only as a social right but as a means to promote political participation and enhance civil liberties.

I. CONCLUSION OF A COLLECTIVE AGREEMENT

The notion that industrial action is permissible only when aimed at the conclusion of a collective agreement is one which still dominates German labour law.[3] It is also a view which certain judges of the European Court of Human Rights seem to take. An example is the decision on admissibility taken by a Chamber of the Court in *UNISON v UK*.[4] In that case, a strike had been called which sought to influence the terms under which an undertaking in the health sector was to be transferred to the private sector. In particular, the union was seeking to protect existing terms and conditions, not just for present members but for future employees. The employer sought and was granted an injunction, on the basis that the objectives of the strike were unlawful. The European Court of Human Rights upheld the findings of the UK courts, stating that there had been no violation of Article 11 of the European Convention on Human Rights (ECHR). Given that current employees could take industrial action to secure a collective agreement if their terms and conditions did indeed come under threat, their right to strike had not been unduly affected and their application was considered to be 'manifestly unfounded'. The Court's decision recognized only the 'occupational interests' of those workers employed by the transferor at present. It was said that the legitimate aims of a strike would not extend to a protest against privatization or protection of other workers.

In *Gustafsson v Sweden*,[5] the European Court of Human Rights seemed to take a more generous view of the legitimate objectives of a strike. This was a case in which an employer, Gustafsson, claimed that industrial action called by a trade union (to which none of his workers belonged) had breached his entitlement to negative freedom of association under Article 11 of the ECHR. The action was taken by people supplying goods to his youth hostel and restaurant. A narrow majority of the Court found that there had been

---

[3] ECSR, *Conclusions II*, 28; *Conclusions XV-1, Second Addendum (Germany)*, 27.

[4] App. No. 53574/99, Decision of 10 Feb. 2002, not yet reported. See also Chap. 9 above, at 231.

[5] (1996) 22 EHRR 409. See again Chap. 9 above, at 234–7.

no violation of the employer's right not to associate under Article 11, pointing to 'the legitimate character of collective bargaining' and the entitlement of workers to engage in solidarity action.[6] In doing so, the majority judgment seemed to endorse legal protection of secondary action. However, it should still be remembered that the aim of the strikes in question was to persuade the employer to sign a collective agreement, which would improve the terms and conditions of Gustafsson's workers. The judgment of the Court can, therefore, be regarded as consistent with the later decision taken in the *UNISON* case, for it also establishes the principle that the objectives of a strike will be legitimate where they are concerned with the conclusion of a collective agreement.

A comparable approach was also evident in the reasoning of Advocate General Jacobs when he provided his opinion in *Albany International*.[7] His view was that 'the right to take collective action' was protected by Community law, 'in so far as it is indispensable for the enjoyment of freedom of association'.[8] He did not link this explicitly to the central issue at stake in that case, namely the scope of EC competition law, but it is evident that he took a narrow view of the subject-matter of a collective agreement which could constitute a legitimate exception to standard competition rules. He observed that the collective agreement should deal only with 'core subjects of collective bargaining such as wages and working conditions' and should not 'directly affect third parties or markets'.[9] His views do not bode well for protection of industrial action which aims at the achievement of more far-reaching objectives.

These approaches have however been rejected as being too narrow, both by the European Committee of Social Rights within the Council of Europe and by ILO supervisory bodies. The ECSR has focused on the role of the right to strike in 'collective bargaining' generally, while ILO supervisory bodies consider that workers are entitled to strike in defence of their economic and social interests.

II. COLLECTIVE BARGAINING

Under Article 6 of the ESC, the right to strike is viewed as an aspect of 'the right to bargain collectively' which may be exercised where 'conflicts of interest' arise.[10] Yet, despite this apparent limitation on the exercise of industrial action, the ECSR has adopted a broad interpretation of these terms:

---

[6] (1996) 22 EHRR 409, para. 53.

[7] Case C–67/96 *Albany International BV v Stichting Bedrijfsfonds Textielindustrie* [1999] ECR I–5751.

[8] *Ibid.*, Opinion, para. 159.

[9] *Ibid.*, Opinion, paras. 193–194, discussed in Chap. 10 above, at 257.

[10] ECSR, *Conclusions I*, 38.

There are many circumstances which, apart from any collective agreement, call for 'collective bargaining', such as when dismissals have been announced or are contemplated by a firm and a group of employees seeks to prevent them or to serve the re-engagement of those dismissed. Any bargaining between one or more employers and a body of employees (whether '*de jure*' or '*de facto*') aimed at solving a problem of common interest, whatever its nature may be, should be regarded as 'collective bargaining' within the meaning of Article 6.[11]

The ECSR considers that strike action may be taken to challenge any decision which could be the subject of collective negotiation, including 'entrepreneurial decisions (rationalisation, closing down of plants, decisions of investment) and the demand for co-determination'.[12] It has been suggested that this view is consistent with the ECSR assertion that the right to strike is an individual right, available to all workers.[13] On this basis, German limitations on the lawful aims of industrial action have been held by the ECSR to be in breach of Article 6(4) and a Recommendation has been issued to Germany in this regard.[14]

It also follows from this construction of Article 6(4) that sympathy strikes and secondary action should be regarded as legitimate. This was Kahn-Freund's view before the ECSR made any comment on the point. His argument was that 'a strike may be designed to improve the future collective bargaining position of the strikers even though its purpose is to secure an advantage from an individual employer who is not himself a bargaining party'.[15] This prediction was borne out by ECSR criticism of the withdrawal of trade union immunity for secondary action in the UK.[16] The Committee has expressed concern at a general ban on secondary action, observing that where trade unions are permitted to take action only against 'their' employer, this may make it 'impossible for them to take action, inter alia, against the company which is their true "employer" but which may hire the workers through an intermediary company'.[17]

This concentration of ECSR jurisprudence on 'collective bargaining' does not readily appear to provide scope for endorsement of the legitimacy

[11] ECSR, *Conclusions IV*, 50. See also *Conclusions II*, 28; *Conclusions VIII*, 95–6; *Conclusions XIII-1*, 155; *Conclusions XIII-4*, 361.

[12] Fabricus, F., *Human Rights and European Politics: The Legal-Political Status of Workers in the European Community* (Oxford/Providence, RI: Berg, 1992), 96.

[13] Samuel, L., *Fundamental Social Rights: Case Law of the European Social Charter* (Strasbourg: Council of Europe, 1997), 164–7; and Casey, N., *The Right to Organise and Bargain Collectively: Protection within the European Social Charter* (Strasbourg: Council of Europe, 1996), 62–4.

[14] Committee of Ministers Recommendation R ChS (98)2, discussed in ECSR, *Conclusions XV-1, Second Addendum (Germany)* 27, which notes that despite the resistance of the German government to changing the law, a judgment of the Gelsenkirchen Labour Court of 13 Mar. 1998 expressed doubts that the right to strike should be restricted in this fashion.

[15] Kahn-Freund, O., 'Labour Relations and International Standards: Some Reflections on the European Social Charter' in *Miscellanea W.J. Ganshof van der Meersch* (Paris/Brussels: Librarie Générale de Droit et Jurisprudence/Establissements Emile Bruylant, 1972), 152.

[16] ECSR, *Conclusions XII-1*, 130–2.

[17] Cf. ECSR, *Conclusions I*, 183; *Conclusions XII-1*, 131. See also Chap. 4 above, at 76–7.

of strikes aimed at challenging government policy. This issue has not been explicitly addressed by the ECSR, but was considered in two cases which came before courts in the Netherlands.

The first of these was *NV Dutch Railways v Transport Unions FNV, FSV and CNV*,[18] in which unions representing railway workers had organized short strikes to protest against a government announcement that the salaries of certain public employees would be reduced unilaterally. The final decision given by the Supreme Court (or *Hoge Raad*) accepted that Article 6(4) of the ESC was a 'self-executing provision of international law, which was binding on every one in the Netherlands'.[19] The right to strike was therefore directly enforceable in the national courts, but the court observed that it was difficult to determine how to deal with strikes which involved a 'political element'. The judgment grappled with this problem and concluded that:

if such actions concern labour conditions which usually are (or should be) the subject of collective negotiation, and are directed against the government, they are (still) covered by art. 6, para. 4; however if such actions are aimed at other kinds of government decision, they fall outside the scope of the article, in which case there is a purely political strike.[20]

In this case, it made no difference that the strike was directed against the government, as it was carried out 'in defence of the right to collective bargaining about conditions of employment'.[21]

Another comparable case has since been decided by the Dutch Supreme Court,[22] concerning a strike which was called to protest against government plans to reduce social security benefits relating to sick leave and disability. An injunction had been granted to prevent the strike taking place, but the union claimed that it had been issued in contravention of Article 6(4). The Supreme Court found that the ESC did cover strikes of this nature, although it was essential that they were concerned with issues that directly affected collective agreements. The ECSR has referred to this case but has not (yet) explicitly criticized this finding, which is curious given that it would seem to be inconsistent with the Committee's more generous interpretation of what constitutes 'collective bargaining'.[23]

Both these cases suggest that workers can strike against government policies which affect either their terms and conditions of employment or

---

[18] (1986) 6 International Labour Law Reports (ILLR) 3.

[19] By virtue of the Dutch Constitution of 1956, which gives provisions of international treaties 'which, according to their nature, are capable of binding the citizens' precedence over national law. In this respect, the Netherlands may be seen as a 'monist' State. Cf. Chap. 1 above, at 29. See also Betten, L., and Jaspers, T., 'Implementation of the European Social Charter: The Netherlands' in Jaspers, A.P.C.M., and Betten, L. (eds.), *25 Years: The European Social Charter* (Deventer: Kluwer, 1988).

[20] (1986) 6 ILLR 3 at 6–7.

[21] *Ibid.*, 7.

[22] NJ 1995/152, decided 11 Nov. 1994, discussed in ECSR, *Conclusions XIV-1*, 555–6.

[23] See above, at 287–8. See also ECSR, *Conclusions XV-1, Addendum (Netherlands)*, 91–5.

their benefit and leave entitlements. There is, however, little apparent scope for protest against other government policies, which cannot so readily be linked to collective bargaining (or the conclusion of a collective agreement). This reveals the limitation inherent in the ECSR formula for determining the permissible objectives of a strike, which stems from the restrictive wording of Article 6.[24] It is an approach which can be contrasted with that taken by ILO supervisory organs.

III.   ECONOMIC AND SOCIAL INTERESTS

Article 10 of Convention No. 87 states that the purpose of workers' organizations is to be understood as 'furthering and defending the interests of workers'. It was logical that the CFA would see the right to strike as a means by which organizations could further such interests. The question that was not immediately settled is what the nature of these legitimate interests would be.

The jurisprudence of ILO supervisory bodies on this issue has evolved over time. Between 1952 and 1985, workers' legitimate interests were described as only 'occupational', 'professional', or 'economic' in nature.[25] However, from 1985 onwards, the CFA has stated that '[t]he right to strike should not be limited solely to industrial disputes that are likely to be resolved through the signing of a collective agreement; workers and their organizations should be able to express in a broader context, if necessary, their dissatisfaction as regards economic and social matters affecting their members' interests'.[26] Indeed, the right to strike is regarded as 'one of the essential means by which workers and their organizations may promote and defend their *economic and social interests*'.[27] This is a 'socio-economic' right, but is recognized as being connected to workers' civil liberties and entitlement to democratic participation.

The CFA's initial intention to protect only strike action in pursuit of 'occupational' interests is evident from *Case No. 170 (France–Madagascar)*,[28] decided in 1959. The Central Trade Unions of Madagascar had lodged a complaint alleging that trade union rights had been violated when the government declared illegal a strike protesting against government economic policy. The government policy in question related to family allowance rates and minimum wages. The CFA decided that, as the strike

[24] See Chap. 6 above, at 142–3.

[25] *Freedom of Association: Digest of Decisions and Principles of the Freedom of Association Committee of the Governing Body of the ILO* (Geneva: ILO, 1972), hereafter '*CFA Digest of Decisions*', para. 246. The same statement is repeated in *CFA Digest of Decisions* (2nd edn., Geneva: ILO, 1976), 112, para. 300.

[26] *CFA Digest of Decisions* (3rd edn., Geneva: ILO, 1985), para. 388; *CFA Digest of Decisions* (4th edn., Geneva: ILO, 1996), para. 484 (my emphasis). For recent reference to this principle see *Case No. 2094 (Slovakia)*, 326th Report of the CFA (2001), para. 478 at para. 491.

[27] *CFA Digest of Decisions* (1985), n.26 above, para. 363; *CFA Digest of Decisions* (1996), n.26 above, para. 475 (my emphasis).

[28] *Case No. 170 (France–Madagascar)*, 37th Report of the CFA (1959), para. 12.

'was not apparently called for the purpose of securing better terms and conditions of employment from the employers but was directed against the policy of the government', there was no infringement of trade union rights.[29]

The CFA was, however, prepared to recognize the legitimacy of strikes associated generally with collective bargaining. For example, the CFA has found that workers should be able to call a strike for recognition of a trade union. In *Case No. 1622 (Fiji)*, reviewing Fijian labour legislation, the CFA noted that a ban on strikes related to recognition disputes was 'not in conformity with the principle that recourse to strike action is a legitimate means available to workers and their organisations for the promotion and defence of their occupational interests'.[30]

In addition, the CFA has found that workers are entitled to call strikes in support of multi-employer collective agreements. It has also been said that it is important that employees should have the means by which to promote industry-wide bargaining, where their bargaining power would otherwise be undermined by the fact that they worked in small undertakings.[31] The CEACR has taken a similar view, stating that denial of a right to strike in the negotiation of multi-employer, industry-wide, or national-level agreements 'excessively inhibits the right of workers and their organizations to promote their economic and social interests'.[32] On this basis, it seems that secondary action aimed at securing a multi-employer collective agreement, such as that confronted by Gustafsson,[33] would be considered by the CFA to be a legitimate exercise of trade union powers.

ILO supervisory bodies have further indicated that a general prohibition of sympathy strikes could lead to abuse, and that workers should be able to take such action, provided that the initial strike they support is lawful.[34] This is a 'two-pronged test', albeit one which is problematic in that 'logically, only one or the other can be applied'.[35] As Paul Germanotta has observed, the attention of ILO supervisory bodies has been directed towards the first rather than the second prong of the test. Nevertheless, recent

---

[29] *Ibid.*, para. 47.

[30] *Case No. 1622 (Fiji)*, 284th Report of the CFA (1992), at para. 696. See also *Case No. 1792 (Kenya)*, 295th Report (1994), para. 519.

[31] *Case No. 1698 (New Zealand)*, 295th Report of the CFA (1994), paras. 253–261; 311th Report (1998), para. 66 at para. 68; and 316th Report (1999), para. 69 at para. 71. Cf. Chap. 4 above, at 76–7.

[32] CEACR, *Individual Observation concerning Convention No. 87 (Australia)* (Geneva: ILO, 2001).

[33] Although in that case the employer was given the additional option of entering into a single collective agreement with the union. See *Gustafsson v Sweden* (1996) 22 EHRR 409, discussed in Chap. 9 above, at 234–7 and above, at 286–7.

[34] *CFA Digest of Decisions* (1996), n.26 above para. 486; Committee of Experts on the Application of Conventions and Recommendations, *General Survey on Freedom of Association and Collective Bargaining* (Geneva: ILO, 1994), hereafter '*CEACR General Survey*', para. 168; CEACR, *Individual Observation concerning Convention No. 87 (Turkey)* (Geneva: ILO, 2002); and CEACR, *Individual Observation concerning Convention No. 87 (Australia)* (Geneva: ILO, 2001).

[35] Germanotta, P., *Protecting Worker Solidarity Action: A Critique of International Labour Law* (London/Geneva: Institute of Employment Rights/Global Labour Institute, 2002), esp. at 10–11.

statements by ILO bodies indicate the capacity for further development of this jurisprudence.

For example, the CEACR has stated that 'workers should be able to take industrial action in relation to matters which affect them even though, in certain cases, the direct employer may not be party to the dispute'.[36] On this basis, the CEACR has criticized the UK ban on secondary action, especially given the tendency of employers to transfer work to associated companies and restructure businesses so as to make primary action secondary. It is evident that this Committee shares the concern of the ECSR that such practices, within the present UK legal framework, will allow the 'real' employer, with whom workers are in dispute, to shelter behind subsidiaries.[37]

Moreover, the CEACR seems to perceive the necessity for greater global solidarity and the implications that this may have for collective bargaining. This is apparent from the Committee's comments on the need workers may feel for secondary action 'because of the move towards concentration of enterprises, the globalization of the economy and the delocalization of work centres'.[38] Trade unions may well hope for further elaboration of this principle, in support of attempts to negotiate international framework agreements which regulate the conduct of multinational companies.[39] In particular, Germanotta has made the case for ILO principles which explicitly endorse transnational industrial action.[40]

ILO protection of secondary action could also be linked to Article 5 of ILO Convention No. 87, which sets out the right of workers' organizations to establish or join federations or confederations and thereby to engage in broader-based solidarity than workplace, enterprise, or even sectoral-level organization would permit. In *Case No. 1884 (Swaziland)*,[41] the government wished to introduce a piece of legislation designed to prevent recourse to sympathy and general strikes. The CFA noted the right to form federations and confederations, adding that the prohibition on the calling of strikes by federations and confederations was not compatible with Convention No. 87. Whether this principle extends to international federations has yet to be conclusively determined.

---

[36] CEACR, *Individual Observation concerning Convention No. 87 (UK)* (Geneva: ILO, 2000). See also *Individual Observations concerning Convention No. 87 (UK)* issued by the CEACR in 1989, 1990, 1991, 1993, 1995, 1997, and 1999. This principle was reiterated in CEACR, *Individual Observations concerning Convention No. 87 (Nicaragua)* and *(Peru)* (Geneva: ILO, 2001).

[37] See above, at 288.

[38] *CEACR General Survey*, n.34 above, para. 168.

[39] These include, e.g., agreements entered into by the International Federation of Chemical, Energy, Mine, and General Workers' Unions (ICEM) with Statoil and the Freudenberg Group, by the International Union of Food, Agriculture, Hotel and Restaurant, Catering, and Tobacco and Allied Workers' Association (IUF) with France-based Danone, and by the International Federation of Building and Wood Workers (IFBWW) with Ikea. See Germanotta, P., and Novitz, T., 'Globalisation and the Right to Strike: The Case for European-level Protection of Secondary Action' (2002) 18 *IJCLLIR* 67 at 70. See also Chap. 15 below, at 346–7.

[40] See Germanotta, n.35 above, 49–51.

[41] *Case No. 1884 (Swaziland)*, 306th Report of the CFA (1997), para. 619.

The recognition of an entitlement to strike to promote and defend workers' economic and social interests has enabled ILO supervisory bodies to reach the conclusion that industrial action aimed at influencing government policy does, in certain circumstances, merit protection. An example of the CFA's treatment of this issue can be found in *Case No. 1777 (Argentina)*.[42] In that case, the Congress of Argentine Workers had organized a strike, the objectives of which included preparation of a national employment policy, job stability and protection, free education, and a public health system. The Ministry of Labour had declared the strike illegal and the government defended the declaration on the grounds that the strike 'was clearly of a political nature, since it did not involve the defence of particular or specific interests of workers in a given activity, but was the expression of pure and simple opposition to the social policy of the Government'.[43] The CFA had no sympathy for this defence, and reminded the government that 'trade union organizations should have the opportunity to call for *protest strikes* particularly with a view to exercising criticism of the social and economic policy of governments'.[44] Future 'protest strikes' of this nature were not to be declared illegal.[45]

This reference to 'protest strikes' is reminiscent of Macfarlane's distinction between 'coercive' and 'protest' strikes. Macfarlane's view was that workers should be able to use industrial action aimed at expressing their opposition to government policy, but that only 'protest' strikes should be permitted. Protest strikes are 'designed merely to draw attention to the extent or depth of feeling against a particular, government law or policy'; they will not depose the government.[46]

CFA interest in protection of industrial action concerning social and economic policy has been shared by the CEACR, which has stated that:

> Organizations responsible for defending workers' socio-economic and occupational interests should, in principle, be able to use strike action to support their position in the search for solutions to problems posed by major social and economic policy trends which have a direct impact on their members and on workers in general in particular as regards employment, social protection and the standard of living.[47]

It seems that the CEACR contemplates that such strikes are legitimate in so far as they are concerned with matters which directly affect workers'

---

[42] *Case No. 1777 (Argentina)*, 300th Report of the CFA (1995), para. 58.

[43] *Ibid.*, paras. 64–65.

[44] *Ibid.*, para. 71 (my emphasis).

[45] *Ibid.* See for similar decisions *Case No. 1851 (Djibouti)*, 304th Report of the CFA (1996), para. 255 at para. 280; *Case No. 1884 (Swaziland)*, 306th Report (1997), para. 619; and *Case Nos. 1851, 1922 and 2042 (Djibouti)*, 318th Report (1999), para. 188 at para. 204.

[46] Macfarlane, L.J., *The Right to Strike* (Harmondsworth: Penguin Books, 1981), 149, discussed in Chap. 3 above, at 64.

[47] CEACR, *Individual Observation concerning Convention No. 87 (Sao Tome)* (Geneva: ILO, 2002); citing *CEACR General Survey*, n.34 above, para. 165.

interests. This is reminiscent of the view put forward by Albertyn on the legitimate objectives of South African 'political stay-aways'.[48]

In part, this approach of the ILO supervisory bodies can be linked to the perception of the right to strike as a social right, for government policies on social and economic issues are 'bound to have consequences on the situation of workers (remuneration, holidays, working conditions)'.[49] It is also arguable that the principles advocated in the ILO stem from an appreciation of workers' entitlement to democratic participation and freedom of speech. These speculations seem to be confirmed by the treatment of other strikes alleged to be 'purely political'.

IV. PROHIBITION OF 'PURELY POLITICAL STRIKES'

The ECSR has stated that governments are free to prohibit political strikes because they are 'obviously quite outside the purview of collective bargaining' and therefore exceed the scope of Article 6(4) of the ESC.[50] ILO supervisory bodies also agree that 'strikes that are purely political in character do not fall within the scope of freedom of association'.[51] However, while the ECSR has never considered in any detail what is a 'political strike', the ILO has not been so successful in skirting this issue. The CFA and the CEACR have acknowledged that it is often difficult to distinguish, in practice, between the illegitimate political strike and legitimate industrial action which is concerned with the workers' 'economic and social' interests.[52]

Chapter 3 of this book suggested various reasons for characterization of a strike as 'political'. One is common to all industrial action, for every strike challenges the traditional social order, within which an employee is subservient to an employer. This is clearly not what the ECSR or ILO supervisory bodies mean by a political strike; for if it were, there would be no right to strike. However, there are also two further senses in which industrial action may be regarded as 'political' in character.[53]

The first is where industrial action has no direct connection to workers' self-interest, but is designed to challenge some other aspect of management

---

[48] See Albertyn, C., 'Political Strikes' (1993) 10(2) *Employment Law* (South Africa) 40, at 41, discussed in Chap. 3 above, at 64.

[49] *CFA Digest of Decisions* (1996), n.26 above, para. 30. Cf. Hyman, R., *Strikes* (4th edn., London: Macmillan, 1989), 176–7.

[50] ECSR, *Conclusions II*, 27. See also ECSR, *Sixth Report on Certain Provisions of the Charter which have not been Accepted* (Strasbourg: Council of Europe, 1998), 49: 'political strikes are not covered by Article 6 which is designed to protect the right to bargain collectively'.

[51] *CEACR General Survey*, n.34 above, para. 165; *CFA Digest of Decisions* (1996), n.26 above, para. 481. See also *Case No. 23 (Sudan)*, 2nd Report of the CFA (1952), para. 49; *Case No. 25 (Gold Coast)*, 2nd Report (1952), para. 57; *Case No. 1067 (Argentina)*, 214th Report (1982), para. 208.

[52] *Cases Nos. 698 and 749 (Senegal)*, 147th Report of the CFA (1975), at para. 88; and *Case No. 920 (UK–Antigua)*, 197th Report (1979), para. 136; *CEACR General Survey*, n.34 above, para. 165.

[53] See Chap. 3 above, at 56–7.

policy on ideological grounds. Examples include action taken to object to an employer's environmental policy or choice of trading partners. This is difficult to justify under the tests established by the ECSR or the ILO supervisory bodies. Strikes motivated by these objectives cannot readily be linked to collective bargaining or workers' direct economic and social interests.

The second is where industrial action is designed to affect the operation of government. In this sense, a 'political' strike is that which is aimed at deposing a government, reducing its credibility, dictating the policies it should follow, or merely seeking to influence the policy formation process. Strikes associated with a *coup d'état*, which entirely undermine social stability, are not considered to be legitimate as they create a 'state of emergency'.[54] However, we have seen that industrial action aimed at challenging government policy is likely to be regarded as permissible under the ESC, in so far as it is concerned with matters which could arise in the context of collective bargaining. In the ILO, supervisory bodies are prepared to defend the use of 'protest strikes' taken to contest aspects of government policy which directly affect workers' economic and social interests.

The objection commonly raised in response to advocacy of 'political' strikes is that they are anti-democratic, in that they allow workers to use economic muscle to impose their views on government to the detriment of other interest groups.[55] To some extent, this objection is undermined where the government lacks democratic credentials and, in any case, does not respond to any interests other than those of its members. Where workers are excluded from voting and denied other fundamental human rights, there are stronger arguments for a strike to have more far-reaching objectives. This issue has yet to be confronted in the Council of Europe, where a precondition of entry as a member is observance of certain 'democratic' principles.[56] However, it is a matter which has been raised before ILO supervisory bodies.

This chapter concludes by considering the extent to which supervisory bodies in the ILO have taken steps to protect ideological strikes against an employer's policies and strikes that challenge policies adopted by repressive regimes. The focus here is on ILO jurisprudence, since neither the ECSR nor the UN Committee on Economic, Social, and Cultural Rights has addressed these issues. The response of ILO organs to these types of 'political strikes' seems to reveal their appreciation of the relationship between exercise of right to strike, political participation, and the enjoyment of civil liberties such as freedom of speech.

A.   Ideological Strikes Against Employer Policies

While the ILO CFA has always regarded the right to strike as a fundamental right of workers and of their organizations, it has regarded it only as a means

---

[54] See Chap. 13 below, at 313–15; and Chap. 14 below, at 322–3.
[55] See Chap. 3 above, at 62 ff.
[56] See Chap. 6 above, at 127.

for the promotion and defence of workers' direct economic and social interests.[57] Ideologically motivated strikes against an employer's policies cannot readily be justified in these terms.

Nevertheless, the decision of the CFA in *Case No. 1647 (Côte d'Ivoire)* indicates that the Committee may intervene to protect participants in ideologically motivated strikes aimed at changing an employer's policies.[58] The CFA found that a strike called by university teachers to protest against acts of repression against students came within the framework of legitimate trade union activities.

The university teachers were not taking industrial action in respect of their own terms and conditions of employment, but in order to express their abhorrence at the way in which their employer, the government, had treated students. This was disinterested action taken for the benefit of others, on ideological or humanitarian grounds. Nevertheless, the CFA found the strike to be legitimate.[59] What is unfortunate is that the reasons for its conclusion were not given.

One option open to the Committee in the *Côte d'Ivoire* case was to find some connection between the strikers' aims and their own interests as workers. The government's treatment of the students obviously had some effect upon the teachers' workplace. This would be consistent with the CFA statement in the *Digest of Decisions* that workers should be able to express their dissatisfaction as regards economic and social matters affecting their members' interests.[60]

Alternatively, the CFA could have explained its decision in *Côte d'Ivoire* in terms of freedom of speech, emphasizing the importance of allowing teachers a voice with which to protest against what was happening both in their workplace and within society at large. This would also be consistent with the general endorsement of freedom of speech within CFA jurisprudence.

The CFA has long been prepared to condemn government action which impinges upon workers' freedom of speech. Examples include two cases referred to the Committee from Morocco. In the first case, the Moroccan government took action against a trade union which distributed pamphlets calling for a boycott of the referendum on the draft constitution. The CFA criticized the arrest of trade union leaders and confiscation of trade union property, on the basis that workers were entitled to enjoy freedom of opinion and expression.[61] In a later case, two trade union leaders who had made certain statements antagonistic to the Moroccan government received prison sentences; one for slander and libel, the other for blasphemy. The

---

[57] Cf. *CFA Digest of Decisions* (1996), n.26 above, paras. 473 and 474.
[58] *Case No. 1647 (Côte d'Ivoire)*, 287th Report of the CFA (1992), para. 442.
[59] *Ibid.*, para. 462.
[60] *CFA Digest of Decisions* (1996), n.26 above, para. 484.
[61] *Case No. 1671 (Morocco)*, 287th Report of the CFA (1992), paras. 486–487.

Committee again stressed that freedom of opinion and expression was 'essential to the normal exercise of trade union rights'.[62] This is consistent with the general principle that workers' organizations should be able 'to express publicly their opinion regarding the Government's economic and social policy';[63] and the assertion that States should allow workers freely to enjoy the right to peaceful demonstrations without unreasonable restrictions.[64]

Yet, while it is difficult to explain the *Côte d'Ivoire* decision in any other way, it is too early to say that ILO supervisory bodies endorse ideological strikes against employer policies on free speech grounds. The CFA has yet to make explicit the link between protection of freedom of speech and the legitimacy of certain forms of industrial action.

B. STRIKES THAT CHALLENGE GOVERNMENT POLICY IN REPRESSIVE REGIMES

There is little doubt that the ILO CFA is critical of totalitarian and repressive regimes. 'The Committee has considered that a system of democracy is fundamental for the free exercise of trade unions rights'; and has stated that 'a genuinely free and independent trade union movement can only develop where fundamental human rights are respected'.[65] Nevertheless, even though in practice workers' organizations have been prominent opponents of such regimes,[66] ILO supervisory bodies have been reluctant to give their wholehearted support to engagement in politically motivated industrial action. They see the primary objective of the trade union movement as 'the economic and social advancement of the workers', not advocacy of wider political objectives.[67]

The principles developed in the ILO on 'political strikes' do not distinguish between repressive regimes and democratic government. Instead, the only relevant distinction is regarded as being that between strikes which protest against a government's social and economic policy (which are legitimate) and 'purely political strikes' (which are not).

However, strikes often have mixed motives, their aims being in part to change government policies which have a direct impact upon the lives of working people, but also to change the very nature of the political regime

---

[62] *Ibid.*, para. 607.

[63] *CFA Digest of Decisions* (1996), n.26 above, paras. 450 and 455. See *Case No. 2129 (Chad)*, 328th Report of the CFA (2002), para. 596 at para. 604; and *Case No. 2005 (Central African Republic)*, 318th Report (1999), para. 172 at para. 180.

[64] E.g., *Case No. 2143 (Swaziland)*, 328th Report of the CFA (2002), para. 583 at paras. 593–594; and *Cases Nos. 2023 and 2044 (Cape Verde)*, 323rd Report (2000), para. 49. See also CEACR, *Individual Observation concerning Convention No. 87 (Swaziland)* (Geneva: ILO, 2002).

[65] *CFA Digest of Decisions* (1996), n.26 above, paras. 32–44.

[66] As discussed in Chap. 1 above, at 12; and Chap. 3 above, at 61–2.

[67] *Case No. 1930 (China)*, 316th Report of the CFA (1999), para. 341 at para. 361.

which introduced and is implementing these policies.[68] In fact, it would be unusual to find that government policies had no bearing on the economic and social interests of workers. ILO supervisory bodies have taken advantage of this overlap in order to uphold the legitimacy of strikes against governments whose actions have infringed essential human rights, or whose policies can be characterized as anti-democratic. The use of this tactic is evident in several cases where an ILO organ[69] has concluded that, despite the mixed motives of the strikers, the industrial action in question pursued legitimate objectives and that therefore government intervention in the strike should be condemned.

The first of these cases concerns industrial action taken in Poland in the early 1980s by the trade union, Solidarity. Its objectives included wage claims, formulation of a national economic policy, dismissal of government officials, free national elections to Parliament, and a national referendum to elect a non-Communist government and to redefine military relations with the Soviet Union. The Polish government considered these objectives to be 'political', and responded by instituting martial law, under which trade union activists were prosecuted and detained.

The *ad hoc* Commission of Inquiry established by the ILO Governing Body found some, but not all, of the strike's objectives to be political. It gave no detailed reasons for this conclusion. Any overtly political objectives were described as insignificant on the basis that most of the points in Solidarity's programme concerned 'normal activities of a workers' organisation furthering and defending the interests of its members, especially in countries *where the State is the principal employer*'.[70]

Of course, the Polish state was not only the principal but the *sole* employer, and as there were at that time no other independent trade unions functioning in a communist state, one may wonder how the Commission decided on what trade unions' 'normal activities' should be.[71] No explanation was given, but sympathy with the democratic Solidarity movement seems understandable, given the repressive nature of the regime in question. This case seems to indicate that where a trade union strikes in pursuit of democratic goals, against a government which lacks democratic credibility, the ILO will recognize the strike as legitimate, as long as some link can be made between the trade union's actions and the broad economic and social objectives which the ILO has deemed legitimate.

---

[68] As was acknowledged by Prof. Sinay at a *Symposium on the European Social Charter and Social Policy Today* (Strasbourg: Council of Europe, 1977), 38.

[69] Whether it be an *ad hoc* Commission of Inquiry, the Fact-Finding and Conciliation Commission on Freedom of Association (FFCC), or the CFA.

[70] *Report of the Commission instituted under Article 26 of the Constitution of the ILO to Examine the Complaint on the Observance By Poland of Conventions Nos. 87 and 98* (Geneva: ILO, 1984), para. 491 (my emphasis).

[71] *Ibid.*, Annex I, Communication dated 24 June 1983 from the Permanent Representative of the Polish People's Republic in Geneva to the Director General of the ILO. The Polish government argued that the very establishment of the Commission reflected a Western democratic bias.

A similar approach was taken in the *Report of the Fact-Finding and Concili-ation Commission on Industrial Relations in the Republic of South Africa*. In 1988, the Congress of South African Trade Unions (COSATU) presented allegations against the government of South Africa, to both the United Nations and the ILO. In 1991, the South African government consented to the referral of this complaint to the FFCC. By that time, certain matters complained of had been remedied. For example, the Labour Relations Amendment Act 1988 had been repealed, largely due to the collective action organized by COSATU and the National Council of Trade Unions (NACTU). Accordingly, the Commission took on a more general role. In its view, its 'essential task' was 'to examine the trade union and labour relations situation in South Africa against the established ILO standards and principles in this field'.[72]

In particular, COSATU requested that the Commission consider whether the government's treatment of strikes aimed at altering South African social and economic policy was in breach of ILO principles. The stay-aways intended to force repeal of the Labour Relations Amendment Act 1988 had been regarded as illegal under South African law, but COSATU sought ILO assurance that workers' direct interest in labour legislation entitled them to take such action. Another more difficult ques-tion was whether workers were entitled to strike, not only to challenge labour legislation, but also to end apartheid government, which had a considerable impact on their daily lives, both as workers and as citizens.

It seems from the South African Report that industrial action aimed at objecting to a piece of labour legislation, such as the 1988 Amendment Act, will be legitimate. The South African government was not entitled to try to prevent that strike from taking place. As regards the use of strikes to challenge the policy of apartheid, which affected workers' lives in their capacity not only as employees but as citizens, the Report observed that the standard ILO prohibition on 'political strikes' had to be considered 'in the very special context of South Africa', where a non-democratic govern-ment had placed extensive restrictions on free speech.[73] However, little more was said on this subject. As a whole, the Report appeared critical of the legislation which had restricted industrial action in opposition to apart-heid; but its recommendations were limited to advocating amendment of the national legislation, namely sections 1(1) and 65(1A) of the Labour Relations Act 28 of 1956, so as to 'safeguard the legality of strikes over social and economic issues affecting workers' and trade union rights'. Notably, the Commission failed to express its view on what issues came within this umbrella definition.[74]

---

[72] *Report of the Fact-Finding and Conciliation Commission on Freedom of Association concerning the Republic of South Africa* (Geneva: ILO, 1992), 8.
[73] *Ibid.*, 175.
[74] *Ibid.*, 52 ff.

Similar issues have been raised in other cases which came before the CFA. Two examples are given below. The CFA conclusions reached in these, and indeed other cases[75] demonstrate that the Committee is prepared to condemn governments' attempts to restrict strikes which have 'mixed motives', even where their aims include political objectives.

In *Case No. 1793 (Nigeria)*,[76] the strike in question had two aims. Trade unions had taken industrial action, protesting both against the situation in the oil industry and the fact that the military regime had annulled the results of the June 1993 elections. The strike was followed by mass dismissals, as well as intimidation, arrest, and the detention of trade unionists. The government responded to the trade unions' complaint by pointing out 'the political nature of the strike',[77] but the CFA was reluctant to allow this to excuse the government's conduct. While the Committee conceded that strikes of a purely political nature would not fall within the scope of the principles of freedom of association, it found that 'in this case, it would appear that a substantial part of the [strikers' claims] were of a social and an economic nature, in particular as concerns the situation in the oil industry'.[78] The Nigerian situation was also considered by the ILO Conference Committee on the Application of Standards in 1995, which agreed unanimously that the government's allegations that the strike was political was 'merely a smokescreen' for violation of human and trade union rights. It was concluded that there were flagrant violations of Convention No. 87.[79]

In *Case No. 1884 (Swaziland)*,[80] the Swaziland Federation of Trade Unions (SFTU) had presented the government with a list of issues for negotiation which became known as 'the 27 demands'. These included the introduction of a minimum wage; the establishment of a national social security system; creation of maternity pay; an end to victimization of journalists; no privatization of water supply services; as well as demands for a more democratic and representative society. The SFTU then held a series of stay-aways in support of the twenty-seven demands. These were met with police violence and arrests. Legislation was passed imposing severe sanctions on office-holders or organizers of industrial action.

The government argued that the SFTU was trying to bring about 'political transformations under the guise of labour issues', but the CFA was not impressed by this argument. It acknowledged that 'it is only in so far as trade unions do not allow their occupational demands to assume a clearly political aspect that they can legitimately claim that there should be no interference

---

[75] See, e.g., *Case No. 1669 (Chad)*, 287th Report of the CFA (1992), para. 330; *Case No. 1562 (Colombia)*, 279th Report (1991), para. 518; *Case No. 1713 (Kenya)*, 291st Report (1993), para. 555.

[76] *Case No. 1793 (Nigeria)*, 295th Report of the CFA (1994), para. 567.

[77] *Ibid.*, at para. 593.

[78] *Ibid.*, at para. 602.

[79] *Record of Proceedings* (Geneva: ILO, 1995) ILC, 82nd Session, 24/89.

[80] *Case No. 1884 (Swaziland)*, 306th Report of the CFA (1997), para. 619.

in their activities', but observed the difficulty of distinguishing between what was 'political' and what was 'trade union' in character. In the present case, the CFA found that the issues in question concerned 'the exercise of legitimate trade union activities' which did not 'cross the line into purely political activities'. The Committee did not elaborate on how it reached this conclusion, but added that:

the Committee would recall that a system of democracy is fundamental for the exercise of trade union rights and that all appropriate measures should be taken to guarantee that trade union rights are exercised in normal conditions with respect for basic human rights and in a climate free of violence, pressure, fear and threats of any kind.[81]

ILO supervisory bodies have not however gone so far as to state that protest against a repressive regime is a legitimate objective of industrial action.

ILO reluctance openly to endorse industrial action of a political character taken against repressive regimes may well stem from pragmatism in the sphere of international relations. In the attempt to preserve 'universality', 'politicization' has long been treated as an evil to be avoided.[82] Accordingly, ILO supervisory bodies have retreated from assessing the democratic nature of particular governments. This has been viewed as a task for the political organs of the United Nations.[83] Moreover, in practice, it may be difficult to distinguish between democratic and other forms of government.[84] One method of overcoming this difficulty could be for the CFA to declare openly that it regards the protection of human rights and civil liberties as coming within the scope of its official functions. It could then be possible to decide cases with reference to certain non-controversial democratic rights and freedoms commonly recognized at international law, such as those set out in the Universal Declaration of Human Rights or the 1966 ICCPR and ICESCR. A list of these rights could be recognized in a multilateral treaty, in an ILO Convention, or by ILO supervisory bodies of their own accord. Whether a tripartite Committee such as the CFA is prepared to take such a step will depend upon the support of government and employer representatives. In the meantime, the awkward process of assessing 'mixed motives' will continue.

[81] *Ibid.*, para. 684. Cf. *CFA Digest of Decisions* (1996), n.26 above, paras. 34 and 36. The comments of the CFA which follow up on developments in Swaziland do not repeat, but also do not detract from, this statement. They merely comment on proposed legislative changes and two individual cases arising from the 1996 stay-away. See *Case No. 1884 (Swaziland)*, 310th Report of the CFA (1998), para. 576 at para. 591. For general support from the Committee of Experts see CEACR, *Individual Observation concerning Convention No. 87 (Swaziland)* (Geneva: ILO, 2002), which criticizes the lengthy procedure and excessive balloting requirements for a peaceful protest action and the withdrawal of immunity for civil liability in respect of such action. See for repetition of this statement by the CEACR in another context CEACR, *Individual Observation concerning Convention No. 87 (Guatemala) 2002* (Geneva: ILO, 2002).

[82] See Chap. 5 above, at 101–2.

[83] E.g., the CFA, in its First Report of 1952, para. 29, noted the opinion of the Governing Body that it is inappropriate for the Governing Body to make recommendations to the UN regarding political issues directly related to international security. To do so would be 'inconsistent with its traditions and prejudicial to its usefulness in its own sphere'.

[84] On controversy over what constitutes a 'democracy' see Chap. 1 above, at 14–22.

What it seems that ILO supervisory bodies will not do is merely accept a government's assertion that a strike is 'political' without further investigation. A government may fear that a strike will have 'political impact' because it is taken in the public sector or that, because an action causes inconvenience to consumers, it will reduce the government's popularity.[85] This is not regarded as a sufficient justification for the restriction of the right to strike.[86] Instead, international and European supervisory bodies carefully evaluate the public welfare considerations raised in the particular circumstances of the case. The detailed principles which are applied are outlined in Chapter 13.

---

[85] Discussed in Chap. 4 above, at 85–6.

[86] See, e.g., on the desire to restrict general strikes *per se*, *CFA Digest of Decisions* (1985), n.26 above, para. 373. See also *Case No. 1381 (Ecuador)*, 248th Report of the CFA (1987), para. 381; *Case No. 1773 (Kenya)*, 297th Report (1995), para. 484 at paras. 532–533. Treatment of general strikes is also discussed briefly in Chap. 13 below, at 313–14.

13

Responses to Public Welfare Considerations

Industrial action usually causes consumers a degree of inconvenience or annoyance.[1] This is not considered by any international or European supervisory body to be, in itself, a sufficient reason for a State to prevent or restrict workers' exercise of the right to strike. More is required, namely that serious public welfare considerations are raised by the action in question.

The standard response of the supervisory bodies in the International Labour Organization (ILO) to public welfare considerations may be summarized as follows:

The right to strike may only be restricted or prohibited in the following cases:

(1) in the public service only for public servants exercising authority in the name of the State;

(2) in essential services in the strict sense of the term (that is, services the interruption of which would endanger the life, personal safety or health of the whole or part of the population); or

(3) in the event of an acute national emergency and for a limited period of time.[2]

These principles are also applied by the UN Committee on Economic, Social, and Cultural Rights when assessing compliance with Article 8 of the International Covenant on Economic, Social, and Cultural Rights 1966 (ICESCR).

Some minor differences have arisen between the approach taken under the European Social Charter 1961 (ESC) and within the ILO. In part, this is due to the influence of decisions reached under the European Convention on Human Rights (ECHR) which have a considerable persuasive effect.[3]

---

[1] See Chap. 4 above, at 79–80.

[2] *Case No. 1581 (Thailand)*, 327th Report of the CFA (2002), para. 107 at para. 111, citing *Freedom of Association: Digest of Decisions and Principles of the Freedom of Association Committee of the Governing Body of the ILO* (4th edn., Geneva: ILO, 1996), hereafter 'CFA Digest of Decisions', paras. 474, 475, 526, and 527. Also, see CEACR, *Individual Observation concerning Convention No. 87 (Burkina Faso)* (Geneva: ILO, 2001), citing Committee of Experts on the Application of Conventions and Recommendations, *General Survey on Freedom of Association and Collective Bargaining* (Geneva: ILO, 1994), hereafter 'CEACR General Survey', paras. 152, 158, and 159.

[3] See Chap. 9 above, at 240–3.

Other disparities may be attributed to the obstructive role which was played by the Governmental Committee within the ESC supervisory process until 1991.[4] Certain remaining deviations from ILO standards can be explained in terms of the text of the ESC. For example, Article 6(4) can be interpreted as permitting exercise of the right to strike only in so far as this does not contravene any collective agreement.[5]

Nevertheless, the conclusions reached by the European Committee of Social Rights (ECSR) are, in many respects, remarkably similar in various respects to that espoused by the ILO Committee on Freedom of Association (CFA) and Committee of Experts on the Application of Conventions and Recommendations (CEACR). Their jurisprudence even seems to be developing in a compatible manner, especially as regards their treatment of essential services and alleged 'economic crises'.

I.   PUBLIC SECTOR STRIKES

Under both international and European law, there is consensus that States may place legal restrictions on the ability of members of the police and the armed services to take industrial action. There is no obligation to allow such persons to exercise the right to strike. This was a conclusion reached at the International Labour Conferences of 1948 and 1949, has been established by the ECSR,[6] and is reflected in Article 8(2) of the ICESCR.

What is more controversial is the extent to which 'public servants' are entitled to strike. For example, Article 6 of ILO Convention No. 98 states specifically that 'this Convention does not deal with the position of public servants engaged in the administration of the State', although this is not to be construed as 'prejudicing their rights or status in any way'.[7] In its 1973 *General Survey*, the Committee of Experts stated that recognition of the freedom of association of public officials did not necessarily imply the right to strike.[8] To some extent, Convention No. 151 Concerning Protection of the Right to Organize and Procedures for Determining Conditions of Employment in the Public Service, adopted in 1978, remedied this situation.

---

[4]   See Chap. 9 above, at 218–9; and Chap. 11 above, at 276–7.

[5]   See Chap. 11 above, at 284.

[6]   ECSR, *Conclusions I*, 38–9. The principle was most recently confirmed by the ECSR under the collective complaints procedure. See *Complaint No. 2/1999 European Federation of Employees in Public Services (EUROFEDOP) v France*, ECSR decision on the merits adopted on 4 Dec. 2000. For similar decisions see *Complaint No. 3/1999 EUROFEDOP v Greece*, decision on admissibility of 13 Oct. 1999; *Complaint No. 4/1999 EUROFEDOP v Italy*, ECSR decision on the merits of 4 Dec. 2000; and *Complaint No. 5/1999 EUROFEDOP v Portugal*, ECSR decision on the merits adopted on 4 Dec. 2000. These decisions have been upheld by the Committee of Ministers: Resolution ResChS(2001)2–4, adopted by the Committee of Ministers on 7 Feb. 2001.

[7]   ILO Convention No. 98 concerning the Right to Organize and Collective Bargaining 1949, Art. 6.

[8]   Committee of Experts on the Application of Conventions and Recommendations, *General Survey on Freedom of Association and Collective Bargaining* (Geneva: ILO, 1973), 116.

Article 4 of Convention No. 151 states that public employees 'shall enjoy adequate protection from acts of anti-union discrimination in respect of their employment', while Article 9 provides that 'public employees shall have, as other workers, the civil and political rights which are essential for the normal exercise of freedom of association, subject only to the obligations arising from their status and the nature of their functions'.

In the ILO, the scope of the public sector exception to the right to strike is determined by reference to whether the employees in question are exercising 'authority in the name of the State'. Under the ICESCR and the ESC, the test is whether workers are engaged in the 'administration of the State'. These are two formulae that could be expected to be roughly approximate in effect. All expert supervisory bodies at the international and European levels have, for example, criticized German law which precludes all '*Beamte*', designated civil servants, from exercising the right to strike. However, the peculiarities of the ESC supervisory procedure meant that Germany was long able to evade criticism by the Committee of Ministers.

A.   PUBLIC EMPLOYEES EXERCISING THE 'AUTHORITY OF THE STATE' OR ENGAGED IN THE 'ADMINISTRATION OF THE STATE'

ILO supervisory bodies have indicated that, while restrictions may be placed on industrial action in the public sector, this exception to the right to strike is narrowly defined.[9] For example, in *Case No. 1762 (Czech Republic)*,[10] the CFA commented that 'a too broad definition of the concept of a public servant is likely to result in a very wide restriction of the right to strike for these workers'. The Committee therefore asked the Czech government to deny the right to strike only to public servants 'exercising the authority of the state'.[11]

This exception seems to extend only to civil servants engaged in public administration, such as officials in ministries and comparable bodies.[12] The CFA has observed that teachers, in particular, should not come within the civil servant exception as they 'do not carry out tasks specific to officials in the State administration; indeed, this kind of activity is also carried out in the private sector'.[13]

---

[9] See, e.g., *Cases Nos. 1648 and 1650 (Peru)*, 291st Report of the CFA (1993). A large number of others are provided below. *CEACR General Survey*, n.2 above, para. 158.

[10] *Case No. 1762 (Czech Republic)*, 297th Report of the CFA (1995), para. 272.

[11] *CEACR General Survey*, n.2 above, para. 158. The ILO CFA adopted this formula in Nov. 1994, having previously referred to 'public servants acting as agents of the public authority'; as discussed in *CFA Digest of Decisions*, n.2 above, para. 492, n 1. See for application of these principles by the ILO Committee on Freedom of Association, *Case No. 1762 (Czech Republic)*, 297th Report of the CFA (1995), para. 272 at para. 284(c); and *Case No. 1865 (Republic of Korea)*, 327th Report (2002), para. 447 at para. 485. See for recent reiteration of this principle by the Committee of Experts CEACR, *Individual Observation concerning No. 87 (Turkey)* (Geneva: ILO, 2002).

[12] *CFA Digest of Decisions*, n.2 above, paras. 794 and 200.

[13] *Case No. 1820 (Germany)*, 302nd Report of the CFA (1996), para. 80 at para. 109.

The only other ground for restriction of the access of public servants to the right to strike is where they provide 'essential services the interruption of which would endanger the life, personal safety or health of the whole or part of the population'.[14] Moreover, the ILO view is that any restriction should be proportionate. In borderline cases where a total or prolonged stoppage could result in serious consequences for the public or in services of public utility of 'fundamental importance', introduction of a 'minimum service' may be appropriate, rather than a total ban on strikes in the public sector.[15]

A similar position has been adopted by the UN Committee on Economic, Social, and Cultural Rights,[16] which considers that only those workers engaged in 'the administration of the State' can legitimately be excluded from the entitlement to strike. This is by virtue of the wording of Article 8(2) of the ICESCR. This Committee has, for example, adopted the ILO view that it is illegitimate to exclude teachers from access to the right to strike.[17]

Article 11(2) of the European Convention on Human Rights 1950 (ECHR) also allows for restrictions to be placed on freedom of association by members 'of the administration of the State'. This provision was given a generous construction in the *CCSU* case which came before the European Commission of Human Rights, in which UK exclusion of trade unions from Government Communication Headquarters (GCHQ) was considered to be justified, despite ILO criticism of this action.[18] There is no such express test under Article 31 of the ESC, but the ECSR followed the Commission's lead in finding that the workers at GCHQ could be deprived of trade union membership. It did so by adopting a generous interpretation of Article 31 which allows restrictions or limitations to be placed, *inter alia*, on the right to strike 'for the protection of the rights and freedoms of others or for the protection of public interest, national security, public health [etc]'.[19] In this, the persuasive power of ECHR case law was to prevail over guidance provided by the ILO.[20] Despite the divergent application of this principle in that case, the ECSR has agreed with the ILO that, while it may be permissible for governments to restrict the right to strike of certain categories of public servants, they cannot 'prohibit all civil servants from striking

---

[14] CEACR, *Individual Observation Concerning Convention No. 87 (Egypt) 2002* (Geneva: ILO, 2002).

[15] *CEACR General Survey*, n.2 above, paras. 158–159. See for principles relating to introduction of a 'minimum service' in the context of essential services below, at 312–3.

[16] *Concluding Observations of the Committee on Economic, Social and Cultural Rights: Australia*, 1 Sept. 2000, E/C.12/1/Add.50, para. 29, where particular reference is made to ILO Convention No. 87.

[17] *Concluding Observations of the Committee on Economic, Social and Cultural Rights: Denmark*, 14 May 1999, E/C.12/1/Add.34, para. 29; and *Concluding Observations: Korea*, 21 May 2001, E/C.12/1/Add.59, para. 19.

[18] *Council of Civil Service Unions v UK* (1988) 10 EHRR 269, discussed in Chap. 9 above, at 228–9.

[19] ECSR, *Conclusions X-1*, 68–9. See also Ewing, K.D., 'Social Rights and Human Rights: Britain and the Social Charter—the Conservative Legacy' [2000] *EHRLR* 91, at 100.

[20] See Chap. 9 above, at 239.

because not all of them do work to which Article 31 will apply'.[21] The Committee also tends to invite governments to introduce a 'minimum service' in consultation with workers, rather than introduce an outright ban.[22] In this respect, their approaches seem to be broadly similar, although, as we shall see, application of this principle has been constrained by the peculiarities of the ESC supervisory process.

B.   AN EXAMPLE: GERMAN TREATMENT OF THE 'BEAMTE'

The general correspondence between the principles espoused by the ILO, the UN Committee on Economic, Social, and Cultural Rights, and the ECSR is borne out by their condemnation of German treatment of the 'Beamte', designated civil servants who are precluded from taking industrial action. The ESC supervisory process has been hampered by extensive State control, which has meant that the influence of the ECSR in this field has been comparatively weak. However, revision of the ESC control mechanism has led to renewed criticism of this aspect of German law.

The ILO considers that German exclusion of a broad group of public sector workers from the right to strike is not defensible.[23] The arguments from the German government to the effect that a strike would be incompatible with the special duties owed by these workers to the State and 'would run counter to the purpose of a professional civil service' have also been rejected by the UN Committee on Economic, Social, and Cultural Rights, which notes that the German interpretation of 'the administration of the State' exceeds 'the more restrictive interpretations by the Committee [and] the ILO (Convention No. 98)'.[24]

In addition, the ECSR found that the treatment of the Beamte was in breach of the right to strike contained in Article 6(4) of the ESC,[25] but the Governmental Committee did not take the same view. The Governmental Committee claimed that it was clear from the travaux préparatoires that the Committee of Ministers considered that Article 31 'would permit a government to take measures depriving certain functionnaires and other

---

[21] Harris, D.J., *The European Social Charter* (Charlottesville, Vir.: University Press of Virginia, 1984), 78; ECSR, *Conclusions I*, 39; and *Conclusions III*, 36.

[22] ECSR, *Conclusions XII-1*, 128; *Conclusions XIII-1*, 155; *Conclusions XIII-3*, 135; Casey, N.A., *The Right to Organise and to Bargain Collectively: Protection within the European Social Charter* (Strasbourg: Council of Europe Publishing, 1996), 65. Cf. above, at 306.

[23] *Case No. 1820 (Germany)*, 302nd Report of the CFA (1996), para. 80 at para. 109; and CEACR, *Individual Observation concerning Convention No. 87 (Germany)* (Geneva: ILO, 2001).

[24] *Concluding Observations of the Committee on Economic, Social and Cultural Rights: Germany*, 24 Sept. 2001, E/C.12/1/Add.68, para. 22. See also *Concluding Observations of the Committee on Economic, Social and Cultural Rights: Germany*, 4 Dec. 1998, *E/C.12/Add.29*, para. 19.

[25] ECSR, *Conclusions I*, 184–5; *Conclusions II*, 28; *Conclusions III*, 37; *Conclusions IV*, 56; *Conclusions V*, 49; *Conclusions VI*, 39. For similar criticism of Danish restrictions on rights to strike in the public sector see *Conclusions V*, 47; *Conclusions VI*, 38; and *Conclusions XIV-1*, 180–1.

persons employed in the public service of the right to strike'.[26] The Governmental Committee has also pointed out that Germany was in a special situation because, 'before ratifying the Charter, the Federal government sent a declaration to the Secretary-General and the governments of all Member States of the Council of Europe setting out its attitude regarding the right to strike of the *"Beamte"* '.[27] This raised the interesting question of what should be the legal status of declarations under the ESC, given that States already have the opportunity to choose between the provisions by which they will be bound.[28] As Betten has commented, 'the Charter itself does not provide for the possibility to accept a provision while at the same time making a reservation as to its wording and/or possible implications'.[29] Nevertheless, it seems that the Committee of Ministers was amenable to accepting such a reservation; and the view of the Governmental Committee was that, in any case, 'Article 31 should be given a wide interpretation'. Moreover, 'within a group of people enjoying the same status, it was sometimes difficult to decide which were really in positions of authority'.[30]

The Council of Europe Parliamentary Assembly preferred the findings of the ECSR to those of the Governmental Committee, commenting that the obligations of a State could not 'be determined by any declaration made by the State prior to ratification'.[31] However, the Assembly was unsuccessful in persuading the Committee of Ministers to adopt this position. By the seventh round of supervision, the ECSR accepted that its repeated comments on this issue would go unheeded, and said it would not revert to this issue, although it continued to maintain the same view.[32] The ECSR was true to its word for a significant period of time, until events in the Netherlands revived the issue.

The Netherlands' ratification of the Charter in 1980, was made with an express reservation as regards limitations placed on industrial action by civil servants in the Netherlands.[33] While this may have been acceptable to the Governmental Committee and Committee of Ministers, the Dutch courts recognized that this situation was untenable. Article 6(4) and Article 31 are directly applicable in Dutch law.[34] In the cases that came before them, the courts ignored their government's reservations and, in a number of cases, recognized the *prima facie* right of civil servants to strike.[35]

---

[26] See ESC Governmental Committee, *1st Report*, Observation by the Federal Republic of Germany. Committee of Ministers/Del/Concl. (61) 96.

[27] ESC Governmental Committee, *2nd Report*, 13, para. 54. See also the Declaration made by the government of the Federal Republic of Germany on 28 Sept. 1961.

[28] See Chap. 5 above, at 132.

[29] Betten, L., *The Right to Strike in Community Law: The Incorporation of Fundamental Rights in the Legal Order of the European Communities* (Amsterdam: North-Holland, 1985), 196.

[30] ESC Governmental Committee, *5th Report*, 9.

[31] Council of Europe, Parliamentary Assembly Report, Doc. 3276 (1973).

[32] ECSR, *Conclusions VII*, 39.

[33] Betten, n.29 above, 195.   [34] See Chap. 12 above, at 289.

[35] Betten, n.29 above, 88–9.

Following this development, the ECSR again criticized governments for denying the right to strike to all public servants. For example, the Icelandic government provided the ECSR with a list of civil servants prevented from striking. These included 'not only personnel whose presence is indispensable ... but also other categories, such as janitors, cooks and telephone operators'. The Committee's response was to ask for an explanation as to why 'workers in apparently non-essential positions were denied the right to strike'.[36] Nonetheless, the Governmental Committee continued to defend the stance taken by Iceland in respect of public sector workers, stating that the restrictions imposed by the Icelandic government were consistent with Article 31.[37]

More recently, the changes made to the Governmental Committee's role in the supervision of the Social Charter appear to have had an impact.[38] When in the thirteenth round of supervision, the ECSR criticized Danish legislation which banned strikes in the civil service,[39] the Governmental Committee decided by eight votes to four (with five abstentions) to propose that a recommendation be addressed to Denmark, asking it to end the general prohibition on strikes by public servants and to bring the right to strike into line with Article 31.[40] This recommendation was issued by the Committee of Ministers in 1995.[41]

A revival of interest in criticism of German law is evident from the concern expressed by the ECSR at requisitioning of civil servants to replace striking state employees and manual workers. This is considered to be a breach of Article 5 (the right to organize) as well as the right to strike under Article 6(4).[42] The Committee stressed that 'the requisitioning of civil servants was such as to seriously restrict the right of workers to strike as a means of defending their professional and economic interests, and that requisitioning of any kind could be justified only in the light of Article 31 of the Charter'.[43] The ECSR later observed that the German Constitutional Court had decided that requisitioning of workers was incompatible with the German Constitution, unless the matter was expressly regulated by law. On these grounds, the ECSR recommended that any law made in this field should be compatible with Article 31 of the Charter.[44] Lately, the ECSR has

---

[36] ECSR, *Conclusions XII-1*, 128–9. For more recent condemnation of the legal position in Iceland see *Conclusions XIV-I (Iceland)*, 390.

[37] ESC Governmental Committee, *Report 11(1)*, 52.

[38] See Chap. 9 above, at 219–20.

[39] ECSR, *Conclusions XIII-1*, 153.

[40] ESC Governmental Committee, *Report 13(1)*, 91.

[41] Committee of Ministers Recommendation No. R ChS (95) 2 (Denmark). This is compatible with ILO criticism of restrictions placed by Danish legislation on the access of teachers to the right to strike. See *Case No. 1950 (Denmark)*, 311th Report of the CFA (1998), para. 430 at paras. 454–461; ECSR, *Conclusions XV-1*, 149–57.

[42] ECSR, *Conclusions X-2*, 98–9. See also Chap. 9 above, at 241.

[43] ECSR, *Conclusions XII-2*, 90 and 113–14; *Conclusions XIII-4*, 362.

[44] ECSR, *Conclusions XIII-2*, 282; and *Conclusions XIII-4*, 362.

criticized German exclusion of employees in newly privatized companies, in the railway and postal sectors, from the right to strike.[45] It therefore seems that application of Article 6(4) of the ESC to German treatment of public sector workers is coming into line with recommendations made by the ILO and the UN Committee on Economic, Social, and Cultural Rights.

II. STRIKES IN ESSENTIAL SERVICES

Strikes in essential services have the capacity to cause the public significant harm, in terms of injury to their lives or liberties.[46] The right to strike may, accordingly, be restricted on this ground. We shall see that international and European supervisory bodies evaluate the threat to an 'essential service' in a similar fashion and tend to arrive at similar findings. The ECSR seems to be aware of decisions taken by the ILO CFA.[47] The only key difference in their approaches stems from the wording of Article 6(4) which has led the ECSR to defer to the content of collective agreements.

ILO supervisory bodies accept that strikes may be restricted or prohibited on the basis that an 'essential service' is concerned, but only in 'the strict sense of the term', that is where there is 'a clear and imminent threat to the life, personal safety or health of the whole or part of the population'.[48] The UN Committee on Economic, Social, and Cultural Rights also uses this test.[49] The ECSR has determined that governments may prohibit industrial action in essential services, in so far as this is compatible with Article 31 of the ESC.[50] Whether a restriction is compatible 'depends on the extent to which the life of the community depends on the services involved'.[51] This is to be decided on a case-by-case basis.[52]

ILO supervisory bodies have had difficulty developing any hard and fast rule governing categorization of a given enterprise or activity as an 'essential service'. Ultimately, this will depend upon the circumstances prevailing in a particular country.[53] Nonetheless, the CEACR has stressed that the na-

---

[45] ECSR, *Conclusions XV-1, Second Addendum (Germany)*, 29–30.

[46] Macfarlane, L.J., *The Right to Strike* (Harmondsworth: Penguin, 1981), 136–40 and 179. See Chap. 4 above, at 79–80.

[47] This may be due to the presence of an ILO observer on the ECSR, as well as its recourse to ILO matters when assessing State compliance. See Chap. 9 above, at 217–18.

[48] *CFA Digest of Decisions*, n.2 above, paras. 526, 540, and 542. See also *Case No. 2135 (Chile)*, 326th Report of the CFA (2001), para. 245 at para. 266; and CEACR, *Individual Observation concerning Convention No. 87 (Colombia) 2002* (Geneva: ILO, 2002).

[49] See *Concluding Observations: Azerbaijan*, 22 Dec. 1997, E/C.12/1/Add.20, para. 32: 'The Committee agrees with the views of the ILO Committee of Experts that the categories of workers prohibited from exercising their right to strike should be limited to only those fields where a strike could result in life-threatening situations.'

[50] ECSR, *Conclusions I*, 38.

[51] *Ibid.*, 34.

[52] ECSR, *Conclusions X-2*, 77; Casey, n.22 above, 67, para. 203.

[53] *Case No. 1438 (Canada)*, 265th Report of the CFA (1989), at para. 398.

tional legislature is not to define essential services in too broad a manner.[54] Transport, broadcasting, education, and banking are not usually considered to constitute essential services.[55] Hotels certainly are not, regardless of how this industry might be categorized by national legislation.[56] Workers in the agricultural sector also do not come within this category.[57] Whether a strike in the transport sector affects 'essential services' may depend on what is transported. Restrictions may, for instance, be placed on industrial action which has an impact on the transport of medicine.[58]

Also, the extent or length of a strike in what are strictly speaking 'non-essential' services may provide sufficient reason for a government to intervene.[59] For example, where communities living on islands along the Norwegian coast were dependent upon ferry services, the CFA found that government intervention in a strike was appropriate, where it continued for a long period.[60] However, a Norwegian strike by oil workers, which was said by the government to have significant social and economic implications, was not considered to come within the 'essential services' exception, by either the ILO CFA or the ECSR. This strike had continued for only thirty-six hours before compulsory arbitration was imposed on the parties. This was considered too short a period of time for the industrial action to cause substantial harm to the public.[61]

A more difficult question is how governments should best respond to strikes in essential services. Both the ILO CFA and the ECSR agree that it may be appropriate to impose additional procedural requirements upon strikes in such industries. The ECSR is willing to contemplate a 'cooling off' period of up to three weeks where 'the strike affects vitally important functions or causes serious harm to the public good'.[62] The CFA has reached the decision that a forty-day period is not contrary to the principle of freedom of association, as it allows the parties a 'period of reflection'.[63]

---

[54] CEACR General Survey, n.2 above, para. 159; and CEACR, Individual Observation concerning Convention No. 87 (Antigua) (Geneva: ILO, 2001). See for a similar view expressed by the Committee on Economic, Social, and Cultural Rights Concluding Observations: Trinidad and Tobago, 17 May 2002, E/C.12/1/Add. 80, para. 20.

[55] CFA Digest of Decisions, n.2 above, para. 545; e.g. Case No. 1937 (Zimbabwe), 318th Report of the CFA (1999), para. 89 at para. 91; and CEACR, Individual Observation concerning Convention No. 87 (Ethiopia) (Geneva: ILO, 2002).

[56] Case No. 2120 (Nepal), 328th Report of the CFA (2002), para. 530 at para. 540; and Case No. 1890 (India), 316th Report (1999), para. 66 at para. 68.

[57] CEACR, Individual Observation concerning Convention No. 11 Right of Association (Agriculture) 1921 (Syrian Arab Republic) (Geneva: ILO, 2001); and CEACR, Individual Observation concerning Convention No. 141 Rural Workers' Organisations 1975 (Costa Rica) (Geneva: ILO, 2001).

[58] Case No. 1971 (Denmark), 317th Report of the CFA (1999), para. 4 at para. 57.

[59] CFA Digest of Decisions, n.2 above, para. 541; and ILO, CEACR General Survey, n.2 above, paras. 159–160.

[60] Case No. 1680 (Norway), 291st Report of the CFA (1993), para. 155.

[61] See ECSR, Conclusions XIII-1, 158–9; discussed in Chap. 11 above, at 280–1.

[62] ECSR, Conclusions XIV-1, 219.

[63] CFA Digest of Decisions, n.2 above, para. 505.

Where a State imposes a complete prohibition on industrial action in essential services, workers 'should enjoy adequate protection to compensate them for the limitation placed on their freedom of action'. Restrictions on the right to strike should be accompanied by impartial and speedy dispute resolution.[64]

Where there is not an 'essential service' in the strict sense of the term, but a total or prolonged stoppage could result in serious consequences for the public, both ILO supervisory bodies and the ECSR favour the establishment of a 'minimum service'.[65] Such a service may also be imposed in relation to public services of fundamental importance.[66] The minimum service 'should be confined to operations that are strictly necessary to avoid endangering the life or normal living conditions of the whole or part of the population'.[67] It should still be possible to maintain the effectiveness of the pressure brought to bear by strike action. In this context, a service which maintained 70 per cent of the city transport operation could not be regarded as coming within this bare minimum and therefore contravened ILO Convention No. 87.[68] The requirement of 50 per cent of personnel to provide a minimum service has also been considered to be excessive.[69]

These supervisory bodies also agree that workers should be involved in determining what would be a reasonable minimum service.[70] This will 'help to ensure that the scope of the minimum service does not result in the strike becoming ineffective in practice because of its limited impact, and to dissipate possible impressions in the trade union organisations that a strike has come to nothing because of excessive and unilaterally fixed minimum services'.[71] In the event of a failure to agree, this difference of opinion should be resolved by an independent body.[72]

Worker involvement in the process of determining what would constitute a sufficient minimum service arguably reflects another principle which is

---

[64] *Ibid.*, paras. 544–547; discussed in *Case No. 2127 (Bahamas)*, 327th Report of the CFA (2002), para. 174 at para. 192 and *Case No. 1999 (Canada)*, 318th Report of the CFA (1999), para. 119 at para. 166. See also CEACR, *Individual Observation concerning Convention No. 87 (Bulgaria)* (Geneva: ILO, 2001).

[65] *CFA Digest of Decisions*, n.2 above, para. 556; ICESCR, *Individual Observation concerning Convention No. 87 (Dominica)* (Geneva: ILO, 2002); ICESCR, *Individual Observation concerning Convention No. 87 (Mexico)* (Geneva: ILO, 2001); and ECSR, *Conclusions XII- 2*, 117.

[66] *CFA Digest of Decisions*, n.2 above, para. 556. See also above, at 306–7.

[67] *Case No. 1971 (Denmark)*, 317th Report of the CFA (1999), para. 4 at para. 57; CEACR, *Individual Observations concerning Convention No. 87 (Belarus)* (Geneva: ILO, 2002); citing *CEACR General Survey*, n.2 above, paras. 160–161.

[68] CEACR, *Individual Observations concerning Convention No. 87 (Guinea)* (Geneva: ILO, 2001).

[69] CEACR, *Individual Observations concerning Convention No. 87 (Panama)* (Geneva: ILO, 2001).

[70] *CFA Digest of Decisions*, n.2 above, paras. 558–560; *CEACR General Survey*, n.2 above, para. 161. See also ECSR, *Conclusions XII-2*, 117; and *Conclusions XIII-1*, 154.

[71] *Case No. 1782 (Portugal)*, 299th Report of the CFA (1995), para. 285, at para. 325; *Case No. 1679 (Argentina)*, 292nd Report (1994), para. 92 at para. 97.

[72] *Cases Nos. 2023 and 2044 (Cape Verde)*, 323rd Report of the CFA (2000), para. 49; CEACR, *Individual Observation concerning Convention No. 87 (Belarus) 2002* (Geneva: ILO, 2002); ECSR, *Conclusions XIII-3*, 280–1; and *Conclusions XV-1*, 475–82.

fundamental to the ILO, namely that workers are entitled to participate in decisions which affect their daily lives.[73] It is therefore interesting to see that it has also been adopted, as noted above, by the ECSR.

Nevertheless, where there is a collective agreement in place which places particular restrictions upon strikes in essential services, it seems that all the principles that the ECSR otherwise espouses fall away. Restrictions stemming from such an agreement, covering the relevant parties, may legitimately extend beyond those which a government would be permitted to impose on industrial action.[74] In this key respect, the ECSR deviates from ILO jurisprudence.

III. STATES OF EMERGENCY AND ECONOMIC CRISES

ESC and ILO supervisory bodies accept that industrial action may be restricted or prohibited where it would either create or exacerbate a state of emergency.[75] For example, the CFA found that in the event of an attempted *coup d'état* against the constitutional government, restrictions on trade union activity and freedom of speech did not violate freedom of association. However, a general prohibition of strikes 'can only be justified . . . for a limited period of time'.[76]

Restrictions placed on strikes and the sanctions for violation of those restrictions must be proportionate to the harms done. For example, requisitioning of military and other workers to break a strike is not permissible, unless this is done to maintain essential services in 'circumstances of the utmost gravity'; otherwise the State may be considered to have violated the prohibition against forced labour.[77]

When defending their actions, certain governments have attempted to make creative use of this exception, but the CFA has been sparing in its application. When the Sri Lankan government attempted to link its restriction of the right to strike in the garment industry to the incidence of terrorism in the country, the CFA's response was to call for the immediate reinstatement of participants in the strike.[78]

The mere fact that a strike affects essential services or the public sector will not by itself constitute a state of emergency;[79] nor will a general strike

---

[73] See Declaration of Philadelphia 1944, Art. I(d). See also Chap. 5 above, at 99–100.

[74] ECSR, *Conclusions VIII*, 98. See Chap. 11 above, at 284.

[75] ECSR, *Conclusions I*, 38; *CFA Digest of Decisions*, n.2 above, paras. 526, 527, and 529.

[76] See *Case No. 1626 (Venezuela)*, 284th Report of the CFA (1992), paras. 90 and 91.

[77] *CFA Digest of Decisions*, n.2 above, paras. 573–577; ECSR, *Conclusions V*, 6; *Conclusions XIV-1*, 452–3; *Conclusions XV-1*, 121–3 and 366–9. Cf. ILO Conventions Nos. 29 and 105 on the Elimination of All Forms of Forced and Compulsory Labour (1930 and 1957); and Art. 1(2) ESC. See also Casey, n.22 above, 68 at para. 205.

[78] *Case No. 1621 (Sri Lanka)*, 286th Report of the CFA (1993), para. 189.

[79] *CFA Digest of Decisions*, n.2 above, para. 530.

which remains peaceful. Industrial action cannot be rendered illegal merely by virtue of the number of workers who engage in the action.[80] For example, a Danish legislative act in 1998, designed to end a strike of more than ten days involving more than 40,000 workers, was considered by the ECSR to be inappropriate. This is because there was no evidence to the effect that the situation had yet developed into an emergency.[81]

States have also claimed that where industrial action could lead to an 'economic' emergency, they should be able to prohibit recourse to industrial action.[82] Both the ECSR and the CFA have accepted this claim in principle,[83] but have tended to view its application with some scepticism.[84] Certainly, 'the viability or productivity of an enterprise must not be a precondition for the guarantee of fundamental rights of freedom of association'.[85] The crucial question is how severe the danger to the national economy must be.

This argument first arose in respect of public sector strikes. It was argued that a State, facing an economic crisis or unmanageable fiscal constraints, should be allowed to restrict collective bargaining or industrial action in the public sector, under the general exception for 'emergency measures'. ILO supervisory bodies and the ECSR have indicated that they are prepared to accept that this may be a legitimate exception to the right to strike, but that they will closely examine the reasons for such claims and will not allow there to be an indefinite ban on strikes in the public sector.[86]

For example, in *Cases Nos. 1715 and 1722 (Canada)*, both the Manitoba and Ontario governments had imposed a ban on industrial action in the public sector, and had unilaterally altered the terms and conditions of civil servants. They claimed, in their defence, that these measures would assist in economic recovery, after a severe recession. The CFA expressed dissatisfaction with the measures taken, but did not condemn these measures, asking merely that this policy be reviewed as the economic situation improved.[87] However, when the legislation in Manitoba and Ontario was extended for a further two years, the Committee considered that it could no longer be

---

[80] *Ibid.*, paras. 494–495; *Case No. 1783 (Paraguay)*, 300th Report of the CFA (1995), para. 272.

[81] ECSR, *Conclusions XV-1*, 149–57.

[82] CEACR, *Individual Observation concerning Convention No. 87 (Australia)* (Geneva: ILO, 2001).

[83] In addition to the provision made for conciliation and voluntary arbitration in Art. 6(3) of the European Social Charter. See ECSR, *Conclusions I*, 38.

[84] CEACR, *Individual Observation concerning Convention No. 87 (Australia)* (Geneva: ILO, 2001). For concern expressed both by the ECSR and the ESC Governmental Committee, as regards an alleged 'economic emergency' warranting the prohibition of strikes in Iceland, see *Report 12(1)*, 61, paras. 264–270.

[85] *CFA Digest of Decisions*, n.2 above, para. 186; and *Case No. 2006 (Pakistan)*, 323rd Report of the CFA (2000), para. 408 at para. 427.

[86] ECSR, *Conclusions X-1*, 74–5; *CFA Digest of Decisions* (3rd edn., Geneva: ILO, 1985), para. 391; *Case Nos. 1779 and 1801 (Canada–Prince Edward Island)*, 297th Report of the CFA (1995), para. 264.

[87] *Cases Nos. 1715 and 1722 (Canada)*, 292nd Report of the CFA (1994), paras. 146 and 511.

'classed as an exceptional measure'.[88] While the CFA was prepared to acknowledge the validity of economic as well as other emergencies, it would not allow labour standards, such as the right to strike, to be compromised in the long term, as a means by which to achieve economic recovery.

More recently, in relation to Canadian legislation, the CFA has reiterated that 'repeated recourse to statutory restrictions on freedom of association and collective bargaining can only, in the long term, have a detrimental and destabilizing effect on industrial relations, as it deprives workers of a fundamental right and means of defending and promoting their economic and social interests'.[89] As the CFA Digest states, 'the solution to the social and economic problems of any country cannot possibly lie in the suppression of important sections of the trade union movement'.[90]

Comparable economic arguments have been made by States as regards labour standards in Export Processing Zones (EPZs).[91] In Nigerian Export Processing Zones, workers have no right to strike for a period of ten years following the commencement of operations within a zone. The reason given for this treatment of workers is the urgent need to stimulate economic activity in the country and attract foreign investment. This has not won approval from the ILO Committee of Experts which has requested that the Nigerian government provide further information relating to 'the measures taken or envisaged to ensure that workers, including those in export processing zones, have the right to establish organizations of their own choosing and that such organizations have the right to organize their activities and to formulate their programmes without interference by the public authorities'.[92] The Committee considers that 'workers in EPZs should have the same rights as other workers'.[93] An identical position has been taken by the UN Committee on Economic, Social, and Cultural Rights.[94]

Finally, even when a government is entitled to prohibit industrial action on the basis of an acute national 'emergency', the sanctions which can be applied to strikers and strike organizers are also circumscribed by international and European law. The guidance given by supervisory bodies on this matter is outlined in Chapter 14.

---

[88] Case No. 1758 (Canada), 297th Report of the CFA (1995), para. 225. See similar cases in which an identical approach was taken: Case No. 1800 (Canada), 299th Report (1995), para. 155; Case Nos. 1733, 1747, 1748, 1749 and 1750 (Canada–Quebec), 299th Report (1995), para. 187; and Case No. 1802 (Canada–Nova Scotia), 299th Report (1995), para. 248.

[89] Case No. 2145 (Canada), 327th Report of the CFA (2002), para. 260 at para. 310.

[90] CFA Digest of Decisions, n.2 above, para. 31.

[91] Cf. Chap. 1 above, at 25–6.

[92] CEACR, Individual Observation concerning Convention No. 87 (Nigeria) (Geneva: ILO, 2002); and CEACR, Individual Observation concerning Convention No. 87 (Nigeria) (Geneva: ILO, 2001).

[93] CEACR, Individual Observation concerning Convention No. 87 (Bangladesh) (Geneva: ILO, 2001); see also CEACR, Individual Observation concerning Convention No. 87 (Namibia) (Geneva: ILO, 2001), in which the Committee takes note of the Government's intention to repeal legislation prohibiting strikes in an EPZ.

[94] Concluding Observations of the Committee on Economic, Social and Cultural Rights: Dominican Republic, 12 Dec. 1997, E/C.12/1/Add.16, para. 20.

14

Sanctions for Industrial Action

The basic tenet, to which all supervisory bodies subscribe, is that those who organize and participate in industrial action should not be unduly penalized for their role in a legitimate strike.[1] In such circumstances, States have an obligation to ensure that employers do not dismiss strikers. Moreover, civil liability should not arise where industrial action was called and taken legitimately; the issue of an injunction preventing such action is regarded as wrong. State powers, such as enactment of legislation criminalizing industrial action, policing of pickets, and imprisonment of strikers, are subject to additional constraints. Even where a strike does not meet the standard criteria for legitimacy, criminal penalties must be proportionate. Peaceful protest does not merit a violent response. Also, when sanctions are imposed by the State, fundamental human rights such as the right to a fair trial, freedom from torture, and freedom from forced labour must be respected.

On these principles there is general agreement between international and European supervisory bodies. The UN Committee on Economic, Social, and Cultural Rights responsible for application of the International Covenant on Economic, Social, and Cultural Rights 1966 (ICESCR) follows guidance provided in the ILO on these matters. The findings of the European Committee of Social Rights (ECSR) under the European Social Charter (ESC), while far from comprehensive, also tend to replicate those of ILO supervisory organs. Divergence from this consensus arises only by virtue of the involvement of the Governmental Committee in the ESC supervisory process and the authoritative role of the European Court of Human Rights. In particular, the Court's finding that it is not a breach of Article 11 of the European Convention on Human Rights (ECHR) for an employer to discriminate between those who participated in a strike and those who did not seems to have led to the silence of the ECSR on this point.

ILO jurisprudence on this issue is more detailed and developed than that which has been generated by other control mechanisms, and therefore receives greater attention in this chapter than the findings of supervisory bodies in other organizations. In part, this may be due to concern with the individual situations of particular workers and union organizers, which are highlighted in cases brought before the ILO Committee on Freedom of

---

[1] The criteria for legitimacy being those set out in Chaps. 11 to 13 above.

Association (CFA). This is not usually achieved under the reporting processes or even the new ESC collective complaints procedure.[2] In addition, when assessing whether State sanctions are appropriate, ILO supervisory bodies also demonstrate an extensive interest in the protection of fundamental human rights. This may be attributed to the extremity of the situations on which they are asked to comment, such as the killing and 'disappearance' of trade unionists in Colombia.[3] This approach may also be due to ILO recognition of the potential link between the right to strike and protection of civil liberties, such as freedom of association, freedom of speech, and freedom from forced labour.[4]

I.   CONSTRAINTS ON EMPLOYER POWERS

When industrial action takes place, an employer may wish to retaliate in various ways. The employer may, for example, seek to dock wages, paying striking workers only for the hours worked. A second possibility is that the employer will, at least on a temporary basis, want to hire replacement labour so as to maintain some level of production or the delivery of services. A more extreme measure is the actual dismissal of those who participate in or organize a strike. Finally, the employer may not go so far as to dismiss such workers, but may decide to give bonuses or other benefits to workers who did not go on strike.

Supervisory bodies in the ILO and the Council of Europe agree that an employer is entitled to dock wages for the days during which a strike took place, whether the action is legitimate or not.[5] The State may enact legislation to this effect, if the national laws do not otherwise provide for such a penalty. This is the traditional means by which States and employers have sought to deter participation in strikes, given how significant the loss of wages is likely to be to workers.[6] Nevertheless, deductions of pay must be proportionate to the length of the strike.[7] There is not to be an additional financial penalty for industrial action. The limited efficacy of the present ESC control mechanism is demonstrated by the fact that, despite repeated violations by the French government of this principle, the Governmental

---

[2] See Chap. 9 above, at 221–2.

[3] *Cases Nos. 1787 and 2968 (Colombia)*, 328th Report of the CFA (2002), para. 84 ff.; see also CEACR, *Individual Observation concerning Convention No. 87 (Colombia) 2002* (Geneva: ILO, 2002).

[4] Cf. Chaps. 3 and 5 above.

[5] *Case No. 1863 (Guinea)*, 304th Report of the CFA (1996), para. 321 at para. 363; and ECSR, *Conclusions XIII-1*, 153.

[6] See Chap. 1 above, at 6–7.

[7] *Freedom of Association: Digest of Decisions and Principles of the Freedom of Association Committee of the Governing Body of the ILO* (4th edn., Geneva: ILO, 1996), hereafter 'CFA Digest of Decisions', paras. 595 and 570–574. ECSR, *Conclusions XIII-1*, 27 and 135; *Conclusion XIV-I*, 258–9; and *Conclusion XV-I*, 254–7.

Committee recently voted against issuing a warning to France in this regard.[8]

The hiring of workers to break a legitimate strike in any industry, other than an essential service (and then in the strict sense of the term), has been found by the ILO CFA to be 'a serious violation of freedom of association'. States have been requested to repeal national legislation that permits this practice, unless the statutory provisions come within the limited essential services or public sector exceptions outlined in Chapter 13.[9] The ECSR has yet to comment directly on replacement of strikers, except in the context of Germany, where the *Beamte* were requisitioned as civil servants to replace other workers on strike in the State sector.[10] It seems most probable that the ECSR would regard national laws which permit the hiring of alternative labour during legitimate industrial action to be a *prima facie* breach of Article 6(4), which may be saved under Article 31 to the extent that they meet the criteria set out in that provision.

ILO supervisory bodies, the UN Committee on Economic, Social, and Cultural Rights, and the ECSR have found that employers should not be allowed to dismiss workers on grounds of their participation in or organization of a legitimate strike, without further cause. 'It is irrelevant for these purposes whether the dismissal occurs during or after the strike.'[11] National laws which treat such conduct as a breach of the contract of employment and, thereby, sufficient reason to terminate that employment have therefore been criticized. Particular concern has been expressed as regards the UK, which allows participation in a legitimate strike to be treated by an employer as grounds for dismissal.[12]

The reason given by the ILO CFA for this principle is that the net result of such dismissals would be 'to deprive workers of the capacity lawfully to take

---

[8] See ESC Governmental Committee, *Report 15(1)*, 58, para. 231. For reiteration of this principle by the ECSR, even though it was not directly relevant to the complaint made, see also *Complaint No. 9/2000 Confédération française de l'Encadrement CFE-CGC v France*, ECSR decision on the merits adopted on 13 Sept. 2001, paras. 46–50.

[9] *CFA Digest of Decisions*, n.7 above, paras. 570–571. See also *Case No. 2005 (Central African Republic)*, 318th Report of the CFA (1999), para. 172 at para. 183.

[10] Discussed in Chap. 13 above, at 309–10.

[11] *CFA Digest of Decisions*, n.7 above, para. 593; and *Case No. 2141 (Chad)*, 327th Report of the CFA (2002), para. 312 at para. 324.

[12] *Case No. 1540 (UK)*, 277th Report of the CFA (1991), para. 47 at para. 90; CEACR, *Individual Observation concerning Convention No. 87 (UK)* (Geneva: ILO, 1999); *Concluding Observations of the Committee on Economic, Social and Cultural Rights: UK*, 4 Dec. 1997, E/C.12/1/Add.19, para. 11; and *Concluding Observations: UK*, 17 May 2002, E/C.12/1/Add.79, para. 16; ECSR, *Conclusions I*, 39; *Conclusions II*, 29; *Conclusions XI-1*, 90; *Conclusions XII-1*, 130–1; and *Conclusions XV-I*, 637–41. The Committee of Ministers has issued two recommendations to the UK in respect of this aspect of national laws: Recommendations Nos. R ChS (93)3 and R ChS (97)3. See also for criticism of Irish law in this regard ECSR, *Conclusions XV-I Addendum (Ireland)*, 26–7; ESC Governmental Committee, *Report 15(1)*, 59 at para. 243; and Recommendation RecChS(2001)2.

strike action to promote and defend their economic and social interests'.[13] Moreover, the dismissal of a worker because of a strike, which is a legitimate trade union activity, is said to constitute discrimination outlawed under Convention No. 98.[14] Governments are to provide not only for financial compensation for dismissal in such circumstances but reinstatement. It is only if reinstatement is no longer remotely feasible, for example, six years after the dismissals have occurred, that full financial compensation can be regarded as satisfactory; and, even then, the CFA will be critical of the handling of the workers' claims.[15]

The CFA has also expressed its concern that 'it may often be difficult for a worker to furnish proof of an act of anti-discrimination of which he or she has been the victim'.[16] So, it seems that the burden of proof should lie with the employer to demonstrate that the strike was not the cause of the dismissal. Lengthy delay in judicial proceedings relating to dismissal for industrial action is also regarded as unacceptable, for this constitutes a denial of justice and trade union rights.[17] In this respect, the CFA has asked States to keep it informed of the outcome of court actions relating to particular dismissals following industrial action.[18] This is an example of the Committee's interest in the personal circumstances of those workers represented by trade union complaints.[19]

Where there are no dismissals, but the employer is permitted by law to discriminate against those involved in legitimate industrial action, the CFA has considered that a State is in breach of freedom of association. Even where special bonuses have been paid to workers who have not taken part in a strike, the CFA has taken the view that 'such discriminatory practices constitute a major obstacle to the right of trade unionists to organize their activities'.[20] The ECSR has not commented on this practice. Its silence on this point may be due to the judgment of the European Court of Human Rights in *Schmidt v Dahlström*, which stated that a collective agreement

[13] *CFA Digest of Decisions* (3rd edn., Geneva: ILO, 1985), para. 363; *Case No. 1511 (Australia)*, 277th Report of the CFA (1991), para. 151 at para. 236.

[14] *CFA Digest of Decisions*, n.7 above, paras. 591–592; *Case No. 2116 (Indonesia)*, 326th Report of the CFA (2001), para. 321 at para. 356; and *Case No. 1937 (Zimbabwe)*, 323rd Report (2000), para. 106 at para. 109.

[15] *CFA Digest of Decisions*, n.7 above, para. 707; *Case No. 2116 (Indonesia)*, 326th Report of the CFA (2001), para. 321 at para. 356; and *Case No. 1719 (Nicaragua)*, 318th Report (1999), para. 63 at para. 65.

[16] *CFA Digest of Decisions*, n.7 above, paras. 590 and 740; *Case No. 1934 (Cambodia)*, 311th Report of the CFA (1998), para. 111 at para. 127; and 316th Report (1999), para. 196 at para. 211.

[17] *Case No. 1978 (Gabon)*, 327th Report of the CFA (2002), para. 58 at para. 60; *Case No. 1914 (Philippines)*, 327th Report (2002), para. 101 at para. 103; *Case No. 1890 (India)*, 326th Report (2001), para. 96 at para. 98; and *Case No. 1937 (Zimbabwe)*, 323rd Report (2000), para. 106 at para. 110.

[18] *Case No. 1992 (Brazil)*, 323rd Report of the CFA (2000), para. 32 ff.

[19] Cf. the collective complaints procedure under the ESC, discussed in Chap. 9 above, at 220–4.

[20] *Ibid.* See also *Case No. 2096 (Pakistan)*, 326th Report of the CFA (2001), para. 419 at para. 446.

which rewarded people who had not gone on strike did not constitute a breach of freedom of association.[21] Given the superior status of the Court within the Council of Europe, it would be difficult for the ECSR to contradict the jurisprudence established under Article 11 of the ECHR.[22] There may however be scope for change of this position, given the judgment of the European Court of Human Rights in *Wilson, the NUJ and others v UK*, in which it was held discriminatory to give additional pay to workers who opted out of collective bargaining.[23]

II.   CIVIL LIABILITY AND INJUNCTIONS

An employer or a third party potentially inconvenienced by a strike may wish to seek an order to prevent the strike from taking place or to claim financial compensation for the loss suffered. The ILO CFA has been critical of legislation 'which makes any trade union or official thereof who instigates such breaches of contract liable in damages . . . and . . . enables an employer faced with such action to obtain an injunction'. The reason given is that, if trade unions were always held liable for workers' breach of contract, they would lack the financial resources to organize industrial action in workers' interests. Accordingly, 'the imposition of penalties for economic losses that might be linked to strike action and/or peaceful protest action constitutes a serious restriction of the right to strike'.[24] Further, if injunctions were readily available strikers could be forced to return to work under threat of criminal sanctions. All these outcomes have been declared unacceptable.[25]

The ECSR has also expressed concern when employers make frequent recourse to the courts to prevent industrial action occurring.[26] The Governmental Committee has also agreed that it is inappropriate to impose civil liability upon either trade unions or workers for legitimate industrial action. Where a strike comes within the ambit of Article 6(4), it should not be possible for an employer to take legal action against participants in or organizers of strikes, in respect of economic loss caused by the strikes.[27]

In particular, the ECSR has been critical of 'the erosion of immunities from civil liability provided to trade unions, their officials and members in the UK';[28] and of UK legislation which makes it possible for third parties to bring

[21] *Schmidt and Dahlström v Sweden*, 1 EHRR 632 (1979).

[22] See Chap. 9 above, at 240–3.

[23] App. Nos. 30668/96, 30671/96 & 30678/96, judgment of 2 July 2002, unreported. See Chap. 9 above, at 227.

[24] *Case No. 2116 (Indonesia)*, 328th Report of the CFA (2002), para. 325 at para. 368.

[25] See Chap. 13 above.

[26] ESC, *Conclusions XV-I*, 80–3.

[27] ESC Governmental Committee, *Report 10(1)*, 13–15.

[28] See Casey, N.A., *The Right to Organise and to Bargain Collectively: Protection within the European Social Charter* (Strasbourg: Council of Europe Publishing, 1996), 70, at para. 212; *Conclusions XII-1*, 131–2; *Conclusions XIII-1*, 159–60; and *Conclusions XIII-3*, 144.

an action where an unlawful strike has deprived them of enjoyment of goods or services.[29] In this context, it cited the report of the ILO Committee of Experts on the Application of Conventions and Recommendations (CEACR), which stated that this 'provides yet another obstacle to the exercise of the right to strike by opening the industrial action of trade unions to constant attack from an infinite number of potentially deprived third parties'.[30] The present UK government has not repealed this statutory provision, but has removed public funding of such actions. The ECSR still considers that this is inadequate and recommends further legislative reform.[31] More generally, the ECSR has commented that under Article 31 of the ESC, damage caused to third parties and financial loss caused to the employer should not *per se* be sufficient grounds for an injunction. These factors should be taken into account only in exceptional circumstances.[32]

III.   CONSTRAINTS ON THE EXERCISE OF STATE POWERS AND IMPOSITION OF CRIMINAL PENALTIES

It is also conceivable that the powers of the State could be exercised to prevent or penalize industrial action, where this action conflicts with government interests. These powers may include deployment of the police, security forces, or the army, who may be required to take action against trade unions and other participants in a strike. The State may also wish to enact legislation criminalizing industrial action and providing for such sanctions as confiscation of trade union assets or imprisonment of strikers. International and European supervisory bodies agree that the exercise of such powers and the imposition of criminal penalties are inappropriate in the context of legitimate, peaceful industrial action.[33] A government may not refuse to register or dissolve a trade union merely on the grounds that it has organized such action.[34] Moreover, dissolution of a trade union on the basis of a peaceful picket has been said by the CEACR to be in violation of freedom of association.[35]

The CFA has added that there must be a serious threat to law and order before there is government intervention. A mere allegation that a strike is

---

[29] ESC, *Conclusions XIII-2*, 144.   [30] *Ibid.*, 144–5.

[31] ESC, *Conclusions XV-I*, 637–41.

[32] ESC, *Conclusions XIII-I*, 158 and *Conclusions XIV-I*, 555.

[33] Committee of Experts on the Application of Conventions and Recommendations, *General Survey on Freedom of Association and Collective Bargaining* (Geneva: ILO, 1994), 177; *Case No. 2068 (Colombia)*, 328th Report of the CFA (2002), para. 125 at para. 128; *Concluding Observations of the Committee on Economic, Social and Cultural Rights: Egypt*, 23 May 2000, E/C.12/1/Add.44, para. 18; *ECSR Conclusions I*, 38–9.

[34] *Case No. 1777 (Argentina)*, 300th Report of the CFA (1995), para. 58.

[35] CEACR, *Individual Observations concerning Convention No. 87 (Belarus) 2002* (Geneva: ILO, 2002).

causing a 'disturbance of the peace' will not suffice.[36] Heavy policing, large-scale arrests, and a failure peacefully to resolve labour disputes are said only to 'aggravate industrial disputes'.[37] States have also been criticized for interference with trade union property and premises. For example, in *Case No. 1849 (Belarus)*, the CFA condemned the actions of the government after it had authorized a search by police of trade union offices, the cutting of telephone wires, removal of property from the offices, and the freezing of union bank accounts, following a peaceful strike.[38] The Committee considers that such a response from a government reveals 'a lack of sufficient and effective machinery to enable solutions to be rapidly found' and, in these circumstances, the CFA has indicated that the technical assistance of the International Labour Office is available to a State, should it desire to establish 'a more effective system for the settlement of labour disputes'.[39]

Criminal penalties may be imposed on those who have participated in unlawful and illegitimate industrial action, but such penalties should be proportionate to the offence. There is no doubt that an 'abuse' of the right to strike, such as vandalism or violent acts in the course of industrial action, can be punished as it would be otherwise.[40] However, arrest, detention, or any other form of imprisonment is not regarded as appropriate where there has been no criminal offence. On this basis, the Philippine penalty of 'reclusion perpetual' to death for organizers or leaders of any pickets held by labour groups to protest against Government action is considered by the ILO CEACR to be unacceptable.[41] As the CFA has stated, 'authorities should not have recourse to measures of imprisonment for the mere fact of organizing or participating in a peaceful strike'.[42] This is a principle which the UN Committee on Economic, Social, and Cultural Rights has since adopted and applied.[43]

In addition, when assessing the criminal sanctions imposed on strike organizers and participants, ILO organs regard the protection of civil liberties as a legitimate aspect of their function. They condemn arbitrary detention and the use of torture, regardless of whether the trade unionists have organized or participated in political strikes.[44] For example, in *Case No.*

[36] *Case No. 1954 (Côte d'Ivoire)*, 311th Report of the CFA (1998), para. 366 at para. 408.

[37] *Case No. 1865 (Republic of Korea)*, 327th Report of the CFA (2002), para. 447 at para. 505; see also *Case No. 2096 (Pakistan)*, 306th Report of the CFA (2001), para. 419 at para. 445.

[38] *Case No. 1849 (Belarus)*, 302nd Report of the CFA (1996), para. 161 at para. 214.

[39] See *Case No. 2082 (Morocco)*, 328th Report of the CFA (2002), para. 464 at para. 470.

[40] *CFA Digest of Decisions*, n.7 above, para. 598; see also ECSR, *Conclusions XIII-1*, 156; decision approved by the Governmental *Report 13(1)*, 95, para. 463.

[41] CEACR, *Individual Observation concerning Convention No. 87 (Philippines)* (Geneva: ILO, 2002).

[42] *CFA Digest of Decisions*, n.7 above, para. 599; and CEACR, *Individual Observation concerning Convention No. 87 (Ghana) 2002* (Geneva: ILO, 2002).

[43] *Concluding Observations of the Committee on Economic, Social and Cultural Rights: Syrian Arab Republic* 24 Sept. 2001, E/C.12/1/Add.63, para. 21.

[44] See, e.g., *Case No. 2048 (Morocco)*, 323rd Report of the CFA (2000), para. 384 at para. 387(a); and *Case No. 1586 (Nicaragua)*, 281st Report (1992), para. 420.

1831 (Bolivia),[45] there had been widespread industrial action combined with violent street protests, all aimed at challenging the government's social policies. The government had responded by declaring a state of emergency. However, the CFA condemned the arrests, detention, beatings, and exile of trade unionists, even though the trade unionists had exceeded the legitimate scope of the right to strike.

The ILO CEACR has since condemned Bolivian penal sanctions for industrial action on the ground that they violate, not only ILO Convention No. 87, but ILO Convention No. 105 on Abolition of Forced Labour 1957.[46] This is presumably on the ground that such extreme sanctions effectively prevent workers from choosing to withdraw their labour, forcing them to work. Imposition of 'compulsory' or 'forced' labour is also considered to be an inappropriate penalty for participation in industrial action. Similar recommendations have been issued to Colombia, Cyprus, Morocco, and Turkey.[47] This is also an issue which has been taken up by the UN Committee on Economic, Social, and Cultural Rights in respect of Iraq.[48] This concern with forced labour is also reminiscent of ECSR and ILO concerns relating to requisitioning of workers to replace striking workers in the context of public sector workers and essential services.[49]

In this manner, ILO supervisory bodies have incorporated into their reports a broad concern with civil liberties which reflects the relationships between different categories of civil, political, and social rights. In doing so, they have accumulated a rich, consistent jurisprudence which has the potential to provide far-reaching protection for those involved in industrial action, to the extent that States (and employers) are prepared to heed the principles that they advocate. They have also seemingly influenced the findings of control mechanisms in operation under the ICESCR and the ESC.

---

[45] *Case No. 1831 (Bolivia)*, 300th Report of the CFA (1995), para. 371.

[46] CEACR, *Individual Observation concerning Convention No. 105 Abolition of Forced Labour 1957 (Bolivia)* (Geneva: ILO, 2001).

[47] CEACR, *Individual Observations concerning Convention No. 105 Abolition of Forced Labour 1957 (Colombia), (Cyprus), (Morocco), and (Turkey)* (Geneva: ILO, 2001).

[48] *Concluding Observations of the Committee on Economic, Social and Cultural Rights: Iraq*, 12 Dec. 1997, E/C.12/1/Add.17, para. 15.

[49] See Chap. 13 above, at 309; see also above, at 319.

Conclusion: Textual and Contextual Limitations on the Scope of the Right to Strike

In Part II, it was suggested that the scope of the right to strike would be determined by the extent to which particular rationales for the legal protection of the right to strike were regarded as compelling. Its ambit would also be circumscribed by the weight given to reasons for its restriction. This hypothesis seems to be confirmed by this study of international and European jurisprudence. Nevertheless, it should be noted that it is not only principle that is reflected in the findings which arise in this context. The political and institutional contexts within which these decisions are made also seem to be relevant, as are the texts of international instruments to which supervisory bodies must refer.

ILO supervisory bodies began by regarding the right to strike as a socio-economic right, which was to play a role in bargaining over collective agreements. This was merely a 'collective right', which States could require was exercised by a trade union rather than an individual employee. However, there was no precise ILO instrument which sought to circumscribe the scope of the right to strike; instead, ILO jurisprudence is based on protection of 'freedom of association' in the ILO Constitution and the general terms of ILO Conventions Nos. 87 and 98. The result was that, as the tripartite Committee on Freedom of Association (CFA) gained in experience and confidence, its case law evolved to encompass an entitlement of broader scope than that initially envisaged. Soon its members could not accept that the right to strike was concerned solely with collective bargaining over terms and conditions of employment. Instead, this right came to be seen as an essential means by which workers could promote and defend their more broadly defined 'economic and social interests'. Arbitration could not suffice as an alternative to such a right, which could be exercised to protest against government policy as well as decisions of the employer. The Committee has accepted that there are exceptions to the right to strike: procedural preconditions that may be prescribed, 'purely political' strikes that may be excluded from legal protection, as well as restrictions in the public service, essential services, and national emergencies. However, each of these exceptions has been narrowly defined and carefully demarcated.

The Committee of Experts on the Application of Conventions and Recommendations (CEACR) has endorsed and elaborated upon the findings of the CFA. In their scrutiny of State conduct, both supervisory bodies have demonstrated a concern with the promotion of participatory democracy and the protection of civil liberties, such as freedom of speech and freedom from forced labour.

These ILO principles have subsequently had a significant influence on the observations made by the UN Committee on Economic, Social, and Cultural Rights. This body has commented only briefly and sparingly on violations of the right to strike, but has done so with explicit reference to the views of the ILO CEACR and the content of ILO Convention No. 87. This is owing to the text of Article 8 of the International Covenant on Economic, Social, and Cultural Rights, which in paragraph 3 states that 'nothing in this Article shall authorize State Parties to the [ILO] Convention of 1948 concerning Freedom of Association and Protection of the Right to Organize to take legislative measures which would prejudice, or apply the law in such a manner as would prejudice, the guarantees provided for in that Convention'. It is therefore not surprising that, while the UN Committee's comments on this point have not been extensive, there is no notable discrepancy between these and the guidance provided by ILO supervisory bodies.

The European Committee of Social Rights (ECSR) is a 'Committee of Independent Experts' which provides a technical evaluation of compliance with those provisions of the European Social Charter 1961 (ESC) adopted by each State Party. In its work, the ECSR has reference to both reports by ILO supervisory bodies and information supplied to the Committee by an ILO representative. Its conclusions might therefore be expected to be consistent with those of the ILO on similar cases. We have seen that this is generally the case, but is not exclusively so. There are both contextual and textual reasons for a difference of approach.

First, the authority of ECSR findings has been undermined by the hesitance of the Governmental Committee to criticize State conduct. Examples include the reluctance of the Governmental Committee to regard the right to strike as an individual right, its refusal to contest a wide-ranging prohibition of public sector strikes in Germany, and its resistance to making a recommendation on lawful deductions from pay. In this respect, changes to the ESC supervisory process introduced in 1991 have been significant, as the influence wielded by government representatives in the interpretation of the Charter has diminished, allowing the ECSR greater scope to develop standards which, if not entirely free from political pressures, are at least rooted in principle.

Secondly, the ECSR has to contend with the existence of a parallel control mechanism which pronounces on the extent of State compliance with 'freedom of association', guaranteed under Article 11 of the European Convention on Human Rights 1950. The European Court of Human

Rights appears to envisage a much more limited role for industrial action than does the ILO. Its judgments indicate that members of the Court tend to view the right to strike solely as a narrowly defined socio-economic right which arises in the context of bargaining over the content of a collective agreement. Moreover, ECHR jurisprudence indicates that the exception to freedom of association for workers engaged in the 'administration of the State' should be broadly construed; an interpretation which the ECSR subsequently applied in the *CCSU* case. The Court has also held that it is permissible for an employer to reward workers who have not participated in industrial action, which may explain the silence of the ECSR on the subject of anti-union discrimination in this context.

These are the contextual constraints placed on the ECSR. The other key constraint is the actual text of the ESC. In particular, the wording of Article 6, with its reference to 'collective bargaining', explains why the ECSR has adopted neither the ILO formulation of the right to strike ('to promote and defend workers' economic and social interests') nor the more restrictive approach advocated by the European Court of Human Rights. This allows less scope for protection of protest strikes aimed at challenging government policy. Moreover, Article 6(4) states that the right to take collective action is 'subject to obligations that might arise out of collective agreements previously entered into'. On this basis, the ECSR considers that it is permissible for a collective agreement to give rise to extensive limitations on the right to strike, even if these would be considered unacceptable when imposed directly by legislation.

This text is not always the source of shortcomings. For example, it has allowed the ECSR to advocate protection of an individual right to strike. Nevertheless, these textual and contextual limitations have combined to the extent that, while the ECSR often adheres to the principles advocated by the ILO, this supervisory body has not simply transposed ILO jurisprudence into a European setting.

15

Conclusion: Past Sources of Divergence and Prospects for Future Developments

'Traditional theory divided the legal universe into international law and national law simply.'[1] However, this is too simple. Distinct legal orders co-exist at the international and European levels. This book has focused on three different organizations, the International Labour Organization (ILO), the Council of Europe, and the European Union (EU), providing a comparative study of their treatment of the right to strike. It has also addressed, to the extent that these are relevant, provisions contained in the United Nations (UN) human rights Covenants of 1966.

These legal orders are not entirely independent, as is apparent from reference to ILO Convention No. 87 in the 1966 Covenants, the assistance provided by the ILO in the drafting of the European Social Charter 1961 (ESC), and the influence of the ILO Ohlin Report on the content of the Treaty of Rome 1957. Shared histories, together with contemporary communication between these organizations, have helped to shape the content of the norms which they now seek to protect. Nevertheless, these connections have not led to the creation of a uniform international and European set of standards relating to industrial action.

To some extent, this is appropriate, as one would expect regional organizations to elaborate upon and develop international norms, in a manner which reflects the particular social circumstances within that geographical area. Their role is more complex than merely that of 'local carriers of a global message'.[2] Moreover, the two European organizations must, in order to co-exist, demarcate their roles as standard-setting and enforcement agencies. There is no pretence here that in any comparison between these organizations one is comparing like with like.

Differences in approach are problematic only to the extent that regional organizations have the capacity to undermine the authority and application of global minimum standards. This may occur where a State is faced with an apparent conflict between its obligations as a Member of the ILO and those

---

[1] *Proceedings of the Colloquy about the European Convention on Human Rights in relation to other International Instruments for the Protection of Human Rights* (Strasbourg: Council of Europe, 1979), 32.

[2] Vincent, R.J., *Human Rights and International Relations* (Cambridge: CUP, 1986), 101.

which arise by virtue of commitments undertaken within the Council of Europe or European Union. A State may then be at a loss how to respond or may consider that, as a law does not appear to contravene one organization's standards, it is free to ignore the violation of another.[3] Moreover, the ability of the ILO to promote workers' rights depends upon its ability to embarrass Member States when they deviate from these standards. This ability may be lost, or greatly diminished, where supervisory mechanisms within regional organizations tell a State that, despite condemnation by the ILO, its actions are acceptable. As Fawcett and Hurrell have recognized, 'far from slotting nicely into a neat pattern of global subsidiarity, regionalism and regional co-operation may form the political framework for conflict over the definition of human rights and over the means by which they should be enforced internationally'.[4]

This final chapter summarizes the differences between the ILO, the Council of Europe, and the European Union as regards their respective attempts to promote protection of the right to strike; and suggests that these are potentially problematic. It is contended that the sources of these differences can be understood as being threefold: theoretical, structural, and contextual. First, they may stem from divergent understandings of the function of the right to strike within a 'democratic' society. In particular, the distinction drawn in the Council of Europe between civil and political rights on the one hand and socio-economic rights on the other does not correspond to the view taken in the International Labour Organization. Secondly, divergent norms are likely to arise from divergent structures of governance. The disparate standard-setting and supervisory mechanisms in operation within the ILO, Council of Europe, and EU are likely to disseminate disparate standards. For example, tripartite processes, in which workers' and employers' voices are heard, are likely to produce different outcomes from processes dominated by States. Thirdly, the constitutional values and governance mechanisms utilized in any given organization have to be placed in their social, political, and historical contexts. In particular, the balance of power at any given time between States, labour, and capital will be relevant.

The last section of this chapter considers the prospects for more consistent or coherent protection of the right to strike by these organizations. It suggests that changes in the nature of work, post cold-war 'democratization' and rapid expansion in globalization of markets may also prompt changes in international legal norms. The question for workers is the direction that such change will take: will it be for their benefit, that of capital, or conceiv-

---

[3] Morris, G.S., 'Freedom of Association and the Interests of the State' in Ewing, K.D., Gearty, C.A., and Hepple, B. (eds.), *Human Rights and Labour Law* (London: Mansell, 1994), 30.

[4] Fawcett, L., and Hurrell, A., *Regionalism in World Politics: Regional Organization and International Order* (Oxford: OUP, 1995), 324.

ably for the mutual benefit of all civil society? This is likely to depend on who takes the decisions on these matters. Here, current debates over the appropriate forms of governance within international and European organizations become pertinent. Also, 'codes of conduct' and corporate social governance have been viewed as attractive propositions, so it seems worth considering what they could contribute. This chapter concludes by considering the particular concerns of the ILO, as well as issues faced by European organizations, and discusses how these could affect future developments in this field.

I. A SUMMARY OF THE DIFFERENCES BETWEEN PROTECTION OF THE RIGHT TO STRIKE IN INTERNATIONAL AND EUROPEAN ORGANIZATIONS

There is no ILO instrument which provides explicit, systematic, and detailed protection of the right to strike. Nevertheless, ILO supervisory bodies, such as the Committee on Freedom of Association (CFA), the Fact-Finding and Conciliation Commission (FFCC), and the Committee of Experts on the Application of Conventions and Recommendations (CEACR), have found that the right to strike is an essential aspect of 'freedom of association', guaranteed under the ILO Constitution, as well as, *inter alia*, ILO Conventions Nos. 87 and 98.[5]

A different view has been taken within the Council of Europe. 'Freedom of association' is guaranteed under Article 11 of the European Convention on Human Rights 1950 (ECHR), but the right to strike is not regarded as necessary to the exercise of that freedom. The European Commission and Court of Human Rights have stated that the right to strike is one important means by which union members may protect their occupational interests, but that there are also other avenues. As this is not an entitlement expressly enshrined in Article 11 they have found that industrial action can be subjected by national law to regulation that limits its exercise. A generous 'margin of appreciation' is applied. In no case brought under Article 11 has the State been found to be in violation of freedom of association by virtue of restrictions placed on the right to strike. Article 11 has been interpreted with a view to protecting individual liberty rather than collective action. The result has been that findings under the ECHR on the subject of the freedom of association deviate considerably from those of the ILO.[6]

Instead, within the Council of Europe, the right to strike is guaranteed only under a separate instrument, the European Social Charter 1961 (ESC).[7] This is an instrument that is, in many respects, inferior in status to the ECHR. While the ECHR guarantees civil and political rights,

---

[5] See Chaps. 5 and 8 above.   [6] See Chaps. 6 and 9 above.   [7] ESC, Art. 6(4).

the ESC merely promotes the protection of socio-economic rights. Under the Charter, States can select from a minimum 'core' of provisions, so that they may become Contracting Parties without being obliged to protect the right to strike. The obligations that they do adopt extend under the original Social Charter only to citizens of Contracting Parties. Refugees and stateless persons also have claims under the Revised Social Charter of 1996, but third-country nationals do not. Not 'everyone within their jurisdiction' can rely on these rights, which is the test applied under the ECHR.[8] Furthermore, the judgments of the European Court of Human Rights on trade union rights under Article 11 of the ECHR are likely to have greater influence than those determinations reached by the European Committee of Social Rights (ECSR), a Committee of Independent Experts, under the European Social Charter. This is unfortunate, given that it is the ECSR that has technical expertise in this field, makes reference to ILO reports and is able to consult with an ILO observer on the conclusions that it reaches.

The adoption of these two distinct human rights instruments within the Council of Europe served as a precedent. The United Nations followed this lead when, in 1966, the General Assembly adopted its own two human rights instruments: the International Covenant on Civil and Political Rights (ICCPR) and the International Covenant on Economic, Social, and Cultural Rights (ICESCR). Protection of freedom of association was guaranteed under Article 22 of the former; a right to strike was explicitly recognized in Article 8(1)(d) of the latter. The Human Rights Committee, responsible for supervising implementation of the ICCPR, in a controversial majority decision considered that it cannot have been the intention of the Contracting Parties that Article 22 should encompass protection of the right to strike. The Committee on Economic, Social, and Cultural Rights, which presents observations to ECOSOC on State compliance with the ICESCR, has achieved less influence than its counterpart under the ICCPR. What is promising is that, as regards protection of the right to strike, this Committee sees its role as being to reiterate and reinforce the findings of the ILO Committee of Experts. This is consistent with Article 8(3) of the ICESCR which explicitly requires that State Parties continue to honour their obligations under ILO Convention No. 87; and also the 'principle of speciality' which indicates that other UN bodies should defer to ILO expertise in this field.[9]

By contrast, the jurisprudence emerging from the Council of Europe on the subject of the right to strike is not entirely consistent with guidance given by ILO supervisory bodies. An example is the definition of the permissible objectives of a strike. In the ILO, it is recognized that workers are entitled to strike in 'their economic and social interests', so as to challenge both employer and government policy. This is not the view taken by the Euro-

---

[8] See Chap. 6 above, at 132.   [9] See Chap. 1 above, at 1 and 30.

pean Court of Human Rights, which considers that such action is appropriate solely in the context of negotiation over conclusion of a collective agreement. The European Committee of Social Rights (ECSR) takes a slightly more generous approach, namely that industrial action need not be taken for the purpose of concluding a collective agreement in order to be legitimate, but must be connected to some form of broadly defined 'collective bargaining'. The ECSR does not, however, go so far as to adopt the ILO formulation.[10] The ECSR is not to blame, so much as the text of Article 6 of the European Social Charter, for it is there that the limitation arises. Article 6 as a whole is concerned solely with 'collective bargaining'. In addition, the supervisory mechanism established under the ESC has given States a degree of control which does not arise in the ILO. Even in circumstances where the principles espoused by the ECSR accord with those of the ILO, such as in relation to restrictions placed on strikes in the public sector, the Governmental Committee has resisted criticism of State conduct.[11] Nevertheless, it is possible to detect a gradual trend towards application of ILO jurisprudence on the part of both the ECSR and the Governmental Committee.

The European Union has acknowledged the importance of the right to strike under the Community Charter of the Fundamental Social Rights of Workers 1989 (CCFSRW),[12] an instrument which is now referred to in Article 136 of the EC Treaty alongside the European Social Charter 1961. The EU Charter of Fundamental Rights 2000 (EUCFR) also recognizes a 'right of collective bargaining' and 'strike action'.[13] However, the possibility of a directive on this subject appears to be precluded by Article 137(6) of the EC Treaty. Instead, issues relating to protection of the right to strike will be considered only in so far as they constitute an exception to the application of other principles of EC law. While the European Court of Justice (ECJ) has acknowledged that 'freedom of association' is a fundamental right,[14] the Court has made no definitive statement on the right to strike. The ECJ has tended to pay attention to protection of civil and political rights, and be fairly circumspect on the subject of socio-economic entitlements. It is only in the staff cases, and in the opinion of Advocate General Jacobs, that one can detect any interest in this issue. This creates potential for erosion of national laws protecting industrial action, owing to the application of EU free movement and competition laws.[15] Nevertheless, the EU has demonstrated an interest in the enforcement of 'core' ILO standards outside its borders, by inclusion of terms requiring compliance with such standards in

---

[10] Chap. 12 above.
[11] Chap. 13 above, at 307–10.
[12] CCFSRW, point 13.
[13] EUCFR, Art. 28.
[14] Case C–415/93 *Union Royale Belge des Sociétés de Football Association ASBL v Bosman* [1995] ECR I–4921, Judgment, para. 79.
[15] See Chap. 10 above.

trade and aid agreements. These standards include those contained in ILO Conventions Nos. 87 and 98.[16] It is merely within its borders that the EU will not play an active role in the implementation of these Conventions.

II.   SOURCES OF DIFFERENCE

This book has been concerned not only with the identification of differences between the approaches taken by these organizations, but also with their sources. It seems that these can be placed within three broad categories: theoretical, structural, and contextual. To some extent these overlap, for a particular institutional structure will lead to the preferences of certain actors prevailing over others, thereby explaining the theoretical approach adopted. Moreover, institutional frameworks and theoretical constructs do not emerge in a vacuum, but can be linked to the social and political developments that are taking place at any point in time. Indeed, they tend to reflect the balance of power between States and also between government, capital, and labour. The tentative conclusions reached in the course of this study are briefly set out here.

A.   THEORETICAL: RIGHTS AND THEIR PLACE WITHIN A 'DEMOCRATIC' FRAMEWORK

As was observed in Chapter 1, the extent to which civil, political, and socio-economic rights should be protected turns on one's conception of what constitutes a genuine 'democracy'.[17] It is generally accepted that there should be protection of 'civil liberties' and 'political rights' which allow an electoral system to be effective. These include freedom of speech, freedom of association, freedom from slavery (or forced labour), and a right to vote. There is less agreement on the kinds of socio-economic rights which should be respected in a 'representative' democracy and the extent to which they should be allowed to impinge on contractual freedoms and property rights.

Nevertheless, a 'right to strike' is commonly acknowledged, in some form, by virtually all governments which could be described as 'representative' and democratically elected. This may well be due to the influence of workers as voters within such States. Still, there remain deviations in the scope of the right protected. Certain States view this entitlement as merely an adjunct to collective bargaining and therefore socio-economic in character, whereas others consider the right to be closely linked with political participation or the exercise of civil liberties.

Chapter 2 examined the implications of categorizing the right to strike as a civil, political, or socio-economic right under international law. The aim was to highlight the reasons given for divergent treatment of such rights; but

---

[16] Chap. 7 above, at 167–70.   [17] Chap. 1 above, at 14–22.

also to rebut those which do not necessarily apply to the right to strike. It has been claimed that 'social rights' are too vague to be justiciable, 'collective' in nature, lacking in universality, and 'positive' in that they impose a financial burden on the State. The adequacy of this analysis is questionable. While there may be room for argument on the scope of the right to strike, this entitlement is readily definable, can be claimed by an individual (as an aspect of personal autonomy even though it is to be exercised in conjunction with others), applies to all persons in employment (just as a right to a fair hearing would apply to all persons appearing before the courts), and imposes no additional financial burden on the State beyond the standard costs of law enforcement.

Nevertheless, socio-economic rights continue to receive less protection under instruments such as the ESC and the ICESCR than do civil and political rights guaranteed in the ECHR and the ICCPR. In the Council of Europe and under the 1966 Covenants, the right to strike has been treated as a socio-economic right and therefore distinct from (and inferior to) the civil liberty that is 'freedom of association'. This is not, however, the approach which has been taken by the ILO. ILO supervisory bodies have concluded that a socio-economic right (the right to strike) may flow from a fundamental civil liberty (freedom of association), and that both may be linked to rights of participation in the workplace and the public sphere. This interpretation of 'freedom of association' accords with the content of the ILO Constitution, which transcends distinctions between these categories of rights. It is also consistent with the recent reiteration of constitutional principles in the 1998 ILO Declaration on Fundamental Principles and Rights at Work.

B.   STRUCTURAL: FORMS OF INTERNATIONAL AND EUROPEAN GOVERNANCE

When, in 1951, the ILO entered into an agreement with the Council of Europe designed to facilitate co-operation between the two organizations, it was feared that the different structures of the two organizations could lead to discrepancies in the setting and enforcement of labour standards. One employer representative on the ILO Governing Body noted that:

Collaboration was comparatively easy between organisations having a similar structure; this did not, however, apply in the case of the Council of Europe, an organisation which was composed essentially of Governments, Ministers and parliamentarians and which did not have a tripartite character.[18]

It has been argued in this book that these structural differences between the ILO and other organizations have led to divergent approaches to

---

[18] *Minutes of the 115th Session of the Governing Body* (Geneva: ILO, 1951) Third Sitting, 29, per Mr Waline (Employers' Group).

protection of the right to strike. They have been significant both in the context of standard-setting and supervisory mechanisms.

1. Standard-setting Mechanisms

The tripartite aspect of the ILO standard-setting mechanism is its distinctive feature. The inclusion of employer and worker representatives in the drafting and adoption of standards ensures that these reflect their interests as well as those of States. These interests may extend to resisting the adoption of an ILO Convention which does not achieve their objectives. In this they try to win support from governments to achieve an effective veto. Chapter 5 investigated the reasons the ILO had not adopted any ILO Convention or Recommendation devoted to the subject of the right to strike. It was argued that this was attributable to the specific dynamics of ILO standard-setting mechanisms.

For some considerable period of time, the workers' group within the ILO sought to achieve the adoption of a Convention which would set minimum standards in respect of both freedom of association and the right to strike. Standard-setting on both these subjects was resisted by the employers' group, which sought to dilute the strength of those standards. The response of the workers was to withdraw their support from any initiative which did not reflect their basic objectives. After the Second World War, there was an implicit threat that if the ILO did not adopt a convention relating to freedom of association, the UN General Assembly would act on its own initiative. ILO Conventions Nos. 87 and 98 were adopted swiftly, in 1948 and 1949 respectively. The issue of the right to strike was left to one side, and commentators do not agree upon whether this entitlement was at that time considered to be implicit in these Conventions.

What followed was the finding by the ILO Committee on Freedom of Association that such a right arose from not only Conventions Nos. 87 and 98, but also the guarantee of freedom of association contained in the ILO Constitution. This view was subsequently adopted by the CEACR and other ILO supervisory bodies, and has only recently been challenged by the employers' group within the Conference Committee on the Application of Conventions and Recommendations. Their aim seems to be to initiate the adoption of a new ILO Convention on dispute resolution, which would reduce the scope of legitimate industrial action and enhance protection of the lock-out.[19] Employers' proposals to place this matter on the International Labour Conference agenda have been opposed by the workers' group, which may have feared that, in the current political climate, protection of the right to strike could be curtailed rather than enhanced.[20]

---

[19] The latter receives little attention at present from the CFA or the CEACR. See Chap. 8 above, at 200–3.

[20] Chap. 5 above, at 120–3.

Within the Council of Europe and the European Union, the situation is more straightforward. The decision to adopt an instrument concerning the right to strike lies in the hands of the Member States, not the Parliamentary Assembly or the social partners. In the Council of Europe, consent from Member States was forthcoming, but the right to strike protected in the text of the ESC was carefully circumscribed and, arguably, unduly limited.[21] The EU can adopt a binding directive on the right to strike only if the necessary competence is ceded to the Union by Member States. No such competence is readily apparent, although it remains possible that the matter may be tackled as a subsidiary issue, for example in the sphere of free movement of goods.[22] The instruments adopted which specifically recognize the right to strike, namely the CCFSRW and the EUCFR, do not appear to place binding obligations upon Member States to alter domestic law; but instead defer to national regulation of industrial action.[23] It is apparent that the interests of States, rather than those of workers or even employers, have dominated the content of instruments relating to industrial action adopted within both these European organizations.

2.   Supervisory Mechanisms

Part III of this book examined the institutional design of supervisory mechanisms within the ILO, Council of Europe, and European Union and their implications for protection of the right to strike. These mechanisms may be categorized according to whether they involve the assessment of State reports or the hearing of complaints relating to State violations of norms. Both forms have advantages and disadvantages. A 'reporting' mechanism relies on State co-operation, which is not always forthcoming, but is a non-confrontational way in which to promote reflection by governments on their attempts to address violations of relevant norms. A 'complaints' mechanism highlights the concerns and grievances of persons affected by State acts or omissions, attracts public attention, and may prompt swift action. However, such a procedure places the onus on victims to confront the State and presupposes that they possess the resources to do so. It may be preferable for a combination of both procedures to be utilized simultaneously, as is the case under the ICCPR and within the ILO.

The way in which the reporting or complaints mechanism in question is designed is also important to its efficacy. For example, the standard supervisory procedure in place under the European Social Charter has permitted substantial delays, involving many lengthy stages of review, and has allowed States substantial control over assessment of compliance (through the

---

[21]   Chap. 6 above, at 142–4.

[22]   Council Regulation 2679/98 [1998] OJ L337/8, Art. 2. Note also the vague potential for industrial action to be addressed in the context of dispute resolution mechanisms, following the Laeken Council Presidency Conclusions, discussed briefly in Chap. 7 above, at 163.

[23]   See Chap. 7 above.

respective roles played by the Governmental Committee and the Committee of Ministers).[24] Its utility has been questioned, and reforms have been made to its operation. Whether these are sufficient to enhance its reputation and influence has yet to be seen. In this respect, the introduction of a supplementary Collective Complaints Protocol is to be welcomed. However, the limitations of this Protocol also need to be recognized, for it creates a complaints mechanism with a peculiar proviso, namely that the individual circumstances of persons affected by the breach cannot be raised in the complaint. Such a procedure lacks the capacity to highlight the actual harms caused by the breach, and therefore is less likely to attract attention than individual complaints adjudicated on by the European Court of Human Rights, or even the collective complaints which are the subject of recommendations by the ILO Committee on Freedom of Association.[25]

The form that the supervisory body itself takes is also likely to be significant. Its authority is derived from an expectation that its members possess the necessary expertise to scrutinize State conduct and that the body is impartial and independent. In labour relations, impartiality is often questioned. A tripartite constitution may therefore be useful in allaying fears of bias. Involvement of government, employer, and worker representatives may also ensure that expertise criteria are met, because each will be able to apply their practical experience in industrial relations. In this they could be assisted by an independent chair person, who possesses potentially useful legal expertise.

It has been contended here that the tripartite constitution of the ILO Committee on Freedom of Association, which is not replicated in other international or European supervisory bodies, has lent authority to its conclusions. The CFA view that 'freedom of association' encompasses a right to strike was adopted by other ILO supervisory bodies, because it reflected a consensus which had been reached between government, employer, and worker representatives on this point. That this view was not accepted by other supervisory bodies would seem to be due to the creation of discrete instruments for the protection of civil and political rights on the one hand and socio-economic rights on the other. This was a barrier to acceptance of this principle both by the Human Rights Committee under the ICCPR and the European Court of Human Rights under the ECHR.

An alternative approach is to imbue the supervisory body with the title of a 'court', which denotes that its status is comparable to that of national institutions with the same designation. There is no doubt that the European Court of Human Rights in the Council of Europe and the European Court of Justice in the European Union both wield considerable authority, despite the fact that they cannot entirely replicate the functions of domestic courts. This book has, however, questioned whether the members of these courts

---

[24] Chap. 9 above, at 217–20.   [25] Chap. 9 above, at 220–4.

possess the expertise in industrial relations that would enable them to make the most appropriate decisions on matters relating the right to strike. Their orientation has been towards the protection of individual rather than collective rights and, especially in the case of the ECJ, property rights. I have suggested that, in both the Council of Europe and the European Union, it may be useful to establish a 'Court of First Instance' (or division of the same) with a tripartite structure, assisted by an independent chair person, exercising special powers in the field of labour law. This is not, however, currently under consideration in either organization.[26]

C.   CONTEXTUAL: BALANCE OF POWER BETWEEN STATES, CAPITAL, AND LABOUR

This last potential explanatory category is more speculative than the others. It is difficult to determine precisely how economic, social, and political circumstances have affected the content of decisions made in the ILO, Council of Europe, and EU. However, to ignore entirely their explanatory potential seems foolish. This book has sought to place decisions taken on constitutional issues, standard-setting, and supervision of international instruments in the specific context in which they arise.

For example, the creation of the International Labour Organization in 1919 can be understood against the background of the Russian revolution; its founders hoped to make capitalism palatable to workers and to resist the extension of communism.[27] This led to some concessions being made to workers which were then contested when the Cold War ended,[28] one of these being the right to strike. It is notable that employers' proposals for a new ILO Convention relating to 'dispute resolution' emerged only in the last decade, as did the challenge made by some members of the employers' group to the jurisprudence of the CEACR on the right to strike. This post-Cold War shift in the balance of power between States has, therefore, also been experienced as a shift in the relative influence of workers and employers within the ILO.

The conceptual division between 'civil' and 'political' rights and 'socio-economic' rights, reflected in the separation of the European Convention on Human Rights from the European Social Charter, seems to have been a manifestation of the Cold War. It was not apparent in the texts of the ILO Constitution 1919, the Declaration of Philadelphia 1944, or the Universal Declaration of Human Rights 1948. By contrast, from 1950 onwards, the Members of the Council of Europe, as part of a Western European alliance,

---

[26] See Chap. 9 above, at 243; and Chap. 10 above, at 259–60.

[27] Chap. 5 above, at 97.

[28] See on this period of transition after the end of the Cold War and the threat to ILO standards generally Nußberger, A., 'Is the International Labour Organization in a State of Transition?' in von Maydell, Baron, and Nußberger, A. (eds.), *Social Protection by Way of International Law: Appraisal, Deficits and Further Developments* (Berlin: Duncker & Humblot, 1996), 214.

sought actively to prioritize civil liberties and rights of political participation which symbolized respect for individual liberty and capitalist enterprise. Social and economic entitlements had become associated implicitly with the perils of Communism.[29] This was also a battle played out in the UN ECOSOC and General Assembly, in the drafting and adoption of the ICCPR and the ICESCR.[30]

Initially, protection of the right to strike under EC law was considered to be unnecessary for the achievement of the limited market objectives envisaged in the Treaty of Rome 1957. However, the range of subject-matter in which the EU is interested has extended considerably, so that exclusion of 'the right of association, the right to strike or the right to impose lockouts' now seems anomalous. Such an exclusion was not, for example, envisaged by the Commission when composing the first draft of the Agreement on Social Policy appended to the Maastricht Treaty on European Union.[31] It is difficult to explain why States have been unwilling to contemplate any European regulation on this subject. It may be that concerns with subsidiarity and respect for legitimate differences between domestic industrial relations underlie this refusal. It may also be that certain Member States are wary of placing this matter within the scope of EC law, which is so much more effective than international law, because they know themselves to be in breach of the latter. In particular, Germany and the UK stand out as being particularly recalcitrant in this respect.[32] Their relative strength in bargaining power within the EU means that their views on this issue may take precedence over those of other countries which do not have such concerns. Nevertheless, the present position is not unalterable.

III. HOW IS THE CONTEXT CHANGING?

This book has endeavoured to set out the contemporary state of international and European law relating to protection of the right to strike. Nevertheless, there is potential for change to the current position. This section identifies particular factors which may trigger further legal evolution. It also suggests ways in which the ILO, Council of Europe, and European Union could respond to new challenges.

The section begins by considering changes in work and modes of production. It is possible that these may have implications for the ability of

---

[29] See Fuchs, K., 'The European Social Charter: Its Role in Present-Day Europe and its Reform' in Drzewicki, K., Krause, K., and Rosas, A., *Social Rights as Human Rights: A European Challenge* (Åbo: Åbo Akademi University Institute for Human Rights, 1994), 151; Council of Europe Parliamentary Assembly, *Additional Protocol to the European Convention on Human Rights Concerning Fundamental Social Rights*, 23 Mar. 1999, Doc. 8357, Explanatory Memorandum by Mrs Pulgar, paras. 18–19.

[30] Ben-Israel, R., *International Labour Standards: The Case of Freedom to Strike* (Deventer: Kluwer, 1988), 43–6; see also Chap. 5 above, at 115–20.

[31] See Chap. 7 above, at 160.   [32] See Chaps. 11–14 above.

workers to organize collectively, co-ordinate bargaining, and take industrial action. One might therefore expect some acknowledgement of and response to these developments in international and European legal norms.

The transformation of global economic relations, following the end of the Cold War, also merit further investigation. These have been described as a facet of 'democratization'. An interesting question is the extent to which democracy and globalization have, in actuality, been realized simultaneously. While the breadth of this question is such that it cannot be answered here in full, I shall seek to explain its pertinence to protection of the right to strike.

Another concern of increasing significance relates to the issue of 'governance', raised in Chapter 1. It has been suggested that attempts to impose labour standards by international or European law are misplaced; and that we should instead look towards regulation through codes of conduct which allow for ethical corporate self-governance. The benefits and potential problems associated with this strategy are also considered below.

Apart from these generalizable issues, the ILO, the Council of Europe, and the European Union each face their own specific challenges. These are highlighted here, for they may also shape the outlook for future protection of the right to strike.

A.   CHANGES IN WORK

Over the last twenty years, the experiences and interests of workers have diversified. The number of women in the workforce has grown rapidly, and this development has been linked to trends towards part-time, casual, and temporary work, as well as greater use of out-sourcing and home work. The introduction of new modes of working may be attributable to the preferences of some women and the lack of available child care for others; but it also coincides with an employer emphasis on 'flexibility' and preference for readily expendable labour.[33] The increasing incidence of these forms of work has diminished conventional modes of access to union representation and support. It may be difficult to make contact with other workers from home or when working intensively during anti-social hours. In addition, workers from immigrant communities which have also been used as cheap expendable labour tend to be particularly vulnerable. Their need to find stable employment swiftly, combined with concerns over their immigration status, may mean that they are more hesitant to challenge poor employment practices.[34]

---

[33] Cf. Rubery, J., and Fagan, C., 'Does Feminisation Mean a Flexible Workforce?' in Hyman, R., and Ferner, A. (eds.), *New Frontiers in European Industrial Relations* (Oxford: Blackwell, 1994).

[34] On the increasing incidence of economic migration see Parisotto, A., 'Economic Globalisation and the Demand for Decent Work' in Blanpain, R., and Engels, C. (eds.), *The ILO and the Social Challenges of the 21st Century: The Geneva Lectures* (Deventer: Kluwer, 2001), 6–7.

Overall, job security has been eroded by demands of 'flexibilization' and unemployment has made it more difficult for workers to take effective industrial action. There is often a surplus of alternative labour. Firms have also tended to restructure to enhance 'efficiency'. This has involved devolving responsibility for areas of production to subsidiaries and 'sub-contracting' work, where to do so would reduce costs. The opportunities to negotiate collectively at the national level or even under a corporate umbrella have, in some States, diminished considerably.[35]

A key question is how legal protection of labour standards should be adjusted in response to these alternative modes of work. Recent studies of these changes in the workplace have said little on the subject of the right to strike.[36]

One argument is that, as union representation, collective bargaining and industrial action are antiquated and anachronistic, legal protection of these mechanisms should be abolished in favour of worker representation in more co-operative information and consultation mechanisms. However, as was observed in Chapter 1, unions have demonstrated a willingness to adapt to these new challenges and are actively seeking to represent potential new members.[37] They are also seeking to form alliances with not only those in traditionally defined 'work' but other 'grassroots and community' contacts in civil society.[38] It seems too early to sound their death knell. Also, as discussed in Chapter 3, such a response ignores the very limited capacity of existing non-union 'participation' mechanisms to allow workers a voice in the management of the enterprise.[39] ILO interest in promoting *Your Voice at Work*[40] makes it improbable that the International Labour Conference would be swayed by an argument for rejection of the right to strike. Moreover, it is unlikely that these changes in work relations would generate the political will to amend the texts of the ESC and ICESCR, which recognize this entitlement.

Leaving aside abolition of the right to strike, how then could international and European legal norms be adjusted in recognition of workers' experiences? It is possible that restrictions may be placed on the right to strike so as

[35] Chap. 1 above, at 8–9. See also Blanpain, R., 'The Social Challenges of the XXIst Century and Fundamental Social Rights' in Blanpain, R. (ed.), *The Council of Europe and the Social Challenges of the XXIst Century* (Deventer: Kluwer, 2001), in (2001) 38 *Bulletin of Comparative Labour Relations* 1 at 11–12.

[36] Collins, H., 'Regulating the Employment Relationship for Competitiveness' (2001) 30 *ILJ* 17; Supiot, A., *Beyond Employment: Changes in Work and the Future of Labour Law in Europe* (Oxford: OUP, 2001).

[37] Chap. 1 above, at 9–10.

[38] Waterman, P., 'The New Social Unionism: A New Union Model for a New World Order' in Munck, R., and Waterman, P. (eds.), *Labour Worldwide in the Era of Globalization: Alternative Union Models in the New World Order* (London: Macmillan, 1999), 261.

[39] Chap. 3 above, at 57–9.

[40] This was the global report produced on 'freedom of association and collective bargaining' under the ILO Declaration on Fundamental Principles and Rights at Work 1998 'follow-up' procedure in 2000.

to realize employers' quest for flexibility. This has been the trend in the UK.[41] Nevertheless, there remain other possibilities for actual enhancement of international protection of the right to strike in response to changing working conditions.

For example, there seems to be an even stronger case for treatment of the right to strike as an individual as well as a collective entitlement. We have seen that this is the position taken by the European Committee of Social Rights under the ESC, but has yet to be expressly endorsed by ILO supervisory bodies.[42] Given relatively isolated working conditions and a lack of access to union representation, if workers are to be able to take industrial action they should be able to do so spontaneously on matters which are of importance to them (and those workers with whom they do have contact). If workers are required by national law to form a union before calling a strike, they will need to be able to do so swiftly without any great cost or delay, so that their exercise of the right to strike is not impaired. While it might be preferable in terms of enhanced bargaining power for workers to join an existing union, it is arguable that this should not be a requirement. First, such a precondition would unduly restrict the right to strike where unions lack access to the workplace (or worker) for trade union recruitment purposes. Secondly, workers who believe that they can wield sufficient bargaining power to achieve their immediate objectives through industrial action should be able to do so without recourse to larger bureaucratic structures. This view has been resisted by those who seek to avoid the creation of fragmented identity-based organizing and seek cosmopolitan trade unionism.[43] However, it is arguable that principles of effective participation in workplace decision-making and subsidiarity should come to the fore here. Affiliation to another trade union federation or confederation may be more useful later, as workers come to appreciate what can be achieved by greater solidarity with other groups.

It is already an established principle that, in the exercise of the right to strike, workers should not be penalized in ways which affect their livelihood.[44] There is a case for this principle to be extended so as to prohibit, for example, the imposition of sanctions on workers which relate to their immigration status. It has yet to be explicitly stated that where the employer or the State does impose such a penalty, this amounts to discrimination on grounds of trade union membership and activities, in violation of ILO

[41] See Chap. 1 above, at 8–11.   [42] See Chap. 11 above, at 275–8.

[43] Selmi, M., and McUsic, M., 'Difference and Solidarity: Unions in a Postmodern Age' in Conaghan, J., Fischl, R.M., and Klare, K. (eds.), *Labour Law in an Era of Globalization: Transformative Practices and Possibilities* (Oxford: OUP, 2002). Cf. Munck, R., 'Labour Dilemmas and Labour Futures' in Munck and Waterman, n.38 above, 8–10 and 16–20.

[44] Chap. 14 above, at 318–21.

Convention No. 98 and Article 11 of the ECHR.[45] Yet this issue is one which is likely to arise, especially in Europe, and is one to which supervisory bodies may wish to direct their attention. Changes in the nature of work may thereby provide scope for expansion of ILO and other jurisprudence on the right to strike, as opposed to its contraction. Whether this expansion comes about may be due to other factors set out below.

B.   Post-Cold War Democratization and Globalization

The implosion of the Soviet empire and the collapse of planned economies in the Eastern bloc have been viewed by some as vindicating the capitalist ideal. Almost all Member States of the ILO have now embraced 'democracy' and the principles of the market economy. The Members of the European Union and Council of Europe pride themselves on having done so.

For some time, 'democracy' and 'capitalism' seemed to be regarded as interchangeable. The introduction of 'free elections' was to be accompanied by uncritical acceptance of neo-liberal 'free market' doctrines. Development aid and loans were made contingent on compliance with both principles, in accordance with the 'Washington consensus' advocated by both the World Bank and the IMF.[46] Will Hutton observes that substantial pressure was simultaneously placed upon States to 'open their financial systems to American participation under the rubric of liberalisation'.[47] In this way, the movement towards democratization was linked to the acceleration of globalization.

A straightforward definition of 'globalization' is difficult to provide. As was observed in Chapter 1, 'globalization of markets' has a multitude of facets, which include an increase in international trade, currency transactions, foreign direct investment, increased manufacturing in developing nations, expanded migration, the expansion of communication technology, and the emergence of the multi-national enterprise (MNE).[48]

The MNE is a corporation or group of corporations whose investments, production, or activities traverse national boundaries. There are over 60,000 MNEs, as compared to 7,000 in the 1970s. They directly employ seventy-three million people worldwide, produce 25 per cent of manufac-

---

[45] This should also be regarded as an infringement of Art. 5 of the ESC, the only problem being that this entitlement does not extend to anyone other than a citizen of a Contracting Party, or (under the Revised Social Charter) a person with refugee status. See Chap. 6 above, at 132.

[46] For analysis of the limitations of the 'Washington consensus' see Stiglitz, J., 'Towards a New Paradigm for Development: Strategies, Policies, and Processes', 1998 Prebisch Lecture at UNCTAD, 19 Oct. 1998, available on www.worldbank.org/html/extdr/extme/jssp101998. htm. See for discussion of the application of IMF and World Bank policies in India and their anti-democratic tendencies Swaminathan, R., 'Regulating Development: Structural Adjustment and the Case for National Enforcement of Economic and Social Rights' (1998) 37 *Columbia Journal of Transnational Law* 161.

[47] Hutton, W., *The World We're In* (London: Little, Brown, 2002), 196 ff.

[48] Chap. 1 above, at 17.

tured goods and account for two-thirds of world trade. Of the 200 wealthiest economic entities in the world, approximately 160 are corporations and only forty are States.[49] As one commentator has observed, 'we are witnessing not just the globalization but the corporatization of trade'.[50]

There is an obvious asymmetry of bargaining power between the MNE and a small, poor developing State. In such circumstances, an MNE can influence the policies of the representative elected government, by using threats to withdraw capital or by promising future investment. An example commonly given is the role played by Shell in Nigeria.[51] Yet, it is also important to recognize that, while globalization has the capacity to challenge and diminish State action, this is not a uniform phenomenon. Certain States, and here the USA springs to mind, have been responsible for fostering the global economy and legitimizing certain market demands.[52] However, this is the prerogative of only the most affluent industrialized nations.

Despite the accolades that greeted the end of the Cold War, globalization and liberalization of markets have threatened to undermine the social policies of elected governments.[53] This was eventually recognized by the World Bank which in 1997, under new leadership and with the advice of its chief economist Joseph Stiglitz, sought to change tack. World Bank programmes began to place a new emphasis on 'good governance', including open participatory democracy and investment in public services. Stiglitz, in particular, gave his express support to ILO standards, including the rights to organize and to bargain collectively.[54] However, this did not have a dramatic influence on the policies pursued by the IMF.[55]

Globalization cannot readily be halted, but this phenomenon (or combination of phenomena) can be 'shaped and controlled'.[56] The strategic response has been described as obvious: 'if business and capital go global, then government and labour should follow suit'.[57]

---

[49] See Hepple, B., 'A Race to the Top? International Investment Guidelines and Corporate Codes of Conduct' (1999) 20 *Comparative Labor Law and Policy Journal* 347 at 351; Parisotto, n.34 above, 4; and Valaskakis, K., 'Globalization as Theatre' (1999) 160 *International Social Science Journal* 142.

[50] Thorpe, V., 'Global Unionism: The Challenge' in Munck and Waterman, n.38 above, 219.

[51] Symonides, J., 'Globalization and Human Rights' (2000) 4 *Mediterranean Journal of Human Rights* 145, at 151; Smith, J., Bolyard, M., and Ippolito, A., 'Human Rights and the Global Economy: A Response to Meyer' (1999) 21 *Human Rights Quarterly* 207 at 208. For discussion of Nigerian labour relations see Chap. 12 above, at 300.

[52] See Blackett, A., 'Global Governance, Legal Pluralism and the Decentered State: A Labor Law Critique of Codes of Conduct' (2001) 8 *Indiana Journal of Global Legal Studies* 401, 427.

[53] McCorquodale, R., and Fairbrother, R., 'Globalization and Human Rights' (1999) 21 *Human Rights Quarterly* 735, at 737–9.

[54] Stiglitz, J., 'Democratic Development as the Fruits of Labor', Keynote Address to the Industrial Relations Research Association, Boston, Mass., Jan. 2000, at 22.

[55] Stiglitz, J., *Globalization and its Discontents* (New York: W.W. Norton, 2002), esp. chaps. 4 and 8; Hutton, n.47 above, chap. 6.

[56] Symonides, n.51 above, 160.

[57] Breitenfellner, A., 'Global Unionism: A Potential Player' (1997) 136 *ILRev.* 531 at 532.

It is possible that States could combine to create institutions which set basic rules for the operation of markets. The World Trade Organization (WTO) could, for example, be a mechanism by which to achieve these ends, but has so far resisted the creation of a 'social clause' which would link trade access to protection of labour standards.[58] Controversy over the terms of the proposed Multilateral Agreement on Investment, especially as regards the inclusion of environmental and labour standards, has also led to the collapse of negotiations.[59] The difficulty lies in the very different position of those States with industrialized market economies in the 'North' from that of those developing countries in the 'South'. A divergence in their vested interests, combined with the fear of 'protectionism', has meant that they have failed to reach agreement.[60] This lack of trust seems to have led to the growth of negative regulatory competition rather than bold combined initiatives. The emergence of the Export Processing Zone (EPZ) illustrates this tendency. An EPZ allows for processing and production without the goods concerned entering the domestic economy, thereby avoiding customs payments and often evading application of national labour laws. Workers within these zones seldom possess the right to strike or even to organize collectively.[61]

In contrast to States, and in spite of the pressures placed upon them to compete, many trade unions have responded to globalization by trying to extend international co-operation. This is the explicit policy of the International Confederation of Free Trade Unions (ICFTU).[62] Workers' organizations have sought to enter into joint negotiations in the same or related industries or inter-related companies. In doing so, they have endeavoured to establish transnational standards and practices.[63] There is a strong tradition of internationalism in the labour movement, but the realization of these objectives is challenging. It requires representation of workers having diverse interests, living in separate countries, and speaking different languages. Communication has been aided by e-mail and internet facilities,[64]

---

[58] Chap. 1 above, at 30; and Chap. 7 above, at 167–70. See also Blackett, A., 'Whither Social Clause? Human Rights, Trade Theory and Treaty Interpretation' (1999) 31 *Columbia Human Rights Law Review* 1; and Summers, C., 'The Battle in Seattle: Free Trade, Labor Rights, and Societal Values' (2001) 22 *University of Pennsylvania Journal of International Economic Law* 61.

[59] Compa, L., 'The Multilateral Agreement on Investment and International Labour Rights: A Failed Connection' (1998) 31 *Cornell International Law Journal* 683.

[60] See Chap. 1 above, at 25–6; and Chap. 5 above, at 104–5. This scepticism has been fuelled by the conduct of the IMF, discussed by Hutton, n.47 above and Stiglitz, n.55 above.

[61] *Record of Proceedings* (Geneva: ILO, 2001) ILC, 89th Session, 19/1 at 19/50; and *General Report of the CEACR 1999* (Geneva: ILO, 1999), para. 110. See also Chap. 13 above, at 315.

[62] See *A Trade Union Guide to Globalisation* (Brussels: ICFTU, 2001).

[63] *Building Workers' Rights into the Global Trading System* (Brussels: ICFTU, 1999), 66. See also Pochet, P., 'Monetary Union and Collective Bargaining in Europe: An Overview' in Pochet, P. (ed.), *Monetary Union and Collective Bargaining in Europe* (Brussels: PIE Lang, 1999), 269–78.

[64] Lee, E., *The Labour Movement and the Internet: The New Internationalism* (London: Pluto Press, 1997); and Lee, E., 'Trade Unions, Computer Communications and the New World Order' in Munck and Waterman, n.38 above, who advocates use of a 'global labour net'.

as well as by the sectoral works councils established by the International Trade Secretariats (since January 2002 renamed 'Global Union Federations').[65] The achievement of collective objectives has, however, been hampered by the existing legal framework in many States.

Not all governments accept the rights of workers to take 'secondary action', that is, in support of claims made against another employer. This means that many workers are subject to lawful sanctions when they take industrial action in solidarity with workers employed by another employer, even when that employer is a related company or the industry concerned is connected to that in which they work. This is a substantial barrier to collective negotiation across national boundaries.

ILO supervisory bodies, together with the European Committee of Social Rights under the European Social Charter, have indicated that secondary action should be protected by law. Nevertheless, their recommendations have yet to be accepted by States such as the UK. Together with Paul Germanotta, I have argued elsewhere that the status quo remains unsatisfactory, especially as regards the realization of European-level collective bargaining and that it is time for the EU to take action on this issue.[66] It would be helpful were ILO supervisory bodies to elaborate on sparing comments made to date on the subject of secondary and transnational industrial action.[67]

Globalization also has significance generally for international law, the architecture of which is not designed for the emergence of a powerful non-State actor like the MNE. The MNE can claim itself to be a victim of a violation of human rights, for example as regards violation of property or speech rights, but cannot be called to account or admonished as a perpetrator.[68] 'The distinction between individuals as the holders of rights and States as the holders of duties was premised on a notion of the State as the ultimate guardian of its population's welfare.'[69] Such a premise is no longer entirely appropriate. This is not to say that the State is powerless, but that MNEs are now often at least as powerful.

---

[65] Breitenfellner, n.57 above, 544; see also Moody, K., *Workers in a Lean World: Unions in the International Economy* (London/New York: Verso, 1997).

[66] Germanotta, P., and Novitz, T., 'Globalisation and the Right to Strike: The Case for European-Level Protection of Secondary Action' (2002) 18 *IJCLLIR* 67.

[67] Germanotta, P., *Protecting Worker Solidarity Action: A Critique of International Labour Law* (London/Geneva: Institute of Employment Rights/Global Labour Institute, 2002); Ewing, K.D., and Sibley, T., *International Trade Union Rights for the New Millennium* (London: Institute of Employment Rights, 2000); and Ewing, K.D., 'Modernising International Labour Standards: Globalisation, Multinational Companies and International Trade Union Rights' (2000) 50 *Federation News* 109, at 112–13. See also Chap. 12 above, at 291–2.

[68] Addo, M.K., 'The Corporation as a Victim of Human Rights Violations' in Addo, M.K. (ed.), *Human Rights and the Responsibility of Transnational Corporations* (The Hague: Kluwer, 1999).

[69] Jochnik, C., 'Confronting the Impunity of Non-State Actors: New Fields for the Promotion of Human Rights' (1999) 21 *Human Rights Quarterly* 56 at 59.

MNEs do not inevitably abuse their powers. Their conduct is not necessarily worse than that of national companies or local employers.[70] However, the potential for breach of human rights and labour standards remains, given that their objectives are likely to be economic rather than humanitarian. MNEs have been advised that their long-term economic interests lie in the protection of labour standards, especially those relating to freedom of association and collective bargaining, but evidence of global practice suggests that some MNEs are willing to breach such standards where they perceive this to be in their short-term interests.[71]

C.   Codes of Conduct and Corporate Social Governance

Concern over 'the spread, scale and reach of multinational enterprises' has led to new initiatives for scrutiny of their activities.[72] The United Nations, the OECD, and the ILO have sought to encourage MNEs to respect labour standards by the adoption of non-binding recommendations which provide a code of conduct. In addition, many MNEs have adopted their own global codes of conduct, which are intended to operate as a guarantee to consumers that fair labour practices are observed.[73] These initiatives can be regarded as a new mode of international governance, in so far as they are directed towards regulation of the conduct of non-State actors. They are also significant in that they are extra-legal mechanisms for the promotion of workers' rights.[74]

Nevertheless, the responsibilities that are actually imposed on MNEs by this means tend to be limited in two notable respects. First, they are limited in terms of content, in that there is no express recognition of the right to strike in any of these codes. At best, they replicate the general terms of the 1998 ILO Declaration.[75] Secondly, difficulties associated with supervision of other international instruments, which were identified in Part III, are

---

[70] As is acknowledged by the ICFTU in *A Trade Union Guide to Globalisation* (Brussels: ICFTU, 2001), 35–6.

[71] OECD, *Trade, Employment and Labour Standards: A Study of Core Workers' Rights and International Trade* (Paris: OECD, 1996); OECD, *International Trade and Core Labour Standards* (Paris: OECD, 2000).

[72] Murray, J., 'A New Phase in the Regulation of Multinational Enterprises: The Role of the OECD' (2001) 30 *ILJ* 255 at 255; see also Jochnik n. 69 above, at 65–8.

[73] I have focused on public international and private corporate developments, rather than codes promulgated at the national level, such as the Sullivan Principles (1977), the MacBride Principles (1984), and the UK Ethical Trading Initiative. For further detail on these see McCrudden, C., 'Human Rights Codes for Transnational Corporations: What can the Sullivan and MacBride Principles Tell Us?' (1999) 19 *OJLS* 167. The extent of EU interest in 'corporate social responsibility' is discussed briefly later in below at 363–4.

[74] See also for advocacy of 'non-legal solutions' and 'benchmarking' Charny, D., 'Regulatory Competition and the Global Coordination of Labour Standards' in Esty, D., and Geradin, D., *Regulatory Competition and Economic Integration: Comparative Perspectives* (Oxford: OUP, 2001), 328–9.

[75] See Chap. 5 above, at 104–5.

replicated and even exaggerated in this context. While codes may be a useful supplement to the protection of a right to strike under international and European law, they are of questionable efficacy.

1. Codes Initiated by International Organizations

There are three recent initiatives that have been taken by international organizations concerning corporate conduct. These are the 1999 'Global Compact', the 2000 Revised OECD Guidelines on Multinational Enterprises, and the 2001 Revised ILO Tripartite Declaration of Principles concerning Multinational Enterprises and Social Policy. Each sets out a code to be respected by MNEs when conducting business and negotiating with labour. The content of each of these instruments is discussed here alongside their means of implementation.

The Global Compact was initiated by Kofi Annan under UN auspices, and is designed to promote observance of labour, human rights, and environmental standards by corporations.[76] The Compact has the advantage of simplicity. It invites 'world business leaders' to 'embrace and enact' nine principles, of which four relate to the core labour standards set out in the ILO Declaration on Fundamental Principles and Rights at Work 1998. Given the deliberations of the Group of Experts under the Declaration 'Follow-up' procedure, the provision for protection of 'freedom of association and the effective recognition of the right to collective bargaining', which is set out in 'Principle 3', might seem to extend to protection of the right to strike; but this has yet to be settled definitively.[77]

The obligations placed on MNEs which wish to participate in the Global Compact are not onerous. They are to issue a clear statement of support for the Global Compact and, once a year, provide a concrete example of progress made for posting on the Global Compact website. Corporate participants are listed on the site, alongside labour and civil society organizations which have given their support. The role of States appears to be negligible, despite the statement that there is 'no substitute for action by governments'.[78] There is no scope for independent investigation of MNE practices; nor is there any opportunity for criticism or complaint. Managerial prerogative is preserved. What this initiative achieves is an ideological shift, away from viewing the success of an enterprise purely in economic terms and towards a shared understanding of what it means to be a socially responsible 'good employer'.

The OECD Guidelines for Multinational Enterprises, originally approved in 1976 and revised in 2000, are more complex.[79] Their 'text,

---

[76] See http://65.214.34.30/un/gc/unweb.nsf/.   [77] Chap. 8 above, at 203–6.

[78] Blackett, n.52 above, at 444.

[79] See www.oecd.org/. See also Picciotto, S., 'What Rules for the World Economy?' in Picciotto, S., and Mayne, R. (eds.), *Regulating International Business: Beyond Liberalization* (London: Macmillan, 1999), 16–17.

commentary and clarifications' extend to over fifty pages. The OECD Guidelines set out non-binding recommendations made by governments to MNEs operating in or from OECD States, as well as Argentina, Brazil, and Chile. The substantive content of the Guidelines is set out in Part I, of which Chapter IV relates to 'Employment and Industrial Relations'. The provisions which are contained therein have been revised so as to 'echo' relevant provisions of the 1998 ILO Declaration. It is anticipated that the 2001 Revised ILO Tripartite Declaration may also be of use in their elaboration.[80]

There is no explicit mention of the right to strike in the text of the Guidelines. Instead, there is recognition in paragraph 1 of 'the right of employees to be represented by trade unions and other bona fide representatives ... and engage in negotiations ... with a view to reaching agreement on employment conditions'. Under paragraph 2, facilities are to be provided to worker representatives as may be necessary to assist the development of collective agreements. This is a more limited view of the legitimate role of trade unions than that endorsed by the ILO, which considers that workers are entitled through their representatives to promote and defend broader 'economic and social interests'.[81] Nevertheless, given the deference to ILO standards in the commentary, principles developed by that organization may well be used in the interpretation of these provisions. The content of national laws will also be relevant, for the revised OECD Guidelines preserve the longstanding obligation to 'observe standards of employment and industrial relations no less favourable than those observed by comparable employers in the host country'.[82] In addition, it is notable that paragraph 7 states that 'in the context of bona fide negotiations with representatives of employees on conditions of employment, or while employees are exercising a right to organise' the MNE is not to 'threaten to transfer the whole or part of an operating unit from the country concerned nor transfer employees from the enterprise's component entities in other countries in order to influence unfairly those negotiations or to hinder the exercise of a right to organise'.

The most obvious weakness of the OECD Guidelines lay, in the past, with the procedures created for their implementation. Even after its revision, this instrument is not legally binding on States or MNEs.[83] This was due to the lobbying of the Business and Industry Advisory Committee

---

[80] Working Party on the OECD Guidelines for Multinational Enterprises, *The OECD Guidelines for Multinational Enterprises: Text, Commentary and Clarifications* (Paris: OECD, 2001), Part I, Chap. IV, Commentary, para. 20.

[81] Cf. the position taken by the ILO, discussed in Chap. 12 above, at 290–4.

[82] Working Party on the OECD Guidelines for Multinational Enterprises, *The OECD Guidelines for Multinational Enterprises: Text, Commentary and Clarifications* (Paris: OECD, 2001), Part I, Chap. IV, Text, para. 4(a).

[83] Murray, n.72 above, 264–5.

(BIAC) which resisted a sanctions regime, 'by arguing that the proper focus should be on promoting business awareness of its self-interest'.[84] The Trade Union Advisory Committee (TUAC), aligned with other NGOs, sought to reform the supervisory mechanism attached to the OECD Guidelines, so as to heighten its influence, but was largely unsuccessful.

'National Contact Points' (NCPs) provide scrutiny of State and MNE implementation of the OECD Guidelines. The constitution of an NCP is a matter for the State concerned. There is, for example, no obligation that it be tripartite in its structure.[85] Its role is to raise awareness of the Guidelines and to respond to 'enquiries' from interested persons and organizations. The NCP is also to 'offer good offices' to resolve issues relating to the Guidelines. Each NCP reports annually to the Committee on International Investment and Multinational Enterprises (CIME) which will clarify the appropriate interpretation of the Guidelines. In doing so, CIME may consult with other experts, such as ILO officials.[86] Finally, this Committee may make unanimous recommendations, although these are primarily directed to the appropriate conduct of NCPs rather than MNEs. The identity of the MNE concerned is to be kept confidential.[87] The potential to embarrass a corporation which does not comply with the Guidelines is thereby lost. BIAC claimed that 'the possibility of disclosure of the identity of a party would fetter the free and effective communication of information to the NCP because of the need to protect the ability to eventually defend legal rights'.[88] However, this also means that consumers are not given full disclosure of the conditions under which goods are being made or supplied.

The ILO Tripartite Declaration concerning Multinational Enterprises and Social Policy is another non-binding declaratory instrument.[89] Its provisions are more detailed than Chapter IV of the OECD Guidelines, especially as regards protection of freedom of association and the right to organize, although once again there is no express mention of the right

[84] Tully, S., 'The 2000 Review of the OECD Guidelines for Multinational Enterprises' (2001) 50 *ICLQ* 394 at 396.

[85] *The OECD Guidelines for Multinational Enterprises: First Annual Meeting of the National Contact Points: Summary Report of the Chair of the Meeting on the Activities of National Contact Points* (Paris: OECD, 2001), 3.

[86] See Salzman, J., 'Labor Rights, Globalization and Institutions: The Role and Influence of the Organization for Economic Cooperation and Development' (2000) 21 *Michigan Journal of International Law* 769 at 795.

[87] Working Party on the OECD Guidelines for Multinational Enterprises, *The OECD Guidelines for Multinational Enterprises: Text, Commentary and Clarifications* (Paris: OECD, 2001), 'Commentary on the Implementation Procedures of the OECD Guidelines for Multinational Enterprises', para. 19. See also Tully, n.84 above, 401.

[88] BIAC, 'Contribution on the Employment and Industrial Relations Chapter of the OECD Guidelines for Multinational Enterprises' in Blanpain, R. (ed.), *Multinational Enterprises and the Social Challenges of the XXIst Century* (Deventer: Kluwer, 2000), in (2000) 37 *Bulletin of Comparative Labour Relations*, 105.

[89] This decision was taken by the ILO Governing Body: see GB.279/12. See also ILO, *Report of the Director-General: Reducing the Decent Work Deficit—A Global Challenge*, ILC, 89th Session (Geneva: ILO, 2001), 26.

to strike.[90] There is also a provision, virtually identical to that set out in the OECD Guidelines, recommending that MNEs not threaten withdrawal of capital or replacement of existing labour 'in the context of bona fide negotiations with the workers' representatives on conditions of employment, or while workers are exercising the right to organize'.[91]

States are required to provide responses to periodic surveys on the implementation of the Tripartite Declaration and, since 1990, representative employers' and workers' organizations have also had the opportunity to respond to questionnaires. Their views are considered by a Working Group of the Committee on Multinational Enterprises, which then reports to the Governing Body. The response rate has been high and breaches of the Tripartite Declaration, for example threats to relocate, have been identified. The Working Group has also received information which has led it to question the effectiveness of the application of the Tripartite Declaration in EPZs. However, the conclusions of the Working Group have been aimed only at further research and study of trends.[92] There is no naming and shaming of particular MNEs. Only five cases requesting interpretation of the Tripartite Declaration have been entertained under the Procedure for the Examination of Disputes. The ICFTU attributes this to 'the resistance of the employers' organisations to consider any questions involving the behaviour of specific companies'.[93] In the 'summary of holdings' relating to these cases, which is made available on the ILO website, the States and the workers' organizations involved are named, but not the MNE concerned.[94] Despite efforts to generate interest in implementation of the Tripartite Declaration,[95] such limitations cast doubt on the utility of this mechanism.

2.   Unilateral Action by Private Corporations

Nevertheless, while an MNE may not be criticized under the Global Compact, the OECD Guidelines, or the ILO Tripartite Declaration, it may be embarrassed by media publicity relating to its employment practices. This may deter consumers from purchasing its goods. An example was the experience of Nike in the 1990s, which had become 'synonymous with

---

[90] Conventions Nos. 87 and 98 are however explicitly referred to. See ILO Tripartite Declaration of Principles Concerning Multinational Enterprises and Social Policy 2001, paras. 41–59. Following revision in 2001, the Tripartite Declaration also recommends that governments, workers, employers, and MNEs should contribute to the realization of the 1998 ILO Declaration (see para. 8).

[91] *Ibid.*, para. 53.

[92] *Seventh Survey on the Effect given to the Tripartite Declaration of Principles Concerning Multinational Enterprises and Social Policy: Analytical Report of the Working Group on the Reports Submitted by Governments and by Employers' and Workers' Organizations* (Geneva: ILO, 2001), GB.280/MNE/1/1, paras. 196–203.

[93] *A Trade Union Guide to Globalisation* (Brussels: ICFTU, 2001), 127, App. IV.

[94] See www.ilo.org/public/english/employment/multi/case.htm.

[95] Such as the Tripartite Forum held at the ILO on 25–26 Mar. 2002: see www.ilo.org/public/english/employment/multi/forum.htm.

slave wages, forced overtime and arbitrary abuse', as its management itself observed.[96] Corporations have, for such reasons, endeavoured to demonstrate their ethical conduct to consumers by the unilateral adoption of their own specific code. On this basis, MNEs may seek to apply 'social labels' to their goods to show that they are good employers.[97]

Such codes may vary as regards their content. Some appear to be mere publicity exercises, being extremely limited in the range of labour standards which they recognize. For example, only 15 per cent of codes investigated by the ILO (out of 215) explicitly protected freedom of association.[98] Chris Engels has observed that, even where private codes mention ILO Conventions Nos. 87 and 98 or state that an MNE will respect the right to organize and bargain collectively, it is unlikely that there will be explicit endorsement of the right to strike:

> While strikes may be condoned, it is an entirely different thing as a company to unilaterally declare to support the right to strike of its employees in a voluntary unilateral code of conduct. It could reasonably be presumed that most—if not all—American multinational companies that have adopted a Code of Conduct would not support the right to strike and the meaning the ILO case law has given to it.[99]

This suggests that MNE codes of conduct are not a useful avenue by which to seek protection of the right to strike in accordance with ILO standards.

Procedural mechanisms for the enforcement of codes also vary. There is often only in-house assessment of compliance, allowing an MNE the opportunity to issue false information about its conduct.[100] At a time at which corporate fraud is a major issue, this mode of monitoring MNE behaviour is not likely to convince consumers of their ethical stance.[101] Moreover, there is frequently no sanction for a failure to comply.[102]

[96] Sabel, C., O'Rourke, D., and Fung, A., 'Open Labor Standards: Towards a System of Rolling Rule Regulation of Labor Practices', Discussion Paper presented at the Annual Meetings of the World Bank Seminar on Labor Standards, 28 Sept. 1999, 6.

[97] See, e.g., 'Rugmark' and 'Ecoflor', discussed by van Liemt, G., 'Production Conditions and International Trade: Protection or Protectionism?' in Cuyvers, L., and Kerremans, B., *The International Social Issue: Social Dumping and Social Competition in the Global Economy* (Antwerp/Groningen: Intersentia Economische Wetenschappen, 1998), 101–2.

[98] See the ILO review of codes and social labelling programmes in *Overview of Global Developments and Office Activities Concerning Codes of Conduct, Social Labelling and Other Private Sector Initiatives Addressing Labour Issues* (Geneva: ILO, 1998), GB.23/WP/SDL/1, esp. at para. 50. This is discussed also by Hepple, n.49 above, 357–8; and Tsogas, G., *Labor Regulation in a Global Economy* (Armonk, NY/London: M. E. Sharpe, 2001), 63–4.

[99] Engels, C., 'Codes of Conduct: Freedom of Association and the Right to Bargain Collectively' in Blanpain, n.88 above, 231.

[100] On the paucity of information where in-house staff monitor compliance see the review of codes carried out by the OECD, Working Party of the Trade Committee, *Codes of Corporate Conduct: An Inventory* (Paris: OECD, 1999), and Hepple, n. 49 above, 357–60.

[101] 'How Auditor Found $4bn Black Hole: Corporate Fraud Uncovered by Second Female Whistleblower', *Guardian*, 28 June 2002; 'Crisis in Corporate America: Fraud Charges Highlight Enron Relationships', *Financial Times*, 1 July 2002.

[102] Colucci, M., 'Implementation and Monitoring of Codes of Conduct: How to Make Codes of Conduct Effective?' in Blanpain, n.88 above, 285–8.

The best of these codes establish an internal complaints procedure to which NGOs and trade unions have access, and involve some external verification of their implementation. Nike, Mattel, the MacArthur Foundation, and the World Bank have recently established a 'Global Alliance for Workers and Communities' which is seeking to develop an internationally applicable programme of assessment and monitoring.[103]

The ICFTU has responded to individual MNE initiatives by presenting its own 'Basic Code of Conduct Covering Labour Practices' which is to operate as a tool for evaluation of the adequacy of corporate codes.[104] The attitude of the ICFTU to the use of individual corporate codes is best described as sceptical. It notes that 'the purpose of the new codes does not include protection of the sovereignty of governments but is to address situations created by the failure of national governments and of the international community to adopt or enforce acceptable labour standards'. However, it is accepted that 'where they are truly applied, codes may end some of the worst exploitation and abuse'.[105]

The ICFTU envisages that a corporate 'code of conduct' may be negotiated between the corporation and the appropriate 'Global Union Federation', but this is to be done with caution. The ICFTU advises that national trade unions should not seek to negotiate a global code on behalf of workers elsewhere, unless there is a foreign trade union which has requested assistance and is consulted at each stage. 'The moral obligation of all trade unions towards unorganised workers is to assist them in joining or forming their own trade unions and to prevent or discourage others—whether they be governments, political parties, employers or NGOs—from claiming to speak for them.' Recognition of participatory democracy is reflected in its stance on this issue. Unsurprisingly, the ICFTU litmus test for the adequacy of a corporate code is whether it promotes freedom of association and the right to engage in collective bargaining. 'Companies should not use codes as a means of avoiding trade unions.' Finally, the ICFTU accepts that in certain circumstances social labels are appropriate, but recommends that trade unions do not support these 'before accredited systems of independent verification are established and proven effective and reliable'. Unions may then play a role in scrutinizing the application of the code.[106]

One of the benefits of corporate codes of conduct is that they may gradually achieve a change in business attitudes, whereby protection of

---

[103] See, e.g., the *Nike: Corporate Responsibility Report: Labour Practices* (2002) at www. nike.com/nikebiz/nikebiz.jhtml?page=29, which considers the causes of industrial action taken in Mexico but does not mention explicitly a right to strike. Nike's conduct is also discussed in Sabel, O'Rourke, and Fung, n.96 above, 18. Note in addition the role played by the Fair Labor Association, SA8000, the Clean Clothes Campaign, and the Ethical Trading Initiative.

[104] *A Trade Union Guide to Globalisation* (Brussels: ICFTU, 2001), 129, App. V.

[105] *Ibid.*, 133–5, App. VI.

[106] *Ibid.*, 136–42, App. VI.

labour standards is regarded as a 'matter of course, not altruism'.[107] This seems to be the hope of the ICFTU, which will continue to work towards enhancing consumer awareness of issues so that pressure may be placed on MNEs to maintain and develop the applications of such codes.

Nevertheless, codes of conduct do not appear to be the most appropriate means by which to ensure compliance with labour standards. To promote this strategy to the exclusion of all others is to ignore the role that many States may still be able to play in the protection of labour standards through national and international lawmaking, and to entrench limited regulatory action.[108] Moreover, we have yet to see whether the codes are a short-term response by MNEs to bad publicity or whether they constitute a long-term commitment to ethical trade. At present, the often limited content of codes, especially when combined with the difficulty of verifying compliance, suggests that they cannot be relied upon as a means by which to secure protection of workers' rights generally and, in particular, the right to strike. They are more likely to provide a useful supplement to other attempts to promote labour standards.

D. ISSUES FACING THE ILO

At the close of the Cold War, it became imperative for the ILO to reassess its role and consider reform of standard-setting and supervisory mechanisms. 'For nearly half a century the ILO was in the firing zone between the superpower blocs.'[109] Its focus on labour standards had made it the debating forum where communism and capitalism could meet. Today the organization needs to demonstrate its relevance in other ways. This has led to review of four crucial issues which are raised here: mechanisms for promotion of labour standards, participation in ILO standard-setting, revision of supervisory procedures, and enforcement of workers' rights. Their potential impact upon the protection of the right to strike is also discussed below.

1. Arguments for Reform

Since 1990, the employers' group has questioned the relevance and utility of many existing ILO standards. This has been combined with resistance to the adoption of new conventions and recommendations (other than in the field of dispute resolution).[110] ILO standards have been said to 'consist of

---

[107] Compa, L.A., and Hinchcliffe Darricarrère, T., 'Private Labor Rights Enforcement Through Corporate Codes of Conduct' in Compa, L.A., and Diamond, S.F., *Human Rights, Labor Rights and International Trade* (Philadelphia, Penn.: University of Philadelphia Press, 1996), 195.

[108] Blackett, n.52 above, 446.

[109] Myrdal, H.-G., 'The ILO in the Cross-Fire: Would it Survive the Social Clause?' in Sengenberger, W., and Campbell, D., *International Labour Standards and Economic Interdependence* (Geneva: IILS, 1994), 340–2.

[110] See Chap. 5 above, at 102–3; and above, at 339.

rigid, detailed and often obsolete rules which can serve as an obstacle to economic and social progress'.[111] Employers argue for a concentration on legal protection of only the most basic, essential labour standards. Their view is that other social objectives can be promoted by more flexible means. For example, employer members of the Conference Committee on the Application of Standards and Recommendations have argued for 'campaigns to raise public awareness, declarations, codes of conduct and technical assistance' as alternative mechanisms by which to achieve agreed objectives. They have even suggested that, in the most extreme cases, 'trial standards' could be adopted which would be implemented for a limited time only.[112] This is consistent with the global trend towards flexibility and deregulation identified above.[113] Workers, by contrast, have expressed concern 'at the proliferation of initiatives seeking to call into question the universal scope, the application, even the existence of standards'.[114] Instead, they are interested in the revitalization of existing standards. For example, a study initiated by the International Centre for Trade Union Rights suggests that it is important for there to be a restatement of principles relating to freedom of association in a single Convention, which would encompass ILO jurisprudence on this subject.[115]

At the same time, the governance of the ILO has been called into question by virtue of its 'tripartite' structure. While this structure creates a balance of vested interests, it has been argued that the range of interests represented is too narrow. The changes in the workplace outlined above have led to accusations that existing worker representation in the ILO protects only the interests of those participating in the formal labour market. The unemployed or children, women, and migrant labour in informal labour markets are allegedly left without representation. For these reasons, there are demands for the ILO to allow greater participation from civil society, namely non-governmental organizations (NGOs), in the design of programmes and setting of norms.[116] Neither the workers' nor the employers' group has voiced any great enthusiasm for such suggestions, which is not surprising given that their role within the ILO could be threatened by such changes.

Alongside these challenges have come requests from government representatives for an urgent review of supervisory mechanisms.[117] The administrative burden of reporting is viewed as being too great, as it entails the provision of a number of separate reports at different intervals. Keeping

---

[111] Myrdal, n.109 above, 356.

[112] *Report of the Committee on the Application of Standards* (Geneva: ILO, 2000), paras. 37–38.

[113] See above, at 341–2.

[114] *Report of the Committee on the Application of Standards* (Geneva: ILO, 2001), para. 42.

[115] Ewing, n.67 above, 110–11.

[116] Cooney, S., 'Testing Times for the ILO: Institutional Reform for the New International Political Economy' (1999) 20 *Comparative Labor Law and Policy Journal* 365 at 371–3 and 390–3. See also Blackett, n.52 above, 436–40.

[117] *Report of the Committee on the Application of Standards* (Geneva: ILO, 2000), para. 42.

track of ILO requirements and preparing reports in advance, if these are to be meaningful, is a time-consuming activity. Sean Cooney has argued that the failure of certain States to comply with reporting requirements is due to their complexity and the sheer workload that they entail.[118] It has been suggested by Steven Oates that 'radical simplification' of the reporting system would be appropriate: 'a system where each government would owe just one report each year but that report would include all *necessary* information on problems that might arise under *all* ratified Conventions is quite conceivable'.[119] This would have the benefit of analysis from a 'country-centred' rather than a 'Convention-centred' perspective, but would not easily allow for the comparative analysis possible under the present system.

Workers' demands are different again. Their response to the erosion of State regulatory power is to seek stronger mechanisms for enforcement of ILO standards. In particular, the ICFTU has campaigned for a link to be made between trade, investment, development aid, and compliance with labour standards. Its focus is on those 'core' workers' rights set out in the 1998 ILO Declaration. The ICFTU considers that, in the face of the challenges presented by globalization, the 'toothless' recommendations made by ILO supervisory bodies are inadequate.[120] Such an initiative is opposed by governments of many developing States, by the employers' group, and even by some trade unions.[121]

2. The ILO Response

The International Labour Organization has struggled to provide responses to these conflicting demands which will satisfy all these interested actors. It is a near impossible task. The International Labour Office has accepted the need to review standards and to explore alternative mechanisms for their promotion. There is also agreement to review of the supervisory procedure. Yet it is less likely that there will be any fundamental change to the ILO's tripartite structure or introduction of a 'social clause'. Instead, the Director-General will try to use other means to achieve inclusion of civil society in ILO decision-making and the implementation of ILO standards.

Owing to recent constitutional reform, a significant number of existing ILO instruments have been declared 'outdated' and no longer binding upon States.[122] The focus of ILO attention will be the standards identified in the

---

[118]   Cooney, n.116 above, 374.

[119]   Oates, S., 'International Labour Standards: The Challenges of the 21st Century' in Blanpain and Engels, n.34 above, 100.

[120]   *A Trade Union Guide to Globalisation* (Brussels: ICFTU, 2001), 31–3; and Ewing, n.67 above, 114–17.

[121]   See Myrdal, n.109 above; and Potter, E., 'International Labour Standards, the Global Economy and Trade' in Sengenberger and Campbell, n.109 above. See also Chap. 1 above, at 25–6; and above, at 346.

[122]   For the conclusions of the Working Party on Policy regarding the Revision of Standards established in 1995, see www.ilo.org/public/english/standards/norm/comefrom/uptodate/ revise2.htm.

1998 Declaration. There will also be frequent monitoring of the eight 'fundamental' or 'core' conventions and an additional four 'priority' conventions, which are elevated above other ILO instruments.[123] The rate of standard-setting is decreasing. Only three ILO conventions were adopted by the International Labour Conference (ILC) in the last five years. This decline can be compared to the peak of activity in 1946 when thirteen conventions were adopted in a single year.

In a report on *Decent Work* in 1999, the incoming Director-General, Juan Somavia, indicated that he was less interested in traditional standard-setting and more in a multi-faceted approach to the promotion of 'decent work'. He has defended the notion of 'decent work' both in humanitarian terms and as a 'productive factor', reflecting employers' economic concerns. His four strategic goals have been the protection of fundamental rights, employment promotion, social protection, and social dialogue. Issues of gender and development are acknowledged as spanning these themes, and broad-based programmes have been established to realize these objectives.[124] An evaluation of these programmes was provided in the Director-General's report to the 2002 ILC.[125]

This programmatic focus may have stemmed from the success of the experimental International Programme for the Elimination of Child Labour (IPEC).[126] It is also consistent with the 'follow-up procedure' attached to the 1998 Declaration, which is concerned not so much with a legalistic assessment of compliance with fundamental workers' rights but with identifying potential recipients of technical assistance.[127] However, the Director-General has been adamant that 'normative action is an indispensable tool to make decent work a reality'. Standards clarify the meaning of the concept (principles and rights) and the process by which it can be achieved (social dialogue). Moreover, standards are 'a stern indicator of progress towards the achievement of ILO objectives, not through lip-service but in law and in practice'. It seems therefore that the International Labour Office is not willing to abandon standard-setting entirely, although it is prepared to contemplate the use of a variety of methods to improve conditions of work.[128]

The Director-General has sought a compromise position on the inclusion of 'civil society' in ILO decision-making. In a report delivered to the ILC in

[123] See Chap. 8 above, at 187.

[124] *Report of the Director-General: Decent Work* (Geneva: ILO, 1999), chaps. 1 and 2; *Report of the Director-General: Reducing the Decent Work Deficit: A Global Challenge* (Geneva: ILO, 2001), chaps. 1 and 2.

[125] *Report of the Director-General: ILO Programme Implementation 2000–1* (Geneva: ILO, 2002).

[126] For further information on the origins and development of this programme see www.ilo.org/public/english/standards/ipec/index.htm.

[127] See Chap. 5 above, at 105; and Chap. 8 above, at 203–6.

[128] *Report of the Director-General: Reducing the Decent Work Deficit: A Global Challenge*, n.124 above, chap. 3.2.

2001, he stated that tripartism 'is under no threat', and that there can be no question of any erosion of 'the constitutional and policy-making prerogatives' of workers and employers. Civil society organizations would not displace their representation in the ILC or ILO committees. The reason given was the difficulty of assessing the democratic mandate of NGOs. A further unstated reason may be that the inclusion of other elements of civil society in standard-setting and supervisory procedures could disrupt the delicate political balance within the ILO. The Director-General does however consider it unfortunate that 'within the ILO, there continues to be reticence and insecurity about engaging outside actors', especially since NGOs may be able to represent people and families in the informal sector. The Director-General is interested in hearing the views of civil society organizations and including them in deliberation on matters in which they have expertise.[129] Such a strategy has been described elsewhere as 'tripartite-plus representation', for it maintains the fundamental structure of tripartism but allows participation in deliberation to 'shift and broaden according to the issues and interests concerned'.[130] The statements of the Director-General on this issue have been tentative, and no detailed plans have as yet been presented to the International Labour Conference or Governing Body on this matter.

There appears to be agreement on the need to revise supervisory mechanisms and this also is reflected in the Director-General's 2001 Report. He accepts that:

The supervisory system needs to be modernized to make it less cumbersome, more efficient and more effective in solving problems. We need to enhance the reporting and legal procedures with a proactive capacity to help solve the problems through other instruments at the disposal of the ILO as a whole.[131]

There is less consensus on how this is to be achieved. The matter is currently under review before the Governing Body,[132] but the Committee of Experts also intends to submit a report setting out its views on appropriate reforms.[133] A more direct linkage of findings to technical assistance would, it seems, be welcomed by the CEACR, but radical revision of its methods may be resisted.

---

[129] *Ibid.*, chaps. 2.2 and 3.4.

[130] Blackett, n.52 above, 438; see also Trebilcock, A., 'Tripartite Consultation and Cooperation in National Level Economic and Social Policy-Making: An Overview' in Trebilcock, A. (ed.), *Towards Social Dialogue: Tripartite Cooperation in National Economic and Social Policy-Making* (Geneva: ILO, 1994), 29, 35, and 44.

[131] *Report of the Director-General: Reducing the Decent Work Deficit: A Global Challenge*, n.124 above, chap. 3.2.

[132] ILO Governing Body, *Examination of Standards-Related Reporting Arrangements*, GB.282/LILS/5; *Reports of the Committee on Legal Issues and International Labour Standards: International Labour Standards and Human Rights* (Geneva: ILO, 2001), GB.282/8/2.

[133] *General Report of the Committee of Experts on the Application of Conventions and Recommendations* (Geneva: ILO, 2002), para. 16.

Finally, the Director-General also appreciates that 'new routes to governance of globalization must emerge', but has not endorsed the introduction of a social clause. Instead, the ILO is investigating other means by which to place 'a social floor under the global economy'.[134] A World Commission on the Social Dimension of Globalization was created in 2002 to address this issue and is due to report back in 2003. It will be interesting to see what conclusions this Commission reaches, for one of its members is Joseph Stiglitz.[135] In the meantime, the ILO seeks to extend its influence through co-operation with other influential international organizations, such as the WTO, the World Bank, and the IMF. The aim is to ensure that those organizations in their trade rules, grants of development aid, and loan conditionality do not undermine ILO standards. The Director-General has observed that 'this is a more formidable task than it should be, because... habits of fragmentation and defensive "turf protection" have made the system an archipelago of basically unconnected islands'. Nevertheless, he has come to the conclusion that 'it would be a form of "multiple schizophrenia" if each organization, with essentially the same membership, should behave as if its sole responsibility were to discharge its own mandate irrespective of others'.[136] An international symposium was held on 24–28 September 2001 designed to promote the co-operation that has been lacking to date.[137] The International Labour Office has contributed to the drafting of Poverty Reduction Strategy Papers used by the IMF and World Bank, but has not yet been as successful in collaboration on social security and other objectives.[138] The most promising initiative in this regard was the agreement on co-operation reached, at least in principle, at the Global Employment Forum held in November 2001. Nevertheless, the mechanics of co-operation have yet to be finalized.[139]

3.   Implications for Protection of the Right to Strike

What then are the implications of these trends for protection of the right to strike? The strength of the employer lobby is evident from this overview. Nevertheless, the ongoing review of ILO conventions and recommendations has not led to any diminution in the status of ILO Conventions Nos. 87 and 98 but, rather, their elevation as core labour standards. Revision of reporting procedures poses no immediate threat to the Committee of

---

[134] *Report of the Director-General: Reducing the Decent Work Deficit: A Global Challenge*, n.124 above, chap. 3.1.

[135] See this Chap. above, at 345; and www.ilo.org/public/english/wcsdg/index.htm.

[136] *Report of the Director-General: Reducing the Decent Work Deficit: A Global Challenge*, n.124 above, chap. 3.4.

[137] See www.ilo.org/public/english/bureau/inf/pr/2001/30.htm.

[138] *Report of the Director-General: Reducing the Decent Work Deficit: A Global Challenge*, n.124 above, chap. 2.

[139] *Report of the Director-General: ILO Programme Implementation 2001–2* (Geneva: ILO, 2002), 22.

Experts' present constitution, and there is no indication that these will be so radically changed as to have an impact on jurisprudence concerning the right to strike. There could even be scope for the potential development of existing principles.[140] However, it may be difficult for this supervisory body to maintain protection of industrial action under Conventions Nos. 87 and 98 in the face of continued opposition from the employer lobby in the Conference Committee. We will have to see whether employer opposition subsides, or whether there is revision of the freedom of association conventions which leads to express protection of a right to strike.

As regards the other issues raised here, it is likely that representatives from civil society will play an increasing role within the ILO, at least as advisors on various programmes, but there is no indication that this need have particular implications for the right to strike, especially as NGOs have often been allied with trade union action.[141] The ILO endeavour to co-operate with the WTO and Bretton Woods institutions is likely to be welcomed by workers, in so far as this remains 'co-operation' rather than 'co-option'.[142] If the latter occurs, then the right to strike, as defined at present by the ILO, may come under threat, but there is no present indication that such a situation is likely to arise.

E. ISSUES FACING EUROPEAN ORGANIZATIONS

The European Union and Council of Europe have also been grappling with issues relating to ideal forms of governance. The European Union in particular is in the process of another constitutional review, this time against the background of imminent enlargement involving East and Central European States.[143] There is a desire on the part of the Commission to enhance the popularity of the EU by addressing the concerns of 'European citizens' and redesigning European governance.[144] Member States are also interested in avoiding legal standard-setting which impinges on the autonomy of national social policy. This trend towards governance by 'soft law' and its implications for potential protection of the right to strike are considered here. The role of the EU in 'global social governance' has also been the subject of a recent Commission proposal, the implications of which are discussed below.

---

[140] Such as recognition of the right to strike as an individual as well as a collective entitlement and elaboration on the subject of secondary action, discussed above, at 343 and 346–7.

[141] See, e.g., action taken in Zimbabwe, discussed in Chap. 1 above, at 12. The ETUC has also been allied with the Platform for Social NGOs in Brussels. See, e.g., joint policy documents submitted to the 'Convention' established for drafting the EUCFR, referred to in Chap. 7 above, at 166; and, generally, Fonteneau, G., 'European Trade Unionism and the European Social Charter' in Blanpain, n.35 above, 244.

[142] See *Report of the Committee on the Application of Standards* (Geneva: ILO, 2001), para. 63 for the views of work representatives from Brazil, France, India, and Pakistan.

[143] 'The Future of the EU: Declaration of Laeken', Dec. 2001 available at www.eu2001.be/.

[144] EC Commission, *European Governance: A White Paper*, COM(2001)428, 25 July 2001.

By contrast, the Council of Europe is less interested in radical constitutional change, having fairly recently undergone a process of rapid enlargement, the pressures of which have left the European Court of Human Rights in crisis. Reform of the ECHR control system therefore appears to be its prime objective; and no alterations to the Social Charter mechanisms are yet envisaged. The Council of Europe does not have the same cohesive character as the EU and has resisted playing any significant role in foreign policy, other than to reprimand its members and neighbours for violations of human rights.[145] Its chief concern is to demarcate its competence and maintain co-operative relations with the EU.

1.   Policy Avenues Contemplated by the European Union

There is no protection of freedom of association and the right to strike under EU law, and no immediate prospect of Member States' agreement to such protection. This is not likely to change on enlargement, given that there will be more States which will have to consent to this extension of competence under the EC Treaty.[146] The only hope for workers is that such a right becomes part of the EU *acquis*, by virtue of incorporation of the EUCFR into the Treaties. There is controversy over whether this will, or even should, be the outcome of the Constitutional Convention.[147]

There may be other ways in which the EU could promote these 'core labour standards', namely through 'soft law' mechanisms which do not impinge so directly upon the prerogatives of Member States. There are two possibilities which seem to arise: the 'open method of co-ordination' (OMC) and 'corporate social responsibility'.

In a conference held in November 2001 on 'The European Social Agenda and the EU's International Partners', Commissioner Diamontopoulou suggested that 'Member States no longer regarded social policy as a purely domestic matter'. The reason was the use of the OMC, which allowed them to develop social measures in concert with each other.[148] The OMC is a mechanism which was originally developed in order to co-ordinate the employment policies of Member States. Since 1997, annual guidelines for State conduct have been issued by the Commission and agreed by the European Council. Each year, Member States have drawn up a National Action Plan, in consultation with business, unions, and other interested parties, indicating how they have responded to those guidelines and what progress has been made. In the light of assessment of this information, State

[145] See, e.g., the stance taken on Chechnya in Parliamentary Assembly, Recommendation No. 1499 on the Conflict in Chechnya (2000).

[146] See Chap. 7 above, at 170.

[147] *Ibid.*, at 163–7.

[148] 'The European Social Agenda and the EU's International Partners', conference held on 20–21 Nov. 2001, Brussels, summary of papers and debates, 2.

conduct is reviewed, recommendations are made, and the guidelines are reformulated.[149] This procedure has now been formally incorporated into the EC Treaty,[150] and has been extended in its application beyond the field of employment promotion to the fields of social protection and social inclusion.[151]

There may be scope under Article 140 (ex Article 118c) EC for the Commission to 'encourage co-operation between the Member States' and to 'facilitate the co-ordination of their action' in terms of the right of association and the right to strike. However, this does not as yet extend to the benchmarking and process of review under the OMC, and there is no indication that such progression is envisaged by the Commission or Member States. Moreover, it could be argued that EU use of the OMC is not so very different from the forms of reporting already utilized by the ILO. Both involve the setting of broadly phrased targets and benchmarks, in which social practice is as important to compliance as legal enactments. Both involve regular review of State reports and the sharing of 'best practice'. For both there is scrutiny by not only experts but their peers (governments, unions, and employers' organizations). One may wonder whether there is any point in the EU essentially replicating existing ILO procedures, especially when the only sanction in either case is potential embarrassment for the State concerned, which is not always effective. There would seem to be a stronger case for freedom of association and the right to strike to be protected by the EU in a more traditional legalistic fashion, so that directives can provide a reference point for the workers affected.

Also, while respect for core labour standards is one aim of the Commission's proposed European 'corporate responsibility' strategy,[152] this seems unlikely to provide a means for effective implementation of a right to strike within the EU. Business is reluctant to support the introduction of a code of conduct by the EU, particularly in the light of recent international initiatives.[153] The corporate lobby has therefore asked that the Commission work

[149] For analysis of the operation of this procedure see Ball, S., 'The European Employment Strategy: The Will but not the Way?' (2001) 30 *ILJ* 353; Szyszczak, E., 'The New Paradigm for Social Policy: A Virtuous Circle?' (2001) 38 *CMLRev.* 1125; and Trubek, D.M., and Mosher, J.S., 'New Governance, EU Employment Policy and the European Social Model' in Joerges, C., Meny, Y., and Weiler, J.H.H. (eds.), *Symposium: Responses to the European Commission's White Paper on Governance* (Florence: European University Institute, 2001). For further elaboration of the co-operative role to be played by the social partners in this process see the *Barcelona Council Presidency Conclusions*, 16 Mar. 2002, paras. 22, 29, and 32.

[150] Arts. 125–130 ECT.

[151] On these recent initiatives see Syrpis, P., 'Legitimising Europe—Taking Subsidiarity Seriously within the Open Method of Coordination,' (2002) EUI Working Paper Series LAW 2002/10 (Florence: EUI, 2002). They have received official recognition in Art. 137(2) ECT, post amendment by the Treaty of Nice 2001.

[152] EC Commission Green Paper, *Promoting a European Framework for Corporate Social Responsibility*, COM(2001)366 final, 18 July 2001, 14–15.

[153] See above, at 348–52.

only towards facilitating consensus on points of dispute;[154] and this view seems to have determined the Council's response to Commission proposals. The Council Resolution 2001 on 'Corporate Responsibility' acknowledged a role for the EU in promoting initiatives aimed at exchange of good practice, training in this field, and provision of information on the economic advantages of social responsibility. However, the Council asked the Commission to 'query carefully the added value of any new action proposed at European level' and emphasized 'the importance of the social partners' contribution to the consultation process at national and European level'.[155] It is therefore difficult to see how EU initiatives on corporate social responsibility will promote effective protection of the right to strike, if this is otherwise excluded from EC regulation.[156]

What seems more likely is that there will be further elaboration of EU foreign policy, which encourages non-Member States to abide by ILO standards. In July 2001, the Commission issued a Communication proposing more extensive EU promotion and enforcement of fundamental workers' rights. Its aim is to enhance the current system of trade preferences under GSP, by widening the trade preferences under incentive schemes, increasing the transparency and streamlining procedures and making effective enforcement of all core labour standards a precondition for receipt of incentives.[157] In line with existing ILO practice, the intention is to accompany these conditions with technical assistance to help countries achieve these goals. Also, the Commission proposes that unilateral suspension of development co-operation or GSP benefits should take place only after an ILO complaints procedure relating to breach of core labour standards has been followed.[158] Co-operation with the ILO is likely to be welcomed by the ETUC, which has long campaigned for utilization of ILO expertise in the implementation of the labour dimension of development programmes.[159] There are also indications that such an initiative would be welcomed by the International Labour Office and ILO Director-General as a means by which

---

[154] See CEEP, *Opinion on the European Commission Green Paper, 'Promoting a European Framework for Corporate Social Responsibility'*, Dec. 2001, CEEP.2001/AVIS.21 at 8: 'It is at this stage not feasible to set up a comprehensive European framework as the development of CSR strategies is still undergoing a learning process'. See also UNICE, *Corporate Social Responsibility: UNICE Position*, Dec. 2001, and ICC, *Comments on the European Commission Green Paper, 'Promoting a European Framework for Social Responsibility'*, 20 Dec. 2001, SB/am.

[155] Council Resolution on Follow-up to the Green Paper on Corporate Social Responsibility, 3 Dec. 2001, available on http://europa.eu.int/comm/employment_social/soc-dial/csr/council_en_011203.htm.

[156] Novitz, T., ' "A Human Face" for the Union or More Cosmetic Surgery? EU Competence in Global Social Governance and Promotion of Core Labour Standards' (2002) 9(3) *Maastricht Journal of European and Comparative Law* 3.

[157] EC Communication from the Commission to the Council, the European Parliament, and the Economic and Social Committee, *Promoting Core Labour Standards and Improving Social Governance in the Context of Globalization*, COM(2001)416 final, 18 July 2001, 16–17.

[158] *Ibid.*, 14.

[159] Fonteneau, n.141 above, 248.

to extend influence over *de facto* enforcement of core labour standards.[160] The result might even be that protection of the right to strike becomes a feature of EU trade and development policy.[161] Nevertheless, there has yet to be any explicit endorsement of this policy by the Council.

2. Potential for Reform within the Council of Europe

While the EU is anticipating enlargement of its membership, the Council of Europe has already experienced a significant increase in numbers of members. As an active advocate of democracy in Central and Eastern Europe during the 1980s, arrangements were made by the Council of Europe for newly independent States to become members, once they had adopted a democratic constitution. On 6 November 1990, Hungary was the first of these States to join. Prior to that date there were twenty-three members. There are now forty-four members.[162]

One result of the Council's expansion has been tremendous strain on the European Court of Human Rights. It was hoped that this could be alleviated by the implementation of Protocol 11 which created a new permanent Court, streamlining judicial procedures relating to admissibility and final determination of cases.[163] Nevertheless, even then, there were doubts whether the reformed Court could respond adequately to the sheer burden of its case-load.[164] The Court is confronted with a steadily rising volume of applications, which grew by over 500 per cent between 1993 and 2000.[165] The Committee of Ministers has indicated that it considers further reform of the ECHR supervisory system to be imperative, but no decision has been made on how this is to be achieved. Both the Court and the Steering Committee for Human Rights (CDDH) are in the process of examining this issue.[166]

What this will mean for the further development of the Court's jurisprudence cannot be predicted, although it is evident that great care will be taken to ensure that its reputation is preserved. In this context, the Committee of Ministers has the opportunity to consider the use of Courts of First Instance to hear particular types of cases, including the creation of a

[160] See the 2001 Exchange of Letters on the terms of co-operation between the ILO and the EU: http://europa.eu.int/comm/employment_social/news/2001/jun/letter1_en.html.

[161] See Chap. 7 above, at 167–70.

[162] For further historical details see www.coe.int.

[163] Discussed in Chap. 9 above, at 212–15.

[164] Mahoney, P., 'Speculating on the Future of the Reformed Court of Human Rights' (1999) 20 *Human Rights Law Journal* 2.

[165] *Report of the Evaluation Group to the Committee of Ministers on the European Court of Human Rights* (Strasbourg: Council of Europe, 2001), EG Court (2001)1, Preface.

[166] See Committee of Ministers, *Declaration on the Protection of Human Rights in Europe: Guaranteeing the Long-Term Effectiveness of the European Court of Human Rights* 8 (Strasbourg: Council of Europe, 2001); and Steering Committee for Human Rights (CDDH), *Reflection Group on the Reinforcement of the Human Rights Protection Mechanism (CDDH-GDR)* (Strasbourg: Council of Europe, 2001), CDDH-GDR (2001)010.

specialized (even tripartite) Chamber to consider labour-related issues.[167] This option has not however been considered by the CDDH or the Evaluation Group advising the Committee of Ministers.

Present preoccupation with reform of the European Court of Human Rights does not bode well for reform to the content or supervisory procedures of the European Social Charter. The role of the Governmental Committee is to be left unaltered; and amendment of Article 6(4) of the Charter does not seem to be contemplated. Moreover, for as long as there is a significant backlog of cases brought under the ECHR, it is unlikely that the Parliamentary Assembly Recommendations proposing inclusion of certain 'social rights' in the ECHR will be adopted.[168] This is not a time at which the Committee of Ministers will wish to expand the Court's jurisdiction. This may disappoint the ETUC, which has expressed concern that 'the inadequate resources of the Council of Europe' for promotion of the Social Charter 'place in jeopardy' the effectiveness of rights and access to them.[169]

What is also left uncertain is the relative demarcation of authority between the Council of Europe and the European Union. The Parliamentary Assembly, in particular, feared that the adoption of the EUCFR by the EU would undermine the status of the ECHR.[170] To some extent these fears have been alleviated by EU adoption of an instrument which is ostensibly not legally binding.[171] Nevertheless, the content of the EUCFR may constitute a conceptual challenge to the modes in which civil, political, and social rights have been promoted within the Council of Europe. The reference to indivisibility of rights in the preamble to the EUCFR, reflected by the decision to place freedom of association and the right to strike in the same instrument, is arguably significant. There also remains potential for some clash of competence in the event of incorporation of the EUCFR into the EU Treaties. The Committee of Ministers has therefore commissioned a study by the CDDH to consider 'the legal and technical issues that would have to be addressed by the Council of Europe in the event of possible accession by the European Communities/European Union to the European Convention on Human Rights, as well as other means to avoid a contradiction between the legal system of the European Convention on Human Rights'. The Steering Committee is to report back by December 2002.[172]

---

[167] See Chap. 9 above, at 243; and above, at 339.

[168] See Chap. 9 above, at 224.

[169] Fonteneau, n.141 above, 246.

[170] Parliamentary Assembly, *Recommendation 1479 on the Charter of Fundamental Rights of the European Union* (Strasbourg: Council of Europe, 2000).

[171] Decision of the Committee of Ministers (Deputies), *Charter of Fundamental Rights of the European Union—Parliamentary Assembly Recommendation 1479 (2000)* CM/Del/ Dec(2001)744/2.58.06.01, 'Appendix: Opinion of the CDDH' (Strasbourg: Council of Europe, 2001), para. 1.

[172] *Ibid.*, para. 3.

This may yet have implications for protection of the right to strike in Europe.

IV. THE OUTLOOK

What then is the outlook for change to international and European protection of the right to strike? It should be evident from the range of factors outlined above that this is difficult to predict.

There appears to be a theoretical shift towards acceptance of the principle of indivisibility of human rights. This is evident from the preamble of the EU Charter of Fundamental Rights[173] and statements made by the Council of Europe's Committee of Ministers.[174] The Cold War ideological clash which led to the creation of divisions between civil and political rights on the one hand and socio-economic rights on the other has ended. All these rights are said to play a legitimate role in legitimate democratic governance, although there remains some ambiguity as to the precise nature of this role. There is therefore scope to appreciate that justifications for industrial action may encompass civil liberties and rights of political participation as well as the socio-economic interests. It has been argued here that this could lead to protection of a right to strike which is of broader scope than that contemplated at present by the Council of Europe; namely that provided by the ILO.

Yet significant structural reform is needed to achieve this end. There would have to be a fusion of two separate instruments, the European Convention on Human Rights and the European Social Charter. Revision of their texts and changes to supervisory machinery would also have to accompany such reform. In addition, some longstanding accommodation would have to be reached between the Council of Europe and the European Union to ensure that EC law protects, or at least cannot undermine, fundamental human rights, including workers' rights. This would be the path towards compliance with ILO standards relating to the right to strike.

Resistance to such structural change comes from the business community, comprising MNEs, national corporations, and smaller enterprises, which see socio-economic rights as potentially costly. They accept that protection of workers' rights should be recognized in principle, but do not wish these to be enforced by legal sanctions. Resistance also comes from States which are currently competing to attract trade and investment. Despite the efforts of OECD and other economists to explain how labour standards may sustain rather than diminish productivity, it seems that more needs to be done to convince business and government that this is so. In the meantime, their concerns are reflected in increasing pressure placed upon the ILO to reduce regulatory burdens upon States.

---

[173] Chap. 7 above, at 164.   [174] Chap. 2 above, at 46.

In this context, protection of the right to strike under ILO Conventions Nos. 87 and 98 has been called into question; and there are calls for a new instrument relating to 'freedom of association' or 'dispute settlement' which would establish the ambit of protection of such a right. There is no challenge to protection of a right to strike *per se*; there is only debate about the form that such protection should take. Nevertheless, this debate is significant. ILO supervisory bodies have developed principles relating to industrial action, upon which workers' organizations rely. These are not perfect, and a case can be made for their improvement in response to contemporary developments, but were their authority to be diminished a carefully reasoned, coherent body of jurisprudence reached through tripartite consensus could be lost.

There have, however, been additional 'wild cards' recently thrown into the pack, which may yet turn the tables in favour of ILO standards. One is the exposure of large-scale corporate fraud, which may generate increasing scepticism regarding effective self-regulation by business. Codes of conduct are likely to be seen as an inadequate substitute for legal intervention. In addition, the 'grass-roots' movements and NGOs which have grown in opposition to economic globalization are likely to support protection of protest, whether by industrial action or other means. Inclusion of NGOs in international and European-level decision-making may not necessarily be at the expense of workers' interests, as some have feared, but may provide workers with a useful ally. Much depends on which NGOs are selected as worthy of participation in this sphere. The outstanding question is therefore what role NGOs will play in international and European governance, given current interest in legitimizing decision-making by the inclusion of 'civil society'.

Future protection of industrial action under international and European law therefore depends on the interplay of all these factors. Protection of the right to strike stands on the cusp of change. There is potential for the divergent approaches taken by the ILO, the Council of Europe, and the European Union to be brought into alignment, so that they complement each other rather than conflict. What will be the eventual content of any consensus reached on this issue remains uncertain, but there remains scope for endorsement of ILO principles, based on appreciation of the right to strike as a civil, political, and socio-economic entitlement.

Appendix 1: ILO Convention No. 87 on Freedom of Association and Protection of the Right to Organise 1948

(Miscellaneous provisions relating to implementation excluded)

The General Conference of the International Labour Organisation,

Having been convened at San Francisco by the Governing Body of the International Labour Office, and having met in its Thirty-first Session on 17 June 1948,

Having decided to adopt, in the form of a Convention, certain proposals concerning freedom of association and protection of the right to organise, which is the seventh item on the agenda of the session,

Considering that the Preamble to the Constitution of the International Labour Organisation declares 'recognition of the principle of freedom of association' to be a means of improving conditions of labour and of establishing peace,

Considering that the Declaration of Philadelphia reaffirms that 'freedom of expression and of association are essential to sustained progress',

Considering that the International Labour Conference, at its Thirtieth Session, unanimously adopted the principles that should form the basis for international regulation,

Considering that the General Assembly of the United Nations, at its Second Session, endorsed these principles and requested the International Labour Organisation to continue every effort in order that it may be possible to adopt one or several international Conventions,

Adopts this ninth day of July of the year one thousand nine hundred and forty-eight the following Convention, which may be cited as the Freedom of Association and Protection of the Right to Organise Convention, 1948.

Part I.   Freedom of Association

Article 1

Each Member of the International Labour Organisation for which this Convention is in force undertakes to give effect to the following provisions.

Article 2

Workers and employers, without distinction whatsoever, shall have the right to establish and, subject only to the rule of the organisation concerned, to join organisations of their own choosing without previous authorisation.

Article 3

1. Workers' and employers' organisations shall have the right to draw up their constitutions and rules, to elect their representatives in full freedom, to organise their administration and activities and to formulate their programmes.
2. The public authorities shall refrain from any interference which would restrict this right or impede the lawful exercise thereof.

Article 4

Workers' and employers' organisations shall not be liable to be dissolved or suspended by administrative authority.

Article 5

Workers' and employers' organisations shall have the right to establish and join federations and confederations and any such organisation, federation or confederation shall have the right to affiliate with international organisations of workers and employers.

Article 6

The provisions of Articles 2, 3 and 4 hereof apply to federations and confederations of workers' and employers' organisations.

Article 7

The acquisition of legal personality by workers' and employers' organisations, federations and confederations shall not be made subject to conditions of such a character as to restrict the application of the provisions of Articles 2, 3 and 4 hereof.

Article 8

1. In exercising the rights provided for in this Convention workers and employers and their respective organisations, like other persons or organised collectivities, shall respect the law of the land.
2. The law of the land shall not be such as to impair, nor shall it be applied as to impair, the guarantees provided for in this Convention.

Article 9

1. The extent to which the guarantees provided for in this Convention shall apply to the armed forced and the police shall be determined by national laws or regulations.

2. In accordance with the principle set forth in paragraph 8 of article 19 of the Constitution of the International Labour Organisation the ratification of this Convention by any Member shall not be deemed to affect any existing law, award, custom or agreement in virtue of which members of the armed forces or the police enjoy any right guaranteed by this Convention.

Article 10

In this Convention the term 'organisation' means any organisation of workers or of employers for furthering and defending the interests of workers or of employers.

Part II.   Protection of the Right to Organise

Article 11

Each Member of the International Labour Organisation for which this Convention is in force undertakes to take all necessary and appropriate measures to ensure that workers and employers may exercise freely the right to organise.

Appendix 2: ILO Convention No. 98 on the Right to Organise and Collective Bargaining 1949

(Final provisions relating to implementation excluded)

The General Conference of the International Labour Organisation,

Having been convened at Geneva by the Governing Body of the International Labour Office, and having met in its Thirty-second Session on 8 June 1949, and

Having decided upon the adoption of certain proposals concerning the application of the principles of the right to organise and to bargain collectively, which is the fourth item on the agenda of the session, and

Having determined that these proposals shall take the form of an international Convention,

Adopts the first day of July of the year one thousand nine hundred and forty-nine, the following Convention, which may be cited as the Right to Organise and Collective Bargaining Convention, 1949:

Article 1

1. Workers shall enjoy adequate protection against acts of anti-union discrimination in respect of their employment.
2. Such protection shall apply more particularly in respect of acts calculated to—
   (a) make the employment of a worker subject to the condition that he shall not join a union or shall relinquish trade union membership;
   (b) cause the dismissal of or otherwise prejudice a worker by reason of union membership or because of participation in union activities outside working hours or, with the consent of the employer, within working hours.

Article 2

1. Workers' and employers' organisations shall enjoy adequate protection against any acts of interference by each other or each other's agents or members in their establishment, functioning or administration.
2. In particular, acts which are designed to promote the establishment of workers' organisations under the domination of employers or employers' organisations, or

to support workers' organisations by financial or other means, with the object of placing such organisations under the control of employers or employers' organisations, shall be deemed to constitute acts of interference within the meaning of this Article.

Article 3

Machinery appropriate to national conditions shall be established, where necessary, for the purpose of ensuring respect for the right to organise as defined in the preceding Articles.

Article 4

Measures appropriate to national conditions shall be taken, where necessary, to encourage and promote the full development and utilisation of machinery for voluntary negotiation between employers or employers' organisations and workers' organisations, with a view to the regulation of terms and conditions of employment by means of collective agreements.

Article 5

1. The extent to which the guarantees provided for in this Convention shall apply to the armed forces and the police shall be determined by national laws or regulations.

2. In accordance with the principle set forth in paragraph 8 of article 19 of the Constitution of the International Labour Organisation the ratification of this Convention by any Member shall not be deemed to affect any existing law, award, custom or agreement in virtue of which members of the armed forces or the police enjoy any right guaranteed by this Convention.

Article 6

This Convention does not deal with the position of public servants engaged in the administration of the State, nor shall it be construed as prejudicing their rights or status in any way.

Appendix 3: International Covenant on Civil and Political Rights 1966, Article 22 and International Covenant on Economic, Social and Cultural Rights 1966, Article 8

INTERNATIONAL COVENANT ON CIVIL AND POLITICAL RIGHTS 1966

Article 22

1. Everyone shall have the right to freedom of association with others, including the right to form and join trade unions for the protection of his interests.

2. No restrictions may be placed on the exercise of this right other than those which are prescribed by law and which are necessary in a democratic society in the interests of national security or public safety, public order (ordre public), the protection of public health or morals or the protection of the rights and freedoms of others. This article shall not prevent the imposition of lawful restrictions on members of the armed forces and of the police in their exercise of this right.

3. Nothing in this article shall authorize States Parties to the International Labour Organisation Convention of 1948 concerning Freedom of Association and Protection of the Right to Organize to take legislative measures which would prejudice, or to apply the law in such a manner as to prejudice, the guarantees provided for in that Convention.

INTERNATIONAL COVENANT ON ECONOMIC, SOCIAL AND CULTURAL RIGHTS 1966

Article 8

1. The States Parties to the present Covenant undertake to ensure:

(a) The right of everyone to form trade unions and join the trade union of his choice, subject only to the rules of the organization concerned, for the promotion and protection of his economic and social interests. No restrictions may be placed on the exercise of this right other than those prescribed by law and which are necessary in a democratic society in the interests of national security or public order or for the protection of the rights and freedoms of others;

(b) The right of trade unions to establish national federations or confederations and the right of the latter to form or join international trade-union organizations;

(c) The right of trade unions to function freely subject to no limitations other than those prescribed by law and which are necessary in a democratic society in the interests of national security or public order or for the protection of the rights and freedoms of others;

(d) The right to strike, provided that it is exercised in conformity with the laws of the particular country.

2. This article shall not prevent the imposition of lawful restrictions on the exercise of these rights by members of the armed forces or of the police or of the administration of the State.

3. Nothing in this article shall authorize States Parties to the International Labour Organisation Convention of 1948 concerning Freedom of Association and Protection of the Right to Organize to take legislative measures which would prejudice, or apply the law in such a manner as would prejudice, the guarantees provided for in that Convention.

Appendix 4: European Convention on Human Rights 1950, Article 11

Article 11: Freedom of Assembly and Association

1. Everyone has the right to freedom of peaceful assembly and to freedom of association with others, including the right to form and to join trade unions for the protection of his interests.

2. No restrictions shall be placed on the exercise of these rights other than such as are prescribed by law and are necessary in a democratic society in the interests of national security or public safety, for the prevention of disorder or crime, for the protection of health or morals or for the protection of the rights and freedoms of others. This Article shall not prevent the imposition of lawful restrictions on the exercise of these rights by members of the armed forces, of the police or of the administration of the State.

Appendix 5: European Social Charter 1961, Articles 5, 6, 31, and Appendix

Article 5: The Right to Organise

With a view to ensuring or promoting the freedom of workers and employers to form local, national or international organisations for the protection of their economic and social interests and to join those organisations, the Contracting Parties undertake that national law shall not be such as to impair, nor shall it be so applied as to impair, this freedom. The extent to which the guarantees provided for in this article shall apply to the police shall be determined by national laws or regulations. The principle governing the application to the members of the armed forces of these guarantees and the extent to which they shall apply to persons in this category shall equally be determined by national laws or regulations.

Article 6: The Right to Bargain Collectively

With a view to ensuring the effective exercise of the right to bargain collectively, the Contracting Parties undertake:

1. to promote joint consultation between workers and employers;

2. to promote, where necessary and appropriate, machinery for voluntary negotiations between employers or employers' organisations and workers' organisations, with a view to the regulation of terms and conditions of employment by means of collective agreements;

3. to promote the establishment and use of appropriate machinery for conciliation and voluntary arbitration for the settlement of labour disputes;
and recognise:

4. the right of workers and employers to collective action in cases of conflicts of interest, including the right to strike, subject to obligations that might arise out of collective agreements previously entered into.

Article 31: Restrictions

1. The rights and principles set forth in Part I when effectively realised, and their effective exercise as provided for in Part II, shall not be subject to any restrictions or limitations not specified in those parts, except such as are prescribed by law and are necessary in a democratic society for the protection of the rights and

freedoms of others or for the protection of public interest, national security, public health, or morals.

2. The restrictions permitted under this Charter to the rights and obligations set forth herein shall not be applied for any purpose other than that for which they have been prescribed.

Appendix to the Social Charter

Article 6, paragraph 4

It is understood that each Contracting Party may, insofar as it is concerned, regulate the exercise of the right to strike by law, provided that any further restriction that this might place on the right can be justified under the terms of Article 31.

Appendix 6: Community Charter of the Fundamental Social Rights of Workers 1989, Articles 11–14

Article 11

Employers and workers of the European Community shall have the right of association in order to constitute professional organisations or trade unions of their choice for the defence of their economic and social interests.

Every employer and every worker shall have the freedom to join or not to join such organisations without any personal or occupational damage being thereby suffered by him.

Article 12

Employers or employers' organisations, on the one hand, and workers' organisations, on the other, shall have the right to negotiate and conclude collective agreements under the conditions laid down by national legislation and practice.

The dialogue between the two sides of industry at European level which must be developed, may, if the parties deem it desirable, result in contractual relations, in particular at inter-occupational and sectoral level.

Article 13

The right to resort to collective action in the event of a conflict of interests shall include the right to strike, subject to the obligations arising under national regulations and collective agreements.

In order to facilitate the settlement of collective disputes the establishment and utilisation at the appropriate levels of conciliation and arbitration procedures should be encouraged in accordance with national practice.

Article 14

The internal legal order of the Member States shall determine under which conditions and to what extent the rights provided for in Articles 11 to 13 apply to the armed forces, the police and the civil service.

Appendix 7: EU Charter of Fundamental Rights 2000, Articles 12, 28, 51, and 52

Article 12
Freedom of assembly and of association

1. Everyone has the right to freedom of peaceful assembly and to freedom of association at all levels, in particular in political, trade union and civic matters, which implies the right of everyone to form and join trade unions for the protection of his or her interests.

2. Political parties at Union level contribute to expressing the political will of the citizens of the Union.

Article 28
Right of collective bargaining and action

Workers and employers, or their respective organisations, have, in accordance with Community law and national laws and practices, the right to negotiate and conclude collective agreements at the appropriate levels and, in cases of conflicts of interest to take collective action to defend their interests, including strike action.

Article 51
Scope

1. The provisions of this Charter are addressed to the institutions and bodies of the Union with due regard for the principle of subsidiarity and to the Member States only when they are implementing Union law. They shall therefore respect the rights, observe the principles and promote the application thereof in accordance with their respective powers.

2. This Charter does not establish any new power or task for the Community or the Union, or modify powers and tasks defined by the Treaties.

Article 52
Scope of guaranteed rights

1. Any limitation of the exercise of the rights and freedoms recognised by this Charter must be provided for by law and respect the essence of those rights and freedoms. Subject to the principle of proportionality, limitations may be made

only if they are necessary and genuinely meet objectives of general interest recognised by the Union or the need to protect the rights and freedoms of others.

2. Rights recognised by this Charter which are based on the Community Treaties or the Treaty on European Union shall be exercised under the conditions and within the limits defined by those Treaties.

3. In so far as this Charter contains rights which correspond to rights guaranteed by the Convention for the Protection of Human Rights and Fundamental Freedoms, the meaning and scope of those rights shall be the same as those laid down in the said Convention. This provision shall not prevent Union law providing more extensive protection.

Appendix 8: Supervisory Cycles of the European Social Charter

This appendix indicates the date at which each cycle of supervision under the European Social Charter commenced and was concluded. For example, *Conclusions I* of the Committee of Independent Experts (now the European Committee of Social Rights) and the *1st Report of the Governmental Committee* come within the first cycle of supervision.

First Cycle of Supervision	commenced 1961
	concluded 1971
Second Cycle of Supervision	commenced 1968
	concluded 1974
Third Cycle of Supervision	commenced 1970
	concluded 1975
Fourth Cycle of Supervision	commenced 1972
	concluded 1978
Fifth Cycle of Supervision	commenced 1974
	concluded 1980
Sixth Cycle of Supervision	commenced 1976
	concluded 1982
Seventh Cycle of Supervision	commenced 1978
	concluded 1983
Eighth Cycle of Supervision	commenced 1980
	concluded 1985

In 1984 (366th meeting of the Deputies), the Committee of Ministers provisionally decided to divide the States which had ratified the Charter into two groups for the presentation of their biennial reports, under Article 21 of the ESC. This arrangement was given permanent status in 1989.

Ninth Cycle of Supervision	commenced 1982
First Group of States	concluded 1988
Second Group of States	concluded 1988
Tenth Cycle of Supervision	commenced 1984
First Group of States	concluded 1989
Second Group of States	concluded 1990
Eleventh Cycle of Supervision	commenced 1986–7
First Group of States	concluded 1991
Second Group of States	concluded 1992

Twelfth Cycle of Supervision   commenced 1988–9
First Group of States   concluded 1993
Second Group of States   concluded 1994

Following a proposal by CHARTE-REL, the Committee of Ministers adopted in 1992 (479th meeting of the Deputies) for a period of four years an amendment to the reporting system provided under Article 21 of the Charter. The parties were to submit an annual report on selected provisions of the Charter to allow for comparison of national situations.

Thirteenth Cycle of Supervision   commenced 1990–2
First Selected Charter Provisions   concluded 1995
Second Selected Charter Provisions   concluded 1996
Third Selected Charter Provisions   concluded 1996
Fourth Selected Charter Provisions   concluded 1997
Fifth Selected Charter Provisions   concluded 1998

In 1996, the Committee of Ministers adopted by unanimous decision a new system, which was to be implemented from June 1997. Under this new procedure, States would all report on the same provisions, with the same reference periods. Reports on hard-core provisions would be submitted by 30 June of uneven years (with the previous two years as a reference period) and reports on provisions outside the hard core would be submitted by 31 March of even years (and would refer each time to half of the provisions concerned within a reference period of four years).

Fourteenth Cycle of Supervision   commenced 1993–6
Hard Core Provisions   concluded 1999
Other Provisions   concluded 1999

Fifteenth Cycle of Supervision   commenced 1997–8
Hard Core Provisions   concluded 2001
Other Provisions   not yet concluded

Bibliography

AALTONEN, J., *International Secondary Industrial Action in the EU Member States* (Espoo: Metalli, 1999).

AARON, B., and WEDDERBURN, LORD (eds.), *Industrial Conflict: A Comparative Legal Survey* (London: Longmans, 1972).

ABBOTT, K.W., and SNIDAL, D., 'International "Standards" and International Governance' (2001) 8 *Journal of European Public Policy* 345.

ACKERS, P., and PAYNE, J., 'British Trade Unions and Social Partnership: Rhetoric, Reality and Strategy' (1998) 9 *International Journal of Human Resource Management* 529.

ADDISON, J.T., and SIEBERT, W.S., *The Market for Labor: An Analytical Treatment* (Santa Monica, Cal.: Goodyear Publishing Co. Inc., 1979).

—— and—— 'The Social Charter of the European Community: Evolution and Controversies' (1991) 44 *Industrial and Labor Relations Review* 597.

ADDO, M.K. (ed.), *Human Rights and the Responsibility of Transnational Corporations* (The Hague: Kluwer, 1999).

ALBERTYN, C., 'Strike Rules' (1992) 9(3) *Employment Law* (South Africa) 106.

—— 'Political Strikes' (1993) 10(2) *Employment Law* (South Africa) 40.

ALCOCK, A., *History of the International Labour Organisation* (London: Macmillan, 1971).

ALEXY, R., *Coherence Theory of Law* (Lund: Jurisfolaget, 1998).

ALSTON, P., 'US Ratification of the Covenant on Economic, Social and Cultural Rights: The Need for an Entirely New Strategy' (1989) XXVIII *International Legal Materials* 365.

—— (ed.), *The United Nations and Human Rights: A Critical Reappraisal* (Oxford: Oxford University Press, 1992).

—— 'The Myopia of the Handmaidens: International Lawyers and Globalization' (1997) 8 *EJIL* 435.

—— (ed.), *The European Union and Human Rights* (Oxford: Oxford University Press, 1999).

—— and TOMASEVSKI, K. (eds.), *The Right to Food* (Utrecht: Martinus Nijhoff, 1984).

AMAN, A.C., 'Symposium: Globalization, Accountability, and the Future of Administrative Law: Introduction' (2001) 8 *Indiana Journal of Global Legal Studies* 341.

ANDERSON, A., and KRAUSE, L., 'Interest Arbitration: The Alternative to the Strike' (1987) 56 *Fordham Law Review* 153.

ANDERSON, K., 'The Ottawa Convention Banning Landmines: The Role of International Non-Governmental Organisations and the Idea of Civil Society' (2000) 11 *EJIL* 95.

ANON., 'The First Year of the International Labour Organisation' (1921) 1 *ILRev.* 23.

—— *The International Labour Organization: The First Decade* (London: Allen & Unwin, 1931).

—— 'The European Social Charter and International Labour Standards' (1961) 84 *ILRev.* 354.

—— 'Partnership at Work' (1997) 645 *IRS Employment Trends* 3.

—— 'Trade Unions—Right to Strike' [1998] *EHRLR* 773.

ATKINSON, J., *Flexibility, Uncertainty and Manpower Management* (Brighton: Institute of Manpower Studies, 1984).

ATLESON, J.B., 'Reflections on Labor, Power and Society' (1985) 44 *Maryland Law Review* 841.

AUER, P., *Social Dialogue and Employment Success: Europe's Employment Revival: Four Small European Countries Compared* (Geneva: ILO, 1999).

AUERBACH, S., *Legislating for Conflict* (Oxford: Clarendon Press, 1990).

BAECHLER, J., *Democracy: An Analytical Survey* (Paris: UNESCO, 1995).

BALL, C.A., 'The Making of a Transnational Capitalist Society: The Court of Justice, Social Policy, and Individual Rights under the European Community's Legal Order' (1996) 37 *Harvard International Law Journal* 307.

BALL, S., 'The European Employment Strategy: The Will but not the Way?' (2001) 30 *ILJ* 353.

BARENDT, E., *Freedom of Speech* (Oxford: Clarendon Press, 1989).

BARNARD, C., *EC Employment Law* (2nd edn., Oxford: Oxford University Press, 2000).

BARNES, G.N., *History of the International Labour Office* (London: Williams and Norgate, 1926).

BARROW, C., *Industrial Relations Law* (London: Cavendish, 1997).

BARTOLOMEI DE LA CRUZ, H.G., 'International Labour Law: Renewal or Decline?' (1994) 10 *IJCLLIR* 201.

BASKIN, J., *Striking Back: A History of Cosatu* (London: Verso, 1991).

BASSET, P., *Strike Free: New Industrial Relations in Britain* (London: Macmillan, 1987).

BATSTONE, E., BORASTON, I., and FRENKEL, S., *The Social Organization of Strikes* (Oxford: Blackwell, 1978).

BEAN, R., *Comparative Industrial Relations: An Introduction to Cross-National Perspectives* (London/New York: Routledge, 1985).

BEATTY, D., and KENNETT, S., 'Striking Back: Fighting Words, Social Protest and Political Participation in Free and Democratic Societies' (1988) 67 *The Canadian Bar Review* 573.

BEAUMONT, P.B., *Public Sector Industrial Relations* (London: Routledge, 1992).

BEDDARD, R., and HILL, D.M. (eds.), *Economic, Social and Cultural Rights: Progress and Achievements* (London: Macmillan, 1992).

BEINER, R. (ed.), *Theorizing Citizenship* (New York: State University of New York Press, 1995).

BELLACE, J., 'Regulating Secondary Action: The British and American Approaches' (1981) 4 *Comparative Labor Law Journal* 115.

—— 'ILO Fundamental Rights at Work and Freedom of Association' (1999) 50 *Labor Law Journal* 191.

—— 'The ILO Declaration of Fundamental Principles and Rights at Work' (2001) 17 *IJCLLIR* 269.

BENDEL, M., 'The International Protection of Trade Union Rights: A Canadian Case Study' (1981) 13 *Ottawa Law Review* 169.

BENDINER, B., *International Labour Affairs: The World Trade Unions and Multinational Companies* (Oxford: Clarendon Press, 1987).

BENEDICTUS, R., 'The Use of the Law of Tort in the Miners' Dispute' (1985) 14 *ILJ* 176.

BEN-ISRAEL, R., 'Is the Right to Strike a Collective Human Right?' (1981) 11 *Israel Yearbook of Human Rights* 195.

—— *International Labour Standards: The Case of Freedom to Strike* (Deventer: Kluwer, 1988).

BENJAMIN, P. (ed.), *Strikes, Lock-outs and Arbitration in South African Labour Law: Proceedings of the Labour Law Conference 1988* (Cape Town: Juta, 1989).

—— 'The Big Ban Theory: Strikes in Essential Services' (1989) 6 *Employment Law* (South Africa) 44.

BERCUSSON, B., *Fundamental Social and Economic Rights* (Florence: EUI, 1989).

—— 'The European Community's Charter of Fundamental Social Rights of Workers' (1990) 53 *MLR* 624.

—— *European Labour Law* (London: Butterworths, 1996).

—— *European Works Councils: Extending the Trade Union Role* (London: Institute of Employment Rights, 1997).

BERENSTEIN, A., 'Economic and Social Rights: Their Inclusion in the European Convention on Human Rights: Problems of Formulation and Interpretation' (1981) 2 *Human Rights Journal* 257.

BERLIN, I., *Four Essays on Liberty* (Oxford: Oxford University Press, 1969).

BERMANN, G., 'Taking Subsidiarity Seriously: Federalism in the European Community and the United States' (1994) 94 *Columbia Law Review* 331.

BERNITZ, U., and NERGELIUS, J. (eds.), *General Principles of European Community Law* (The Hague: Kluwer, 2000).

BETTEN, L., *The Right to Strike in Community Law: The Incorporation of Fundamental Rights in the Legal Order of the European Communities* (Amsterdam: North-Holland, 1985).

—— 'Towards a Community Charter of Fundamental Social Rights' (1989) 1 *NQHR* 77.

—— *International Labour Standards: Selected Issues* (Deventer: Kluwer, 1993).

—— 'Committee of Ministers of the Council of Europe Call for Contracting States to Account for Violations of the European Social Charter' (1994) 10 *IJCLLIR* 147.

—— 'Current Developments: European Law: Human Rights' (2001) 50 *ICLQ* 690.

—— 'The EU Charter on Fundamental Rights: A Trojan Horse or a Mouse?' (2001) 17 *IJCLLIR* 151.

—— HARRIS, D., and JASPERS, T. (eds.), *The Future of European Social Policy* (Deventer: Kluwer, 1989).

—— and MACDEVITT, D. (eds.), *The Protection of Fundamental Social Rights in the European Union* (The Hague: Kluwer, 1996).

BLACKBURN, R. (ed.), *Rights of Citizenship* (London: Mansell, 1993).

—— and TAYLOR, J. (eds.), *Human Rights for the 1990s: Legal, Political and Ethical Issues* (London: Mansell, 1991).

BLACKETT, A., 'Whither Social Clause? Human Rights, Trade Theory and Treaty Interpretation' (1999) 31 *Columbia Human Rights Law Review* 1.

—— 'Global Governance, Legal Pluralism and the Decentered State: A Labor Law Critique of Codes of Corporate Conduct' (2001) 8 *Indiana Journal of Global Legal Studies* 401.

BLANDY, R., and NILAND, J. (eds.), *Alternatives to Arbitration* (London/Sydney: Allen & Unwin, 1986).

BLANPAIN, R. (ed.), *International Encyclopaedia for Labour Law and Industrial Relations* (Deventer: Kluwer, 1977–).

—— (ed.), *Comparative Labour Law and Industrial Relations in Industrialized Market Economies* (4th edn., Deventer: Kluwer, 1990).

—— 'European Social Policies: One Bridge Too Short?' (1999) 20 *Comparative Labor Law and Policy Journal* 497.

—— (ed.), *Multinational Enterprises and the Social Challenges of the XXIst Century* (Deventer: Kluwer, 2000), in (2000) 37 *Bulletin of Comparative Labour Relations*.

—— (ed.), *The Council of Europe and the Social Challenges of the XXIst Century* (Deventer: Kluwer, 2001), in (2001) 38 *Bulletin of Comparative Labour Relations*.

—— and ENGELS, C. (eds.), *Comparative Labour Law and Industrial Relations in Industrialized Market Economies* (5th edn., Deventer: Kluwer, 1993).

—— and—— (eds.), *The ILO and the Social Challenges of the 21st Century: The Geneva Lectures* (The Hague: Kluwer, 2001).

—— and WEISS, M. (eds.), *The Changing Face of Labour Law and Industrial Relations: Liber Amicorum in Honour of Professor Clyde Summers* (Baden-Baden: Nomos Verlagsgesellschaft, 1993).

BODANSKY, D., 'The Legitimacy of International Governance: A Coming Challenge for International Environmental Law' (1999) 93 *AJIL* 596.

BOSANQUET, N., *After the New Right* (London: Heinemann, 1985).

BOTCHWAY, F.N., 'Good Governance: The Old, the New, the Principle and the Elements' (2001) 13 *Florida Journal of International Law* 159.

BOWLES, S., and GINTIS, H., *Democracy and Capitalism: Property, Community and the Contradictions of Modern Social Thought* (London: Routledge and Kegan Paul, 1996).

BRASSEY, M., *Labour Relations under the New South African Constitution* (Cape Town: Labour Law Unit, 1994).

BREITENFELLNER, A., 'Global Unionism: A Potential Player' (1997) 136 *ILRev.* 531.

BRIDGE, J. (ed.), *Fundamental Rights* (London: Sweet and Maxwell, 1973).

BRINK, D.O., 'Semantics and Legal Interpretation (Further Thoughts)' (1989) II *Canadian Journal of Law and Jurisprudence* 184.

BRITTAN, S., *The Economic Consequences of Democracy* (Philadelphia, Penn.: Temple Smith, 1977).

BROWN, D., and McCOLGAN, A., 'UK Employment Law and the International Labour Organization: The Spirit of Co-operation?' (1992) 21 *ILJ* 265.

BROWN, L.N., and KENNEDY, T., *Brown and Jacobs: The Court of Justice of the European Communities* (5th edn., London: Sweet & Maxwell, 2000).

BROWN, W., 'The Contraction of Collective Bargaining in Britain' (1993) 31 *BJIR* 189.

BRUUN, N., *Trade Union and Fundamental Rights in the EU: A Discussion Document on Strategies for the Future* (Stockholm: TCO, 1999).

BULMER, M., and REES, A.M. (eds.), *Citizenship Today: The Contemporary Relevance of T.H. Marshall* (London: UCL Press, 1996).

BURCHELL, B., DEAKIN, S., and HONEY, S., *The Employment Status of Workers in Non-Standard Employment* (London: Department of Trade and Industry, 1999).

BURCHILL, R., 'The Developing International Law of Democracy' (2001) 64 *MLR* 123.

BURGESS, M., *Federalism and the European Union: The Building of Europe 1950–2000* (London and New York: Routledge, 2000).

BURKITT, B., 'Excessive Trade Union Power: Existing Reality or Contemporary Myth?' (1981) 12 *Industrial Relations Journal* 65.

BUTLER, E., *Hayek: His Contribution to the Political and Economic Thought of our Time* (Philadelphia, Penn.: Temple Smith, 1983).

BUTLER, H., 'Albert Thomas, the First Director' (1932) 26 *ILRev.* 1.

—— *The International Labour Organization* (Oxford: Oxford University Press, 1939).

BYERS, M. (ed.), *The Role of Law in International Politics* (Oxford: Oxford University Press, 2000).

CALLAGHAN, B., *Meeting Needs in the 1990s: The Future of the Public Service and the Challenge for Trade Unions* (London: Institute of Public Policy Research, 1990).

CAMPBELL, D., and SENGENBERGER, W. (eds.), *Creating Economic Opportunities: The Role of Labour Standards in Economic Restructuring* (Geneva: IILS, 1994).

CAPPELLETTI, M. (ed.), *New Perspectives for a Common Law of Europe* (Leiden: EUI/ Sijthoff, 1978).

CAPPUYNS, E., 'Linking Labor Standards and Trade Sanctions: An Analysis of their Current Relationship' (1998) 36 *Columbia Journal of Transnational Law* 659.

CARBY-HALL, J.R. (ed.), *Studies in Labour Law* (Bradford: MCB Books, 1976).

—— 'Industrial Conflict: the Civil and Statutory Immunities of Trade Unions and their Officials' (1987) 29 *Managerial Law* 1.

CARLEY, M., *The Regulation of Industrial Conflict in Europe: Strikes and Lock-Outs in Fifteen European Countries* (London: Industrial Relations Service, 1989).

CARPI, F., and ORLANDI, C.G. (eds.), *Judicial Protection of Human Rights at the National and International Level: International Congress on Procedural Law for the Ninth Centenary of the University of Bologna September 22–24 1998* (Bologna: University of Bologna, 1999).

CARTY, H., 'Intentional Violation of Economic Interests: The Limits of Common Law Liability' (1988) 104 *LQR* 250.

CASEY, N.A., *The Right to Organise and to Bargain Collectively: Protection within the European Social Charter* (Strasbourg: Council of Europe Publishing, 1996).

CHAPMAN, J.W., and SHAPIRO, I. (eds.), *Democratic Community: Nomos XXXV* (New York: New York University Press, 1993).

CHARNEY, J.I., 'Universal International Law' (1993) 87 *American Journal of International Law* 529.

CHARNOVITZ, S., 'Trade, Employment and Labour Standards: The OECD Study and Recent Developments in the Trade and Labor Standards Debate' (1997) 11 *Temple International and Comparative Law Journal* 131.

—— 'Two Centuries of Participation: NGOs and International Governance' (1997) 18 *Michigan Journal of International Law* 183.

CHISHOLM, A., *Labour's Magna Charta: A Critical Study of the Labour Clauses of the Peace Treaty and of the Draft Conventions and Recommendations of the Washington International Labour Conference* (London: Longmans, Green & Co., 1925).

CHODOSH, H.E., 'Neither Treaty nor Custom: The Emergence of Declarative International Law' (1991) 26 *Texas International Law Journal* 87.

CHURCHILL, R., and ULFSTEIN, G., 'Autonomous Institutional Arrangements in Multilateral Environmental Agreements: A Little-Noticed Phenomenon in International Law' (2000) 94 *The American Journal of International Law* 623.

CLAUWAERT, S., *Fundamental Social Rights in the European Union: Comparative Tables and Documents* (Brussels: ETUI, 1998).

CLEMENTS, L.J., MOLE, N., and SIMMONS, A., *European Human Rights: Taking a Case under the Convention* (2nd edn., London: Sweet & Maxwell, 1999).

CLUTTERBUCK, R., *Industrial Conflict and Democracy: The Last Chance* (London: Macmillan, 1984).

COATES, K., and TOPHAM, T., *Trade Unions and Politics* (Oxford: Blackwell, 1986).

COHEN, J., and ROGERS, J. (eds.), *Associations and Democracy* (London/New York: Verso, 1995).

COHEN, R., HENDERSON, J., and MICHAEL, D., *Contested Domains, Debates in International Labour Studies* (London: Zed, 1991).

COLLINS, H., 'Market Power, Bureaucratic Power and the Contract of Employment' (1986) 15 *ILJ* 1.

—— 'Independent Contractors and the Challenge of Vertical Disintegration of Employment Protection Laws' (1990) 10 *OJLS* 353.

—— 'Regulating the Employment Relation for Competitiveness' (2001) 30 *ILJ* 17.

COMPA, L., 'The Multilateral Agreement on Investment and International Labour Rights: A Failed Connection' (1998) 31 *Cornell International Law Journal* 683.

—— 'Workers' Freedom of Association in the United States under International Human Rights Standards' (2001) 17 *IJCLLIR* 289.

—— and DIAMOND, S.F. (eds.), *Human Rights, Labor Rights and International Trade* (Philadelphia, Penn.: University of Pennsylvania Press, 1996).

—— and HINCHCLIFFE-DARRICARRERE, T., 'Enforcing International Labour Standards Through International Codes of Conduct' (1995) 33 *Columbia Journal of Transnational Law* 663.

CONAGHAN, J., 'Critical Labour Law: The American Contribution' (1987) 14 *Journal of Law and Society* 334.

—— FISCHL, R.M., and KLARE, K. (eds.), *Labour Law in an Era of Globalization: Transformative Practices and Possibilities* (Oxford: Oxford University Press, 2002).

COOMANS, F., and VAN HOOF, F. (eds.), *The Right to Complain About Economic, Social and Cultural Rights: Proceedings of the Expert Meeting on the Adoption of an Optional Protocol to the International Covenant on Economic, Social and Cultural Rights held 25–28 January 1995* (Utrecht: Netherlands Institute of Human Rights, 1995).

COONEY, S., 'Testing Times for the ILO: Institutional Reform for the New International Political Economy' (1999) 20 *Comparative Labor Law and Policy Journal* 365.

COPP, D., HAMPTON, J., and ROEMER, J.E. (eds.), *The Idea of Democracy* (Cambridge: Cambridge University Press, 1993).

CORBY, S., 'Limitations on Freedom of Association in the Civil Service and the ILO's Response' (1986) 15 *ILJ* 161.

CORDOVA, E., 'Some Reflections on the Overproduction of International Labour Standards' (1993) 14 *Comparative Labor Law Journal* 138.

COX, L., 'The International Labour Organisation and Fundamental Rights at Work' [1999] *EHRLR* 451.

COX, R., 'Social Policy and Labour Policy in the EEC' (1963) 1 *BJIR* 5.

—— *International Organisation: World Politics, Studies in Economic and Social Agencies* (London: Macmillan, 1969).

—— *Labor and Transnational Relations* (Geneva: International Institute for Labour Studies, 1971).

—— *The Anatomy of Influence: Decision-Making in International Organisations* (New Haven, Conn.: Yale University Press, 1973).

—— *Production, Power and World Order* (New York: Columbia University Press, 1987).

CRAIG, G. (ed.), *Jobs and Community Action* (London: Routledge and Kegan Paul, 1979).

CRAIG, P., and DE BÚRCA, G. (eds.), *The Evolution of EU Law* (Oxford: Oxford University Press, 1999).

—— and ——, *EU Law: Text, Cases and Materials* (3rd edn., Oxford: Oxford University Press, 2002).

—— and HARLOW, C. (eds.), *Lawmaking in the European Union* (The Hague/London: Kluwer, 1998).

CRANSTON, M., *What are Human Rights?* (London: Bodley Head, 1973).

CRAVEN, M., *The International Covenant on Economic, Social and Cultural Rights: A Perspective on its Development* (2nd revd. edn., Oxford: Clarendon Press, 1998).

CROUCH, C., *Industrial Relations and European State Traditions* (Oxford: Clarendon Press, 1993).

—— and PIZZORNO, A. (eds.), *The Resurgence of Class Conflict in Western Europe Since 1909* (New York: Macmillan, 1978).

CROW, B., and HENDY, J., *Reclaim Our Rights: Repeal the Anti-Union Laws* (London: Organising Committee of Reclaim our Rights, 1999).

CULLY, M., WOODLAND, S., O'REILLY, A., and DIX, G., *Britain at Work: As Depicted by the 1998 Employee Relations Survey* (London and New York: Routledge, 1999).

CURRIE, J., and MCCONNELL, S., *Strikes and Arbitration in the Public Sector: Can Legislation Reduce Dispute Costs?* (London: Centre for Labour Economics, London School of Economics, 1989).

CUYVERS, L., and KERREMANS, B. (eds.), *The International Social Issue: Social Dumping and Social Competition in the Global Economy* (Antwerp: Intersentia Economische Wetenschappen, 1998).

DAHL, R.A., *A Preface to Economic Democracy* (Cambridge, Polity Press, 1985).

—— *Democracy and its Critics* (New Haven, Conn., and London: Yale University Press, 1989).

DASHWOOD, A., and JOHNSTON, A. (eds.), *The Future of the Judicial System of the European Union* (Oxford: Hart Publishing, 2001).

DÄUBLER, W., 'Co-determination: The German Experience' (1975) 4 *ILJ* 218.

—— 'The Employee Participation Directive—A Realistic Utopia?' (1977) 14 *CMLRev.* 457.

DAVIES, P., and FREEDLAND, M., *Labour Law: Text and Materials* (2nd edn., London: Weidenfeld and Nicolson, 1984).

—— and —— *Labour Legislation and Public Policy* (Oxford: Oxford University Press, 1992).

—— LYON-CAEN, A., SCIARRA, S., and SMITH, S., *European Community Labour Law: Principles and Perspectives: Liber Amicorum Lord Wedderburn of Charlton* (Oxford: Oxford University Press, 1996).

DAVIS, D.M., 'Social Power and Civil Rights: Towards a New Jurisprudence for South Africa' (1991) 108 *South African Law Journal* 453.

DE BÚRCA, G., 'Reappraising Subsidiarity's Significance After Amsterdam' (Cambridge, Mass.: Harvard Law School, 1999) Harvard Jean Monnet Working Papers 7/99.

—— 'The Drafting of the European Charter of Fundamental Rights' (2001) 26 *ELRev.* 126.

—— 'Human Rights: The Charter and Beyond' (Cambridge, Mass.: Harvard Law School, 2001) Harvard Jean Monnet Working Papers 10/01.

DE TOCQUEVILLE, A., *Democracy in America* (London: Fontana, 1968).

DE WITTE, B., 'The Legal Status of the Charter: Vital Question or Non-Issue?' (2001) 8 *Maastricht Journal of European and Comparative Law* 81.

DEAKIN, S., 'Legal Change and Labour Market Restructuring in Western Europe and the US' (1991) 15 *New Zealand Journal of Industrial Relations* 109.

—— and WILKINSON, F., 'The Law and Economics of the Minimum Wage' (1992) 19 *Journal of Law and Society* 379.

—— and—— 'Rights vs Efficiency? The Economic Case for Transnational Labour Standards' (1994) 23 *ILJ* 289.

DIAMOND, L., and PLATTNER, M.F. (eds.), *The Global Resurgence of Democracy* (2nd edn., Baltimore, Mld., and London: The Johns Hopkins University Press, 1996).

DIEBOLD, W., *The Schuman Plan: A Study in Economic Co-operation 1950–1959* (New York: Praeger, 1959).

DRYZEK, J.S., *Democracy in Capitalist Times: Ideals, Limits and Struggles* (New York/Oxford: Oxford University Press, 1996).

—— *Deliberative Democracy and Beyond: Liberals, Critics, Contestations* (Oxford: Oxford University Press, 2000).

DRZEMCZEWSKI, A., 'The European Human Rights Convention: Time for a Radical Overhaul?' (1987) 10 *Boston College International and Comparative Law Review* 9.

—— 'A Major Overhaul of the European Human Rights Convention Control Mechanism: Protocol 11' (1995) VI(2) *Collected Courses of the Academy of European Law: The Protection of Human Rights in Europe* 206.

—— 'The European Human Rights Convention: A New Court of Human Rights in Strasbourg as of November 1, 1998' (1998) 55 *Washington and Lee Law Review* 697.

DRZEWICKI, K., KRAUSE, C., and ROSAS, A., *Social Rights as Human Rights: A European Challenge* (Åbo: Institute for Human Rights, Åbo Akademi University, 1994).

DUNNING, H., 'The Origins of Convention No. 87 on Freedom of Association and the Right to Organize' (1998) 137 *ILRev.* 149.

DUPUY, R.-J. (ed.), *Mélanges en l'honneur de Nicolas Valticos* (Paris: Editions A. Pedone, 1999).

DUVIGNEAU, J.L., 'From Advisory Opinion 2/94 to the Amsterdam Treaty: Human Rights Protection in the European Union' (1999) 25 *Legal Issues of European Integration* 61.

DUXBURY, N., *Patterns of American Jurisprudence* (Oxford: Oxford University Press, 1997).

DWORKIN, R., *Taking Rights Seriously* (London: Ducksworth, 1977).

—— 'Law as Interpretation' (1982) 12 *Michigan Journal of International Law* 371.

EASTERBROOK, F.H., 'Implicit and Explicit Rights of Association' (1987) 10 *Harvard Journal of Law and Policy* 91.

EBSEN, I., 'Social Policy in the European Community Between Competition, Solidarity and Harmonization: Still on the Way from a Free Trade Area to a Federal System' (1996) 2 *Columbia Journal of European Law* 421.

EDWARDS, P. (ed.), *Industrial Relations: Theory and Practice in Britain* (Oxford: Blackwell, 1995).

EDWARDS, R., GARONNA, P., and TODTLING, F., *Unions in Crisis and Beyond: Perspectives from Six Countries* (Beckenham: Croom Helm, 1986).

EICKE, T., 'The European Charter of Fundamental Rights—Unique Opportunity or Unwelcome Distraction' [2000] *EHRLR* 280.

EIDE, A., 'Realization of Social and Economic Rights and the Minimum Threshold Approach' (1989) 10 *Human Rights Journal* 35.

——KRAUSE, C., and ROSAS, A. (eds.), *Economic, Social and Cultural Rights: A Textbook* (Dordrecht: Martinus Nijhoff, 1995).

EISTREICHER, S. (ed.), *Employee Representation in the Emerging Workplace: Alternatives/Supplements to Collective Bargaining* (Boston, Mass./The Hague: Kluwer, 1998).

ELDRIDGE, J.E., *Industrial Disputes: Essays in the Sociology of Industrial Relations* (London: Routledge and Kegan Paul/New York: Humanities Press, 1968).

ELGAR, J., and SIMPSON, B., *Industrial Ballots and the Law* (London: The Institute of Employment Rights, 1996).

EMPLOYMENT POLICY INSTITUTE, *Implementing a National Minimum Wage in the UK* (London: EPI, 1997).

ENDERWICK, P., 'Strike Costs and Public Policy' (1982) 2 *Journal of Public Policy* 347.

——*Multinational Business and Labour* (London and Sydney: Croom Helm, 1985).

ENGELS, C., 'Who is Who in the Eastern European Industrial Landscape: Identifying Proper Collective Bargaining Partners in Reforming Socialist Systems through the Application of ILO Conventions 87 and 98' (1992) 13 *Comparative Labor Law Journal* 167.

—— 'The European Charter of Fundamental Rights: A Changed Political Opportunity and its Normative Consequences' (2001) 7 *ELJ* 151.

ENGLAND, G., 'Some Thoughts on Constitutionalizing the Right to Strike' (1988) 13 *Queen's Law Journal* 168.

EPSTEIN, R.A., 'A Common Law for Labor Relations' (1988) 92 *Yale Law Journal* 1357.

ERICKSON, C.L., and MITCHELL, D.J.B., 'Labor Standards in International Trade Agreements: The Current Debate' (1996) 47 *Labor Law Journal* 763.

——and—— 'Labor Standards and Trade Agreements: US Experience' (1998) 19 *Comparative Labor Law and Policy Journal* 145.

ESTY, D., and GERADIN, D., *Regulatory Competition and Economic Integration: Comparative Perspectives* (Oxford: Oxford University Press, 2001).

EUROPEAN TRADE UNION INSTITUTE, *Strike and Structural Change: The Future of the Trade Unions' Mobilisation Capacity in Europe* (Brussels: ETUI, 1993).

EVANS, E.W., and CREIGH, S.W. (eds.), *Industrial Conflict in Britain* (London: Frank Cass, 1977).

EVJU, S., 'Collective Agreements and Competition Law: The *Albany* Puzzle, and *van der Woude*' (2001) 17 *IJCLLIR* 165.

EWING, K., *Trade Unions, the Labour Party and the Law* (Edinburgh: Edinburgh University Press, 1982).

—— 'The Right to Strike' (1986) 15 *ILJ* 143.

—— 'Rights and Immunities in British Labour Law' (1988) 10 *Comparative Labour Law Journal* 1.

—— 'Economics and Labour Law in Britain: Thatcher's Radical Experiment' (1990) 28 *Alberta Law Review* 632.

—— *The Right to Strike* (Oxford: Clarendon Press, 1991).

—— *Britain and the ILO* (2nd edn., London: Institute of Employment Rights, 1994).

—— 'Democratic Socialism and Labour Law' (1995) 24 *ILJ* 103.

—— (ed.), *Working Life: A New Perspective on Labour Law* (London: Institute of Employment Rights, 1996).

—— 'Freedom of Association and the Employment Relations Act 1999' (1999) 28 *ILJ* 283.

—— 'Social Rights and Constitutional Law' [1999] *Public Law* 105.

—— 'Dancing with the Daffodils?' (2000) 50 *Federation News GFTU* 1.

—— 'Modernising International Labour Standards: Globalisation, Multinational Corporations and International Trade Union Rights' (2000) 50 *Federation News GFTU* 109.

—— 'Social Rights and Human Rights: Britain and the Social Charter—the Conservative Legacy' [2000] *EHRLR* 91.

—— (ed.), *Human Rights at Work* (London: Institute of Employment Rights, 2000).

—— (ed.), *Employment Rights at Work: Reviewing the Employment Relations Act 1999* (London: Institute of Employment Rights, 2001).

—— GEARTY, C.A., and HEPPLE B.A. (eds.), *Human Rights and Labour Law* (London: Mansell, 1994).

—— and SIBLEY, T., *International Trade Union Rights for the New Millenium* (London: Institute of Employment Rights, 2000).

FABRICUS, F., *Human Rights and European Politics: The Legal-Political Status of Workers in the European Community* (Oxford/Providence, RI: Berg, 1992).

FAHLBECK, R., 'Reflections on Industrial Relations' (1996) 12 *IJCLLIR* 289.

FALK, R.A., 'International Regimes Progress and Problems' (1993) 87 *American Society of International Law Proceedings* 422.

FARNER, A., *Changing Public Sector Industrial Relations in Europe* (Warwick: Industrial Relations Research Unit, 1991).

FAWCETT, L., and HURRELL, A. (eds.), *Regionalism in World Politics: Regional Organization and International Order* (Oxford: Oxford University Press, 1995).

FIELDS, G.S., 'International Labour Standards and Economic Interdependence' (1996) 49 *Industrial and Labor Relations Review* 571.

FIGUEIREDO, J.B., and SHAHEED, Z. (eds.), *Reducing Poverty through Labour Market Policies* (Geneva: IILS, 1995).

FINKIN, M., 'Bridging the Representation Gap' (2001) 3 *University of Pennsylvania Journal of Labor and Employment Law* 391.

FINNIS, W., HIMSWORTH, C.M.G., and WALKER, N., *Edinburgh Essays in Public Law* (Edinburgh: Edinburgh University Press, 1991).

FISH, S., 'Fish v Fiss' (1984) 36 *Stanford Law Review* 1325.

FISHER, I.W., and McDONALD, J.J., 'State Anti-Strikebreaker Laws: Unconstitutional Interference with Employers' Right to Self-help' (1985) 3 *Hofstra Labor Law Journal* 59.

FISHER, W.W., and HORWITZ, M.J. (eds.), *American Legal Realism* (Oxford: Oxford University Press, 1993).

FISS, O., 'Objectivity and Interpretation' (1982) 34 *Stanford Law Review* 739.

FITZPATRICK, B., 'Straining the Definition of Health and Safety?' (1997) 26 *ILJ* 115.

FLANDERS, A., *Management and Unions* (London: Faber and Faber, 1970).

FORBATH, W.E., 'The Constitution and the Obligations of Government to Secure the Material Preconditions for a Good Society: Constitutional Welfare Rights: A History, Critique and Reconstruction' (2001) 69 *Fordham Law Review* 1821.

FORDE, M., 'The European Convention on Human Rights and Labor Law' (1983) 31 *American Journal of Comparative Law* 301.

—— 'Citizenship and Democracy in Industrial Relations: The Agenda for the 1990s' (1992) 55 *MLR* 241.

FORREST, H., 'Political Values in Individual Employment Law' (1980) 43 *MLR* 361.

FOSH, P., MORRIS, H., MARTIN, R., SMITH, P., and UNDY, R., 'Politics, Pragmatism and Ideology: The "Wellsprings" of Conservative Union Legislation (1979–1992)' (1993) 22 *ILJ* 14.

FOSTER, J.W., 'Meeting the Challenges: Renewing the Progress of Economic and Social Rights' (1998) 47 *University of New Brunswick Law Journal* 197.

FOWERAKER, J., and LANDMAN, T., *Citizenship Rights and Social Movements: A Comparative and Statistical Analysis* (Oxford: Oxford University Press, 1997).

FOX, A., *Industrial Sociology and Industrial Relations* (London: Royal Commission Research Paper 3, HMSO, 1966).

—— *Man Mismanagement* (2nd edn., London: Hutchinson, 1985).

FOX, G.H., and NOLTE, G., 'Intolerant Democracies' (1995) 36 *Harvard International Law Journal* 1.

—— and ROTH, B.R. (eds.), *Democratic Governance and International Law* (Cambridge: Cambridge University Press, 2000).

FRANCK, T., 'The Emerging Right to Democratic Governance' (1992) 86 *AJIL* 46.

—— *Fairness in International Law and Institutions* (Oxford: Clarendon Press, 1995).

FRANKEL PAUL, E., MILLER, F.D., and PAUL, J. (eds.), *Economic Rights* (Cambridge: Cambridge University Press, 1992).

FRANZOSI, R., *The Puzzle of Strikes: Class and Strategies in Post War Italy* (Cambridge: Cambridge University Press, 1995).

FREDMAN, S., 'The Right to Strike: Policy and Principle' (1987) 103 *LQR* 176.

—— 'The New Rights: Labour Law and Ideology in the Thatcher Years' (1992) 12 *OJLS* 24.

—— and MORRIS, G., *The State as Employer: Labour Relations in the Public Services* (London: Mansell, 1986).

—— and —— 'Freedom of Association' (1988) 17 *ILJ* 105.

—— and —— 'The State as Employer: Is it Unique?' (1990) 19 *ILJ* 142.

—— and —— 'Public or Private? State Employees and Judicial Review' (1991) 107 *LQR* 298.

—— and —— 'Is there a Public/Private Labour Law Divide?' (1993) 14 *Comparative Labor Law Journal* 115.

FREEMAN, M., 'Is a Political Science of Human Rights Possible?' (2001) 19 *Netherlands Quarterly of Human Rights* 123.

FRIEDMAN, M., *Capitalism and Freedom* (Chicago, Ill.: Phoenix Books, 1962).

FUKUYAMA, F., *The End of History and the Last Man* (New York: Free Press, 1992).

FULCHER, J., *Labour Movements, Employers and the State: Conflict and Co-operation in Britain and Sweden* (Oxford: Clarendon Press, 1991).

GALL, G., 'A Review of Strike Activity in Western Europe at the End of the Second Millennium' (1999) 21 *Employee Relations* 357.

GASTIL, J., SMITH, M.A., and SIMMONDS, C., 'New Directions in Direct Democracy: There's More than One Way to Legislate: An Integration of Representative, Direct and Deliberative Approaches to Representative Democratic Governance' (2001) 72 *University of Colorado Law Review* 1005.

GAUNTLET, J.J., and SMUTS, D.F., 'Boycotts: The Limits of Lawfulness' (1990) 11 *Industrial Law Journal* (South Africa) 937.

GEARY, R., *Policing Industrial Disputes: 1893–1985* (Cambridge: Cambridge University Press, 1985).

GERMANOTTA, P., *Protecting Worker Solidarity Action: A Critique of International Labour Law* (London/Geneva: Institute of Employment Rights/Global Labour Institute, 2002).

—— and NOVITZ, T., 'Globalisation and the Right to Strike: The Case for European-Level Protection of Secondary Action' (2002) 18 *IJCLLIR* 67.

GERNIGON, B., ODERO, A., and GUIDO, H., 'ILO Principles Concerning the Right to Strike' (1998) 137 *ILRev.* 441.

——, —— and —— *ILO Principles Concerning the Right to Strike* (Geneva: ILO, 1998).

——, —— and —— *Collective Bargaining: ILO Standards and the Principles of the Supervisory Bodies* (Geneva: ILO, 2000).

GETMAN, J.G., and KOHLER, T.C., 'The Common Law, Labor Law and Reality: A Response to Professor Epstein' (1983) 92 *Yale Law Journal* 1418.

GHEBALI, V., *The International Labour Organisation: A Case-Study on the Evolution of UN Specialised Agencies* (Dordrecht: Martinus Nijhoff, 1989).

GIDDENS, A., *Beyond Left and Right: The Future of Radical Politics* (London: Polity Press, 1994).

GOLDTHORPE, J.H. (ed.), *Order and Conflict in Contemporary Capitalism: Studies in the Political Economy of Western European Nations* (Oxford: Clarendon Press, 1984).

GOMIEN, D., HARRIS, D., and ZWAAK, L., *Law and Practice of the European Convention on Human Rights and the European Social Charter* (Strasbourg: Council of Europe Publishing, 1996).

GORMAN, R., *Labor Law: Unionization and Collective Bargaining* (St Paul, Minn.: West Publishing Co., 1976).

GOULD, G.C., *Rethinking Democracy* (Cambridge: Cambridge University Press, 1988).

GRABER, M., 'Social Democracy and Constitutional Theory: An Institutional Perspective' (2001) 69 *Fordham Law Review* 1969.

GRANT, B., 'Political Stay-aways: The Dismissal of Participants' (1990) 11 *Industrial Law Journal* (South Africa) 944.

—— 'Political Stay-aways and the Labour Appeal Court' [1992] *South African Mercantile Gazette* 88.

GREEN, K., 'Labor Standards in the European Union: The Effects on Multinationals' (1996) 18 *Houston Journal of International Law* 497.

GREEN, L., 'Two Views of Collective Rights' (1991) IV *Canadian Journal of Law and Jurisprudence* 315.

GREENBERG, S.B., *Legitimating the Illegitimate: State, Markets and Resistance in South Africa* (Berkeley, Cal.: University of California Press, 1987).

GRIEG, J.W., 'Reflections on the Role of Consent' (1992) 13 *Australian Yearbook of International Law* 125.

GRIFFITHS, R.T., *Europe's First Constitution: The European Political Community 1952–1954* (London: Federal Trust, 2000).

GROSS, J.A., 'A Human Rights Perspective on United States Labor Relations Law: A Violation of the Right to Freedom of Association' (1999) 3 *Employee Rights and Employment Policy Journal* 65.

GUEST, D.E., and PECCEI, R., 'Partnership at Work: Mutuality and the Balance of Advantage' (2001) 39 *BJIR* 207.

GUNNING, I., 'Modernizing Customary International Law: The Challenge of Human Rights' (1991) 31 *Virginia Journal of International Law* 211.

GUTTO, S.B.O., 'Beyond Justiciability: Challenges of Implementing/Enforcing Socio-Economic Rights in South Africa' (1998) 4 *Buffalo Human Rights Law Review* 79.

HAAS, E., *Beyond the Nation-State: Functionalism and International Organisation* (Stanford, Cal.: Stanford University Press, 1964).

HABERMAS, J., *Between Facts and Norms: Contributions to a Discourse Theory of Law and Democracy* (trans. Rehg, W., Boston, Mass.: MIT, 1997).

HAIN, P., *Political Strikes: The State and Trade Unionism in Britain* (London: Viking, 1986).

HALBERSTAM, M., 'The Use of Legislative History in Treaty Interpretation' (1991) 12 *Cardozo Law Review* 1645.

HALL, M., 'Beyond Representation and EU Law' (1996) 25 *ILJ* 15.

HAMLIN, A., and PETTIT, P. (eds.), *The Good Polity: Normative Analysis of the State* (Oxford: Blackwell, 1989).

HANAMI, T., and BLANPAIN, R. (eds.), *Industrial Conflict Resolution in Market Economies: A Study of Australia, the Federal Republic of Germany, Italy, Japan and the USA* (2nd edn., Deventer: Kluwer, 1989).

HANSENNE, M., 'The Declaration of Philadelphia' [1994] *Labor Law Journal* 454.

HANSENNE, M., 'The 75th Anniversary of the International Labour Organisation' (1994) 10 *IJCLLIR* 195.

HANSLOWE, K.L., and ACIERNO, J.L., 'The Law and Theory of Strikes by Government Employees' (1982) 67 *Cornell Law Review* 1055.

HANSON, C., and MATHER, G., *Striking out Strikes: Changing Employment Relations in the British Labour Market* (London: Institute of Economic Affairs, 1988).

HARRIS, D.J., 'The European Social Charter' (1964) 13 *ICLQ* 1076.

—— *The European Social Charter* (Charlottesville, Vir.: University Press of Virginia, 1984).

—— 'A Fresh Impetus for the European Social Charter' (1992) 41 *ICLQ* 659.

—— and JOSEPH, S. (eds.), *The International Covenant on Civil and Political Rights and United Kingdom Law* (Oxford: Clarendon Press, 1995).

HARTNEY, M., 'Some Confusions Concerning Collective Rights' (1991) IV *Canadian Journal of Law and Jurisprudence* 293.

HAYEK, F.A., *Studies in Philosophy, Politics and Economics* (London: Routledge and Kegan Paul, 1967).

—— *Law, Legislation and Liberty: A New Statement of the Liberal Principles of Justice and Political Economy* (London: Routledge and Kegan Paul, 1976).

—— *1980s Unemployment and the Unions: Essays on the Impotent Price Structure of Britain and Monopoly in the Labour Market* (2nd edn., London: Institute of Economic Affairs, 1984).

—— *The Fatal Conceit: The Errors of Socialism* (London: Routledge, 1988).

HEALY, G., and KIRTON, G., 'Women, Power and Trade Union Government in the UK' (2000) 38 *BJIR* 343.

HECKSCHER, C., *The New Unionism: Employee Involvement in the Changing Corporation* (Ithaca, NY: ILR Press, 1996).

HEENAN, J., *Trade Liberalisation and ILO Labour Standards: Some Future Directions*, LLM thesis, European University Institute, Florence (unpublished, 1999).

HEERE, W. (ed.), *International Law and Its Sources: Liber Americorum Maarten Bos* (Deventer: Kluwer, 1988).

HEFFERNAN, L., 'A Comparative View of the Individual Petition Procedures under the European Convention on Human Rights and the International Covenant on Civil and Political Rights' (1997) 19 *Human Rights Quarterly* 78.

HEINZE, E., 'Principles for a Meta-Discourse of Liberal Rights: The Example of the European Convention on Human Rights' (1999) 9 *Indiana International and Comparative Law Review* 319.

HELD, D., *Democracy and the Global Order: From the Modern State to Cosmopolitan Governance* (Cambridge: Polity Press, 1995).

—— *Models of Democracy* (2nd edn., Cambridge: Polity Press, 1996).

HENDY, J., 'The Human Rights Act, Article 11 and the Right to Strike' [1998] *EHRLR* 582.

—— *Every Worker Shall Have the Right to be Represented at Work by a Trade Union* (London: Institute of Employment Rights, 1998).

—— and WALTON, M., 'An Individual Right to Union Representation in International Law' (1997) 26 *ILJ* 205.

HENKIN, L., 'Economic-Social Rights as "Rights": A United States Perspective' (1981) 2 *Human Rights Law Journal* 223.

HEPPLE, B. (ed.), *The Making of Labour Law in Europe: A Comparative Study of Nine Countries up to 1945* (London/New York: Mansell, 1986).

—— '25 Years of the European Social Charter' (1989) 10 *Comparative Labor Law Journal* 460.

—— 'The Role of Trade Unions in a Democratic Society' (1990) 11 *Industrial Law Journal* (South Africa) 645.

—— *European Social Dialogue—Alibi or Opportunity?* (London: The Institute of Employment Rights, 1993).

—— 'The Future of Labour Law' (1995) 24 *ILJ* 303.

—— 'New Approaches to International Labour Regulation' (1997) 26 *ILJ* 353.

—— 'A Race to the Top? International Investment Guidelines and Corporate Codes of Conduct' (1999) 20 *Comparative Labor Law and Policy Journal* 347.

—— 'The EU Charter of Fundamental Rights' (2001) 30 *ILJ* 225.

HIBBS, D.A., *The Political Economy of Industrial Democracies* (Boston, Mass.: Harvard University Press, 1987).

HIGGINS, R., *Problems and Process: International Law and How We Use It* (Oxford: Clarendon Press, 1994).

HILLER, E.T., *The Strike: A Study in Collective Action* (Chicago, Ill.: University of Chicago Press, 1928).

HIRSCHMAN, A.O., *Exit, Voice and Loyalty: Responses to Decline in Firms, Organizations and States* (Boston, Mass.: Harvard University Press, 1970).

HODGES-AEBERHARD, J., and DE DIOS, O., 'Principles of the Committee on Freedom of Association Concerning Strikes' (1987) 126 *ILRev.* 543.

HOSLI, M., 'Coalitions and Power: Effects of Qualified Majority Voting on the Council of the European Union' (1996) 34 *JCMS* 255.

HUDSON, M.O., *The Permanent Court of International Justice 1920–42* (New York: Macmillan, 1945).

HUTT, W.H., *The Theory of Collective Bargaining* (revd. edn., London: Institute of Economic Affairs, 1975).

HUTTON, W., *The State We're In* (London: Jonathan Cape, 1995).

—— *The World We're In* (London: Little, Brown, 2002).

HYDE, A., 'Economic Labor Law v Political Labor Relations: Dilemmas for Liberal Legalism' (1981) 60 *Texas Law Review* 1.

HYMAN, R., *Strikes* (4th edn., London: Macmillan, 1989).

—— and FERNER, A. (eds.), *New Frontiers in European Industrial Relations* (Oxford: Blackwell, 1994).

IMBER, M., *The USA, ILO, UNESCO and IAEA: Politicization and Withdrawal in the Specialised Agencies* (London: Macmillan, 1989).

INGHAM, G., *Strikes and Industrial Conflict, Britain and Scandinavia* (London: Macmillan, 1974).

INGLOTT, P.S., 'The Subjects of Human Rights, Human Individuals and the Human Community' (2000) 4 *Mediterranean Journal of Human Rights* 105.

JACHTENFUCHS, M., 'The Governance Approach to European Integration' (2001) 39 *JCMS* 245.

JACOBI, O. (ed.), *Economic Crisis, Trade Unions and the State* (London: Croom Helm, 1986).

JACOBS, A., 'Towards Community Action on Strike Law' (1978) 15 *CMLRev.* 133.

JACOBS, F.G., 'The Extension of the European Convention on Human Rights to Include Economic, Social and Cultural Rights' (1978) 3 *Human Rights Review* 166.

—— and WHITE, R.C.A., *The European Convention on Human Rights* (2nd edn., Oxford: Oxford University Press, 1996).

JACOBS, L.A., 'Bridging the Gap Between Individual and Collective Rights With the Idea of Integrity' (1991) IV *Canadian Journal of Law and Jurisprudence* 375.

JACOBY, S.M., 'Employee Representation and Corporate Governance: A Missing Link' (2001) 3 *University of Pennsylvania Journal of Labor and Employment Law* 449.

JANIS, M., 'Individuals as Subjects of International Law' (1984) 17 *Cornell International Law Journal* 61.

—— 'The Challenge of Universality: The Common Law Tradition' (1989) 83 *American Society of International Law Proceedings* 547.

—— KAY, R., and BRADLEY, A., *European Human Rights Law* (Oxford: Oxford University Press, 1995).

JASPERS, A.P.C.M., and BETTEN, L. (eds.), *25 Years: European Social Charter* (Deventer: Kluwer, 1988).

JEFFERY, K., *States of Emergency: British Governments and Strikebreaking since 1919* (London: Routledge and Kegan Paul, 1983).

JENKS, C.W., 'Co-ordination in International Organization: An Introductory Survey' (1951) 28 *BYBIL* 29.

—— *The International Protection of Trade Union Freedoms* (London: Stevens & Sons, 1957).

—— 'The Challenge of Universality' (1959) 53 *American Society of International Law Proceedings* 85.

—— *Human Rights and International Labour Standards* (London: Stevens & Sons, 1960).

—— *Social Justice in the Law of Nations: The ILO Impact after 50 Years* (London: London University Press, 1970).

—— *The International Labour Organization in the UN Family* (New York: United Nations Institute for Training and Research, 1971).

JOCHNICK, C., 'Confronting the Impunity of Non-State Actors: New Fields for the Promotion of Human Rights' (1999) 21 *Human Rights Quarterly* 56.

JOERGES, C., and NEYER, J., 'From Intergovernmental Bargaining to Deliberative Political Processes: The Constitutionalisation of Comitology' (1997) 3 *ELJ* 273.

—— and —— 'Transforming Strategic Interaction Into Deliberative Problem-Solving: European Comitology and the Foodstuffs Sector' (1997) 4 *Journal of European Public Policy* 609.

—— and VOS, E. (eds.), *European Committees: Social Regulation, Law and Politics* (Oxford: Hart Publishing, 1999).

JOHNSON, J.L., 'Public-Private-Public Convergence: How the Private Actor can Shape Public International Law Standards' (1998) 24 *Brooklyn Journal of International Law* 291.

JOHNSTON, G.A., *The International Labour Organization: Its Work for Social and Economic Progress* (London: Europa/Europa Publications, 1970).

JOHNSTONE, I., 'Treaty Interpretation: The Authority of Interpretive Communities' (1991) 12 *Michigan Journal of International Law* 371.

JONES, K., 'Everywhere Abroad and Nowhere at Home: The Global Corporation and the International State' (1984) 12 *International Journal of Social Law* 84.

JONES, R., 'The OECD Multilateral Agreement on Investment: Key Concepts and Trade Union Response', Trade Union Advisory Committee to the OECD (TUAC) Unpublished Discussion Paper (1998).

—— 'Multilateral Agreement on Investment—Unions Seek Safeguards' (1998) 5 *International Trade Union Rights* 19.

JONES, T., 'The Devaluation of Human Rights under the European Convention' [1995] *Public Law* 430.

KAHN-FREUND, O., *Labour and the Law* (London: Stevens & Sons, 1972).

—— 'Labour Relations and International Standards: Some Reflections on the European Social Charter' in *Miscellanea W.J. Ganshof van der Meersch* (Brussels: Librairie Générale de Droit et de Jurisprudence, Paris/Etablissements Emile Bruylant, 1972).

—— *The Right to Strike: Its Scope and Limitations* (Strasbourg: Council of Europe, 1974).

—— *Labour and the Law* (2nd edn., Stevens & Sons, London, 1977).

—— 'On Uses and Misuses of Comparative Law' (1974) 37 *MLR* 1; also reproduced in O. Kahn-Freund, *Selected Writings* (London: Stevens & Sons, 1978).

—— DAVIES, P., and FREEDLAND, M., *Labour and the Law* (3rd edn., London: Stevens & Sons, 1983).

—— and HEPPLE, B., *Laws Against Strikes: International Comparisons in Social Policy* (London: The Fabian Society, 1972).

KELLERSON, H., 'The ILO Declaration of 1998 on Fundamental Principles and Rights: A Challenge for the Future' (1998) 137 *ILRev.* 223.

KELLY, J., *Trade Unions and Socialist Politics* (London/New York: Verso, 1988).

KELSEN, H., and TUCKER, R.W., *Principles of International Law* (2nd edn., New York: Holt, Rinehart and Winston, 1966).

KELSO, W.A., *American Democratic Theory: Pluralism and Its Critics* (Westport, Conn./ London: Greenwood Press, 1978).

KENNEDY, D., 'The Forgotten Politics of International Governance' [2001] *EHRLR* 117.

KENNY, T., *Securing Social Rights Across Europe: How NGOs Can Make Use of the European Social Charter* (Strasbourg: Council of Europe Publishing, 1997).

KHAN, A., 'A Theory of Universal Democracy' (1997) 16 *Wisconsin International Law Journal* 61.

KILGOUR, J.G., 'Can Unions Strike Anymore? The Impact of Recent Supreme Court Decisions' (1990) 41 *Labor Law Journal* 259.

KILPATRICK, C., 'Production and Circulation of EC Nightwork Jurisprudence' (1996) 25 *ILJ* 169.

—— NOVITZ, T., and SKIDMORE, P. (eds.), *The Future of Remedies in Europe* (Oxford: Hart Publishing, 2000).

KNELL, J., *Partnership at Work* (London: DTI, 1999).

KOCHAN, T., and OSTERMAN, P., *The Mutual Gains Enterprise: Forging a Winning Partnership among Labor, Management and Government* (Boston, Mass.: Harvard Business School Press, 1994).

KOH, H.H., and SLYE, R.C. (eds.), *Deliberative Democracy and Human Rights* (New Haven, Conn.: Yale University Press, 1999).

KORNHAUSER, A., DUBLIN, R., and ROSS, A.M. (eds.), *Industrial Conflict* (New York: McGraw-Hill, 1954).

KORPI, W., *The Democratic Class Struggle* (London: Routledge and Kegan Paul, 1983).

KROPP, S.H., 'Rethinking the Labor and Employment Law Curriculum: Legal Education's Belated Response to the Demise of Collective Bargaining and the Rise of Individual Rights' (1991) 60 *University of Cincinnati Law Review* 433.

KUPFERBERG, S., 'Political Strikes, Labor Law and Democratic Rights' (1985) 71 *Virginia Law Review* 685.

KYLOH, B. (ed.), *Mastering the Challenge of Globalization* (Geneva: ILO, 1998).

LADEUR, K.-H., 'Towards a Legal Theory of Supra-Nationality—The Viability of the Network Concept' (1997) 3 *ELJ* 33.

LANDMAN, A.A., 'Freedom of Association in South African Labour Law' (1990) 31 *Acta Juridica* 89.

LANDY, E.A., *The Effectiveness of International Supervision: Thirty Years of ILO Experience* (London: Stevens & Sons, 1966).

LANGILLE, B., 'Eight Ways to Think About International Labour Standards' (1997) 31 *Journal of World Trade* 27.

—— 'The ILO and the New Economy: Recent Devlopments' (1999) 15 *IJCLLIR* 229.

LANNUNG, H., 'Human Rights and the Multiplicity of European Systems for International Protection' (1972) 5 *Human Rights Journal* 651.

LAPPING, B. (ed.), *Laws Against Strikes: International Comparisons in Social Policy* (London: Fabian Society, 1972).

LASKI, H.J., *Liberty in the Modern State* (London: Faber & Faber, 1930).

—— *A Grammar of Politics* (4th edn., London: Faber & Faber, 1938).

—— *Trade Unions in the New Society* (London: Allen & Unwin, 1950).

LAUTERPACHT, H., *International Law* (Cambridge: Cambridge University Press, 1970).

LAWRY, M., 'Jacksonville Bulk Terminals: The Norris–La Guardia Act and Politically Motivated Strikes' (1983) 44 *Ohio State Law Journal* 821.

LAWSON, R., and DE BOIS, M. (eds.), *The Dynamics of the Protection of Human Rights in Europe: Essays in Honour of Henry J. Schermers* (Dordrecht/Boston, Mass./London: Martinus Nijhoff, 1994).

LEADER, S., *Freedom of Association, A Study in Labour Law and Political Theory* (New Haven, Conn./London: Yale University Press, 1992).

LEARY, V.A., 'The WTO and the Social Clause: Post- Singapore' (1997) 8 *EJIL* 118.

LEE, E., 'Globalization and Employment: Is Anxiety Justified?' (1996) 135 *ILRev.* 485.

—— 'Globalization and Labour Standards: A Review of the Issues' (1997) 136 *ILRev.* 173.

—— *The Labour Movement and the Internet: The New Internationalism* (London: Pluto Press, 1997).

—— 'Trade Union Rights: An Economic Perspective' (1998) 137 *ILRev.* 313.

LEE-CHING, D., 'Labor Law I: Judicial Intervention in Politically Motivated Work Stoppages' [1983] *Annual Survey of American Law* 411.

LENAERTS, K., 'Fundamental Rights to be Included in a Community Catalogue' (1991) 16 *ELRev.* 367.

—— 'Fundamental Rights in the European Union' (2000) 25 *ELRev.* 575.

—— and DE SMIJTER, E., 'A "Bill of Rights" for the European Union' (2001) 38 *CMLRev.* 273.

LEUPRECHT, P., 'Innovations in the European System of Human Rights Protection: Is Enlargement Compatible with Reinforcement' (1998) 8 *Transnational Law and Contemporary Problems* 313.

LEWIS, G.D., 'The International Labor Organization and the Polish Independent Labor Organization' (1982) 22 *Virginia Journal of International Law* 555.

LEWIS, R. (ed.), *Labour Law in Britain* (Oxford: Blackwell, 1986).

—— 'Reforming Industrial Relations: Law, Politics and Power' (1991) 7 *Oxford Review of Economic Policy* 60.

LEWIS-ANTHONY, S., *The Right to Freedom of Peaceful Assembly and to Freedom of Association as Guaranteed by Article 11 of the European Convention on Human Rights* (Strasbourg: Council of Europe, 1992).

LIISBERG, J.B., 'Does the EU Charter of Fundamental Rights Threaten the Supremacy of Community Law?' (2001) 38 *CMLRev.* 1171.

LIPSET, S.M. (ed.), *Unions in Transition: Entering the Second Century* (San Francisco, Cal.: ICS Press, 1986).

LO FARO, A., *Regulating Social Europe: Reality & Myth of Collective Bargaining in the EC Legal Order* (Oxford: Hart Publishing, 2000).

LOCKE, R., KOCHLAN, T., and PIORE, M., 'Reconceptualizing Comparative Industrial Relations: Lessons from International Research' (1995) 134 *ILRev.* 139.

LONEY, M. (ed.), *The State or the Market: Politics and Welfare in Contemporary Britain* (London: Sage Publications, 1987).

LORENZ, E.C., 'The Search for Constitutional Protection of Labor Standards, 1924–1941: From Interstate Compacts to International Treaties' (2000) 23 *Seattle University Law Review* 569.

LUKES, S., *Essays in Social Theory* (London: Macmillan, 1977).

MACBRIDE, S., 'The Enforcement of the International Law of Human Rights' [1981] *University of Illinois Law Review* 385.

MACDONALD, R. St J., JOHNSTON, D.M., and MORRIS, G.L. (eds.), *The International Law of Policy and Human Welfare* (Alphen aan den Rijn: Sijthoff and Noordhoff, 1978).

—— MATSCHER, F., and PETZOLD, H. (eds.), *The European System for the Protection of Human Rights* (Dordrecht: Martinus Nijhoff, 1993).

MACFARLANE, L.J., *The Right to Strike* (Harmondsworth: Penguin Books, 1981).

MACKEN, J.J., *Australian Industrial Laws: The Constitutional Basis* (2nd edn., Sydney: Law Book Company Ltd, 1980).

MACMILLAN, J., 'Employment Tribunals: Philosophies and Practicalities' (1999) 28 *ILJ* 33.

MADURO, M.P, *We the Court: The European Court of Justice and the European Economic Constitution* (Oxford: Hart Publishing, 1998).

MAGUIRE, P.R., 'Political General Strikes' (1977) 28 *Northern Ireland Legal Quarterly* 269.

MAHONEY, P., 'Speculating on the Future of the Reformed Court of Human Rights' (1999) 20 *Human Rights Law Journal* 2.

MANCINI, G.F., 'The Making of a Constitution for Europe' (1989) 26 *CMLRev.* 595.

MANN, M., *The Sources of Social Power: The Rise of Classes and Nation States 1760–1914* (Cambridge: Cambridge University Press, 1993).

MANZINI, P., 'The Priority of Pre-Existing Treaties of EC Member States within the Framework of International Law' (2001) 12 *EJIL* 781.

MARCEAU, G., 'A Call for Coherence in International Law: Praises for the Prohibition Against "Clinical Isolation" in WTO Dispute Settlement' (1999) 33 *Journal of World Trade* 87.

MARKS, G., and DIAMOND, L. (eds.), *Reexamining Democracy* (London: Sage, 1992).

MARKS, S., *The Riddle of all Constitutions: International Law, Democracy and the Critique of Ideology* (Oxford: Oxford University Press, 2000).

MARSHALL, R., *Unheard Voices: Labor and Economic Policy in a Competitive World* (New York: Basic Books, 1987).

MARSHALL, T.H., *Citizenship and Social Class* (Cambridge: Cambridge University Press, 1950).

—— and BOTTOMORE, T., *Citizenship and Social Class* (London: Pluto Press, 1992).

MARTÍNEZ, G.P., 'Fundamental Rights: Between Morals and Politics' (2001) 14 *Ratio Juris* 64.

MATSCHER, F., and PETZOLD, H. (eds.), *Protecting Human Rights: The European Dimension: Studies in Honour of Gerald J. Wiarda* (2nd edn., Cologne/Berlin/Bonn: Carl Heymanns Verlag KG, 1990).

McCARTHY, W. (ed.), *Legal Intervention in Industrial Relations* (Oxford: Blackwell, 1992).

McCORQUODALE, R., with FAIRBROTHER, R., 'Globalization and Human Rights' (1999) 21 *Human Rights Quarterly* 735.

McCRUDDEN, C., 'Human Rights Codes for Transnational Corporations: What can the Sullivan and MacBride Principles Tell Us?' (1999) 19 *OJLS* 167.

—— 'The Future of the EU Charter of Fundamental Rights' (Cambridge, Mass.: Harvard Law School, 2001) Harvard Jean Monnet Working Papers 10/01.

—— and DAVIES, A., 'A Perspective on Trade and Labour Rights' (2000) 21 *Journal of International Economic Law* 43.

McDOUGAL, M.S., LASSWELL, H.D., and MILLER J.C., *The Interpretation of International Agreements and World Public Order: Principles of Content and Procedure* (New Haven, Conn.: New Haven Press, 1994).

McGEE, R.W., 'The Right to Not Associate: The Case for an Absolute Freedom of Negative Freedom of Association' (1992) 23 *University of West Los Angeles Law Review* 123.

McKAY, S., *The Law on Industrial Action under the Conservatives* (London: Institute of Employment Rights, 1996).

McKEE, J., 'Legalism in Industrial Tribunals' (1986) 15 *ILJ* 110.

McMAHON, J.F., 'The Legislative Techniques of the International Labour Organization' (1965–66) 41 *BYBIL* 1.

McNAIR, LORD, *The Law of Treaties* (Oxford: Clarendon Press, 1961).

MERON, T. (ed.), *Human Rights in International Law: Legal and Policy Issues* (Oxford: Oxford University Press, 1984).

MERTUS, J., 'From Legal Transplants to Transformative Justice: Human Rights and the Promise of Transnational Civil Society' (1999) 14 *American University International Law Review* 1335.

MEUNIER, D., and NICOLAIDIS, K., 'Who Speaks for Europe? The Delegation of Trade Authority in the EU' (1999) 37 *JCMS* 477.

MEYER, W.H., 'Human Rights and MNCs: Theory versus Quantitative Analysis' (1996) 18 *Human Rights Quarterly* 368.

MICHELMAN, F., 'Law's Republic' (1988) 97 *Yale Law Journal* 1493.

—— 'Democracy-Based Resistance to a Constitutional Right of Social Citizenship' (2001) 69 *Fordham Law Review* 1893.

MIDWOOD, L., and VITACCO, A., 'The Right of Attorneys to Unionize, Collectively Bargain, and Strike: Legal and Ethical Considerations' (2000) 18 *Hofstra Labor and Employment Law Journal* 299.

MILL, J.S., *Utilitarianism* (Warnock, M. (ed.) Glasgow: Fontana Press, 1962).

MILLER, K., and WOOLFSON, C., 'Timex: Industrial Relations and the Use of Law in the 1990s' (1994) 23 *ILJ* 209.

MILLER, V., 'Human Rights in the EU: The Charter of Fundamental Rights' (2000) House of Commons Research Paper 00/32.

MISCHKE, C., 'The Significance and Practical Effect of ILO Standards—A View from the Outside' (1993) 14 *Industrial Law Journal* (South Africa) 63.

MOBERG, A., 'The Nice Treaty and Voting Rules in Council' (2002) 40 *JCMS* 259.

MONOGHAN, K., *Challenging Race Discrimination at Work* (London: Institute of Employment Rights, 2000).

MOODY, K., *Workers in a Lean World: Unions in the International Economy* (London/ New York: Verso, 1997).

MORGENSTERN, F., *Legal Problems of International Organizations* (Cambridge: Grotius, 1986).

MORGENTHAU, H.J., *Politics Among Nations* (5th edn., New York: Knopf, 1973).

MORRIS, A., and O'DONNELL, T. (eds.), *Feminist Perspectives on Employment Law* (London: Cavendish, 1999).

MORRIS, G., *Strikes in Essential Services* (London: Mansell, 1986).

—— 'Industrial Action: Public and Private Interests' (1993) 22 *Industrial Law Journal* 194.

—— 'The Employment Relations Act 1999 and Collective Labour Standards' (2001) 17 *IJCLLIR* 63.

—— and ARCHER, T., *Collective Labour Law* (Oxford: Hart Publishing, 2000).

MOWER, A.G., *International Co-operation for Social Justice: Global and Regional Protection of Economic/Social Rights* (London/Westport, Conn.: Greenwood Press, 1985).

MTHOMBENI, R., 'The Right or Freedom to Strike: An Analysis from an International and Comparative Perspective' (1990) 23 *Comparative International Law Journal of South Africa* 337.

MUNCK, R., and WATERMAN, P. (eds.), *Labour Worldwide in the Era of Globalization: Alternative Union Models in the New World Order* (London: Macmillan, 1999).

MURRAY, J., *Transnational Labour Regulation: The ILO and EC Compared* (The Hague: Kluwer, 2001).

—— 'A New Phase in the Regulation of Multinational Enterprises: The Role of the OECD' (2001) 30 *ILJ* 255.

NAFZIGER, J.A.R., 'The International Organization and Social Change: The Fact-Finding and Conciliation Commission on Freedom of Association' (1969) 2 *New York University Journal of International Law and Politics* 1.

NAPIER, B., 'Unions and Political Strikes' (1974) 33 *Cambridge Law Journal* 71.

NARVESON, J., 'Collective Rights?' (1991) IV *Canadian Journal of Law and Jurisprudence* 329.

NEAL, A.C., 'Public Sector Industrial Relations—Some Developing Trends' (2001) 17 *IJCLLIR* 233.

NEUWAHL, N.A., and ROSAS, A. (eds.), *The European Union and Human Rights* (The Hague: Kluwer/Martinus Nijhoff, 1995).

NICOD, J., 'Freedom of Association and Trade Unionism: An Introductory Survey' (1924) 9 *ILRev.* 467.

NINO, C.S., *The Ethics of Human Rights* (Oxford: Clarendon Press, 1991).

—— *The Constitution of Deliberative Democracy* (New Haven, Conn., & London: Yale University Press, 1996).

NOLAN, D.R., 'RIP: Compulsory Labour Arbitration in New Zealand (1894–1984)' (1991) 12 *Comparative Labour Law Journal* 411.

NOLAN, J., and POSNER, M., 'International Standards to Promote Labour Rights: The Role of the United States Government' [2000] *Columbia Business Law Review* 529.

NOVITZ, T., 'New Zealand Industrial Relations and the International Labour Organisation: Resolving Contradictions Implicit in Freedom of Association' (1996) 21 *New Zealand Journal of Industrial Relations* 119.

—— 'Negative Freedom of Association' (1997) 26 *ILJ* 79.

—— 'Freedom of Association and "Fairness at Work"—An Assessment of the Impact and Relevance of ILO Convention No. 87 on its Fiftieth Anniversary' (1998) 27 *ILJ* 169.

—— 'International Promises and Domestic Pragmatism: To What Extent will the Employment Relations Act 1999 Implement International Labour Standards Relating to Freedom of Association' (2000) 63 *MLR* 379.

—— 'Are Social Rights Necessarily Collective Rights?—A Critical Analysis of the Collective Complaints Protocol to the European Social Charter' [2002] *EHRLR* 50.

—— ' "A Human Face" for the Union or More Cosmetic Surgery? EU Competence in Global Social Governance and Promotion of Core Labour Standards' (2002) 9(3) *Maastricht Journal of European and Comparative Law* (forthcoming).

—— and SKIDMORE, P., *Fairness at Work: A Critical Analysis of the Employment Relations Act 1999 and its Treatment of Collective Rights* (Oxford: Hart Publishing, 2001).

NOWAK, M., *UN Covenant on Civil and Political Rights: CCPR Commentary* (Kehl/ Strasbourg/Arlington, Vir.: Engel, 1993).

ODINKALU, C.A., 'Analysis of Paralysis or Paralysis by Analysis? Implementing Economic, Social, and Cultural Rights Under the African Charter on Human and Peoples' Rights' (2001) 23 *Human Rights Quarterly* 327.

OECD, *Trade, Employment and Labour Standards: A Study of Core Workers' Rights and International Trade* (Paris: OECD, 1996).

—— *International Trade and Core Labour Standards* (Paris: OECD, 2000).

O'HIGGINS, P., 'Political Strikes' [1974] *Haldane Soc. Bulletin* 9.

O'KEEFFE, D., and TWOMEY, P. (eds.), *Legal Issues of the Amsterdam Treaty* (Oxford: Hart Publishing, 1999).

OLIVIER, M., 'Labour Relations Legislation for the Public Service: An International and Comparative Perspective' (1993) 14 *Industrial Law Journal* (South Africa) 1371.

OLNEY, S., *Unions in a Changing World: Problems and Prospects in Selected Industrialized Countries* (Geneva: International Labour Office, 1996).

OPPENHEIM, L., and LAUTERPACHT, H., *International Law: A Treatise* (8th edn., London: Longmans Green, 1955), i.

ORLANDINI, G., 'The Free Movement of Goods as a Possible "Community" Limitation on Industrial Conflict' (2000) 6 *ELJ* 341.

OSIEKE, E., 'The Exercise of the Judicial Function with respect to the International Labour Organization' (1974–1975) LXVII *BYBIL* 315.

PALMER, G., 'New Ways to Make International Environmental Law' (1992) 86 *AJIL* 259.

PATEMAN, C., *Participation and Democratic Theory* (Cambridge: Cambridge University Press, 1970).

PATTON, W.W., and LATZ, S., 'Severing Hansel from Gretel: An Analysis of Siblings' Association Rights' (1994) 48 *University of Miami Law Review* 745.

PELLET, A., 'The Normative Dilemma: Will and Consent in International Law-Making' (1992) 12 *Australian Yearbook of International Law* 22.

PELLING, H., *A History of British Trade Unionism* (London: Macmillan, 1992).

PETERSMANN, E.-U., 'How to Constitutionalize International Law and Foreign Policy for the Benefit of Civil Society?' (1998) 20 *Michigan Journal of International Law* 1.

—— 'Human Rights and International Economic Law in the 21st Century: The Need to Clarify their Inter-relationships' (2001) 22 *Journal of International Economic Law* 3.

PICCIOTTO, S., and MAYNE, R. (eds.), *Regulating International Business: Beyond Liberalization* (London: Macmillan, 1999).

PIGOU, A.C. (ed.), *Memorials of Alfred Marshall* (London Macmillan, 1925).

PIORE, M., *Beyond Individualism* (Cambridge, Mass.: Harvard University Press, 1995).

PLANT, R., *Labour Standards and Structural Adjustment* (Geneva: ILO, 1994).

POCHET, P. (ed.), *Monetary Union and Collective Bargaining in Europe* (Brussels: PIE Lang, 1999).

POLLACK, M.A., and SHAFFER, G.C. (eds.), *Transatlantic Governance in the Global Economy* (Lanham, Mld.: Rowman, 2001).

POPE, J.G., 'Labor and the Constitution: From Abolition to De-industrialization' (1987) 65 *Texas Law Review* 1071.

—— 'Labor-Community Coalitions and Boycotts: The Old Labor Law, the New Unionism and the Living Constitution' (1991) 69 *Texas Law Review* 889.

—— 'Labor's Constitution of Freedom' (1997) 106 *Yale Law Journal* 941.

POSNER, R., *The Economics of Justice* (Boston, Mass.: Harvard University Press, 1983).

—— 'Some Economics of Labor Law' (1984) 57 *University of Chicago Law Review* 988.

POUYAT, A.J., 'The ILO's Freedom of Association Standards and Machinery: A Summing Up' (1982) 121 *ILRev.* 287.

POWERS MCGUIRE, J., 'A Comparison of the Right of Public Employees to Strike in the United States and Canada' (1987) 23 *Labor Law Journal* 304.

RAPHAEL, D. (ed.), *Political Theory and the Rights of Man* (London: Bodley Head, 1967).

RAWSON, D.W., 'The Law and the Objects of Federal Unions' [1981] *The Journal of Industrial Relations* (Australia) 295.

RAZ, J., 'Liberalism, Autonomy and the Politics of Neutral Concern' (1982) 8 *Midwest Studies in Philosophy* 89.

—— *The Morality of Freedom* (Oxford: Clarendon Press, 1986).

RHODES, M., 'The Future of the "Social Dimension": Labour Market Regulation in Post-1992 Europe' (1992) 30 *JCMS* 23.

RIS, M., 'Treaty Interpretation and ICJ Recourse to *Travaux Préparatoires*: Towards a Proposed Amendment of Articles 31 and 32 of the Vienna Convention on the Law of Treaties' (1991) 14 *Boston College International and Comparative Law Review* 111.

RISSE, T., ROPP, S.C., and SIKKINK, K. (eds.), *The Power of Human Rights: International Norms and Domestic Change* (Cambridge: Cambridge University Press, 1999).

ROBERTSON, A.H., 'The European Convention for the Protection of Human Rights' (1950) 27 *BYBIL* 145.

—— 'The European Political Community' (1952) 29 *BYBIL* 383.

—— *The Council of Europe as an Organ of Inter-governmental Co-operation* (Strasbourg: Council of Europe, 1954).

—— *The Council of Europe* (2nd edn., London: Stevens & Sons, 1961).

—— *European Institutions* (3rd edn., London: Stevens & Sons, 1973).

—— and MERRILLS, J.G., *Human Rights in the World: An Introduction to the Study of the International Protection of Human Rights* (4th edn., Manchester: Manchester University Press, 1996).

ROGOWSKI, R., and WILTHAGEN, T. (eds.), *Reflexive Labour Law* (Deventer/Boston, Mass.: Kluwer, 1994).

ROSENAU, J.N., and CZEMPIEL, E.-O. (eds.), *Governance Without Government: Order and Change in World Politics* (Cambridge: Cambridge University Press, 1992).

ROTHSCHILD, J., 'Obscuring But Not Reducing Managerial Control: Does TQM Measure up to Democracy Standards?' (1999) 20 *Economic and Industrial Democracy* 583.

ROWBOTHAM, S., and MITTER, S. (eds.), *Dignity and Daily Bread: New Forms of Economic Organising among Poor Women in the Third World and the First* (London: Routledge, 1994).

RUBINSTEIN, S., 'A Different Kind of Union: Balancing Co-Management and Representation' (2001) 40 *Industrial Relations* 163.

RYAN, B., 'Unfinished Business? The Failure of Deregulation in Employment Law' (1996) 23 *Journal of Law and Society* 506.

—— 'Pay, Trade Union Rights and European Community Law' (1997) 13 *IJCLLIR* 305.

SABEL, C., O'ROURKE, D., and FUNG, A., 'Open Labor Standards: Towards a System of Rolling Rule Regulation of Labor Practices', Discussion Paper presented at the Annual Meetings of the World Bank Seminar on Labor Standards, 28 September 1999.

SACHS, A., *Protecting Human Rights in a New South Africa* (Cape Town: Oxford University Press, 1990).

—— *Perfectability and Corruptibility: Preparing Ourselves for Power* (Cape Town: University of Cape Town, 1992).

SALZMAN, J., 'Labor Rights, Globalization and Institutions: The Role and Influence of the Organization for Economic Co-operation and Development' (2000) 21 *Michigan Journal of International Law* 769.

SAMUEL, L., *Fundamental Social Rights: Case Law of the European Social Charter* (Strasbourg: Council of Europe Publishing, 1997).

SANDS, P., and KLEIN, P., *Bowett's Law of International Institutions* (5th edn., London: Sweet & Maxwell, 2001).

SANDU, G., and KUOKKANEN, M., 'On Social Rights' (1990) 3 *Ratio Juris* 89.

SARRA, P., 'Politically Motivated Labor Actions in the United States and England: A Comparison of Judicial and Legislative Treatment' (1984) 7 *Boston College International and Comparative Law Review* 91.

SARTORI, G., *The Theory of Democracy Revisited* (Chatham, NJ: Chatham House Publishers Inc, 1987).

SASSEN, S., *Losing Control? Sovereignty in an Age of Globalization* (New York: Columbia University Press, 1996).

SCHACHTER, O., and JOYNER, C.C. (eds.), *United Nations Legal Order* (Cambridge: Cambridge University Press, 1995), i.

SCHERMERS, H.G., *International Institutional Law* (Alphen aan den Rijn: Sijthoff and Noordhoff, 1986).

—— 'Is There a Fundamental Right to Strike? (Right to Fair Conditions)' (1989) 9 *Yearbook of European Law* 225.

—— 'The Eleventh Protocol to the European Convention on Human Rights' (1994) 19 *ELRev.* 367.

—— 'Human Rights in the European Union after the Reform of 1 November 1998' (1998) 4 *EPL* 335.

—— '*Matthews v United Kingdom*' (1999) 36 *CMLRev.* 673.

SCHIAVONE, G., *International Organizations* (3rd edn., London: Macmillan, 1992).

SCHLOSSBERG, S.I., 'United States Participation in the ILO' (1989) 11 *Comparative Law Journal* 48.

SCHOLTEN, I. (ed.), *Political Stability and Neo-Corporatism: Corporatist Integration and Social Cleavages in Western Europe* (London: Sage, 1987).

SCHREGLE, J., 'Collective Bargaining and Workers' Participation: The Position of the ILO' (1993) 14 *Comparative Labor Law Journal* 431.

SCHWARTZ, H., 'Do Economic and Social Rights Belong in a Constitution?' (1995) 10 *American University Journal of International Law and Policy* 1233.

SCIARRA, S. (ed.), *Labour Law in the Courts: National Judges and the European Court of Justice* (Oxford: Hart Publishing, 2001).

—— 'Market Freedom and Fundamental Social Rights' (Florence: EUI, 2002) EUI Working Paper Series LAW 2002/3.

SCOTT, C., 'Reaching Beyond (Without Abandoning) the Category of "Economic, Social and Cultural Rights"' (1999) 21 *Human Rights Quarterly* 633.

—— and MACKLEM, P., 'Constitutional Ropes of Sand or Justiciable Guarantees? Social Rights in a New South African Constitution' (1992) 141 *University of Pennsylvania Law Review* 1.

SCOTT, S., 'International Law as Ideology: Theorizing the Relationship Between International Law and International Politics' (1994) 5 *EJIL* 313.

SEADY, H.M., and BENJAMIN, P.S., 'The Right to Strike and Freedom of Association: An International Perspective' (1990) 11 *Industrial Law Journal* (South Africa) 439.

SEDLER, R.A., 'The Institutional Protection of Freedom of Religion, Expression and Association in Canada and the United States: A Comparative Analysis' (1988) 20 *Case Western Reserve Journal of International Law* 577.

SENGENBERGER, W., and CAMPBELL, D. (eds.), *International Labour Standards and Economic Interdependence* (Geneva: IILS, 1994).

SERVAIS, J., 'ILO Standards on Freedom of Association and their Implementation' (1984) 123 *ILRev.* 765.

SHANKS, M., 'The Social Policy of the European Communities' (1977) 14 *CMLRev.* 375.

SHAPIRO, M., 'Administrative Law Unbounded: Reflections on Government and Governance' (2001) 8 *Indiana Journal of Global Legal Studies* 369.

SHAW, J. (ed.), *Social Law and Policy in an Evolving European Union* (Oxford: Hart Publishing, 2000).

SHENFIELD, A., *What Right to Strike? With Commentaries by Cyril Grunfeld and Sir Leonard Neal* (London: Institute of Economic Affairs, 1986).

SHEPPARD, T., 'Liberalism and the Charter: Freedom of Association and the Right to Strike' (1996) 5 *Dalhousie Journal of Legal Studies* 117.

SHOTWELL, J.T., *The Origins of the International Labour Organization* (New York: Columbia University Press, 1934).

SIEGHART, P., *The International Law of Human Rights* (Oxford: Clarendon Press, 1983).

SILVIA, S.J., 'The Social Charter of the European Community: A Defeat for European Labor' (1990–91) 44 *Industrial and Labour Relations Review* 626.

SIMMA, B., and ALSTON, P., 'The Sources of Human Rights Law: Custom, Jus Cogens and General Principles' (1992) 12 *Australian Year Book of International Law* 82.

SIMPSON, B., 'The Labour Injunction, Unlawful Means and the Right to Strike' (1987) 50 *MLR* 506.

—— *The Right to Strike and the Law in Britain, with Special Reference to Essential Services* (London: Centre for Economic Performance, London School of Economics, 1993).

—— 'Freedom of Association and the Right to Organise: The Failure of an Individual Rights Strategy' (1995) 24 *ILJ* 235.

SKOGLY, S., *The Human Rights Obligations of the World Bank and the International Monetary Fund* (London: Cavendish, 2001).

SLAUGHTER, A.-M., 'The Real New World Order' (1997) 76 *Foreign Affairs* 183.

SLAUGHTER BURLEY, A., 'International Law and International Relations Theory: A Dual Agenda' (1993) 87 *AJIL* 205.

SMISMANS, S., 'An Economic and Social Committee for the Citizen or a Citizen for the Economic and Social Committee' (1999) 5 *EPL* 557.

SMITH, G.F., 'From Consensus to Coercion: the Australian Air Pilots Dispute' (1990) 32 *The Journal of Industrial Relations* (Australia) 238.

SMITH, J., BOLYARD, M., and IPPOLITO, A., 'Human Rights and the Global Economy: A Response to Meyer' (1999) 21 *Human Rights Quarterly* 207.

—— and ZWAAK, L. (eds.), *International Protection of Human Rights: Selected Topics* (Utrecht: Netherlands Institute of Human Rights/Studie- en Informatiecentrum Mensentrechten, 1995).

SMITH, K.E., 'The Use of Political Conditionality in the EU's Relations with Third Countries' (Florence: EUI, 1997) EUI Working Paper Series SPS 97/7.

SPAAK, P.-H., *Strasbourg: The Second Year* (London: Oxford University Press, 1952).

SOLOW, R.M., *The Labor Market as a Social Institution* (Oxford: Blackwell, 1990).

STEIN, E., 'International Integration and Democracy: No Love at First Sight' (2001) 95 *AJIL* 489.

STIGLITZ, J., 'Towards a New Paradigm for Development: Strategies, Policies, and Processes', 1998 Prebisch Lecture at UNCTAD, 19 October 1998.

—— 'Democratic Development as the Fruits of Labor', Keynote Address to the Industrial Relations Research Association, Boston, Mass., January 2000.

—— *Globalization and its Discontents* (New York: W.W. Norton, 2002).

STOTZKY, I.P., 'Establishing Deliberative Democracy: Moving from Misery to Poverty with Dignity' (1998) 21 *University of Arkansas at Little Rock Law Review* 79.

—— 'Substantive Self-Determination: Democracy, Communicative Power and Inter/National Labor Rights: Suppressing the Beast' (1999) 53 *University of Miami Law Review* 883.

STRANGE, S., *The Retreat of the State: The Diffusion of Power in the World Economy* (Cambridge: Cambridge University Press, 1996).

STREEK, W., and SCHMITTER, P., 'From National Corporatism to Transnational Pluralism: Organised Interests in the Single European Market' (1991) 19 *Politics and Society* 133.

SUMMERS, C., 'Public Employee Bargaining: A Political Perspective' (1974) 83 *Yale Law Journal* 1156.

—— 'Lord Wedderburn's New Labour Law: An American Perspective' (1991) 20 *ILJ* 157.

—— 'Review of Sheldon Leader's Freedom of Association: A Study in Labor Law and Political Theory' (1995) 16 *Comparative Labour Law Journal* 262.

—— 'The Battle in Seattle: Free Trade, Labor Rights, and Societal Values' (2001) 22 *University of Pennsylvania Journal of International Economic Law* 61.

SUPIOT, A., *Beyond Employment: Changes in Work and the Future of Labour Law in Europe* (Oxford: Oxford University Press, 2001).

SWABEY, J., and GROUSHKO, M., *Secondary Industrial Action: The Right to Strike and to Take Secondary Action in the EU Member States* (Brussels: Watson Wyatt, 1996).

SWAMINATHAN, R., 'Regulating Development: Structural Adjustment and the Case for National Enforcement of Economic and Social Rights' (1998) 36 *Columbia Journal of Transnational Law* 161.

SWEPSTON, L., 'Supervision of ILO Standards' (1997) 13 *IJCLLIR* 327.

—— 'Human Rights and Freedom of Association: Development through ILO Supervision' (1998) 137 *ILRev.* 169.

SWIATKOWSKI, A., 'Current Developments in Labor Law and Labor Relations in Poland' (1990) 12 *Comparative Labour Law Journal* 35.

SYMONIDES, J., 'Globalization and Human Rights' (2000) 4 *Mediterranean Journal of Human Rights* 145.

—— (ed.), *Human Rights: Concept and Standards* (Brookfield, Vt.: Ashgate, 2000).

SYRPIS, P., 'Legitimising Europe—Taking Subsidiarity Seriously within the Open Method of Coordination' (Florence: EUI, 2002) EUI Working Paper Series LAW 2002/10.

SZYSZCZAK, E., 'The New Paradigm for Social Policy: A Virtuous Circle' (2001) 38 *CMLRev.* 1125.

TAJGMAN, D., *International Labour Standards in Southern Africa* (Cape Town: Labour Law Unit, 1994).

TAYLOR, R., *The Trade Union Question in British Politics: Government and the Unions since 1945* (Oxford: Blackwell, 1993).

TENNJFORD, F., 'The Social Charter—An Instrument of Social Collaboration in Europe' [1962] *European Year Book* 71.

TESON, F.R., 'Interdependence, Consent and the Basis of International Obligation' [1989] *American Society of International Law Proceedings* 547.

THOMAS, A., 'The International Labour Organisation: Its Origins, Development and Future' (1921) 1 *ILRev.* 5.

THOMAS, P., *Taming the Corporate Jungle* (Sydney: New South Wales Branch of the Australian Building Construction Employees and Builders' Labourers' Federation, 1973).

THUSING, G., 'Recent Developments in German Labour Law: Freedom of Association, Industrial Action and Collective Bargaining' (1998) 9 *Indiana International and Comparative Law Review* 47.

TOMKINS, A., 'The Committee of Ministers: Its Roles under the European Convention on Human Rights' [1995] *EHRLR* 49.

TOYE, J., *Structural Adjustment and Employment Policy: Issues and Experience* (Geneva: International Labour Office, 1995).

TREBILCOCK, A. (ed.), *Towards Social Dialogue: Tripartite Cooperation in National Economic and Social Policy-Making* (Geneva: ILO, 1994).

—— 'Structural Adjustment and Tripartite Consultation' in ILO, *Labour Law and Labour Relations Briefing Note 1* (Geneva: ILO, 1995).

TRIMBLE, P., 'Globalization, International Institutions, and the Erosion of National Sovereignty and Democracy' (1997) 95 *Michigan Law Review* 144.

TRUBEK, D.M., and MOSHER, J.S., 'New Governance, EU Employment Policy and the European Social Model' in Joerges, C., Meny, Y., and Weiler, J.H.H. (eds.), *Symposium: Responses to the European Commission's White Paper on Governance* (Florence: European University Institute, 2001).

TSOGAS, G., *Corporate Codes of Conduct and Labor Standards in Global Sourcing* (London: IDS, 1998).

—— 'Labour Standards in the Generalized Systems of Preferences of the European Union and the United States' (2000) 6 *European Journal of Industrial Relations* 349.

—— *Labor Regulation in a Global Economy* (Armonk, NY/London: M.E. Sharpe, 2001).

TULKINS, F., 'Towards a Greater Normative Coherence in Europe: The Implications of the Draft Charter of Fundamental Rights of the European Union' (2000) 21 *Human Rights Law Journal* 329.

TULLY, S., 'The 2000 Review of the OECD Guidelines for Multinational Enterprises' (2001) 50 *ICLQ* 394.

TURNER, B.S., *Citizenship and Capitalism: The Debate Over Reformism* (London: Allen & Unwin, 1986).

TWINE, F., *Citizenship and Social Rights: The Interdependence of Self and Society* (London: Sage, 1994).

UNDY, R., FOSH, P., MORRIS, H., SMITH, P., and MARTIN, R., *Managing Trade Unions: The Impact of Legislation on Trade Union Behaviour* (Oxford: Oxford University Press, 1996).

UNGER, R.M., 'The Critical Legal Studies Movement' (1982) 96 *Harvard Law Review* 561.

UTZ, A.F., 'Is the Right to Strike a Human Right?' (1987) 65 *Washington University Law Quarterly* 732.

VALASKAKIS, K., 'Globalization as Theatre' (1999) 160 *International Social Science Journal* 142.

VALTICOS, N., 'International Labour Standards and Human Rights: Approaching the Year 2000' (1998) 138 *ILRev.* 135.

VAN ALSTINE, M.P., 'Dynamic Treaty Interpretation' (1998) 146 *University of Pennsylvania Law Review* 687.

VAN DIJK, P., and VAN HOOF, G.J.H., *Theory and Practice of the European Convention on Human Rights* (Deventer: Kluwer, 1984).

VANDAMME, F., 'The Revision of the European Social Charter' (1994) 133 *ILRev.* 635.

VEDDER, C., and FOLZ, H., 'A Survey of Principal Decisions of the European Court of Justice Pertaining to International Law in 1993' (1994) 5 *EJIL* 448.

VERCUIL, P.R., 'Whose Common Law for Labor Relations?' (1983) 92 *Yale Law Journal* 1409.

VIERDAG, E.W., 'The Legal Nature of the Rights Granted by the International Covenant on Economic, Social and Cultural Rights' (1978) 9 *Netherlands Year Book of International Law* 69.

VILLIGER, M., *Customary International Law and Treaties: A Study of their Interactions and Interrelations with Special Consideration of the 1969 Vienna Convention on the Law of Treaties* (Dordrecht: Martinus Nijhoff, 1985).

VINCENT, R.J., *Human Rights and International Relations* (Cambridge: Cambridge University Press, 1986).

VINCENT-DAVIS, D., 'Human Rights Law: A Research Guide to the Literature—Part III: the International Labour Organization and Human Rights' (1982) 15 *New York University Journal of International Law and Politics* 211.

VITORINO, A., 'The Charter of Fundamental Rights as Foundation for the Area of Freedom, Security and Justice', Exeter Paper in European Law No. 4 (Exeter: Centre for European Studies, University of Exeter, 2001).

VON BOGDANDY, A., 'The European Union as a Human Rights Organization? Human Rights and the Core of the European Union' (2000) 37 *CMLRev.* 1307.

VON MAYDELL, B., and NUβBERGER, A. (eds.), *Social Protection by Way of International Law: Appraisal, Deficits and Further Development* (Berlin: Duncker & Humblot, 1996).

VON PRONDZYNSKI, F., 'Freedom of Association and the Closed Shop: The European Perspective' (1982) 41 *Cambridge Law Journal* 256.

—— *Freedom of Association and Industrial Relations: A Comparative Study* (London: Mansell, 1987).

VOSKO, L.F., 'Legitimizing the Triangular Employment Relationship: Emerging International Labour Standards from a Comparative Perspective' (1997) 19 *Comparative Labor Law and Policy Journal* 43.

VOUSDEN, S., 'Albany, Market Law and Social Exclusion' (2000) 29 *ILJ* 181.

WALDRON, J., *Theories of Rights* (Oxford: Oxford University Press, 1984).

WALLACE, H., and YOUNG, A. (eds.), *Participation and Policy-Making in the European Union* (Oxford: Clarendon Press, 1997).

WATERMAN, P., *Social-Movement Unionism: A New Model for a New World* (The Hague: Institute of Social Studies, 1991).

WEBB, J.F., 'Political Boycotts and Union Speech: A Critical First Amendment Analysis' (1988) 4 *The Journal of Law and Politics* 579.

WEDDERBURN OF CHARLTON, LORD, 'Multi-national Enterprise and National Labour Law' (1972) 1 *ILJ* 12.

—— *The Worker and the Law* (3rd edn., London: Sweet and Maxwell, 1986).

—— *The Social Charter, European Company and Employment Rights: An Outline Agenda* (London: Institute of Employment Rights, 1990).

—— *Employment Rights in Britain and Europe: Selected Papers in Labour Law* (London: Lawrence and Wishart/Institute of Employment Rights, 1991).

—— *Freedom of Association and Community Protection: A Comparative Enquiry into Trade Union Rights of the European Community and into the Need for Intervention at the Community Level* (Luxembourg: European Commission, 1992).

—— *Labour Law and Freedom: Further Essays in Labour Law* (London: Lawrence and Wishart, 1995).

—— 'Consultation and Collective Bargaining in Europe: Success or Ideology?' (1997) 26 *ILJ* 1.

—— 'Underground Labour Injunctions' (2001) 30 *ILJ* 206.

—— LEWIS, R., and CLARK, J., *Labour Law and Industrial Relations: Building on Kahn-Freund* (Oxford: Clarendon Press, 1983).

—— and MURPHY, W.T. (eds.), *Labour and the Community: Perspectives for the 1980's* (London: Institute of Advanced Legal Studies, 1982).

—— ROOD, M., LYON-CAEN, A., DÄUBLER, W., and VAN DER HEIJEN, P., *Labour Law in the Post-Industrial Era* (Dartmouth: Aldershot, 1994).

WEIL, G.L., *The European Convention on Human Rights: Background, Development and Prospects* (Leyden: A.W. Sythoff, 1963).

WEILER, J.H.H., 'The Transformation of Europe' (1991) 100 *Yale Law Journal* 2403.

—— 'European Democracy and its Critique' (1995) 18 *Western European Policy* 4.

—— 'To Be a European Citizen—Eros and Civilization' (1997) 4 *Journal of European Public Policy* 495.

—— 'Editorial: Does the European Union Truly Need a Charter of Rights?' (2000) 6 *ELJ* 97.

—— (ed.), *The EU, the WTO and the NAFTA* (Oxford: Oxford University Press, 2000).

WEINBURG, R., 'Enjoining Political Protest Strikes' (1981) 38 *Washington and Lee Law Review* 1285.

WEIR, T., 'A Strike Against the Law?' (1986) 46 *Maryland Law Journal* 133.

WEISS, M., 'Fundamental Social Rights for the European Union' (1997) 18 *Industrial Law Journal* (South Africa) 417.

WELCH, R., *The Right to Strike: A Trade Union View* (London: Institute of Employment Rights, 1991).

—— 'Judges and the Law in British Industrial Relations: Towards a European Right to Strike' (1995) 4 *Social and Legal Studies* 174.

WERHANE, P.H., *Persons, Rights and Corporations* (Englewood Cliffs, NJ: Prentice-Hall, 1985).

WHEELER, H.N., 'Employee Rights as Human Rights' (1994) 28 *Bulletin of Comparative Labour Relations* 9.

WILTHAGEN, T. (ed.), *Advancing Theory in Labour Law and Industrial Relations in a Global Context* (Amsterdam: Royal Netherlands Academy of Arts & Sciences, 1998).

WIRTH, D.A., 'Trade Union Rights in the Workers' State: Poland and the ILO' (1983) 13 *Denver Journal of International Law and Policy* 269.

WOOD, J., 'International Labour Organisation Conventions: Labour Code or Treaties?' (1991) 40 *ICLQ* 649.

WRONKA, J., *Human Rights and Social Policy in the 21st Century* (Lanham, Mld./New York/London: University Press of America, 1992).

YOUROW, H.C., *The Margin of Appreciation Doctrine in the Dynamics of European Human Rights Jurisprudence* (The Hague/Boston, Mass./London: Kluwer, 1996).

ZELANTIN, G., 'The Economic and Social Committee' (1962) 1 *JCMS* 22.

ZURCHER, A.J., *The Struggle to Unite Europe, 1948–1958: An Historical Account of the Development of the Contemporary European Movement from its Origin in the Pan-European Union to the Drafting of Treaties for Euratom and the European Common Market* (New York: New York University Press, 1958).

ZÜRN, M., 'Governance Beyond the Nation-State: The EU and Other International Institutions' (2000) 6 *European Journal of International Relations* 183.

Index